African American Mental Health

Cobb & Henry Titles of Related Interest

Advances in African American Psychology. Reginald L. Jones (Editor)

African American Identity Development. Reginald L. Jones (Editor)

African American Children, Youth, and Parenting. Reginald L. Jones (Editor)

Black Adolescents. Reginald L. Jones (Editor)

Black Adult Development and Aging. Reginald L. Jones (Editor)

Black Psychology, 3rd Edition. Reginald L. Jones (Editor)

Handbook of Tests and Measurements for Black Populations. (Volume 1)
Reginald L. Jones (Editor)

Handbook of Tests and Measurements for Black Populations. (Volume 2)
Reginald L. Jones (Editor)

Psychoeducational Assessment of Minority Group Children: A Casebook.
Reginald L. Jones (Editor)

Forthcoming

Racial Socialization: Ecologies of Child and Adolescent Development.
Deborah Johnson and Andrea G. Hunter (Editors)

Spirituality and Well-being: African American Perspectives.
John Rogers (Editor)

African American Mental Health

Reginald L. Jones, Editor
Hampton University

1998
Cobb & Henry Publishers, Hampton, VA

For information, contact:

Cobb & Henry Publishers
1 Sutton Place
Hampton, VA 23666
Telephone: (757) 827-7213
Fax: (757) 827-1060

Printed in the United States of America.

Library of Congress Cataloging-in-Publication Data

African American mental health / edited by Reginald L. Jones
     p.   cm.
    Includes bibliographical references and index.
    IBSN 0-943539-12-9
    1. Afro-Americans—Mental Health. 2. Cultural psychiatry—United States.   I. Jones, Reginald Lanier, 1931- .
    RC451.5.N4A375 1998
    616.89 ' 0089 ' 96073—dc21   97-20436
                                            CIP

Contents

Preface

African American Mental Health and several volumes nearing completion have a long evolutionary history. This book was developed in response to my request of colleagues, more than a decade ago, for their innovative psychological theory, research and intervention with African American individuals that would be included as chapters in a series of books entitled *Advances in Black Psychology*. Contributors were identified through nomination by valued colleagues and my review of the literature and conference proceedings. I received many chapters and placed them in three categories: theory, research and intervention. My idea was that each volume would include chapters in each of these categories. Upon reflection, and following consultation with wise colleagues, I decided to develop topical volumes. My new plan, informed by colleagues, was that most scholars and practitioners would prefer to read work that was directly related to their professional interests. Following this reasoning, four volumes were conceptualized from the contributions submitted: (1) *African American Mental Health* (present volume), (2) *African American Identity Development*, (3) *African American Children, Youth and Parenting*, and (4) *Advances in African American Psychology*. In several instances, especially for the present volume, I solicited additional chapters in order to present a broad view of the subject, but even with additions, the volumes do not comprehensively cover the subject represented by the title. Rather, individual chapters, while part of a whole, are meant to stand alone as representative of some of the best thinking on the subject now available.

The present volume is unique in at least two respects: its attention to Afrocentric perspectives, and its focus on intervention techniques and approaches. Some of the work reported herein was conceptualized more than a decade ago and has been updated and refined. Other work is of relatively recent origin. Whether old or new, however, virtually all contributions reported herein represent fresh and forward thinking approaches to the definition of psychological health for African Americans, substantive research and perspectives that bear on African American mental health, and innovative and sometimes controversial approaches to psychotherapeutic intervention. Some very traditional approaches (i.e., psycho-pharmacology and behavior modification) are presented and evaluated alongside interventions thought to be uniquely appropriate for African Americans (for example, a cognospiritual model of psychotherapy and special techniques for families and black males). Controversial topics (psychoanalytic psychotherapy with African American clients and Rootwork and Voodoo in diagnosis and treatment) are also included. Because questions have been raised about their efficacy for African American clients, scholars and practitioners of diverse orientations have been invited to respond to these chapters. Each author of the focal chapter then responds to the critiques. A rich mixture of perspective and points of view come out of these interchanges and will be invaluable for those who wish to be informed about psychoanalytic psychotherapy and Rootwork and Voodoo with African American clients.

I am indebted to a number of individuals who made completion of this volume possible. First are the chapter authors. These talented and creative scholars and practitioners are helping to break the chains of Eurocentric hegemony in psychology by developing fresh theories, analyses, constructs and interventions that are especially suited for understanding and addressing the mental health needs of African Americans. Completion of the volume was also facilitated by the assistance of Drs. Faheem Ashanti, Aubrey Escoffery, Howard King, Jacqueline Mattis, Linda James Myers and Daryl Rowe who provided critical evaluation of individual chapters. Every chapter they reviewed has been improved as a result of their input and suggestions. Katasha Harley, Michelle Lacy, and Elise Vestal were most competent in maintaining contact with authors, keeping records, and word processing. Figures and tables were ably prepared with the assistance of Jan Miller Graphics, and proofreading was done with competence and care by Carol Brooks and Pamela Reilly. Final preparation of the manuscript for printing was handled by Wesley Kittling, computer expert and wizard. All of the aforementioned persons were indispensable in completing this book and I am most grateful to them for their assistance. Finally, I express my love and appreciation for the support of my wife, Michele, for her patience and understanding as I took time from our personal lives to complete yet another project.

Reginald Jones,
Hampton, VA

Contributors

Na'im Akbar, Ph.D.
Research Assistant in Clinical Psychology, Florida State University and Executive Director, Mind Productions and Associates, Inc., Tallahassee, Florida

Norman B. Anderson, Ph.D.
Director, Office of Behavioral and Social Science, National Institutes of Health, Bethesda, Maryland

Kwabena Faheem Ashanti, Ph.D.
Professor of African American Studies and Counselor, North Carolina State University, Raleigh, North Carolina, Licensed Member of the Ghanaian National Association of Traditional Healers, and African American Rootdoctor

W. Curtis Banks, Ph.D.
Deceased, was Professor, Department of Psychology, Howard University, Washington, DC

Lula Beatty, Ph.D.
Chief, Special Populations Officer, National Institute on Drug Abuse, National Institutes of Health, Bethesda, Maryland

Jacqueline Booth, M.S.
Graduate Student, Department of Psychology, Howard University, Washington, DC

Nancy Boyd-Franklin, Ph.D.
Professor, Graduate School of Applied and Professional Psychology, Rutgers University, Piscataway, New Jersey

Renee Brown
Graduate Student, Department of Psychology, Virginia Tech, Blacksburg, Virginia

Linda Hart Davis, M.S.
Graduate Student, Department of Psychology, Howard University, Washington, DC

Mary Davis
Graduate Student, Department of Psychology, Virginia Tech, Blacksburg, Virginia

Karen Lenore Edwards, Ph.D.
Associate Professor, Department of Psychology, Coordinator, Multi-Ethnic/Cross-Cultural Psychological Services, Psychological Services Center, University of Cincinnati, Cincinnati, Ohio

Anderson J. Franklin, Ph.D.
Professor, Ph.D. Program in Clinical Psychology, The City College and Graduate School of the City University of New York.

Bernadette Jeffrey Fletcher, Ph.D.
Assistant Professor, University of Pittsburgh, Pittsburgh, Pennsylvania

W. Henry Gregory, M.A.
Clinical Director, Progressive Life Center, Washington, DC

Cheryl Grills, Ph.D.
Associate Professor, Department of Psychology, Loyola Marymount University, Los Angeles, California

Maisha Hamilton-Bennett, Ph.D.
President and CEO, Hamilton Wholistic Health Care, Ltd., Chicago, Illinois

Jules P. Harrell, Ph.D.
Professor, Department of Psychology, Howard University, Washington, DC

Sherlyn Harrison
Department of Psychology in Education, University of Pittsburgh, Pennsylvania

Huberta Jackson-Lowman, Ph.D.
Assistant Professor, Department of Psychology, Florida A & M University, Tallahassee, Florida

Rossell Jeffries
Graduate Student, Department of Psychology, Virginia Tech, Blacksburg, Virginia

Adelbert Jenkins, Ph.D.
Associate Professor, Department of Psychology, New York University, New York, New York

Arthur C. Jones, Ph.D.
Senior Clinical Professor of Psychology, University of Denver, Denver, Colorado

Enrico E. Jones, Ph.D.
Professor, Department of Psychology, University of California, Berkeley; Faculty, San Francisco Psychoanalytic Institute; and Private Practice, Berkeley, California

Reginald L. Jones, Ph.D.
Distinguished Professor of Psychology, Hampton University, Hampton, Virginia; and Professor Emeritus, University of California, Berkeley, Berkeley, California.

Russell T. Jones, Ph.D.
Professor, Department of Psychology, Virginia Tech, Blacksburg, Virginia

Jimalee Kalu
Graduate Student, Department of Psychology, University of Virginia, Charlottesville, Virginia

Kobi K. K. Kambon, Ph.D. (a.k.a. Joseph A. Baldwin)
Professor and Chairman, Department of Psychology, Florida A & M University, Tallahassee, Florida

S. M. Khatib, Ph.D.
State University of New York at New Paltz, New Paltz, New York

Howard King, Ph.D.
Assistant Professor, Department of Psychology, Hampton University, Hampton, Virginia

William B. Lawson, Ph.D., M.D.
Chief, Roudebush VAMC, Psychiatric Service, Indianapolis, Indiana

Jacqueline S. Mattis, Ph.D.
Assistant Professor of Psychology and Women's Studies, University of Michigan, Ann Arbor, Michigan

Marcellus M. Merritt, Ph.D.
Postdoctoral Fellow, Duke University Medical School, Durham, North Carolina

Carolyn B. Murray, Ph.D.
Associate Professor, Department of Psychology, and Principal Investigator, African American Family Research Project, University of California, Riverside, Riverside, California

Hector F. Myers, Ph.D.
Professor of Psychology, University of California, Los Angeles (UCLA), and Director, Biobehavioral Research Center, Charles R. Drew University of Medicine and Science, Los Angeles, California

Chioma Obiechina
Graduate Student, University of Pittsburgh, Pittsburgh, Pennsylvania

Frederick B. Phillips, Psy.D.
President, Progressive Life Center, Inc., Washington, DC

Jerilyn Pope, B.S.
Student, Department of Psychology, Howard University, Washington, DC

Howard P. Ramseur, Ph.D.
Psychologist, Psychiatry Service of the Medical Department, Massachusetts Institute of Technology, and Private Practitioner, Cambridge, Massachusetts

John A. Rogers, Ph.D.
Director of Extension Services, Center for Family Excellence, Inc., Pittsburgh, Pennsylvania

Daryl Rowe, Ph.D.
Associate Professor, Pepperdine University, Culver City, California

Uma Shenoy
Graduate Student, University of Pittsburgh, Pittsburgh, Pennsylvania

Tony L. Strickland, Ph.D.
Associate Director, Biobehavioral Laboratory and Associate Professor, Department of Psychiatry and Human Behavior, Charles R. Drew University of Medicine and Science, Los Angeles, California

Jerome Taylor, Ph.D.
Director, Center for Family Excellence, Pittsburgh, Pennsylvania

Cheryl J. Thompson, Ph.D.
Associate Professor, Clinical Psychology, Seton Hall University, South Orange, New Jersey

Samuel M. Turner, Ph.D.
Professor, Department of Psychiatry and Behavioral Sciences, and Director, Anxiety Prevention and Treatment Research Center, Medical University of South Carolina, Charleston, South Carolina

African American Mental Health: Introduction and Overview

Reginald L. Jones

The present volume, *African American Mental Health*, is one of several books on the subject that has been written during the past two decades. Enrico Jones and the late Sheldon Korchin edited *Minority Mental Health* (1982), a volume that contained many important insights into African American mental health in the areas of theory, research and intervention. However, only a few of the book's fourteen chapters focused specifically on African American mental health issues. In discussing the rationale undergirding their book, Jones and Korchin indicated that the cross-cultural perspective was adopted because this perspective "views the behavior and problems of minority persons as expressions of their history and life conditions that can be best understood in terms of the customs and values of each of their cultures in a pluralistic society." The present volume embraces a similar view but focuses solely upon African Americans. My belief is that if we are to understand mental health research and intervention with African Americans, then African Americans must be the focus of our theories, research, and intervention strategies.

Three more recent volumes are also noteworthy. The first, edited by Dorothy Ruiz (1990) (*Handbook of Mental Health and Mental Disorder Among Black Americans*), includes chapters devoted to epidemiology, research and mental health, legal and policy issues, definitions of positive mental health for African Americans, and psychiatric diagnosis and treatment, among other topics. Unlike the present volume, however, the many valuable and insightful chapters in Ruiz's volume rarely address intervention approaches and strategies directly. Willie, Rieker, Kramer, and Brown (1995) edited a volume entitled *Mental Health, Racism, and Sexism,* and while this volume includes many generic and provocative chapters, no chapter addresses specific treatment or psychotherapeutic interventions with African Americans.

Neighbors and Jackson (1996) edited *Mental Health in Black America*, a volume of empirical studies on the emotional and psychological well-being of adult African Americans. The book is unique in that all chapters are based on statistical analysis of data in a single study, the National Survey of Black Americans (NSBA). NSBA is a national probability household survey of non-institutionalized African

Americans. In describing the contents of the book, Neighbors and Jackson write: "...this is a book that details the self-reported stress of being Black in America while at the same time documenting the cultural resources African Americans draw on to overcome adversity and maintain a positive, healthy perspective on life." The focus of the book is "on the social and psychological correlates of coping with serious personal problems, the distribution of psychological distress, and help-seeking, including the use of special mental health care, general medical care, and informal social support networks" (p. xii). Like the other books noted, this volume is an important contribution to developing and revisionist thinking about African American mental health. In addition to the edited volumes noted, many theoretical and empirical articles and chapters that addresses African American mental health issues have also been written. Many of these writings are summarized by authors of individual chapters in the present volume.

African American Mental Health presents up-to-date treatment of some of the areas covered in the aforementioned volumes but departs from them in at least two respects: (1) its introduction of Afrocentric approaches to the mental health of African Americans; and (2) its emphasis upon therapeutic intervention from a wide variety of perspectives. While there are a plethora of theories, paradigms, perspectives, perceptions, admonitions and orientations to mental health intervention with African Americans, few examples are found in the literature which show, through case studies, how these ideas are implemented in actual clinical practice. A noteworthy feature of the present volume is that specific approaches to treatment that derive from many of the perspectives and paradigms presented in early chapters of the book are described; 19 chapters are devoted to actual interventions or critique and evaluation of case studies and intervention approaches. The 30 chapters included in this volume represent a rich mixture of theory, research and practice. Existing literature on important mental health topics is summarized, new concepts and conceptualizations are highlighted, and controversial and promising therapeutic interventions are reviewed, evaluated, and illustrated through use of vignettes and case studies.

The book is organized around six parts that move from theory and research to intervention. An overview of each chapter is presented below.

Part I. Perspectives and Paradigms

Four chapters are included in *Part 1* that presents perspectives and paradigms related to African American mental health. While some of the authors in *Part 1* draw upon mainstream literature in advancing their formulations, for most authors mainstream views are simply a point of departure for understanding and defining African American mental health from diverse and expanded perspectives, with a focus upon Afrocentric ideas.

In the first chapter, Ramseur ("Psychologically Healthy African American Adults") reviews theory and research on psychological health among African American adults by discussing the social/cultural situation of Black Americans, "universal" models of psychological health, and theories of Black personality and identity that have psychological health implications. Ramseur then turns to empirical research and associated theorizing in areas that have been linked to African American's mental health and, finally, examines the implications of recent theory and empirical research for creating models of African American adult psychological health.

While Ramseur draws upon mainstream literature and the work of African American scholars in developing his views on psychologically healthy African Americans, Kambon, Jackson-Lowman, and Grills and Rowe advance a more patently Africentric approach. Kambon ("An African-Centered Paradigm for Understanding the Mental Health of African Americans") proposes an African-centered paradigm of African mental health "that is not only applicable to the American context of Africans, but also to the Continental African context where Eurasian cultural domination prevails there as well as throughout the Diaspora." Using the American context as the prototype for the African psycho-cultural condition of oppression, Kambon articulates the "normal-natural" condition of African personality and the adverse impact of Eurasian cultural oppression on distorting its natural psychodynamics. Kambon continues his discussion by proposing Africentric nosology which addresses the appropriate reconceptualization of this phenomenon which is intended to "challenge the African world community to reconceptualize its standards of normalcy ...."

Using three questions posed by Frantz Fanon—Who am I? Am I really who I am? Am I all I ought to be?—Jackson-Lowman ("Sankofa: A Black Mental Health Imperative for the 21st Century") offers an Afrikan-centered analysis of the importance of the issues of identity, authenticity, and purpose for the retrieval of Black mental health. Jackson-Lowman believes that these questions direct us to the fundamental ground from which the traditional Afrikan worldview emerges, the spiritual nature of all life, and provide the framework for the development of models of mental health for Afrikan people which must embrace our spiritual and communal nature. Finally, the author expands upon her view that rituals, beginning prenatally and continuing to death, are integral to the cultivation and expression of each person's unique purpose within family, community, and society.

The major premise of Grills and Rowe's chapter ("African Traditional Medicine: Implications for African-Centered Approaches to Healing") is that traditional African medicine and science can serve as the basis for understanding African American mental health. Support for this view is provided through a brief examination of the limitations of theoretical frameworks emergent from the accumulated cultural patterns of Europeans juxtaposed against the cultural origins of African Americans. The authors present ethnographic information on traditional

African healing paradigms (and classifications of healers from four African countries which may have psychological importance for African Americans) and provide a brief discussion of the role of divination as a method for discerning both the nature of afflictions and strategies for restoring health in traditional and contemporary African social systems. Lastly, Grills and Rowe provide information on African conceptualizations of what it means to be human. They also discuss the need for African psychologists to engage in psycho-historical research on Kemetic, Western, Central, Eastern, and Southern African conceptions of health and systems of healing and their transformations throughout the world in order to delineate a more authentic and historically valid framework for apprehending an African-centered psychology.

Taken as a whole, the four chapters in *Part I* broaden our conception of African American mental health. Considerable support is presented for an expanded definition of African American mental health that includes self-esteem and racial identity, the social/cultural context of African Americans, including adapting to racism, and coping resources and styles. Moreover, the promise of Afrocentric approaches to African American mental health, including insights from traditional African medicine, is highlighted.

Part II. Spirituality and Mental Health

As is apparent in *Part I* and as will be noted in a number of chapters throughout this volume, spirituality is believed to be an important dimension of African American mental health. Spirituality and its relationship to African American mental health is explicated in chapters by Rogers and Fletcher in *Part II*. Rogers ("Spirituality: Questing for Well-Being") observes that the connection between the practical application of psychology and the study of human spirituality in relation to the historical and holistic liberation of African Americans is the foundational human questing for well-*being*. Rogers believes that it is insufficient to focus on psychological dynamics without concern for the spiritual ground from which they emerge. This "spiritual ground," from the human side, is a mix of ontological and existential realities that are constituents of human *being*-becoming. For African Americans, this mix compromises the distinctively human questing for well-*being* that has been circumscribed historically by racial oppression-discrimination. The consequence of this circumscribing is the exacerbating of our distinctively human suffering. However, because suffering and *being* are inextricable, suffering provides the gateway for well-*being*. Rogers explores the latter premise through the lens of the historical oppression of African Americans, with a view toward both individual liberation and societal transformation.

Fletcher ("Spirituality, Grieving and Mental Well-Being") further expands upon the relationship between spirituality and mental health by developing her thesis that mental well-being results when persons live in spiritual harmony with the one Creator-God, with the Creator-God's life-force in creation, and with all humanity. For Fletcher, mental well-being extends beyond the physical and principally connects people at a deeper level that, in essence, represents our spirituality. It is a position of balance and harmony of mental, physical, and spiritual aspects of human nature realized ideally through beneficent human interactions in all realms of social existence. This harmonious spiritual dynamic, Fletcher believes, is the foundation of the human experience of community and underpins mental well-being.

Part III. Self Concept

Most conceptions of positive mental health include self-concept as one of the cornerstones of its definition. Important perspectives on the self concept are presented in *Part III*. In the first chapter in this section, "Black Self-Concept Revisited," the late Curtis Banks and his colleagues draw revisionist conclusions from their analysis of more than sixty published reports of research using self report and preference methods, while Jenkins ("The Self Concept in the Psychology of African Americans") presents a humanistic psychological view of the self concept in African Americans that emphasizes the active and "dialectical" intentionality of human beings and relates these ideas to treatment and other matters.

In the final chapter of *Part III* ("Competency and Legitimacy as Organizing Dimensions of the Black Self Concept"), Khatib and Murray place discussion of African American "self-concept" in a comprehensive theoretical framework. They identify *"competency"* and *"legitimacy"* as major dimensions of the self which they view as opposite sides of the same coin, in much the same way as light is viewed as both a particle and a wave. Khatib and Murray pay considerable attention to the "legitimacy" aspect of the African American self, since they believe this has revealed itself as a dominant theme in African American creative writing that has not received as much attention as the competency component. Finally, Khatib and Murray identify potential research questions concerning the legitimacy aspect of the African American self-concept they believe need to be addressed.

Part IV. Stress and Hypertension

Research and perspectives on stress and hypertension are presented in *Part IV*. A comprehensive biobehavioral perspective developed by Myers and his colleagues and Harrell and his associates' conceptualization and review of research on the relationship among racism, stress and disease comprise the two chapters in this section.

Myers, Anderson, and Strickland ("A Biobehavioral Perspective for Research on Stress and Hypertension in African American Adults: Theoretical and Empirical Issues") review and discuss the empirical evidence for biological and psychosocial differences in the possible causes, course, and outcome of hypertensive disease in African Americans and Whites, outline the basic rationale for an integrative, multi-domain, biobehavioral perspective for research on hypertension and the basic components of such a model, and present a brief review of current biobehavioral research addressing the question of African American-White differences in cardio-vascular functioning. Finally, the authors discuss new research directions, and the implications of their findings for improving the health status of African Americans.

In a complementary chapter ("Racism, Stress, and Disease"), Harrell, Merritt, and Kalu survey research and laboratory studies and review two lines of evidence related to the effects of racism and stress on disease among African Americans. They report that the survey research evidence shows personality variables and situational contexts moderate the symptoms African Americans display in racist environments and that laboratory studies support this finding and also demonstrate that gender and personality variables influence the manner in which African Americans respond to psychological stressors in the laboratory.

Part V. Therapeutic Interventions

African American scholars and practitioners are forging psychotherapeutic interventions that are designed to be uniquely appropriate for African American clients and they are also critically evaluating conventional intervention approaches. Innovative approaches to prevention and psychotherapeutic intervention and critical evaluation of selected approaches for their appropriateness with African American clients are presented in *Part V.*

The chapter by Taylor and his colleagues ("Toward a Psychology of Liberation and Restoration: Answering the Challenge of Cultural Alienation") is noteworthy for its focus upon activities that reduce cultural alienation, thereby preventing potentially serious mental health problems. After documenting negative effects of cultural alienation on Black adults, Black youth, and the Black community, Taylor and his colleagues explore strategies intended to liberate Blacks from White racist stereotypes about African Americans and describe a "post liberation agenda" of discovery, engagement, and maintenance activities intended to restore values which promote quality of individual, familial and communal life among African Americans. The authors conclude by examining the development, research, and policy implications of their proposals.

The use of psychotropic medication is an issue of critical importance in the treatment of African Americans. In an enlightening chapter, Lawson ("Psychophar-macology and African American Mental Health") addresses issues related to the inappropriate use of psychotropic medication with African Americans, failure to address cultural considerations in developing medication regimens, and needs for provider and patient education, policy changes, and research on minority patients.

Boyd-Franklin ("A Multisystems Approach to Home and Community Based Interventions with African American Poor Families") presents a multisystems model of home and community based interventions with African American families. Boyd-Franklin notes this is a problem solving approach that allows the therapist to intervene at multiple systemic levels, and is particularly effective with poor, urban families who are experiencing many concrete problems. Boyd-Franklin describes the Rutgers Counseling Project in order to provide examples of application of this model to high risk African American adolescents and their families.

Treatment approaches that have spirituality as a base are the focus of chapters by Edwards and Phillips. Edwards ("A Cognospiritual Model of Psychotherapy") observes that American Psychology "has been fairly consistent in veering away from or minimizing the role of religion/spirituality in addressing the psychological and emotional needs of Blacks in a therapeutic modality" and that "little has been done in applying the notion of spirituality as a power enhancing strategy." Edwards describes a cognospiritual model that combines Jungian and cognitive therapies with Black spirituality as a component of an Afrocentric worldview and the symbolic interactionist notion of "defining situations" to create an orientation which addresses both the spiritual and political/environmental aspects of psychotherapy with African Americans and other oppressed people.

Phillips' approach ("Spirit Energy and NTU Psychotherapy") is rooted in the traditional African philosophy. Phillips reminds us that African philosophy has a singular appreciation of the harmony of life which also undergirds the NTU perspective of force and matter, body and mind, being an integrated whole. This force/matter, known in NTU as spirit-energy, becomes the operational framework through which the therapist-healer both understands and facilitates the healing process. Phillips indicates the goal of NTU psychotherapy is to assist the client system in realignment of their spirit-energy toward a more authentic and healthier process of being within the principles of Nguzo Saba and MAAT. Phillips presents case studies that describe and illuminate NTU principles.

A framework for understanding the psychological issues faced by upwardly mobile African American adults as they struggle to attain an authentic personal identity to accompany their economic success is the focus of Arthur C. Jones' chapter ("Upwardly Mobile African American Adults: Reflections on Rootedness, Psychotherapy and Identity"). Jones suggests that rootedness in African American culture is an important buffer against the personal alienation and emptiness that is often associated with an economic achievement ethic which is not grounded in cultural and spiritual integrity. Jones reviews three recent books by African American authors in order to sketch the specific outlines of the kind of psychological and spiritual grounding which is effective in forging an authentic "success" and discusses lines of future psychological inquiry in this area.

In " Invisibility Syndrome in Psychotherapy with African American Males," Franklin advances the thesis that psychological invisibility, a set of broad personal experiences of not being recognized except when considered threatening, is a significant mental health stressor for Black men. The racial slights experienced by African American men and women as part of everyday racism force each into adaptive behaviors to manage feelings of marginality, confusion, and disillusionment. When personal efforts to counteract this stress fail, dysfunctional behavior emerges as an invisibility syndrome of clustering symptoms such as chronic indignation and internalized rage. Racial identity development is seen as one way to neutralize the effects of invisibility and the toll upon the psychological well being of Black men. Finally, Franklin discusses therapy as an option Black men can use in managing stress related to the invisibility syndrome.

Behavior therapy with African American clients is the focus of the chapter by Russell Jones and his colleagues ("African Americans in Behavior Therapy and Research: The Need for Cultural Consideration"). The authors examine the representativeness of African Americans in behavioral research and therapy, discuss the adequacy of the behavioral and cognitive behavioral conceptualizations for African Americans, review practices related to assessment, treatment and process issues, followed by a discussion of the implications of such practices. Finally, the authors present guidelines to achieve increased participation of African Americans in research and therapy, and chart future directions for research and intervention activities.

Part VI. Symposia on Psychotherapeutic Interventions

Psychoanalytic psychotherapy and Rootwork and Voodoo are therapeutic approaches for treating the mental health problems of African Americans that do not enjoy wide currency among scholars and practitioners, despite the fact that many professionals utilize psychoanalytic concepts in whole or in part in their clinical practices, and in spite of the fact that thousands of individuals in this country believe in Rootwork and Voodoo phenomena. The purpose of this section of the book is to bring these approaches under the spotlight in order to inform scholars and practitioners of their strengths and limitations as potential interventions with African American clients.

The rationale underlying psychoanalytic psychotherapy and Rootwork and Voodoo and case studies illustrating their application with African American clients are presented in *Part VI*. Because these approaches are controversial as potential psychotherapeutic interventions with African American clients, scholars/ practitioners of diverse orientation and persuasion have been invited to respond to papers written by prominent practitioners of psychoanalytic psychotherapy and Rootwork and Voodoo with African American patients.

The focal papers were written by Cheryl Thompson ("Does Insight Serve a Purpose: The Value of Psychoanalytic Psychotherapy with Diverse African American Patients") and by Faheem C. Ashanti ("Rootwork and Voodoo in the Diagnosis and Treatment of African American Patients). The purpose of Thompson's chapter is to present to readers issues that are significant in psychoanalytic psychotherapy with African American patients. Thompson makes a case for the usefulness of psychoanalytic psychotherapy with African American patients and demonstrates how entanglements of racial and neurotic issues impact Black patients in psychotherapy. Thompson presents two case studies that explicate the value of psychoanalytic psychotherapy with African Americans. Four clinicians respond to Thompson's chapter, two of whom share her psychoanalytic perspective (Enrico Jones and W. Henry Gregory) and two who have different clinical orientations (Howard King and Maisha Hamilton-Bennett).

Enrico Jones ("Psychoanalysis and African Americans"), in the first response to Thompson, presents his belief that the value of psychoanalytic treatment as a means for empowering African American patients has been underestimated and that psychoanalysis has been wrongly cast as locating the source of problems only in the individual rather than in societal inequities. Enrico Jones argues that psychoanalysis offers a compelling conceptual framework for understanding and treating many of the psychological problems experienced by African Americans and that psychoanalytically oriented treatments are uniquely suited to address the role of trauma and the experience of racism in the etiology of the emotional problems of African Americans, as well as the difficulties in self-definition that many Black Americans experience.

According to Gregory ("Psychoanalysis into the 21st Century"), the key to optimal mental health is flexible negotiation of the change process. Gregory encourages psychoanalytic psychotherapy to evolve so that it can accommodate the needs and processing styles of diverse populations into the next century. He suggests a pluralist approach that encourages the use of psychoanalytic psychotherapy as part of a continuum of treatment and he recommends the adoption of a more positive view of human nature that supports competency as opposed to the classic view that reinforces pathology.

King and Hamilton-Bennett are not sympathetic to Thompson's approach. In his response to Thompson, King ("The Expansion of Psychoanalytic/Insight Therapy to be More Effective with Diverse African Americans: Africentrism/ DCT)" attempts to address whether or not insight serves a purpose. After questioning psychoanalysis as an approach that is truly applicable to diverse African American groups, he presents an approach he believes is applicable to African Americans despite age, socioeconomic status, whether therapy is individual or family, and whether or not the client is capable of utilizing insight based on the cognitive developmental orientation(s) from which they are operating.

In her response, Hamilton-Bennett ("Healing the African American Collective Requires More than the Psychoanalysis of Individuals)" sees the strengths of Thompson's paper to be the significance which she attaches to the legacy of slavery in explaining interracial relationships in this country, including client/therapist relationships, her assertion that African Americans have a critical need for self definition, cathartic healing, correct insights, and strategic, purposeful use of time; and her optimism that positive changes are possible. However, Hamilton-Bennett challenges Thompson's proposition that psychoanalysis is a highly desirable model for African American clients. She sees the deficiencies of psychoanalysis to derive from its focus on the needs and wants of individuals rather than on the best interests of the group, the length of time that it typically takes to yield limited results, and the fact that there are culturally specific, wholistic models of intervention available which are far more effective with African Americans.

The second focal chapter is by Ashanti ("Rootwork and Voodoo in the Diagnosis and Treatment of Africans"). His coverage includes discussion of Africentric conceptualization of illness, features of African traditional religion, description of symptoms of Voodoo and Rootwork Syndrome, and assessment and treatment procedures.

In the first response to Ashanti's chapter, Akbar ("The Dilemma of Double Consciousness: Understanding Voodoo from An European Perspective") raises important issues about the difficulty of engaging in such a discussion within a Eurocentric paradigm. Akbar invokes the classical dictum by Dr. W.E.B. DuBois regarding the double consciousness of being both African and American and he also raises a question as to whether it is possible to discuss a reality that either does not exist or exists only as a derogatory fact in the thinking of a European paradigm. Finally, Akbar discusses the importance of non-Western scholars taking on the task of describing the reality of their indigenous cultures in a proactive way.

Turner ("The Role of Possession and Other Spiritual Phenomena in Understanding Psychopathological States: Comments on Ashanti") believes that Ashanti's writings serve to: (1) highlight the failure of modern psychology to address the study of powerful cultural belief patterns and the role they play in shaping human behavior; (2) the need for research in this area; and (3) the need to train practitioners who are informed and acquainted with these issues. Turner also provides commentary on Ashanti's thesis and identifies a number of areas in need of conceptual clarity.

In a final response to Ashanti, Mattis ("Bridging Spirituality and Psychotherapy") reminds us that in the academy, discussions of spirituality are often mired in misrepresentations and misunderstandings. The topic of spirituality, particularly of such spiritual healing traditions as Rootwork and Voodoo, induces images of chaotic mysticism and anxieties about evil and malevolence. Given these misrepresentations, Mattis believes it is crucial that any discussion of Rootwork and Voodoo be contextualized. Four points of context are addressed in her response: First, her response is situated in a broad discussion about spirituality. Second, Mattis examines scholarly treatments of Rootwork and Voodoo in the context of the rupture between "spirituality" and psychology. Third, she gives attention to the functional significance of Rootwork and Voodoo as an ethnomedical tradition. Finally, Mattis' response raises what she believes are crucial considerations for psychotherapists who work with victims of Rootwork syndrome and Voodoo poisoning.

Ashanti ("Taking Back Your Mind and Health: A Reaction Paper") responds to the critiques of his chapter that were offered by Akbar, Mattis and Turner. He takes issue with Akbar's application of DuBois' "Double Consciousness" to African Americans, addresses questions stimulated by Turner and Mattis and, finally, recommends strategies for encouraging training and research in African traditional healing.

References

Jones, E., & Korchin, S. J. (Eds.). (1982). *Minority mental health*. New York: Praeger Publishers.

Neighbors, H. & Jackson, J. S. (1996). *Mental health in Black America*. Newbury Park, CA: Sage.

Ruiz, D. S. (Ed.). (1990). *Handbook of mental health and mental disorder among Black Americans*. New York: Greenwood Press.

Willie, C. V., Rieker, P. R., Kramer, B. M. & Brown, B. S. (Eds.). (1995). *Mental health, racism and sexism*. Pittsburgh: University of Pittsburgh Press.

Author

Reginald L. Jones
1 Sutton Place
Hampton, VA 23666
Telephone: (757) 838-1980
Fax: (757) 827-1060
E-mail: CobbHenry@aol.com

Part 1

Perspectives and Paradigms

Psychologically Healthy African American Adults

Howard P. Ramseur

> . . . the Negro has no possible basis for a healthy self-esteem and every incentive for self-hatred (A. Kardiner and L. Ovesey, *The Mark of Oppression,* 1951, p. 297).

> . . . the experience of being Black in a society dominated by Whites does *not,* as is sometimes incorrectly assumed, lead to deep and corrosive personal demoralization. Blacks live with greater stress, but they have the personal and social resources to maintain a perspective which keeps the stress external, does not permit it to become internalized or to disrupt personal integration (J. Veroff, E. Douvan and R. A. Kulka, *The Inner American,* 1981, p. 437)

Overview

What are the psychological and social characteristics of psychologically healthy African American adults? How do these characteristics develop and change over the life cycle? Until now these significant questions have not been comprehensively addressed. They have not been addressed partly because of the lack of consensus and conceptual clarity in the literature about what represents "psychological health" or "healthy development" for adults, African American or White. In addition, the idea that African American adults could be psychologically healthy, however defined, is one that mainstream social scientists and much of the lay public would find unacceptable. The vast literature on African Americans in psychology, sociology, social work, and psychiatry converges on the assumptions embodied in the quote from Kardiner and Ovesey (1951) above. That is, given the social and cultural conditions under which African Americans live, psychological health is an impossibility.

The 1960s and 1970s saw theoretical and empirical challenges to mainstream social science theories, particularly to their predictions that African American adults were self-hating or had self-esteem lower than White Americans. Recently, some social scientists have moved beyond the mainstream view, or simply challeng-

3

ing it, have begun to focus on specific aspects of psychological functioning or development that have been defined as healthy, e.g., high self-esteem, positive racial identity, or adaptive coping styles. While a number of interesting empirical findings have emerged, little general theorizing about African American adult psychological health over the life cycle, or about the implications of these findings for psychological treatment, has occurred.

In this chapter I will review theory and research on psychological health among African American adults by discussing the social/cultural situation of African Americans, "universal" models of psychological health, and theories of African American personality and identity that have psychological health implications. I will then turn to empirical research and associated theorizing in three areas that have been linked to African American psychological health: self-conception (self-esteem and racial identity), the "competent" personality, and African American coping resources and styles. Finally, I will examine the implications of recent theory and empirical research for creating models of African American adult psychological health and for future research.

Models of Psychological Health

How should psychological health be defined? How does it change over the adult life cycle? No theory or model of adult psychological health has achieved a consensus or accumulated a convincing body of empirical evidence to address these questions. In addition, while existing models of psychological health claim to be "universal," that is applicable and explanatory for all persons, in fact, they usually have little or nothing to say about the unique social/cultural circumstances of African Americans and the impact of such circumstances on African American adult psychological health. Existing theories of African American adult psychological health will be reviewed by focusing on the unique social/cultural situation of African Americans and the issues that it raises, and by examining the two existing bodies of theory: "universal" models of psychological health and models of African American personality and identity.

The Social/Cultural Context of African Americans

African American adults must live and adapt to a unique social and cultural environment as well as history in the United States. That environment and the necessity that they adapt to it has implications for any model that claims to define and understand psychological health for African American adults. Certain issues seem important in characterizing the aspects of that environment that are relevant to psychological health: White racism, the need to adapt to White institutions and culture, adapting to the African American community—family, institutions, and culture, and coping with poverty and political powerlessness (see Barbarin, 1983; Cross, 1984; Gary & Weaver, 1991; J. Jones, 1991, 1996; Pierce, 1974; for extended discussions).

Pierce (1974) argues that the overriding psychiatric (psychological) problem for African Americans is the "withering effect of racism" (p. 512). Jones (1991, 1996) and Pierce have extensive discussions of racism and its impact on African Americans and their community. While Pierce defines White racism as behavior that results from the attitude that White skin (and Whites) are always superior to Black skin (and African Americans), Jones has a more detailed discussion of the different levels of racism: individual, institutional and cultural. For Jones, individual racism refers to individual acts of discrimination or violence and attitudes of prejudice and paternalism that grow out of a belief in the genetic inferiority of African Americans to Whites. Institutional racism refers to institutional patterns of resource allocation, entry, expectation, or outcome—that consistently lead to different and more negative status for African Americans than for Whites. Cultural racism refers to the ideologies and values that undergird the other forms of racism; racist values that are perpetuated by the mass media, schools, and churches. While Jones and other writers emphasize different themes, three key racist cultural themes emerge from a survey of the literature: (1) African Americans as unattractive and not socially valuable; (2) African Americans as unable to be effective in the world: unable to achieve, to effectively manage people or events, unable to compete with Whites; and (3) what Pettigrew (1964) calls Id-oriented stereotypes—African Americans as sexually and aggressively impulsive and uncontrolled. These, then, may be key cultural themes of racism to which the African American individual (and community) are forced to adapt.

Most African Americans must adapt to both the African American community and its culture as well as White American culture and institutions. While most African Americans live, have families, social friends and churches within the African American community, they still must adapt to White-run schools, workplaces, military settings, and media; an adaptation that often requires them to juggle different values, behavioral styles and aspirations. This situation has led some social scientists to postulate that many African Americans become bicultural; i.e., able to function in both cultures. There is another aspect of social reality that African Americans must adapt to as well. Cross (1984) exhaustively documents a family poverty rate and an adult unemployment rate for African Americans that are double those for Whites. He notes the family income and wealth gap and lower access to quality medical and other social services that African Americans suffer from as well. Cross also demonstrates the continuing relative political and economic powerlessness of African Americans and the African American community. He links these social conditions to the historic and current discrimination and institutional racism that he sees as continuing constraints and frustrations for African Americans. [Barbarin (1983) points out that these social conditions mean more stressors for African Americans and fewer resources than Whites have to cope with them.]

In summary, African American adults must adapt to racism in its different variants—African American and White cultures, poverty, and political powerlessness. They often have the support of African American families and friends, the African American community and its institutions, and African American culture in their attempts to successfully adapt. Which psychosocial issues and conflicts are the central ones they must adapt to, given the social/cultural context, and which psychosocial characteristics are "adaptive" or "healthy" for African American adults are questions any adequate model of African American adult psychological health must address.

"Universal" Models of Psychological Health

What do existing "universal" models of psychological health contribute to an understanding of African American adult psychological health? This review of existing models will utilize the work of George and Brooker (1984), who analyzed conceptions of psychological health and came up with four categories that grouped them. Modifying their format by drawing on the work of Lazarus (1975) yields six categories which will be used to organize a brief discussion of existing universal models of psychological health. The categories are: (1) freedom from illness; (2) being average; (3) an ideal personality type; (4) using multiple criteria to determine psychological health; (5) a developmental/life-span perspective; and (6) a stress/adaptation approach.

Freedom from symptoms or illness is the most medical model of psychological health. Health is the absence of illness, and implicitly the ability to function adequately. This model has been characterized as inadequate by theorists like Maslow (1968) who stress the importance of "positive" characteristics like creativity, "growth," and self-actualization in healthy psychological functioning. Psychological health defined as being essentially like the average or "modal" member of society, or being "adjusted" to one's social/cultural surroundings were once common models in the literature. However, both concepts are rarely used now. "Adjustment" seems to evoke conformity and blandness for many theorists, and to be a culture-bound notion that they want to transcend.

The "ideal personality" approach has a number of exponents: Freud (1926) and his concept of the "genital character" and Maslow's (1968) model of the "self-actualizer" are the most widely known. Freud is reputed to have said that the healthy person should be able to "love and work;" that is, to make a balanced commitment to a heterosexual love "object" and productive work. The abilities to have unconflicted sexual and emotional expression and to work productively are expressions of the full maturity of the genital character. The final stage of psychosexual development, the genital stage, is reached by those whose sexual, emotional, and interpersonal development was not damaged and fixated at an earlier psychosexual stage. The genital character is an ideal of balanced psychological forces, functioning, and rationality that is never actually attained by any individual.

Maslow (1968), writing from a humanistic perspective, described a healthy person as a self-actualizer, someone who is moving towards fulfilling (or has fulfilled) their unique human potential. We all have an inherent motivation towards growth or self-actualization, Maslow felt, that would flower if society allowed more primitive needs to be satisfied (e.g., hunger, safety). Maslow investigated the personality characteristics of self-actualizers by reviewing biographies of prominent figures and his friends and drawing up a list of common traits. He arrived at fifteen, ranging from the accurate perception of reality, the ability to be intimate with others, and the capacity to have mystical experiences to creativity. Self-actualizers are rare, and probably should be seen as the Olympic athletes of mental health—if they exist.

Marie Jahoda's (1958) classic discussion of the six themes of "positive mental health" perhaps best represents the "multiple criteria" approach to psychological health. Positive mental health refers to the stance that psychological or mental health is more than the absence of symptoms of mental disorder, it involves the presence of "positive," "healthy" characteristics. Based on the social science literature and discussions with colleagues, she came up with six aspects of the healthy person: (1) positive and realistic attitudes towards the self; (2) growth and self-actualization; (3) integration or a balance of psychological forces and consequently stress resistance; (4) autonomy; (5) accurate perception of reality; and (6) environmental mastery—the ability to love, work, and play, efficiency in problem solving, etc. Jahoda did not specify how, or if, the six criteria are interrelated (see also Taylor and Brown, 1988).

Erik Erikson's (1968) elaboration and extension of Freud's model is probably the most sophisticated example of the developmental/lifespan approach to psychological health. Erikson analyzed the human life cycle in terms of eight different stages of ego development. Each stage is a crisis or turning point that involves a basic psychological issue that can have a healthy or pathological outcome that has implications for the next stage of life. Erikson emphasized the role of social and cultural factors on development, as well as sexual and unconscious ones, and analyzed their impact on personality development over the whole life cycle. He postulated that four stages (of eight) are in adulthood: (V) Ego Identity vs. Role Confusion—where the healthy outcome is identity and role confusion the pathological outcome; (VI) Intimacy vs. Isolation; (VII) Generativity vs. Stagnation; and (VIII) Ego Integrity vs. Despair. Erikson states that the outcome of each of these stages is a dynamic balance with health representing a favorable ratio, not perfection. His work is the basis for much of the recent life-span developmental research focusing on mid-life.

A sizeable amount of literature has developed in recent decades that examines the stress/adaptation model and the links between stress, coping mechanisms, and the level of subjective well-being or distress experienced by an individual or group. Stress has been defined in many ways, but all definitions involve an environmental demand to which the person must react, one that is perceived of as at least potentially exceeding the person's ability or resources to meet it. Coping refers to efforts to master environmental demands when a previous response is unavailable or ineffective. The stressor and the coping response(s) are linked by the cognitive appraisal of the stressor and the internal/external resources of the individual. Cognitive appraisal refers to the significance and meaning attached to the stressor. Internal resources are individual factors; i.e., personality traits, racial identification, and cultural beliefs. External resources refer to family or social ties, work relationships, church affiliation, etc. Outcome refers to either short or long-term psychological distress and symptoms or adaptive behavior and subjective health. The model then is: stressor(s), an appraisal of the stressor(s) and the person's internal/external resources which in turn produces a coping response that leads to an adaptive or distressful outcome. There is also feedback between elements of the model; i.e., the outcome can modify the coping response and/or appraisal of the stressor (Barbarin, 1983; see also Cervantes and Castro, 1985 for extended discussions).

While all existing universal models of psychological health fail to meet the criteria for an ideal model of African American adult psychological health, each has its areas of strength and weakness. "Freedom from symptoms" and "being average" or "adjusted" have the virtues of being straightforward and potentially measurable. However, their atheoretical nature, and their "adjustment," culture-bound stance, limit their usefulness. The "ideal personality" model, especially Freud's genital character, has the asset of being tied to personality theory and more general psychological theories. It also presents a unified, detailed picture of the psychologically healthy adult, and in Freud's case a picture of development and pathology. However, the lack of a social/cultural framework for understanding adult psychological health and the neglect of development(s) during the adult years are real weaknesses. The difficulty in empirically defining and investigating the model as well as the implicit assumption that either no actual adult or very few are psychologically healthy limits its usefulness.

The multiple criteria, developmental, and stress models all seem to be more useful in understanding psychological health among African Americans. The multiple criterion approach specifies that psychological health has a number of definable dimensions that may be related, but may also be independent of one another. Implicit in the approach is the idea that the dimensions are measurable and can be empirically investigated. However, variants of this model are often not tied to theory, don't have a developmental or social/cultural perspective, and don't consider gender differences. Because Erikson discusses the whole life cycle, points to the importance of society and culture, and forges clear links to theory, his developmental approach has a number of strengths. He also points out that psychological health is a matter of a "dynamic balance" or a favorable ratio of positive to negative psychological aspects—not perfection—a useful corrective. Unfortunately, relatively little empirical investigation of his work has occurred. The stress/adaptation model has a number of strengths too: it inherently takes the social/ cultural environment of the person into account, can look at different points in the life cycle, is open to empirical measurement and investigation, and is linked to social/psychological theory. However, generally work based on this model has been focused at the group level of analysis, rather than the individual, so that applying findings to assess or describe a psychologically healthy individual is often difficult.

R. Lazarus (1975), in a comprehensive review of existing models and research on psychological health, makes two observations that are important for a discussion of universal models. First, Lazarus points out a central issue: the role of values. The question of why "autonomy" might be considered an essential characteristic of health and not "creativity," confronts the role that the values of the theorist, investigator, or community play in defining psychological health. Lazarus argues that it is impossible to objectively define "optimal," "effective," or healthy functioning because at least implicit in the discussion is a conception of what is a good or desirable behavior, emotion, or way of life. Lazarus argues that theorists and investigators need to explicitly state their position in this inevitable aspect of describing or defining psychological health and attempt to empirically investigate the consequences of favoring one value over another (e.g., autonomy over creativity). Implicit in his discussion is the question of whose values, or which community's perspective, will determine what are healthy or positive characteristics or functioning. Second, Lazarus addresses the issue of the central characteristics of the psychologically healthy person. He does so by surveying the major theorists and attempting to identify areas of consensus on central characteristics. He identifies five: (1) Acceptance of self; (2) The ability to be intimate with others; (3) Competence (Freud's work); (4) Accurate perception of reality; and (5) Autonomy and independence (pp. 16-18). Relating the social/cultural realities facing the African American individual and the central characteristics of the healthy person listed by Lazarus, it seems clear that the social/cultural context facing the African American individual compromises or renders more difficult attainment of a positive status on Lazarus' characteristics. For example, Lazarus lists acceptance of self and a sense of competence as key aspects of the healthy person. Certainly for African Americans, given their unique social/cultural circumstance and its demands, attaining both is a more complex and problematic enterprise than it is for their White American peers. Unfortunately, existing universal models of psychological health give little guidance in understanding that complex process.

Traditional Theories of African American Personality and Identity

While little direct theorizing or research on the topic of psychological health among African American adults occurred in mainstream social science literature, a substantial literature on African American personality and identity was produced. Given the prevailing assumptions and findings about African American personality or African American identity, little needed to be said about psychological health; rather, the focus was on emotional disorder and social pathology among African Americans. A brief review of mainstream work about African American personality will point out the assumed barriers to African American psychological health more clearly and put recent work in context. The mainstream view of African American personality and identity has a number of variants; but the basic model is that living in a racist White society, where African Americans are viewed and treated as inferior, and where they are in poverty in a powerless community, leads African Americans early in life to internalize negative beliefs and negative feelings about themselves and other African Americans. Explanations of exactly how the internalization occurs and its precise impacts vary with the theoretical orientation of the writer (Kardiner and Ovesey, 1951; Karon, 1958; Pettigrew, 1964; Thomas and Sillen, 1972).

The most influential example of the psychological approach has been Kardiner and Ovesey's *Mark of Oppression* (1951). Kardiner and Ovesey were Freudian psychiatrists whose central idea was that a group of people who live under the same institutional and environmental conditions will have similar mental and emotional processes, or a "basic personality" in common. Since African Americans live under similar caste and social class barriers they should possess a basic personality that differs from that of American Whites. To understand "Black personality," they studied 25 African American New York City residents. Their subjects were psychoanalytically interviewed for 20 to 100 sessions and administered the Rorschach and T.A.T. tests. Male and female as well as lower and middle class African Americans were studied; 12 were patients in psychotherapy, 11 were paid subjects, and two volunteered.

Kardiner and Ovesey concluded that African Americans did have a "basic personality" that was different and more damaged than that of White Americans. African American personality was centrally organized around adapting to social discrimination (racism) they argued. Racist behavior by Whites reveals an unpleasant image of the self to the African American individual who internalizes it and feels worthless, unlovable, and unsuccessful. In essence, he or she feels low self-esteem that eventually is elaborated into self-hatred and idealization of Whites. In addition, the frustrations of racist behavior arouse aggression, which cannot be expressed because of the caste situation, so it must be controlled and contained. Kardiner and Ovesey argued that this repressed aggression usually led to low self-esteem, depression, and passivity.

Grier and Cobbs (1969) used a number of elements of this approach in their discussion of African American psychology in the book *Black Rage*. They seem to differentiate between a male and female basic personality. African American male personality revolves around the control of aggression through repression, passivity, or explosion. The family, particularly mothers, socializes males against the direct expression of aggressiveness in childhood and their social roles in adult life reinforce the lesson. African American women have their feminine narcissism (self-love) wounded because they cannot be the White ideal of femininity; their central concern, therefore, becomes maintaining self-esteem. Grier and Cobbs saw turning away from heterosexual life towards maternal functions or becoming depressed as typical ways African American women cope with this dilemma.

Grier and Cobbs (1969) also developed a model of African American psychological health that they called the *Black Norm*. The *Black Norm* is a body of personality traits that all African Americans share. "It also encompasses adaptive devices developed in response to a peculiar environment," which are seen as "normal devices for making it in America" for African Americans (p. 178). The African American norm consists of cultural paranoia, cultural depression and masochism, and cultural anti-socialism. While providing little detail for their formulations, Grier and Cobbs seem to say that African Americans share a mistrust of Whites as individuals, distrust White society's laws, and have each developed a sadness and an "intimacy with misery" in reaction to racism. Grier and Cobbs say little about variation by age, class, gender, or region in these characteristics, nor do they provide any non-clinical empirical evidence for them.

While the "Mark of Oppression" model and traditional social science approaches have substantial theoretical and empirical support (see Baldwin, Brown, & Hopkins, 1991; McCarthy & Yancey, 1971; Taylor, 1976; for reviews), challenges to them have recently developed. Social scientists have questioned the model's assumptions, noting that given the social and cultural diversity of the African American community, postulating one reaction pattern to racism or one set of personality traits seems unreasonable. Some observers have also noted that the African American family, institutions, and community can serve as mediators of the negative messages from White society (Barnes, 1980) and as sources for alternative frames of reference and significant others for African American children and adults (Taylor, 1976). In addition, African American identity need not be negative or only have an insignificant effect on the psychological functioning or behavior of the African American individual (Cross, 1980).

The most striking challenge to this tradition has been the findings of recent studies that run counter to the predicted personality characteristics of African Americans. In fact, African American children and adults have been shown to have equivalent levels of self-esteem when compared with Whites (see Baldwin, Brown, & Hopkins, 1991; Demo & Parker, 1986; Edwards, 1974; Heiss & Owens, 1972; Jensen, White, & Galliher, 1982; McCarthy & Yancey, 1971; Taylor, 1976; Veroff,

Douvan, & Kulka, 1981; for reviews), and to show no more symptoms, diagnoses of psychopathology, or reported psychological distress (with social class controlled) than Whites (see Neighbors, 1984; Veroff, Douvan, & Kulka, 1981; Yancey, Rigsby, & McCarthy, 1972; for reviews). In addition, the prediction of more repressed aggression or more aggression directed against other African Americans rather than Whites receives only limited support in a brief review of studies by Guterman (1972, pp. 231-233).

"Afrocentric" models of African American personality that have implications for psychological heath and healthy functioning for African Americans are becoming increasingly evident in the literature on psychological health (see e.g., Kambon 1997, [a.k.a. J. A. Baldwin, 1991a, b]; Nobles, 1991). Kambon's Africentric model, perhaps the most representative, conceptualizes the "natural state" of the African personality and how it has been "estranged" from its natural condition under the domination of the European "cultural reality structure." Kambon postulates an African personality with two components: an African self-extension orientation (ASEO) and an African self-consciousness (ASC). The ASEO is innate (biogenetically determined), unconscious, and operationally defined by "Spirituality." The ASC is a conscious level expression or dimension of the ASEO; in part biogenetically determined and in part subject to environmental determination. It directs and guides the personality system (the ASEO). The ASC is open to distortion and negative socialization by the "anti-African" Eurocentric worldview. This leads the typical African American to Psychological/Cultural Misorientation—an incorrect (distorted) Eurocentric orientation among African people to their natural (African) cultural reality—for Kambon a grossly psychopathological condition and the basis for the personal and social pathology in the African American community. He calls for "cultural renewal;" that is, for African Americans to rebuild their African cultural infrastructure in order to heal themselves, by adopting African names, religions, rituals, learning African languages, and holding memorials about the "holocaust" of slavery.

Kambon (1997) makes essential points about the importance of congruent and self-affirming cultural values and worldview for African American psychological health. He also agrees with other theorists about the need for African Americans to be rooted in a positive sense of culture and social history. However, his model of the "biogenetically determined" ASEO and more experientially determined ASC, and his notion that the average African American is "mentally disordered" because of Cultural Misorientation exist largely without supporting data.

Positive mental health among African Americans is another emerging model (see for example, Anderson, Eaddy, and Williams, 1990; Franklin and Jackson, 1990; Shade, 1990). This approach is based on Marie Jahoda's (1958) insight that mental health is more than the absence of symptoms, but involves the presence of "positive," i.e., healthy characteristics. Franklin and Jackson (1990) take her definition and six major dimensions and discuss the implications of research and clinical data for African Americans in each dimension. Anderson et al. (1990) focus on psychosocial competence and resiliency as the key positive mental health factors for African Americans. Their brief review of the research literature, in a number of social and psychological areas, highlights these factors in health functioning by African Americans. Shade has the most developed model of what positive mental health means among African Americans. She elaborates four major factors that "facilitate survival and mental health: (1) The possession of a historical sense of the Afro-American community and the adaptational strategies developed over time... (2) A strong grounding in the cultural ethos and norms of the African American community... (3) The development and use of the culturally specific cognitive style which strengthens and emphasizes social cognition and social intelligence...(4) The development of a strong, assertive, active concept of self which helps individuals achieve a sense of identity and a strong belief in their ability to control their lives ... " (1990, p. 286). This emerging model has strong parallels with the literature on competent personality and points to alternative non-pathological outcomes for African Americans as well as specific factors supporting positive developments.

To summarize, how successful are existing theories in explaining and describing African American adult psychological health over the adult life cycle? Clearly no existing theory meets the criteria for an "ideal" model of African American adult psychological health. A number of the universal theories have positive points and ideas; e.g., Erikson's life-cycle perspective, and his idea that health is a dynamic balance, not perfection. However, all of them leave large areas unexplored, often the social/cultural factors that have an impact on health—a crucial lack for a model of African American adult psychological health. While traditional theories addressing African American personality and identity do discuss social and cultural factors, their focus on the "inevitable" pathological outcome and impact for the African American adult, and their assumption of little diversity in reaction to social factors in the African American community limit their explanatory usefulness as well. The emerging Afrocentric and Positive mental health models do point to non-pathological outcomes and factors leading to psychological health diversity in the African American community. This is an encouraging development.

While no existing theory will serve as a satisfactory explanatory or descriptive model of African American adult psychological health, it is possible to synthesize aspects of existing theory, the discussion of the social/cultural situation of African Americans, and Lazarus' "consensus" characteristics to point to central issues an adequate theory would address. Based on the work cited earlier, several psychological issues can be hypothesized as important for the African American individual throughout the adult life cycle: (1) maintaining an overall positive conception of the self; (2) maintaining a positive conception of African Americans as a group and a positive sense of connection and involvement with the African American community and its culture; (3) maintaining an accurate perception of the social environment (including its racism); (4) adapting to both African American and White community/cultures and using effective, non-destructive ways to cope with both; (5) developing and maintaining emotional intimacy with others; and (6) maintaining a sense of competence and the ability to work productively. How successfully an individual confronts these issues and the balance between successful and dysfunctional adaptation may be the measure of psychological health for an African American adult. Certainly, an adequate theory of African American adult psychological health would have to describe and explain how the African American person developed and maintained a positive status on these issues.

Recent Empirical Research

The findings of recent empirical studies of self-esteem and psychological distress cited above stand in stark contrast to the conclusion that no African American adults are able to successfully adapt to the key psychological tasks that face them. Investigations of African Americans in several other areas also challenge the mainstream view and address issues central to African American psychological health as well—specifically studies in the areas of racial identity, the competent personality, and coping with stress. Unfortunately, no general model and little theorizing has emerged from this work. In addition, only scattered work has emerged in other areas related to psychological health, like intimacy and interpersonal relations or involvement in group or individual action to combat racism—an important lack. Existing research will be reviewed in the areas of self-concept, competent personality, and coping with stress in order to assess current findings and draw theoretical implications where appropriate. This review will cite studies that are central to the area discussed or ones that illustrate important trends in the literature. Comments in each area will be based on cited studies as well as a wider reading of the literature.

Self-Concept

Self-concept, variously defined and conceptualized, has been at the heart of much of the research and theorizing done about African Americans. Low self-esteem, self-hatred and a negative racial identity have been the characteristics traditionally attributed to African American children and adults. Recent research on self-esteem and racial identity challenges these traditional findings and offers new evidence about how some African Americans positively adapt to one of the central psychological tasks facing them: establishing and maintaining a positive sense of self—both individually and as a member of a group.

Self-Esteem

Self-esteem is usually defined as the evaluative dimension of the self-concept. The person is thought to have global, i.e., overall, self-esteem that can range from very positive to very negative. Global self-esteem is often thought to be the summing up of the person's self-esteem in a number of specific areas, ranging from physical self to academic self. Adult self-esteem is typically measured using paper and pencil personality or self-esteem inventories or projective tests or, more rarely, interviews.

A number of comprehensive reviews and excellent studies of African American self-esteem have been published in the last 20 years. Perhaps the most comprehensive was done by Cross (1985), who reviewed 161 studies of African American self-concept done between 1939 and 1977, studies conducted using child and adult subjects. Some 101 of these studies involved self-esteem; of those, 71% showed African American self-esteem to be equal to or to exceed that for Whites, 16% found Whites with higher levels of self-esteem, and 13% had mixed results. Taylor (1976) in a comprehensive review of theory and studies of child and adult self-esteem, reached similar conclusions. Large sample studies of African American and White adult self-esteem by Yancey, Rigsby, and McCarthy (1972) and by Heiss and Owens (1972) found that the two groups had essentially equal overall self-esteem. Veroff, Douvan, and Kulka (1981), using national survey data, found African American and White American adults to have equivalent overall self-esteem and equivalent self-esteem in a number of areas. Unfortunately, little information about African American self-esteem at different points in the adult life cycle exists (see also Baldwin, Brown, & Hopkins, 1991; Barbarin, 1993; Demo and Parker, 1986; Spurlock, 1986; Whaley, 1993).

What are the sources of positive African American self-esteem? Discussing children and youth, Taylor (1976) and Gibbs (1985) found that the key factor for the level of an African American child's self-esteem was the general attitude of significant others towards the child. Parents, peers, and teachers are the significant others for African American children. For the vast majority of African American children, and by extension African American adults, these significant others are African American. Therefore, an African American social context is their primary source of social comparisons and self-evaluation—evaluations that are often positive. Barnes (1980) also argues that, under certain conditions, the African American family and community can act as mediators or filters of negative, racist images and messages for the African American child or youth (and adults). McCarthy and Yancey (1971) argue that African American adults use other African Americans as significant others, that they use criteria of worth relevant to the African American community to evaluate themselves, and that a "system-blame" explanation of failure is available to cushion blows to self-esteem. Heiss and Owens (1972) empirically investigated these ideas with a large-sample study of African

American and White adults. They looked at global self-esteem and how these adults evaluated different aspects of the self (e.g., self as parent, intelligent, athlete). While they found rough equality overall between groups, there was variation between each race on different traits (and by the four race-sex groups as well). They argued that their results indicated that variation occurred because of the variations in the type of significant others used by African Americans, likelihood of African Americans using dominant society standards of evaluation (vs. African American community ones), and differences in the availability of a system-blame explanation for each aspect of self-esteem (see also Luster & McAdoo, 1995).

In summary, recent research points out that: (1) African Americans and Whites have equivalent global self-esteem; (2) African Americans often use other African Americans, not Whites, as their significant others; (3) other mechanisms may be available to insulate African American self-esteem, e.g., a system-blame explanation of negative events, or the use of African American cultural (vs. White) standards of evaluation; and (4) African Americans and Whites may not have equivalent evaluations of different aspects of the self.

Racial Identity

Racial identity has been discussed extensively in the social science literature using various terms and measures. African American identity, group identity, group self-concept, "sense of peoplehood," "sense of blackness" are all terms used and measured by workers in the field. No consensus on concept definition, measurement technique, or links to personality theory has emerged, however. Much of the work in the field seems to assume that African American identity is strongly linked to personal self-esteem, but usually makes that link a theoretical postulate rather than empirically demonstrating it.

Cross (1985), in a comprehensive review of 22 studies of "reference group orientation" (group identity, race awareness) done from 1968 to 1977 found that in 68% (15 studies) African American subjects (children and adults), showed positive African American identities, in 27% (6) negative ones, and in 5% (1) a mixed pattern. Surveying studies back to 1939 and one longitudinal study, he argues that "Black parents present both the Black and White worlds to their children . . . . Black children, and perhaps Black people in general, have a dual [Black and White] reference group orientation" (p. 169). Cross sees this dual reference group orientation as adaptive and healthy for African Americans.

Although few studies have investigated the racial identities of African American adults, a number have looked at the racial identities of African American adolescents. Gurin and Epps (1975) investigated African American identity and self-hatred by interviewing 600 southern African American college students in 1965 as part of a larger study. They found what they saw as a typical pattern of

African American identity: a predominantly positive African American identity for most African American students and a small subgroup of students who had a predominantly negative identity. Ramseur (1975) looked longitudinally at the racial identities of African American freshmen and cross-sectionally at a sample of African American upperclassmen at Harvard College. He found two independent dimensions: "Salience of racial issues" and "Acceptance of Black ideology" (separatism, community control). Both dimensions were significantly linked to race-related social/extracurricular activities at college, but not to academic achievement. Gibbs (1974) interviewed 41 African American college student clients at Stanford's Counseling Center and categorized them based on their orientation towards the dominant White culture at the university. Her categories were affirmation, assimilation, separation and withdrawal. Affirmation was the most adaptive mode, involving "movement with the dominant culture." It was a mode marked by "self-acceptance, positive [Black] identity . . . high achievement motivation, and autonomous self-actualizing behavior" (p. 736).

Perhaps the best known and most widely researched model of African American identity and identity development is Cross's (1980, 1991, 1997) model of the conversion from "Negro" to "Black." He has sometimes referred to his (and Charles Thomas') perspective as that of "psychological nigrescence," the process of becoming African American. He describes five stages: (1) Pre-encounter—the person is a Negro and accepts a "White" view of self, other African Americans, and the world. (2) Encounter—some shocking personal or social event makes the person receptive to new views of being African American and the world. This encounter precipitates an intense search for African American identity. (3) Immersion—an emotional period ensues where the person glorifies anything African American and attempts to purge him or herself of their former worldview and old behavior. (4) Internalization—the person makes his/her new values their own and African Americans their primary reference groups. This stage and the next, (5) Internalization-Commitment, are characterized by positive self-esteem, ideological flexibility and openness about one's blackness. In the fifth stage the person finds activities and commitments to express his or her new identity.

Cross clearly sees the person in stage Five-Internalization-Commitment as the "ideal," that is, psychologically healthy African American person. They have made their new pro-African American identity and values their own. They have a "calm, secure demeanor" characterized by "ideological flexibility, psychological openness and self-confidence about one's blackness" (1980, p. 86). African Americans are a primary reference group, but the person has lost his prejudices about race, sex, age and social class. He or she also struggles to translate their values into behavior that will benefit the African American community. Cross seems to see the Negro to African American conversion process as an African American model of self-actualization under oppressive social conditions. African Americans in Stage Five would then be African American self-actualizers. Cross has yet to follow up this idea, and says elsewhere that basic personality structure remains the same after the process. It seems that key aspects of racial identity change, however.

Cross, Parham, and Helms (1997) point to a number of studies that seem to validate his stage model and to say that his stages exist independently and occur in the sequence he describes. However, the family and social conditions that lead all African Americans to the "Pre-encounter" stage or that support the Stage 5—Internalization/Commitment phase are largely unspecified. In addition, class, gender, and regional differences in the prevalence of people at different stages and theorizing about those differences are largely missing from this work as well. This model has produced a large number of empirical studies that link the stages to other personal and social characteristics. Taylor (1997), for example, combines the Cross/Thomas model with those of Milliones and Banks to create 6 stages of "Black cultural conversion." He empirically investigated 4 stages using a scale developed by Milliones (1973), and found that in his college student samples the modal conversion stage was Stage 1—Preconsiousness. He also found that the higher the stage the better his subjects' personal adjustment, and that the stages were linked to functioning in social and cultural areas. Strikingly, Cross, Parham, and Helms (1997) in their review found Stage 1 not generally tied to "poor mental health," and that Personal identity (personality variables like self-esteem) and what they called Reference Group Orientation (racial identity) were largely independent for African Americans (see also Plummer, 1995; who found a sample of African American adolescents to widely endorse internalization attitudes).

In summary, (1) many African Americans have a predominantly positive racial identity, with perhaps a minority having a negative identity; (2) African American identity has links to behavior; (3) African American identity can evolve over time, and change dramatically; and (4) African American identity can have links to other attitudes and personality characteristics. However, the issue of whether an individual's type (positive, negative) of African American identity is linked to their level of personal self-esteem seems unresolved. While Cross (1985), Cross, Parham, and Helms (1991), Clark (1982), and Houston (1984) find little evidence for such a link, Gibbs (1974), Parham and Helms (1985a, 1985b), and Wright (1985) do find substantial empirical evidence for it (see also Clark, 1992; Porter & Washington, 1979).

Competent Personality

M. B. Smith (1968) describes competence as an important aspect of personality functioning. He bases his discussion on the theoretical work of Robert White (1960) and his empirical study of "competent" Peace Corps volunteers. Smith sees the competent person as having views of the self, the world and behaviors that fit together, and are trans-cultural (and trans-racial). The person has positive self-esteem, but more importantly a sense of potency and efficacy in the world—a sense he or she can cause desirable things to happen. The person also has "hope" about the world—an attitude that effort can achieve results in the real world. Smith also describes a behavioral component to competence, since he expects the competent person to set "realistic," moderately challenging goals for himself. Tyler (1978), with a conception of competence similar to Smith's, explored the idea that competence is a configuration of personality traits, attitudes toward the world, and behaviors. Focusing on Rotter's Internal-External control dimension, level of trust (rather than Smith's hope) and an "active coping orientation" that has behavioral attributes like realistic goal setting, he surveyed three samples of college students. He found that the configuration held across the three samples and was independent of social desirability and aptitude.

Unfortunately, studies focusing on competent adult African Americans are sparse. Ramseur (1982), in a study of stress and coping mechanisms among "successful" (competent) African American administrators at White universities, surveyed the literature and interviewed six successful male and female African American administrators. The interviewed administrators were found to have high self-esteem and realism about the self and their work environment. They were also planful and had set career strategies for themselves in ways that pointed to a high sense of internal control. These administrators also seemed to positively identify with being African American and took a pragmatic view of race-related issues and problems they confronted.

A number of studies have had adolescents as their focus. Looney and Lewis (1983) examined 11 competent working-class African American adolescents and 11 upper-middle class White ones. The African American (and White) youngsters were strikingly secure and open, were described as "doers"—active and self-assertive, as generally good students, and as having wide networks of friends. The authors described their competent families, all of whom were two-parent ones, as having open communication, openness with affection, a focus on efficiently solving problems, as encouraging the development of autonomy, and as showing high emotional support of members. Lee (1984, 1985) studied competent African American adolescents in a rural county in the deep South. In his 1984 study of these academically and socially successful students, Lee found them to have "positive, but realistic" views of the self, an internal locus of control, high achievement motivation, and strong social networks outside the family. Students described their families as having a high degree of open communication, and their parents as "strict," or close to it in terms of rules and discipline. Lee rated most of them as having low to moderate levels of "Black consciousness." Griffin and Korchin (1980) initially interviewed 6 junior college faculty members for their descriptions of the ideal competent personality for an adolescent African American male. These faculty members then nominated competent African American male students (13) who were studied along with "average" peers (10) who volunteered for the study.

Faculty members, both African American and White, saw competent male African American adolescents similarly: as able to adapt to many different settings—academic and social; as goal oriented, with realistic flexible goals; and as able to be disciplined and self-confident in the face of difficult conditions. Both competent and average students scored as "well-adjusted" on Offer's self-image questionnaire and in general seemed to be functioning effectively. Competent males, however, were more inner-directed, more ambitious, goal-striving more vigorously, and less concerned with their acceptability to others than were their "average" peers (see also Abatso, 1985; Anderson, Eaddy, & Williams, 1990; Barbarin, 1993; Franklin & Jackson, 1990; Gordon, 1995; Taylor, 1994 for other research in this area).

The ability to draw conclusions from the studies in this area is limited by a number of methodological problems. The differing definitions of "competence" used in the studies, small sample sizes, the usual lack of a contrast group, the focus on adolescents as subjects (see also Edwards, 1976), and the lack of discussion of gender differences combine to limit the force of conclusions that can be drawn. However, trends do emerge: 1) Positive self-esteem, a high sense of efficacy, active coping strategies ("a doer"), being achievement oriented, and having good social relations, are characteristics that seem to regularly occur together; 2) At least a mildly positive identification with African Americans and a pragmatic view of race relations were also regularly present; and 3) Certain family backgrounds seem most common for competent African American individuals: high family stability, both marital and residential, high emotional support generally, and encouragement of academic achievement. Clear rules and regulations at home ("strictness") was another common finding, along with "competents" being first-borns.

Stress/Adaptation

In recent years, a number of studies have looked at links between aspects of stress (appraisal, coping resources, coping styles), and the level of psychological well-being or distress of African American adults. This section will briefly review work on the appraisal of stress, external and internal coping resources, and the coping styles of African American adults.

Appraisal. Do African Americans and Whites differ in their appraisal of the severity or meaning of different stressors? Little systematic information exists on these questions, but there are some suggestive studies. Komaroff, Masuda, and Holmes (1968) compared Whites, African Americans, and Mexican-Americans on their assessment of the amount of adaptation required by certain life-change events (e.g., marriage, moving). The three groups of low income subjects rank-ordered the items in similar fashion, with African Americans and Mexican-Americans in closest agreement. Barbarin (1983) in a review of stress and appraisal among African American families, pointed to three factors that might be important in

African Americans' appraisal of stress: religious orientation, causal attributions of undesirable events to racial discrimination, and "paradoxical" control beliefs. He argued that personal religiosity and involvement in organized religion can enhance coping by providing a basis for optimism and a cognitive framework for understanding stressful episodes. He also found in an empirical study (Barbarin et al., 1981) that African Americans more frequently interpret negative life outcomes in terms of individual and institutional discrimination than do Whites. In addition, based on that 1981 study, he argued that African Americans often have paradoxical control attributions. This means they have a sense of personal efficacy but at the same time the sense that African Americans as a group have little control over their destiny. Overall, then, his work suggests a type or style of appraisal for African Americans that differs from that of White Americans (see also Outlaw, 1993; Wilson-Sadberry, 1993).

External coping resources. A number of researchers have examined the topic of external resources that African Americans use to cope with stress. A quote cited by George and McNamara (1984) summarizes many of the findings well:

We know Black people have a history of being religious and oriented towards their kinship and friendship networks for buffering the stresses of life, but we were surprised by the extent to which the data [from American Blacks] reveal family and church to be essential elements in the lives of our respondents (*ISR Newsletter,* 1983, p. 5-6).

Neff (1985), in a brief review, points out that adjusting for age and social class, African Americans show higher levels than Whites for church attendance, interaction with friends, enjoyment of clubs, and help from both friends and relatives. African Americans also more often had a family member nearby, had contact with relatives living close by, and were somewhat more likely than Whites to perceive relatives as available sources of help.

African Americans have also been found to rely more than Whites on informal social networks (family, friends) than formal ones to cope with stress (Gibson, 1982; Barbarin, 1983). Neighbors, Jackson, Bowman, & Gurin (1983) found that for *all* socio-demographic groups of African American adults in a national survey sample, informal social networks were used first and more substantially than formal sources of help. Gibson (1982), in a reanalysis of national survey data from 1957 and 1976, looked at middle-aged and elderly African American resources and coping styles. She found that African Americans in middle and late life were more likely to seek help from friends (1957) and from a combination of family members (1976) than were Whites. That is, Whites were more likely to only turn to a spouse or one family member with their worries than were African Americans. This difference held even when all social variables were held constant. Gibson also found that African Americans shifted from talking with friends in middle years to multiple family members in later years.

In addition, other studies point to the importance of supportive social and kin networks. For example, Holahan, Betak, Spearly, and Chance (1983) studying working-class African American and White women found that African American women with high social network scores (friends, neighborhood contacts, job) showed mental health levels similar to White women. Those African American women low in social integration showed mental health scores in the pathological range. All measures of social integration showed a much greater relation to mental health scores for African American women than White. Dressler (1985) studied the ability of the extended African American family to buffer stress. He linked recent stressful events, chronic stress, kin and non-kin support, and depression for African American subjects. Those African American adults who perceived their kin to be supportive reported fewer symptoms of depression. The number of kin and non-kin support sources were not related to depression. However, there was no buffering effect for chronic stressors, like economic problems. Dressler defined support as money, information, and help with tasks for both sexes (see also Smith, 1993).

Internal coping resources. Religion has historically played a powerful role in the life of the African American community and for African American individuals. It apparently continues to do so given recent research findings. George and McNamara (1984) note that studies have found African Americans to be more frequent church attendees than Whites. Their re-analysis of 1972-1982 national survey data which looked at religion, subjective life satisfaction, and health produced several striking findings: (1) For African Americans, far more than for Whites, a sense of well-being seems markedly enhanced by religious attendance and by stated strength of religious affiliation, at *all* levels of age, education and income. African American women seem to derive most life satisfaction from church attendance and African American men from stated strength of religious affiliation (religiosity). For both sexes, their respective measures of religious involvement are highly predictive of global happiness, subjective health, and satisfaction with family life.

Bowman (1985) used a national survey sample of African American husbands/ fathers to examine the links between stress (employment difficulties and consequent difficulties fulfilling the provider role in the family), coping resources, and psychological well-being (subjective life happiness.) Bowman examined five coping resources—multiple economic providers, family closeness, non-kin friendship, racial ideology (system-blame), and religious orientation. He found that religious orientation had a much stronger positive effect on the level of life happiness among African American fathers than did family cohesion or any other informal coping resource investigated.

Harrison, Bowman, and Beale (1985) used a national sample of African American working mothers to investigate the links between stress (role strains from being a worker and a mother), coping resources, and psychological well-being. They examined five coping resources—religious orientation, family closeness, best friend, child care availability, and child care advice. They found that religious orientation was the most important coping resource followed by family closeness. They also found that the five coping resources together significantly offset the stress from role strain these African American mothers experienced and therefore positively affected their psychological well-being (see also Barbarin, 1993; Bowman, 1992; Krause, 1992).

Coping styles. Neighbors, Jackson et al. (1983), Barbarin (1983), and Gibson (1982) found prayer to be the most common coping response to worries or stressful episodes for African Americans. Moreover, prayer was used substantially more by African American adults at all age ranges than by Whites. Neighbors found that the coping response ranked "most helpful" by African Americans after prayer was an instrumental one: "Facing the problem squarely and doing something about it." Neighbors found that among subjects with economic difficulties, lower income people were more likely to use prayer as a coping strategy; and that, overall, a majority of African Americans using prayer found that it made economic troubles "easier to bear" (Neighbors & Jackson et al., 1983). Perhaps there is a fusion of external resource (church association) with internal resource (religiosity), and coping style (use of prayer) for many African American adults.

Lykes (1983) studied how 52 "successful" African American women coped with incidents of racial and sexual discrimination over their life histories. The women were 70 or older at the time of the study and Lykes worked from transcripts of their oral histories. The study and findings were complex but, in part, she found that these African American women were discriminating and adaptive in their use of coping responses in response to situational demands and constraints. She also found that directness (confrontation vs. indirect) and flexibility (use of several strategies) of coping were independent dimensions of coping style for these women (see also Myers, Anderson, & Strickland, 1997).

Several findings emerge from these studies of stress and coping: while African American adults may not differ from others in their appraisal of the stressfulness of particular events, they may have a cognitive framework for appraising stress that is significantly different from that of White Americans. In addition, African Americans seem to rely on informal social networks (kin, friends) to buffer stress to a significantly greater degree than White adults. Religious involvement—church attendance, "religiosity"—is also an important factor in buffering stress for many African American adults. There are some suggestive findings that point to typical patterns of coping with stress by African American adults, that is, use of resources and coping styles, that may differ significantly from those of their White peers.

Conclusion

What are the social and psychological characteristics of psychologically healthy African American adults and how do they change over the life cycle? No existing theory or model satisfactorily addresses these questions. While "universal" models of psychological health offer some positive perspectives and ideas, they generally have little to say about the unique social-cultural context of African Americans. Other models that focus on African American personality and identity have generally assumed pathological reactions and a lack of diversity of reaction to the social/cultural context by African Americans. While neither body of theory provides an adequate model, taken together, along with work on the social and cultural situation of African Americans, they do provide a basis for hypothesizing about the central psychological issues for African American adult psychological health. Those issues are: (1) maintaining globally positive self-conception; (2) maintaining a positive group (African American) identity and community connection; (3) maintaining an accurate perception of the social environment—including its racism; (4) effectively adapting to the social environment confronting a individual—coping with its stressors and adapting to both African American and White cultures; (5) developing and maintaining emotional intimacy with others; and (6) maintaining a sense of competence and the ability to work productively.

What are the major findings of recent empirical research in areas important for African American adult psychological health? In the area of self-conception, recent research has pointed out that many African American adults have positive self-esteem, that they use African Americans as significant others, and that they use an African American social context for their social comparisons and self-evaluations. In addition, African American adults may use system-blame explanations of failure to protect their self-esteem. Other studies point out that many African Americans have positive or largely positive racial identities and that racial identity has links to behavior and other personality characteristics. African American adults may also have a cognitive framework for appraising stress that is significantly different from their White peers. They also appear to use different internal and external resources to buffer stress: relying on informal social networks and religious involvement to a greater degree than do Whites. These different types of appraisal and resource use may be tied to unique African American coping styles. Other research on competence indicates that positive self-esteem, a sense of personal efficacy, active coping strategies, achievement orientation, good social relations, and a positive racial identity may regularly occur together to form what might be called a "Black competent personality." Certain family backgrounds and childrearing practices also seem associated with these characteristics.

What are the implications of these theories and recent research? Several central ones stand out: (1) African American adults possess positive or healthy psychological characteristics and functioning. Theories or models that postulate universal pathology or pathological outcomes are clearly unhelpful and do not fit current findings; (2) Particularly in the area of self-esteem, some of the sources and mechanisms that maintain these healthy characteristics are being identified, theorized about, and empirically investigated; (3) Developing new models and expanding current theory is a vital task at this point, particularly outside of the area of self-esteem. For example, a rigorous definition of the dimensions of African American identity and its links to other aspects of self-conception, personality, and behavior would be extremely useful. A clear definition and conceptualization of the African American competent personality would also be helpful. Examining emotional intimacy and interpersonal relations among African Americans would be a valuable addition as well. Forging theoretical links with other traditions and newer theories in psychology and sociology are other necessities. Rutter's (1979) discussion of "protective factors" and more recent discussions of the "invulnerability" of some children in the face of stress have obvious relevance;   (4) Empirical research using adult subjects, with large samples, sophisticated designs and statistical rigor is sorely needed. New research needs to be guided by theory and to be sensitive to gender differences and the diversity by class, region, and home country within the African American community. For example, research that investigated the actual degree of association of the characteristics said to comprise the African American competent personality and that looked at gender, class, and regional differences would be extremely valuable; (5) Perhaps the model of the competent personality has the ability to unite and make sense of recent research findings on self-concept, personality characteristics, and coping styles (see Whaley, 1993 for a discussion of a similar perspective). It also offers a link to a theoretical/research tradition in psychology that has been fruitful. Finally, recent theorizing and empirical findings and the increasing research interest in areas this chapter identified as central to understanding African American adult psychological health mark this as an important and productive period for the field.

References

Abatso, Y. (1985). The coping personality: A study of Black college students. In M. Spencer, G. Brookings, & W. Allen (Eds.), *Beginnings: The social and affective development of Black children* (pp. 131-144). Hillsdale, NJ: Lawrence Erlbaum.

Anderson, L. P., Eaddy, C. L., & Williams, E. A. (1990). Psychosocial competence: Towards a theory of understanding positive mental among Black Americans. In D. S. Ruiz (Ed.), *Handbook of mental health and mental disorder among Black Americans*. New York: Greenwood Press.

Baldwin, J. A. (1991). African (Black) psychology: Issues and synthesis. In R. Jones (Ed.), *Black psychology* (3rd ed.). Berkeley, CA: Cobb and Henry.

Baldwin, J. A., Brown, R., & Hopkins, R. (1991). The Black self-hatred paradigm revisited: An Africentric analysis. In R. Jones (Ed.), *Black psychology* (3rd ed.). Berkeley, CA: Cobb and Henry.

Barbarin, O. (1983). Coping with ecological transitions by Black families: A psychosocial model. *Journal of Community Psychology, 11,* 308-322.

Barbarin, O. (1993). Coping and resilience: Exploring the inner lives of African American children. *Journal of Black Psychology, 19*(4), 478-492.

Barbarin, O., Maish, K., & Shorter, S. (1981). Mental health among Blacks. In O. Barbarin, P. Good, O. Pharr, & J. Siskind (Eds.), *Institutional racism and community competence.* Rockville, MD: U.S. Department of Health and Human Services (DHHS Publication #ADM81-907).

Barnes, E. J. (1980). The Black community as a source of positive self-concept for Black children: A theoretical perspective. In R. Jones (Ed.), *Black psychology* (pp. 106-138). New York: Harper & Row.

Bowman, P. (1985). Black fathers and the provider role: Role strain, informal coping resource, and life happiness. In W. Boykin (Ed.), *Proceedings.* Seventh Conference on Empirical Research in Black Psychology, 9-21. Rockville, MD: National Institute of Mental Health.

Bowman, P. (1992). Coping with provider role strain: Adaptive cultural resources among Black husband-fathers. In A. Burlew, K. Hoard, W. C. Banks, H. P. McAdoo, & D. A. Azibo (Eds.), *African-American psychology: Theory, research and practice.* Newbury Park, CA: Sage Publications.

Cervantes, R. C., & Castro, F. G. (1985). Stress, coping, and Mexican American mental health: A systemic review. *Hispanic Journal of Behavioral Sciences, 7*(1), 1-73.

Clark, M. L. (1982). Racial group concept and self-esteem in Black children. *Journal of Black Psychology, 8(2),* 75-89.

Clark, M. L. (1992). Racial group concept an self-esteem in Black Children. In A. Burlew, W. C. Banks, H. P. McAdoo, & D. A. McAdoo (Eds.), *African American psychology: Theory, research and practice.* Newbury Park, CA: Sage Publications.

Cross, T. (1984). *The Black power imperative: Racial inequality and the politics of nonviolence.* New York: Faulkner Books.

Cross, W. E. (1980). Models of psychological nigrescence: A literature review. In R. Jones (Ed.), *Black psychology.* New York: Harper & Row.

Cross, W. E. (1985). Black identity: Rediscovering the distinction between personal identity and reference group orientation. In M. Spencer, G. Brookings, & W. Allen (Eds.), *Beginnings: The social and affective development of Black children* (pp.155-173). Hillsdale, NJ: Lawrence Erlbaum Associates.

Cross, W. E., Parham, T. S., & Helms, J. E. (1991). The stages of Black identity development: Nigresence models. In R. Jones (Ed.), *Black psychology* (3rd ed.). Berkeley, CA: Cobb and Henry.

Cross, W. E., Parham, T. S., & Helms, J. E. (1997). Nigresence revisited: Theory and research. In R. L. Jones (Ed.), *African American identity development.* Hampton, VA: Cobb and Henry.

Demo, D. H., & Parker, K. D. (1986). Academic achievement and self-esteem among Black and White college students. *Journal of Social Psychology, 127*(4), 345-355.

Dressler, W. W. (1985). Extended family relationships, social support, and mental health in a southern Black community. *Journal of Health and Social Behavior,* 26, 39-48.

Edwards, D. W. (1974). Blacks versus Whites: When is race a relevant variable? *Journal of Personality and Social Psychology,* 29(1), 39-49.

Edwards, O. L. (1976). Components of academic success: A profile of achieving Black adolescents. *Journal of Negro Education,* 45, 408-422.

Erickson, E. (1968). *Identity, youth, and crisis.* New York: Norton.

Franklin, A. J., & Jackson, J. S. (1990). Factors contributing to positive mental health among Black Americans. In D. S. Ruiz (Ed.), *Handbook of mental health and mental disorder among Black Americans.* New York: Greenwood Press.

Freud, S. (1926). Inhibitions, symptoms, and anxiety. *Standard Edition, 20,* 77-175. London: Hogarth Press.

Gary, L. E. (Ed.). (1978). *Mental health: A challenge to the Black community.* Philadelphia: Dorrance & Co.

Gary, L. E., & Weaver, G. D. (1991). Mental health of African Americans: Research trends and directions. In R. Jones (Ed.), *Black psychology* (3rd ed.). Berkeley, CA: Cobb and Henry

George, A., & McNamara, P. (1984). Religion, race and psychological well-being. *Journal for the Scientific Study of Religion, 23*(4), 351-363.

George, J. C., & Brooker, A. E. (1984). Conceptualization of mental health. *Psychological Reports, 55,* 329-330.

Gibbs, J. (1974). Patterns of adaptation among Black students at a predominantly White university: Selected case studies. *American Journal of Orthopsychiatry, 44,* 728-740.

Gibbs, J. (1985). City girls: Psychosocial adjustment of urban Black adolescent females. *Sage, 2(2),* 28-36.

Gibson, R. (1982). Blacks at middle and late life: Resources and coping. *Annals of the American Academy of Political and Social Science, 464,* 79-90.

Gordon, K. A. (1995). Self-concept and motivation patterns of resilient African American High School Students. *Journal of Black Psychology, 21*(3), 239-255.

Grier, W., & Cobbs, P. (1969). *Black rage.* New York: Basic Books.

Griffin, Q. D., & Korchin, S. J. (1980). Personality competence in Black male adolescents. *Journal of Youth and Adolescence, 9(3),* 211-227.

Gurin, P., & Epps, E. (1975). *Black consciousness, identity, and achievement: A study of students in historically Black colleges.* New York: John Wiley & Sons, Inc.

Guterman, S. (1972). *Black psyche: The modal personality patterns of Black Americans.* Berkeley, CA: Glendessary Press.

Harrison, A. O., Bowman, P., & Berale, R. (1985). Role strain, coping resources and psychological well-being among Black working mothers. In W. Boykin (Ed.), *Proceedings.* Seventh Conference on Empirical Research in Black Psychology, 21-29. Rockville, MD: National Institute of Mental Health.

Heiss, J., & Owens, S. (1972). Self-evaluations of Blacks and Whites. *American Journal of Sociology, 78,* 360-370.

Holahan, C. J., Betak, J. F., Spearly, J. L., & Chance, B. J. (1983). Social integration and mental health in a biracial community. *American Journal of Community Psychology, 11(3),* 301-311.

Houston, L. (1984). Black consciousness and self-esteem. *Journal of Black Psychology, 11(1),* 1-7.

Institute for Social Research (1983). Black Americans surveyed. *I.S.R. Newsletter* 5-6. Ann Arbor: Institute for Social Research.

Jahoda, M. (1958). *Current concepts of positive mental health.* New York: Basic Books.

Jensen, G. F., White, C. S., & Galliher, J. M. (1982). Ethnic status and adolescent self-evaluations: An extension of research on minority self-esteem. *Social Problems, 30(2),* 226-239.

Jones, E. E., & Korchin, S. J. (1982). *Minority mental health.* New York: Praeger.

Jones, J. M. (1996). *Prejudice and racism.* Reading, MA: Addison-Wesley Publishers.

Jones, J. M. (1991). Racism: A cultural analysis of the problem. In R. Jones (Ed.), *Black psychology* (3rd ed.). Berkeley, CA: Cobb and Henry.

Kambon, K. K. K. (1997). An African-centered paradigm for understanding the mental health of Africans in America. In R. Jones (Ed.), *African American mental health.* Hampton, VA: Cobb and Henry

Kardiner, A., & Ovesey, L. (1951). *The mark of oppression: Explorations in the personality of the American Negro.* New York: World Books.

Karon, B. P. (1958). *The Negro personality: A rigorous investigation of the effects of culture.* New York: Springer.

Komaroff, A. C., Masuda, M., & Holmes, T. H. (1968). The social readjustment rating scale: A comparative study of Negro, Mexican, and White Americans. *Journal of Psychosomatic Research 12(2),* 121-128.

Krause, N. (1992). Stress, religiosity, and psychological well-being among older Blacks. *Journal of Aging & Health, 4(3),* 412-439.

Lazarus, R. (1975). The healthy personality—A review of conceptualizations and research. In L. Levi (Ed.), *Society, stress and disease (Vol.* 2). *Childhood and adolescence* (pp. 6-35). New York: Oxford University Press.

Lee, C. C. (1984). An investigation of psychosocial variables related to academic success for rural Black adolescents. *Journal of Negro Education, 53(4),* 424-434.

Lee, C. C. (1985). Successful rural Black adolescents: A psychosocial profile. *Adolescence, 20(77),* 129-142.

Looney, J. G., & Lewis, J. M. (1983). Competent adolescents from different socioeconomic and ethnic contexts. *Adolescent Psychiatry, 2,* 64-74.

Luster, T., & McAdoo, H. P. (1995). Factors related to self-esteem among African American Youth: A secondary analysis of the High/Scope Perry preschool data. *Journal of Research on Adolescence, 5*(4), 451-467.

Lykes, M. B. (1983). Discrimination and coping in the lives of Black women: Analyses of oral history data. *Journal of Social Issues, 39(3),* 79-100.

Maslow, A. (1968). *Towards a psychology of being* (2nd ed.). Princeton, NJ: Van Nostrand.

McCarthy, J., & Yancey, W. (1971). Uncle Tom and ML Charlie: Metaphysical pathos in the study of racism and personal disorganization. *American Journal of Sociology, 76,* 648-672.

Milliones, J. (1973). *Construction of the developmental inventory of consciousness.* Doctoral Dissertation, University of Pittsburgh.

Myers, H. F., Anderson, N. B., & Strickland, T. L. (1997). Biobehavioral Perspective for research on stress and hypertension in Black adults: Theoretical and empirical issues. In R. Jones (Ed.), *African American mental health.* Hampton, VA: Cobb and Henry.

Neff, J. (1985). Race and vulnerability to stress: An examination of differential vulnerability. *Journal of Personality and Social Psychology, 49(2),* 481-491.

Neighbors, H. W. (1984). The distribution of psychiatric morbidity in Black Americans: A review and suggestions for research. *Community Mental Health Journal, 20(3),* 169-181.

Neighbors, H., Jackson, J., Bowman, P., & Gurin, G. (1983). Stress, coping, and Black mental health: Preliminary findings from a national study. *Prevention in Human Services, 2,* 1-25.

Nobles, W. W. (1991). Extended self: Rethinking the so-called Negro self-concept. In R. Jones (Ed.), *Black psychology* (3rd ed.). Berkeley, CA: Cobb and Henry.

Outlaw, F. H. (1993). Stress and coping: The influence of racism on the cognitive appraisal processing of African Americans. *Issues in Mental Health Nursing, 14*(4), 399-409.

Parham, T., & Helms, J. (1985a). Relations of racial identity attitudes to self-actualization and affective states of Black students. *Journal of Counseling Psychology, 32(3), 431-440.*

Parham, T., & Helms, J. (1985b). Attitudes of racial identity and self-esteem of Black students: An exploratory investigation. *Journal of College Student Personnel, 26,* 143-147.

Pettigrew, T. W. (1964). *A profile of the Negro American.* Princeton, NJ: Van Nostrand.

Pierce, C. (1974). Psychiatric problems of the Black minority. In A. Arieti (Ed.), *American Handbook of Psychiatry* (2nd ed., pp. 524-534).

Plummer, D. L. (1995). Patterns of racial identity development of African American adolescent males and females. *Journal of Black Psychology, 21(2),* 168-180.

Porter, J., & Washington, R. (1979). Black identity and self-esteem: A review of studies of Black self concept 1968-1978. *Annual Review of Sociology, 5,* 53-74.

Ramseur, H. (1975). *Continuity and change in Black identity: Black students at an interracial college.* Cambridge, Mass: Unpublished doctoral dissertation, Harvard University.

Ramseur, H. (1982). Major sources of stress and coping strategies of Black administrators at White universities. *Proceedings.* First National Conference on Black Administrators at White Universities. Cambridge: Massachusetts Institute of Technology Black Administrators Association.

Rutter, M. (1979). Protective factors in children's responses to stress and disadvantage. In M. Kent & J. Rold (Eds.), *Primary Prevention of Psychopathology, 3,* 49-79. Hanover, NH: University Press of New England.

Shade, B. J. (1990). Coping with color: The anatomy of positive mental health. In D. S. Ruiz (Ed.), *Handbook of mental health and mental disorder among African Americans.* New York: Greenwood Press.

Smith, J. M. (1993). Function and supportive roles of church and religion. In J. S. Jackson, J. Sidney, L. Chatters, & R. J. Joseph (Eds.), *Aging in Black America.* Newbury Park, CA: Sage Publications.

Smith, M. B. (1961). "Mental health" reconsidered: A special case of the problem of values in psychology. *American Psychologist, 16,* 299-306.

Smith, M. B. (1968). Competence and socialization. In J. Clausen (Ed.), *Socialization and society* (pp. 270-320). Boston: Little, Brown and Co.

Smith, W. D., Burlew, A. K., & Mosley, M. H. (1978). *Minority issues in mental health.* Reading, MA: Addison-Wesley.

Spurlock, L. (1986, Janurary). Development of self-conception in Afro-American children. *Hospital and Community Psychiatry, 37(1),* 66-70.

Stock, W. A., Okun, M. A., Haring, M. J., & Witter, R. A. (1985). Race and subjective well-being in adulthood: A Black-White research synthesis. *Human Development, 28,* 192-197.

Taylor, J. (1997). Cultural conversion experiences: Implication for mental health research and treatment. In R. L. Jones (Ed.), *African American identity development*. Hampton, VA: Cobb and Henry.

Taylor, R. D. (1994). Risk and resilience: Contextual influences on the development of African American adolescents. In M. C. Wang & E. W. Gordon (Eds.), *Educational resilience in inner-city America: Challenges and prospects*. Hillsdale, NJ: Lawrence Elbaum Associates, Inc.

Taylor, R. L. (1976). Psychosocial development among Black children and youth: A reexamination. *American Journal of Orthopsychiatry, 46(2),* 4-19.

Thomas, A., & Sillen, S. (1972). *Racism and psychiatry.* Secaucus, NJ: Citadel Press.

Thomas, C. S., & Comer, J. (1973). Racism and mental health services. In C. Willie, B. Kramer, & B. Brown (Eds.), *Racism and mental health.* Pittsburgh: University of Pittsburgh Press.

Tyler, F. (1978). Individual psychosocial competence: A personality configuration. *Educational and Psychological Measurement, 38,* 309-323.

Veroff, J., Douvan, E., & Kulka, R. A. (1981). *The inner American: A self-portrait from 1957 to 1976.* New York: Basic Books.

Whaley, A. L. (1993). Self-esteem, cultural identity, and psychosocial adjustment in African American children. *Journal of Black Psychology, 19*(4), 406-422.

White, R. (1960). Competence and the psychosexual stages of development. In M. Jones (Ed.), *Nebraska symposium on motivation* (pp. 97-141). Lincoln: University of Nebraska Press.

Wilcox, C. (1973). Positive mental health for Blacks. In C. Willie, B. Kramer, & B. Brown (Eds.), *Racism and mental health.* Pittsburgh: University of Pittsburgh Press.

Wilson-Sadberry, K. R. (1993). Staying alive: Stress, coping, and personal resources along African American men. *Challenge: A Journal of Research on African American Men, 4*(1), 18-36.

Wright, B. (1985). Effects of racial self-esteem on personal self-esteem of Black youth. *International Journal of Intercultural Relations, 9(1),* 19-30.

Yancey, W. L., Rigsby, L., & McCarthy, J. D. (1972). Social position and self-evaluation: The relative importance of race. *American Journal of Sociology, 78,* 338-359.

Author

Howard P. Ramseur
MIT/E23-361
77 Massachusetts Avenue
Cambridge, MA 02139
Telephone: (617) 253-2916
Fax: (617) 253-0162
E-mail: hpram@mit.edu

An African-Centered Paradigm for Understanding the Mental Health of Africans in America

Kobi K. K. Kambon (aka Joseph A. Baldwin)

Introduction

Since the 1960s, we have been increasingly bombarded with reports and allegations of escalating rates of conventional forms of mental illness (e.g., neurotic and psychotic reactions, drug addiction and abuse, suicidal behavior, deviant sexual behavior, and emotional stress generally) and "so-called" anti-social behaviors among Africans in America (Baldwin, 1984). Contemporary estimates suggest that approximately one of every 20-25 urban African Americans is likely to encounter one of the traditional "Eurocentric" American treatment or correctional institutions each year. When these alarming statistics are combined with the widely acknowledged observation of the continuing dismal social-economic and political plight of the African world today—in Africa, the United States, and throughout the rest of the world—most if not virtually all of which have profound psychological content, ramifications and implications,they bring a much needed additional perspective to the construction of a truly comprehensive analysis of contemporary African/ African American mental health issues.

In this light, it would no doubt represent an understatement to observe that the African community in America (North as well as South America) is probably under a broad scale "mental health siege" by the Eurocentric forces of racial-cultural oppression (Akbar, 1981; Ani, 1994; Baldwin, 1984, 1985; Fanon, 1967; Hare, 1965; Kambon, 1992, in press a ; McGee, 1973; Nascimento, 1978; Nobles, 1976b; Russell, Wilson & Hall, 1992; Williams, 1976). Since the beginning of the "Maafa/ African Holocaust" of 300-500 years of Eurasian enslavement of Africans (and the more than 1,200 years of continuous violent encroachment), African people have been, and continue to this day to be oppressed (physically, psychologically and culturally speaking) by the forces of European culture throughout the world. African Americans are almost totally economically dependent on Europeans for their life support resources, education and knowledge about the world and about themselves. African Americans are thus almost totally controlled by Europeans/the European worldview (Ani, 1994; Baldwin, 1984, 1985; Ben-Jochannon, 1982; Clark, 1991; Kambon, 1992, 1995;Williams, 1976; Woodson, 1969). As a result of the miseducation imposition of this European cultural oppression over virtually the entire African world community, most African people throughout the African diaspora in particular lack true racial-cultural consciousness (do not manifest a "conscious African identity"). The "so-called" educated Africans are almost totally intellectually dependent upon Europeans, and the general (personal, social, etc.) values and attitudes of Africans in America as well as their politics and "so-called" leadership itself are all Eurocentric in orientation. Hence, the general lifestyle of Africans under Eurocentric cultural oppression, just as the ideas and knowledge systems utilized by Africans, are merely "imitative" of the European philosophy-worldview (Ani, 1994; Baldwin, 1985; Kambon, 1992, in press a).

Despite the African world community being practically on the verge of total self-destruction as a racial-cultural collective (i.e., as a national/international community having cultural sovereignty), most Africans in both Africa and the United States seem virtually uninformed, "unconcerned," and unalarmed. Most Africans, on the surface at least, seem to feel quite comfortable with this insidious form of collective/racial psychopathology, and genocide, or what has even been referred to as a "Mentacidal" condition (Wright, 1979), i.e., the psychological equivalent of "genocide." Notwithstanding that the true cause of this dismal African predicament is rarely acknowledged, it is virtually certain to have consisted of the almost total cultural devastation of African people's normal way of life and functioning resulting from the Maafa or African Holocaust (Kambon, 1996; Lester, 1968). It is most peculiar that the obvious psychologically destructive impact of the cultural-dismantling of African civilization and African national consciousness (at least to the extent that it existed) that have resulted from the African Holocaust/ Maafa has never been appropriately addressed within the context of mental health analysis (notwithstanding the late Frantz Fanon's struggle with some aspects of this issue). As I have argued repeatedly (Baldwin, 1980b, 1984, 1985, 1991; Kambon, 1992, in press a), all forms of dysfunctional behaviors among Africans the world over, and especially in Africa and the United States, require a much broader paradigm of African mental health analysis than that offered by conventional models of "abnormal behavior" or maladaptive and dysfunctional behaviors that derive from Eurocentric psychology (see Coleman, 1992). The social-economic and political behaviors of Africans living in a world besieged by Eurasian supremacy domination are surely just as abnormal and dysfunctional as any Eurocentric-type of mental disorder that Africans may suffer from through their (forced) over-identification with the European world-view/the European Survival Thrust (Akbar, 1981; Azibo, 1989; Baldwin, 1984, 1985; Fanon, 1967; Kambon, 1992, in press a; Nobles, 1976b).

Given the complex psychological predicament which this dangerous trend in self-destructive psychological functioning and behaviors among African Americans represents, it should now be rather obvious that we must begin to generate some basic psychological models of the African reality structure which allows us to explain as fully as possible the sociocultural forces which account for such a dangerous phenomenon as is the current state of African mental health throughout the world. Additionally, we need models that explain the psychological forces which actually define the phenomenon of African mental health, its nature, function/operation, and those cultural-defined preventive-intervention mechanisms and processes that are required to correct this problem of African self-destructive functioning where it is appropriate and to otherwise eradicate it by any means necessary when warranted.

An "African-centered" view of contemporary African behavior and functioning throughout the world thus brings into clear focus just how potent and devastating a psychological force European cultural oppression of Africans has been in almost totally destroying the psychological resilience and adaptativeness of African people. It also illustrates just how far African American people's behaviors have departed from the normal-healthy realm of functioning without any widespread recognition of such a basic contradictory (race-cultural survival-threatening) mental health state of affairs. In other words, it is clear that when the concept of "abnormal/maladaptive" or "mentally disordered behavior" is extended to incorporate those behaviors which pose a basic threat to the racial-cultural survival (physical-psychological, individual-collective) of African people, then the true prevalence of disorder and abnormality in African behavior becomes clearer indeed (Baldwin, 1984, 1985; Kambon, 1992, in press a and b).

Thus, more and more African psychologists are beginning to recognize two critical concerns in their work: (1) the absolutely critical importance of broadening the context of African/African American mental health to encompass those more sociopolitical behavior patterns which have clear psychological (mental health) implications where the welfare and survival of the African American community are concerned (Akbar, 1974, 1981; Baldwin, 1980a, 1980b, 1981; X[Clark], McGee, Nobles, & X[Weems], 1975; Nobles, 1976b; Wright, 1979); and (2) the need to develop an African-centered conception/reinterpretation of the more conventional types of mental disorders as they occur among Africans in America (Akbar, 1981; Azibo, 1989).

In advancing an African-centered paradigm applicable to these concerns, I will address two basic considerations: (1) Is there a culturally relevant model of the African/African American personality? and if so, (2) How does such a model enable us to explain African mental health and mental disorder, and the appropriate preventive-intervention strategy that will effectively address the problem?

Models of African Personality

At least two meaningful categories can be constructed around models of African personality which provide the conceptual foundation for models of African mental health. Those models, more recent in occurrence, which are developed within the framework of the African world-view are called Africentric Models, while those which have grown out of the traditional conceptual framework of European-centered psychology are referred to as non-Africentric Models (Baldwin, 1984; Kambon, 1992). Thus, the few Africentric models of African American personality in existence (see Kambon, in press b) represent African worldview-centered analyses, while the preponderance and long standing tradition of non-Africentric models represent European worldview-centered analyses. Within this context, one of the crucial differences between these models, the non-Africentric models (NAM) and the Africentric models (AM), is that the NAM tend to conceptualize the African personality as more or less the net result of the protracted European racial-cultural oppression of Africans (i.e., emphasis on European-centered reality in the nature and operation of African American personality), while the AM point to the natural and fundamental cultural condition (African world-view orientation) of the African American personality.

Briefly, non-Africentric models of African personality are distinguished by the following characteristics: (a) reliance on the conceptual framework of the European world-view; (b) a negative energy and reactive motivational emphases; and (c) emphasis on abnormality and deficiency as the core of African mental health. Contrastingly, the distinguishing characteristics of the Africentric models are: (a) reliance on the African worldview as the conceptual framework for understanding African mental health; (b) a positive-affirmative energy and proactive motivational emphasis; and (c) an emphasis on the normalcy/naturalness or African-centeredness as the core of African mental health (Kambon, 1992, in press b).

The Africentric models thus allow us to not only conceptualize the natural-normal condition of African personality, but also the extent to which the African personality has become estranged from its natural condition under the "unnatural" negative anti-African influence of the European world-view (cultural reality structure) which dominates American society (Baldwin, 1980b, 1984, 1985; Kambon, 1992, in press b; Nobles, 1976b). Of the Africentric theories, the model proposed by Kambon is the most representative and will be employed to explain the issue of African/African American mental health in the modern-day Eurocentric dominated world, and in Eurocentric American society in particular.

Kambon's Africentric Model of Black Personality

According to Kambon's (1992; Baldwin, 1976, 1980a, 1981) model, African personality consists of a core system called the African Self-Extension Orientation and African Self-Consciousness, and a number of basic traits emanating from the core. The African Self-Extension Orientation (ASEO) is the foundation of the African personality. It is the organizing principle of the entire system. ASEO is innate (biogenetically determined), unconscious, and operationally defined by the concept of "Spirituality"—a dynamic energy which allows the self to merge (extend) into the totality of phenomenal experience. African Self-consciousness (ASC) derives from the African Self-extension Orientation and is essentially an "undifferentiated process" from the ASEO under normal natural conditions. It is the "conscious level" expression or dimension of the ASEO. Being a derivative of the ASEO, ASC is in part biogenetically determined, and because it is "conscious" by nature, it is also subject in part to environmental determination as well. (This, of course, is because consciousness evolves through experience, at least in part). ASC thus directs and guides the personality system (the ASEO). The former gives conscious direction and meaning to the latter. In other words, ASC directs/focuses the African survival thrust inherent in the ASEO. Thus, the ASEO defines and energizes the African personality system, while ASC directs or focuses the system toward the fulfillment and maintenance of African survival (Kambon, 1992). Given the seemingly omnipresent anti-African Eurocentric (sociopolitical) forces surrounding contemporary African existence, the ASC dimension of the African personality system is extremely important to the effective and/or adaptive functioning of African people even under the enormous psychological weight of the culturally oppressive condition of Eurasian supremacy domination (Kambon, 1992).

Based on Kambon's model, it should be clear that the ASEO (its biogenetic foundation) is immutable as the basic core of the African personality. By the same token, however, it should also be clear that the same condition does not hold for the ASC dimension given its more basic dependence on experiential development. For example, variability in the actual manifestation of the African personality among African people is explained in terms of experiential variability among individual African Americans. That is, it is dependent on the extent to which early socialization experiences and/or significant institutional-systemic processes actively nurture and reinforce the African personality system. In a heterogeneous racial-cultural context or a high socially mobile context (where an "alien worldview" is likely to dominate the reality orientation of African American people), socialization processes which nurture and reinforce the active (and especially the conscious level) operation of this natural African disposition are likely to be lessened-distorted by such potentially mitigating circumstances, whereas a strengthening-reinforcing effect would be expected in a homogeneous racial-cultural context, and perhaps in low socially mobile contexts as well (Kambon, 1992). Of course, a variety of psychologically distorting-indoctrinating circumstances of an institutional-systemic nature may also interact with and in some cases override ambiguous individual socialization conditions (such as in a multi-racial-cultural society where most of the basic institutional-systemic processes outside of the family are controlled-determined by an alien racial-cultural group's worldview).

African Self-Consciousness and African Mental Health

There are many circumstances which can and do interfere with and distort normal functioning of the African (American) personality. These circumstances, where they do occur, are usually sociocultural in nature and typically involve the operation of institutionalized anti-African forces (Baldwin, 1985; Kambon, 1992, in press a). In other words, such mitigating circumstances typically occur in a sociocultural context whereby the African (American) personality—its African reality structure—is superimposed upon by an alien and anti-African reality structure. The context of American society is one of the best examples of this process where the cultural oppression of African people is pervasive and fundamental to all of the basic societal institutions (Baldwin, 1979, 1985). In such an unnatural sociocultural context for the African American personality, the conscious level functioning of African American personality (that is, African Self-Consciousness) in particular is subject to weakening and distortion from the superimposed influence of the alien/anti-African European worldview (Baldwin, 1980b, 1984, 1985).

Given the importance of African Self-Consciousness to defining and directing the African survival thrust (i.e., in actualizing the African survival thrust potential of the African [American] personality system), then the crucial relationship between this construct and the phenomenon of African mental health should also be clear. This is because the condition of "disorder" in African personality occurs at the level of African self-consciousness, not at the level of the African Self-Extension Orientation. In other words, where socialization and/or experiential indoctrination processes are reflective of an alien (Eurocentric) worldview (as has always been the case for Africans in America), to the extent that such an experience is experientially dominant for the African person (i.e., in the forms of both significant and generalized significant others, see Baldwin, 1985; Kambon, 1992), then African Self-Consciousness is vulnerable to distortions by the alien influence. As I noted earlier, when the alien worldview is in fact anti-African in its basic survival thrust, as in European-American society where the dominant world-view is naturally the "European world-view" (Baldwin, 1985; Kambon, in press a), then the nature of the distorting and misdirecting influences on African Self-Consciousness becomes "anti-African" as well (Kambon, 1992).

In short, then, under such conditions of "disorder" in the African personality, the natural African survival thrust of African Self-Consciousness becomes distorted into a self-destructive "alien/anti-African survival thrust" (Baldwin, 1984, 1985; Kambon, in press a). In the case of Africans in America specifically, a pseudo European/Eurocentric self-consciousness comes to dominate over their natural

Figure 1
The ASEO and ASC as the Basic Core of African Personality

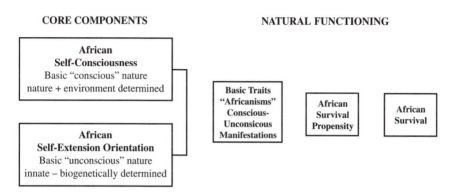

AFRICAN PERSONALITY

CORE COMPONENTS   NATURAL FUNCTIONING

African
Self-Consciousness
Basic "conscious" nature
nature + environment determined

Basic Traits
"Africanisms"
Conscious-
Unconsicous
Manifestations

African
Survival
Propensity

African
Survival

African
Self-Extension Orientation
Basic "unconscious" nature
innate – biogenetically determined

Basic Characteristics: Self-knowledge; Oneness-harmony with nature;
Communalism; We'ness; Group survival; Self-reinforcing-enhancing/Africentric
values, beliefs, attitudes and behaviors.

African Self-Consciousness (i.e., dominate the personality system at the conscious level of functioning). This "abnormal" psychological circumstance creates a contradictory intrapsychic condition in the African personality (i.e., unconscious level Africanity and conscious level Eurocentrism). It thus manifests itself in the contradiction of African functioning (cognitive and behavioral functioning) reflecting the European survival thrust, a most unnatural and paradoxical outcome indeed. This complex condition of disorder in African personality based on Kambon's model is illustrated in the contrasting of Figures 1 and 2.

The solid lines in Figure 1, as contrasted with the broken lines in Figure 2, indicate the normal-natural organization and functioning of the African personality structure. That is, the unity/undifferentiation of functioning between the African Self-Extension Orientation (ASEO) and African Self-Consciousness (ASC). The broken lines in Figure 2, on the other hand, indicate the unnaturalness and weakening in the unity of functioning between ASC and the ASEO. Order exists in the African (American) personality system when the normal and natural relationship of unity or undifferentiated form is maintained between the ASEO and ASC. In contrast, disorder occurs in the African personality system whenever the normal and natural relationship of unity or undifferentiated form no longer maintains (i.e., these basic processes become "differentiated"). Consequently, when an "abnormal unnatural" relationship (incongruence or differentiation) characterizes the operation of the core components of the African personality system, we have a case of basic African mental disorder. Given the fundamental "oppositional" nature of the

Figure 2
Disorder in African Personality at the Level of ASC

AFRICAN PERSONALITY

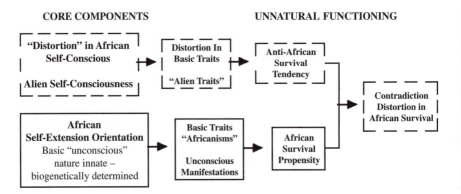

CORE COMPONENTS   UNNATURAL FUNCTIONING

Basic Characteristics: Individualism; Materialism; Conflict with nature;
Self-as-object orientation; I'ness; Me'ness survival; Self-Alienating-Negating Values,
Beliefs, Attitudes and behaviors.

African and European world-views (Ani, 1994; Baldwin, 1980a, 1985; Baldwin &
Hopkins, 1990; Kambon, 1992, in press b; Nobles, 1976a or b; Richards, 1989), then
under conditions where the European world-view achieves dominance over the
natural African worldview orientation of African people, as in American society,
this results in a condition of personlity disorder. Thus, where disunity/incongruence
exists between the operation of African Self-Consciousness and that of the African
Self-Extension Orientation, this signifies the presence of basic personality disorder
within the African personality.

Kambon's model of African (American) personality thus provides us with an
entirely different framework for conceptualizing the phenomenon of "African
(including "African American") mental health." Here the notion of mental health
is clearly grounded in the fundamental primal motive or universal principle of
"Organismic Survival Maintenance" (Baldwin, 1980b, 1984, 1985), which assumes that all functionally normal organisms strive to secure, protect, maintain and
advance their own survival. Given that African personality is naturally couched in
interconnectedness-collectivism, then African survival maintenance naturally is
couched in Africans striving to secure, protect, maintain and advance African
"collective" survival.

Cultural Misorientation in African Personality Disorder

Specifically, the condition of African personality disorder described in the foregoing discussion represents a phenomenon which I refer to as "Psychological/ Cultural Misorientation" (Baldwin, 1980a, 1980b; Kambon, 1992, in press a). Hence, the Eurocentric distortion in African Self-Consciousness referred to earlier manifests itself in terms of Cultural Misorientation (CM). Cultural Misorientation refers to an incorrect (and distorted) orientation among African people to their natural (African) cultural reality. It appears functionally normal within the framework of the European worldview/European social reality which dominates African existence in America because all of the social cues, institutional support systems, etc. throughout European-centered (American, etc.) society reinforce only the European survival thrust. Thus, Africans in America who suffer from this condition may not typically experience any overt anxiety, confusion or conflict over their identity or their sense of psychological normalcy, since all of the basic institutional processes in American society reinforce such psychopathology in African people. Hence, Cultural Misorientation refers to a grossly psychopathological condition in African Americans masquerading as functional normalcy or as optimal mental health.

As I have noted elsewhere (Kambon, 1992), while the condition of Cultural Misorientation is psychological in nature and therefore is certainly appropriately called "psychological misorientation" in terms of its content, as was my initial statement of this construct (Baldwin 1980b), it is at the same time more meaningfully interpreted in terms of "cultural reality" (Baldwin, 1985; Baldwin & Hopkins, 1990; Kambon, 1992, in press a). Thus, in terms of its cultural and social reality meaningfulness, I subsequently adopted the terminology of "Cultural Misorientation." This construct was used in an attempt to account for the widespread incidence of a form of mental disorder common among African people that is sanctioned, nurtured and reinforced by the institutional network of European-American culture and Eurasian society in general (Akbar, 1981; Azibo, 1989; Baldwin, 1984, 1985; Kambon, 1992, in press a; Nobles, 1976b).

Thus, I have begun to employ the concept of Cultural Misorientation as the most appropriate label for designating the widespread contradictory psychological condition among Africans in America reflecting an incorrect cultural orientation that is "Eurasiancentric" in its basic nature or worldview framework (Kambon, 1992, in press a). As has been noted, then, Cultural Misorientation in effect consists of the existence of a Eurocentric (or Arabcentric/Asiancentric) self-consciousness in African people which is consistent with and thereby supported and reinforced (in American society) by European-American culture itself (or another alien anti-African culture). Because Africans are obviously not Europeans, and therefore the European (or Eurasian) worldview does not and cannot foster self-affirmative and efficacious functioning in African people as a culturally distinct group (i.e., "as

African people" rather than as "Black-skinned Eurasians" for example), it is indeed an illness, a mental illness (Baldwin, 1984, 1985). It is a mental disordered condition because it leads African people to literally culturally self-destruct! It is thus a severe and gross condition of mental disorder/psychopathology in Africans.

This construct therefore means that a cultural specific mental disorder exists among African people victimized by Eurasiancentric (European, Arab, Asian) cultural oppression which is not recognized, and in fact cannot be recognized by the traditional American psychiatric nosologies which dominate our conceptions of mental health and illness (see Coleman, 1992). This occurs because the traditional American (Eurocentric) psychiatric nosologies are in reality cultural specific to the European cultural reality, although they are purported erroneously to represent "universal" or "cross-cultural" conditions (Coleman, 1992; Thomas & Sillen, 1972).

In previous work (Baldwin, 1984; Kambon, 1992), I have argued that this African-centered model of African American mental health allows us to explain nearly all of the distortions, pathologies, and self-destructive tendencies that are so prevalent in African behavior today. For example, the vivid psychopathologies among African Americans as captured by Woodson (1969), Frazier (1957), Hare (1965), Fanon (1967), Grier and Cobbs (1968, 1971), Smith (1975), Braitwaite et al. (1979), Malcolm X's autobiography (among many others), and the countless volumes of novels that depict various hypothetical and/or fictitious portrayals of self-destructive behaviors in contemporary African life in America (albeit most are actually based on real life situations), all serve to confirm the existence of severe distortions in African Self-Consciousness among African American people. One can readily observe manifestations of Cultural Misorientation in African political life, where the emphasis is placed almost obsessively on voting, integration, and simply participation in European-American social systems rather than on activities grounded in the cardinal principle of "African self-determination." It is also clearly manifested in (so-called) African religious life, where we absurdly worship God and other deities in the images of our enemies, among other gross contradictions of sanity and historical facts, and in the so-called educational life of Africans in America, where all aspects of formal knowledge and intellectual-type skills that Africans acquire from American education are controlled by the European worldview. In all of these cases, as in others not mentioned, the blatant pattern of distortion in African American people's African Self-Consciousness is overwhelmingly clear. In fact, the very nature of African people's "blanked dependency" on Europeans for psychological-intellectual existence as well as for physical-material existence clearly reveals that Africans in America, by and large, have assumed a European Self-Consciousness (an anti-African self-consciousness). This Eurocentric/anti-African Self-Consciousness has been superimposed upon and thereby has severely distorted our natural African Self-Consciousness (Akbar, 1981, 1984; Azibo, 1989;

Baldwin, 1979, 1980a, 1980b, 1984, 1985; Kambon, 1992, in press a; McGee, 1973; Nobles, 1976b; Smith, 1975; Wright, 1979).

The utility of this model in explaining Africans' blatant self-destructive patterns of mental health is therefore clearly supported by the mass of data all around us. In particular, Kambon's model enables us to understand and explain most of the basic pathologies that are manifested in African mental health (see Kambon, in press a). To reiterate the basic conclusion of this paradigm, the Cultural Misorientation model proposes that Eurocentric cultural distortions in African Self-consciousness define the basic nature of "disorder in the African personality in America," and thus poses one of the greatest threats to African mental health in America and elsewhere throughout the Eurasian dominated world.

In previous work (Baldwin, 1985; Kambon, 1992, in press a), I have identified a number of major areas of collective (institutional-organized) life activities of Africans, particularly in America, where cultural oppression operates to create the condition of Cultural Misorientation. Chief among these are the areas of education, religion, economics, media-communications, cultural icons and other symbols and imagery, political activity, and social activity, among others. These all represent regular, if not everyday areas of African collective life activity penetrated by the imposition of the European worldview. Perhaps there is no more critical area of everyday African functioning in America under White supremacy domination than the blatantly self-destructive manifestations which predominate African "self-presentation" behaviors. I will briefly discuss four commonly occurring examples of anti-African self-presentation behaviors that characterize the contemporary African experience in America.

Examples of Anti-African Self-Presentation Behaviors in the American Context

1. The widespread maintenance of European names and personal labels by Africans in America is one of the fundamental manifestations of anti-African self-presentation behavior. The pervasive linguistic condition of virtual illiteracy among Africans in America in any of the traditional African languages (such as Twi, Yoruba, etc) is also related. Africans in America continue religiously, since the so-called emancipation from physical enslavement, to practice the selection of European names intergenerationally for their newborn children. The overwhelming majority are also monolingual as a rule (English is our only language), and ironically, when we do become bilingual, we adopt a Eurasian second language. Hence, Africans in America suffering from CM do not experience any contradiction in this form of anti-African behavior. Some groups even perceive themselves as progressive and revolutionary when they reject the European name inherited from one condition of enslavement and then, paradoxically, exchange it for an Arab name

and learn the Arab language. All of this so-called "revolutionary" activity occurs under the banner, slogan or guise of African "liberation" and "self-determination" (i.e., moving from African American Christian to African American Muslim).

2. A second fundamental manifestation of this phenomenon occurs in Africans maintaining a death-like grip and pathological dependency on European-centered/ anti-African religions that were imposed upon their great-great-great grandparents through terrorizing murder, rape and naked brutality (i.e., during our enslavement) Africans adhere to the religions of their enemies and conquerors so intensely and through such internalized intimidation that they will defend the alien beliefs even against their own people's/their own culture's survival. Such victimized Africans will fight, kill and even willingly die over these religions as well. In Christianity, Islam, and Judaism the Creator is assigned a foreign/non-African name (i.e., names that are not indigenous to any African language/ethnicity, etc.), yet Africans subscribed to these non-African languages as if they really were indigenous African languages.

3. A third example of fundamental manifestations of anti-African self-presentation behavior consists of the widespread ritual among African Americans of cooking their hair to achieve the straight and looping curly hair look (perms and Jerri curl looks). This condition of White supremacy-induced anti-self pathology among African Americans is so deeply ingrained that even when some Africans seemingly can generate accurate intellectual insights into our cultural pathology and our great need for "re-Africanization," they do not connect it with this vital aspect of their own self-presentation behavior.

4. A fourth and final example of this phenomenon consists of the widespread practices associated with the Mulatto Hypothesis among Africans in America which manifests itself in terms of skin color conflicts and prejudices, and facial and physical features denigration rituals. It is common-place for African American parents and other significant others and generalized significant others for African children to denigrate wooly hair, broad noses and lips, and dark skin color in relation to their children, while concurrently praising degrees of physical features departing from those identified in other African children. Furthermore, it is generally a fact that light complexioned African women consistently enjoy higher status and special psychological and material privileges among African Americans (are given more positive-favored treatment) than their darker complexioned sisters enjoy. Most darker complexioned African American men of high accomplishment according to the European American standards select as spouses African American women who are of lighter complexions than themselves, or of a similar hue if they are of lighter skin color. This phenomenon, no matter what it's conscious rationale may be, literally defies statistical prediction of normal-natural variability in mate selection among African American men.

African-Centered Intervention and Prevention Strategies

Where implications for the treatment and prevention of these types of disorders in African personality and mental disorders among Africans are concerned, Kambon's model suggests that the primary focus lies in the area of reawakening and enhancing or strengthening African Self-Consciousness. The evidence clearly suggests that most Africans in America exhibit severe distortions in their African Self-Consciousness as a result of their basic acceptance/internalization of the "anti-African" survival thrust of the European worldview (cultural assimilation/psychological internalization-identification with Eurocentric culture). Thus, Africans in America are in serious need of innovative African-centered therapeutic intervention that is directed toward reestablishing the natural-harmonious relationship between the ASEO and ASC within the African personality system.

I have proposed elsewhere (Baldwin, 1984, 1985; Kambon, 1992) that African-centered (functionally relevant) preventive intervention for African mental health in America must involve the implementation of Africentric social-communal level therapeutic procedures. This preventive intervention must occur in terms of the creation of institutional level processes which define, support and reinforce African Self-Consciousness, i.e., the creation of Africentric institutions. Specifically, I have proposed that functionally relevant African mental health preventive intervention/healing must involve the rebuilding and reinstitutionalizing of the African cultural infrastructure that was virtually destroyed by the 500-700 year Maafa/African Holocaust. At the very spiritual center of this cultural destruction has been the disruption of the continuity of our African cultural memory, the loss of our recognition and acknowledgment of our African ancestry, from Africa through the period of enslavement and right into the present day, and the loss of our fundamental sense of obligations and responsibilities to them. In essence, we lost our fundamental African identity in the psychological trauma of the Maafa, and to this day have not been able to set into motion the appropriate cultural healing procedures or methodology that is required to restore that psycho-cultural infrastructure that has been lost from our culture self-consciousness. The healing methodology to address our fragmented cultural self-consciousness must be specific to our traditional African culture and our contemporary sociopolitical (mental health) circumstance. We need healing rituals that specifically acknowledge our historical (communal/ancestral) experience of the Maafa, the destruction and pain that it inflicted, and our resolve to reconnect with our cultural ancestral continuity (accountability, cultural obligations and responsibilities).

In previous work (Kambon, 1992), I have proposed the following Africentric healing/preventive intervention activities that are relevant to African mental health under European cultural domination. They are as follows:

1. Every African in America should participate in an African Identity Reclamation Rite that involves the resumption of traditional African names for ourselves, our children,

etc. This formally initiates the purging and cultural healing-renewal process for African people emerging spiritually-holistically from the Maafa of Eurasian enslavement.

2. Africans in America should participate in an Annual Maafa Rite commemorating our ancestors who struggled through this great physical and sociocultural calamity or holocaust. It is a way of remembering and renewing our historical African ties and sense of cultural continuity (reciprocity, accountability, etc.).

3. The utilization of African-centered calendars of rituals, rites and ceremonies must become an essential part of every African's daily life in America. These calendars will guide our daily lives and allow us to continually reaffirm our cultural-ancestral connect-edness and our victorious vision of reestablishing African cultural-political empowerment throughout the world. This practice also allows for the renewal of our historical ties and sense of cultural continuity, but in a much more intense and fuller sense given its regularity.

4. Africans in America should "reclaim" an African language by becoming "bilingual or multi-lingual," learning at least one African language system in addition to the English that we speak, be it Akan (Twi), Tuni (Ashante), Yuroba, Zulu, Kiswhilli, or other Bantu or Fonte language systems as well as others. This practice also represents a very powerful and ultimately necessary part of the African cultural renewal process.

5. Africans in America should require the use of an African language form in all rituals and ceremonies in our community, in our homes and in our close social circles.

6. Africans in America should practice African-centered rituals in our private/personal lives when we are away from the context of the European societal situations that we often must function in daily. Our private-personal space should be treated as sacred cultural space and kept separate from the other more "multicultural" or intercultural space that we often encounter outside of our personal circles in life.

The reader should clearly recognize that this is not a fad that is being proposed here. We have developed African-like fads in the past because we didn't have (we weren't operating from) a larger more substantive African-centered framework to place such activities and practices within, in order to give them substantive cultural recovery/renewal meaningfulness. In the sense that these procedures are employed here, they are very practical acts that are firmly grounded in the African world-view and Africentric models of African mental health. The paradigm articulated in this manuscript clearly denotes the relevance and significance of this critical cultural renewal procedure.

African Mental Health in Perspective

This model has attempted to demonstrate that under the socio-cultural conditions of White/Eurasian supremacy rule and domination over African people, virtually all behavior/actions not only have major mental health significance, but also have significant "political" import for African people, either strengthening or weakening African empowerment, self-determination, affirmation, etc. This must not be overlooked in psychological analysis of African mental health under conditions such as those characterizing the American context, as well as the broader diasporian and continental African contexts. Thus, whether it is Africans' religious practices/spiritual system-expressions, our naming ourselves, our hair preparation and physical presentation, our clothing, our economic and political practices, or our entertainment and recreational preferences and activities, etc., it must all be defined and practiced from an African cultural centered framework if it is to reinforce our African survival thrust, and thus reflect positive/optimal African mental health.

It has been said that for African people, our psychological-spiritual health, our energy and our strength comes from our cultural foundation; our cultural rituals, customs and practices which symbolize and reaffirm our ancestral linkage (Richards, 1989, 1990a). Thus, the weakening of our psychological-spiritual health occurs in our movement away from our African cultural foundation—our African cultural values, rituals and customs. Hence, African mental health depends on our closeness to or the continuity that we Africans maintain to our cultural origins, to our ancestors, etc., through our practice of our traditional values and rituals. ASC, therefore, represents that natural disposition in the African personality which allows African people to consciously value and participate in African self (cultural)-reaffirmation through the practice of African cultural values, rituals and practices (the African worldview) modified for our contemporary circumstance.

Conclusion

This analysis of African mental health asserts that there is indeed an African reality system that is not only indigenous to Africans in America, but that most Africans in America are almost totally unaware of it and how it determines our very lives. It further asserts that this African worldview/reality system is "superior" (in fact "optimal") for African people to the European American reality system (the European worldview), to which Africans have been forced to assimilate and internalize (through the American societal institutional arrangement) in order to enjoy whatever the rewards American life are supposed to offer (psychological, social, material rewards, etc.). It thus argues that optimal African functioning/ mental health lies outside of the "alleged" superior/optimal quality of European reality, i.e., the false assertion of the European worldview as "universal" and of the African worldview as primitive and inferior.

This analysis also asserts that the "average" African in America operates/ functions in a mentally disordered state, on a daily basis, engendered by the institutional imposition of Eurasian culture (White/Eurasian supremacy domination) over our African cultural reality here in America. This is because Africans are forced through White supremacy miseducation and Eurasian cultural indoctrination to function psychologically, behaviorally, etc., as a European person in Black skin (Fanon, 1967; Hare, 1965; Kambon, 1992, in press a). Such a condition, then, is literally one of "cultural based mental disorder unique to Africans," which the American (European controlled) societal system itself supports and reinforces in African people. Hence, not only is it the criminal and homicidal Africans, the suicidal and drug/substance addicted-abuse Africans, and the ghetto dwelling, school dropout, and unskilled and unemployed Africans who suffer from this pervasive form of African personality disorder, but it is also the so-called average-everyday Africans as well (the "hard-working, bills-paying, family-oriented, church-going, apple-pie-eating, etc. Africans). This condition of pervasive "cultural" (mental) disorder thus affects the vast majority of the African population in America (Kambon, 1992, in press a).

Finally, this analysis asserts, among other things, that in order for Africans to heal themselves from this unprecedented predicament of pervasive cultural/mental disorder, we must revive our ASC and rebuild our African cultural infrastructure throughout the diasporian African community. (This approach to mental health intervention is also applicable to continental Africans as well.) This will entail our revitalizing and reinstitutionalizing our African cultural traditions, some of which will need to be modified based on contemporary African knowledge. It thus challenges us as well as directs our mental health preventive-intervention efforts toward the serious work of Pan-African Nation-building/rebuilding and mainte-nance of our own cultural infrastructures (again, traditional African values, beliefs, rituals, practices, etc.) shaped or informed by the historical continuity of African knowledge. In concluding, then, this Africentric model of African mental health recognizes that the full recovery of the African personality victimized by Eurasian supremacy domination requires a massive dosage of African cultural renewal (Kambon, 1992), which will entail the rebuilding and revitalization of the African cultural infrastructure throughout African communities of the diaspora and the African world community as well.

References

Akbar, N. [aka Luther X (Weems)] (1974). Awareness: The key to Black mental health. *Journal of Black Psychology, 1*, 30-37.

Akbar, N. (1981). *Mental disorder among African-Americans. Black Books Bulletin, 7*(2), 18-25.

Akbar, N. (1984). *Chains and images of psychological slavery.* Jersey City, NJ: New Mind Productions.

Azibo, D. A. (1989). African-centered theses on mental health and a nosology of African American/African personality disorder. *Journal of Black Psychology, 15*(2), 173-214.

Baldwin, J. A. (1976). Black psychology and Black personality. *Black Books Bulletin, 4*(3), 6-11, 65.

Baldwin, J. A. (1979). Education and oppression in the American context. *Journal of Inner City Studies, 1*(1), 62-85.

Baldwin, J. A. (1980a). *An Africentric model of Black personality.* In Proceedings of the Fourteenth Annual Convention of the Association of Black Psychologists. Washington, DC: ABPsi.

Baldwin, J. A. (1980b). The psychology of oppression. In M. Asante & A. Vandi (Eds.), *Contemporary Black thought.* Beverly Hills, CA: Sage Publishers.

Baldwin, J. A. (1981). Notes on an Africentric theory of Black personality. *The Western Journal of African American Studies, 5*(3), 172-179.

Baldwin, J. A. (1984). African self-consciousness and the mental health of African-Americans. *The Journal of Black Studies, 15*(2), 177-194.

Baldwin, J. A. (1985). Psychological aspects of European cosmology in American society. *The Western Journal of Black Studies, 9*(4), 216-223.

Baldwin, J. A. (1989). The role of Black psychologists in African liberation. *The Journal of Black Psychology, 16*(1), 67-76.

Baldwin, J. A. (1991). An African-centered model of the health and social behavior of African-American males. In L. Gary (Ed.), *The health and social behavior of African-American males.* Washington, DC: The Urban Research Institute, Howard University.

Baldwin, J. A., & Hopkins, R. (1990). African-American and European-American cultural differences as assessed by the worldviews paradigm: A theoretical and empirical analysis. *The Western Journal of Black Studies, 14* (1), 38-52.

Braitwaite, H., Taylor, K., & Black, H. (1979). *Survival manual: First aid for the mind* (2nd ed.). Atlanta, GA: Private Printing.

Coleman, J. S. (1992). *Abnormal Psychology* (4th ed.). New York: John Wiley & Sons.

X(Clark), C., McGee, D., Nobles, W., & X(Weems), L. (1975). Voodoo or IQ: An introduction to African psychology. *Journal of Black Psychology, 1*(2), 9-29.

Fanon, F. (1967). *Black skin, white masks.* New York, NY: Grove Press.

Frazier, E. F. (1957). *Black bourgeoise.* Glencoe, IL: The Free Press.

Grier, W., & Cobbs, P. (1968). *Black rage.* New York, NY: Basic Books.

Grier, W., & Cobbs, P. (1971). *Jesus bag.* New York, NY: McGraw-Hill.

Hare, N. (1965). *The Black anglo-saxons.* New York, NY: Collier Books.

Kambon, K. K. K. (1992). *The African personality in America: An African-centered framework.* Tallahassee, FL: Nubian Nations Publications.

Kambon, K. K. K. (in press a). Towards the assessment of cultural misorientation among Africans in America. *The Journal of Black Psychology.*

Kambon, K. K. K. (in press b). *African psychology in the American context: An introduction.* Tallahassee, FL: Nubian Nations Publications.

Karenga, M. R. (1965). *Nguzo saba.* San Diego, CA: Kawaida Pubs.

Karenga, M. R. (1978). *Essays on struggle.* San Diego, CA: Kawaida Pubs.

Madhubuti, H. (1973). *From plan to planet.* Chicago, IL: Third World Press.

McGee, D. P. (1973). White conditioning of Black dependency. *The Journal of Social Issues, 29,* 53-56.

Nascimento, Abdias do (1978). *Mixture or massacre: The genocide of a people.* Buffalo, NY: Afrodiaspora Press.

Nobles, W. W. (1976a). African science: The consciousness of self. In L. M. King (Ed.), *African philosophy: Assumptions and paradigms for research on Black persons.* Los Angeles, CA: Fanon Center.

Nobles, W. W. (1976b). Black people in White insanity: An issue for Black community mental health. *Journal of Afro-American Issues, 4,* 21-27.

Richards, D. M. (1989). *Let the circle be unbroken: African spirituality in the diaspora.* Trenton, NJ: Red Sea Press.

Richards, D.M. (1990). The development, transformation and healing of the African Self. Keynote address to The 22nd Annual Convention of ABPsi, Ocho Rios, Jamaica, WI.

Russell, K., Wilson, M., & Hall, R. (1992). *The color complex: The politics of skin color among african americans.* New York: Anchor Books.

Smith, P. M., Jr. (1975). Lets psyche 'em? *Journal of Black Psychology, 1*(2), 42-52.

Thomas, A., & Sillen, S. (1972). *Racism and psychiatry.* Secaucus, NY: Citadel Press.

Williams, C. (1976). *The destruction of black civilization.* Chicago: Third World Press.

Woodson, C. G. (1933). *The mis-education of the Negro.* Washington, DC: Associated Publishers.

Wright, B. (1979, September). *Mentacide.* Paper presented at the First Annual Conference of the Black Psychology Task Force. SREB, Atlanta, GA.

Author

Kobi K. K. Kambon
Dept. of Psychology, GECC #302
Florida A&M University
Tallahassee, FL 32307
Telephone: (904) 599-3014/3468
Fax: (904) 561-2540

Sankofa: A Black Mental Health Imperative for the 21st Century

Huberta Jackson-Lowman

Introduction

A persisting mark of the oppression of Afrikan people is manifested in our struggle to experience, reflect upon, define, interpret, and recreate reality from our perspective—that is, grounded in our world-view, our history, and our cultural requirements for our collective well-being. Trapped in a "500 year room" of European domination (I. Van Sertima, speech at Community College of Allegheny College, Pittsburgh, PA, 1992), Afrikan people have lost contact with the reality that we knew for thousands of years before EuroAsian intrusion. In the context of the Afrikan world view and the history of Afrikan peoples, the fact that we have adopted the standard European criteria for evaluating contact with reality literally means that we are disoriented in regard to time, person, and place; or, as Wilson (1993) puts it, we are "out of our minds." The dislocation that has ensued from this disorientation has profoundly affected our mental health and well-being. "To the extent that the individual feels isolated or detached from a meaningful sociocultural and spiritual context, he or she is at risk for a variety of pathological conditions ranging from depression and apathy to more severe forms of pathology such as murder and self-destruction" (Ghee, 1990, p. 91).

That Afrikan American communities are aggrieved with aberrant conditions heretofore relatively uncommon among us is indisputable. Our efforts to remedy these conditions have inadequately addressed the bases for the growing sense of isolation and detachment that prevails in Afrikan American neighborhoods (but also in European American neighborhoods) and the lack of meaning that we find in the sociocultural and spiritual contexts in which Afrikan Americans exist. Our challenge as Somé (1994) asserts is to recognize that "there is more than one version of 'reality' . . . . To exist . . . each culture has to have its own version of what is real" (p. 8). What is missing for Afrikan Americans is our own consensually validated constructions of reality. This lack daily whittles away at our ability to fully appreciate and be who we really are and live out our divine purpose.

51

In this essay I contend that there is a distinct Afrikan American view of reality based upon our Afrikan and Afrikan American historical and cultural experiences. Using the three questions posed by Frantz Fanon (Karenga, 1988)— *Who am I? Am I really who I am? Am I all I ought to be?*—as the lens for this exploration, I will examine critical dimensions of the issues of identity, authenticity, and purpose within the context of the Afrikan world view. Fundamental to all Afrikan world views is the belief in the spiritual nature of life; thus, this formulation, through its focus on these three essential life questions, embraces the inseparability of mental health and spiritual orientation. For Afrikan people imbued with a Western/ Eurocentric world view, the potential for becoming disoriented, dislodged, and dislocated as we struggle with these basic human questions, is practically a given. The omnipresence of our historically oppressive conditions has perverted and distorted our experience of our identity, forced us into the assumption of inauthentic ways of being, and denied us opportunity to fully reveal our traditional greatness.

To begin this analysis some understanding of the underlying assumptions of Western/Eurocentric models of mental health that make them wholly insupportable for Afrikan people is necessary. The next section summarizes these understandings.

Rationale for Redefining Mental Health

Models of mental health conceived in Western terms carry assumptions that run counter to indigenous Afrikan experiences of reality. First, these models constrict the definition of valid experience. Second, the constraints of a Western/ Eurocentric world-view delimit the methods acceptable for assessing our experience. Third, the kinds of explanations that are considered valid within a Western/ Eurocentric world view emanate from these prior assumptions, which means that only certain aspects of our existence are considered relevant and worthy of focus. However, rarely are issues of world view the subject of analysis.

The field of psychology, which relies on a Western/Eurocentric world view in its construction of theories of human development and behavior, rarely, if ever, articulates the assumptions associated with this world view. Therefore, redefining mental health for Afrikan people is utterly compelled by the recognition that Western psychology's understanding both of what psychology is and who Afrikan people are originates from foundations that assert reductionism, compartmentalism, dualism, and racism (Nobles, 1986). Several examples of the extent to which these ideas and their related assumptions pervade and underlie the philosophy of Western psychology will suffice.

Reductionism is the assumption that things should be expressed and understood in the simplest possible terms. The use of a metaphysical explanation to account for certain "natural" phenomena would be unacceptable within this framework. Rather, emphasis is placed on explanations that embrace materialistic conceptualizations of matter. Ani (1994) clearly articulates the inherent difficulties with this assumption: "The tyranny of mechanical causation in European thought precludes the perception of cosmic interrelationship, identification, meaningful coincidence, complementarity, and the 'circle'" (p. 67). Thus, within a reductionistic framework, in the case of a plague biological variables are typically pursued as the causal agents, while metaphysical theories that posit nonmaterial or spiritual factors would be considered untenable and unnecessary—a perspective which for Afrikan people is extremely perplexing and incapacitating. The traditional Afrikan worldview interprets life as an "eternal cycle . . . that offers the possibility of transcendence, of harmonious interrelationship, of wholeness, integration, and authentic organicity" (Ani, 1994, p. 67).

Compartmentalism, the process of dividing things up into component parts which are studied separately as if they were independent, provides the structure for Western knowledge production and dissemination both within and across disciplines. Consequently, within the "academy," it is possible to demarcate psychology and religion and spirituality, which is impossible in everyday lived experience. Furthermore, within psychology, it is possible to study the individual, the family, the neighborhood or community as if these entities had an existence apart from the contexts in which we find them.

Dualism is often expressed in the ongoing mind-versus-body or nature-versus-nurture controversies that persist in Western psychology. A significant number of studies have been undertaken to identify the amount of variance attributable to genetic versus learned experience. This debate operates within the either-or context of Western/Eurocentric thought, which has difficulty comprehending the diunital nature of experience and admitting that both dimensions are necessary and essential for understanding phenomena associated with human development and functioning.

Thomas and Sillen (1972) expound extensively on the infusion of racism in the study of Afrikan people throughout psychology and psychiatry since its earliest development. Assumptions of mental deficiency and extraordinary physical prowess are profuse and provide the basis for interaction with and treatment of Afrikan peoples (Bevis, 1921; Hall, 1904; Jensen, 1969; Jung, 1928, 1930; McDougall, 1908; Terman, 1916). Most recently these notions have found expression once again in the highly popular book *The Bell Curve* (Hernstein & Murray, 1994).

While the above conceptual differences might suffice as explanations for seeking and developing alternative approaches to the understanding of mental health, more fundamental is the fact that Western models of mental health are derived both from theories of pathology and normative studies primarily of the majority European American community (Akbar, 1991; Baldwin, 1976; Thomas & Sillen, 1972). The assumption that health is simply the absence of disease undergirds this activity. Furthermore, to rely upon normative definitions of mental health— what Akbar (1991) refers to as "democratic sanity"—maintains the oppression of Afrikan Americans, given that racism is enshrined in the consciousness of most

European Americans. The contrasting assumptions undergirding this essay are; (1) the processes that support health are distinctly different from those that support disease, and (2) normative definitions of mental health, subject as they are to the social and political exigencies of the empowered group, are inadequate for establishing an acceptable definition of mental health. Therefore, models of health that emerge from the highest values and principles known to humanity are essential and must be developed for the promotion, maintenance, and enhancement of mental health. Examples of these values and principles are evident throughout the continent of Afrika, the earliest known expression being the Maat (Karenga, 1988).

Another difficulty with Western/Eurocentric definitions of mental health lies in how they are applied. Although these definitions of mental health are primarily generated from studies of European Americans or their theories, more often of middle class status and male gender, they are applied to persons of a variety of cultures, ethnicities, and socioeconomic status. Two problems are inherent: (1) Their application to persons of different race/ethnic groups, gender, and classes; and (2) the focus on the individual rather than the group. The first issue has already been discussed both here and in other works (Adebimpe, 1981; Willie, Rieker, Kramer, & Brown, 1995); however, little attention has been given to the second issue. World view is integrally connected to the selection of the *unit* or *entity* upon which one focuses to evaluate mental health. Zimbardo (1985) indicates that in some Afrikan societies mental health is viewed not as a characteristic of the individual but as "part of the ecological relationship." By implication, then, the notion of the individual is an illusion, for no one can be understood apart from the context in which he or she exists both historically and contemporarily. Thus, the ground on which this formulation of mental health stands assumes that mental health is a dynamic process vested in a society or group, rather than in individuals, and is subject to the same universal laws and principles that govern and support all living things. Therefore, models that are based in pathology and disease, normatively generated, and embedded with Western/Eurocentric values can do little to facilitate the understanding or appreciation of what mental health is for Afrikan people.

Concept of Self

The Western notion of self as "individual" is perhaps the most fundamental source of distortion for Afrikan people (Baldwin, 1985; Baldwin, Brown, & Hopkins, 1991; Nobles, 1991). An acceptance of the concept of the individual as an appropriate starting point undergirds discussions of self-concept and identity that are foundational to Western psychological theories. "Self-concept includes both what the person perceives himself/herself to be in reality, and the conception of what he/she would like to be ideally" (Ghee, 1990, p. 90). In this definition, self is unidirectional and locked within the time boundaries of the physical self. From an

Afrikan-centered perspective, embracing this definition of self results in alienation, disconnectedness, and confusion, and ultimately contributes to increased suffering (Rogers, 1996).

An Afrikan analysis of self is provided by Ogbonnaya (1994), who discusses the concept of self as community. He summarizes the views of many different Afrikan societies and suggests that Afrikans view the individual as a "community of selves." These selves minimally and variously include a totem self, an ancestral self, a contemporary self, a mischievous self, an emergent self, a not-yet self, and a divine self. Each person must have access to all aspects of self to be in balance. Furthermore, this community of selves must be well integrated for the individual to function in a healthy manner. The integration of each aspect of self is viewed as essential to personal and communal equilibrium and is a requirement for healing when disequilibrium exists. Thus, for the Afrikan mind, connection to others is not an abstract phenomenon, nor is it only a result of self- or other-initiated actions. Rather it is inborn and integral to human nature. This distinction is not merely semantical, for it implies that each person incorporates within himself or herself the whole world and the Divine and suggests that our connection to self is reflected in our connection to others.

Within this community of selves the physical body serves as the environment for the interplay among these selves. The *ancestral self* contains the embodiment of the past, representing our connection to our ancestors through our blood lines and our collective unconscious. As described by Kambon (1992, p. 50), it is characterized as African Self-Extension Orientation (ASEO), "a cumulative pool of African ancestral knowledge . . . will and intent . . . locked away . . . the deeply rooted, unconscious spiritual process through which each new generation of Africans continually moves towards their essence."

The *totem self* acknowledges the spiritual and genetic bond with one's group, composed of members of the extended family, clan, and tribe. The totem that a particular group selects to represent it is typically identified as an animal that manifests those characteristics associated with the group. It incorporates the most valued qualities to which the group aspires. It links humanity with the natural kingdom acknowledging their interdependence. In many Afrikan societies, people may be first identified by the totem to which they belong, emphasizing the collective sense of their identity. Akbar (1982, p. 15) speaks of this as "tribal knowledge":

> Why do we need knowledge of ourselves as a tribe? Because knowledge of ourselves as a tribe is what gives us the strength to cultivate what we are as an individual. Knowledge of ourselves as a tribe is what gives us the power to move against oppositional forces that are seeking to destroy us individually and collectively. Knowledge of ourselves as a tribe is that superpower that makes people willing to stand up, go to war and to die to protect their families, protect their institutions, protect their culture, protect what they stand for as a people.

Thus, the totem self, manifested as the relationship with the group, promotes what Karenga (1988, p. 47) calls *Umoja,* or unity, defined as "a principled and harmonious togetherness in the family, community, nation and world African community." It provides a sense of brotherhood and sisterhood which encourages commitment to the collective physical, mental, and spiritual well-being of the group.

From the *mischievous self* we come to understand that aspect of self which through curiosity, playfulness, trickery, and ingenuity brings us to the brink of disaster as we stumble over our Achilles heel. On the other hand, it also helps to bring into being the *not-yet self* as we discover new dimensions of who we are. For the Yoruba this force—the mischievous self—is referred to as *Elegba*, god of the crossroads, one who opens the doors, and presents us with choices. This force is recognized and identified in many different Afrikan cultures by various names.

The *contemporary self* recognizes the influence of family, friends, community, and environment on how we manifest our personality at any given point in time; while the *emergent self* captures the dynamic aspect of our development, stressing the natural growth orientation that exists within us. In the *not-yet self* we see the image of possibility—the recognition that we can become something of which we have no visible evidence today. And the *divine self* communicates the sense of destiny that lies within us, pointing us always towards that which we are meant to be in the eyes of the Creator. Encoded in the *divine self* is the sense of purpose that allows us to evolve according to the unique plan of the Creator.

In drawing out these different aspects of self (others can also be identified), the intent is not to engage in categorization but to acknowledge that self is not an independent, individually guided or initiated construction, but deeply rooted in an historical, cultural, and sociopolitical context that is full of meaning. When the very notion of self communicates multiple levels of connectedness, then outcomes on the interpersonal, political, and economic levels are quite likely to look different from those which emerge from Western constructions of self. The questions— *Who am I? Am I really who I am? Am I all I ought to be?* —assume a different level and order of significance when self is defined as extended.

Identity: Who Am I?

The first and most critical question that any group of people must pose of itself in the quest for self- and group actualization is *Who am I?* Contained in this question are the *who, where, what, why,* and *how* of existence, which define the ontology of being (Ghee, 1990). Because of the potential political, economic, and social implications associated with issues of identity, the most significant liberatory act that a group of people can undertake is self-definition. Ghee extensively examines the importance of this question in his analysis of the significance of the name change that Afrikan Americans have recently made:

Who you are links the self with the past and the present (from Africa to America). Where you are identifies your current coordinates on the planet (America). What you are indicates your species and your biology (dominant African gene). Why you are indicates your spiritual orientation and justification for human existence. How you are indicates your present state of being and affect. (p. 85)

The act of naming ourselves is an act of self-determination or *Kujichagulia,* one of the Seven Principles (*Nguzo Saba)* defined by Karenga (1988). It requires both historical and cultural self-knowledge. Oppression cannot be easily maintained when a group of people is fully cognizant of their identity. Consequently, one of the key components of oppression is creating a system of myths and images about who the oppressed are that maintains oppression. This mythology must then be systematically incorporated into all arenas of human activity—politics, economics, labor, education, religion, entertainment, military warfare, sexuality. Thus, the process of oppression in its most sophisticated form is designed to be all-inclusive and self-contained. A fundamental and radical shift in one's perspective or world view is therefore required to liberate oneself from this intricately interwoven conceptually incarcerating set of beliefs, images, policies, laws, models, and theories. It is imperative that the oppressed have little real knowledge of who they are and that whatever knowledge they have be proffered through the eyes of the oppressor if oppression is to be sustained. In this light the vociferous attacks on the Afrocentric movement that have characterized the early 1990s can be interpreted as efforts by our oppressors to mitigate threats to the continued oppression of Afrikan people.

For Afrikan people, the work of defining who we are has been impeded significantly by our immersion in the oppression of white supremacy for 500 years. The result of this process has been a great disruption in our connectedness to our earliest source of nurturance, Mother Afrika. In not knowing Mother Afrika, in having Mother Afrika presented to us through the tainted eyes of our oppressors, we are prevented from fully knowing who we are. No group of people that lacks self-knowledge can expect to attain mental health.

Identity, how one defines self in relation to others, nature, the world, and the cosmos, profoundly impacts every dimension of human being and functioning. Ancient Afrikans from many different cultures recognized the importance of consciously taking steps to ensure an integrated and connected sense of self. On the other hand, American social requirements, based as they are in a Western/Eurocentric worldview, highlight individualism, materialism, hedonism, and radical autonomy (Hill, 1995; Rogers, 1994). Consequently, the search for identity leads to disconnection in the quest for internal integration. There is an obsessive and constrictive focus upon the individual—what makes *me* feel good—and an almost hysterical rejection of connections with those who are closest in many instances. The search for autonomy often is construed as a quest for separateness, uniqueness, and independence which are strategies that fall short of the recognition of our interdependence and connectedness. Demonstrating one's autonomy is a core part of the search for identity in this society; and it is considered achieved when one displays the capacity to "stand on one's own two feet" without reliance on others. This conceptualization of autonomy is especially ruinous for Afrikan Americans, when internalized, for it has historically been our capacity to rely on each other, while standing on our own two feet, that has enabled us to thrive in the midst of overwhelmingly oppressive conditions.

Afrikan Americans have been conceptually incarcerated by definitions of identity grounded in Western/Eurocentric thinking, with disastrous consequences for our mental health and well-being. Such thinking has resulted in our children being forced into the world without appropriate preparatory rites and rituals, has led to the erroneous application of psychiatric diagnoses (Adebimpe, 1981), has scattered families and their members all over the country in search of better fortunes, and has led us to reject the wisdom and guidance of our elders as we pursue "advancement." Those things that have been vital to our well-being have been deserted in the face of what appears to be the more compelling Western dogma presented to us in our schools, by the media, by our employers, and through the policies of our government.

Recognizing the intrinsic problems associated with conceptualizations of identity within a Western/European framework for Afrikan Americans, the question then becomes "What is a healthy identity within an Afrikan-centered context?" If self is extended, embracing aspects of experience that extend before and beyond our present existence, then an essential aspect of healthy identity is connectedness—backward, lateral, and forward (Taylor, 1996b). Backward connectedness is implied by the Yoruba proverb "However far the stream flows, it never forgets its source." Forward connectedness is understood from the image of the stream, which does not flow backwards but flows purposely towards something. To dam it up (oppression) would obstruct the stream in its quest to be what it is meant to be (purpose) and eventually would lead to its destruction. A similar image is suggested by the Wolof proverb "The split tree still grows." Again, what becomes clear is that the split tree retains its connections to its roots, which enables it to sustain its life. And as the roots of the tree seek to extend themselves downward ever deeper, the branches strive to extend themselves both outward (lateral connectedness) and upward (forward connectedness), seeking to reach the heavens, each in its own unique way.

Having access to that part of identity referred to as the ancestral self—backward connectedness—at the collective level compels the joining of our post-enslavement experiences as Afrikan Americans with our experiences prior to (precolonial) and during our enslavement. The psychological and spiritual impact of the Maafa (catastrophe beyond human comprehension) on the psyche of Afrikan peoples has been practically denied by Afrikans as well as Europeans. We neither celebrate the sacrifices of our ancestors nor mourn their suffering and losses. As I discuss in the next section, linkage with the ancestral self or backward connectedness is essential for the reconstruction of self as an authentic being.

One aspect of our effort to understand who we are—the identity question—is the fervent attempts of many Afrikan Americans to identify and locate their ancestors through genealogical exploration. Searching for our roots has become an occupation for many Afrikan Americans and is indicative of our deep desire to reconnect with our ancestral and totem selves. Collectively, this search has resulted in extensive archaeological work designed to enhance our knowledge of the history and cultures of our cultural ancestors and to promote reconnection with the values, ethics, and wisdom that they represent.

While the above tasks are necessary, they are not sufficient to fully engage the question *Who am I?* A second requirement in relation to the identity question is a full understanding of our *essence*. The Afrikan worldview recognizes that human beings are spiritual beings with physical/material manifestation. Our spiritual nature is frequently acknowledged in statements that comment on the religious nature of Afrikan people. For Afrikan people, comprehending our essence as spiritual beings goes beyond the constraints that are placed upon us by a Western frame of reference. It compels the awareness that everything has a spiritual basis. It refuses the compartmentalization of mind, body, and spirit in approaches to healing. Furthermore, the communalistic nature of Afrikans leads to the embracing of the suffering of other members of the community, as exhorted in the third principle of the *Nguzo Saba—Ujima* (collective work and responsibility), defined as making the problems of our sisters and brothers our problems and solving them together (Karenga, 1988). In other words, if the essence of self is spiritual and is fundamentally not separate from others within our group, then any concept of mental health for Afrikan people must be both spiritually grounded and communal. Only when we truly know who we are are we positioned to evaluate ourselves as authentic beings.

Authenticity: Am I Really Who I Am?

As indicated above, a prerequisite of authenticity is understanding who we are and recognizing the dynamic nature of our identity. With this knowledge in hand, the integration of the many facets of self into a harmonious and balanced whole characterizes the process of authenticity. Many obstacles collaborate to thwart this dynamic and creative process of continuous harmonizing and balancing among Afrikan Americans. Most prominent are racism and oppression, which are integrally connected to and supported by a Western/Eurocentric world-view that fosters compartmentalization and fragmentation. Racism, particularly in its institutionalized forms, constantly presents us with images of ourselves designed to maintain our oppression by promulgating false, distorted, and pejorative beliefs about our identity—past, present, and future—and promoting disunity and disaffection among those who look like us and share our history. When racism is internalized, it results in cultural alienation. Taylor and Obiechina's review of numerous studies of cultural identity and mental health (Brown, 1976; Denton, 1986; Franklin, 1986; Taylor, 1996a, 1996b; Taylor, Henderson, & Jackson, 1991; Taylor & Jackson, 1990a, 1990b; Taylor & Jackson, 1991; Tomes, Brown, Semenya, & Simpson, 1990; Tong, 1993) convincingly illustrate the debilitating effects of cultural alienation on the mental and physical health of Afrikan Americans. The findings from these studies reveal that culturally alienated persons exhibit "greater risk of personal maladjustment . . . fewer ties to future generations . . . doubt of their ability to lead . . . emptiness in their future . . . low self-esteem . . . impaired access to their 'true feelings' . . . more alcohol consumption and general mental health symptoms including depression" (in press). Thus, the first task required in our efforts to be authentic is, as Freire (1990) suggests, to locate the oppressor within us and externalize this presence so that we can become authentic beings.

The consequences of oppression are internalized and manifested at all levels of self. At the level of *totem self*, the internalization of oppression promotes disunity and disaffection between Afrikan people, thereby diminishing our capacity for *Umoja* (Unity) and *Ujima* (Collective Work and Responsibility). People with a damaged totem self experience difficulty offering adequate protection to their families and children in the face of highly oppressive conditions. At the level of *ancestral self* oppression impairs emotional empathy for the pain and suffering of other Afrikan people, moderates the capacity to experience pride and joy in our historical triumphs, and lessens utilization of the lessons and wisdom of our ancestors. Pain and suffering—the sequelae of oppression—unacknowledged, become monsters that haunt and torment us, leading to the destruction of our children and families. Feeling no legitimate claim to the triumphs, lessons, and wisdom of our ancestors as viable contemporary assets for dealing with present challenges, Afrikan Americans are easy prey for the disposable culture promulgated by Western society and, therefore are unable to seek the assistance of our ancestors in the continued struggle against oppression.

At the level of *mischievous self* internalized oppression often results in taking on racist concepts of self projected by this oppressogenic society. Enticed by the images, rewards, and privileges which this offers, the mischievous self, disconnected from other aspects of self, is easily led down the path of hedonistic pursuits. Thus, conceptions of our physical giftedness are exaggerated in overemphasis on sports and entertainment and displaced sexuality, while our intellectual giftedness, emotional maturity, and highly developed morality of ancient proportions are dissociated from us through the repression of our history and culture. The loss of totem, ancestral, and mischievous selves to the effects of oppression has especially deleterious effects for other aspects of self. And furthermore, without this protection, Afrikan Americans are extremely vulnerable to the regular attacks on our already fragile and weak self-concept. Thus, oppression subverts our connection with our totem and ancestral selves which consequentially means that the contemporary self will be defined, not from the basis of the depth and wealth of experiences which emerge from the totem and ancestral selves, but only from an ill-conceived, disconnected mischievous self. As a result the ongoing manifestation of *emergent, not-yet,* and ultimately *Divine selves* will be prematurely foreclosed or underdeveloped. The latter is exemplified in the decrement in our sense of hope and faith or *Imani,* and the sheer sense of "giving up" which is observed in many of our communities. Locked into oppressogenic images of ourselves we perpetuate our oppression and contribute to the promulgation of images which prevent our individual and collective evolution and the manifestation of emergent, not-yet, and Divine selves.

Western civilization and culture regularly evoke the denial of aspects of self through their ahistorical emphasis and the operation of both selective and distorted memory. "Natal alienation" (Thomas, 1993) is fundamental to the continued oppression of Afrikan people. Most Afrikans in America have little knowledge even of our history within this country except through the eyes of our oppressors, and still less knowledge of our Afrikan past. Consequently, except through collective unconscious recollection, without significant historical research, we are doomed to persist in a state of inauthenticity, a state prescribed for us by the oppressogenic characteristics of our environment.

The demands of Western civilization for inauthentic behavior further contribute to the disorientation of Afrikan people. The very act of fully being who we are not only threatens the consciousness assumed by oppressed people, but often is life-threatening as well. Our authenticity thwarts the agenda of those institutions that perpetuate our oppression and challenges the consensus that exists among our oppressors about the identity of Afrikan people. Authenticity directly confronts internalized racism or oppression, for it requires that we have access to and foster integration among all aspects of self—totem self, ancestral self, mischievous self, contemporary self, emergent self, not-yet self, and Divine self. As specified in the proverb "The split tree still grows" constant balancing of backward, lateral, and forward connectedness expressed by delving deeper into our history and maintaining connections with our ancestors; nurturing our relationships with family, community, and nation; and maintaining a clear sense of our direction is required.

Although the grounding for authenticity comes out of a fundamental connection to our extended self in its backward, forward, and lateral dimensions, this knowledge is insufficient for psychological wholeness, for it is possible to have such knowledge and not act on it. So, authenticity further implies the need for *Kujichagulia,* the capacity that people demonstrate to name themselves, define themselves, create for themselves, and speak for themselves rather than being named, defined, created for, and spoken for by others (Karenga, 1988). Thus, after externalizing the oppressor within us, the first act of a mentally healthy group of people must be *Kujichagulia* (self-determination). To do less is to accept the definitions of our oppressors of who we are and to remain inauthentic beings trapped by the nefarious images presented us by them. The frequent name changes that Afrikan Americans in this country have and continue to undergo represent our quest to define ourselves in ever more authentic ways.

Intimately bound up with our efforts to externalize the oppressor within us is the full acknowledgment of the deep wounds that we as Afrikan people have suffered as a result of our Maafa. In a demonstration of *Kujichagulia,* our collective voice is vociferously asserting itself around this issue throughout Afrikan America in a plethora of research and literature that articulates the impact of the trauma of American enslavement and White supremacy on the sociopsychological and economic functioning of Afrikan Americans (Akbar, 1984; Ani, 1994; Asante, 1988; Hill, 1992; Kambon, 1992; Kunjufu, 1991; Myers, 1988; Nobles, 1991; Taylor & Obiechina, in press; Wilson, 1993). The Maafa, whose most prominent feature is the continuation of the denial of the humanity of Afrikan people (Nobles, 1994), had its inception in events that included the EuroAsian invasion of Afrika, the Middle Passage, and the institution of American enslavement. It survives through institutionalized racism present in every arena of American life and through the litany of micro-aggressions experienced by Afrikan Americans in today's society. In Thomas' analysis (1993) of the institutions of American Enslavement and the Jewish holocaust, he suggests that for a people to be psychologically whole it is eminently important for social discourse to occur about trauma that is experienced individually or collectively. By implication, the efforts that Afrikan Americans are making to have dialogues about our collective trauma, both past and present, are, in essence, an attempt to achieve psychological wholeness—to weave together extricated parts of self repressed not only because of the pain and suffering associated with them but also because of the disapproval that acknowledgment and open dialogue generates from our oppressors. To become authentic beings we must confront the pain and suffering that we have experienced—in our collective past and that continues in the present—through the enactment of rituals and activities that engage us physically, mentally, emotionally, and spiritually.

Finally, it is essential, if we are to be authentic beings, that we create our own Africentric space characterized by the values, traditions, rituals, practices, and aesthetics of Afrikan people and designed to unabashedly and uncompromisingly affirm who we really are with consistency, commitment, and integrity. Through ritual, Afrikan people of many different cultures created the processes for reminding, binding, and enlivening the true essence of members of their tribes, villages, and societies. Somé (1993) stresses that a community without ritual cannot exist. The recreation and reconstruction of our rituals and traditions to meet contemporary needs, and based in an Afrikan narrative, must become the holding environment for the promotion of the psychological wholeness of Afrikan Americans.

Summing up, authenticity requires; (1) knowing our extended communal identity, (2) externalizing the oppressor within, (3) confronting our collective trauma, (4) continuosus harmonizing and balancing all aspects of self, and (5) exercising *Kujichagulia* so that the Africentric space necessary to nurture our full extended communal identity can be created.

Purpose: Am I All I Ought to Be?

In posing the question *Am I all I ought to be?* Fanon (1967) recognized the constraints encountered by oppressed Afrikans in our efforts to achieve our full potential. Oppression systematically distorts the inner and outer vision of the oppressed by substituting the oppressor for the "Supreme Being." It stifles our creativity which differentiates living from merely surviving (Y. Gampel, "Can these wounds be healed?" speech at Family Resources, Pittsburgh, PA, April 18, 1996). Thus, being all we ought to be is defined in terms consistent with the oppressors' projections that we have assumed as a part of the oppressogenic process. Images, roles, rewards, privileges, and punishments are presented to Afrikan Americans to ensure our continued cooperation with the enactment of scripts that define how our potential is to be expressed consistent with the maintenance of our oppressed status. Therefore, to unravel this dilemma requires a return to the issues of identity and authenticity, without which there can be no discussion of purpose. One cannot be all one ought to be if one has no knowledge of and is prevented from being one's true self.

One of the most painful encroachments that Afrikan people experienced as a result of American Enslavement was the loss of our sense of *Kujichagulia*. Thomas (1993) astutely characterizes American enslavement as having the intent of bringing about the "utter dependence of blacks upon slaveowners." Having achieved this aim through public and cultural policies that prevailed in this country legally until 1964 (and in actuality that persist by virtue of the failure to implement laws), and through the neglect of the development of sociopsychological processes for remedying the consequences of this legacy, along with ongoing attempts to reverse whatever gains have been secured, the result is no less than the "glass ceiling" that Afrikan Americans regularly encounter in our individual and collective pursuits of individual and group actualization. In Western Eurocentrically defined spaces, we must regularly reshape ourselves to fit Western European models if we are to benefit from rewards issued by them. Being so utterly dependent upon our oppressor and exhibiting a "fear of freedom" (Freire, 1990), we permit ourselves only to bask in the light of the oppressor's sun.

By posing the question *Am I all I ought to be?* not only are we brought back to the question of identity, or true self; we also are thrust into a discussion of what our possibilities are—a question that cannot be separated from the issue of authenticity, for achieving our possibilities is thwarted if we are inauthentic beings. In our efforts to unpack this issue of purpose, we must declare three primary assumptions: (1) Life is a dynamic process of change and transformation; (2) there are particular patterns that characterize a healthy process of development for all living beings; and (3) there is a destiny unique to each person that helps to fulfill the larger humanizing mission of life.

The first assumption reminds us that continuous growth and change is the order of life. When this process ends in this existence, better known as death, then we simply move into another form of existence—often referred to as afterlife, of which little is known. From the second assumption we recognize that, as Akbar (1995) relates in his analogy of the transformation of the caterpillar, change is planful and orderly. Even though there are many possible outcomes in the lives of every person, certain limitations—prescribed by genetics, history, culture, and sociopolitical variables—constrain the range of outcomes. The Akan proverb "No man's path crosses another man's" supports the third assumption by suggesting that each person has a unique destiny or purpose. As the proverb implies, since every person is given a distinct path or purpose, there is no need for competition with others in the expression of it. In the Wolof proverb mentioned earlier, "The split tree still grows," this sense of purpose is expressed in the forward connectedness exhibited by each branch reaching upwards in its own creative way. This can be likened to our efforts to fulfill our personal destinies; and, as the proverb indicates, we do so by maintaining our connections to the body of the tree. From the above assumptions, it becomes apparent that change is normative. We are challenged to consider how we manage these normal and expected events or changes that have potential for facilitating or inhibiting our individual and collective movement towards becoming "all we ought to be."

The analogy that Akbar (1995) presents in his metaphor about human transformation is appropriate for guiding this analysis of purpose. Examining the transformation of the caterpillar from its lower wormlike form to its more beautiful and evolved form as a butterfly through the medium of the cocoon, Akbar illustrates the relationship between self and society. It is apparent that the transformation of the caterpillar is reliant not only upon internally driven processes, which have been genetically transmitted from generation to generation, but also upon the capacity of the cocoon to support the needs of the caterpillar, allowing it to eventually emerge as a butterfly. It is equally apparent that there is a vision or sense of purpose that guides the caterpillar in its evolution to butterfly. Although all caterpillars do not successfully emerge as butterflies—and for those that do emerge, not all look alike, nor are they equally attractive to different human eyes—no caterpillars emerge from their cocoons in the same wormlike state, nor do they become flies, mosquitoes or flowers. While the transformational process is perhaps most dramatic in the case of the butterfly, observation of any living form consistently reveals that change occurs in a systematic, planful manner that is generally supportive of the continuation of the species and the unity of life. Afrikan-centered principles of living affirm these universal laws as a guide for human development. Rather than perceiving human beings as outside of or above the universal laws to which other forms of life are subject, Afrikan people view themselves as integrally connected to the universe and therefore strive to be in harmony, balance, and rhythm with it. Afrikan models of spirituality utilize nature as the gigantic classroom that the Creator has given to teach us how to live in harmony and balance. From this perspective, human beings have an ecological relationship with nature and are meant to neither dominate nor control her but to collaborate with her in the achievement of our divine purpose.

Within both human and natural contexts (the human is actually a part of the natural context), rituals and structures for facilitating transformation are standard. Our ancestors of Akan, Dogon, Dagara, Ibo, and Yoruba descent, to name a few, understood their importance in the human evolutionary process and thus constructed rituals through which transformation could be realized. Rituals often began prior to birth to bring forth the needed spirit. Shortly after birth, the ritual of naming occurred, which was based on the awareness that names contain purpose, continue the narrative of a family and people, provide direction, and link the newly arrived member with older members of the family and village. Concisely said, "A person's life project is inscribed in the name s/he carries" (Somé, 1994, p. 1). Imbued in these naming rituals are the seeds that the elders recognized would bear the fruit needed by that family, village, and people for its continued development.

At adolescence an exceedingly important ritual took place, thus preparing the young man or woman to become an adult within the society. In Dagara society, failure to participate in the adolescent rites of passage relegated a person to the status of adolescent permanently, regardless of age (Somé, 1994). For the Dagara this exceedingly complex and life-challenging ritual necessitated the removal of the youth to be initiated from the community and placing them in the hands of elders who guided them through a transformational process that left no part of their original selves untouched and unchanged. Following the adolescent rites of passage, the youth were paired with mentors specially selected to assist them in the further development and expression of their unique talents and abilities. So, it is clear that at least among the Dagara, the challenge of becoming "all one ought to be" was handled with great seriousness and caution, and the adolescent rite of passage was a critical transitional point in the achievement of one's purpose.

Later the ritual of marriage would consecrate the male-female bond as a vital one to the family, village, and society. Still later, the ritual of eldership would proclaim the significant status of elders within the village. The final ritual of transition was viewed as an acknowledgment of the circular process of life joining birth (where souls enter from the realm of the ancestors) with death (where they return to that realm). Foundational to each of these rituals occurring at critical points of transition is the awareness that there is a larger collective purpose for which we must be groomed and ultimately transformed that will uplift the family and the society. Thus, the question "Am I all I ought to be?" assumes a different direction when self is perceived as communal and becoming more human is the goal. These rituals focus on the humanization process—a process dependent upon transformation—which is viewed as the capacity to relate, connect, and support each other in being the best we can be.

One's sense of purpose, then, is given shape by family and society, history and culture. No separation exists here. Once we acknowledge our fundamental connectedness to our families, our history, nature, and the Divine, our role in pursuing the legacy of helping Afrikan people becomes "mo' better" (W. W. Nobles, speech at "Family Affair" conference, Pittsburgh, PA, April, 1993) becomes eminently visible. Purpose never occurs outside of our sociohistorical context; and by allowing our oppressors to overcome us with the seduction of Western/Eurocentric values and customs, we have been lured away from our purpose. The necessity for rituals and institutions (not unlike the cocoon on which the caterpillar depends) that can assist us in becoming our true Afrikan selves in the larger context of our families, our communities, and our nations (a destiny that if not liberating is not authentic) is the task facing Afrikan people. We acknowledge this understanding in the growing focus on *Sankofa,* based upon the Akan deity symbolized as a bird whose head turns back in a circle entreating us, "Go back and retrieve that which we have lost."

Conclusion

Addressing the questions *Who am I? Am I really who I am?* and *Am I all I ought to be?* within an Afrikan-centered context is fundamental to achieving health, well-being, and liberation for Afrikan people. This work is personal, communal, national, and most importantly spiritual, for it demands healing at all levels within the African American community to overcome the insidious and debilitating effects of the Maafa. Because we have been entrapped in a Western/Eurocentric world view, our efforts to create strategies to remove ourselves from the bondage of our oppression have been fruitless and have often resulted in further entrapment. Now, in the light of a growing body of research and literature supportive of the significance of world view as a starting point for analysis, we can no longer deny the necessity of retrieving, reconnecting, and reconstructing African reality so that we can become all we ought to be. Concretely, the retrieval of black mental health requires that we face into the tasks of: (1) fully acknowledging who we are as Afrikan people; (2) restoring and adapting rituals, customs, and traditions that foster harmony and balance, and personally and collectively promote healing of the wounds from our collective trauma, and nurture the possibilities within us; and (3) building social, political, and economic institutions that are reflective of the holistic and integrated nature of our world view.

References

Adebimpe, V. (1981). Overview: White norms and psychiatric diagnosis of Black patients. *American Journal of Psychiatry, 138,* 279–285.

Akbar, N. (1982). *From miseducation to education.* Jersey City: New Mind Productions.

Akbar, N. (1984). *Chains and images of psychological slavery.* Jersey City: New Mind Productions.

Akbar, N. (1991). Mental disorder among African Americans. In R. L. Jones (Ed.), *Black psychology* (3rd ed., pp. 339–352). Berkeley, CA: Cobb & Henry.

Akbar, N. (1995). *Natural psychology and human transformation.* Tallahassee, FL: Mind Productions.

Ani, M. (1994). *Yurugu: An African-centered critique of European cultural thought and behavior.* Trenton, NJ: Africa World Press.

Asante, M. K. (1988). *Afrocentricity: Theory of social change.* Trenton, NJ: Africa World Press.

Baldwin, J. A. (1976). Black psychology and Black personality. *Black Books Bulletin, 4*(3), 6–11.

Baldwin, J. A. (1985). Psychological aspects of European cosmology in American society. *Western Journal of Black Studies, 9*(4), 216–223.

Baldwin, J. A., Brown, R., & Hopkins, R. (1991). The Black self-hatred paradigm revisited: An Africentric analysis. In R. L. Jones (Ed.), *Black psychology* (3rd ed., pp. 141–165). Berkeley: Cobb & Henry.

Bevis, W. M. (1921). Psychological traits of the Southern Negro with observations as to some of his psychoses. *American Journal of Psychiatry, 1,* 69-78.

Brown, A. B. (1976). *Personality correlates of the developmental inventory of Black consciousness.* Unpublished master's thesis, University of Pittsburgh.

Denton, S. E. (1986). *A methodological refinement and validation analysis of the developmental inventory of Black consciousness.* Unpublished doctoral dissertation, University of Pittsburgh.

Fanon, F. (1967). *Black skins, white masks.* New York: Grove Press.

Franklin, A. T. (1986). *Influence of economic, social, religious and cultural factors on depression in single Black women with male friends.* Unpublished doctoral dissertation, University of Pittsburgh.

Freire, P. (1990). *Pedagogy of the oppressed* (Rev. ed.). New York: Continuum.

Ghee, K. L. (1990). The psychological importance of self definition and labeling: Black versus African American. *Journal of Black Psychology, 17*(1), 75–93.

Hall, G. S. (1904). *Adolescence.* New York: Appleton.

Hernstein, R. J., & Murray, C. (1994). *The Bell Curve: Intelligence and class structure in American life.* New York: Free Press.

Hill, P. (1995). *Male rites of passage.* Workshop sponsored by Pittsburgh Coalition against Substance Abuse, Pittsburgh, PA.

Hill, P. (1992). *Coming of age.* Chicago: African American Images.

Jensen, A. R. (1969). How much can we boost IQ and scholastic achievement? *Harvard Educational Review, 39,* 1-123.

Jung, C. G. (1928). *Contributions to analytical psychology.* New York: Harcourt, Brace.

Jung, C. G. (1930). Your Negroid and Indian behavior. *Forum, 83,* 193-199.

Kambon, K. K. K. (1992). *The African personality in America.* Tallahassee, FL: Nubian Nation Publications.

Karenga, M. (1988). *The African American holiday of Kwanzaa: A celebration of family, community, and culture.* Los Angeles, CA: University of Sankore Press.

Kunjufu, J. (1991). *Black economics.* Chicago, IL: African American Images.

McDougall, W. (1908). *Social psychology.* New York: Luce.

Myers, L. J. (1988). *Understanding an Afrocentric world-view: Introduction to an optimal psychology.* Dubuque, IA: Kendall/Hunt.

Nobles, W. W. (1986). *African psychology: Towards its reclamation, reascension and revitalization.* Oakland, CA: Institute for the Advanced Study of Black Family Life and Culture.

Nobles, W. W. (1991). African philosophy: Foundations for Black psychology. In R. L. Jones (Ed.), *Black psychology* (3rd ed., pp. 47–63). Berkeley, CA: Cobb & Henry.

Nobles, W. W. (1991). Extended self: Rethinking the so-called Negro self-concept. In R. L. Jones (Ed.), *Black psychology.* (3rd ed., pp. 295–304). Berkeley, CA: Cobb & Henry.

Nobles, W. W. (1994). *The Maafa.* Unpublished manuscript.

Ogbonnaya, A. O. (1994). Person as community: An African understanding of the person as an intrapsychic community. *Journal of Black Psychology, 20*(1), 75–87.

Rogers, J. A. (1994). *Reflections on suffering.* Unpublished manuscript.

Rogers, J. A. (1996). Spirituality: Questing for well-being. In R. L. Jones (Ed.), *African American mental health.* Hampton, VA: Cobb & Henry.

Somé, M. P. (1993). *Ritual: Power, healing, and community.* Portland, OR: Swan/Raven.

Somé, M. P. (1994). *Of water and the spirit: Ritual, magic, and initiation in the life of an African shaman.* New York: Putnam.

Taylor, J. (1996a). Cultural conversion experiences: Implications for mental health research and treatment. In R. L. Jones (Ed.), *African American identity development.* Hampton, VA: Cobb & Henry.

Taylor, J. (1996b). The Pittsburgh Project, Part III: Toward A purposeful systems approach to parenting. In R. L. Jones (Ed.), *African American children, youth, and parenting.* Hampton, VA: Cobb & Henry.

Taylor, J., Henderson, D., & Jackson, B. B. (1991). A holistic model for understanding and predicting depression in African American women. *Journal of Community Psychology, 19,* 306–320.

Taylor, J., & Jackson, B. B. (1990a). Factors affecting alcohol consumption in Black women: Part I. *International Journal of the Addictions, 25,* 1279–1292.

Taylor, J., & Jackson, B. B. (1990b). Factors affecting alcohol consumption in Black women: Part II. *International Journal of the Addictions, 25,* 1407–1419.

Taylor, J., & Jackson, B. B. (1991). Evaluation of a holistic model of mental health symptoms in African American women. *Journal of Black Psychology, 18,* 19–45.

Taylor, J., & Obiechina, C. (in press). Cultural alienation: Analytical and empirical implications. *Journal of Black Studies.*

Terman, L. M. (1916). *The measurement of intelligence.* Boston, MA: Houghton, Mifflin.

Thomas, L. M. (1993). *Vessels of evil.* Philadelphia, PA: Temple University Press.

Thomas, A., & Sillen, S. (1972). *Racism and psychiatry.* New York: Brunner/Mazel.

Tomes, E., Brown, A., Semenya, K., & Simpson, J. (1990). Depression in Black women of low socioeconomic status: Psychological factors and nursing diagnosis. *Journal of National Black Nurses Association, 4,* 37–46.

Tong, L. (1993). *Impact of cultural, social, physical, and stress factors on the mental health of urban, elderly Afro-American women.* Unpublished doctoral dissertation, University of Pittsburgh.

Willie, C. V., Rieker, P. P., Kramer, B. M., & Brown, B. S. (Eds.). (1995). *Mental health, racism, and sexism.* Pittsburgh, PA: University of Pittsburgh Press.

Wilson, A. (1993). *The falsification of Afrikan consciousness: Eurocentric history, psychiatry and the politics of white supremacy.* New York: Afrikan World InfoSystems.

Zimbardo, P. (1985). *Psychology and life.* Glenview, IL: Scott, Foresman.

Author

Huberta Jackson-Lowman, Ph.D.
Florida A&M University
Department of Psychology
GEC-C, Room 302
Tallahassee, FL 32307
Telephone: (904) 599-3014/3524
Fax: (904) 561-2540

African Traditional Medicine: Implications for African-Centered Approaches to Healing

Cheryl Grills and Daryl Rowe

Intellectuals ought to study the past not for the pleasure they find in so doing, but to derive lessons from it or, if necessary, to discern those lessons in full knowledge of the facts . . . . Classical psychology argues that human nature is essentially universal. This is because it wants to see the triumph of humanism. For the latter to become possible, man must not be by nature impervious to any manifestation of feeling, etc., on the part of his fellow man. His nature, his consciousness and his spirit must be capable of assimilating through education everything which is initially foreign to him (Diop, 1989, p. 3).

The story of African survival in the U.S. is a story of transformation—the capacity to transform through experiencing all that initially was foreign while maintaining the essential African core. It has been that capacity to "make way out of no way" which characterizes how Africans in America have approached and apprehended mental health. The task confronting us now is to study the past, the African past to discern the essential lessons for both the present and the future.

The core of African mental health has its basis in traditional African medicine or spiritual systems. Those of us involved in the study of these issues must critically examine the philosophical, conceptual, methodological and ethical foundations of existing ideas regarding health and, by extension, mental health. The Association of Black Psychologist's (Nobles, King & James, 1995) definition of health which has been applied in its work with the Center for Disease Control states that health is a dynamic process resulting in the capacity to maintain, adapt, and creatively refine (change, integrate, evolve, correct) one's quality of life, at least to the status of effective, if not to optimal and maximal functioning. Nobles et al. assert that health—the capacity to experience optimal and maximal functioning—is the ever-present ability to adapt and evolve toward a more complex, integrated and creative structure or being. They argue that health is connected to the spirit, the energy, force

71

or power that is both the inner essence and outer envelope of human beingness. As such, "good health" is not a thing to be available and accessible like a market commodity. It is a process of ongoing relations with the person and between the person and the environment informed by an ethical society. From this perspective, persons are unified wholes consisting of spiritual/cultural, physiological, emotional, and social/behavioral elements in continuous relation with each other. Nobles et al. (1995) conclude that any effort to improve health care and health behaviors which are inclusive of indigenous practices and models must be attentive to the dynamic interactions which occur within each of these dimensions.

Consequently, the single most critical issue facing the science and profession of psychology is how to address the cultural, spiritual, economic, social, historical and political factors which influence conceptions of human beingness, features of human functioning and methods for restoring healthy order to humans throughout the world. For psychology to maintain its heuristic value, it must begin to survey the broader population of humans to which it attempts to generalize its findings. It must substantively incorporate the various contexts out of which humans emerge, understand themselves, and adapt to a constantly changing world. To date psychology has failed to do this (Rowe & Grills, 1996).

Unfortunately, African American mental health specialists have generally relied on the systems of meaning emerging out of the cultural traditions of Europeans. These systems have been used as the philosophical, conceptual, methodological and ethical standards to direct and inform the majority of work relating to the promotion, prevention and intervention of health concerns for African persons throughout the diaspora. The purpose of this chapter is to locate the discussion regarding African mental health outside of the parameters of Eurocentric psychology and inside the accumulated cultural patterns of African people.

To this end, we will: (1) provide a brief critique of western European and European American conceptions of human psychology and mental health; (2) address the cultural origins of Africans in the United States; (3) examine the value of traditional African medicine and its contemporary manifestations (both diasporan and continental) as the cosmological, ontological and epistemic frame for explicating African American mental health; (4) explicate many features and philosophical perspectives regarding traditional African medicine, with particular attention on divination; and (5) describe examples of the work ahead for African centered psychology.

Eurocentric Foundations of Psychology

As a discipline, professional psychology is ill-equipped to serve as the theoretical foundation for examining the mental health needs of Africans and African

Americans due to its assumptions of universality, tendency towards reductionism, overemphasis on pathology, overreliance on the Western European scientific method, and inclination toward an etic versus emic approach to understanding human behavior (Rowe & Grills, 1993).

Central to the western European scientific method is the assumption that the observations, upon which theories are developed, hypotheses generated and predictions confirmed or disconfirmed, are representative of the population(s) to which the information will be applied. In other words, phenomena must be explainable based upon underlying laws. Unfortunately, psychology has consistently undervalued the contributions of thinkers or healers from nonwestern cultures (Bernal & Enchauteguide-Jesus, 1994; King, Moody, Thompson, & Bennett, 1983; Suarez-Balcazar, Durlak, & Smith, 1994; Trimble, Mackey, Lafromboise & France, 1983; Weinstein, 1994; Wong, Kim, Lim, & Morishima, 1983), while it has simultaneously overvalued the perspectives about human behavior and mental processes derived from studying European and Euro-American populations (Lonner & Malpass, 1994). Euro-American concepts of adaptive behavior and dysfunction have simply been assumed to exist in other sociocultural environments and measured using categories developed in the context of Euro-American culture (Obeyesekere, 1985; cf. Rowe & Grills, 1996). Africans and African Americans have been excluded as contributors to theory and paradigm development which could amplify the understanding of human behavior and mental processes.

Thus, because of the over reliance on European thinkers, philosophies and methodologies, many problems have occurred in professional psychology and mental health which stem directly from efforts to understand human variability through a Eurocentric conceptual system (Speight, Myers, Cox, & Highlen, 1991).

Cultural Origins of African Americans

The cultural heritage of African Americans is based on numerous West and Central African cultures brought together from Senegambia (Serer, Goree, Wolof, Mandingo, Malinke, Bambara, Fulani, Papel, Limba, Bola and Balante), the Sierra Leone coast (Temne and Mende), the Liberian coast (Vai, De, Gola, Kisi, Bassa and Grebo), the Guinea coast (Yoruba, Ibo, Nupe, Benin, Fon, Ewe, Akan, Ga, Popo, Edo-Bini and Fante), the Niger Delta (Efik-Ibibio, Ijaw, Ibani, and Igbos), and the Central African coast (Bakongo, Malimbo, Bambo, Ndungo, Balimbe, Badongo, Luba, Loanga, Luango and Ovimbundu) (Holloway, 1990).

It has been argued that Africans experienced multiple acculturation processes (Stuckey, 1987; Mulira, 1990). The first process occurred during the Middle Passage, when through the common horrors of mistreatment, contact and interaction, the various African ethnic groups, e.g., the Fulani, Mende, Ga, Igbo and

Bakongo, were melded into Africans with blended customs and practices. The retention of cultural identity was expressed through religion, philosophy, folklore, folkways, storytelling, naming practices, home economies, art, kinship, music, and conceptions of health and healing (see Creel, 1988 for a fuller discussion of these issues). This blending allowed for the synthesis of cultural patterns, ways of knowing, and rules for behaving which have contributed to the expression of a distinctive African character. The opportunity to exist in relative isolation helped these various Africans maintain a strong sense of unity, retain a cultural vitality and has served as the foundation for the expression of African American culture. The second process involved contact with the emerging hybrid European American (EA) culture, wherein Africans sought to reinterpret EA cultural patterns through their own African cultural lenses. These processes are critical for understanding African American mental health.

There has been a long-standing tendency to assume that unless physical manifestations of African-constructed artifacts survived the middle passage, that the cultural lens through which Africans apprehended reality self, others and the world resulted solely from the atrocities of enslavement and the ensuing Maafa[1]. Furthermore, customary wisdom suggests that there is a fundamental difference in the Africanity of continental versus diasporan Africans; hence we hear many references to African retentions, residuals or artifacts throughout the diaspora (DuBois, 1969; Holloway, 1990; Richards, 1989; Snow, 1993).

We argue, as do others (Creel, 1988; Hall, 1990; Stuckey, 1987), that such a perspective is much too limited in scope and depth. Physical manifestations of phenomena simply reflect the articulation of subjective realities. Furthermore, given the centuries of European cultural imperialism and colonialism impressed upon continental Africans, it is likely that diasporan African cultural patterns are as distinctively African as continental African cultural patterns. In other words, the manifestation of any physical objects or cultural patterns must cohere with a conceptualization of the form, design, function and utility of that object or pattern in order for it to be brought into being, or represented. According to Hall (1990):

> . . . what we see is not necessarily what the craft worker has in his or her head. It is, rather, the end product of an interaction among the craftperson's image of the cultural tradition or ideal; the materials available to work with; and the craftperson's skill, practice, and ability to shape the materials in conformity with the ideal image. The ideal image is a mental image carried, not in the hands or on the backs of the African bondsmen, but in their heads (p. 107).

If one substitutes diasporan African for craft person, beliefs for "image," and European or European-American-influenced social system for "materials to work with," a very different perspective might be realized about the import of examining traditional African medicine as a frame for apprehending the mental health of Africans in the United States. Finally, if we broaden Hall's reference to "head" to more holistically refer to heart and spirit, one may come to a clearer position about the value of exploring alternative African healing systems. Thus the articulation of culture is not represented solely through its external manifestations. Culture is best seen as being contained in the spirits or hearts of a people.

The Persistence of Traditional African Medicine and Science

As a science and a system of health care, thousands of years old, traditional African medicine represents one of the clearest examples of the persistence of the African worldview. It reflects an approach to health care which is patterned after institutions, beliefs, and practices which are indigenous to Africa's varied yet commonly held paradigm of human functioning (Ackah, 1990; Amponsah, 1977; Aryee, 1978; Barrett, 1974; Fink, 1989; Mbiti, 1970; Mullins, 1984; Twumasi, 1975). As a form of healing based upon a concept of health and disease that does not rely on western technology or ideology, it encompasses a range of therapeutic interventions and techniques, which might be referred to in western lexicon as: herbal medicine, therapeutic fasting and dieting, hydrotherapy, radiant heat therapy, venisection, surgery and bone setting, spinal manipulation and massage, psychotherapy, divination and preventive medicine (Tella, 1977). Each of these practices is born out of African philosophy and beliefs about the meaning of life, health, illness, disease, development, nature, spirituality, and cosmology .

Typically, traditional African medicine and healing practices have been studied by North American and European anthropologists. As a result, important knowledge concerning African healing phenomena has been lost or distorted due to their inability to suspend cultural biases regarding epistemology, concepts of science, the scope of African people's "sources of knowledge and ways of knowing," prejudices against divination, and prejudices against non-western forms of healing. Unfortunately, negative portrayals of divination and other African healing methods by European and American anthropologists and theologians are plentiful (Lambo, 1976).

In spite of these negative depictions, studies have found that Africans use both systems or methods of care (Aryee, 1978; Twumasi, 1975). For example, in Ghana, Senegal, Mali, Nigeria, Ivory Coast, Burkina Faso, South Africa, Zimbabwe, Benin, in fact in all of Africa, traditional medical practitioners continue to be accepted, recognized, and sanctioned healers by the indigenous African community.

Despite significant beliefs among African Americans in "traditional ways," "folk methods" or "home remedies," many may be reluctant to share this information even with people within the African American community. Snow (1993) in her summation of twenty years of study on African American practices in traditional medicine, convincingly argues that "traditional health beliefs can and do coexist with orthodox medicine here in the U.S." (p. xiv). But do we, as mental health and medical professionals, ever have the benefit of accessing and utilizing these beliefs? Landrine and Klonoff (1994) found that popular freeform methodologies for gathering information (i.e., asking subjects to generate causes for illnesses) inhibit non-White ethnic group respondents from expressing their beliefs about the supernatural causes of illnesses. However, when asked to rate the significance of "supernatural" causes of illnesses, non-White ethnic groups rated supernatural causes significantly more important than did Whites. The implications for African Americans are clear. People's beliefs about the causes of illness may be important mediators of health related behavior and illness outcomes (Landrine & Klonoff, 1994). Causal attributions which reflect the client's cultural (private) worldview can remain censored, depending on how information is assessed and whether the worldview is shunned or demeaned by the broader social perspective.

Culture and the Practice of Traditional Medicine

Traditional medicine is concerned with prevention and the restoration and preservation of health by facilitating a return to normal functioning following illness. It is closely tied to spiritual systems of belief which form the vital essence of this healing system. God is seen as the sole power or source of all things. Certain people (i.e., priests and healers) are endowed with special knowledge and gifts that permit them to tap into the sacred sources of this energy. The general belief is that knowledge of medicine comes directly from God, operates through the intermediate spirits, and is dispensed through the rituals, incantations, practices and herbs of the traditional healer (Quarcoopome, 1987). In fact, unconsecrated medicine (medicine practiced in the absence of ritual, rituals derived from spirituality or religion) has no meaning (Opoku, 1978).

Traditional medicine is often prescribed with the instruction that it must be used at specified times, under set conditions, accompanied by particular rituals or gestures (often repetitive), and with certain incantations. The holistic configuration of healing practices—the combination of herbs, behaviors, utterances, and temporal and spatial settings—yields a form of treatment which is contrary to the western European notion of healing which emphasizes the isolation of "curative" aspects of treatment.

In the African worldview, illness and disease are not purely a physical, biological or psychological phenomena as they are prone to be characterized in the Western tradition. They are also a social, cultural, and spiritual fact. As Opoku (1978) states "nothing can be well with men in society if good relations are not maintained between them and their fellow human beings and between them and the powers that control the universe . . . Broken relationships may result in sickness or even the death of an individual" (p. 149).

In treating illnesses, both the organic and spiritual aspects of the disease are considered and addressed in traditional African medicine and will oftentimes occur within a social context. Views of illness and health are intimately tied to African religion or spirituality (through a system of beliefs, ceremonies and rituals) and African philosophy (through attitudes, logic, and perception which frame the manner in which African people think, act and speak in various situations). The concepts of God, spirituality, time, elders, ancestors, the social roles and expectations of interconnectedness, harmony between body and soul, morality, and proper social relationships are some of the central aspects of this worldview which inform beliefs and practices about illness and well-being (Ademuwagun, 1980; Appiah-Kubi, 1981; Aryee, 1978; Barrett, 1974; Field, 1960; Mbiti, 1970). In this way, Africans' believe that humans are a composite of both material and immaterial substances, making the balance between the material and spiritual a condition for sound human health.

Given that there is no conceptual separation between the physical and the spiritual, there is an inclination to view illness as a more functional than pathological phenomenon. In this functional analysis, people set their minds, not on future things, but on what has taken place (Mbiti, 1970). Therefore, when an illness, death or some other misfortune occurs, the first question posed is Why? Why has this happened to me? The answer to "why" is the key to resolution of the illness or problem. The client will seek out the healer or diviner to determine why the affliction happened to her or him and not to someone else. A ritual might have been neglected, a relative disrespected, an ancestor neglected, or a neighbor insulted. Through an understanding of the past, the present is discerned. It is also understood that harmonious relationships between past and present permit good health (Aryee, 1978). In the traditional schema, there is no room for a purely naturalistic notion of illness; whereas, in western medicine's schema, there is a conceptual hierarchy and negation, between the natural and the spiritual (Opoku, 1978; Quarcoopome, 1987; Twumasi, 1975). Herein lies an important distinction. The western system places more emphasis on the somatic level, while the traditional African system weaves the somatic within the social and spiritual.

Types of Traditional Healers and Their Respective Healing Paradigms

While there is a metatheoretical continuity across African ethnic groups regarding illness and healing, a number of ethnically distinct manifestations can be found in both types of practitioners and elaborations of their guiding paradigms. As a brief overview, examples are provided here from four African countries, Ghana, Angola, Senegal and Nigeria.

There are several "types" of traditional healers in Ghana. Among them are: (a) herbalists (those who use plants); (b) spiritualists (whose use of plants is limited, their treatment being primarily metaphysical); (c) divination spiritual healers (who generally do not use plants, but rely upon incantations and rites); (d) diviners (herbalists who practice divination and are specialists in metaphysical diagnosis); (e) the traditional birth attendants; and (f) the bone-setters (who function as orthopedic doctors). The general Akan term for healer is *asofo* (*osofo*, Sing.). The two main groups of *asofo* are the akomfo (okomfo, Sing., the priest, priestess, religious specialist, priest-healer) and the *nnunsinfo* (dunsini Sing., the herbalists). Within these two broad categories of priesthealers are further subtypes (Fink, 1989; Grills, 1995).

As part of their profession, the Akan healers must acquire knowledge in a number of areas: the classificatory system of diseases; the physiological under-standing of the structure and functioning of the human body; knowledge of medicinal herbs, leaves, roots, barks and grasses; the medicinal uses of various kinds of minerals and animal parts; preparing plant medicines in the form of powder, saps, and ointments; diagnostic techniques to identify diseases of the body (*onipadua*) including divination; divination diagnosis while under spirit possession; causes of diseases and ways of curing them; characteristics of spirits and spiritual forces and how to deal with them; and a variety of "secrets" which have to do with the properties of physics, chemistry, astronomy, magnetic energy and vibration, to name a few. Their formal training typically requires a minimum of three years, however tutelage under some form of apprenticeship can last for 10-15 years. It is not uncommon, particularly for herbalists, to specialize in the treatment of specific disorders such as *awoo* (sterility), *twe* (epilepsy), *soro* (convulsions), *ananasono* (children's diarrhea), *ntonkomada* (sleeping sickness), *babaso* (venereal disease), *awodene* (midwifery), *abunu* (malarial fever), *brompete* (chicken pox) or *dam* (mental diseases). Particularly among the *akomfo* it is not uncommon that they specialize in the treatment of various mental illnesses (Grills, 1995). Treatment emphasizes the resolution of illnesses associated with both natural and preternatural causes and determining "why" the person has been afflicted. Today, elements of several Akan systems are practiced by African Americans in different parts of the U.S. (i.e., there are U.S. established shrines and devotees based on the Akonedi shrine in Larteh, Ewe trained practitioners of Ifa and herbal practitioners who base their practice on the Akan system and knowledge).

Among the BaKongo of Angola and Zaire, a different traditional system of healing and typology of healers is in operation. The BaKongo healers believe in the perfect equalizing of the energy of the world of the living with the discernment of the world of the dead. The primary means for effecting such a balance has been through the media of charms, talismen, and medicines (Thompson, 1983). The

BaKongo peoples developed and utilized a complex system of *Nkisi* (pl. *minkisi*), or sacred medicines to effect proper alignment. According to MacGaffey (1991), a *nkisi* is a personalized energy from the world of the dead, which has been either chosen or been impelled to submit itself to human[2] influence through ritual actions. *Nganga* (pl. *banganga*) is the generic title of the healer who performed the rituals, ranging from highly elaborate processes—including whole villages, taking years to complete—to simple procedures, requiring the participation of one person for a few minutes. Most rituals have included behavioral restrictions, special settings or spaces and some combination of songs/chants and dances/movements. In addition, materials have included the bodies of the *nganga* and the client/patient, articles of clothing, and usually a focal object—which has come to be associated as the *nkisi* itself. The *nkisi* is best considered to be the totality of the materials, energies, places and persons, which when combined in appropriate ways, effects healing. It is the configuration of ritual features which imbued the nganga with healing power and effected healing, not the presence of any particular artifact. Because of this holistic apprehension of spiritual energy, Africans have been able to substitute artifacts and still effect healing (cf. Zahan, 1979, p. 54).

There are various ritual experts or *banganga*. Some invoke ancestral spirits— *banganga simbi*—spiritual beings imbued with the power to influence community and environmental processes. Other BaKongo traditional practitioners healed with charms— *the banganga nkisi,* and roots and herbs— *banganga mbuki*. Still others were diviners, (*banganga ngombo*), who attended to the needs of their "clients" by discerning the presence and influence of intermediate spirit forces. These and other forms of African healers known in the U. S. as "conjurors" and "root doctors" have been retained.

Yet another system which has captured the rich similarity of essence yet the distinctiveness of elaboration across different African healing practices is the Lebou/Wolof system in Senegal. In the Lebou system, pathological behavior in the realm of mental illness is considered to be the consequence of visible signs of an aggression coming from some external source such as: (1) the ancestral spirits (the *tuur* or *rabs*); (2) other celestial spirits *(jinne)*; (3) the witches (*seytane* or *domm*); or from (4) the practice of sorcery *(liggeey)*. These four levels of interpretation constitute a system of opposition and correlations (Zempleni, 1969).

The Wolof and Lebou have four types of *fajkat* (healers); the *marabout* or *serin*. the *jabarkat*, the *bilejo*, and the *boroom tuur* or *ndepkat*. The *marabout* or *serin* fulfills important religious, political, economic and social functions as well as a therapeutic one. He heals mainly with Koranic words which are written down as part of the healing procedure and with the Koranic verses he recites and says on his rosary. The traditional healer called *jabarkat*, is an important rival of the marabout, who employs the use of pharmacopeia and magical rituals as a predominant part of his therapeutic system. The witch hunter called *bilejo* is in an ambivalent position because of his ties with the world of witchcraft. He or she is exclusively devoted to detecting the handwork of the *domm* (witches). Finally, the priest or priestess (*boroom tuur* or *ndepkat*) who officiates over matters related to the Ancestral Spirits exercises his/her therapeutic functions either inside the lineage from which he/she inherits his *tuur* or within congregational groups organizing the rites of possession (Zempleni, 1969).

To each of these levels of interpretation or methods of healing is associated a series of therapeutic techniques and procedures. For example, healing (of mental or physical afflictions) associated with the rabs as causal agents will consist of the rite of possession (*ndop* and *samp*). This rite is performed to offer an alliance between the client and the Ancestral Spirit which is named for afflictions due to the *domm* (witches) the *bilejo's* cure consists of offering to locate and name the witch, to obtain his/her confessions and to make him restore the client's vital principal (*fit*) that the *domm* has tried to devour. In afflictions caused by the *jinne* (spirits) the marabout's cure is also the return of the client's *fit* that has "escaped" during the *jommi* (process of seeing a *jinne*).

The *jommi* results in a state of terror, stupor and lethargy caused by the view of the monstrous appearance of the *jinne*. But more than restoring the vital principal, the *serin* seeks to break the links by *liggeey* (sorcery) whether it is treated by the *marabout* or the *jabarkat*, treatment between the victim of the *jommi* and the cause (the jinne) by purifying the victim and by exorcising the *jinne* by means of Koranic words. Finally in afflictions caused by liggeey (sorcery) whether it is treated by the marabout or the jabarkay, treatment is aimed at a restoration of functioning through interventions which focus on issues associated with the etiology, not the symptomatology, of the affliction. Features of the Lebou interpretation of a patient's mental disorder are noteworthy. The interpretation of the disorder (and in fact, the determination of patient improvement) is not an external sovereign judgement of the therapist healer. Diagnosis and assessment of improvement are both the result of the consensus judgement of the healer/therapist, the patient and the patient's circle of family and friends; it is their quasi collective experience of the patient's illness and their collective speech about the patient determinations and assessments of client improvement. Through this "reason of the circle of family and friends to the ideas or to the delivering of the patient" (Zempleni, 1969), the healer is assisted in a determination of the etiology of the patient's problem. In other words, his/her examination is focused neither on clinical nor nosographic signs but on etiological signs. It is a fundamental principle of the traditional cure. In concrete terms, the therapist/healer has knowledge of all the signs likely to determine the identity and the intentions of the persecutory authority. In the treatment process, the *fajkat* does not ask the client and his/her family to reconstruct the story of the presenting mental disorder, to talk about the case history, or to depict the pre-morbid personality of the patient as the psychiatrist would do. He/she rather invites them to reveal the signs that can guide him/her in the etiological quest using divination (i.e., through the use of cowry shell) as a tool to uncover these signs.

His/her questions are concerned with the precise circumstances of the "starting point" of the disorders; more precisely about the place and the time symptoms began on one hand, and on the activity of the patient and her/his circle of family and friends on the other hand. The inaugural moment will interest him/her because certain months, certain days, certain hours are traditionally associated with the activity of one or several persecutory authorities: October-November (harvest, abundance of food, loosening of the social control) is associated with witchcraft; Monday and Thursday (cult days) with the *rabs*; the *yor-yor* hour (1:00 p.m. - 2:00 p.m.) is associated with activity by the *jinnes*; and *timis* (sunset) is associated with witchcraft, *jinnes*, and certain other processes.

The place reveals even better who may be responsible for the disorders; in the bush pond surrounded by foliage (the *rabs*); near a "pile" of garbage (*seytane* - Satan or negative forces), at the market (a sorcerer) etc. Thus, as opposed to diagnosing problems based primarily on the personal history of thoughts, feelings, and behaviors of individual clients and the occurrence of external temporally related circumstances, the causal theory and resultant diagnostic focus, emphasizes more social-communal activity and contextual issues—specific times and locations of clients at the onset of disturbance.

Among the Yoruba of Nigeria, the premier healer is known as the Babalawo (male) or Iyanifa (female) of which there are many degrees or levels and the Onisegun (herbalists only). To become a Babalawo or Iyanifa, one must undergo an extensive apprenticeship and initiation process. Central to the Yoruba conceptualization of healing, is the notion of inner essence which directly impacts the classification of disease. Ayoade (1979) explains that everything animate or inanimate is endowed with a spirit or power within it. Everything animate and inanimate has a double presence; it is both corporeal and incorporeal. The object, in effect, possesses a spirit that has latent powers. The soul represents a spiritual double which fuses with the organism it animates. That which the soul/spirit has fused with in some way represents its essence. So, the spirits of rocks are stationary, strong and dependable. The latent powers of all object/organisms can be harnessed or evoked in typically one of two ways; through the power of the spoken word and secondly, through the combination of the spirit forces in different objects.

Following from this belief system comes a classification of diseases. The Yoruba distinguish between three types of illnesses; diseases, afflictions, and sacred illness. The distinction is based on whether they have supernatural or non-supernatural causes. Diseases (mental and physical) have non-supernatural causes and can often be discerned with mere observation of the syndrome of manifest symptoms. Afflictions have supernatural causes and require the employment of divination to be diagnosed. Sacred illnesses are caused by divine intervention (God himself) with the diagnosis occurring through divination, observation, experience, and the patient's resistance to traditional and western methods of treatment which have shown utility in the past.

The overt symptom is not necessarily indicative of the nature of the illness. For example, Ayoade (1979) points out the cause of the headache in one patient may be non-supernatural while that of another patient is supernatural. Likewise, the headache of a patient may be non-supernatural in the morning but supernatural in the evening. One reason this can be so is the Yoruba believe that to be in the state of *ill* health increases one's vulnerability to a supernatural ailment. Ultimately, "a non-supernatural and a supernatural ailment are only different points along the same continuum."

This system of diagnosis is based upon what Ayoade (1979) refers to as a *preter-rational* (verses rational) medicine. "Preter" is a prefix meaning "beyond" or "more than" or past. Preter-rational medicine, then, means beyond mere rational methods and is based upon processes which are indicative of a higher mind and society. Preter-rational medicine serves three functions: curative, causative, or protective. "Protective" is used in this system rather than the term "preventive" from western medicine because preventive medicine "produces the effect of cure and prevention because of the pharmacological qualities of its components." Protective medicine performs its function because "of the inner spirit of the recipe" (p. 50).

Finally, preter-rational African medicine as expressed in the Yoruba system is based upon such central principles as similarity, contact, and transferability (Ayoade, 1979). Through these principles, the vital force in an object can be distilled through the expertise of the *Babalawo*. *Similarity* is based upon the understanding that similarity between an act which is performed and the expected result inevitably brings forth the desired result. "Like begets like and like poles attract" (p. 54). Incantation (the power of the word) adds to the potency of this process. In the case of *contact*, the distillation of the object's inner force can be through contagion. The individual's inner force can be transmitted through to his belongings like clothes and personal objects. "Since a person breathes his spirit into anything with which he comes into contact, his spirit could be harnessed through such objects . . . "(p. 54). *Transferability* reflects the belief that these forces can be harnessed and transferred to different objects and in different directions. Recalling the analogy of the rock, an individual could hypothetically be imbued with the essential nature of a rock: dependability, strength and endurance through the transference process.

Given the tenets of this Yoruba system one can more clearly appreciate the significance and meaning of their concept of *alafia*—the Yoruba term and concept for health. Literally, *alafia* means peace. What the term embraces, however, is "the totality of the individual's physical, social, emotional, psychological, and spiritual well-being in his total environment setting" (Ademuwagun, 1978, p. 89). *Alafia* or good health results from the dynamic interaction of these factors. In this global concept of *alafia*, a person can be sick in one of two mutually *inclusive* ways: (1) physical sickness *(ilera)* describing physical health and the factors which predispose one to possess good/poor physical or mental health; and (2) socio-psychological sickness which includes illnesses caused by social problems (unemployment, financial duress, strained interpersonal relations or community relations etc.).

Within the *alafia* schema, the (*babalawo* or *iyanifa*) initiates a set of diagnostic procedures, divinatory and standard diagnostic interviewing (including a review of symptoms), to determine whether the person is truly sick and to identify the causal factors. The diagnostic process is concerned with both the actual sickness and the predisposing factors. Social forces (people in the client's social world who would harbor ill will toward the client), natural forces (snake bites, fire, environmental pollution), or supernatural forces (offense to a divinity—known as an *orisha*; the ancestors—*egun* or *egungun*; the witches—*aje*; or one's personal spiritual guide—ori) are all considered as possible causative agents. Recognizing the power of inner essence discussed earlier, the Yorubas recognize that even sheer jealousy or hatred is enough for one individual to negatively affect another in the absence of overt actions to that effect.

The Practice and Function of Divination

"With few exceptions, African systems of divination have not been carefully studied, though diviners are found in almost every community" (Mbiti, 1970, p. 232). Divination is the practice of discovering the personal, familial, or communal human significance of future, present or past events. It is a skill and gift employed by many traditional healers to diagnose, treat, and prevent mental and physical affliction. Much of science itself has evolved from forms of divination and may be said to continue certain aspects of it (Edinche, 1986). Divination is particularly concerned with uncovering the hidden causes of ills. It is the disclosure of what has been previously concealed and is unlike revelation which is the manifestation of what resists conceptualizastion in the linguistic terms available to people. Divination is a mode of analysis and a taxonomic system while revelation is a prehension of experience taken as a whole (Turner, 1975). The way diviners interpret their divinatory symbols reveals deep insight into both the structure of their own society, their conception of human nature, and their ability to engage in preter-rational processes.

Modes of divination are regarded as both lie-detecting and truth discovering processes. The major thrust is revealing the hidden. The process of *cure* is essentially a way of "making known and visible or symbolic in guise" the unknown and invisible agents of affliction. Within this uncovering process the diviner acts as a consultant providing the necessary formula, principles, insights, and approaches for both understanding and resolving problems. Even though they may be specialists, the diviner must be a generalist in the sense that s/he must also have an understanding of a wide variety of associated factors (i.e., physiology, psychology, social, political, historical, cultural and religious phenomena). In this capacity, diviners are simultaneously guardians of this array of knowledge and utilizers of it.

Within the practice of his/her healing function, the diviner does not act alone. This is particularly true within the initial consultation for services. Within the consultation process, the family representative or family advisor[3] of the afflicted may play a critical role. Furthermore, it is not uncommon among some African ethnic groups that several consultations on the same matter are sought. The verification and integrity of the healer's diagnosis and prescription can sometimes be an important part of the consultation process. In the initial consultation with a diviner, the family advisor typically may not provide details such as who the afflicted person is or the history of the illness as a method of ascertaining the legitimacy of the diviner. If the diviner cannot accurately answer questions regarding the details of the case, the advisor knows that he or she may have to question the proposed solutions. Thus, diviners are always evaluated on the accuracy of their knowledge.

The problem of consultants sometimes giving incorrect advice is acknowledged by members of the society of healers and by the consultants themselves. For example, among the Batammaliba of Tog, diviners perform a ritual at the funeral of deceased diviners in which they sing the phrase "It is the consultant who is the liar; he consults to eat." Through this process consultants acknowledge publicly the difficulties and potential problems, ethical and otherwise, associated with the work of their profession.

Divination is utilized to determine the etiology, diagnosis, course, treatment and prognosis of various biopsychosocial disorders. It represents perhaps the most powerful method of healing in traditional medicine. It is therefore important that we try to understand the essence of divination, from the standpoint of the people who practice and subscribe to it, and from the standpoint of its processes and products. Only through an understanding of the process and context, grounded in its own epistemological and cosmological reference points, can we appreciate the products and their meanings. Through the process of divination one is more likely to glean the essential truths inherent in this system of healing and more fundamentally, one can learn about the essential truths of our African science. If in fact divination is core and central to African life then the truths of the people are embodied within the divination process. They are embodied there and protected there. One could argue then, that the divination systems represent ways for discerning the nature of human beingness, the features of human functioning and the restoration of normal and natural functioning which have been referred to as the cornerstones of African psychology (cf. Rowe, 1994). Furthermore, its presence, absence, or denial, in the lives of African Americans becomes an issue worthy of examination, particularly in discourse about their psychological functioning or the development of African-centered models of mental health. The use, products, and processes of divination require the attention of African and African American scholars.

African Conceptualizations of Human Beingness and Functioning

This discussion of African traditional medicine would be incomplete without some discussion of African conceptualizations of what it means to be human; what influences the behavior, personality, and functioning of the individual; and African theories regarding dynamic processes which operate to influence behavior, thought, and feelings.

Almost every concept in African thought is onto-theological. In other words, it is dense with religiosity (Dukor, 1993). Any conceptualization of human psychological and behavioral functioning will reflect this basic postulate. Consequently, spirit features prominently in African psychology. The mind as defined in western thought is the "element or complex of elements within the individual that feels, perceives, thinks, wills, and especially reasons"; it reflects "the conscious mental events and capabilities in the organism" (Merriam-Webster, 1995).

Within an African conceptualization, the mind is the combined influence of the soul/spirit (i.e., *emi* or *nkrabea*) and the guardian spirit (i.e., *ori* or *okra*). Furthermore, in this conceptualization, spirit is as important as the physical manifestation of self and spiritual processes which are not immediately discerned by the ordinary physical senses represent environmental forces which are as critical as "concrete" manifestations of environmental influences on behavior and development. In all respects, there must be harmony and balance between the physical and spiritual at the level of person and environment. These spiritual processes influence, guide, and protect human functioning; influence positively or negatively human development; influence personality development and traits; and are central to all forms and stages of healing.

As depicted in Table 1, African conceptualizations fully incorporate these spiritual processes into their models of human functioning. A useful resulting heuristic for mapping human functioning within the context of psychology is to look at behavior, cognition, affect, personality etc. as manifestations of or derivatives of both essence and manifestation. Essence reflects the essential nature, operating principles, substance, heart, gist, crux or core of who we are as persons; that which makes us human. Manifestation is the expression, evidence, indication, exhibition, tangible presentation, or articulation of that essence which makes us human. Western conceptualizations have been restricted primarily to the examination of manifestation only. The African has long recognized that this is but a mere representation of what really is. This is why in African theory, it is commonly accepted that existence (in the form of essence) precedes manifestation (the state of being alive) and that death is merely an end to the current manifestation and an important transition for the continued existence of one's unique essence.

Table 1
Conceptualization of the Elements of Human Beingness

Kemetic - Conceptualization/Kemet Wade Nobles (1986) and Na'im Akbar (1994)		Lebou Conceptualization/Senegal Maam Fatou Seck (1985)	
Ka	(body/container-synthesizer of spiritual energy) A. Divine Ka - original Ka of the creator B. Intermediate Ka - nature's minerals, vegetables, and animal life C. Inferior Ka - personal body (strive to transform from the inferior to the Divine)	**Fit**	(vital energy/life force/ soul; it represents the spiritual heart) The main part of your essence as a human being; if you lose it, you can lose your mind; severe fear/ anxiety can cause one to lose it
Ba	(breath of the soul; the activating life)	**Roo**	(breath of life - leaves body at death) Given by God (Suñu Boron); the part of the individual that gives him/ her physical life
Khaba	(shade or covering soul - ghost; produces emotion and motion, maintains rhythms, circulation, etc.; stimulated by the drum)	**Takandeer**	(shadow/shade) Given by God; one's companion/protects the individual, is always present; upon death it leaves the person
Akhu	(seat of intelligence, rational function, and perception; the navigator but in the service of the Divine Ka)	**Xel**	(intelligence)
		Sago	(reason, rationality)
Seb	(the self-creative power of being which does not manifest itself until puberty)	**Jiko**	(personality/traits)
		Raab	(ancestral spirits which guide, protect, and can harm/influence/shape personality) In addition, a person's behavior and well being is also affected by other spirits: a pantheon of deities (jines), angels (malaka), and negative forces (seyfane)
Putah	(the intellectual soul of the first intellectual father, the ability to teach others)		
Atum	(the divine or eternal soul)		

Table 1 (continued)
Conceptualization of the Elements of Human Beingness

Akan Conceptualization/Ghana Kofi Asare Opoku (1978)		Yoruba Conceptualization/Nigeria Dr. M. Dukor (1993)	
Okra	(soul, given by Nyame, the spiritual force of your conscience, influences your actions, good and ill luck associated with it; the bearer of one's destiny)	**Ori Inu**	(inner head/personal spirit given by Olodumare; influences personality; carrier of one's destiny; guardian self)
		Ori	(physical head)
Kradin	(the soul's name given to the child and represents the day of the week on which you are born)	**Emi/Muo**	(Breath of life; soul; returns to Olodumare when person dies)
Nkrabea	(destiny, before the okra leaves heaven it takes its nkrabea with it)	**Iwaju**	(soul at the forehead)
		Iwaju/atari	(soul at the crown)
		Ipako	(soul at the occiput)
Sunsum	(spiritual element in person; accounts for one's personality, disposition and intelligence; can change, i.e., from weak to strong, can leave the body at night and what is involved with dreams; it is what is attacked by evil forces)	**Ara**	(body molded by the orisa Obatala)
		Eje	(the blood/animates life)
		Okan	(physical heart)
		Egbe	(inner heart)
Mogya	(blood/bloodline - through Mother, one's physical self)	**Iye**	(inner heart that denotes the mind) (Okan/Obi)
Ntoro	(personality life force which comes from one's father, it is also immaterial, transmitted through the father's sperm, spiritually bonds the child to the father)	**Ojiji**	(shadow; follows the individual; represents a higher phenomenon that is unseen)
		Iwa	(one's fate/destiny/charater)
Suban	[one's character; must co-operate to make one's destiny successful by acquiring and practicing good character (Suban-pa)]	**Ewo**	(one's personal taboos)

The conceptualizations of what makes the person a living, functioning human being endowed with all the capacities commonly recognized as features of human functioning (i.e., intellect, will, emotion, and social functioning) are in fact very rich. For example, in the Akan conceptualization, the features of human functioning are not simply described as man consisting of a complex of physical features and a mind influenced by spiritual or divine forces. Rather, the features of human beingness first include the presence of the individual's okra which is their soul, given to them by *Nyame* (God) before incarnation into the physical world. The *okra* is the spiritual force of the individual's conscience. It influences actions, good and ill fortune, and is also the bearer of destiny. In addition, there is the *kradin* which is the soul's name given to the child and represents the day of the week on which the child is born. Who one is, including personality, lot in life and talents, skills, etc. are further influenced by other features of one's being or essence such as their nkrabea (destiny; before the *okra* leaves heaven it takes its *nkrabea* with it); *sunsum* (a spiritual element in each person; accounts for their personality, disposition and intelligence; can change i.e., from weak to strong; can leave the body at night; is what is involved with dreams and is what is attacked by evil forces); *mogya* (the physical blood/bloodline—through one's mother; reflects the person's physical self); *ntoro* (the personality life force which comes from one's father; it is also immaterial and transmitted through the father's sperm; spiritually it bonds the child to the father); *suban* (one's character; this feature must co-operate to make one's destiny successful by acquiring and practicing good character known as *suban-pa*) (Opoku, 1978).

Not too dissimilar from the Akan conceptualization, is the Yoruba concept of human beingness. According to the Yoruba schema the individual is a manifestation of a complex set of features which includes their: *emi* (breath of life), it returns to *Olodumare* (God) when the person dies; *ori* (the physical head); the *ori inu* (the real essence of being)which is the individual's inner head—it is their personal spirit given by *Olodumare* and it forms consciousness without being conscious. The individual does not control it, rather it controls personality and the whole being of the person. One can have good or bad *ori*. Good *ori* can be spoiled by one's character, society, *aje* (witches) and wicked people and bad *ori* can be modified and improved through *ebo* (sacrifice) and rituals. Bad *ori* can be changed to good and good to bad based upon individual character, choice and ebo. Hence, the Yoruba proverb: "Ori inu re ti ba ti ode je—his inner head has spoiled the outer one." There are three souls in the head: *iwaju* (soul at the forehead); *awuje/atari* (soul at the crown); and *ipako* (soul at the occiput); *ara* (body molded by *Orisanla*—a Yoruba *orisa* or spirit); *owo* and *ese* (hands and feet crafted by *Ogun*—a Yoruba *orisa* or spirit); *eje* (the blood which animates life); *okan* (the physical heart; when blood passes through it, it stimulates the egbe); *egbe* (the inner heart); *iye* (the inner heart that also denotes what the western world refers to as the mind); *ojiji* (the shadow whose primary function is to follow the individual); *oro* (the manifestation of the power of the word); *iwa* (the individual's fate or destiny/character); and *ewo* (the individual's personal taboos that if broken could spoil a good destiny) (Dukor, 1993; Elebuibon, 1996).

What is clearly discernable in African conceptualizations, is the centrality of a metaphysical component to the person which requires of him/her certain social and natural "obligations" which are accompanied by rituals (rhythms in life). We, as human beings, do not exist alone in the universe, but are always interacting with and under the influence of other forces (Dukor, 1993). Nature provides rules for living peacefully in society and death does not put an end to existence. Death is not the end of life; it is a transition to the "after life." The soul joins the community of the spirits of the departed (the ancestors), and, eventually revisits the material world. Spiritual forces also influence, guide and protect human functioning. They influence personality, can facilitate or impede destiny and can protect and guide. They can operate at the level of the individual, family, community, or entire town. Ademuwagun (1978) argues that if even one aspect of this complex system of health and healing is neglected or omitted, the client remains psychologically without *alafia* or health. This reflects the metaphysical basis of the Yoruba belief system. "Philosophy, theology, politics, social theory, land law, medicine, psychology, birth and burial, all find themselves logically concentrated in a system so tight that to subtract one from the whole is to paralyze the structure of the whole" (Adesanya, 1958).

Conclusion and Implications

An understanding of culture and its role in shaping the nature of human interaction, interpersonal as well as intrapersonal, has more recently led to intensive investigation of the influence of culture for specific ethnic groups. As we have begun to document, there is now converging evidence that many elements of African culture are present in the patterns, practices and beliefs of African American individuals, families, and communities.

One area of investigation already underway has been the African-centered movement among African American scholars attempting to explicate the role of African based epistemology, cosmology, and ontology to explain African and African American life and behavior (Akbar, 1995; Ani, 1994; Grills & Nobles, 1995; Kambon, 1992; Nobles, 1986; Rowe & Grills, 1993). They advocate for paradigm adaptations or alternative culturally specific mental health paradigms of relevance to various African ethnic groups that are based upon African principles. The need for this area of investigation is long overdue particularly considering the questionable effectiveness of standard practices of intervention for African American populations (Longshore, Hsieh, Anglin, & Annon 1992; Wallen, 1992). In fact, it has been argued that the existing treatment system lacks ascribed and achieved credibility for African American populations, the consequences of which include underutilization of services, high attrition rates, and limited effectiveness (Rowe & Grills, 1993; Sue & Zane, 1987).

Considerable work lies ahead for those concerned with the development of African-centered models of mental health and well being. We need to engage in intensive investigation of West, Central, Eastern, and Southern African science as well as Kemetic science and knowledge and their transformations here in the U.S. in the form of root medicine in the south; voodoo, vodu and hoodoo in the south and the Caribbean; Santeria in Cuba; Obea in Jamaica; Candomble in Brazil etc.

Notwithstanding the enormous amount of work yet to be done, there are some things we do know about traditional African medicine. The following facts bear reiteration: (1) Throughout Africa traditional healers continue to be the primary caregivers not only for medical patients but for psychiatric patients as well (Edgerton, 1980). In the edited volume "African Therapeutic Systems" Ademuwagun, Ayoade, Harrison, and Warren (1979) compile an extensive series of articles on traditional healing practices, however, very little of what is presented empirically demonstrates the utility of these practices alone, in contrast with Western approaches, or across various African ethnic groups. In addition, a number of limitations have been noted with the existing research on this topic. For example, insufficient attention has been given to the psychological analyses of divination emphasizing its therapeutic functions (i.e., reduction of anxiety, resolution of depressive symptomatology, and alleviation of stress). (2) In terms of psychiatric concerns, the most studied topic has been the frequency of occurrence of schizophrenia-like symptoms while less emphasis has been placed on the meaning and causes of the constellations of symptoms within the respective systems (WHO, 1979). (3) Traditional healers have generations of accumulated knowledge of clinical patterns and treatments. The "witchdoctor system is much more organized than was previously believed" and has distinct differentiations as to type of healer, scope of practice, and illness specialization (Conco, 1972; Finch, 1992; Stott & Brown, 1973). (4) Commonly found among a number of African ethnic groups is the belief that psychiatric disorders are caused by a variety of spirits including familial, ancestral and witchcraft. In addition, however, is the recognition that there are also social and psychological causes as well, what Conco (1972) refers to as the dualist theory of naturalist and supernatural causation of disease (Gelfand, 1964). (5) African therapeutic systems tend to be characterized by holism. For example, there may be no segmentation of physiological, anatomical or mental disease (Zeller, 1979). (6) Medicine and treatment are often intertwined with spirituality. In fact, spirituality is a major cornerstone to the practice of healing in all of its phases (Ayoade, 1979; Opoku, 1978); and (Zeller, 1979). (7) In several systems, categories of mental illness are defined by criteria that are based far less upon symptoms than they are upon etiology and prognosis (Edgerton, 1980). (8) To become a traditional healer, whether this means diviner, herbalist, medium, bone setter, or fetish man requires extensive training and apprenticeship (on average ten to twenty years). In addition, several striking similarities and stark contrasts have been noted between the African and Euro-American "systems" in the areas of healer prestige and status, the "calling" to become a healer, specializations within the field, and the existence of professional organizations (Finch, 1992; Harrison, 1974). (9) Traditional healing practices have been found to be effective and in some instances to have a faster recovery rate and fewer recurrent symptoms than Western strategies (Ademuwagun, 1980; Lancet, 1964). Aryee (1978) surmises that this occurs in part because the patient is often not separated from their families or the things that have always been important to them. Within this traditional system of care, "Churches, shrines, priests, herbalists and the continuity of community life all contribute to a successful therapy" (Lambo,1981). In fact, there are a wealth of psychotherapeutic strategies within the village that are not typically found within the hospital or other institution. (10) To be accepted, a diagnosis must address not only the "what" and "how" but also the "why" of the patient's illness (Ayoade, 1979; Seck, 1995; Zempleni, 1969). The diviner concerns him/herself with just those matters in the diagnosis of the problem. In fact, the answer to why a particular ailment impacts an individual is essential to the prescriptions for cure which is contrasted with the Western approach, even as practiced in Africa, where the emphasis is on the diagnosis of the disease (some organ dysfunction) and not the illness (not "feeling well") (Simmons, 1980). (11) Sickness and health can often times be seen as a matter of corporate social concern (Janzen, 1978). While concerned about the well being of the afflicted individual, it is recognized that the reason for the disorder may have derived from the family or clan so the well being of all is at stake. (12) Various groups use a process referred to as kinship based therapy management. The kinship system consists usually of relatives who rally together to support the identified patient to sift through information, lend moral support, make decisions, and arrange the details of the therapeutic relationship. They in effect act as a broker/intermediary between the client and the traditional healer (Aryee, 1978; Turner, 1975). (13) In the context of traditional African medicine, the power of words is enormously important. Words, used in incantations and amulets derive from the healer's special understanding of the nature of things to which these words are associated in time, space and essence (Ayoade, 1979; Gbedemah, 1995; Makinde, 1988).

Thus, two primary aims of traditional medicine are to restore humans to their proper social and spiritual relationships, even in matters of physical or mental health. Social complexities are central and pressing and must be dealt with before handling the attendant physical or mental/emotional issues. Furthermore, the spiritual issues are of paramount importance. Nothing can happen in a positive vein until all supernatural blocks to good health have been removed. The physical cure can now proceed and disharmonious social relations can resolve themselves as the spirit realm is addressed. What emerges in this explication of the science of African medicine is its holistic features—its fundamental reliance on the cohesion of the social, physical, psychological, and spiritual.

Serious consideration must be given to a reexamination of the usefulness of western paradigms of human functioning, illness, and healing. While one would not want to throw the "baby out with the bath water," likewise, one would not want to bathe their most precious gift of life in the used bathwater of another family. For example, we must examine whether the philosophical, ontological, epistemological and axiological assumptions of western paradigms of psychology are sufficient or appropriate for describing the behavior of people with a distinctive African character.

In an oral community, such as has been the case with African Americans, many of the beliefs or ideas about optimal human functioning have been passed down from generation to generation through various proverbs and "wise sayings." For African Americans, many of those proverbs have been embodied in both the songs (spirituals, gospel, blues, soul) which have evolved out of our unique experiences as well as the "wise sayings" memorialized in the "things grandma said." It is time for psychologists to examine those media to reclaim and explicate the conceptual frames for understanding African American functioning, for within those 'sayings" lie both the remembrances of African ways—the cosmological, philosophical and ontological principles which define optimal human functioning—and the rules for promoting and achieving health and healing (Bacon, 1895; Blake, 1984; Crell, 1990; Deas-Moore, 1987; Hurston, 1995; Jones, 1993; Snow, 1974; and Watson, 1984).

It is not enough to simply identify them, however. The more critical work is to resurrect their regulatory or aligning spiritual functions. Only then can we begin to develop more authentic African-centered approaches for understanding human beingness, delineating features of functioning and articulating and developing mechanisms for restoring order to our behavior.

We submit that essential to such an approach is the recognition of the essentiality of spirit, out of which physical, psychological and moral features manifest. Developing authentic African-centered approaches to healing requires us to study the details or remembrances of ways of being and their African roots. We can only understand and articulate behavior by acknowledging how and under what conditions the behavior was learned .

The tendency in the U.S. and other western countries is to dismiss African traditional medicine as nothing more than unscientific primitive beliefs. With great assistance from the Maafa, the credibility of traditional African medicine is often questioned by Euro and African Americans. Given that culturally specific interventions, by definition, are grounded in the cultural tenets of specific populations, it is important that interventions are couched within the cultural heritage of the group. For African Americans, this entails a grounding of African centered interventions within the framework of African beliefs and practices of human behavior, functioning and healing. In other words, prior to the Maafa, what were our indigenous African principles and techniques for healing?

As we examine traditional African precepts of healing, several key questions must be explored. From an African world view: (1) What are the elements or essential features of health? (2) What constitutes illness? (3) What, if any, are the differences among and between physical illness and mental illness? (4) What are the causative factors in the occurrence of mental illness? and (5) How are individuals, defined as ill, altered or impacted in ways which promote or reestablish healthy human functioning?

We must carefully study the principles and strategies of African traditional healing practices as used in the treatment of mental health concerns. The goal is to understand and determine the utility of these principles and strategies in the ongoing development of culturally specific treatment and prevention programs for African American youth, adults, and families. We can then generate a schema of traditional healing which reflects an African epistemological framework.

The approach we take to learn about and explore this area of our heritage must be handled with the utmost care and acumen. For example, it is apparent that African divination practices do not correspond easily to Western epistemology. Consequently, the dynamic quality, the essence, the very meaning of the process over which we seek to gain epistemological mastery is lost or diminished when subjected to standard western empirical methods of investigation. It is important, therefore, that the essence of the spiritual foundation, the employment of rituals, the involvement of community, and the practice of divination be understood from the standpoint of its practitioners and users with an emphasis first on the process and later on its products. In other words, we must attempt to define this process *a posteriori* and not with the *a priori* paradigm of illness and nosology characteristic of western theories and practice of psychology and psychiatry. Consider the metaphorical question: "how do you assess the essential qualities of a river?" The western trained mind would likely take a sample of the water and analyze it; yet the essential piece that makes a river a river, is that it flows. Yes, that analyzed sample will tell you about the chemical composition of the water that makes up the river. It will also be true that the essential nature of that body of water is obscured by the constraints of our methods for answering the question, a method that forces us to take the phenomena out of its context resulting in a circumscribed and distorted image.

In the investigation of traditional healing practices we must study with an African mind and heart: (a) the cultural systems of knowledge; (b) theories of mental illness and health; (c) the relationship of divination practices to the larger context of decision making and the cultural ethos of African life; (d) the various diagnostic systems and practices; (e) theories of illness etiology and method of divining causality; (f) healer prevention and intervention techniques and procedures; (g) the nature of the client-healer relationship; (h) the diviner's role in society; (i) the efficacy of treatment including the vitality of herbal medicine; and (j) diviner training. Examining the training of healers is important because it exposes both the minimum requirements for what is considered mastery in the practice of healing and the axiology, the true value, assigned to healing and its various components. In this way, we can begin to understand how people view what healer/diviners do.

We must identify the metatheoretical constructs underlying the various African systems of healing and explore their implications for mental health interventions with African people. What is the all-embracing, metatheoretical basis to African traditional healing and divination practices. Perhaps Gelfand (1964) was correct when he observed that "running throughout all these researches (on African healing) we notice a basic pattern and a basic philosophy." Can we articulate this philosophy and its implication for African centered psychological praxis in the United States?

The responsibility facing African-centered psychology is to expand the reference base of theories and methods of legitimate "healing" beyond European and American paradigms. This new base must include African concepts, constructs, and methods of knowing. It must be instrumental in the delineation of an alternative conceptual framework and accompanying praxis for culturally specific mental health interventions for African Americans based on and informed by an appreciation of core African centered beliefs regarding adaptive and maladaptive functioning, and the fulfillment of personal, familial and communal destiny.

As Ayi Kwei Armah (1978) wrote in his book The Healers: "Those who learn to read the signs around them and to hear the language of the universe reach a kind of knowledge healers call the shadow." As African American healers in search of our mother's garden (African reality), perhaps we can find our own (the blend of our African and African American realities) and become consciously imbued in shadow.

Notes

1. The Maafa is a great disaster and misfortune of death and destruction beyond human convention and comprehension. Its critical feature is the denial of the validity of African people's humanity, reflected in the ever-present complete and total disregard and disrespect for the African and people of African ancestry's right to exist. It includes the on-going, sophisticated continuous process in the support of worldwide White supremacy (Nobles, 1994).

2. A word of caution is in order. Mac Gaffey notes that much of the understanding of BaKongo systems of healing have been misinterpreted because of the lack of understanding of the integrated system of spirituality. He reports that even in his attempts to document the compilations regarding BaKongo healing artifacts, many of the original texts had been dissected, abbreviated, sorted and fused, then

translated, in such a way that it was impossible to verify who was saying what and with what authority. His comments suggest that the imposition of linear and reductionistic European cultural and intellectual frames to interpret African culture and spirituality have led to the loss of meaning of the richness, breadth and depth of these ideas (cf. Ani, 1994).

3. The family advisor is typically someone selected by the family because of their knowledge of the family, of the community, of the language of divination, and because s/he is serious. In particular, the family advisor comes to the consultation with basic knowledge about the problem, its history, and its potential causes. In part, their role includes determining the veracity of the information given.

4. Adapted from Alice Walker (1974) who wrote: "In search of my mother's garden, I found my own."

References

Ackah, F. E. (1990). *Comprehension notes on West African traditional religion for advanced level (Vol. 1).* Legon: University of Ghana Bookshop.

Ademuwagun, Z. A. (1976). The challenge of co-existence of orthodox and traditional medicine. *The East Africa Medical Journal, 53*(1), 21-32.

Ademuwagun, Z. A. (1978). "Alafia"—the Yoruba concept of health: Implications for health education. *International Journal of Health Education, 21*(2), 89-97.

Ademuwagun, Z. A. (1980). Problem and prospect of legitimizing and integrating aspects of traditional health care systems and methods in the modern medical therapy: The IgboOro experience. *Nigerian Medical Journal, 5*(2),182-190.

Ademuwagun, Z. A., Ayoade, J. A. A., Harrison, l. A., & Warren, D. M. (1979). *African therapeutic systems.* Los Angeles, CA: Crossroads Press.

Adesanya, A. (1958). Yoruba metaphysical thinking. *Odu, 5, 39.*

Akbar, N. (1995). *Natural psychology and human transformation.* Tallahassee, FL: Mind Productions & Associates, Inc.

Amponsah, K. (1977). *Topics on West African traditional religion (Vol.1).* LegonAccra, Ghana: Adwinsa Publication Limited.

Ani, M. (1994). *Yurugu: An African centered critique of European cultural thought and behavior.* Trenton, NJ: Africa World Press, Inc.

Appiah-Kubi, K. (1981) *Man cures, God heals: Religion and medical practice among the Akans of Ghana.* New York: Friendship Press.

Armah, A. K. (1979). The healers. London: Heinemann.

Aryee, A. (1978). *The coexistence of traditional and modern medicine in Nigeria: An example of transitional behavior in the developing world.* Unpublished doctoral dissertation, Boston University.

Ayoade, J. A. A. (1979). The concept of inner essence in Yoruba traditional medicine. *African Therapeutic Systems*, 49-55.

Barrett, L. E. (1974). *Soul-force: African heritage in Afro-American religion.* New York: Doubleday .

Bernal, G., & Enchautegni-de-Jesus, N. (1994). Latinos and latinas in community psychology: A review of the literature. *American Journal of Community Psychology, 22*(4), 531-557.

Conco, W. Z. (1972). The African Bantu traditional practice of medicine: Some preliminary observations. *Social Science and Medicine, 6,* 283-322.

Creel, M. W. (1988). *"A Peculiar people": Slave religion and community-culture among the Gullahs*: New York University Press.

Diop, C. A. (1989). *The cultural unity of Black Africa: The domains of matriarchy and patriarchy in classical antiquity.* London: Kamak House.

DuBois, W. E. B. (1969). *The souls of Black folk. New York:* Signet.

Dukor, M. (1993, July). African concept of man. *Orunmilism, 2,* 27-34.

Edgerton, R. B. (1980). Traditional treatment for mental illness in Africa: A review. *Culture, Medicine, and Psychiatry, 4,* 167-184.

Elebuibon, l. (1996). *Interview with Dr. Cheryl Grills.* Oshogbo, Nigeria.

Field, M. J. (1960). *Search for security: An ethnopsychiatric study of rural Ghana* (p. 149). London: Faber and Faber

Finch, C. (1992). *Knowledge, attitudes and practices survey of traditional healers in Fatick, Senegal.* Final Report (USAID): Grant #685-0281-G-00-1254-00.

Fink, H. (1989). *Religion, disease and healing in Ghana: A case study of traditional dormaa medicine.* Germany: Trickster Wissenschaft.

Gbedemah, G. K. K. (1995). *Interview with Dr. Cheryl Grills in her capacity as president of the Ghana Psychic and Traditional Healer's Association.* Mankrong Junction, Ghana.

Gelfand, M. (1964). Psychiatric disorders as recognized by the Shona. In A. Kiev (Ed.), *Magic, faith, and healing* (pp.156-173). New York: The Free Press.

Ghana Ministry of Health. (1994). *Traditional medicine 1994 report.* Accra: Ghana Ministry of Health.

Grills, C., (1995*). Research interviews held with traditional healers in Ghana, Senegal, Mali and Nigeria.* Unpublished research; work in progress.

Grills, C. & Nobles, W. (1995). A covenant with destiny: The ABPsi African healers project. *Psych Discourse, 26*(6) ,11-12.

Hall, R. L. (1990). African religious retentions in Florida. In J. E. Holloway, *Africanisms in American culture* (pp. 98-118). Bloomington: Indiana University Press.

Harrison, I. E. (1974). Traditional healers: A neglected source of health manpower. *Rural Africana, 26*, 197-201.

Holloway, J. E. (1990). *Africanisms in American culture*. Bloomington: Indiana University Press.

Hurston, Z. N. (1995). Zora Neale Hurston: Folklore, memoirs and other writings. In Cheryl Wall (Ed.), NY: *The Library of America*.

Janzen, J. M. (1978). *The quest for therapy in lower Zaire*. Berkeley, CA: University Press.

Jones, A. C. (1993). *Wade in the water: The wisdom of the spirituals*. Maryknoll, NY: Orbis Books.

Kambon, K. K. K. (1992). *The African personality in America: An African-centered framework*. Tallahassee, FL: Nubian Nation Publishers.

King, L. M., Moody, S., Thompson, O., & Bennett, M. (1983). Black psychology reconsidered: Notes toward curriculum development. In J. C. Chunn II, P. J. Dunston, & F. RossSheriff (Eds.), *Mental health and people of color: Curriculum development and change* (pp.322). Washington, DC: Howard University Press.

Lambo, J. O. (1976). The impact of colonialism on African cultural heritage with special reference to the practice of herbalism in Nigeria. In Singer (Ed.), *The Conch, 8, (1- 2), 123-135*. Traditional Healing: New Science or New Colonialism. *Conch Magazine Limited*.

Lancet. (1964). The Village of Aro. *Lancet: Leading Articles*, 513-514.

Landrine, H., & Klonoff, E. A. (1994). Cultural diversity in causal attributions for illness: The role of the supernatural. *Journal of Behavioral Medicine, 17*(2),181-193.

Longshore, D., Hsieh, S., Anglin, M. D., & Annon, T. A. (1992). Ethnic Patterns in Drug Abuse Treatment Utilization. *The Journal of Mental Health Administrations, 19(3)*, 268-277.

Lonner, W. J., & Malpass, R. (1994). *Psychology and culture*. Needham Heights, MA: Allyn and Bacon.

MacGaffey, W. (1991). *Art and healing of the BaKongo commented by themselves: Minkisi from the Laman collection*. Stockholm, Sweden: Folkens Museum-Etnografiska.

Makinde, M. A. (1988). African Philosophy, culture and traditional medicine. Athens: Ohio University Center for International Studies.

Mbiti, J. S. (1970). *African religions and philosophies*. Garden City, NY: Anchor/Doubleday.

Merriam-Webster, Inc. (1995). *Merriam-Webster's Collegiate Dictionary*. Springfield, MA: Merriam-Webster, Inc.

Mulira, J. G. (1990). The case of voodoo in New Orleans. In J. E. Holloway (Ed.) *Africanisms in American culture* (pp. 34-68). Bloomington: Indiana University Press.

Mullins, L. (1984). *Therapy, ideology, and social change: Mental healing in urban Ghana.* Berkeley: University of California Press,

Nobles, W. W. (1986). *African psychology: Towards its reclamation, reascension and revitalization.* Oakland, CA: Institute for the Advanced Study of Black Family Life and Culture.

Nobles, W. W. (1994a). Healing the rupture and extending the splendor. *Psych Discourse, 25*(9), 8-13.

Nobles, W. W., King, L., & James, C. B. (1995). *Health promotion and disease Prevention: Strategies in the African American community.* African American professionals health promotion and disease prevention focus group report submitted to the Congress of National Black Churches. Washington, DC: The Association of Black Psychologists.

Obeyesekere, G. (1985). Depression, Buddhism, and the work of culture in Sri Lanka. In A. Klejuman & B. Good (Eds.), *Culture and depression: Studies in the anthropology and cross-cultural psychiatry of affect and disorder* (pp. 134-152). Berkeley and Los Angeles: University of California Press.

Opoku, K. A. (1978). *West African traditional religion.* Accra: FEP International Private Limited .

Peek, P. M. (1991). African divination systems: Non-normal modes of cognition. In P. M. Peek (Ed.), *African Divination Systems* (pp. 193-212). Bloomington: Indian University Press.

Quarcoopome, T. N. O. (1987). *West African traditional religion.* Ibadan, Nigeria: African Universities Press.

Richards, D. M. (1989). *Let the circle be unbroken: The implications of African spirituality in the diaspora.* Westport, CT: Greenwood Press.

Rowe, D. M. (1994). *The African psychology institute's conceptual overview: A working draft.* Presented at the Association of Black Psychologist's National Convention. Philadelphia, PA.

Rowe, D., & Grills, C. (1993, January-March). African-centered drug treatment: An alternative conceptual paradigm for drug counseling with African American clients. *Journal of Psychoactive Drugs, 25*, 21-33.

Rowe, D. M., & Grills, C. N. (1996). *Eurocentric foundations of psychology: Implications for the future.* Paper presented at the National Council for Schools of Professional Psychology. Orlando, FL.

Seck, F. (1995). Interview with Dr. Cheryl Grills. Rufisque, Senegal.

Simmons, R. E. (1980). *Integrated health care, traditional and modern.* Unpublished Manuscript.

Snow, L. (1974). Folk medical beliefs and their implications for care of patients. *Annals of Internal Medicine, 81*, 82-96.

Snow, L. F. (1993). *Walking over medicine.* San Francisco: Westview Press.

Speight, S. L., Myers, L. J., Cox, C. I., & Highlen, P. S. (1991). A redefinition of multicultural counseling. *Journal of Counseling and Development, 70*, 29-36.

Stott, N. C. H., & Browne, W. M. (1973). Do witchdoctors practice clinical pattern recognition? *South African Medical Journal*, 334-335.

Stuckey, S. (1987). *Slave culture.* New York: Oxford University Press.

Suarez-Balcazar, Y., Durlak, J. A., & Smith, C. (1994). Multicultural training practices in community psychology programs. *American Journal of Community Psychology, 22*(6), 785-798.

Sue, S., & Zane, N. (1987). The role of culture and cultural techniques in psychotherapy. *American Psychologist, 42*, 37-45.

Tella, A. (1977). *African traditional medicine and healing practices: Prospects of integrating them into modern health services.* Presented at Second World Black and African Festival of Arts and Culture. Lagos, Nigeria.

Thompson, R. F. (1983). *Flash of the spirit: African and Afro-American art and philosophy.* NY: Vintage Books, a division of Random House.

Trimble, J. E., Mackey, D. H., Lafromboise, T. D., & France, G. A. (1983). American Indians, psychology and curriculum development: A proposed reform with reservations. In J. C. Chunn II, P. J. Dunston, & F. Ross-Sheriff (Eds.), *Mental health and people of color: Curriculum development and change* (pp. 43-64). Washington, DC: Howard University Press.

Tumer, V. (1975). *Revelation and Divination in Ndembu Ritual.* Ithaca: Comeh University Press.

Twumasi, P. A. (1975). *Medical systems of Ghana.* Tema: Ghana Publishing Corporation.

Wallen, J. (1992). Providing culturally appropriate mental health services for minorities. *The Journal of Mental Health Administrations, 19*(3), 288-295.

Watson, W. H. (1984). Central tendencies in the practice of folk medicine. In W. H. Watson, *African American folk medicine: The therapeutic significance of faith and trust.* New Brunswick, NJ: Transaction Books.

Weinstein, R. S. (1994). Pushing the frontiers of multicultural training in community psychology. *American Journal of Community Psychology, 22*(6), 811-820.

Wong, H. Z., Kim, L. l., Lim, D. T., & Morishima, J. K. (1983). The training of psychologists for Asian and Pacific American communities: Problems, perspectives and practices. In J. C. Chunn II, P. J. Dunston, & F. Ross-Sheriff (Eds.), *Mental health and people of color: Curriculum development and change* (pp. 23-41). Washington, DC: Howard University Press.

World Health Organization. (1976). African traditional medicine. Afrotechnical Report Series, No.1, Brazzaville.

World Health Organization. (1979). *Schizophrenia: An International follow-up Study.* New York: John Wiley and Sons .

Zahan, D. (1979). *The religion, spirituality, and thought of traditional Africa.* Chicago, IL: The University of Chicago Press.

Zeller, D. L. (1979). Traditional and western medicine in Buganda: Coexistence and complement. *African Therapeutic Systems*, 251-256.

Zempleni, A. (1969). La therapie traditionnelle des troubles mentaux chez les Wolof et les Lebou (Senegal). *Social Science and Medicine, 3,* 191-205.

Author

Daryl M. Rowe
Pepperdine University
Grad. School of Ed. in Psych.
Pepperdine University Plaza
400 Corporate Pointe
Culver City, CA 90230
Telephone: (310) 568-5673
Fax: (310) 568-5755
E-mail: dr@pepperdine.edu

Part 2

Spirituality

Spirituality: Questing for Well-Being

John A. Rogers

Introduction

In this essay I use foundational constructs related to human spirituality to consider issues related to the well-being of African Americans, deliberately situating myself within the community of historically oppressed peoples with a transformational and liberationist orientation. My aim is to provide a framework for the recovery of the creative voice that is radically linked with our suffering as an historically oppressed people, which I see as coincident with the inevitable suffering of all human "being-becoming." The recovery of this voice is critical, not just for our well-being as African Americans but also for the well-being of all with whom we are co-creators.

Spirituality is not an abstract premise about human being. Rather, spirituality centers on concrete matters of individual and corporate living and dying. So in speaking of human spirituality, I wrestle with the questions of our own living and dying as African Americans, an oppressed minority forcibly transported to and embedded in a world not of our choosing and radically inimical to our prior modes of being. I struggle to find a ground wherein to root myself because the prevailing dispositions and values that inform (non-)being in the dominant culture are not consonant with my deepest being, my most profound aspiring.

As an historically oppressed people, we African Americans were hindered from wrestling with ultimate concerns without interference. We were not free to encounter "normal" living and dying, but lived and died at the discretion of others. In effect, our oppressors determined the contexts and questions surrounding our living and dying and then provided pseudo-answers to their own pseudo-questions. But the answers of the oppressors were designed to maintain their positions of power, to take us away from our own lived experience and impress their world-view upon us.

Liberation, as the wresting of being from the grip of non-being, demands that as an historically oppressed people, we return to our own more foundational experiences so that we can construct our own questions and find our own answers. Apart from this return, we remain lost in the wilderness created by our oppressors, in many cases even taking on their oppressive character. This is the thrust of our fundamental struggle for being over non-being as an historically oppressed people. However, as I suggest later, given the integral nature of all human being-becoming, our foundational struggle is part of the struggle of all to affirm being over non-being.

This essay, then, attempts to; (1) consider the sociohistorical context for the African-American struggle for being over non-being, (2) describe the fundamental nature of this struggle for African Americans in terms of the "suffering of being," and (3) explore the essential priority of suffering for truthful knowing and being.

Finally, it is necessary for me to acknowledge at the outset that in this essay I only speak of the human expression of spirituality primarily in relation to suffering. I do not attempt to explicate the other primary facets of human spirituality— intimacing and aspiring. Nor do I address the issue of the ultimate sources of human spirituality. Though critical, I simply did not have time and space to consider them. In this regard, what I attempt here is somewhat prolegomenous. Still the experiential priority of suffering to human being-becoming makes this narrow focus a legitimate starting point.

Being Versus Non-Being

From the time that European immigrants set foot on this continent, people of color—those already here and those imported from Africa—were treated as dispensable. The record of the treatment of African Americans is well-documented; and the impact of that treatment continues through the present moment. Throughout most of the history of this nation, the living and dying of people of color has not been important for the majority of European Americans. The problems that dispropor-tionately plague African Americans (Jaynes & Williams, 1989; Livingston, 1994) are largely the result of this historical indifference—and antipathy—to the well-being of people of color.

Making this connection contradicts the view—held even by some African Americans, historically and contemporaneously—that the problems that African Americans experience in this country are primarily the result of our failure to appropriate our freedom and to choose and act wisely and responsibly. To the contrary, the problems that we African Americans have faced historically are not primarily the consequence of our misuse of individual freedom but of oppression. The oppressive character of these problems represents the extension and internal-ization of a prior oppression that goes back to the importation of Africans as slaves and continues through the present in the racist stereotyping that is manifest throughout the society. The oppressive processes that formed the foundation and much of the superstructure of this nation have not disappeared (Bell, 1987, 1992; Coner-Edwards & Spurlock, 1988; Cose, 1993; Franklin, 1993; Orfield & Ashkinaze, 1991; West, 1993).

Recognizing the connection between this historical indifference and antipathy toward people of color and the current problems that plague African Americans accurately reflects the continuity of human processes. Contrarily, the affirmation of radical individualism—wrongly associated with the assumption of radical freedom (that people ultimately make of themselves whatever they choose)—tends to make people forget that they are part of human processes that have ongoing effects. Persons then focus on the choosing and not on the critical limits of what they choose or how they choose. Thus they fail to recognize the continuity of their being with those who have preceded them, those who are contemporaneous with them, and those who will follow them (Cushman, 1990; DeBerry, 1993, chap. 5; Doherty, 1995; Guisinger & Blatt, 1994; McCombs, 1985; Noel, 1990; Paris, 1995, chap. 5; Tarnas, 1991, chap. 7; Taylor, 1991).

Associated with this more disintegrating and objectifying view of person is the belief that human well-being is measured primarily in materialistic terms; not with the progression or extension of human virtue, but with the production, consumption, and acquisition of material goods or the extension of personal power over others (Ani, 1994, chap. 9). This materialistic orientation is coincident with the historical tendency to view African Americans as expendable. Moreover, it is at the heart of the disproportionate incidence of disease, dysfunction, and maladaptation among African Americans, because all ultimately reflect the historical devaluing and dehumanizing of African Americans.

There is no way to escape this as a problem of the human spirit—not just a social, economic, political, or legal problem. To say that someone is expendable is to devalue the life, the being, of another. This is more than a question of valuing in the sense of assessing someone's worthiness according to some arbitrary criteria. Most fundamentally it means to cut oneself off from that person, to sever the essential ties of humanity; to say that the life of another is without meaning or significance for one's well-being, that one can exist apart from the other. It is to affirm an impossibility—namely, that human being is fundamentally disconnected (cf. Zohar, 1990).

Yet the principle of expendability has been, and continues to be, near the heart of this nation. It is part of its spirituality, part of its heart and soul. What was perpetrated and perpetuated against African Americans did not emerge *ex nihilo*. The devaluing of human life was part of the mindset of the European Americans who radically devalued African-Americans (Ani, 1994, chap. 7), making us convenient targets, scapegoats, thereby diverting this devaluing away from European Americans and providing a convenient means of avoiding having to face into the character of their own heart and soul. Thus they advanced the myth of the depravity of people of African descent. They mis-spoke of our animalistic qualities, our absence of true religion, our lack of civility (Berkhofer, 1972; Jordan, 1968). But their own behaviors indicated that they actually were describing themselves—they were depraved; they behaved as animals; they lacked truthfulness in their religion; they were most uncivil. (As Erikson [1968, p. 304] notes, "The oppressor has a vested interest in the negative identity of the oppressed because that negative identity is a projection of his own unconscious negative identity.")

European Americans saw African Americans as expendable likely because at a very deep level they experienced themselves as radically expendable, radically worthless, meaningless, and without value. They then acquired *pseudo*-worth, *pseudo*-meaning, and *pseudo*-value by displacing their own sense of worthlessness, meaninglessness, and valuelessness onto people of African descent, as well as onto the indigenous people of the "new world" they had discovered. By distancing themselves from these others, but more importantly from their own truest selves, European Americans seemed to acquire worth or value. But, of course, this was an illusion, because the displacement of one's sense of worthlessness onto others does not diminish one's own *experience* of worthlessness; it actually exacerbates it, because one then encounters one's own worthlessness always in the other.

Projection. . . is essentially a neurotic device, and does not fundamentally relieve the sufferer's sense of guilt or establish a lasting self-respect. The hated scapegoat is merely a disguise for persistent and unrecognized self-hatred. A vicious circle is established. The more the sufferer hates himself, the more he hates the scapegoat. But the more he hates the scapegoat, the less sure he is of his logic and his innocence, hence the more guilt he has to project (Allport, 1958, pp. 365–366).

Just as issues of meaning ultimately are not abstract theories about life and death but rather about the connections that one has with the world, the experience of worthlessness really has to do with disconnection. Persons who experience life as disconnected and disconnecting have no meaning; and ultimately those persons become sick or die or become purveyors of death, destruction, or violence for others (Glass, 1989; Sagan, 1987, chap. 7). Similarly, disconnected persons experience no *essential* valuation as human being. This is the dynamic that characterized the treatment of African Americans by European Americans—radical disconnection with the accompanying attribution of worthlessness.

The devaluing of others for the pseudo-valuation of self was not applied just to African Americans and Native Americans. To some extent this *modus vivendi* seemed to characterize the entire economic-political system. In the absence of a sense of connection, or in the face of the radical affirmation of disconnection, wealth becomes a primary alternative. Persons begin to relate to each other primarily around the exchange of commodities or services for monetary remuneration. The more fundamental relationship of shared being is displaced by a common desire to maximize wealth. Eventually one's primary relationship, or focus of concern, is with one's wealth, rather than the community with whom one constitutes societal reality—along with animals and plants and the overarching planetary, galactic, and universal environments that sustain all life as we know it. Thus although a sense of worthlessness is not *essentially* linked to material poverty, in this country they are very much related. Worth and wealth have become intertwined in the American psyche (Etzioni, 1988; Kanner & Gomes, 1995; Katz, 1989; Postman, 1992).

A major consequence of this shift in relational focus is the further demise of a sense, or experience, of community. The values that are necessary to accumulate wealth are not necessarily precipitative of the virtues that enhance personal community. So a result is a decrease in human virtues with the constant escalation of material wealth (Durning, 1995).

Where the sense of personal relatedness is lost, there is little apparent need for virtue (cf. Bellah, Madsen, Sullivan, Swidler, & Tipton, 1985; Carter, 1993; Wilson, 1993), because the essence of virtue is being for the well-being of all—human and nonhuman. The problems plaguing African Americans can be understood as a consequence of the decline of virtue—moral-spiritual direction and strength—which, again, is rooted in the absence of relatedness, first by those who imported and enslaved Africans in this country and then by those persons of African descent who lost their sense of relatedness to each other and to the larger cosmic community. Because the majority of people of European descent were not able to connect with the humanity of African peoples, they could not act virtuously toward us. Instead, they denied our humanity—which, as stated earlier, was a reflection of their own inhumanity, their own absence of virtue. This absence of virtue and the resulting viciousness have been part of the dominating spiritual orientation of this nation since its founding. Each fundamental dynamic of human spirituality, which all people, individually and collectively, have to face—how one relates to others (the issue of meaning), how one engages human mortality (the issue of suffering), and what one chooses as ultimately valuable (the issue of aspiration) (cf. Naylor, Willimon, & Naylor, 1994, chap. 5; Tillich, 1952, chap. 2)—reflects this underlying viciousness.

Rather than radically and virtuously embracing their own suffering, their own experiences of meaninglessness and worthlessness, to varying degrees the majority population displaced their suffering onto people of African descent through slavery and other forms of discrimination. Rather than affirming the radical interrelatedness of all human life, the majority emphasized separateness, uniqueness, and dominance in relating to African Americans. Rather than affirming moral virtues that were significantly broader than individual predisposition and power, the majority defined their experiences and perspectives as normative without regard for the lived experiences of African Americans. This aptly describes the historical maltreatment of African Americans by European Americans and exemplifies the underlying disintegrating spiritual orientation, which precipitates disproportionate levels of dysfunction, maladaptation, underachievement, and even physical ailment among African Americans. And because this dominating disintegrating spiritual orientation impacts what is perceived as possible for correcting societal problems, the solutions that are proffered by the dominant social institutions not only reflect but also perpetuate that orientation, attempting to absorb the disaffected into the systemic apparatus or to move them further toward the fringes by labeling them as aberrant or recalcitrant. By no means is the fundamental nature of the system to be examined; so primary disintegrating patterns do not change (Ellah et al., 1985; Popenoe, 1994).

The significance of virtue for human being-becoming is related to the distinctively human questing for meaningfulness that arises from our awareness of our living and dying. Our experience of meaningfulness is tied to our freedom, capacity, and willingness to face into, or embrace, the reality of our mortality (Kass, 1985). Through the virtuous wrestling with our mortality, potentially we discover the larger framework of our being-becoming, which ideally issues forth in relating more virtuously to the world around us.

The refusal of European Americans to virtuously wrestle with their own mortality not only hindered their acting virtuously toward African Americans (and Native Americans); it also affected the emergence of virtue among us because the acts of our oppressors separated us from our normal rhythms of living and dying. Because we were forced to live and die in relation to the whims, values, and worldviews of our oppressors, the deeper questing for meaningfulness was displaced by issues of mere physical survival. The most fundamental issues of being were displaced by issues of accommodating the non-being of our oppressors (cf. Kraft, 1974; May, 1983, chap. 6). Thus the most fundamental wellspring of virtue was diverted.

Since context and being are integral (Schrag, 1969), the removal of the foundational contexts that co-constitute being, or the introduction of factors that make those contexts chaotic, represents the jeopardizing of being. For oppressed African Americans, the foundational contexts of our being-becoming were stripped away and replaced with contexts of non-being. That which anchored our being-becoming was removed and replaced with that which was not intended to anchor. So in a twofold way our being-becoming was put at risk, and the deepest wellsprings of aspiration and creativity were tainted with desperation and destructiveness. Rather than being-becoming being enhanced out of the distinctive yet universal virtuous wresting of meaning from exigency, our being was disintegrating— individually and communally (see Anderson, 1994; Shakoor & Chalmers, 1991).

A concrete example of the replacing of (virtuous) being with non-being is reflected in an issue that African Americans have had to deal with from the very beginning of our enslavement in this country—invisibility, that is, the tendency of the oppressive majority to ignore our being and the accompanying demand to be inconspicuous, to not call attention to our being. Ralph Ellison (1952) eloquently articulated this reality in the prologue to his novel *Invisible Man*:

> I am an invisible man. No, I am not a spook like those who haunted Edgar Allan Poe; nor am I one of your Hollywood-movie ectoplasms. I am a man of substance, of flesh and bone, fiber and liquids—and I might even be said to possess a mind. I am invisible, understand, simply because people refuse to see me. Like the bodiless heads you see sometimes in circus sideshows, it is as though I have been surrounded by mirrors of hard, distorting glass. When they approach me they see only my surroundings, themselves, or figments of their imagination—indeed, everything and anything except me.
>
> Nor is my invisibility exactly a matter of a biochemical accident to my epidermis. That invisibility to which I refer occurs because of a peculiar disposition of the eyes of those with whom I come in contact. A matter of the construction of their inner eyes, those eyes with which they look through their physical eyes upon reality. I am not complaining, nor am I protesting either. It is sometimes advantageous to be unseen, although it is most often rather wearing on the nerves. Then too, you're constantly being bumped against by those of poor vision. Or again, you often doubt if you really exist. You wonder whether you aren't simply a phantom in other people's minds. Say, a figure in a nightmare which the sleeper tries with all his strength to destroy. It's when you feel like this that, out of resentment, you begin to bump people back. And…you feel that way most of the time. You ache with the need to convince yourself that you do exist in the real world, that you're a part of all the sound and anguish, and you strike out with your fists, you curse and you swear to make them recognize you. And, alas, it's seldom successful (p. 3).

The oppressive majority not only refused to see, to know, our being as African Americans; they also demanded that we not call attention to our being, which meant that eventually we had to ignore our being. To survive we had to refuse our own being (Connor, 1995; Majors & Billson, 1992), which corresponded to the refusal of the oppressor—not only in relation to us, but also in relation to their fundamental refusal to know their own being, or non-being (Kovel, 1984). Eventually we could not recognize the non-being of the oppressive majority because the broader context of our being had been stripped away. The consequence was a radical lostness, being cut off from the deepest movements of meaningful existence, gradually yet relentlessly moving toward, even embracing, the non-being of those who oppressed us (Alschuler, 1992). (It is important to recognize this as a statement of the negative principle that undergirded oppression, not as the absolute historical reality of the whole of African American experience. The history of African American resistance is as clear as the history of compliance and subjugation.)

In the presence of their refusal to *see*, in the midst of demanding inconspicu-ousness by the oppressed, the oppressing majority made inconspicuousness impos-sible by defining the oppressed primarily in terms of skin color. In essence they said, "Be visible always, while being invisible always"—which, of course, is the status of *object*. This became the primary vehicle for not knowing, or ignoring—for the oppressing and the oppressed. Emphasizing color became the way for the oppress-ing majority to not know either themselves or those they oppressed. They objecti-fied dynamic persons on the basis of color (Omi & Winant, 1994; San Juan, 1992; Webster, 1992); and in the process of objectifying, they also dis integrated, cut themselves off, from a fundamental part of their being. Just as they refused to see the reality of their own deepest being, they also refused to see the reality of the being of the other. The failure to face their own non-being resulted in the extension of non-being to others (Buber, 1958; Fromm, 1976; Naylor, Willimon, & Naylor, chaps. 4–5).

But the dynamics of colorization also potentially disoriented African Ameri-can being-becoming toward non-being. Having stripped away the foundational contexts that made African American being meaningful, the oppressors made themselves in their paleness the focus of desirability, which ultimately was centered in the illusion of escaping suffering. The promise was that if we African Americans became like our oppressors, we would experience being. But, of course, this was an impossibility. We African Americans could never be what we were told to become. At best we could imitate, but we could never *be*. (The essential paradox here should not go unnoticed. The (pseudo) being of the oppressing is actually non-being; so the promise of the oppressing is that you can be through non-being—a radical and essential impossibility.)

> The centuries of racial dictatorship. . . defined "American" identity as white, as the negation of racialized "otherness"—at first African and indigenous, later Latin American and Asian as well. This negation took shape in both law and custom, in public institutions and in forms of cultural representation. It became the archetype of hegemonic rule in the U.S. It was the successor to the conquest as the "master" racial project

> . . . racial dictatorship organized. . .the "color line" rendering it the fundamen-tal division in U.S. society. The dictatorship elaborated, articulated, and drove racial division not only through institutions, but also through psyches, extend-ing up to our time the racial obsessions of the conquest and slavery periods (Omi & Winant, 1994, p. 66).

An eventual consequence was that both the oppressed and the oppressing ceased to know themselves and the other. Both were trapped in seeing primarily the externals. Neither was privy to the deepest movements of the other; and eventually neither was privy to the deepest movements of their own being-becoming. Non-being became the illusion of being. Both the powerful and the powerless, the oppressing and the oppressed, were caught up in the dance of non-being, which represents the denial of our most fundamental encounters with living and dying. The aspirations of authentic being-becoming were radically corrupted and disoriented toward non–being-becoming (Alves, 1972; Berman, 1981; Bruner, 1990; Schaef, 1987, 1992).

This suggests that the liberation of the oppressed actually entails moving from non-being to being. It is not a matter of 'equal participation' in the non-being of the oppressing. Liberation ultimately means transcending the non-being of the oppressing. But where oppression is most effective, the oppressed look to the oppressing for validation of their existence. In so doing, they put their being-becoming at risk, because they seek validation from non-being. But since non-being only validates itself, to be validated by non-being demands that the oppressed embrace non-being. They must become what they are not, which reflects the great tragedy of oppression: it is always the extension of non-being.

Rubem Alves states well the potential constraints of oppressing contexts, articulating clearly how the ultimate longing for being is overwhelmed and held hostage by the proximate possibilities—or, more accurately, the proximate impossibilities—of non-being:

Suppose that you find yourself locked in a room with no windows or doors. No matter how nice the room is, you will very soon experience a boredom which turns into the panic of claustrophobia. There is no way out. Inevitably after a while, you will begin to plan your escape. You will start probing the walls and looking for tools with which to break your way to liberty.

Now imagine that you find yourself in a castle with 1001 luxurious rooms filled with surprises, pleasures, and unexpected experiences. As you get tired of one room you move to the next. And so on, indefinitely. So absorbed will you be that you will not notice that the castle, just like that other single room, has neither doors nor windows. You are equally a prisoner, but you will grow old without ever realizing your own condition, and will assume all along that you are free. Thus you will never look for a way out, and your imagination will be kept in thrall to the expectation of what the next room has in store for you.

This is the first principle for control of the imagination: create so many objects of desire that the mind will be kept moving from one to another, without ever being able to move beyond them (Alves, 1972, p. 26; cf. Wilmore, 1983).

This radical circumscribing of oppressed peoples gradually leads to incorporation and a deep existential confusion of being:

The oppressed suffer from the duality which has established itself within their innermost being... Although they desire authentic existence, they fear it. They are at one and the same time themselves and the oppressor whose consciousness they have internalized. The conflict lies in the choice between being wholly themselves or being divided; between ejecting the oppressor within or not ejecting him; ... between acting or having the illusion of acting through the action of the oppressors; between speaking or being silent, castrated in their power to create and re-create, in their power to transform the world (Freire, 1968, pp. 32–33).

Over ninety years ago, William Edward Burghardt Du Bois (1903) pointed toward these potentially disintegrating and chaotic dynamics of being oppressed in his classic work *The Souls of Black Folk:*

The Negro is... born with a veil, and gifted with second-sight in this American world,—a world which yields him no true self-consciousness, but only lets him see himself through the revelation of the other world. It is a peculiar sensation, this double-consciousness, this sense of always looking at one's self through the eyes of others, of measuring one's soul by the tape of a world that looks on in amused contempt and pity. One ever feels this twoness,—an American, a Negro; two souls, two thoughts, two unreconciled strivings; to warring ideals in one dark body, whose dogged strength alone keeps it from being torn asunder (p. 45).

How, then, does an historically oppressed people find authentic freedom or experience transcendence within a radically constraining context that has intentionally worked toward the destruction of our being-becoming? How do we experience meaningfulness within such contexts? Is the only option to become like the oppressing, to become the oppressing? What happens to imagination when surrounded by such a wasteland? Do real creative possibilities appear as illusions and therefore get dismissed? How do the oppressed determine what is real and what is illusion?

For an historically oppressed people immersed in a context of non-being, what are the possibilities for the recovery of being? Is it possible to break from the web of non-being, which has circumscribed our existence for an extended time? Having been forcefully engrafted into a system of non-being and suffused and infused with its characteristic *élan vital*, a foundational aspect of which has been the intentional denial of the our being, is there any possibility that frees and protects us from the toxins that ultimately disintegrate and destroy?

The answer to these seemingly impossible, yet critical and unavoidable, questions, which are at the center of our questing for well-being, may already be present in our lived experience as an historically oppressed people, which is the "suffering of being." Even when we adopt the non-being of the oppressor, we are

never far removed from our suffering. Despite generations of trying to accommodate dominant social norms, the suffering that derives from the negating of our being
continues. So it may be that the movement into the center of the suffering of being
is the key to our transcending.

The Suffering of Being

Of the three foundational expressions of human spirituality—how one relates
to others (the issue of meaning; reflecting the human need and capacity for
integrating), how one engages human mortality (the issue of suffering; reflecting the
distinctively human capacity for intentionally disintegrating relative to the rest of
life), and what one chooses as ultimately valuable (the issue of aspiration; reflecting
the distinctively human capacity for choosing between integrating and disintegrating, based in the equally distinctive human capacity and need for believing)—
perhaps the most difficult to wrestle with in this individualistic and materialistic
society is suffering. Reducing personal suffering through material advancement
(particularly as increased production and consumption) fuels the engine of this
social system. Every new innovation is touted as making one's life easier and,
thereby, better. Entire industries, not necessarily related to medicine, are geared
toward helping people escape suffering. For example, athletes and entertainers
provide regular means of ignoring or refusing the inevitable, and they are paid well
for it. We do not see into their hearts and minds; they just play a role for us. We
connect with them so that we can disconnect from ourselves. They become our
means of escape; they become our addictions. One sees the *good life* consistently
portrayed in terms of physical and emotional gratification. Suffering is to be
avoided at all costs.

However, if one believes that all life is interconnected, and that the rending of
connections results in suffering, then suffering is integral to human being, because
the human journey is one of constantly rending and reweaving life's connections
(Viorst, 1986). The most fundamental processes of human emergence, or development, are accompanied by some level of suffering—dislocation, disorientation,
alienation, severing, dying—as a continuous passage from 'old' to 'new' (Kegan,
1982). Grieving over the loss of something or someone and the distinctively human
characteristic of anxiety, or care (Becker, 1973, chap. 4; May, 1983, chap. 7), are
present in all human societies. So is the displacing of suffering onto others to
alleviate or escape one's own suffering (e.g., Bullard, 1990, 1993, 1994).

If persons do not understand suffering in terms of disconnecting and reconnecting, or rending and reweaving our most fundamental linkages or bonds with
other humans, with other life forms, and with the earth and the universe, then likely
they will not see suffering as bound to fundamental relational dynamics that result

from a particular world-view—our implicit way of being toward the world, comprising our experiences of intimacing, suffering, and aspiring. Thus they will treat it as an object to be disposed. Consequently, especially within radically individualistic and materialistic—that is, radically disintegrating—contexts, deep personal suffering is mixed with an equally deep ignoring or denying of that suffering. The unavoidable, distinctively human experience of suffering is not matched with a distinctively human understanding—intellectual and experiential comprehension that comes from the discipline of *standing under* the inherent constraints of a situation—of suffering, the conscious affirmation that "I suffer" or "I am sufferer" (Krishnamurti, 1954, pp. 168–171; 1977, chap. 8; Macquarrie, 1985, chap. 17; Starck & McGovern, 1992). Rather, it often is matched with the contrary affirmation "I am not suffering" or "I should not be suffering." The consequence then is to try to bring the truthful experience of suffering in line with the false affirmation of "not suffering."

But to deny one's own suffering leads to distorting one's view of and disorienting oneself in relation to oneself and to all of life. To refuse suffering and displace it onto others disturbs the rhythms of being and points the creation in the direction of chaos (Postel, 1994). The end of this process is not the alleviation of suffering but its extension and exacerbation, as reflected in dysfunction, maladaptation, and violence against self and others. And the dissonance and chaos that result and resound from the denial of suffering become a cacophony of discord and destruction.

There is no purely individual suffering; it is fundamentally systemic. The vast majority of suffering represents a rending of the social fabric, the fabric of life—not just in the present moment, but throughout all the moments of history. When I am suffering, my part in the fabric of life is being stretched and torn; and because I am part of a fabric, my suffering is also the suffering of others, and vice versa. So the historical suffering of African Americans is not just the suffering of particular individuals. Nor is it just the suffering of the communities where we live. No, it is the suffering of a system that began with European emigrants who were trying to lessen their own suffering but who did so by displacing that suffering onto others. So social problems excessively concentrated among African Americans reflect to a large degree the refusal of suffering that has been inherent to the social system from its inception. It is the suffering of a system conceived, birthed, nurtured—and perhaps dying—in and through the denial and displacement of suffering onto others.

In disintegrating materialistic contexts that suggest "You suffer alone," suffering becomes debilitating and destructive when persons have no moral-relational network to leverage suffering. In the literature that deals with the nature of suffering, it is constantly related to the threat or actual experience of disintegrating as the web of interconnections that comprise meaningfulness is broken. This disintegrating is not an instantaneous act; it is a dynamic that may become a mode of non-being—the unrelenting rending, or unraveling, of the fabric of being. It is as though one knows no other way of being. At the deepest levels, one's being is disintegrating; and the most basic dynamic that one then brings to others is disintegrating. And this applies societally as well as individually.

The view of spirituality undergirding this essay suggests that the key to arresting, and perhaps reversing, this disintegrating dynamic is moral-relational reintegrating, which I refer to as "embracing suffering." But what does that look like and how does that happen in a social context that seems centered on moral-relational disintegrating? Does this mean that one takes a fatalistic approach to suffering and just overlays it with moral platitudes about the virtue of suffering? What does this do for the underlying disintegrating that precipitates suffering? Or is it possible to embrace suffering in ways that lead to liberation and empowerment because they lead to reintegrating?

The focus here is the relationship between embracing and reintegrating. Does embracing suffering equate with embracing disintegrating? What does it mean to embrace disintegrating? This articulation gets to the heart of the issue because it clearly connotes bringing together countervailing dynamics—embracing and dis-integrating. And the key here is whether these countervailing dynamics can coexist, especially when one of those dynamics—embracing—is intentional. Speaking in images, the embracing would seem to arrest the unraveling, the rending, and by its very nature set in motion reintegrating.

The key, as mentioned earlier, is that suffering is not some *thing* that one experiences; one's being—perhaps all being—is suffering. And suffering is not just a signifier of disintegrating; it is one's being—all being—disintegrating. So when one embraces one's suffering, one embraces one's whole being, including one's disintegrating; and this embracing is an act of integrating, or reintegrating. It is as though one focuses on the point of unraveling; and, in doing so, one begins reweaving. This is particularly significant if, in fact, the dominant movement of the social system is toward dis integrating. And it gains even more potential signifi-cance if one is able to make the affirmation that at some level one's suffering is coincident, though not coextensive, with the suffering of all being—and perhaps being.

This latter affirmation is important because then embracing suffering repre-sents more than individuals simply caring for themselves. It is, rather, the radical engaging of being with non-being. Essentially, this is not an optional movement of being; it is the way in which being is renewed. Apart from this movement, being is overwhelmed by non-being. Rubem Alves (1972) provides a helpful perspective in relation to this:

> How can we enjoy the song of the wind, of the birds and the flowing brooks, if the groaning of men, women, and children fills the space and time in which we live? Only those who close their eyes and ears—only those who have

become insensitive—can feel at home in the world as it is. Because we see and hear, we have to say, "I do not belong here." Man discovers that he suffers from an incurable disease, which will follow him wherever he goes: homelessness. He is an exile in the world. . . .

Strange as it may appear. . . man becomes whole and free only after his roots are cut off and he is an exile. There is no way out. If we are not already blind, if we are still able to understand and feel, how can we avoid the conclusion that the present order of things is absurd?. . .

Thus suffering is not accidental to personality. It belongs to its very essence. It is an indication that we are in touch with the world, a sign both of our presence and of our rebellion—of our being in the world without being domesticated by it. . . It is not possible for freedom and happiness to go together. Freedom is creativity. How can the happy create? By the very fact that they are content they must be committed to the preservation of things as they are. Creativity is born out of an infinite loathing for what makes man suffer. How can one create if one does not know what suffering is? "In a certain sense personality is suffering," remarks Berdyaev. "The struggle to achieve personality presupposes resistance, it demands a conflict with the enslaving power of the world, a refusal to conform to the world. Pain in the human world is the birth of personality. And freedom gives rise to suffering. Refusal of personality, acquiescence in dissolution in the surrounding world can lessen the suffering, and man easily goes that way. . . " (Nikolai Berdyaev, *Slavery and Freedom* (1944), p. 28).

Why do I suffer? I suffer when I feel that our social order is structured in such a way that it has to destroy the values which are the ultimate concern of my personality. . .

Suffering arises when we discover that there is an insurmountable opposition between our own values and those of the world we live in. It is born in the moment when we come to the conclusion that we are homeless. It is the experience of meaninglessness, or our world's irreducible absurdity, of the futility of all efforts to make sense of it. . . .

What makes personality suffer? Is it because it is inwardly deranged? Or because it contains a bundle of contradictory tendencies? Hardly. The essential and irreducible suffering of personality results from the fact that it is much more realistic than the realists. It knows the world in a way it is seldom consciously known. It knows that reality makes no room for its values—that the reasons of the heart have been displaced by the facts of power—and that the rationalization of power makes the creative act impossible. It knows the world from the vantage point of the future it envisages, and it hears the verdict clearly: those values must be aborted. To be happy in an unfriendly world is to be insane. The price of contentment, in such a situation, is to exchange reality for illusion....

We may now understand the reason why personality clings to its suffering. It suffers because it refuses false solutions—i.e., those that do not involve any change in reality but only a change in consciousness (pp. 132–137).

Alves not only accurately portrays the suffering of oppressed peoples but also provides a liberating—transcending—normative framework for understanding all suffering. Implicit in his words is the perspective that the being of the oppressed *is* suffering, which can be extrapolated to "all human being is suffering." Therefore, in embracing suffering, we embrace being. And in embracing being, we break the cycle of denying, or refusing, being. Additionally, in embracing the suffering of being, it becomes the hermeneutic for reinterpreting our existing. We have the potential to see, to know, reality in light of our suffering, our being, which, as Alves suggests, indicates that something is not right with the world in which we live.

But this knowing through suffering may not necessarily lead to liberation or transformation, because the effects of oppressing (non-being) may be so ingrained that the response may simply be its extension. In this case, the oppressed becomes the oppressing. No one is actually liberated. Non-being overwhelms being.

Almost always, during the initial stage of the struggle, the oppressed, instead of striving for liberation, tend themselves to become oppressors, or "sub-oppressors." The very structure of their thought has been conditioned by the contradictions of the concrete, existential situation by which they were shaped. Their ideal is. . . is to be oppressors. This is their model of humanity. This phenomenon derives from the fact that the oppressed, at a certain moment of their existential experience, adopt an attitude of "adhesion" to the oppressor. Under these circumstances they cannot "consider" him sufficiently clear to objectivize him—to discover him "outside" themselves. . . Their perception of themselves as oppressed is impaired by their submersion in the reality of oppression. . . Their perception of themselves as opposites of the oppressor does not yet signify engagement in a struggle to overcome the contradiction; the one pole aspires not to liberation, but to identification with its opposite pole.

In this situation the oppressed do not see the "new man" as the man to be born from the resolution of this contradiction, as oppression gives way to liberation.

For them, the new man is themselves become oppressors. Their vision of the new man is individualistic; because of their identification with the oppressor, they have no consciousness of themselves as persons or as members of an oppressed class. It is not to become free men that they want agrarian reform, but in order to acquire land and thus become landowners—or, more precisely, bosses over other workers. It is a rare peasant who, once "promoted" to overseer, does not become more of a tyrant towards his former comrades than the owner himself. This is because the context of the peasant's situation, that is, oppression, remains unchanged (Freire, 1968, p. 30).

This raises the deeper question of the nature of liberation and its connection to suffering. The beginning of the answer is to acknowledge that liberation denotes a dynamic rather than a state. If one holds to a dynamic and integrated view of reality, then one understands such concepts in terms of the whole rather than the condition of any one part. So it is inaccurate to speak of one part as existing in a state of liberation while other parts exist in a state of oppression. Indeed, this is the meaning of suffering: the interrelatedness of all life. So, then, liberation does not mean an end to suffering; it actually means the freedom to suffer.

If, as noted above, being—particularly the being of the oppressed—is suffering, then the freedom to suffer is the freedom to *be*. This becomes clear when one realizes that in most situations of oppression, the oppressed are not allowed to express their suffering. Often they have to feign a visage that is opposite to what they feel—who they *are*—most deeply. Again, they must become what they are not. (In this regard, note the historical characterizations of African Americans in the television industry in this country. Even to this day, the dominant representation is comedic.) And those who oppress demand this because suffering (being) subverts non-being. In some radical way, suffering may circumvent the non-being of those who oppress and encounter their residual being; and those who oppress do not wish to encounter their being precisely because being is suffering. (Does the trivializing of suffering and dying that often occurs in the mass entertainment market represent a form of immunization against being? Similarly does the constant barrage of advertising that suggests that life can be a never-ending creating and consuming of new things tend to anesthetize us to the urgency of being?) So in place of being, those who oppress provide illusions:

Do you suffer? It is because you are still seeking. Give up your dreams. Adapt yourself to the pattern of the present world. All restlessness will disappear, and you will find yourself at home. There is no easier way of solving the feeling of discomfort and pain than by adapting oneself?…Why knock our heads against reality in a hopeless attempt to transform it, if the emotional result attendant on the creative act can be achieved by a so much simpler and painless change of consciousness? Become adjusted and you will find happiness (Alves, 1972, p. 138).

Within oppressive situations, suffering often is displaced by illusion. (Might one also affirm that where suffering is displaced by illusion there is oppression?) The dynamic of creating and maintaining illusions becomes the addiction for human suffering. Illusion provides an *apparent* stability that replaces the *apparent* instability of suffering. This is the function of the collective illusion known as realism—the way in which a particular social system may try to escape suffering (Alves, 1972, chaps. 3, 9). So, for example, the illusory promise of Western patterns of development—individual, corporate, national—is that suffering will decrease as power increases. But the illusion does not specify under what conditions, at what cost, and for whom power seems to reduce suffering. The illusion does not specify where suffering increases so that suffering can decrease someplace else.

The critical connection between illusion and suffering is that illusions are not just false ideas or notions that people hold in their minds. Illusions are lived realities, ways of non-being. Though the term *illusion* often denotes an inaccurate apprehending, a distorting, of reality, illusion is not just a matter of inaccuracy in perceiving; it also is a matter of what one chooses—consciously or unconsciously—to ignore. Perception and apprehension are not just technical competencies; they are also experiences of valuing, of selecting. So, illusion is not something I have; it is something I live. One could even say that it is who I am. In that I am disoriented or disintegrating, I am an illusioning.

This helps to explain the obduracy of illusions and the necessity of suffering to subvert them. Just as illusion is ultimately nonspecific, so is suffering—even though within atomistic contexts it does not appear to be so. Suffering does not touch just one aspect of life; it touches the whole being. Embracing suffering is critical to liberation because suffering undermines illusion and transcends what Alves refers to as mere shifts in consciousness that do not change external conditions. Because suffering is grounded contextually, it cannot be ameliorated unless the dynamics of the context(s) change. So for oppressed persons, the embracing of suffering is essential for liberation—for "suffering prepares the soul for vision" (Alves, 1972, p. 201). But this also explains why the oppressed often become oppressors and simply displace their suffering onto others. Changes of consciousness are significantly easier than radically transforming the world where one lives. It seems easier to become addicted to illusion than to suffer consciously for a lifetime.

Additionally, though embracing suffering may be liberating, it also may have chaotic consequences. Suffering may undermine the structures of a persons' primary spheres of involvement and identity and send shock waves reverberating throughout the surrounding field. The longer the oppressed hold onto their suffering, the greater the tension and ultimate undoing of the lines that hold the oppressed in place. Eventually all of the structures of meaning associated with oppression may be called into question. The chaotic dimension is that within oppressive situations, the oppressed are often disconnected from any structures of meaningfulness apart from those sanctioned by those who oppress. So when suffering releases the oppressed from those structures, the result may be a radical meaninglessness, a state in which all one has to hold onto is the suffering. In the worst case, one is set adrift on a raft of suffering in a sea of impossibilities. In the more normal scenario, the suffering is alleviated by adopting social illusions, with the consequence that the context that precipitated the suffering continues to operate normally and normatively. In light of this reality, the question becomes, Can suffering take on a normative character and undermine the authority of illusion?

The opposite of illusion is certainty. The certainty of oppressed persons is their suffering. That they suffer is not a question. But their suffering is not *just* their suffering. They are the locus of suffering, of the disintegrating, of social systems (Zohar & Marshall, 1994, chap. 9). In this regard, their suffering also is a certainty about the world in which they live. It is not a fiction; it is not an illusion. It is real—despite the attempts of those who oppress to dismiss it, to explain it away as personal fault or failure. In this regard, it has experiential authority as truthful representation of the dynamics of their immediate context and the broader world. But it also has authority as truthful representation about human being—to be human is to suffer.

The experiential authority of suffering as truthful representation of reality also becomes clear when one considers the application of the illusory antithesis of " not suffering." As noted above, what is perceived as not suffering most often is the displacing and disproportionate concentrating of suffering among those who are most vulnerable. Accompanying this displacing, one finds chaos, disintegrating, addiction, violence, and death. Where *not suffering* is affirmed as normative, *net* suffering is not reduced. In fact, often it is increased because those onto whom suffering is displaced do not have the capacity to offset it; so the consequences are devastating for the immediate generations and are compounded for future generations.

Though suffering has an experientially authoritative function as grounding, as anchoring, in reality, the more difficult issue is whether suffering has a nurturing function. Does the embrace of suffering lead to transcendence, or is it just a limiting function that has no impact on the overarching contexts for human being-becoming? If only the oppressed embrace their suffering and not the oppressing, do the overall disintegrating dynamics change, or do the oppressed just continue to be the dumping ground for those who oppress? In such situations, the embracing of suffering would seem to become a fatalistic and quietistic approach to being, which becomes non-being.

The critical issue is that embracing suffering is not just the embracing of individual suffering; it is the embracing of communal suffering. When persons embrace suffering, they embrace being. But the being that they embrace is not just their own; it is the being of others as well. When suffering clarifies vision, those who embrace suffering see everything more clearly, even those who oppress them. Ideally this embracing of suffering leads to compassion, not as sentimentality, but as deep longing, deep aspiration, for the well-being of all (Alves, 1972, chap. 11; Merton, 1955, chap. 5).

What, then, does it mean to say to a historically oppressed people to embrace their suffering? Does it mean that one stops resisting oppression or discrimination? Does one become fatalistic or quietistic? While in a context where the displacement of suffering is normative these would seem to be the only options, the power of embracing suffering is that it represents a stance that is the opposite of those who oppress. In this regard, it opens the way for release from the illusions of the oppressing because suffering and being are synonymous. There is no human being without suffering; and where persons try to be without suffering, the result is non-being. So when oppressed persons embrace their suffering, they open the door for radically truthful being for themselves and others.

Suffering, Knowing, and Well-Being

Parker Palmer (1983) insightfully writes of the "passionate" sources of knowledge:

> Knowledge contains its own morality. . . it begins not in a neutrality but in a place of passion within the human soul. Depending on the nature of that passion, our knowledge will follow certain courses and head toward certain ends. From the point where it originates in the soul, knowledge assumes a certain trajectory and target—and it will not easily be deflected by ethics once it takes off from that source. . . If we are worried about the path on which our knowledge flies and about its ultimate destination, we had better. . . deal with the passions that fuel and guide its course.

> History suggests two primary sources for our knowledge. . . One is curiosity; the other is control. The one corresponds to pure, speculative knowledge, to knowledge as an end in itself. The other corresponds to applied science, to knowledge as a means to practical ends.

> We are inquisitive creatures, forever wanting to get inside of things and discover their hidden secrets. Our curiosity is piqued by the closed and wrapped box. We want to know its contents, and when the contents are out we want to open them too—down to the tiniest particle of their construction. We are also creatures attracted by power; we want knowledge to control our environment, each other, ourselves. Since many of the boxes we have opened contain secrets that have given us more mastery over life, curiosity and control are joined as the passion behind our knowing.

> Curiosity sometimes kills, and our desire to control has put deadly power in some very unsteady hands. We should not be surprised that knowledge

launched from these sources is heading toward some terrible ends, undeflected by ethical values as basic as respect for life itself. Curiosity is an amoral passion, a need to know that allows no guidance beyond the need itself. Control is simply another word for power, a passion notorious not only for its amorality but for its tendency for corruption. If curiosity and control are the primary motives for our knowing, we will generate a knowledge that eventually carries us not toward life but death (pp. 7–8).

Spirituality fundamentally is about identifying the "passion within the human soul." And passion, at its root, denotes suffering—as does compassion. So our knowing reflects our suffering—whether embraced or displaced. That is, we may know through our suffering; or we may *not know*—we may ignore being—through the denial of our suffering. And to *not know* points toward the production of untruthful knowledge (Palmer, 1983, chap. 4).

The untruthful knowledge produced by those who oppress, or those who live or know primarily through the denial of suffering, is a knowledge based in ignoring the suffering of those who are oppressed or underprivileged. But since historically the suffering of the oppressed is in large part the displaced suffering of those who oppress them, this ignoring is more fundamentally an ignoring by the oppressing of their own suffering. This ignoring becomes the trajectory for future knowledge for those who oppress—and for those whom they oppress (Myers, 1991). Thus ignorance becomes the norm for knowledge, which suggests that knowledge potentially becomes synonymous with not knowing, or ignoring.

However, another kind of knowledge is available to us, one that begins in a different passion and is drawn toward other ends. This knowledge can contain as much sound fact and theory as the knowledge we now possess, but because it springs from a truer passion it works toward truer ends. This is a knowledge that originates not in curiosity or control but in compassion, or love—a source celebrated not in our intellectual tradition but in our spiritual heritage.

The goal of a knowledge arising from love is the reunification and reconstruction of broken selves and worlds. A knowledge born of compassion aims not at exploring and manipulating creation but at reconciling the world to itself. The mind motivated by compassion reaches out to know as the heart reaches out to love. Here, the act of knowing is an act of love, the act of entering and embracing the reality of the other, of allowing the other to enter and embrace our own. In such knowing we know and are known as members of one community, and our knowing becomes a way of reweaving that community's bonds

. . . the origin of knowledge *is* love. The deepest wellspring of our desire to know is the passion to recreate the organic community in which the world was first created.

The minds we have used to divide and conquer creation were given to us for another purpose: to raise to awareness the communal nature of reality, to overcome separateness and alienation by a knowing that *is* loving, to reach out with intelligence to acknowledge and renew the bonds of life. The failure of modern knowledge is not primarily a failure of ethics, in the application of what we know. Rather, it is the failure of our knowing itself to recognize and reach for its deeper source and passion, to allow love to inform the relations that our knowledge creates—with ourselves, with each other, with the whole animate and inanimate world (Palmer, 1983, pp. 8–9).

Palmer points toward a knowing that is rooted in suffering—in shared suffering, or compassion; and the deeper issue inherent in Palmer's perspective is whether there can be truthful knowing apart from a rooting in suffering. Though this seems to be an obvious possibility, this obviousness is suspect; for it may be that the fundamental impetus for all searching for knowledge, for truth, is human suffering (cf. Grudin, 1990, chap. 9)—the rending of the fabric of life and the inherent desire or longing that is the consequence. Even the production of pseudo-knowledge, the means for ignoring being, is at root a response to life's inherent longing. However, it is the addictive response rooted in denial and rejection, and the consequence is the increase in the breadth and depth of the dominating and appealing illusions that promise life without suffering.

If truthful knowing is rooted in suffering, then it is essential that the voice of suffering be heard. Since the suffering of the oppressed is the suffering of being (and *BEING*), their voice is necessary to comprehend the full scope of being (and *BEING*). There can be no truthful knowing, no knowing that is full of truth, apart from the knowing, the speaking, of the oppressed. Any knowing that ignores the suffering of the oppressed is, in fact, ignorance.

This understanding of knowing helps to clarify the limitations of the pseudo-knowing of those who oppress, which is rooted in illusion, the objectifying of ignoring. The fundamental dynamic of the ignoring of those who oppress is moving within and extending illusion. The trajectory of ignoring becomes the trajectory of knowledge. To be knowledgeable is to be immersed in ignoring the radical being-becoming dimensions of knowing-that-embraces-suffering. This knowledge disintegrates being, reflecting a radical human arrogance that derives from our distinctively human capacity to willfully ignore.

Knowing truthfully, like all dimensions of truthful being, entails suffering. The *essential* suffering of being is the pivot of truthful knowing. So "to know" demands the embrace of suffering—individually *and* collectively. And when the illusion of the possibility of *not suffering* holds sway, the consequence always is the increase of suffering through the greater rending of the fabric of life, the ground of societal existence.

Ignored suffering is not the same as *not suffering*, because suffering *is*—and is not to be ignored. Suffering wishes (perhaps demands) to be noticed because being wishes (perhaps demands) to be noticed. Suffering is the call of being (and BEING) for attention rather than ignoring. However, the voice of suffering often is silenced under the illusion that the silencing of suffering is the enhancing of being.

The silencing of suffering is the attempt to silence being. But BEING behind being cannot be silenced, cannot BE silenced. Suffering is the longing of BEING for being, and of being for BEING. So there is a point beyond which all rationalizations and addictions are ineffectual in silencing being. At that point one must hear the voice of being, and BEING, which is suffering, or move inevitably toward chaos and destruction.

The ignoring or refusal of suffering results, not in health or well-being, but in chaos and destruction; and this applies communally as well as individually. Suffering is the grieving of being—and perhaps BEING—at the point where possibility meets impossibility, transcendence meets intransigence, hope meets despair. In this regard, suffering is the place of deepest knowing because it is the place of deepest being. Alves (1972, pp. 132–137) is quite correct when he implies that suffering is the response of our deepest knowing, as is Gibran (1923, "On Pain"), who suggests that our deepest knowing comes through the full embracing of our suffering.

The full embracing of our suffering"—how consistently this premise is applied to certain modes of disease in relation to individuals and how consistently it is not applied to groups who have been historically oppressed or to the dynamics of social systems. So much of contemporary writing on recovery entails the radical embrace of historical suffering that has been repressed or denied. Sometimes this even takes the form of a public embrace. For the oppressed, however, suffering is divorced from historical oppression; it is atomized, radically disconnected from its deepest historical roots. Thus the oppressed often are denied the opportunity to experience the fullness of their being, as are those who oppress.

When the voice of suffering is silenced, the fullness of our humanity is sacrificed. We experience ourselves as less than distinctively human and describe ourselves as other animals, as machines, as commodities. Violence becomes entertaining. Sexuality becomes exhibitionism and voyeurism (Frankl, 1978, pp. 79–85). Love is associated more with desire than with compassion. Quality of life is associated more with possessions than with virtues. The trajectory of human *becoming* becomes increasingly disintegrating and impersonal rather than integrating and personal. The pursuit of eternal youth supplants the quest for ageless wisdom. Religion becomes escape rather than the focus of and avenue for our most radical attention to and interconnection with life (Arterburn & Felton, 1991; Booth,

1991; Cushman, 1984; Halperin, 1982; Saliba, 1985; Stipes, 1985). Habitual reaction prevents significant and heartfelt responses among persons in everyday encounter. Life becomes a series of disconnected moments and chance occurrences rather than a process of intentionally weaving the fabric of meaningful encounters that constitute our living and dying, our being-becoming.

For individuals, communities, societies, and nations to move toward well-being, not only must the voice of suffering be heard; it must actively be sought and uncovered. The addictions that blind us to our suffering must give way to truthful realism—that all suffering is communal and therefore that all health has to be communal; that disintegrating social structures and dynamics cannot produce health and reduce overall suffering because they only displace suffering; that health and well-being are integrally tied to justice in relation to both human and nonhuman environments.

If suffering is integral to being—all being—then giving voice to suffering seems integral to well-being. This is not the same as putting words in the mouth of suffering—to rationalize it—but actually allowing suffering to speak for itself. And the speaking of suffering is not to make it go away but rather to make it more fully present, which is to allow being a fuller presence. This fuller presence of suffering is critical as the primary individual link to communal well-being—because suffering is the entryway to compassion, which is the gateway to justice, which is the opening to well-being.

To hear the voice of suffering requires quieting the noises of non-being. The distractions and enticements of the illusion of *not suffering* are intended to overwhelm the inescapable reality of suffering. These enticements and distractions are addictions because ultimately they attempt to do the impossible. Thus we attempt to avoid the suffering of being, which is grounded in our fundamental interrelatedness, by trying harder and harder to rend the fabric of which we are part, thinking that through separation we can escape what is inescapable. But in the acts of rending, we only exacerbate the suffering that we try to escape. Thus the desire for enticements and distractions increases; and the addictive cycle continues, which makes withdrawal from the disintegrating addictive illusion of *not suffering* increasingly difficult.

Conclusion

As noted at the beginning of this essay, the connection between the practical application of psychology and the study of human spirituality in relation to the historical and holistic liberation of African Americans is the foundational human questing for well-being. My intention has not been to maintain a false distinction between psychological well-being and spiritual well-being but rather to suggest that the latter is the ground for the former and that in this regard they are integral. Apart from considering the deepest dimensions of human being-becoming, historically oppressed peoples whose humanity has been devalued and denied have little foundation for facilitating psychological well-being. Reconnection to the deepest experiential ground of human being-becoming opens the way for transcending the constricted and constricting perspectives and experiences of those who oppress. So though the following summarizing paragraphs speak of spirituality, they also speak to the ground for psychological well-being.

(1) Any reflection on spirituality must reckon with the historical forced invisibility of African Americans and the historical refusal of the suffering of being in this society. These dynamics have placed African Americans in an extremely precarious position in relation to living authentically spiritually, which includes the "revealing of being," the antithesis of which is obscuring being, or non-being, which is the heart of every form of oppression.

(2) Because all being is always integral—non-integral being is an impossibility—the recovery of authentic spirituality as the revealing of being is never just an individual enterprise. It is impossible to speak of revealing being at an individual level while obscuring being at a communal level. That is why much of the popular talk about spirituality in this society is suspect—because it reflects the radical materialistic individualism that historically has been the heart and soul of this nation. It is not rooted in the suffering of being and often represents deliberate attempts to avoid it. Contrarily, the creative and transformative dimensions of authentic spirituality are grounded in embracing the suffering of all being.

(3) Because authentic spirituality, as the revealing of being, is foundationally integral and rooted in the suffering of being, it must wrestle with issues of morality and justice. Spirituality that simply helps me to feel better about my place in the world is disoriented and inauthentic. Authentic or truth-full, spirituality moves one toward, not away from, the suffering of all being—which is why authentic spirituality is radically creative rather than merely imitative. For the same reason, we can speak of the revealing of being as authentic and radically creative only when it moves one toward, not away from, the suffering of all being.

(4) The three preceding points help to clarify the concept of authenticity in relation to human being-becoming in its various dimensions (Doherty, 1995; Paris, 1995, chap. 6; Taylor, 1991). What is authentic: (a) is integral or integrating, rather than non-integral or disintegrating; (b) is revelatory rather than obscuring; and (c) embraces rather than refuses the *essential* suffering of being. These criteria also provide a framework for conceptualizing justice experientially. Justice that is rooted in authentic spirituality at least: reveals being (or, better, allows being to be revealed), is foundationally integrating (rather than disintegrating), and neither begins nor ends in either desire or disdain, but in recognizing and embracing our shared suffering.

(5) Authentic human spirituality is concerned with what it means to be distinctively and truthfully human increasingly over the life cycle in relation to the

being-becoming of all humanity and all creation. This suggests that authentic processes of human being-becoming not only reflect but are deeply rooted in authentic spirituality. Thus the maturing person ought to be becoming increasingly more integrating than disintegrating across the many domains of human being-becoming, progressively realizing and affirming the interconnection of all life. Accompanying this realization should be a growing sense of responsibility as a contributor to and co-creator of well-being, not just for self and those closest to oneself, but ultimately for all with whom we share being-becoming. This foundational expanding of the heart then allows for an expanding capacity to embrace rather than refuse the essential suffering of all being, which becomes the ground for authentic and just creativity throughout the cycle of life.

I end by returning to a quotation from Ralph Ellison's (1952) *Invisible Man* that describes well the dynamics of obscuring being and the deep cry for the revealing of being.

> I am an invisible man. No, I am not a spook like those who haunted Edgar Allan Poe; nor am I one of your Hollywood-movie ectoplasms. I am a man of substance, of flesh and bone, fiber and liquids—and I might even be said to possess a mind. I am invisible, understand, simply because people refuse to see me. Like the bodiless heads you see sometimes in circus sideshows, it is as though I have been surrounded by mirrors of hard, distorting glass. When they approach me they see only my surroundings, themselves, or figments of their imagination—indeed, everything and anything except me.
>
> Nor is my invisibility exactly a matter of a biochemical accident to my epidermis. That invisibility to which I refer occurs because of a peculiar disposition of the eyes of those with whom I come in contact. A matter of the construction of their inner eyes, those eyes with which they look through their physical eyes upon reality. I am not complaining, nor am I protesting either. It is sometimes advantageous to be unseen, although it is most often rather wearing on the nerves. Then too, you're constantly being bumped against by those of poor vision. Or again, you often doubt if you really exist. You wonder whether you aren't simply a phantom in other people's minds. Say, a figure in a nightmare which the sleeper tries with all his strength to destroy. It's when you feel like this that, out of resentment, you begin to bump people back. And. . . you feel that way most of the time. You ache with the need to convince yourself that you do exist in the real world, that you're a part of all the sound and anguish, and you strike out with your fists, you curse and you swear to make them recognize you. And, alas, it's seldom successful (p. 3).

Ellison is describing not just an African American struggle, but the struggle of all being to be revealed. The issue that he is raising, at its deepest dimensions, is at the heart of social existence—being revealed, rather than obscured, as part of an integrated whole. This is the distinctively human cry that unfortunately often is obscured because it seems too painful to endure. It seems easier to embrace non-being, to live in obscurity, than to authentically and creatively engage the struggle to be.

And the revealing of being is never just an individual enterprise, because the obscuring of being is never just an individual enterprise. Being is always integral. Non-integral being is an impossibility. Therefore, healing—as the revealing and reintegrating of being—also must be integral. Non-integral healing also is an impossibility. This perspective potentially provides a framework for struggling with foundational issues of health and healing in relation to both mind and body (Hahn, 1995; Romanucci-Ross & Tancredi, 1987).

- What does it mean to be healthy, to be well?
- What does well-being look like in a society that evaluates persons primarily by the material extensions of their existence; that emphasizes individual creativity without simultaneously emphasizing justice?
- What constitutes healthy being in a society that values eternal youth and external beauty over the ever-increasing development of virtues over the life span; that prizes individuals on their desirability as commodities or as sources of gratification; that emphasizes instrumentality at the expense of wisdom (May, 1985)?
- How do the nurturers-healers of a community or society foster healthy being?
- What does it mean for communities or societies to be well?
- How does one measure the health of a community, a society, a nation, a planet?
- What is the relationship between well-being, health, and disease?

These questions point toward the necessity of evaluating one's understanding of health and well-being in relation to the inescapable reality of suffering. Particularly important are the implications for experiencing health and well-being, individually and collectively, when the underlying assumption of individuals or groups is that the impossibility of *not suffering* is both desirable and possible. If one accepts the view of spirituality presented herein, which suggests that the refusal of suffering represents the obscuring of being, or the frustrating of authentic being-becoming, then there can be no real health or well-being in the presence of the radical affirmation of this impossibility, because there can be no well-being—individually or collectively—when being is obscured.

These questions also point to the need to articulate, to make explicit, the trajectory of human being-becoming that guides individual and communal emergence, to identify the ideas and ideals that shape and direct both societal processes and the intertwined communal, familial, and individual processes of *normal* human development. Such articulation is important because it identifies the wellsprings from which being (non-being) is issuing; it reveals our deepest intimacing and aspiring, which constitute, with suffering, our deepest identities—individual, communal, societal, and global. This revealing potentially is the foundation for reintegrating, remembering (Shore, 1995, pp. 95–104.), human being-becoming.

References

Allport, G. (1958). *The nature of prejudice* (Abridg. ed.). Garden City, NY: Anchor Books.

Alschuler, L. R. (1992). Oppression and liberation: A psycho-political analysis according to Freire and Jung. *Journal of Humanistic Psychology 32(2)*, 8–31.

Alves, R. A. (1972). *Tomorrow's child: Imagination, creativity, and the rebirth of culture.* San Francisco: Harper & Row.

Anderson, E. (1994, May). The code of the streets. *Atlantic Monthly, 273*, 81–94

Ani, M. (1994). *Yurugu: An African-centered critique of European cultural thought and behavior.* Trenton, NJ: Africa World Press.

Arterburn, S., & Felton, J. (1991). *Toxic faith: Understanding and overcoming religious addiction.* Nashville: Oliver-Nelson Books.

Becker, E. (1973). *The denial of death.* New York: Free Press.

Bell, D. (1987). *And we are not saved: The elusive quest for racial justice.* New York: Basic Books.

Bell, D. (1992). *Faces at the bottom of the well: The permanence of racism.* New York: Basic Books.

Bellah, R. N., Madsen, R., Sullivan, W. M., Swidler, A., & Tipton, S.M. (1985). *Habits of the heart: Individualism and commitment in American life.* Berkeley: University of California Press.

Berkhofer, Jr., R. F. (1972). *Salvation and the savage: An analysis of Protestant mission and American Indian response, 1787–1862.* New York: Atheneum.

Berman, M. (1981). *The reenchantment of the world.* Ithaca, NY: Cornell University Press.

Booth, L. (1991). *When God becomes a drug: Breaking the chains of religious addiction and abuse.* Los Angeles: Jeremy P. Tarcher.

Bruner, J. (1990). *Acts of meaning.* Cambridge: Harvard University Press.

Buber, M. (1958). *I and thou (2d ed.).* New York: Charles Scribner's Sons.

Bullard, R. D. (1990). *Dumping in Dixie: Race, class, and environmental quality.* Boulder, CO: Westview Press.

Bullard, R. D. (Ed.). (1993). *Confronting environmental racism: Voices from the grassroots.* Boston: South End Press.

Bullard, R. D. (Ed.). (1994). *Unequal protection: Environmental justice and communities of color.* San Francisco: Sierra Club Books.

Carter, S. L. (1993). *The culture of disbelief: How American law and politics trivialize religious devotion.* New York: Basic Books.

Coner-Edwards, A. F., & Spurlock, J. (Eds.). (1988). *Black families in crisis: The middle class.* New York: Brunner/Mazel.

Connor, M. K. (1995). *What is cool? Understanding Black manhood in America.* New York: Crown Publishers.

Cose, E. (1993). *The rage of a privileged class.* New York: HarperCollins.

Cushman, P. (1984). The politics of vulnerability: Youth in religious cults. *Psychohistory Review, 12(4),* 5–17.

Cushman, P. (1990). Why the self is empty: Toward a historically situated psychology. *American Psychologist, 45(5),* 599–611.

DeBerry, S. T. (1993). *Quantum psychology: Steps to a postmodern ecology of being.* Westport, CT: Praeger.

Doherty, W. J. (1995). *Soul searching: Why psychotherapy must promote moral responsibility.* New York: Basic Books.

Du Bois, W.E.B. (1903/1969). *The souls of Black folk.* New York: New American Library.

Durning, A. T. (1995). Are we happy yet? In T. Roszak, M. E. Gomes, & A. D. Kanner (Eds.), *Ecopsychology: Restoring the earth, healing the mind* (pp. 68–76). San Francisco: Sierra Club Books.

Ellison, R. (1952). *Invisible man.* New York: Random House.

Erikson, E. H. (1968). *Identity: Youth and crisis.* New York: W. W. Norton.

Etzioni, A. (1988). *The moral dimension: Toward a new economics.* New York: Free Press.

Frankl, V. E. (1978). *The unheard cry for meaning: Psychotherapy and humanism.* New York: Simon & Schuster.

Franklin, J. H. (1993). *The color line: Legacy for the twenty-first century.* Columbia, MO: University of Missouri Press.

Freire, P. (1968). *Pedagogy of the oppressed* (M. B. Ramos, Trans.). New York: Seabury Press.

Fromm, E. (1976). *To have or to be?* New York: Harper & Row.

Gibran, K. (1923). *The prophet.* New York: Alfred A. Knopf.

Glass, J. M. (1989). *Private terror, public life: Psychosis and the politics of community.* Ithaca, NY: Cornell University Press.

Grudin, R. (1990). *The grace of great things: Creativity and innovation.* New York: Ticknor & Fields.

Guisinger, S., & Blatt, S. J. (1994). Individuality and relatedness: Evolution of a fundamental dialectic. *American Psychologist, 49(2),* 104–111.

Hahn, R. A. (1995). *Sickness and healing: An anthropological perspective.* New Haven: Yale University Press.

Halperin, D. A. (1982). Group processes in cult affiliation and recruitment. *Group, 6(2),* 13–24.

Jaynes, G. D., & Williams, Jr., R. M. (Eds.). (1989). *A common destiny: Blacks and American society.* Washington, DC: National Academy Press.

Jordan, W. D. (1968). *White over Black: American attitudes toward the Negro 1550–1812.* Baltimore: Penguin Books.

Kanner, A. D., & Gomes, M. E. (1995). The all-consuming self. In T. Roszak, M. E. Gomes, & A. D. Kanner (Eds.), *Ecopsychology: Restoring the earth, healing the mind* (pp. 77–91). San Francisco: Sierra Club Books.

Kass, L. (1985). Mortality. In K. Vaux (Ed.), *Powers that make us human: The foundations of medical ethics* (pp. 7–27). Urbana, IL: University of Illinois Press.

Katz, M. B. (1989). *The undeserving poor: From the war on poverty to the war on welfare.* New York: Pantheon Books.

Kegan, R. (1982). *The evolving self: Problem and process in human development.* Cambridge: Harvard University Press.

Kovel, J. (1984). *White racism: A psychohistory.* New York: Columbia University Press.

Kraft, W. A. (1974). *A psychology of nothingness.* Philadelphia: Westminster Press.

Krishnamurti, J. (1954). *The first and last freedom.* San Francisco: Harper & Row.

Krishnamurti, J. (1977). *Truth and actuality.* San Francisco: Harper & Row.

Livingston, I. L. (Ed.). (1994). *Handbook of Black American health: The mosaic of conditions, issues, policies, and prospects.* Westport, CT: Greenwood Press.

Macquarrie, J. (1985). *In search of humanity: A theological and philosophical approach.* New York: Crossroad.

Majors, R., & Billson, J. M. (1992). *Cool pose: The dilemmas of Black manhood in America.* New York: Lexington Books.

May, R. (1983). *The discovery of being: Writings in existential psychology.* New York: W. W. Norton.

May, W. (1985). Honor. In K. Vaux (Ed.), *Powers that make us human: The foundations of medical ethics* (pp. 29–44). Urbana, IL: University of Illinois Press.

McCombs, H. G. (1985). Black self-concept: An individual/collective analysis. *International Journal of Intercultural Relations, 9(1),* 1–18.

Merton, T. (1955). *No man is an island.* New York: Harcourt Brace Jovanovich.

Myers, L. J. (1991). Expanding the psychology of knowledge optimally: The importance of world view revisited. In R. L. Jones (Ed.), *Black psychology* (3d ed., pp. 15–25). Berkeley: Cobb & Henry.

Naylor, T. H., Willimon, W. H., & Naylor, M. R. (1994). *The search for meaning.* Nashville: Abingdon Press.

Noel, J. A. (1990). Memory and hope: Toward a hermeneutic of African American consciousness. *Journal of Religious Thought, 47*(1), 18–28.

Omi, M., & Winant, H. (1994). *Racial formation in the United States from the 1960s to the 1990s* (2d ed.). New York: Routledge.

Orfield, G., & Ashkinaze, C. (1991). *The closing door: Conservative policy and Black opportunity.* Chicago: University of Chicago Press.

Palmer, P. J. (1983). *To know as we are known: A spirituality of education.* San Francisco: Harper & Row.

Paris, P. J. (1995). *The spirituality of African peoples: The search for a common moral discourse.* Minneapolis: Fortress Press.

Popenoe, D. (1994). The family condition of America: Cultural change and public policy. In H. J. Aaron, T. E. Mann, & T. Taylor (Eds.), *Values and public policy* (pp. 81–112). Washington, DC: Brookings Institute.

Postel, S. (1994). Carrying capacity: Earth's bottom line. In L. R. Brown, et al., State of the world 1994: *A Worldwatch Institute report on progress toward a sustainable society* (pp. 3–21). New York: W. W. Norton.

Postman, N. (1992). *Technopoly: The surrender of culture to technology.* New York: Alfred A. Knopf.

Romanucci-Ross, L., & Tancredi, L. R. (1987). The anthropology of healing. In R. J. Bulger (Ed.), *In search of the modern Hippocrates* (pp. 127–145). Iowa City: University of Iowa Press.

Sagan, L. A. (1987). *The health of nations: True causes of sickness and well-being.* New York: Basic Books.

Saliba, J. A. (1985). Psychiatry and the new cults: Part 2. *Academic Psychology Bulletin 7(3)*, 361–375.

San Juan, Jr., E. (1992). *Racial formations, critical transformations: Articulations of power in ethnic and racial studies in the United States.* Atlantic Highlands, NJ: Humanities Press.

Schaef, A. W. (1987). *When society becomes an addict.* San Francisco: Harper & Row.

Schaef, A. W. (1992) *Beyond therapy, beyond science: A new model for healing the whole person.* San Francisco: Harper San Francisco.

Schrag, C. O. (1969). *Experience and being: Prolegomena to a future ontology.* Evanston, IL: Northwestern University Press.

Shakoor, B. H., & Chalmers, D. (1991). Co-victimization of African-American children who witness violence: Effects on cognitive, emotional, and behavioral development. *Journal of the National Medical Association, 83(3),* 233–238.

Shore, L. I. (1995). *Tending inner gardens: The healing art of feminist psychotherapy.* New York: Haworth Press.

Starck, P. L., & McGovern, J. P. (1992). The meaning of suffering. In P. L. Starck & J. P. McGovern (Eds.), *The hidden dimension of illness: Human suffering* (pp. 25–42). New York: National League for Nursing Press.

Stipes, G. P. (1985). Principles of religious cult indoctrination. *Journal of Psychology and Christianity 4(3),* 64–72.

Tarnas, R. (1991). *The passion of the Western mind: Understanding the ideas that have shaped our world view.* New York: Ballantine Books.

Taylor, C. (1991). *The ethics of authenticity.* Cambridge: Harvard University Press.

Tillich, P. (1952). *The courage to be.* New Haven: Yale University Press.

Viorst, J. (1986). *Necessary losses: The loves, illusions, dependencies and impossible expectations that all of us have to give up in order to grow.* New York: Simon & Schuster.

Webster, Y. O. (1992). *The racialization of America.* New York: St. Martin's Press.

West, C. (1993). *Race matters.* Boston: Beacon Press.

Wilmore, G. S. (1983). *Black religion and Black radicalism: An interpretation of the religious history of Afro-American people* (2d ed.). Maryknoll, NY: Orbis Books.

Wilson, J. Q. (1993). *The moral sense.* New York: Free Press.

Zohar, D. (1990). *The quantum self: Human nature and consciousness defined by the new physics.* New York: William Morrow.

Zohar, D., & Marshall, I. (1994). *The quantum society: Mind, physics, and a new social vision.* New York: William Morrow.

Author

John Rogers, Ph.D.
Center for Family Excellence
1835 Centre Avenue, Room 208
Pittsburgh, PA 15219
Telephone: (412) 434-0391
Fax: (412) 434-0393
E-mail: jarogers@ix.netcom.com

Spirituality, Grieving, and Mental Well-Being

Bernadette Jeffrey Fletcher

Introduction

During most of my years as a clinician working with individuals and families and as a professional educator training graduate social work students, human suffering and grieving have been constant foci. Historically, we African Americans have had more than our share of these fundamentally human experiences because of the oppression we have endured. In the midst of this reality, the religious dimension has been a mainstay for self-help strategies, enabling us to deflect the distortions of the majority toward us. Major movements of liberation also have been deeply rooted within religious centers, where African Americans have experienced the capacity to endure, embrace, and ultimately transform suffering through creative grieving, which has ushered in re-creative activities for individuals and communities.

While suffering and grieving are universal, rarely is a Christian perspective included in current discussions among practitioners and educators, except within specifically religious institutions. Because of the significant adherence to Christianity among African Americans, I believe it is helpful to bring together a Christian perspective toward life, an experientially Afrocentric orientation, and concern for empowering professional help givers and educators as a means toward holistically addressing issues related to mental well-being. The concurrence of Christian faith and the African American experience around issues of suffering and grieving makes this integration potentially generative in relation to both theory and practice. Toward this end, I intend to articulate issues of grieving and healing in relation to mental well-being for African Americans from an Afrocentric Christian perspective.

This is personally important because Christianity has been the ground for my personal and professional emergence over the past twenty years. It has allowed me to understand and use my professional education in a very different and broader way than is often expressed in current discussions about spirituality and mental well-being. Particularly important has been a Christian view of what it means to be human in the context of all being—human, nonhuman, and transhuman. This view of human-being-in-context has implications for understanding human well-being as reflected in concerns related to disease, dysfunction, and healing.

Although historically Christianity has played a significant role in most of our African American communities—and throughout other communities of African peoples of the diaspora and on the continent of Africa—one of the historical issues for Christians of African descent has been the consequences of embracing Christianity for personal and communal well-being. Specifically significant has been the debate around the role of Christian faith in our oppression and liberation. Some have argued that Christianity was brought to Africans as a tool of oppression. Others argue that people of African descent ultimately understood the essence of Christianity as fundamentally liberatory and attempted to live through that essence. The critical need in relation to this essay is to lift this liberatory essence for persons of African descent who have chosen to live within a Christocentric framework and to neutralize those oppressive residuals of a Eurocentric Christian "faith" within the American context.

Here, then, I attempt to present this liberatory essence using a radically Christocentric perspective that emerges from a radically Afrocentric experience whose concern is human liberation. It is intended to enjoin the discussions, particularly among African Americans, of liberation and mental health, attempting to understand the universal implications for fostering individual, communal, and global well-being. The assumption here is that by looking from the point of view of Afrocentric-Christocentric experience, we can identify dynamics that foster healing for African Americans, as well as other communities. This is not to take an exclusionary position. Rather, it attempts to explore the truthfulness of the experience of many African Americans as both "African" and "Christian" in the fullest sense of the terms as a source for truth regarding optimal human being-becoming and to recognize that truth as potentially normative for all persons who are searching for healing.

Well-Being and Grieving

As we approach the next millennium, it is necessary to articulate fresh ways of thinking about human need, healing, and well-being. What is required is a philosophical discussion that includes world view and a shift toward holism, which extends beyond a dehumanizing empiricism on the one hand and a radically individualistic moralizing on the other. Such an approach transcends both a narrow technological view of helping, in which psychopharmacologic techniques are very near the center of the helping episode, and a narrow personalistic view that emphasizes, individual responsibility, conformity, and control. It also facilitates the recovery of the relational dimension, in its deepest human, nonhuman, and transhuman aspects, which is central to healing and well-being. This relational aspect entails a fundamental "attunement" to the spiritual dimension.

While some argue that mental well-being can occur without persons being attuned to the spiritual dimension, I disagree. Spirituality—the life-force of the cosmos originating with and emanating from the one Creator-God—gives ultimate meaning to all the human and nonhuman elements of the universe. At our core, humans are spiritual, distinctively expressing this unifying and integrating life-force that emanates from the one Creator-God. This understanding of human spirituality perceives spirit as the essential and primary component of our humanity, encompassing physical, mental, emotional, and social spheres.

From an Afrocentric Christian perspective, humans not only are distinctive expressions of this life-force but also have a unique stewarding position within the created order (Hall, 1986; Paris, 1995). At the heart of such an understanding is human caring for what has been created in the human and nonhuman environment so that mutual growth, development, and enrichment occur within a context of just relationships. Holding this understanding of our essential nature fosters harmony, mirrored as individual and communal well-being.

Mental well-being is a continuous adapting, growing, evolving dynamic of affect, mentation, and motivation in harmony with the one Creator-God, all humanity, and the Creator-God's life-force in the nonhuman creation. As an axiomatic human dimension, well-being is unlimited, atemporal, and xenophillic. Mental well-being extends beyond the individual to the communal and fosters people connecting at an authentic level, which in essence represents our spirituality. It is an orientation-dynamic that balances and harmonizes mental, physical, and emotional aspects of human nature realized ideally through beneficent human interaction in all realms of social existence. The color spectrum of communities of humans is recognized as reflecting the one Creator-God's light. This harmonious spiritual dynamic is the foundation of the human experience of community and underpins healing processes in relation to humans and nonhumans.

However, people have a distinctive capacity for dis-integration, dis-harmony, and dis-ease within the created order; and these occur whenever people deny, reject, or ignore this foundational orienting dynamic with the Creator-God. The resulting absence of mental well-being cultivates an individual and communal orientation-dynamic of imbalance, maladaptation, and dysfunction in physical and emotional domains and interferes with and erodes healing processes. Individual and communal attempts to achieve a continuous adapting, growing, evolving state of affect, mentation, and motivation without harmony with the one Creator-God jeopardize all humanity, and the nonhuman creation.

Grieving, the individual and collective response to disintegration, is universal; and acknowledging and embracing grieving is normative for individual and collective mental well-being. As such, grieving is not negative, rather it is a positive life sign. It is not a signal of illness, nor should it be avoided, but lived with and through. All human life is supported, settled, comforted, and fulfilled by grieving. It is a dynamic of mutually recognizing, acknowledging, and authenticating our human spiritual condition. Grieving is a public and open acknowledging of suffering in oneself and others that allows our human assembly to strip away "protective masks" that we wear to shield ourselves from awareness of or exposure to our deeply and distinctively human suffering. As an unbounded, unobstructed, communal process, grieving dismantles those barriers we (as individuals and as groups) construct to ward off recognizing and validating suffering in ourselves and others. Grieving only hinders growth, and thereby becomes dysfunctional, when it is refused, denied, or displaced or projected onto others. The displacing of one's grieving onto others is a foundational characteristic of oppression, expressing the desperate and destructive projecting or transferring of non-being onto others (Fogelman, 1991).

Denying or neglecting adversity and distress, reflected in the refusal of grieving, does violence to the human spirit, dehumanizing existence and ascribing non-person status to human being-becoming (Pine, 1990). To understand and to join in with the suffering and grieving of others expresses who we are as fundamentally spiritual persons. Yet, because we are limited by time and space, spiritual connections are incomplete, thereby often increasing human suffering. Over time, controllable and uncontrollable life events intensify our distress. In our attempts to manage and seek relief from this distress, we may deny the spirituality, humanity, and importance of others, thereby setting in motion processes of marginalization and dehumanization that produce mental distress and destabilize us all.

This displacing of grieving ultimately dehumanizes because it contradicts our deepest spiritual connections. It dehumanizes the oppressors because they refuse to recognize and honor shared being, which is the ground of all experiences of suffering (and joy), and rejects grieving as foundationally creative for all being-becoming. This displacing dehumanizes the oppressed because they are forced to assent to non-being as reflected in the oppressor and deflected onto the oppressed (Doka, 1989; DuBois, 1903; Freire, 1970). Thus the creative and aspirational dimensions of grieving often are disoriented toward alleviating the "unnatural" conditions of non-being. Without the willingness (on the part of the oppressor) and the freedom (on the part of the oppressed) to grieve life's ultimate issues in relation to authentic being-becoming, grieving is expressed *desperately* and *destructively* for oppressing and oppressed.

This desperate and destructive grieving is found in all situations of oppression (Allport, 1958), including the maltreatment of people of African descent both on the continent and in the diaspora. The intractable prejudices against African Americans throughout the history of this nation were possible because one people failed to recognize their true spiritual essence and thereby controverted the reality that all humans are equally valued and equally part of a bigger picture. The refusal of the oppressors to grieve authentically resulted in desperate and destructive acts against all people of color on this land and even against the land itself (Deloria, 1969; Kovel, 1984). This refusal also contributed to the unbroken thread of violence in the national psyche and character, which continues through the present and seems to spread with the extension of Western values of materialistic individualism.

When any human community engages in self-destructive behavior, all persons in contact with that community are impacted. When the well-being of any community is deliberately put at risk, well-being for all is jeopardized. Just as individuals do not exist in isolation from one another, neither do communities. The dynamics within any community both impact and reflect the dynamics of other communities with whom there is intercourse—whether conscious and preconscious, immediate or remote, direct or indirect.

The Western values of materialistic individualism provided a framework for misunderstanding humanity, mental health, and well-being. This overarching framework "transformed" people of African descent into commodities and "redefined" the one Creator-God, not as universal creating, sustaining, and liberating Spirit, but as celestial capitalist that valued objects and things (Ani, 1994; Durkheim, 1915). Cultural symbols representing this celestial capitalist invited amassing material possessions and produced a philosophy that marked whole groups of people as objects and disposable property. Consequently all that was human was eroded and all peoples dehumanized. This mis-understanding corrupted connections with others and ushered in a different way of being (non-being). Surviving connections were impoverished—always transitional, color specific, gender specific, power driven, possession defined.

The distinctively human integrating and stewarding capacities, of the oppressed and the oppressing, were further undermined; and all persons embracing this disarticulation of human spirituality—voluntarily or involuntarily—were further dehumanized. This dehumanization exacerbated the rift in the human "spirit" (as communal rather than individual) and became a dominating way of human non-being, which is continually manifest in varieties of biopsychosocial disease among the oppressing, but even more intensively and extensively among the oppressed.

The systematic assault on the spirit of people of African descent has led to the rending of the spiritual fabric of African American communities. The residuals of the diaspora and the Maafa, as reflected in shortened life expectancy, high infant mortality, and a host of other health indicators, inform us that the sustained, traumatic impact of this fundamental way of Americans of European descent towards people of African descent continues to damage African American communities, resulting in the loss of some of the nation's strongest, best, and brightest people (Akbar, 1991). Indices of physical, mental, and social distressors are metaphorical for the sustained, traumatic impact of this fundamental Eurocentric way of non-being.

Moreover, African Americans are continually encouraged to embrace the dehumanization of fellow African Americans (and other humans) by rejecting spirituality and deifying materialism, which results in seeking individual profit at the expense of community. As this tendency spreads, suffering increases as the awareness of communal connections with others is sacrificed. This loss threatens communal mental well-being and could culminate in communal destruction. As African Americans accept the projections and transferals of the oppressing onto themselves, they become increasingly susceptible to self-destructive implosive actions. African American communities bearing the brunt of black-on-black violence manifested as the abuse of women, drugs and related drug culture, abuse of children, exclusion of elders, suicide, and homicide are actually reflecting the disoriented spiritually alien perspective projected onto them by oppression. Harmony with one another and with the larger human and nonhuman world becomes increasingly impossible as disrespect, dishonor, and devaluation of all things—human, nonhuman, and transhuman—metastasizes. If intensifying disorders in African American communities reflect increasing individual and communal acceptance of a projected disoriented spiritually alien perspective, then a spiritual reorientation is needed. Individual and communal disorders among African Americans cannot be fully explicated or remedied without including a world view or perspective that extends to matters beyond the physical dimension of historical trauma to include matters that connect people at a deeper spiritual level.

Grieving and Well-Being in Christian Perspective

The experience of peoples of African descent and the essential tenets of Christianity come together in the central experiences of suffering and grieving, which issue forth in empathy and compassion. To be experientially Afrocentric and experientially and essentially Christian is to be one who suffers (Cone, 1975). But to be experientially Afrocentric and truthfully Christian also is to be part of empathic and compassionate communities that willingly embrace the suffering of others (Ansbro, 1982, pp. 27–29; Murphy, 1983; Paris, 1995; Wolterstorff, 1983). (The dimensions of suffering, empathy, and compassion are integral to, but not exhaustive of, the essence of being Christian.) The results of this embracing of suffering is the renewing of both the individuals who suffer and the larger communities of which they are part. This is reflective of the foundational Christian themes of redemption and renewal.

The Old Testament reverberates with the theme of mutual responsibility for grieving humans, for those who were less fortunate. For example, in the Law, Moses instructed farmers to not fully harvest crops so that oppressed persons and travelers might experience physical and spiritual renewal:

"You must not infringe on the rights of the foreigner or the orphan; you must not take a widow's clothes in pledge. Remember that you were once a slave in Egypt and that Yahweh your God redeemed you from that. That is why I am giving you this order."

"If, when reaping the harvest in your field, you overlook a sheaf in that field,

do not go back for it. The foreigner, the orphan and the widow shall have it, so that Yahweh your God may bless you in all your undertakings."
"When you beat your olive tree, you must not go over the branches twice. The foreigner, the orphan and the widow shall have the rest."
"When you harvest your vineyard, you must not pick over it a second time. The foreigner, the orphan and the widow shall have the rest."
"Remember that you were once a slave in Egypt. That is why I am giving you this order." Deuteronomy 24:17-22 (New Jerusalem Bible)

The Wisdom writings also point toward the compassionate regard for the poor and suffering as normative for individual and communal well-being. A beautiful example comes from Job's defense of his integrity before his three interlocutors:

Have I been *insensible* to the needs of the poor, or let a widow's eyes grow dim? Have I eaten my bit of bread on my own without sharing it with the orphan, whom God has fostered father-like from childhood, and guided since I left my mother's womb? Have I ever seen a wretch in need of clothing, or the poor with nothing to wear, without his having cause to bless me from his heart, as he felt the warmth of the fleece from my lambs? Have I raised my hand against an orphan, presuming on my credit at the gate? If so, let my shoulder fall from its socket, let my arm break off at the elbow! For the terror of God would fall on me and I could not then stand my ground before my majesty. Job 31:16-23 (New Jerusalem Bible)

And, of course, the Prophetic writings repeatedly warn of judgment against leaders and the nation as a whole for their disregard and abuse of the poor, the oppressed, and the vulnerable in their midst:

Listen to the words of Yahweh, King of Judah now occupying the throne of David, you, your officials and your people who go through these gates. Yahweh says this: Act uprightly and justly; rescue from the hands of the oppressor anyone who has been wronged, do not exploit or ill-treat the stranger, the orphan, the widow; shed no innocent blood in this place. For if you are scrupulous in obeying this command, then kings occupying the throne of David will continue to make their entry through the gates of this palace riding in chariots or on horseback, they, their officials, and their people. But if you do not listen to these words, then I swear by myself, Yahweh declares, this palace shall become a ruin! Jeremiah 22:2-5 (New Jerusalem Bible)

This ancient ethic also is found in the corpus of the Christian New Testament. Beginning with John the Baptist, the major transitioner from the "old" to the "new," one hears the familiar refrains:

When all the people asked him, "What must we do then?" he answered.

"Anyone who has two tunics must share with the one who has none, and anyone with something to eat must do the same." There were tax collectors, too, who came for baptism, and these said to him, "Master, what must we do?" He said to them, "Exact no more than the appointed rate." Some soldiers asked him in their turn, "What about us? What must we do?" He said to them, "No intimidation! Be content with your pay!" Luke 3:10-14 (New Jerusalem Bible)

Interestingly in Jesus' Sermon on the Mount, the ethic is reaffirmed in a rather surprising way. He does not begin by enjoining care for those who are the underprivileged; he actually affirms their blessedness: "Blessed are those who mourn" (Matthew 5:5). This paradoxical passage raises the important question of the relationship between mourning and blessing. One translation says that "Blessed are those who mourn" really means "Happy are those with sorrows" (Living Bible). The key to this apparent paradox lies within the rest of the verse: "for they shall be comforted." In the context of the Beatitudes, sorrowing is the first step of embracing the understanding that to be truly human is to mourn, to join in the suffering of others, because it galvanizes and strengthens who we really are. Though it may begin as a private activity, it concludes as a communal experience.

In this sermon that set forth the governing ethics of the new Christian community, Jesus also provided another surprising twist. He stipulated that mere adherence to the letter of the Law would not be adequate because it could not get at the roots of destructive attitudes and behaviors. So, in essence, he set forth principles that prevented the emergence or extension of conflicts that threatened both individuals and the community:

You have heard how it was said, You will love your neighbor and hate your enemy. But I say this to you, love your enemies and pray for those who persecute you; so that you may be children of your Father in heaven, for he causes his sun to rise on the bad as well as the good, and sends down rain to fall on the upright and the wicked alike. For if you love those who love you, what reward will you get? Do not even the tax collectors do as much? And if you save your greetings for your brothers, are you doing anything exceptional? Do not even the gentiles do as much? You must therefore set no bounds to your love, just as your heavenly Fathers sets none to his. Matthew 5:43-48 (New Jerusalem Bible)

Yet another example of this ethic applied is the judgment parable in Matthew 25:31-46, which relates the story of people receiving their eternal reward based on their attitudes and responses to oppressed strangers who had crossed their paths during their earthly lives. Some people formed empathic accepting attitudes and responded with compassion. In sharp contrast, others chose hostile rejecting attitudes and affirmed the oppression of those strangers who had crossed their paths. All persons who, during their lifetimes, lovingly embraced suffering strangers received great eternal rewards; all who did not received eternal punishments.

Despite this foundational ethic of care and inclusion, time and time again the early church had to overcome natural tendencies to maintain barriers between themselves and others from whom they had been estranged historically. Those Jews who embraced Christ still struggled with old animosities toward "strangers" as the early Christian church experienced growth among non-Jews. At those critical moments when the "new community" was threatened by its own exclusive and entropic tendencies, the Spirit of Christ reoriented them toward inclusiveness. The Acts of the Apostles details this "breaking out" process as new ministries were accorded apostolic status to meet the needs of the expanding community in the face of increasing persecution (Acts 6:1-7). As persecution extended the church geographically, the church also was extended ethnically, sometimes with great difficulty (Acts 8:10–11, 15). Still, the character of this emerging new community was mutual care and concern (2 Corinthians 8–9; James 1:9-11, 27–29; 5:1-6).

The elegance of the Revelation story that concludes with a view of human transcendence into a new heaven and a new earth was easily recognizable by African Americans. The new heaven and new earth, interpreted as metaphorical for the restoration of harmony between the Creator and the creation, depict the ultimate state of well-being, in which symphonic activities, relationships, and communication between creation and Creator yield joy, health, and illumination. Humans who, while on earth, connected themselves with the redeeming Christ and through that transformation lived by embracing the grieving and suffering of others at last in heaven transcend human conditions of tears, sorrow, illness, and death (Revelation 21–22).

The quest for restoring intimacy with the Creator-God as the ground for individual, communal, and global well-being has been a central thrust of African Americans since we landed in Jamestown (Cone, 1975; Cooper-Lewter & Mitchell, 1986; Franklin, 1969; Paris, 1995). The historical European American oppression and spiritual disorientation impinging upon that quest has been the parallel undercurrent throughout our history. In specific times and places this disorientation overlay and undermined the truthful expression of Christian faith, resulting in insensitivity and disobedience to human suffering (Lincoln & Mamiya, 1990). And when we were insensitive and disobedient to the deeply and distinctly human experience of suffering and grieving, we succumbed to spiritual entropy, ultimately mirroring the acts and attitudes of our oppressors (Wilmore, 1983). Conversely when we were obedient to the distinctly human experience of suffering and grieving, we were sustained and sustaining as individuals, families, and communities of faith and faithfulness (Harding, 1981). Historically, this view of spirituality immunized African Americans against the disintegrative effect of any oppressive nationalistic strategy that might have induced or aggravated physical experiences of starvation, poverty, incarceration, or even death.

This Christocentric perspective can be identified in the underpinnings of indigenous self-help strategies of African Americans, which focused on adaptive vitality and resiliency of African American people (Ross, 1978; Shannon &

Wilmore, 1985). Those self-help strategies founded or sustained by Christian churches or related religious bodies acknowledged oppression while preaching that individuals and communities should aspire to a higher level of being, universally encouraging strong kinship ties that included elders and children in non–blood-related families. Persons of all ages, whether well-known or newly known, were equally accorded kinship status with the usual rights and privileges of the wel-comed, wanted, and appreciated extended family member (DuBois, 1909; Ross, 1978; Stack, 1974).

Implications

One compelling aspect of Christianity is the raw depiction of the human condition as isolating, alienating, and disconnecting in ways that preclude well-being. A grieving Christ was the consequence of the Creator-God choosing to remain connected with humankind, to retain the possibility of reconciliation across all domains of human experience. His life spoke of the divine intention to renew the human community. His suffering and death encompassed all human suffering that occurs when people attempt to live without being spiritually attuned, spiritually intimate, with the Creator-God. His resurrection and subsequent participation as Spirit within and among the new "fellowship of believers" promised redemptive possibilities for bridging chasms between persons, the Creator-God, and ultimately all creation.

Within a Christian framework, participation in this multidimensional process of redemption-reconciliation is the essence of spiritual reconnection, which be-comes the ground for human well-being. In embracing Christ, we willingly enter onto the path of reconciliation by accepting the reality of human suffering and grieving and ultimately are empowered to settle the matter of breached relationships (Freedman, 1993). It is the settling of the spiritual rift between humankind and the one Creator God through Christ that empowers persons to settle breached relation-ships among persons and between persons and the nonhuman creation. In this context, mental wholeness or well-being expresses itself as the ongoing restoration of harmony to relationships between people and Creator and all creation.

For Christians, the divine initiative "in Christ" is paradigmatic. Therefore, embracing the "grieving of being" (Rogers, 1996) is at the heart of well-being—human and nonhuman; individual, familial, communal, national, and global. Recognition of the redemptive possibilities inherent in suffering—even suffering based in injustice—has served to strengthen and renew African Americans through-out the centuries of our oppression. Historically, our joining in the suffering and grieving of others is not a pessimistic, sadistic, or destructive process, but rather a spiritually liberatory, transforming, regenerative process that really restores bal-ance and harmony in the human family (Cone 1987; Cooper-Lewter & Mitchell,

1986, pp. 127–140; Harding, 1987; Perkins, 1982). Thus for African Americans to embrace Christianity was not an escape from suffering; rather, it provided the impetus for individual liberation and societal transformation, despite attempts of our oppressors to use "faith" to enforce non-being (Cone, 1986; Paris, 1995; Sernett, 1985; Wilmore, 1983; Wilmore & Cone, 1979; Woodson, 1972). Therefore, to move toward healing and well-being at this point in time requires the recovery of these essential dimensions of African-Christian being—namely, an embracing of suffering that issues forth in redemptive and creative grieving.

At any time, expected and unexpected life events may impact daily activities in ways that precipitate situations for which persons require specific and significant aid from others. From a Christian point of view, at the nexus of help giving is a spiritual encounter in which helper and helpee are confronted with suffering and grieving, which ultimately are born of human attempts to live without being spiritually attuned, spiritually intimate, with the one Creator-God. The healing encounter centers on embracing suffering and grieving as an unavoidable part of human life, as an integral part of who we are individually and collectively, that can be creatively transformed by becoming spiritually re-attuned with the one Creator-God. The experience of healing itself is precisely wrestling through this integral dialectic of reckoning with who I am (we are) while realizing that I am (we are) still becoming. The "suffering of being" (Rogers, 1996) is, at least in part, the tension between the implicit desire of being to continue becoming while we struggle to avoid the uncertainty that is inherent to that process. In fact, much of the disease that we experience reflects the refusal of this creative dialectic—individually and collectively.

Martin and Martin (1995) begin to explore this struggle with the suffering, mourning, and aspirations of African Americans in their discussion of social work practice. Although social workers have long recognized the link between the sorrow and suffering of African American clients and oppressive societal dynamics, they have not always understood the resulting need for mourning as a means of cleansing the pollutions that were an inherent part of that oppression. Within this mourning were the seeds of renewal and recreation, which were watered by their tears of grief and joy, thereby producing the roots of hope. The authors further suggest that when African Americans lose their ability to engage this "mourning work," they also lose their capacity for healing. So, for example, as persons moved from rural settings to urban areas, they lost sight of the creative dimensions of this mourning:

> Caught up in the commercialism, individualism, and materialism of urban culture, they began to privatize their troubles and camouflage their pain. Without strong social support and strong institutions of mourning, the old psychologies of cultural sickness, cultural paranoia, and cultural claustrophobia began to rise to unprecedented heights and even showed signs of leading to the most destructive psychology of all, the psychology of cultural terminal illness (p. 196).

This perspective reorients helping and healing beyond personal adaptation to a social system to redemptive reconciliation across all domains of human experience. In contrast, helpers who are insensitive to or deny this universal spiritual dimension may create help-giving episodes that are conducted in a myopic disintegrating manner that obscures or blocks contemplating this fundamental orienting and grounding reality, consequently thwarting genuine help giving, hindering connections, and possibly introducing non-help (Doherty, 1995; Sheridan, Bullis, Adcock, Berlin, & Miller, 1992; Siporin, 1985). Under these circumstances, repeated help-giving attempts potentially endanger both helpee and helper as both increase their own vulnerability through increased spiritual disorientation.

Precisely what is often lost in current discussions of empowerment (Riger, 1993) is the spiritual dimension, which permits psychosociopolitical empowerment within the African American, or any other, community. Without the spiritual dimension, empowerment cannot be achieved or sustained:

> Although contemporary social work practice tends to be primarily a secular profession, this can be said categorically: there can be no social work based on the African American experience that does not consider both the secular and the sacred world of African American people. Thus, African American experience-based social work is primarily a secular practice with a deep spiritual emphasis. It does not operate from a theological framework, but it recognizes that African American people historically are a spiritual people; not only in the religious sense but also in terms of the role of historical empathy, ancestral connectedness, and faith and hope. African American experience-based social work advances the idea that it is imperative for any social worker working with African American people to recognize the primary role and important function of the sacred as well as the profane in African American life (Martin & Martin, 1995, p. 200).

Through this spiritual empowerment, persons attain greater awareness of and sensitivity to the human community and consider communal expressions of vital movements—conceiving, birthing, growing, mating, maturing, aging, dying—as having essential consequences for our well-being. If life is considered to be spiritual, then conceiving and birthing are sacred and are to be valued, cherished, and honored. If growing is understood to be spiritual, then children are to be nurtured, supported, and sustained. If mating is understood to be spiritual, then marriage is to be venerated as life-sustaining, lasting, and secure. If maturity is understood to be spiritual, then it is treasured as providing essential opportunities for intergenerational caring and nurturing. If aging is understood as spiritual, then the aged are appreciated and honored as sources of wisdom, knowing what and how to do with what is known, and living with humility in the face of what cannot be known. Ultimately, if death is understood to be spiritual, it is reverenced as a sacred passage from one spiritual realm to another.

Summary

A reaffirmation of spirituality will contribute to the redaction of human suffering. Chronic social problems can only be addressed effectively by remembering, reinforcing, and restoring our essential interconnectedness as spirit beings and embracing suffering as an inescapable part of human experience. Participation in this framework, individually and communally, calls forth healing across our diverse communities who share common visions of harmony, unity, wholeness and well-being (Sawyer, 1994). Postmodern western technocratic life cannot provide the means of addressing the deep wounds of people, which if not addressed will continue to fester and exacerbate the decline that many are naming and lamenting. African Americans need not go beyond our historical experience in search of the roots for healing. A spiritual reorientation that acknowledges our historical and foundational wounding and the resulting suffering and grieving is possible within a Christian and Afrocentric perspective. This essay has attempted to provide and example of one possible framework and the implications for speaking to our contemporary quest for mental well-being.

References

Akbar, N. (1991). Mental disorder among African Americans. In R. L. Jones (Ed.), *Black psychology* (3rd ed., pp. 339–352). Berkeley, CA: Cobb & Henry.

Allport, G. (1958). *The nature of prejudice* (Abridg. ed.). Garden City, NY: Anchor Books.

Ani, M. (1994). *Yurugu: An African-centered critique of European and cultural thought and behavior.* Trenton, NJ: Africa World Press.

Ansbro, J. J. (1982). *Martin Luther King, Jr.: The making of a mind.* Maryknoll, NY: Orbis Books.

Cone, J. H. (1975). *God of the oppressed.* New York: Seabury Press.

Cone, J. H. (1986). *A Black theology of liberation* (2nd ed.). Maryknoll, NY: Orbis Books.

Cone, J. H. (1987). Martin Luther King, Jr., and the Third World. *Journal of American History, 74*(2), 455–467.

Cooper-Lewter, N. C., & Mitchell, H. H. (1986). *Soul theology: The heart of American Black culture.* San Francisco: Harper & Row.

Deloria, V. (1969). *Custer died for your sins: An Indian manifesto.* New York: Macmillan.

Doka, K. J. (1989). *Disenfranchised grief: Recognizing hidden sorrow.* Lexington, MA: DC. Heath.

Doherty, W. J. (1995). *Soul searching: Why psychotherapy must promote moral responsibility.* New York: Basic Books.

DuBois, W. E. B. (1909). *Efforts for social betterment among Negro Americans.* Atlanta, GA: Atlanta University Press.

DuBois, W. E. B. (1903/1969). *The souls of Black folk.* New York: New American Library.

Durkheim, E. (1915/1965). *The elementary forms of religious life.* New York: Free Press.

Fogelman, E. (1991). Mourning without graves. In A. Medvene (Ed.), *Storms and rainbows: The many faces of death.* Washington, DC: Lewis Press.

Franklin, J. H. (1969). Puritan masters. In J. H. Franklin, *From slavery to freedom: A history of Negro Americans* (3rd ed.). New York: Vintage Books.

Freedman, S. G. (1993). *Upon this rock: The miracles of a Black church.* New York: Harper Collins.

Freire, P. (1970). *Pedagogy of the oppressed.* New York: Seabury Press.

Hall, D. J. (1986). *Imaging God: Dominion as stewardship.* Grand Rapids, MI: William B. Eerdmans.

Harding, V. (1981). *There is a river: The Black struggle for freedom in America.* New York: Vintage Books.

Harding, V. G. (1987). Beyond amnesia: Martin Luther King, Jr., and the future of America. *Journal of American History, 74*(2), 468–476.

Hyman, M. (1983). *Blacks who died for Jesus.* Nashville, TN: Winston-Dereck Publishers, Inc.

Kovel, J. (1984). *White racism: A psychohistory.* New York: Columbia University Press.

Lincoln, C. E., & Mamiya, L. H. (1990). *The Black church in the African-American experience.* Durham, NC: Duke University Press.

Martin, E. P., & Martin, J. M. (1995). *Social work and the Black experience.* Washington, DC: NASW Press.

Murphy, L. (1983). Howard Thurman and social activism. In H. J. Young (Ed.), *God and human freedom: A festschrift in honor of Howard Thurman* (pp. 150–160). Richmond, IN: Friends United Press.

Paris, P. J. (1995). *The spirituality of African peoples: The search for a common moral discourse.* Minneapolis: Fortress Press.

Perkins, J. (1982). *With justice for all.* Ventura, CA: Regal Books.

Pine, V. R. (Ed.). (1990). *Unrecognized and unsanctioned grief: The nature and counseling of unacknowledged loss.* Springfield, IL: C.C. Thomas.

Riger, S. (1993). What's wrong with empowerment. *American Journal of Community Psychology, 21*(3), 279–292.

Rogers, J. A. (1996). Spirituality: Questing for well-being. In R. L. Jones (Ed.), *African American Mental Health.* Hampton, VA: Cobb & Henry.

Ross, E. (1978). *Black heritage and social welfare.* Metuchen, NJ: Scarecrow Press.

Sawyer, M. R. (1994). *Black ecumenism: Implementing the demands of justice.* Valley Forge, PA: Trinity Press International.

Sernett, M. C. (Ed.). (1985). *Afro-American religious history: A documentary witness.* Durham, NC: Duke University Press.

Shannon, D. T., & Wilmore, G. S. (Eds.). (1985). *Black witness to the apostolic faith.* Grand Rapids, MI: William B. Eerdmans.

Sheridan, M. J., Bullis, R. K., Adcock, C. R., Berlin, S. D., & Miller, P. C. (1992). Practitioners' personal and professional attitudes and behaviors toward religion and spirituality: Issues for education and practice. *Journal of Social Work Education, 28*(2), 190–203.

Siporin, M. (1985). Current social work perspectives on clinical practice. *Clinical Social Work, 13*(3), 198–217.

Stack, C. (1974). *All our kin: Strategies of survival in a Black community.* New York: Harper & Row.

Wilmore, G. S. (1983). *Black religion and Black radicalism* (2nd ed.). Maryknoll, NY: Orbis Books.

Wilmore, G. S., & Cone, J. H. (Eds.). (1979). *Black theology: A documentary history, 1966–1979.* Maryknoll, NY: Orbis Books.

Wolterstorff, N. (1983). *Until justice and peace embrace.* Grand Rapids, MI: William B. Eerdmans.

Woodson, C. G. (1972). *The history of the Negro church* (3rd ed.). Washington, DC: Associated Publishers.

Author

Bernadette Jeffrey Fletcher, Ph.D.
University of Pittsburgh
School of Social Work
Pittsburgh, PA 15260
Telephone: (412) 624-6306
Fax: (412) 624-6323
E-mail: bef2@pitt.edu

Part 3

Self-Concept

Black Self-Concept Revisited

W. Curtis Banks, Lula Beatty, Jacqueline Booth, Jerilyn Pope and Linda Hart Davis

Taylor & Walsh (1979) observed that until the late 1960's it was an axiom of social science that White discrimination and segregation depressed and debilitated the psyche of the average African American person in this country. This "depressed and debilitated psyche" translates into negative self-concept or low self-esteem. It was assumed by most researchers that minority persons could not develop positive self-concepts because of the social rejection and negative labeling they received as a result of living in a society that rejected them (e.g., Kardiner & Ovesey, 1951; Proshansky & Newton, 1968). The belief among researchers, clinicians, and the lay public, that positive self-concept is both desirable and necessary for success in life, coupled with the persistent belief that self-concept in African Americans is negative, compels us to periodically evaluate the status of the scientific evidence and separate cultural fictions from empirical facts.

Perhaps the most noteworthy observation we can make at the outset here is the fact that the fiction, along with a legion of scientific supporters, still exists. Despite considerable evidence and persuasive argument to the contrary, the scientific community has continued its "normal" practice of pushing the construct of negative self-concept into the arena of worthwhile empirical questions. This inertia would, at the least, suggest that perhaps convincing criticisms have still to be advanced. Yet, nothing could be further from the truth.

The theoretical soundness of self-concept in general has been questioned by a number of investigators (e.g., Wells & Marwell, 1976; Wylie, 1961, 1974). Reasons for the questioning include the imprecision and vagueness of the definitions of self-concept, and, even more importantly, the inability of theorists to reliably predict or explain behavior based on their conceptions of the functional relationships between self-concept and other variables (Banks, McQuater, & Ross, 1979). Criticisms pertaining to method have included attacks on the paradigm used to study self-concept, the operationalization of variables and conditions, the choice of materials, and the analysis and interpretation of results. Some have argued that inappropriate statistical procedures were used, creating findings that misrepresented African American subjects' choice behaviors (Banks, 1976; Banks et al., 1979). The racially symbolic stimulus materials used in much of the experimental research have been criticized as being confounded by attractiveness or familiarity (Brand, Ruiz, & Padilla, 1974), leading children potentially to respond to them on

153

grounds other than true racial preference. Failure to control for variations due to age and sex of subjects and stimuli, has also been noted as a limitation. In regards to self-report measures, arguments have been raised concerning the validity of some of the scales used (Baldwin, 1979; Hare, 1977; Porter & Washington, 1979; Wells & Marwell, 1976; Wylie, 1961, 1974).

Another important criticism has been the frequent use of racial comparisons. Concentrating on differences between racial groups on self-concept measures does not, per se, promote knowledge about self-concept within any one group itself. A finding, for example, that African American and White children differ in the extent to which they evaluate varying stimuli, reveals little, if anything, about their self-concent (Baldwin, 1979). Furthermore, using the response patterns of White samples as a baseline or norm has risked the adoption of a standard that may reflect a peculiarity in group response (Banks, 1976) rather than a model of functional adequacy.

On the other hand, it might be argued that, like any corrective intervention into a chronic problem, evaluative criticism into systems of beliefs and practices must be repeated to check the recurrence of a persistent error. And it is in that spirit that we undertake here to reassess the state of research on this vital topic. What we have found, in general, is that not only does the fiction of negative self-concept continue, but the means by which its existence is sustained have shown little innovation or inventive insight. In some respects this seems surprising, but there is actually little reason to expect erroneous old hypotheses to generate creative new methods.

Several years ago we reviewed research on the self-concept as represented in the paradigm of preference (Banks, 1976). Employed by Clark and Clark (1939) in the 1930's, the paradigm presented subjects with stimuli presumably representative of their own and another race. Oral requests designed to elicit evaluations of the stimuli were then made of the children (e.g., "Give me the good doll"). Self identification was similarly measured by making such requests of the children as, "Give me the doll that looks like you." It was usually reported (e.g., Clark & Clark, 1939, 1947; Morland, 1962) that African American children showed a preference for the White stimuli, rejecting themselves and, therefore, revealing negative self-concepts.

The next most popular method of studying self-concept is through what will be called here "self-report measures." These include paper and pencil scales, instruments, and questionnaires that purport to measure self-concept. Findings from these methods were not analyzed in our earlier review, but they contribute to the bulk of the more recent literature on self-concept in African American children and deserve critical attention as well. In that regard, the present revisitation provides an opportunity to broaden our critical task, as well as an opportunity to update it.

Preference Paradigm Studies

Traditionally, in racial preference research African American subjects' choice behaviors are compared to those of White subjects. In most of the early studies African American children chose stimuli similar to their racial group significantly less often than White children chose the racial characteristics of their group. This disparity in choice behaviors was usually interpreted as indicative of African American self-rejection and, consequently, negative self-concept.

Several theorists have argued in one way or another against the validity of the paradigm, suggesting that it measures ethnocentrism rather than self-concept (Brand et al., 1974), that the instrumentation used in the procedures was confounded by uncontrolled factors (Brand et al., 1974), or that the construct was fundamentally inappropriate for studying self-concept in African Americans (Nobles, 1973). We, however, have earlier argued (Banks, 1976) that even assuming the claim that White-preference in African Americans is a measure of self-rejection, the statistical bases used by previous investigators to support such claims were inappropriate. Appropriate statistical analyses would indicate the extent to which subjects consistently chose one stimulus alternative over another, not the extent to which two groups differed in their choice rates. This criterion was employed to evaluate the choice behaviors exhibited by African American subjects in the studies of evaluative- and self-identification-preference conducted more recently. We have found that in these studies the actual frequencies of choices of White and African American stimulus alternatives were not consistently presented for each request made of the subjects. But from the data that have been reported in the literature it can be concluded that African American subjects have continued to show a preponderance of nonpreferential responding.

Non-preference. In an investigation by Moore (1978) low income African American boys and girls, aged 47-76 months, were presented with pictures of African American and White adult females identified as teachers. The children were asked to point to the "nice," and to the "mean" teacher, and to "the teacher you would like next year." There was no overall significant correlation between racial preference and IQ. Furthermore, the overall patterns choices failed to deviate from chance. In response to the "nice teacher" query, 48% of the children chose the White teacher, and 52% chose the African American. In response to the "mean teacher" query, 62% of the children designated the African American teacher, but this level of choice failed to reach the criterion of 63% required to reject the null hypothesis at the .05 level. About half of the children (48%) chose the African American teacher as the one they would prefer, and about half (52%) selected the White teacher.

Rohru conducted a comparative study of African American, White, and Mexican-American children in segregated and integrated classes (1977). She presented her subjects with color photographs of children from each of the three racial groups and asked them to select the one who looked like them, and the one they "would prefer to eat with," "would prefer to play with," and "like best." In response to the question, "Which one looks like you," 56.9% of the African American children indicated the African American stimulus child. Overall, in response to the other queries African American children distributed their choices evenly across the three alternatives, preferentially selecting the African American photograph 29.4%, the Mexican American photograph 39.2%, and the White photograph 31.4% of the time.

In a study of African American and White preschool children in South Africa, Press, Burt, and Barling (1979) asked their subjects to donate a sweet to either a African American or a White child. Fifty-percent of the African American children selected the White child as the recipient of their gift, indicating non-preference.

In a slightly modified replication of Clark and Clark (1947) and Mahan (1976) found that 88% of her African American seven-year-old correctly identified themselves with the African American doll. As the doll they would like to play with, 68% of African American children chose the White doll. As the doll that looks like a nice doll, 44% of the children chose the White doll. As the doll that looks bad, 52% of the children chose the African American doll. As the doll that is a nice color, 52% of the children chose the White doll. All of these frequencies conformed to chance, indicating non-preference.

Schofield (1978) asked African American and White first- and second-graders to draw pictures of human figures using a selection of yellow, red, orange, blue, green, peach, brown, and black crayons. She then classified the completed drawings into seven groups reflecting the inferred racial identity of the figures, ranging from African American to White, with the addition of a group designated "Fanciful." In all, 24% of the African American children produced figures classified at the Black end of the scale, 30% of the African American children produced figures classified as "Indeterminant," and 28% produced figures classified at the White end of the scale. This pattern conforms to chance.

Morland (1980) asked African American preschool and school-aged children to select from a African American or White photographed child the one they "prefer to play with," "look most like," "would most prefer to be." Preschool children demonstrated non-preference in response to each of the queries. Of those who made a choice, 45% chose the African American child and 55% chose the White, as the one they would prefer to play with. Fifty-percent of those choosing selected the African American child as the one they most looked like, and 50% selected the White child. While fully 63% of those choosing selected the photograph of the White child as the one they would prefer to be, this rate of choice conformed to chance at the .05 level, for a sample of 54.

African American-preference. Thirty-percent of Morland's (1980) school-aged sample refused to make a choice in response to the first query. Of the remaining group, 77% chose the African American child to play with, exceeding the 66% required at the .05 level to reject the null hypothesis in the direction of African

American-preference. Likewise, six percent of the school-aged children refused to choose which child they most looked like. But of the remainder, 87% selected the African American child, indicating a significant level of African American preference. Four-percent of the school-aged children refused to choose whether they would rather be the White or the African American child. But 67% of those who chose selected the African American child, exceeding the 64% criterion at the .05 level, and indicating significant African American-preference.

Anderson and Cromwell (1977) found that 82% of their sample of African American high-school children responded positively to the statement that "most Blacks feel Black to be beautiful." Fully 88% of their subjects expressed a preference for being African American. Both these levels of choice were significantly African American-preferential.

Williams-Burns (1980) examined the self-portrait drawings made by African American children in the third-grade, and compared those drawings with actual color photographs of the children. Using a judging procedure that yielded a maximum possible score of 8 for a perfect correspondence between actual and self-portrayed skin color, Williams-Burns found that girls obtained a mean score of 7.4, and boys a mean score of 7.3.

Self-Report Studies

By self-report measures of self-concept or self-esteem we mean those instruments, most often paper and pencil questionnaires or scales, specially constructed to gauge self-reported evaluations in a written verbal format. Respondents are asked to evaluate themselves either globally or on a number of dimensions of the self, such as "body image," "social self," or "academic self." Conservative estimates suggest that such scales number 200 or more, the majority comprised of unvalidated investigator-developed questions that are seldom, if ever, replicated.

While our present view of this research is for the purpose of determining, where possible, the status of self-concept in African Americans, the purposes of the majority of the studies themselves were not as simplistic as this. Most studies attempted to assess the extent to which other factors were implicated in the development or the manifestation of self-concept. To that end, there were investigations that examined social class and self-esteem (Osborne & LeGette, 1982); race, sex and self-esteem (Hendrix, 1980); SES, race, academic achievement, achievement orientation and self-esteem (Hare, 1980); father absence, SES, GPA, and self-concept (Alston & Williams, 1982); self-esteem, locus of control and problem-solving (Horitz, Tetenbaum, & Phillips, 1981); SES, grade, sex and self-esteem (Bledsoe & Dixon, 1980) and locus of control, self-concept, masculinity-femininity, and fear of success imagery (Savage, Stearnes, & Friedman, 1979).

Rarely did reports include a complete disclosure of the data separately for each of the variables under investigation. Among those studies that used subsets of the same factors there was no common convention of reporting the data. This diversity not only of purpose, but in patterns of reporting, makes it difficult to organize or compare studies an any meaningful manner. To be sure, in many cases the actual self-concept scores were not presented because the relationships between those scores and other variables were of primary interest (see e.g., Wilderson, 1976). Nonetheless, it is our aim here to focus upon the question of the empirical status of the attribute under examination. For that purpose we have considered primarily the data associated with African American samples, and we have examined the data, where available, using statistical criteria that compare African American scores with the theoretical null baseline for the measure employed (midpoint of possible score range, or binomial chance).

The most frequently used standardized scales were the Tennessee Self-Concept Scale (e.g., Hines & Berg-Cross, 1981; Bledsoe & Dixon, 1980; King & Price, 1979), the Coopersmith Self-esteem Inventory (e.g., Osborne & LeGette, 1982; Horitz, Tetenbaum, & Phillips, 1981), the Piers-Harris Children's Self Concept Scale (e.g., Osborne & LeGette, 1982; Jegede, 1982; Jegede & Bamgboye, 1982) and the Rosenberg Self-esteem Scale (e.g., Jegede & Bamgboye, 1981; Zuckerman, 1980; Hare, 1980; Jegede, 1982; Jordan, 1981). Semantic differential techniques have been used (e.g., Eato & Lerner, 1981) and many investigators have developed and used their own instruments. For example, Hare (1980) developed an instrument based on the Rosenberg and Coopersmith scales. At about the same time Taylor & Walsh (1979) developed the "African American Self-Concept Scale."

The Non-comparative Research. Among the non-comparative studies of African American self-concept the status of self-concept scores was most often reported as high. Bledsoe (1981), in a study of advantaged and disadvantaged African American youths (using the Tennessee Self-Concept Scale) found that the youths thought highly of their identity, their behavior, physical self, moral/ethical self, personal self, family self, and social self. Moreover, they were overall very "satisfied with themselves." Similarly, Alston & Williams (1982), using the Self-Appraisal Inventory, found African American boys from father-absent and father-present homes were average to above average in self-concept. Within their sample of 35 ninth graders, 46% scored above average and 48% average in their self perceptions of relationships with peers. On general self-concept, 40% scored above average on the inventory, 54% scored in the average range. The overall pattern of scores on the dimension of academic self-concept was average, the children equally distributing themselves across the above average, average, and below average ranges of scoring.

Jegede (1982) administered the Piers-Harris Children's Self-Concept Scale to 1380 Nigerian secondary school students, and reported that the children had high self-concepts. McAdoo (1979) administered the Thomas Self-Concept Values Test to 19 boys and 17 girls from working and middle-class African American families. He reported an overall mean score of 52, just above the midpoint of 50 on that scale. Eato and Lerner (1981) reported that both the female and male samples in their study of 183 African American adolescents expressed relatively high self-esteem on a semantic differential measure. Paul and Fischer (1980) used the African American Identity Questionnaire to assess the degree of racial identity in their sample of 13-14 year old African American adolescents. The mean scores obtained by their sample subgroups ranged from 9.65 to 11.20. Compared to the scale midpoint of 6.0, these means would indicate a level of racial identity that was moderate to high.

The Comparative Research. Among comparative studies of African American self-concept the finding of no difference in self-concept or self-esteem was most often reported. For example, Stephen and Rosenfeld (1978) found no difference in self-esteem scores between African American and White 5th and 6th grade students, although Mexican American children scored lower than both the African American and White children. Using a modified version of Rosenberg's (1965) scale to measure self-esteem, Stephen and Rosenfeld (1979) again investigated differences between African Americans and others. They found that African Americans, with a mean score of 33.5, were not statistically different from either Whites (mean = 34.5) or Mexican-Americans (mean = 32.6).

Heaven and Nieuwoudt (1981) and Momberg and Page (1977) found no difference in self-esteem between South African Blacks and Whites. Lopez (1978) compared employed African American and White adults and found no difference in self-concept. Hare (1980) found that when SES was controlled, there was no difference in self-concept between African American and White fifth-grade children.

Nichols and McKinney (1977) used the Coopersmith Self-Esteem Inventory to investigate self-concept in African American and White elementary school children. They examined separately the scores of children in their sample whose families received Aid to Families with Dependent Children and children whose families did not receive AFDC. Their results showed no differences among any of the groups, including across African American-White comparative samples.

In some of the recent comparative research the findings have indicated more positive self-concepts in African Americans. Higher self-esteem in African American youths than in White youths was found by Simmons and Brown (1978). In their longitudinal study of 768 children, Simmons and Brown found initially that 79% of the African American sample scored in the medium or high range of the scale developed by Rosenberg and Simmons (1972), as compared to 65% of the White sample. In a follow-up with the same samples one year later, 83% of the African American children scored in the high or medium range of the scale, as compared with 68% of the White children.

Using a semantic-differential technique, Chen (1978) obtained self-reports from African American and White college students on dimensions related to "me,"

"African American people," and "ideal self," among others. The range of possible scores for each dimension was from 1 (negative) to 7 (positive). Her results indicated that both African American males and females rated all dimensions above the midpoint of the possible range. Similar results have been reported by other researchers as well (e.g., Stephen & Rosenfeld, 1978, 1979).

In a few instances recent research has revealed lower self-concept in African Americans. Gray-Little and Appelbaum (1979) found no differences in African American and White children when the Tennessee Self-Concept Scale was used, but a higher score in favor of Whites when the Coopersmith Self-Esteem measure was used. African American seventh-graders were found to be lower in self-esteem than White seventh graders on one of several measures used by Hines and Berg-Cross (1981), but higher than Whites on another. African American children scored lower on self-esteem in a study by Osborne and LeGette (1982). Fu (1979) in an investigation of African American, White and Mexican American girls found that White girls scored highest on self-concept, followed by African Americans and Mexican-Americans. It was not clear, however, whether these differences were statistically significant (see also Winnick & Taylor, 1977).

Discussion

One can readily identify over sixty prominent articles on self-concept in African Americans published in the years since 1976. The majority of the studies include African American children as the subjects, but African American college students (e.g., Chen, 1978; Zuckerman, 1980) and adults (e.g., Lopez, 1978) and native Africans (e.g., Heaven & Nieuwoudt, 1981; Jegede & Bamgboye, 1982; Press, Burt, & Barling, 1979) were subjects in a small number of studies. The sample of investigations reviewed here represents those published articles that, for the most part, provide a report of the specific data pertaining to African American subjects, separately for the measures employed to assess self-concept.

Most of the published reports in the literature included new data; and, of these, the majority used direct self-report measures of self-concept. Earlier research had been dominated by the "experimental" paradigm of preference. But one very important limitation of those earlier techniques was their dependence upon a single response from each subject. Consequently, the analysis of the results of earlier research focused upon the frequencies, within and between samples, with which groups of subjects individually responded in one direction or the other. The revelation that the within-group pattern of responding for African American samples had so consistently been nonpreferential (Banks, 1976), therefore, left unanswered whether that pattern represented a majority of individuals acting non-preferentially, or two distinct minorities of individuals each acting preferentially in opposite directions. The quite different implications of these alternative empirical possibilities were important. And for the time-being, they were addressed at a theoretical level by an analysis of the evidence surrounding the criterion and construct validity of African American self-concept as measured primarily within the preference paradigm (Banks et al., 1979).

The use of the multiple queries that constitute most of the standardized instruments provides a more direct answer to the empirical question, "What is the pattern of responding that characterizes African American individuals under repeated sampling, as well as the group taken all together?" It appears that the pattern is anything but one of White-preference, low-esteem, or negative self-concept. When African Americans are sampled alone the resultant pattern of responding is characterized most often as one of high self-esteem or positive self-concept. When they are considered merely as a comparative sample, contrasted with Whites and others, the predominant pattern is characterized as not different. One implication of these findings, when examined against the nonpreferential patterns that dominated earlier research, is simply that some degree of sensitization is introduced by procedures that reiterate the question of racial preference and racial attitudes; and under conditions of sensitization African American subjects increase their own-group preference (McGuire et al., 1978). Another implication could be that since so many of the standardized measures focus upon a more generalized evaluation of self, the racial focus of the preference procedures yields results that are different because the judgments that subjects are making are different. With respect to their own personal self-appraisal, African American individuals hold a reasonably high estimation; however, this does not translate into the ethnocentrism of own-race prejudice that earlier theorists seemed to believe should be considered "normal."

Semaj (1980), on the other hand, has provided a very different explanation. Applying the cognitive-structural framework of Piagetian theory, his analysis suggests that the concept of racial constancy mediates the kinds of judgments elicited in racial preference research. Semaj hypothesized that preoperational children will not have developed the concept of race as a permanent attribute. Consequently, they regard any self-associations with the attributes of race as transient. Older children, he reasoned, whose thinking is characterized by racial constancy, will associate their own identity inseparably with the permanent attributes of their racial group. He hypothesized that younger children will respond randomly to queries regarding the evaluative features of racial identity, while older children will tend to a greater extent to respond systematically, in a self-preferential direction. His research confirmed his hypotheses and helps also to explain some otherwise inscrutable findings from other investigations. At the same time his analysis provides a potential interpretation for the divergence of findings in the preference and self-report paradigms.

The preference paradigms traditionally relied upon a limited iteration of queries perhaps in part because of the ages of the children under examination. That research initially was concerned with early, preschool development of personality (Clark & Clark, 1939, 1947). It required oral presentation of queries to a population presumed to be limited in attention span or comprehension. The standardized measures of self-concept and self-esteem rely more upon longer attention and upon reading comprehension, two factors that extend the range of iteration for experimental queries. Therefore, to some extent the differences observed across paradigms, and even across time (Feinman, 1980), may be the product of age differences in the samples. Future reviews should more precisely examine this interpretation.

Overall, the findings of this review are consistent with earlier discussions (Baldwin, 1979; Porter & Washington, 1979). There is, on the whole, no difference in measured self-concept between African Americans and Whites, with both groups appearing to have reasonably positive self-concepts. Furthermore, when examined through the paradigm of preference, African American self-concept continues to be manifested as neutral and nonpreferential (Banks, 1976). This should come as no surprise. By the mid-nineteen-seventies, forty years of systematic empirical research had already established the fact of African American responding. Beyond the fiction of professional beliefs (Williams & Morland, 1979), there remained little but the redundant to be said. Perhaps the only negative note that may come out of the present examination is just that: the recent past has provided so little new insight into the behavior of African American individuals, apart from the reiteration that the stereotype of African American deficiency is invalid.

From that vantage point it seems superfluous whether the decline in the use of the racial preference paradigm marks a methodological advance. While relevant, it seems rather unimportant to examine the multiplicity of problems, both theoretical and methodological, posed by the proliferation of self-report instruments in this area. Having raised our conceptual sights from the level of racial stereotypes at least to the level of empirical phenomena, it would seem the most appropriate direction for scientific research should be the illumination of the actual behavior of African American populations and the antecedent conditions that elicit it.

References

Alston, D. N., & Williams, N. (1982). Relationship between father absence and self concept of Black adolescent boys. *Journal of Negro Education, 51*(2), 134-138.

Anderson, C., & Cromwell, R. L. (1977). "Black is beautiful" and the color preferences of Afro-Americans. *Journal of Negro Education, 46,* 76-88.

Baldwin, J. A. (1979). Theory and research concerning the notion of Black self-hatred: A review and reinterpretation. *The Journal of Black Psychology 15*(2), 51-77.

Banks, W. C. (1976) White preference in Blacks: A paradigm in search of a phenomenon. *Psychological Bulletin, 83*(6), 1179-1186.

Banks, W.C., McQuater, G.V., & Ross, J.A. (1979). On the importance of white preference and the comparative difference of Blacks and others: Reply to Williams and Morland. *Psychological Bulletin, 86* (1), 33-36.

Bledsoe, J. (1981). Is self-concept a reliable predictor of economic status? *Psychological Reports, 49,* 883-886.

Bledsoe, J. C., & Dixon, C. (1980). Effects of economic disadvantage on self-concepts of urban Black high school students. *Journal of Psychology, 106,* 121-127.

Brand, E. S., Ruiz, R. A., & Padilla, A. M. (1974). Ethnic identification and preference: A review. *Psychological Bulletin, 81,* 776-783.

Chen, K., (1978). Semantic habits and attitudes of Black college students. *Psychological Reports, 42,* 963-969.

Clark, K., & Clark, M. (1939). The development of consciousness of self and the emergence of racial identification in Negro preschool children. *Journal of Social Psychology 10,* 591.

Clark, K., & Clark, M. (1947). Racial identification and preference in Negro children. In T. M. Newcombe & E. C. Hartley (Eds.), *Readings in Social Psychology.* New York: Holt.

Eato, L. E., & Lerner, R. M. (1981). Relations of physical and social environment perceptions to adolescent self-esteem. *The Journal of Genetic Psychology, 139*(1), 143-150.

Feinman, S. (1980). Trends in racial self-image of Black children: Psychological consequences of social movement. *Journal of Negro Education, 10*(3), 488-499.

Fu, V. R. (1979). A longitudinal study of the self-concepts of Euro-American, Afro-American, and Mexican-American preadolescent girls. *Child Study Journal, 9*(4), 279-288.

Gray-Little, B., & Appelbaum, M. (1979). Instrumentality in the assessment of racial differences in self-esteem. *Journal of Personality and Social Psychology, 37,* 1221-1229.

Hare, B. (1977). Black and White child self-esteem. In social science: An overview. *Journal of Negro Education, 46*(2), 141-156.

Hare, B. (1980). Self-perception and academic achievement: Variations in a desegregated setting. *American Journal of Psychiatry, 137,* 683-689.

Heaven, P. L., & Nieuwoudt, J. M. (1981). Black and White self-esteem in South Africa. *The Journal of Social Psychology, 151,* 279-280.

Hendrix, B. L. (1980). The effects of locus of control on the self-esteem of Black and White youth. *Journal of Social Psychology, 112*(2), 301-302.

Hines, P., & Berg-Cross, L. (1981). Racial differences in global self-esteem. *The Journal of Social Psychology, 113*(2), 271-281.

Horitz, J. C., Tetenbaum, T. J., & Phillips, R. H. (1981). Affective correlates in the problem-solving process. *The Journal of Psychology, 109*(2), 265-269.

Jegede, R. O. (1982). A cross sectional study of self-concept development in Nigerian adolescents. *The Journal of Psychology, 110*(2), 249-261.

Jegede, R. O., & Bamgboye, E. A. (1981). Self-concepts of young Nigerian adolescents. *Psychological Reports, 49,* 451-454.

Jegede, R. O., & Bamgboye, E. A. (1982). Psychological children as measured from their drawings. *Perceptual and Motor Skills, 54*(1), 55-58.

Jordan, T. J. (1981). Self-concepts, motivation and academic achievement of Black adolescents. *Journal of Educational Psychology, 73*(4), 509-517.

Kardiner, A., & Ovesey, L. (1951). *The mark of oppression: A psychological study of the American Negro.* New York: Norton.

King, E., & Price, F. T. (1979). Black self-concept: A new perspective. *Journal of Negro Education, 48*(2), 216-221.

Lopez, E. M., & Greenhau, J. H. (1978). Self-esteem, race, and job satisfaction. *Journal of Vocational Behavior, 13*(1), 75-83.

Madon, J. (1976). Black and White children's racial identification and preference. *Journal of Black Psychology, 3(1),* 47-58.

Mahan, J. (1976). Black and white children's racial identification and preference. *Journal of Black Psychology, 3* (1), 47-58.

McAdoo, J. L. (1979). Father child interactions patterns and self-esteem in Black, preschool children. *Young Children, 34*(2), 46-53.

McGuire, W. J., McGuire, C.V., Child, P., & Fujioka, T. (1978). Salience of ethnicity in the spontaneous self-concept as a function of one's ethnic distinctiveness in the social environment. *Journal of Personality and Social Psychology, 36,* 511-520.

Momberg, A., & Page, H. (1977). Self-esteem of colored and White scholars and students in South Africa. *Journal of Social Psychology, 102,* 179-182.

Moore, C. (1978). Racial preference and intelligence. *Journal of Psychology, 100,* 39-43.

Morland, J. K. (1962). Racial acceptance and preference of nursery school children in a southern city. *Merrill Palmer Quarterly of Behavior and Development, 8,* 271-280.

Morland, J. K. (1980). Racial attitudes of children: Perspectives on the structural-normative theory of prejudice. *Phylon, 26,* 267-275.

Nichols, N., & McKinney, A. (1977). Black and White socioeconomically disadvantaged pupils: They aren't necessarily inferior. *Journal of Negro Education, 46,* 443-449.

Nobles, W. W. (1973). Psychological research and the Black self-concept: A critical review. *Social Issues, 29,* 11-31.

Osborne, W. L., & LeGette, H. R. (1982). Sex, race, grade level, and social class differences in self-concept. *Measurement and Evaluation in Guidance, 14*(4), 195-201.

Paul, M., & Fischer, J. (1980). Correlates of self-concepts among Black early adolescents. *Journal of Youth and Adolescence, 9,* 163-173.

Porter, J., & Washington, R. (1979). Black identity and self-esteem: A review of studies of Black self-concept, 1968-1978. *Annual Review of Sociology, 5,* 53-74.

Press, L., Burt, I., & Barling, J. (1979). Racial preferences among South African White and Black preschool children. *Journal of Social Psychology, 107*(11), 125-126.

Proshansky, H., & Newton, P. (1968). The nature and meaning of Negro self-identity. In M. Deutsch, I. Katz, & A. R. Jensen (Eds.), *Social class, race and Psychological development.* New York: Holt, Rinehart & Winston.

Rohru, G. K. (1977). Racial and ethnic identification in young children. *Young Children, 32*(2), 24-33.

Rosenberg, M. (1965). *Society and the adolescent self-image.* Princeton University Press.

Rosenberg, M., & Simmons, R. G. (1972). *Black and White self-esteem: The urban school child.* Washington, DC: American Sociological Association.

Savage, J. E., Jr., Stearnes, A. D., & Friedman, P. (1979). Relationship of internal-external locus of control, self-concept, and masculinity-femininity to fear of success in Black freshmen and senior college women. *Sex Roles, 5*(3), 373-383.

Schofield, J. (1978). An exploratory study of the Draw-A-Person as a measure of racial identity. *Perceptual and Motor Skills, 46,* 311-321.

Semaj, L. (1980). The development of racial evaluation and preference: A cognitive approach. *Journal of Black Psychology, 6* (2), 59-79.

Simmons, R.& Brown, L. (1978). Self-esteem and achievement of Black and White adolescents. *Social Problems, 26* (1), 86-96.

Stephen, W. G., & Rosenfeld, D. (1978). Effects of desegregation on race relations and self-esteem. *Journal of Educational Psychology, 70,* 670-674.

Stephen, W. G., & Rosenfeld, D. (1979). Black self-rejection: Another look. *Journal of Educational Psychology, 71* (5), 708-716.

Williams-Burns, W. (1980). Self-esteem and skin color perception of advantaged Afro-American children. *Journal of Negro Education, XLIX*(4), 385-397.

Taylor, M. C., & Walsh, E. J. (1979). Explanations of Black self-esteem: Some empirical tests. *Social Psychology Quarterly, 42* (3), 242-253.

Wells, L.E, & Marwell, G. (1976). *Self-esteem: Its conceptualization and measurement.* Beverly Hills: Sage Publications.

Wilderson, I.L. (1976). Black awareness, achievement orientation, and school grades. *Journal of Black Psychology, 2*(2), 45-52.

Williams, J.E., & Morland, J.K. (1979). Comment on Banks's "White preference in Blacks: A paradigm in search of a phenomenon." *Psychological Bulletin, 86,* 28-32.

Winnick, R. H., & Taylor, J. A. (1977). Racial preference - 36 years later. *Journal of Social Psychology, 102,* 157-158.

Wylie, R. (1961). *The self-concept.* Lincoln: University of Nebraska Press.

Wylie, R. (1974). *The self-concept* (Vol. I). Lincoln: University of Nebraska Press.

Zuckerman, D. M. (1980). Self-esteem, self-concept and the life goals and sex-role attitudes of college students. *Journal of Personality, 48*(2), 149-162.

Author

W. Curtis Banks, deceased, was Professor
Department of Psychology
Howard University

The "Self" Concept in the Psychology of the African American

Adelbert H. Jenkins

In previous work (Jenkins, 1985, 1995) I have attempted to address issues relating to the psychology of African Americans from a somewhat different perspective than is typical in modern psychology. African Americans are a people that have lived through some frightful historical circumstances in the last 350 years. Although things are more comfortable for some of us now, a large percentage of African Americans remain in America's underclass living in punishing social and economic conditions. Traditional psychological theories have been used effectively to account for some of the impact that such circumstances have on African Americans. Hayes (1991) wrote from a behaviorist psychological perspective, about the environmental contingencies that shaped African American behavior during and after slavery. Pugh (1972) describes in social learning theory terms the behavior patterns of "adaptive inferiority" that African Americans developed to deal with the anxiety engendered by Whites' hostility and oppression.

However, what African American scholars have come to emphasize more and more is that African Americans have done more than just merely survive. Rather they have sustained a set of positive values and have accomplished much in the face of the "meannesses and obstacles imposed upon them," as Ralph Ellison has put it (1964, p. 39). One of the marvels of American history is the way in which a surprising number of African American people have turned adversity into some degree of personal triumph, sometimes in a publicly acknowledgeable way, often in a more modest but still real way. When the old mother in Langston Hughes' poem frankly acknowledges that "Life for me ain't been no crystal stair," she later goes on to tell her son, "But all the time . . . I'se been a-climbin' on . . . and turnin' corners. . . . And sometimes goin' in the dark. . . . Where there ain't been no light"(1926, p. 187). This idea has been summed up in a more modern idiom in a line from one of the first "rap records" of the sixties in which the speaker, meant to represent an ordinary African American reflecting on the positive sense of values and identity he has achieved in spite of the hardships imposed, notes, "I've been treated like a mule and I've turned [myself] into a human being." Even these unsung collective achievements have not gone unnoticed among African Americans and they have had their effect in buoying the spirits and the efforts of African Americans over the generations.

However, many of these accounts of African Americans' overcoming derive from novels and poetry. It seems to me that many of our traditional psychological perspectives on the situation of African American people have not been as adequate as these literary sources to the task of accounting for the quality of persistent and creative self-development under fire. Typically in psychological theory there has been a heavier emphasis on the way in which African Americans have been *re* actors to historical events rather than the ways that they have been *pro* active in those circumstances. We need to find a way of treating the positive, competence-oriented side of the human individual systematically and directly rather than merely seeing such aspects of behavior as a kind of by-product of drives and/or environmental contingencies. Furthermore, even as we attempt to redress some of these problems by identifying the trends in African cultural thinking that have shaped the African American mind, it is important that we remain sensitive the conceptual slant that any such theory might have. All theories rest on one or another assumptive philosophical base. The ones we have relied on in psychology could profitably be supplemented for the sake of psychology in general and certainly for African Americans in particular.

Humanism in Psychology

To characterize this aspect of African Americans, which I think psychology has neglected over the years, I have become convinced that some aspects of "humanistic" psychological thinking are particularly apt. Although this term is used in a variety of contexts, most basically the humanist in psychology sees the human individual as a being who, as the late Isidore Chein (1972) put it:

> . . . tries to generate circumstances that are compatible with the execution of his intentions . . . a being who seeks to shape [the] environment rather than passively permit himself or herself to be shaped by the latter, a being, in short, who insists on injecting himself into the causal process of the [surrounding] world (p. 6).

In general in psychology our emphasis on identifying the external or constitutional forces operating on us and formulating laws to explain how these forces work has taken us away from a study of processes of choice and self-direction that also are an important feature of human behavior (Rychlak, 1979). In social psychology and even in behavioral approaches to personality there is more and more recognition of what are called cognitive—indeed "mental"—processes which dramatically influence our adaptation. However, these features of human psychology are not just "intervening variables," they actually have causal power, as Chein implies. The emergence of these trends in psychological thinking comes at a time when many African American scholars are becoming more vocal about the need for a truly balanced psychological view of our situation. There is no question that African Americans have been buffeted about as if they were passive objects, but something in our human heritage, possibly supported by African cultural traditions, has nurtured the striving of African American individuals to oppose the factors arrayed to oppose us. I believe that the particular humanistic perspective that I have adopted can help us to capture this aspect of our humanity. "The tie binding all humanists," one psychologist notes, "is [the] assumption that the individual 'makes a difference' or contributes to the flow of events" (Rychlak, 1976, p. 128). Let's look more closely for a moment at the conceptual view that I am referring to here.

Intentions as Causes

We can begin by briefly considering the issue of causation. Much of psychology has been cast in a scientific world-view that sees a third-person or what one might call an "extraspective" point of view as the best way of looking at the situations in which people are involved. This is characteristic of the methods that the natural sciences have used successfully in describing and predicting nonhuman events. From this vantage point the primary job is to identify the "causes" acting *on* the individual framed in language appropriate to the postulated force. So we have had hydraulic models and information theory models and computer models of human behavior. While such paradigms have been useful to some extent, in typically mechanistic fashion they tend to view the human individual almost totally from the *observer's* point of view. They assume that the subject's behavior can be accounted for solely in terms of what happens *to* him or her.

The humanistic view requires in addition that when considering *human* behavior we take an "introspective" view of events, from within the frame of reference of the actor. It requires that we take into account how the actor sees things, because what a person intends to do, what purposes and goals s/he holds in mind— "for the sake of" which s/he strives—represent powerful motivating factors in that person's behavior as well. To include such a perspective into our explanatory framework is to add a "telic" or "teleological" perspective on human behavior. While telic concepts have been considered inappropriate to scientific analysis in the natural sciences, humanists consider them perfectly fitting as a part of the investigation of human behavior (Chein, 1972; Rychlak, 1988). So, for example, a student's intention to become a doctor, a plan about the future held in mind in the present, can be a powerful motivating factor influencing the kinds of behaviors that she carries out in the ensuing years and the ways in which she overcomes obstacles placed in her path.

In my formulation of these issues (Jenkins, 1995) I have also highlighted Robert White's (1959, 1963) discussion of "competence" motivation as a particularly intriguing example of *intentionality* as it begins to develop in early infancy and gradually takes self-conscious shape in later life. White suggests that many of the young infant's early interactions with the world are not drive dominated, but reflect its effort to reach out and have a satisfying effect on the world and, in essence, be *effective*. This tendency develops into a lifelong striving to become ever more *competent* in one's transactions with the physical and social world. This is an example of a powerfully motivating intention that governs all people's lives, including those of African American persons.

Dialectical Mentality

A second important point in this humanistic perspective is that people have the capacity to frame things in their minds in terms of the opposite or an alternative of what is given in a particular situation or what is intended by a particular social authority. It is true of course that events within a given culture can be seen to have a conventionally defined and compelling character, but we have the capacity to conceive of those events different from how they seem to be. This has been called a "dialectical" capacity in human thought (Rychlak, 1988). So, to take a very simple example, I see a bird sitting in a tree and, although the bird really is there, while looking at the bird I can imagine alternatives, some of which I may never have seen before. For example, I can imagine that bird sitting on a telephone pole at the moment or I could think of a dog sitting on that limb where the bird is now. That is to say, human mentality has the capacity to transcend conceptually the "actualities" of a given reality and imagine different views about the ways things *could* be. More to the point of our discussion here, White society told African Americans that they were inferior as human beings and incapable of accomplishment. Enforced by brute strength this had a telling effect on many African Americans. At the same time there was a trend within the thinking of African Americans, more or less strong in different people, to resist this point of view (Lester, 1968) and sustain alternative perspectives of self-worth in the face of adversity. This human capacity to envision alternatives that will allow for the expression of competence strivings has been a major factor in the psychological survival of African Americans.

Active Mentality

A third important aspect of the theoretical framework being advanced here is that the human individual is mentally active and conceptually structuring of the things going on around him or her. People actively structure and construe their reality and then respond to the world as they (actively) conceive it. This is true of human mentality from birth—from "jump street," as it were. People are not simply blank slates waiting for the imprint of experience, although of course such input is very important in determining the course of development. The point that I want to emphasize for our purposes is that the human individual does not just accept "givens" as presented but *actively* evaluates and shapes the world in terms of his or her own perspectives. Thus:

> Mentation (cognition, thought, etc.) is selective because at heart it is an arbitrary activity. Human intelligence makes this arbitrariness possible, for it always sees a myriad of possibilities in the continually arising experience of life "... mentation works within this flux of possibility and seeks to." stabilize it in conceptual regularities. . . . There is always more in sensory experience than meets the conceptual eye (Rychlak &Williams, 1983, p. 16).

To sum up, from the particular humanistic perspective that we are employing here behavior is governed partly by the subjectively derived intentions that people set from among the dialectical alternatives presented to them. We come to the world with an active mentality which gradually structures our conception of reality and it is this conception to which we respond. This point of view which emphasizes the person's contribution as a causal factor in his/her life is meant to enrich our view of the human being by supplementing the typical psychological depictions of the individual which characterize him or her as being only a respondent to stimuli. Of course thoughts and actions do partly reflect internal drive and environmental contingency factors not of our own making. But a full picture of human beings includes the view of people as also making important contributions to their experience and their destiny which are independent of such factors. With respect to the African American the point is that they have survived the objectively oppressive circumstances by calling on universal aspects of human psychological capacity. In many instances they have actively and intentionally brought to their lives conceptions of their competence that have been at variance with the judgments made of them by the majority society (Jenkins, 1995).

The Concept of "Self" and the African American

We now turn to the theme that is the topic of this paper, namely, self as it relates to African Americans. An emphasis in this paper so far has been the way in which African Americans as people have been active in their manner of addressing their life circumstances. Their behavior has not been just aimless flailing about nor merely doing rather than thinking about things. African Americans have acted with purposiveness and as much as possible with a sense of direction and identity, demonstrating a sense of self. The term self is usually used in regard to the notion of self-concept, that image that we get as we direct our gaze at what we consider to be "me" and "mine," as William James put it. This is a picture of ourselves as the object of our consideration, the sense of "what I am" (Keen, 1970). In this sense the image of the self can be seen to be complex and multifaceted. There are many components which we hold as a part of our concept of ourselves, some carried at a more conscious level than others and some held with more of a sense of pride and self-acceptance than others.

The aspect of self that I want to emphasize here is not so much this sense of self as object but rather the connotation of the term self reflected in the sense of *agency* we have, the sense not so much of *"what* I am" but rather the sense *"that* I am" (Keen, 1970). A sense of orientation or identity guides a person's choices, giving an apparent "logical thrust" to the perspectives that a person develops in the course of life (Rychlak, 1988, p. 350). A basic motivation for people is choosing and promoting the kinds of activities that they can perceive as enhancing their effectiveness and competence (White, 1959) and which will increase their sense of themselves as being competent, that is, which will increase their self-esteem.

The concept of self does not refer to an entity, something residing somewhere within the person. It is a way of talking about a process or an activity. It is a way of pointing to the fact that we can recognize ourselves as persons who inevitably take action and initiative and make decisions and choices from among the possibilities that confront us. So, self is a way of describing our ability to come to a situation full of possibilities (as most situations are) and make a choice. As we do this we shape the course of our lives. Consider as an example a person who in the course of his development finds himself affirmed more and more by his interests in athletics. He is well-coordinated and strong and is appreciated by family and friends for his abilities. But it is not only that others reward his efforts with their approval, it is also that he recognizes that the rhythm and feel of various athletic activities themselves and the sense of growing mastery of various sports are pleasurable. Many of the choices he makes are governed by the goal of enhancing the direction of this development. From the many options that there may be in the environment around him he selects those that help him coalesce a firm identity. The close friends that he develops are those who share and support his interests; he becomes most knowledgeable about things that will further a potential career in sports and tends to overlook information that would lead him down other occupational avenues; he chooses to engage in activities as much as he can that further the development of his skills, and so on. These choices are reflected in his sense of himself—a sense of orientation and identity, and are possibly reflected in a repeated thought that he holds, "I'm going to become a world class athlete someday." We could similarly return to the example of the student who has the intention of becoming a doctor. Her selection of courses, jobs, and friends may all lead her away from developing her artistic sensitivities and pursuing a career in dance, though she is well-coordinated. Her choices are also making her considerably different in some respects from many of the girls she grew up with back on the block in the low-income neighborhood that her family lives in. As they make their choices from among the options available to them, these young people are actively creating the sense of identity which is central to the sense of purpose which guides them.

While the idea that we have choices may seem to be clearer in the context of the affluent segments of Western society with its apparent options for activity, I would suggest that such a model is meaningful in a simple, so-called "primitive" society as well. Although the range of options is narrower in a stable simple society, still the males in a tribe, for example, become somewhat unique in terms of their affirmation of and identity regarding special skills that they develop. One person may be acknowledged as a superior tracker of game and another a swift runner. Their different abilities are a part of their sense of self and are acknowledged by others as such, and make their individual contributions to the overall good of the tribe. I will have more to say about this later.

One of the implications of this notion is that we bear responsibility, in one sense of the word, for what we become. Based on the intentions which we are trying to advance we choose one set of alternatives, when we could conceivably have chosen others. This idea is captured in Frost's (1964) poem "The Road Not Taken" in which a traveler, a metaphor for the self as conceived here, pauses at a point where the path in a wood diverges. Taking one of the paths, the one less worn by travel, the voyager comes to realize eventually that his choice "has made all the difference." The main point here is that all humans, as seen in the light of the choices they make, are to an important degree self-creating beings (Chein, 1972; Markos and Nurius, 1986).

I believe that African Americans have made use of this principle in promoting their survival. With a kind of native wisdom many African Americans have been about the business of self-creation. Whatever their actions may have seemed like to an observer—sharply resistant in one case, unusually passive in another---such actions were frequently ones which were guided by the intention to sustain some feeling of self-worth and dignity. (It occurs to me as an aside here that Christianity may have caught on among African Americans to an important degree because for some it served as a vehicle for sustaining a sense of self-worth which these people were trying to maintain and enhance. In other words, perhaps it was not so much that religion was experienced as *giving* slaves a sense of value that they had not felt they had, rather the message contained in Christianity e.g., "Blessed are the meek," was attractive because it supported elements of a sense of worth which they already had from their experience with one another in family contexts and personal relationships as well as from prior cultural contexts. That is, Christianity may have been seen as affirming, through the symbols of the new and alien culture, elements of self-worth that the slaves were trying to keep alive.)

The African American Family and "Self-Awareness"

Although the capacity for choice resides with the individual, cultural and environmental factors provide direction and support for such activity. The family is a crucial institution for developing and fostering self-esteem. Some research has suggested that a sense of personal self-worth is as high among African American children as it is among White (Cross, 1991). Although there has been controversy in social science literature about the quality of African American family life, it seems as if the African American family has frequently been an important support of positive direction for the self-creative process that we have been discussing here. As various writers have noted, the African American family, though strained by economic and structural pressures, has more often than is recognized adapted to provide emotional support for its children (Gutman, 1976; Hill, 1990; Stack, 1974; Wilson, 1989).

Our humanistic orientation can provide a further perspective on one way that this process works. Recall that in the view being presented here the self is seen as the individual's tendency to develop a certain pattern of choices from among the alternatives in life. To an important degree the choices made are up to the individual and not fully imposed from without. This is true of us even when we do not realize our role in our affairs. From the perspective being proposed here a goal of development is to become more conscious of the fact that life continually poses alternative possibilities for action, divergent paths as it were, within a given cultural milieu. Our choice of actions is governed to an important degree by our own sense of ourselves. To the extent that the individual does become conscious of the degree to which his or her identity is governing the choices in life, that person is said to be "self-aware" in the vocabulary of the view I am using here (Rychlak, 1988). Self-awareness refers to the (dialectic) recognition that although a person chooses to act or be *this* way in a given circumstance, s/he *could* be another way or do something else in that circumstance. I have suggested (Jenkins, 1995) that one thing that African American families have done for African American youngsters is to help them become "self-aware," that is, help them to realize that experience is full of options and that even within the relative limitations of a racist society *they* inevitably make choices that govern their lives. Thus, one can accept the label one is handed by society—that acceptance is an act, a kind of choice—and be satisfied with finding relatively limited avenues of self-enhancement. Or one could take on the difficult task of developing another more prideful image of self that offers a greater range potentially for self-development.

An example of the latter can be taken from Edwards and Polite (1992) who interviewed a sample of African American men and women, born in the generation from 1935 to 1965, who have achieved a great deal in spite of the obstacles of racism. The authors describe one successful entertainment executive whose characterization of his father's influence aptly illustrates the notion of awareness here. He noted:

> My father always said there's a difference between being poor and being po'. Poor has an "or" in it, which means you always have a choice. Po', on the other hand, means you got no mo'—no more choice. I never believed I was po' (p. 137.

Many African American families have struggled to help their children do the latter by exposing them to varying kinds of educational and cultural opportunities, as well as by giving them knowledge about positive figures from African American history that they would not ordinarily get from the mainstream society.

In addition, families promote this self-awareness by giving emotional support—"sympathy, understanding, friendship and love," as W. E. B. DuBois suggested (in Diggs, 1976), to help sustain the motivation to continue to make the choices that are positively self-enhancing and to realize the role that one plays in doing so. This is poignantly illustrated by Robert Coles (1967) in his quote from an unlettered Mississippi woman who had a sophisticated recognition of her responsibility, particularly as an African American parent living in an area and a time of special racial crisis:

> I tell the children that it's a confusing world, and they have to get used to it. You have to try to overcome it, but you can't hide it from the kids. When they ask me why colored people aren't as good as Whites, I tell them it's not that they're not as good; it's that they're not as rich. Then I tell them that they should separate being poor and being bad, and not get them mixed up. . . . I tell them, and I hope that makes them feel satisfied, so they don't dislike themselves. That's bad, not liking your own self (p. 64).

An important point here is that, to the extent that the child begins to internalize negative aspects of self as a function of what is reflected back by the racist society, the family can give the child alternative views of self and his or her racial group and offer the child conceptions of what s/he can be that allow the child to pursue self-enhancement more fruitfully. Many African American families have attempted to do this kind of thing with their children even when these families were characterized by nontraditional (in middle-class terms) structure, although of course an unfortunate number of African American families have become fragmented under the pressures of a racist society. This kind of negative impact on families has become more of an issue in the current climate of government policy toward the poor. In such circumstances the options for choice for some African American children are very narrow, through no fault of the family, leading to maladaptive adjustment. The point to be underscored here is that while strains on the underclass have always been great it is necessary to recognize the efforts that have been made for generations by many ordinary and sometimes poor African American people to nurture into life a sense of self in their children. A focus on the active strivings that have operated historically in African Americans to sustain a sense of self and self-worth can be a useful supplement to our considerations about the situation of African Americans in the United States.

Self Activity and Mental Health

Let's turn our attention more formally to issues of self and mental health for a moment. As psychologists we have to be particularly aware of the fact that the effort to sustain a healthy and realistic sense of competence has been a struggle for African Americans as it has for many other people as well. African Americans certainly have their share of mental disorder and lowered self-esteem. From one perspective mental disorder can be seen to be disharmony among important strivings within ourselves, each pressing their agendas with equal insistence. An individual thus comes to be in conflict about which program of action to pursue. For example, a young woman's striving for personal intellectual development and occupational advancement is at variance with unconscious wishes not to separate from or rise above her mother (a person of limited educational background), long the mainstay of the family, but now growing more feeble in her older years. A young man's wishes to emulate and be closer with a supportive male teacher run up against a strongly independent self-image which is a buttress against still active but unconscious dependent longings for a long absent father, feelings which have overtones of homosexual wishes for him. Another woman struggles with whether to stay, as she believes is her Christian duty, with a sometimes physically abusive husband who is the father of her children and who is for her, unconsciously, very much like her own father (whom she very much loved and feared), a man whom her mother could never leave.

Thrust into social circumstances where some action seems required, individuals under such pressure experience anxiety, depression, physical symptoms and frequently the special sense of what Frank and Frank (1991) have called "demoralization," the feeling of being "at the end of one's rope," as it were: "conscious of having failed to meet their own expectations or those of others . . . [and feeling] powerless to change the situation or themselves" (p. 35). It is as if there is a sense of confusion about what direction to go to pursue self-enhancement. Scenarios such as these are not unique to African American people. But for African Americans from day to day there is the added assault on the sense of self that coping with personal and institutional racism brings. Most African Americans are able to muster sufficient defensive and adaptive resources based on a solid enough self-esteem and sense of competence to put aside some of the negative feelings stirred by such encounters with society. These confrontations tend to lead to a continuing sense of wariness and vigilance in social situations (Block, 1981; Grier & Cobbs, 1968; Ridley, 1984) and perhaps even to an increased level of mild but persistent sadness (Crain & Weisman, 1972; Grier & Cobbs, 1968).

It seems likely, then, that when African Americans come to psychotherapy they come with an uncertainty about how fairly they will be dealt with by the mental health establishment (Block, 1981). Although coming for help in order to get themselves back on track, they also are concerned about guarding their sense of self-esteem. The literature has suggested that African Americans tend particularly to drop out of therapy early as compared to people from other ethnic groups (Sue, 1977; Sue, S., Fujino, D.C., Li-tze, H., Takeuchi, D.T., & Zane, N.W.S., 1991). Some writers suggest that it is particularly important to work actively in early phases of the treatment to engage the African American client or s/he may leave (Gibbs, 1985; Griffith & Jones, 1979).

Again the humanistic theory adopted here can make some contribution to understanding this phenomenon. This perspective, supported by research, suggests that all persons bring the tendency to evaluate affectively the situations of which they are a part. To the extent that a situation is meaningful to us it includes our "affective assessment" of it as being something we like or something we dislike. Such judgments influence whether we approach and learn more about a given situation or whether we retreat from the event. African Americans and Mexican Americans more often than Whites have been found to bring this natural human tendency forward as a mode of adapting to the world (Rychlak, 1988). This may be true of non-White ethnic minorities because feeling that they are discouraged from readily identifying with the values of the dominant society, they rely on the broadly human capacity "to order experience affectively . . . rather than according to the intellectualized discriminants of the [mainstream] verbal community," (Rychlak, 1978, p. 114). I would suggest that this process might well operate with particular force for African Americans in the early stages of psychotherapy which is usually done in a setting that has the aura of mainstream culture.

Two sets of writings speak to this issue. Jewelle Gibbs (1985), an African American psychologist, provides a good analysis of the dynamics of the beginning phase of a therapy relationship with many African American clients. She notes that African American clients in a consulting or therapeutic relationship tend to take an "interpersonal" rather than an "instrumental" orientation to the encounter initially. That is, they are especially tuned to the interaction process between therapist and client rather than to getting immediately to the task-related aspects of the problem that brought them to therapy. She suggests that one can see this in several "micro-stages" in the first two or three sessions of the treatment process. At first the client, remaining somewhat aloof, warily "sizes up" the therapist; then the client may "check out" the therapist by posing questions and challenges regarding the therapist's values or qualifications. If the therapist doesn't measure up, presumably the client will leave after one or two sessions. If satisfied with the therapist's ability to equalize status differences and show acceptance of the client's cultural concerns and style as well as the personal problems tentatively posed, the client begins to become more self-disclosing. As this interpersonal phase evolves further with the therapist's tactful guidance, the client becomes able to commit him/herself to the task-centered aspects of the treatment.

For our considerations the point of Gibbs' discussion is that the initial somewhat guarded and aloof manner that many African American clients seem to present may not just be defensiveness. From the humanistic perspective, what seems to happen in the early phase of therapy is that African American clients make active use of the broad human capacities for affective assessment that they tend to rely on more in their everyday interaction in this society. That is, having become wary about trusting American institutions and identifying with the dominant cultural style of approaching situations, African Americans make use of a native and universal mode, namely, bringing their affective evaluation capacities into play. Such responses reflect the agency of an actively assessing mentality deciding on what seems to be the best way of understanding what is going on and how to proceed consistent with principles of self-enhancement. Thus, even when African American clients seem relatively passive in the opening moments of an interpersonal phase of therapy, they are actively involved in an evaluation of the therapist. This process reflects the operation of self activity and has an impact on whether therapy will continue.

Gibbs' analysis is consistent with the way that some scholars with other approaches are coming to view the process of psychotherapy generally. From these perspectives, just as human beings generally approach life with the active effort to structure situations effectively, so the psychotherapy client can be seen to be coming to a setting where s/he is prepared to be an active part of the self-repair process. For example such a perspective on the patient's active strivings for greater effectiveness is taken quite literally in the approach to therapy called "Control-Mastery" theory, a variant of psychoanalytic psychotherapy (Sampson, 1976; Weiss & Sampson, 1986). A fundamental tenet of this view is that "a patient's most powerful unconscious motivation is to solve his problems" (Sampson, 1976, p. 257). The patient does this by gradually bringing the disturbing material into consciousness where s/he can get better control over it. From early on the client poses what these writers call unconscious "tests" during the therapy process to gauge the therapist's reaction to the nature of the problem. This ongoing assessment by the client of the therapist's response helps the client to determine whether it is safe to be more self-disclosing and bring the particular problem into the open. If the therapist shows that s/he is not threatened or overly involved with a particular theme that a client is struggling to bring to the surface, the client is more likely to continue with the work. The research program generated by this group seems to have validated this framework to some extent (Weiss & Sampson, 1986).

Again the particular implication of this approach which is relevant to our concerns is that the troubled person is portrayed as taking an active and purposeful role in trying to affect the course of therapy. This activity is quite consonant with the overall goals of therapy. As Sampson and his colleagues describe it, this effort manifests partly through a focus on the relationship between the patient and the therapist. This latter point, in particular, is consistent with what Gibbs proposes. That is, the process of testing the therapist is an effort to see whether s/he really is likely to be an ally, someone sensitive to the social as well as personal circumstances that have contributed to the client's particular situation. This testing, affectively-assessing aspect of the client's behavior is consistent with the depiction of self-processes I have been focusing on here—active agency in adaptation.

The Self in the Group

Now I would like to turn to another issue that has been highlighted in the writing of some African American psychologists. This has to do with the question of what the nature of the sense of self is for African Americans. Perhaps this emphasis on a concept of individual self is not so valid for African Americans. Wade Nobles (1973) in a well-known paper has counterposed Western notions of self with what he believes to be the conception of self that can be derived from African culture and philosophy. He posits that "The African world-view suggests that 'I am because *we* are, and because we are therefore I am.' In so emphasizing, this view makes no real distinction between self and others" (p. 23-24). He goes on to argue that in Western thought self is defined in terms of the separateness and distinctness of the individual from others in *opposition* to rather than in *apposition* to the group. He suggests that the sense of **"we"** added to the **"I"** and **"me"** contributes a sense of "extended self" which is needed to fully describe the experience of the African American.

This idea of the extended self is consistent with the recent re-awakening within the African American community of some pride in group membership. [An emerging critique of the individualized self in western society can be seen in other psychological writings as well (e.g., Cushman, 1995; Sampson, 1988).] The idea of an extended self has ramifications beyond a sense of participation in one's tribal or kinship group. Linda Myers (1988) suggests that at the broadest levels of ontology and epistemology we should see the individual as being embedded in the larger extrasensory spiritual force which generates all life and material phenomena. She argues that such notions were developed and systematized to a high degree of sophistication in ancient African and eventually Egyptian societies and have been a legacy, she asserts, to the great civilizations that came after these societies went into decline. Her Afrocentric model of psychology, which embraces an idea of the oneness of all things, draws on what she argues is an African conception originally. She notes, "As all is spirit individually and uniquely expressed; one is unified with all creation, sharing the same essence (p. 19)." This perspective is consistent with the recognition by many writers that African and African American people are quite spiritual in their orientation. Implicit also in Myers' point of view, as in mine, is a philosophically "constructionist" orientation, that is, one that emphasizes the idea that our perception and knowledge of the world is to an important degree what we make it to be and that we respond to reality as we have conceived it, not simply as it "is."

However, at more mundane levels of discourse we must find specific and viable ways of characterizing our functioning. I would still argue that the idea that the manifold things of the universe are ultimately connected does not rule out the fact that important distinctions can be made between things for certain purposes. The somewhat related perspectives presented by Myers and Nobles, though different in scope, caution us not to lose sight of the whole in our focus on the individual. But as psychologists we know that one aspect of the concept of self refers to the simple fact that all infants must learn that there is an "I" or a "me" that is separate from other literal aspects of the physical and social world that are "not me." From that base the developing child begins to make clear distinctions between other things in the object world. The establishment of that sense of self is an important developmental milestone. A basic sense of self as an individual has to be maintained for healthy psychological functioning in any culture.

What needs to be made clear for the normal individual in the more mature phases of his or her development is that a sense of "we" does not obliterate a sense of "I." To return to the example of the tribal society mentioned in an earlier section of this paper, even within the "we" there were different "mes." Some group members were men with their prescribed roles and tasks; others were women with their particular roles. Although most were competent, some were more expert at some aspects of their gender-linked role than at other aspects of it.

Let's turn to another cultural setting to illustrate this issue further. The importance of group commitment is not unique to African people. Ramirez (1983) describes the "mestizo" cultural perspectives derived from ancient Indian cultures indigenous to North and South America. He notes that in many of these cultures the individual's identity was very much tied to his or her sense of being a member and a representative of the group. "'I am the people' is a statement often made by members of North American Indian groups" (1983, p. 21). But this perspective did not preclude self-knowledge and self-development. In the mestizo tradition the individual was expected to discover his unique talents and develop them to the full through education and self-discipline. Ramirez takes as examples the Nahuatl-speaking people of the Valley of Mexico and the Mayas: "Much of education had as its major goal what the Nahuas referred to as self-admonishment, which meant to know for oneself what one should be" (p. 22). Among these groups of people:

> The ultimate goal was to develop a free will which was not subject to the passions of the individual, but which could serve the individual and his/her people. With a free will, the person could overcome a negative fate or keep from straying from the path of a positive fate. [p. 25]

Thus the non-Western tradition of putting emphasis on the group membership component of identity does not necessarily mean that a sense of individual identity or "free will" is lost. Rather we should be reminded of the fact that the self-concept is a multifaceted and dialectic entity (Jenkins, 1995, Chap. 2). People have varying vantage points on identity from which they direct their approach to the situations that confront them while at the same time they maintain a sense of personal coherence (Cross, 1991). The sense of individual identity and the sense of group identity represent two important perspectives through which people orient themselves to their experience, but these are not mutually exclusive. Nobles (1973) calls to our attention that the ethos of mainstream modern industrial society seems to emphasize development of individual identity at the expense of a sense of group identity. The African American person, however, can be seen (dialectically) as a unique individual who also takes important meaning from group definition.

The research of Gurin and Epps (1975, Chap. 14) suggests the importance of keeping both of these dimensions in view at once. Among a group of African American college students in predominantly Black Southern colleges in the sixties and early seventies Gurin and Epps identified a group of persons who had what seemed to be strong elements of both a clear sense of self and a strong sense of group identity. This group was called the "Committed Achievers." They pointed themselves toward occupations that they experienced as rewarding and which they also felt could potentially make significant contributions to the African American community, such as in law and medicine. On the other hand, another segment of this sample were found to have an equally strong sense of group commitment or "we-ness," as we are using the term here, but who did not have as solid a sense of individual personal identity. The authors labeled them the "Activists." They were less effective in college and not oriented toward moving on to more influential professional positions. Gurin and Epps's data seem to support the idea that an emphasis on the "we" component of group identity is a necessary condition for useful group contributions but it is not necessarily a replacement for a clear sense of self that guides personally meaningful choices.

What we should hope for is the development of individuals whose strong sense of self entails a readiness to choose to commit that uniqueness to the group's needs. "The social norm is a mutual . . . [premise] employed in common affirmation [i.e., by individual choice] by all members of a discernible group . . . lending them a common sense of identity and commitment in life" (Rychlak, 1988, pp. 305-306). The individual who recognizes his or her dialectic tension with the group is a more mature group member and is able to become the group's "loyal opposition" when necessary, that is, perhaps more able to resist the common affirmation when s/he sees it to be folly. From another point of view it can be from the individual's unique experience that creative directions for advancing the group's understanding of their situation can come. For example, it seems likely that Malcolm X had a clear sense of personal identity which was for a time enhanced by the continuing commitment he made to Elijah Muhammed and the Nation of Islam. But for all of his commitment to the group it was probably his own personal sense of what the group's religious ideals should be that led him to his eventual break with the group (Malcolm X, 1965).

Conclusion

What I am suggesting is that in spite of our trials as a people, which have had their crippling psychological effects, there have been consistent strengths in our functioning that have sustained us. While a sense of group identity has been important for many African Americans, I maintain that concomitantly, at the level of individual experience, African Americans have acted individually from a personal sense of agency embodied in a sense self-oriented towards creating the most effective adaptation they could for themselves and their families. The particular humanistic psychological framework presented here takes into account this "introspective" point of view toward human behavior, one which portrays the human being as an actor in the world. It characterizes the person as being capable of imagining alternative meanings in any given object or event. This enables the individual in principle to bring something different to the environmental situation. Such a perspective can supplement those in psychology that only emphasize the effects of social forces acting *on* African Americans.

From early on in their lives African Americans, like all people, reach out purposively to make effective contact with the world. We do not have to instill competence motivation in African American people; we have to provide the circumstances that enhance the inherent process which pushes toward self-development and group welfare. Our interventions must not only bear on what is done with individual African American people but, equally important, also with our social institutions so that the latter will become more supportive of the competence strivings of African Americans.

References

Block, C. G. (1981). Black Americans and the cross-cultural counseling and psychotherapy experience. In A. J. Marsella & P. B. Pederson (Eds.), *Cross-cultural counseling and psychotherapy* (pp. 177-194). Elmsford, NY: Pergamon Press.

Chein, I. (1972). *The science of behavior and the image of man.* New York: Basic Books.

Coles, R. (1967). *Children of crisis: A study of courage and fear.* New York: Dell.

Crain, R. L., & Weisman, C. S. (1972). *Discrimination, personality and achievement: A survey of northern Blacks.* New York: Seminar Press.

Cross, W. E., Jr. (1991). *Shades of Black: Diversity in African-American identity.* Philadelphia: Temple University Press.

Cushman, P. (1995). *Constructing the self, constructing America: A cultural history of psychotherapy.* Reading, MA: Addison-Wesley.

Diggs, I. (1976). DuBois and children. *Phylon, 37,* 370-399.

Edwards, A., & Polite, C. K. (1992). *Children of the dream: The psychology of Black success.* New York: Doubleday.

Ellison, R. (1964). That same pain, that same pleasure: An interview. In R. Ellison, *Shadow and act*. New York: Signet Books.

Frank, J. D., & Frank, J. B. (1991). *Persuasion and healing: A comparative study of psychotherapy* (3rd ed.). Baltimore, MD: Johns Hopkins University Press.

Frost, R. (1964). The road not taken. In *Complete poems of Robert Frost*. New York: Holt.

Gibbs, J. T. (1985). Establishing a treatment relationship with Black clients: Interpersonal vs. instrumental strategies. *Advances in clinical social work* (pp. 184-195). Silver Spring, MD: National Association of Social Workers, Inc.

Grier, W. H., & Cobbs, P. M. (1968). *Black rage*. New York: Basic Books.

Griffith, M. S., & Jones, E. E. (1979). Race and psychotherapy: Changing perspectives. In J. H. Masserman (Ed.), *Current psychiatric therapies* (Vol. 18, pp. 225-235). New York: Grune & Stratton.

Gurin, P., & Epps, E. G. (1975). *Black consciousness, identity and achievement*. New York: Wiley.

Gutman, H. G. (1976). *The Black family in slavery and freedom, 1750-1925*. New York: Harper.

Hayes, W. A. (1991). Radical Black behaviorism. In R. L. Jones (Ed.), *Black psychology* (3rd ed., pp. 65-78). Berkeley, CA: Cobb & Henry.

Hill, R. B. (1990). Research on the African American family: A holistic perspective. *Assessment of the Status of African Americans*. Boston, MA: William Monroe Trotter Institute, University of Massachusetts-Boston.

Hughes, L. (1926). Mother to son. In *Selected poems of Langston Hughes*. New York: Alfred A. Knopf.

Jenkins, A. H. (1985). Attending to self activity in the Afro-American client. *Psychotherapy, 22*, 336-341.

Jenkins, A. H. (1995). *Psychology and African Americans: A humanistic approach* (2nd ed.). Needham Heights, MA: Allyn & Bacon.

Keen, E. (1970). *The three faces of being: Toward an existential clinical psychology*. New York: Appleton-Century-Crofts.

Lester, J. (1968). *Look out Whitey! Black power's gon' get your mama!* New York: Grove.

Malcolm X (1965). *The autobiography of Malcolm X*. New York: Grove.

Markus, H., & Nurius, P. (1986). Possible selves. *American Psychologist, 41*, 954-969.

Myers, L. J. (1988). *Understanding an Afrocentric world view: Introduction to an optimal psychology*. Dubuque, IA: Kendall/Hunt.

Nobles, W. W. (1973). Psychological research and Black self-concept: A critical review. *Journal of Social Issues, 29*, 11-31.

Pugh, R. W. (1972). *Psychology and the Black experience*. Monterey, CA: Brooks/Cole.

Ramirez, M. (1983). *Psychology of the Americas: Mestizo perspectives on personality and mental health.* Elmsford, NY: Pergamon.

Ridley, C. R. (1984). Clinical treatment of the non-disclosing Black client: A therapeutic paradox. *American Psychologist, 39,* 1234-1244.

Rychlak, J. F. (1976). Is a concept of "self" necessary in psychological theory, and if so why? A humanistic perspective. In A. Wandersman, P. J. Poppen, & D. F. Ricks (Eds.), *Humanism and behaviorism: Dialogue and growth* (pp. 121-143). Elmsford, NY: Pergamon Press.

Rychlak, J. F. (1978). The stream of consciousness: Implications for a humanistic psychological theory. In K. S. Pope & J. L. Singer (Eds.), *The stream of consciousness: Scientific investigations into the flow of human experience* (pp. 91-116). New York: Plenum.

Rychlak, J. F. (1979). *Discovering free will and personal responsibility.* New York: Oxford University Press.

Rychlak, J. F. (1988). *The psychology of rigorous humanism* (2nd ed.). New York: New York University Press.

Rychlak, J. F., & Williams, R. N. (1983). *Dialectical human reasoning: Theoretical justification and supporting evidence drawn from the method of triassociation.* Manuscript submitted for publication.

Sampson, E.E. (1988). The debate on individualism: Indigenous psychologies of the individual and their role in personal and societal functioning. *American Psychologist, 43,* 15-22.

Sampson, H. (1976). A critique of certain traditional concepts in the psychoanalytic theory of therapy. *Bulletin of the Menninger Clinic, 40,* 255-262.

Stack, C. (1974). *All our kin.* New York: Harper.

Sue, S. (1977). Community mental health services to minority groups: Some optimism, some pessimism. *American Psychologist, 32,* 616-624.

Sue, S., Fujine, D. C., Li-tze, H., Takeuchi, D.T., & Zane, N. W. S. (1991). Community mental health services for ethnic minority groups: A test of the cultural responsiveness hypothesis. *Journal of Consulting and Clinical Psychology, 59,* 533-540.

Weiss, J., & Sampson, H. (1986). The psychoana lytic process: Theory, clinical observation, and empirical research. New York: Guilford.

White, R. W. (1959). Motivation reconsidered: The concept of competence. *Psychological Review, 66,* 297-333.

White, R.W. (1963). Ego and reality in psychoanalyic theory. *Psychological Issues, 3* (Serial no. 11).

Wilson, M. N. (1989). Child development in the context of the Black extended family. *American Psychologist, 44,* 380-385.

Author

Adelbert H. Jenkins
New York University
Psychology Clinic
715 Broadway
New York, NY 10003
Telephone: (212) 998-7937
Fax: (212) 995-4687E
E-mail:jenkins@px.psych.nyu.edu

Competency and Legitimacy as Organizing Dimensions of the Black Self-Concept

S. M. Khatib and Carolyn B. Murray

Concepts and *values* are the basic components of a society's *culture* (Bowers, 1984; Kuhn, 1963); they enable us to organize our world and make judgments about it. Together they serve to guide behavior along patterns which are more or less predictable. Shared versions of reality—as these are generated by concepts—and shared concerns over means and goals—as these are generated by values—enable us to more or less accurately predict how others will act in a given situation (Fiske & Linville, 1980). This knowledge of how others are expected to behave makes us attempt to realize these expectancies by acting in ways expected of us (Murray & Jackson, 1993). Such reciprocity of expectations—generated by the process of "role-taking"—insures some minimal amount of predictability or non-randomness in human behavior (Darley & Fazio, 1980; Mead, 1934). It thus leads to what we call *social organization.*

Despite occasional entrophic (disorganized) social situations (e.g., "riots"), evidence of patterned behavior and predictability abound in the social universe. Recognizing that such a state of predictability exists does not, however, explain *why* it exists, why mankind prefers this state over others. Why does it appear "natural" for us to avoid situations where we feel that we have "no control" over what may occur; i.e., where predictability is low? Why is that a totalitarian state, where social organization and social control are perhaps at a maximum, is often viewed as preferable to a democratic one, where predictability and control are relatively minimal?

Such preference for predictability appears to stem largely from our need to maintain some stable conception of our own place in the universe; i.e., we use the actions of other people as social coordinates from which we are able to provide self-definitions (Fazio, 1979; Festinger, 1954; Tajfel, 1982; Suls & Miller, 1977; Wilder, 1986). Only by knowing how others will behave can we be sure of our own behavior and, by extension, of our self-conceptions (Tajfel, 1982). Thus, it follows that the type of social organization within which persons find themselves is of paramount importance in determining the nature of their self-conceptions (Wilder, 1986).

In discussing these issues below, the terms *"competency"* and *"legitimacy"* are employed as isomorphic to the terms *"information"* and *"energy."* The selection of the terms *competency* and *legitimacy* is based on the congruence of the former with established usage in the behavioral science field and on the direct relevancy of the latter to the lives and experiences of peoples of African descent. The two concepts are discussed more fully in the paragraphs below in the general context of psychological self-conception.

The Nature of the Self-Concept

The *self-concept* can be conceived of in a literal fashion: the conception a person has of him or herself (Markus & Sentis, 1982; Rogers, Kuiper, & Kirker, 1977; Sneed & Murray, 1993;). A concept is a belief and beliefs are among the fundamental elements of psychological systems.

It is useful to view this belief collection as consisting of two distinct clusters, or "subsystems." One set of beliefs concerns the self as an actor or subject, while the other concerns the self as acted upon or as an object. The beliefs which are characteristic of the former involve feelings of *competency*, or personal adequacy in these actions. The latter involve feelings of *legitimacy*, or the social worth which is bestowed upon the actor by some group of observers.

This dual conception of the self-system bears an obvious relationship to the *"I/Me"* conception formulated by Mead (1934) and to the *"I/Thou"* conception of Buber (1957). Other related formulations include William James' (1968) distinction between the *self as a knower* (as a competency-assessing animal) versus the *self as known* (as an object of legitimation or worth). More generally, the formulation follows the principle of "complementarity" which physicists employ to describe the dual conception of the nature of light (as both a *wave* and a *particle* [Bohr, 1987]).

Social Behavior and the Development of Competence

Robert White (1959) first called modern attention to the psychological significance of competency. He defines competence as "an organism's capacity to interact effectively with its environment." Some organisms, White maintains, are at birth equipped to deal with those parts of the environment which must be (1) recognized as dangerous and defended against; (2) identified as safe and explored; and (3) identified as transformable into material for self-maintenance and growth. Mankind, however, is not one of the animals so endowed; in their case, virtually everything has to be learned. Hence, the importance of educational institutions. Even before entry into such institutions, however, a human organism undergoes much competency-related learning (Bandura, 1982).

It is from this line of thought that Whites stresses the importance of competency. He proposes that activity, manipulation, and exploration are "all pretty much of a piece of the infant" and that they be considered together as aspects of competence. He further suggests that one general motivation principle lies behind them. This principle he calls *"effectance"*—effectance because its most characteristic feature is seen in the production of effects upon the environment. The experience concomitant with these changes in the environment he defines as the feelings of efficacy.

Social Organization: Product and Context of Human Competence

In addition to obvious demonstrations of competency in controlling the physical environment, mankind has had a dramatic effect on the social environment—i.e., structuring of social relationships. This reveals itself in the high degree of behavioral predictability characterizing human behavior (Bowers, 1984; Sagar & Schofield, 1980). The question arises "where does this predictability in social relations originate?" "How do we know how to act in relation to other people?"

While there are numerous factors contributing to the creation of such predictability, one of the most important involves the use of biological (perceptible) differences among people as principles of social organization (Kahneman & Tversky 1972, 1973; Taylor & Falcone, 1982; Wilder, 1986). The following quotation from Talcott Parsons and Edward Shils (1951) is relevant:

> In all societies the ascriptive criteria of sex and age . . . limit the eligibilities for participation in different roles, and hence membership in collectivities. Besides these, the ascription of roles on the basis of the criteria of biological relationship and territorial location of residence plays some significant part in all societies, by virtue of the fact that all have kinship units and kinship units are units of residence . . . the range of allocative results determined by these ascriptive criteria varies enormously in different societies. The maximum application of the "hereditary principle" in, for example, an Australian tribe or the Indian caste system—represents one extreme variation in this respect. *Our own society is considerably removed in the opposite direction* (p. 207).

One might argue, however, that "our own society" is not "considerably removed" from an Indian-like caste system, and it is *race* (which is equivalent to the term "kinship" in this quotation) which is the organizing principle making this so (Ogbu, 1988). The degree to which American society is "considerably removed" from the application of a hereditary principle is, of course, a matter of judgment. And, while there are differences between the Indian caste system and American racial segregation, whether the investigator chooses to heighten the similarities or the differences represents a conscious or unconscious value judgment.

In any case, as indicated in the quotation above, what principles of social organization organize are *roles*—those expected patterns of behavior which create predictability in social relations. While some roles, particularly those relating to occupations, are often *achieved* in American society, many are *ascribed*. This ascription is done, as the quotation above suggests, on the basis of the biological characteristics of *age*, *sex*, and *race*. Because these characteristics are associated with certain roles they enable every individual to predict the pattern of behavior associated with people who are distinguishable by these biological traits. The knowledge that is gained from the mere appearance of a person thus serves to reduce behavioral uncertainty (Hamilton, 1979; Sagar & Schofield, 1980). People act pretty much in accord with how they perceive they are expected to act, and such actions serve to reinforce these expectations in the minds of the observers (Darley & Fazio, 1980; Jussim, 1994; Murray & Jackson, 1982/83; Sneed & Murray, 1993). Statistically speaking, a tremendous amount of *variance* is accounted for by the biological characteristics of individuals. (It is thus hardly surprising that the application of any socially relevant measurement instrument yields differences between men and women and between Whites and Blacks.)

In American society, an individual is able to place other individuals in a kind of three-dimensional social space (age, sex, and race); they are thus able not only to establish the identities of others, but, by so doing, establish their own self-conception. Inkeles (1966) notes:

> It is only by knowing "who he is—that is by knowing his status and role—that (man) discriminates between the massive flow of stimuli from others and selects only those signals to which he must pay attention and perhaps respond, according to his position in the system of interaction . . . a person not only learns who or what he is, but he also acquires a set of attitudes and feelings about himself, especially with reference to that aspect of the self, which is part of his social identity (p. 105). Newspaper stories, for example, tend to identify actors by their age, sex, and race. By so doing, they communicate a high amount of information (reduce a lot of uncertainty) in limited space.

In any case, what is worth emphasizing here is that we have organized our system of social interactions and, as will be specified in more detail below, this organization is both a consequence of and a contributor to psychological feelings of personal competency (Bandura, 1982). To understand how and why this is so, it is necessary to specify what societal effects emerge from a social organization based on age, sex, and race. As suggested in the section below, a direct effect is the creation of distinct patterns of communication (Bowers, 1984); an indirect and related effect is the creation of distinct cultures (Hodge, Struckmann, & Trost, 1975).

Communication, Race and Culture

A direct social consequence of the ascription of people to roles has been the creation of distinct patterns of communication associated with these roles. The process of communication, which involves the transmission of concepts and values, is necessary if people are to make the decisions necessary for their daily existence. We do not merely act; we act on the basis of information. Individuals sharing the same roles, because they share common experiences, exchange messages which are distinctive to them. The messages are "distinctive" in the sense that they concern concepts and values which are more important to these same role performers than to others. Women, for example, have their primary role defined for them in terms of their relationship to their family (Hyde, 1991). From these expectations, women have developed a communication pattern (involving concepts and values) from which men (by choice or habit) are largely excluded. The same phenomenon occurs with respect to racial classification.

The assignment of roles on the basis of biological characteristics thus leads not only to role-specific types of communication patterns but, necessarily in American society, to patterns which are biologically specific; i.e., communication networks are developed which are specific to African Americans as opposed to Whites, men as opposed to women, and old people as opposed to young. This is particularly true with respect to the African American-White dimension where patterns of residential segregation have also served to organize communication in race-specific directions (Hodge, et al., 1975).

To the extent that this communication involves the transmission of shared experiences generated from the sharing of role ascriptions, there develops, in each case, a distinct *culture* (Bowers, 1984). A *culture*, it will be recalled, is defined as *a set of concepts and values common to a specified group of people*. Thus, role ascriptions and communication processes create distinct cultures which are associated with the points of the three-dimensional social space; i.e., there is a " *Black* " as opposed to "*White*" culture, a "*female*" as opposed to "*male culture*," and a "*youth*" as opposed to "*elder*" culture. Such cultures are inevitable occurrences generated by communication processes.

The formation of distinct cultures through distinctive communication patterns also often results in unique perceptions of reality, or what the Germans term *Weltanschauungs*. This, together with the fact that social rewards are distributed unequally with respect to the biologically-based role ascription (men make more money than women, and Whites more than African Americans) accounts for the inherent tensions in the social system. That is to say, people representing the cultures may *perceive* (categorize reality) differently and, on the basis of these perceptions, act differently (Billig & Tajfel, 1973; Brewer & Kramer, 1985). The terms "*racial tension*," "*battle between the sexes*," and "*generation gap*" describe the conflict generated from the inherent tension in those societies which are organized around the principles of age, sex, and race.

It is thus important to emphasize the relevance of culture in sustaining not only role expectations but also *social conflict* (Bonacich, 1984). What is significant in this respect is the extent to which the culture of the White, middle-age male operates as a general societal norm within which all behavior is defined, assessed, and explained (Clark [Khatib], McGee, Nobles, & Akbar, 1976).

The following quotation from Goffman (1963) is relevant and can be generalized to support the above arguments:

> . . . in an important sense there is only one complete unblushing male in America: a young, married, White, urban, northern, heterosexual, Protestant father of college education, fully employed, of good complexion, weight, and height, and a recent record in sports. Every American male tends to look out upon the world from this perspective, this constituting one sense in which one can speak of a common value system in America. . . (p. 128).

In a word, such an American is *competent*. The culture associated with this model contains the values and concepts which, more than any other, are used to define, assess, and account for the behavior of all other Americans (Clark [Khatib] et al., 1976). This is not to say that Goffman's model is the only one representing societal concepts and values; we can appreciate Inkeles' (1966) observation that "every model of competence is . . . specific to some culture" (p. 282). The point is that Goffman's model is the *dominant* one—the one presented most frequently in our educational institutions and institutions of mass communication. The model represents what Hoetink (1967/1971) terms the *"somatic norm image"* of American society.

This brings us, finally, back to the problem of African American feelings of incompetency. In discussing the effects of this "one-dimensional" (White male) culture on feelings of nonwhite incompetency, it is fruitful to focus attention on the two major components of culture: *concepts* and *values*.

The Role of Concepts in Generating Feelings of Incompetency

Concepts, as indicated previously, are the labels we use to classify or codify reality. They are man-made abstractions, used in the interpretation and control of our physical and social environment. The ultimate source of concepts is the experience of those who create them. It is well known, for example, that native Alaskans (Eskimos) have several concepts for what we know as *"snow."* The reason for this is that they need several concepts to exercise control over (i.e., create predictability in) their environment in relation to snow (Whorf, 1956).

A *concept*, then is a convenient *label*—a label whose usefulness can be assessed only in relationship to the environment in which it occurs. Most Americans, for example, have no need for more than one or two concepts relating to "snow." (Note, however, that the same is not true for "corn"). Whether this is important ("relevant") or not depends on how fundamental the phenomena ("corn") is to one's self-conception.

The point of this should perhaps be made more explicit: *concepts which are not descriptive of, or relevant to, the environment shared by a group of people may not be learned and employed as easily as concepts which are.* To the extent that the process of education is nationally uniform in terms of communication content (e.g., textbooks), and to the extent that the transmission of concepts (and values—cf. below) is integral to all social communication, it is clear that the concepts transmitted are likely to be related to some restricted societal culture (Bowers, 1984). Educators recognize, for example, that the "Dick and Jane" reading series is totally alien to the life experiences of many urban youngsters. What is often not yet appreciated, however, is that the feelings of incompetency characterizing many African Americans may be directly related to experiences of failure generated from their being tested with these "foreign" concepts (Medina & Neill, 1988; Montague, 1975).

The Role of Values in Generating Feelings of Incompetency

Values (the second major component of culture) serve as the behavioral means and goals of a group of people (Rokeach, 1969). This distinction between means and goals is important because many school systems tend to stress common goals ("freedom," "security") but a uniqueness of means ("politeness," "friendliness") to achieve them. People representing different points in the three-dimensional social space are expected to aspire to common goals, but are often expected to employ different means for reaching these.

However, to the extent that specific modes of behavior ("*means*") are highly correlated with (or lead to) success in the pursuit of specific goals ("*ends*"), it is clear that those individuals whose repertoire of reinforced modes are restricted will fail in the pursuit of these goals (Ogbu, 1981, 1988).

Summary and General Comments on African American Feelings of Incompetency

The preceding paragraphs have attempted to describe some of the issues related to African American feelings of incompetency, as these are derived from the operation of specific organizing principles in society. Primary emphasis was placed on the desire to exercise control or mastery over our environment. This desire led to the organization of society around principles generated from biological characteristics: age, sex, and race. These principles maintain society by ascribing individuals to specific roles (expecting certain patterns of behavior from them). It was noted also that the organization of society around biologically-based principles creates and sustains distinct communication patterns—patterns which, in turn, create and reinforce distinct cultures (sets of concepts and values). Conflict is generated when individuals representing the various cultures are differentially rewarded in terms of the allocation of societal resources (Murray & Smith, 1995). Finally, to the extent that the concepts and values associated with the dominant culture are employed in the definition, evaluation, and assessment of behavior unique to particular cultures—to that extent nonwhite feelings of incompetency are generated.

Social Behavior and the Development of Legitimacy

The conception of the self-system presented here is, it will be recalled, a dual one—one which stresses the importance of both the *self as an actor*, and the *self as an object*. Accordingly, we have conceptualized the self concept as consisting of two sets of beliefs: one set dealing with the belief that one's actions are, have been, and will be efficacious or competent, and the other dealing with the belief that one's definition and conception by others is a worthy one. Sherif (1968) offers the following definition of the self-concept: Self is developmental formation in the psychological makeup of the individual, consisting of interrelated attitudes that the individual has acquired in relation to his own body and its parts, to his capacities, and to objects, persons, family groups, social values, goals, and institutions, which define and regulate his relatedness to them in concrete situations and activities (p. 157). The present section of this paper concerns that aspect of the self-concept which is determined by the "definition and regulation" of a person's relatedness. The generic term we have used is *legitimacy*.

The Concept of Legitimacy

While an integral part to scientific theorizing in the disciplines of sociology (Weber, 1964), political science (Easton, 1969), economics (Boulding, 1956a), and anthropology (Swartz, 1966), the concept of legitimacy has commanded only limited attention in psychology (Holander & Julian, 1971; Kelman, 1970). As used here, in a social-psychological sense, beliefs of legitimacy are related to the extent that a person feels that he/she is (a) *recognized* and (b) *respected* (Clark [Khatib, 1971).

The importance of recognition (being attended to) should not be underestimated, particularly as it relates to nonwhite individuals. By not recognizing people we decrease their social worth or significance, and this is precisely what, according to many African Americans, has been done (Clark [Khatib] et al., 1976).

While the process of recognition may be *necessary* for legitimation to occur, it is not, however, *sufficient*. The sufficient condition is the communication of respect. Respect or feelings of being respected involve several components: (a) the extent to which one feels that others share or appreciate his/her definitions of reality; (b) the extent to which one feels that one's behavior is assessed fairly (Katz, 1968), and (c) the extent to which one believes that one's achievements (manifestations of competency) are, in general, attributable to oneself, but one's failures (manifestations of incompetency) are not (Katz, 1967; Brown & Rogers, 1991).

The paragraphs below will focus in more detail on these components of legitimacy.

Nonrecognition and Its Effects

In an earlier paragraph we paraphrased a comment by Martin Buber (1957) in connection with legitimation. It is worthwhile to present, in this context, the complete quotation:

> Man wishes to be confirmed in his being by man, and wishes to have a presence in the being of the other. The human person needs confirmation, because man as man needs it. An animal does not need to be confirmed, for it is what it is, unquestionably. It is different with man: sent forth from the natural domain of species into the hazard of the solitary category, surrounded by the air of a chaos which came into being with him, secretly and bashfully he watches for a Yes which allows him to be and which can come to him only from one human person to another (p. 104).

In other words, and in the words of the "Symbolic Interactionalists" (Blumer, 1969; Mead, 1934), the concept of self develops through interaction with others. When this interaction is thwarted, both interactants become, in fact, less human. In summarizing Mead's thinking along these lines, Paul Pfuetze (1961) notes:

> Self-realization requires self-assertion plus recognition and reflected appraisal by others in order to possess those values and qualities which we associated with persons. "Being Known" and, especially, knowing that one is known, is constitutive of self-hood. One has to find one's self in his individual creation as appreciated by others (p. 8).

The nonrecognition of Blacks in America is well-known, if not systematically studied. African American athletes, for example, are still not recognized as much as their achievements would recommend (Blum, 1994; Edwards, 1969, 1982; Rashad, 1995; Young, 1963). African American music, jazz in particular, has only recently become accepted as an American art form, despite long and widespread acceptance in other parts of the world (Harrison, 1978). The entire issue of the role of the African American man in American history is only now beginning to be recognized (Adams, 1995; Bennett, 1968; Van Sertima, 1983).

Themes from African American creative writing have dealt extensively with this issue of nonrecognition or de-legitimation. James Baldwin, for example, claims that *Nobody Knows My Name* (1961). Ralph Ellison speaks of an *Invisible Man* (1952), and African American children talk about *The Me Nobody Knows* (Joseph, 1969).

Considering the more symbolic manifestations of African American de-legitimation, the presence of African Americans in the mass media is a relatively recent occurrence. While there may appear to be significant numbers of African Americans on television, this may be because of the vacuum which is being filled (Greenberg, 1969; Clark [Khatib], 1969). What direct effects this lack of African American recognition in societal institutions has at the psychological level is a question for systematic research. The effects of social isolation (a kind of nonrecognition) have been investigated and are well-known: *hysteria* (White & Watt, 1981), *undirected thinking* (Zuckerman, Persky, & Link, 1968), *lack of sensitivity* (Cole, Machir, Altmern, Haythorn, & Wagner, 1967), *insomnia* and *anxiety* (Gunderson, 1968; Korchin, 1976), and hallucination (Ziskind, 1967). It is distinctly possible that most of the "Black Pathologies" known are the results of general nonrecognition or de-legitimation (Jenkins, 1982).

In the context of the present discussion, the most important effect of social isolation or nonrecognition is a loss of identity or a failure to acquire an adequate sense of identity. The need to be recognized seems so fundamental that its absence is perhaps a sufficient condition for the development of negative self-conceptions. For as Berlinger (1968) suggests, "Human beings cannot exist without distinct points of reference, be these memories of past experience or the distinct states of present social fields of interaction" (p. 98).

The Definition of Social Behavior

Without going into philosophical detail, it is worth noting that the meaning of objects and events is to a large extent a function of the observer. That is, *meanings are in people*; they are not a part of the event or object being perceived (Atkinson, Atkinson, Smith, & Bem, 1990). The same object may generate different meanings within the same group of people (Osgood, Suci, & Tannenbream, 1971).

The lack of commonality in the meaning attached to objects and events has its origins in the different human experiences and behavioral reinforcement patterns characterizing individuals and groups. Hence, it is not surprising that African Americans and Whites often differ in terms of the meaning attached to their definitions of objects and events. One might suspect, in fact, that many of the racial differences reported in the social and educational literature are due to the differences in meanings attached to various objects and events. The importance of this was recently made manifest to the authors when African American respondents to a self-administered questionnaire asked quite explicitly and innocently: "Do we use *their* (i.e., White) or *our* (i.e., African American) definitions in answering these questions?"

That many African Americans recognize differences between themselves and Whites in social perception and definitions of reality is suggested by the term "*put on.*" The term has its origins in plantation life where slaves often "*put on*" a demeanor conducive to safe interaction with the slave master. Its contemporary usage is broader: it refers to all instances where African Americans consciously adopt the definition of reality held by Whites—definitions which are, in such instances, not necessarily held by African Americans themselves.

Returning to a consideration of these issues in relation to the "respect" aspect of legitimation—people have their self-conceptions confirmed or legitimated to the extent that others share or at least appreciate their own definitions of reality.

The Evaluation of Behavior

Individuals require not only some confirmation or recognition of their existence and support for their definitions of reality, they also need "feedback" about the nature of their behavior. This is because human behavior is "goal-directed" and the only way one is able to "steer" him or herself in pursuit of these goals is by receiving some information about one's activity. A major goal directing individual behavior is the maintenance of the self-concept. In this sense, human beings are no different from other systems in their need to generate and maintain a satisfactory "image" (Boulding, 1956a).

In developing a healthier self-concept for people it is thus important that (a) evaluative communication occur and (b) that they not be restricted to either positive or negative feedback. With respect to (a) the tendency to assess seems to be a strong element in the process of ascribing meaning itself (Osgood, et al., 1971). With respect to (b) feedback restriction: people who receive only positive feedback cannot "correct" themselves, whereas those who receive only negative feedback cannot "maintain" themselves. Without some negative feedback, or "punishment," a person will continue a given pattern of behavior—a pattern which may not be in his/her best interest. The person will not know whether he/she is approaching the desired goals or moving away from them. Since a self-conception depends on being able to view one's behavior in relation to some other object or event, a total absence of negative feedback would preclude the very development of a self-conception. As indicated earlier, a self is a dynamic process, a system of interaction. As such, feedback is required for continued elaboration of the system. A self-system receives this through a process of communication which is characterized by a minimal amount of negative evaluations (Murray & Jackson, 1989).

The Explanation of Behavior

To the extent that a person is able to "identify with" or "place himself or herself in the shoes of" another, causality is likely to be attributed in the same manner as the observer would to him or herself (Gilbert & Jones, 1986; Gould & Sigall, 1977; Johnson, Jemmott, & Pettigrew, 1984; Jones & Nisbett, 1971). To the extent that this occurs, the observer maintains the dignity of the individual, or in the terminology preferred here, attributes *respect* to the individual.

The "truth" or "reality" of the situation is irrelevant. What is important is whether or not a person can account for another's behavior with the same degree of respect that she/he would do for their own. Thus, we interpret this attribution as fundamentally one of *self-esteem maintenance* (Zuckerman, 1979); i.e., people maintain self-esteem by inputting blame to their environment for their failures and praise to themselves for success (Baumgardner, Heppner, & Arkin, 1986; O'Malley & Becker, 1984). This being the case, another person's self-esteem can be maintained when observers make the same kind of attribution of the actor's behavior as the actor would make.

It is this process which communicates "respect" or " *legitimacy*" to the actor. And it is this which the American White culture, in general, and the educational institution in particular, have been unwilling to provide for members of the African American culture (Park & Rothbart, 1982; Wilder, 1986).

It should be carefully noted that the reason White Americans are sources for African American legitimation has little to do with the fact that they are White, *per se*; the sources are needed because it is the White culture which guides the operation of the dominant societal institutions (Clark [Khatib], 1971). Conversely, the reason why African Americans cannot rely upon other African Americans for legitimation is because it is not the African American culture which is manifested in dominant societal institutions. In short, the sources of legitimation are based not on skin color but on *competence* (at one level) and *power* (at a more fundamental level). Those who display competence and power—particularly the power to define social reality—become, for better or worse, sources of legitimation (recognition and respect [Myers, 1991]).

Ridicule: The Communication of De-legitimation

Just as social isolation defines the denial of recognition, so does *ridicule* define the denial of respect. The aspect of ridicule which is of relevance here involves the personal attribution of incompetency across invariant environmental conditions. Generally speaking, this attribution is made of people sharing a particular point in the three-dimensional social space discussed earlier (cf. p. 7) and is distributed by the mass media. Often, also, it involves people who possess a socially defined deformity or "*stigma*" (Goffman, 1963). Thus, a common first impulse upon seeing a midget, or an extremely fat person, is to laugh. The dominant culture has taught us, on the basis of physical appearance alone, whether or not a person should be taken "seriously." We have institutionalized the behavior (in the form of a circus) to insure behavioral predictability in such situations.

The social function (not necessarily intent) of ridicule is well-known; it is to control people and thereby create behavioral predictability (Duncan, 1962; Klapp, 1962; Stephenson, 1951). This function of ridicule is related to that of humor in general. Kolaja (1953) notes, in reference to cartoons, that:

> . . . humor functions as a control by ridiculing behavior which deviates from dominant social values and norms and the conflict function of humor consists of ridiculing the opponent, strengthening in such a way the morale of the (individual's) own group (p. 71).

The quotation above also hints at the psychological function of humor. It is this psychological function which has direct relevance to the legitimation component of the self-concept; i.e., one important aspect of the process of African American legitimation has historically involved the ridicule of African American behavior (e.g., "Little Black Sambo" nursery stories, "The Jeffersons" and "Different Strokes" and "Martin" television programs, etc.). Such ridicule has not only served the sociological function of controlling African American behavior, but has frequently served a psychological function of increasing White self-identity and self-esteem at African American expense (Murray & Smith, 1995; Staples & Jones, 1985).

This "superiority" theory of humor is old, articulated by both Hobbes and Rousseau. Hobbes, in fact, described laughter as a kind of "sudden glory" which one obtains through contemplating the infirmity of others. We may laugh at our own follies provided that they are in the past and we are conscious of having surmounted them; i.e., our past selves take the place of other people in order to inflate our present self-esteem. However, in a very real sense, our "past selves" are more frequently represented by "present people" consisting of either "stigmatized" individuals or those clustered in specific points in the three-dimensional social space referred to earlier. That is to say, African Americans are often viewed as children or as individuals in primitive stages of development (Jensen, 1969; 1980); they thus serve as (the White individual's) "past self"—particularly the past self which was incompetent.

Conclusion

This paper has attempted to place discussions concerning the African American "self-concept" in a more comprehensive theoretical framework with the hope that subsequent research on the topic will generate more systematic and meaningful results. Two major dimensions of the self were identified as *"competency"* and *"legitimacy."* These were viewed as opposite sides of the same coin, in much the same way as light is viewed as both a particle and a wave. Considerable attention was paid to the "legitimacy" aspect of the African American self, since this has revealed itself as a dominant theme in African American creative writing and has not received as much attention as the competency component. Potential research questions concerning the legitimacy aspect of the African American self-concept might address such questions as:

1. What are the major *sources* for African American legitimation?

2. What are the *conditions* under which legitimation is transferred from one source to another?

3. How might we *measure* the concept of legitimacy?

4. What are the specific effects of a lack of legitimation on an individual and/or group of individuals?

5. What role does the mass media play in the communication of legitimacy?

6. How does the degree of legitimacy relate to the production of social conflict?

7. What is the relationship between feelings of legitimacy and feelings of competency?

These are just some of the questions which need to be addressed by those psychologists and others interested in the development of positive African American identity.

References

Adams, N. G. (1995, April). What does it mean? Exploring the myths of multicultural education. *Urban Education, 30*(1), 27-39.

Atkinson, R. L., Atkinson, R. C., Smith, E. E., & Bem, D. J. (1990). *Introduction to Psychology,* 10th Edition. San Diego, CA: Harcourt Brace Jovanovich.

Baldwin, J. (1961). *Nobody knows my name.* New York: Dell.

Bandura, A. (1982). Self-efficacy mechanism in human agency. *American Psychologist, 37*(2), 122-147.

Baumgardener, A. H., Heppner, P. P., & Arkin, R. M. (1986). Role of causal attribution in personal problem solving. *Journal of Personality and Social Psychology, 50,* 636-643.

Bennett, L. (1968). *Before the Mayflower.* Baltimore, MD: Penguin.

Berlinger, K. (1968). A psychiatrist looks at loneliness. *Psychosomatics, 9,* 96-102.

Billig, M., & Tajfel, H. (1973). Social categorization and similarity in intergroup behavior. *European Journal of Social Psychology, 3*(1), 27-52.

Blum, D. E. (1994, July 13). "Eyes on the Prize": Black Coaches Association working to eradicate discrimination in college sports. *Chronicle of Higher Education, 40*(45).

Blumer, H. (1969). *Symbolic interactionism.* New Jersey: Prentice-Hall.

Bohr, N. (1885/1962). *Atomic theory and the description of nature.* Woodbridge, CN: Ox Bow Press.

Bohr, N. (1934). *Atomic theory and the description of nature.* New York: The Macmillan Co.

Bonacich, E. (1984, October). *Racism and meritocrary: The poverty of social mobility.* Paper presented at the Landsdowne Fellowship lecture, University of Victoria, B.C.

Boulding, K. (1956a). *The image: knowledge in life and society.* Ann Arbor: Michigan Press.

Boulding, K. (1956b). General systems theory: The skeleton of science. *Management Science, 2*(3), 197-208.

Bowers, C. A. (1984). The promise of theory. *Theoretical foundations of communicative competence* (pp. 31-48). New York: Longman Inc.

Brewer, B., & Kramer, R. M. (1985). The psychology of intergroup attitudes and behavior. *Annual Review Psychology, 36*, 219-243.

Brown, J. D., & Rogers, R. J. (1991). Self-serving attributions: The role of physiological arousal. *Personality and Social Psychology Bulletin, 17*, 501-506.

Buber, M. (1957). Distance relation. *Psychiatry, 20*, 97-104.

Clark [Khatib], C. (1969). Television and social controls. *Television Quarterly, 8*, 18-22.

Clark [Khatib], C. (1971). The concept of legitimacy in Black psychology. In E. Epps (Ed.), *Race relations: Current perspectives (pp. 332-354).* Connecticut: Winthrop.

Clark [Khatib], C., Nobles, W., McGee, P., & Akbar, N. (1976). *Voodoo or I.Q.: An introduction to African psychology.* Chicago, IL: Institute of Positive Education Black Pages.

Cole, J., Machir, D., Altman, I., Haythorn, W., & Wagner, C. (1967). Perceptual changes in social isolation and confinement. *Journal of Clinical Psychology, 23*, 330-333.

Darley, J., & Fazio, R. (1980). Expectancy confirmation processes arising in the social interaction sequence. *American Psychologist, 35*(10), 867-881.

Duncan, H. (1962). *Communication and social order.* London: Oxford University.

Easton, D. (1969). *Children in the political system: Origins of political legitimacy.* New York: McGraw Hill.

Edwards, H. (1969). *The Black athlete.* New York: Macmillan.

Edwards, H. (1982). On the issue of race in contemporary American sports. *The Western Journal of Black Studies, 6*, 138-144.

Ellison, R. (1952). *The invisible man.* New York: Random House.

Fazio, R. H. (1979). Motives for social comparison: The construction-validation distinction. *Journal of Personality and Social Psychology, 37,* 1683-1698.

Festinger, L. A. (1954). *A theory of cognitive dissonance.* Stanford: Stanford University.

Fiske, S. T., & Linville, P. W. (1980). What does the schema concept buy us? *Personality and Social Psychology Bulletin, 6,* 543-557.

Gilbert, B., & Jones, E. E. (1986). Perceiver-induced constraint: Interpretations of self generated reality. *Journal of Personality and Social Psychology, 50*(2), 269-280.

Goffman, E. (1963). *Stigma.* Englewood Cliffs, NJ: Prentice-Hall.

Gould, R., & Sigall, H. (1977). The effects of empathy and outcome on attribution: An examination of the divergent-perspective hypothesis. *Journal of Experimental Social Psychology, 13,* 480-491.

Greenberg, B. (1969). *Communication among the urban poor.* Unpublished manuscript, Michigan State University.

Gunderson, E. (1968). Mental health problems in Antarctica. *Archives of Environmental Health, 17,* 558-564.

Hamilton, D., (1979). A cognitive-attributional analysis of stereotyping. *Advances in Experimental Social Psychology, 12,* 53-84.

Harrison, D. D. (1978, Fall). Jazz: The serious music of Black Americans. *The Western Journal of Black Studies, 2*(3), 196-201.

Hodge, J. L., Struckman, D. K., & Trost, L. D. (1975). *Cultural biases of racism and group oppression.* Berkeley, CA: Two Riders Press.

Hoetink, H. (1971). *Carribean race relations*: A study of two variants [by] H. Hoetink. E. M. Hooykaas (Trans.). New York: Oxford University Press. (Original work published, 1967.)

Hollander, E., & Julian, J. (1971). Studies in leader legitimacy, influence and innovation. In L. Berkowitz (Ed.), *Advances in Experimental Social Psychology,* New York: Academic Press.

Hyde, J. S. (1991). *Half the human experience: The psychology of women* (4th ed.). Lexington, MA: D. C. Heath and Co.

Inkeles, A. (1966). Social structure and the socialization competence. *Harvard Educational Review, 36,* 265-183.

James, W. (1968), The self. In C. Gordon & J. Gergen (Eds.), *The self in social interaction.* New York: Wiley.

Jenkins, A. (1982). *The psychology of the Afro-American.* New York: Pergamon Press.

Jensen, A. R. (1969). How much can we boost I.Q. and scholastic achievement? *Harvard Educational Review, 39,* 449-483.

Jensen, A. (1980). *Bias in mental testing.* New York: The Free Press.

Johnson, J. T., Jemmott, J. B., III, & Pettigrew, T. F. (1984). Causal attribution and dispositional inference: Evidence of inconsistent judgments. *Journal of Experimental Social Psychology, 20,* 567-585.

Jones, E. E., & Nisbett, R. E. (1971). The actor and the observer: Divergent perceptions of the causes of behavior. In E. Jones et al. (Eds.), *Attribution: Perceiving the causes of behavior.* Morristown, NJ: General Learning Press.

Joseph, S. (1969). *The me nobody knows.* New York: Avon.

Jussim, L., Madon, S., & Chatman, C. (1994). Teacher expectations and student achievement: Self-fulfilling prophecies, biases, and accuracy. In L. Heath, R. S. Tindale, J. Edwards, E. J. Posavac, & J. Myers (Eds.), *Applications of heuristics and biases to social issues: Social applications to social issues* (Vol. 3, pp. 303-334). New York: Plenum Press.

Kahneman, D., & Tversky, A. (1972). Subjective probability: A judgment of representativeness. *Cognitive Psychology, 3,* 430-454.

Kahneman, D., & Tversky, A. (1973). On the psychology of prediction. *Psychological Review, 80,* 231-251.

Katz, I. (1967). The socialization of academic motivation in minority group children. In D. Devine (Ed.), *Nebraska symposium on motivation,* University of Nebraska Press, 133-191.

Katz, I. (1968). Academic motivation and equal educational opportunity. *Harvard Educational Review, 38,* 57-65.

Kelman, H. C. (1970). A social-psychological model of political legitimacy and its relevance to Black and White student protest movements. *Psychiatry, 33*(2), 224-245.

Klapp, O. (1962). *Heroes, villains, and fools.* Englewood Cliffs: Prentice-Hall.

Kolaja, J. (1953). American magazine cartoons and social control. *Journalism Quarterly, 30,* 71-74.

Korchin. S. J. (1976). *Modern clinical psychology.* New York: Basic Books.

Kuhn, A. (1963). *The study of society.* Homewood, IL: Dorsey Press.

Markus, H., & Sentis, K. (1982). The self in social information processing. In J. Suls (Ed.), *Psychological perspectives on the self.* Hillsdales, NJ: Erlbaum.

Mead, G. H. (1934). *Mind, self, and society.* Chicago, IL: University of Chicago.

Medina, N., & Neill, D. M. (1988). *Fallout from the testing explosion.* MA: National Center for Fair & Opening Testing.

Montague, A. (1975). *Race and I.Q.* London: Oxford University Press.

Murray, C. B., & Jackson, M. (1982/83). The conditioned failure model of Black educational underachievement. *Humboldt Journal of Social Relations,10*(1), 276-300.

Murray, C. B., & Jackson, J. (1989). The conditioned failure model revisited. In J. O. Smith & C. E. Jackson (Eds.), *Race and ethnicity: A study of intracultural socialization patterns* (pp. 319-355). Iowa: Kendall/Hunt Publishing Co.

Murray, C. B., & Smith, J. O. (1995). White privilege: The rhetoric and the facts. In D. A. Harris (Ed.), *Multiculturalism from the margins: Non-dominant voices on difference and diversity* (pp. 139-155). Westport, CN: Bergin & Garvey.

Myers, L. J. (1991). Expanding the psychology of knowledge optimally: The relationship between categorization and prejudice. *Personality and Social Psychology Bulletin, 8,* 426-432.

Ogbu, J. U. (1981). Black education: A cultural-ecological perspective. In H. P. McAdoo (Eds.), *Black families,* Beverly Hills, CA: Sage Publications.

Ogbu, J. (1988). Black education: A cultural-ecological perspective. In H. P. McAdoo (Ed.), *Black families* (pp. 169-184). Newberry Park, CA: Sage Publications, Inc.

O'Malley, M. N., & Becker, L. A. (1984). Removing the egocentric bias: The relevance of distress cues to evaluation of fairness. *Personality and Social Psychology Bulletin, 10,* 235-242.

Osgood, C., Suci, G., & Tannenbaum, P. (1971). *The measurement of meaning.* Urbana, IL: University of Illinois Press.

Park, B., & Rothbart, M. (1982). Perception of out-group homogeneity and levels of social categorization: Memory for the subordinate attributes of in-group and out-group members. *Journal of Personality and Social Psychology, 42,* 1051-1068.

Parsons, T., & Shils, E. (1951). *Toward a general theory of action.* Cambridge: Harvard University Press.

Pfuetze, P. (1961). *Self, society and existence.* New York: Harper.

Rogers, T. B., Kuiper, N. A., & Kirker, W. S. (1977). Self-reference and the encoding of personal information. *Journal of Personality and Social Psychology, 35,* 677-688.

Rokeach, M. (1969). The role of values in public opinion research. *Public Opinion Quarterly, 32,* 547-559.

Saad, L., & Newport, F. (1995, August). Majority of Americans still believe Simpson is guilty: O. J. Simpson. *Gallup Poll Monthly, 359,* 15.

Sagar, H. A., & Schofield, J. W. (1980). Racial and behavioral cues in Black and White children's perceptions of ambiguously aggressive acts. *Journal of Personality and Social Psychology, 39,* 590-598.

Sherif, M. (1968). Self concept. *International Encyclopedia of the Social Sciences, 14,* 150-159.

Sneed, C., & Murray, C. B. (1993). *The causal direction between self-esteem and achievement for Black male elementary students.* Unpublished manuscript. Riverdale: University of California.

Staples, R., & Jones, T. (1985, May/June) Culture, ideology and Black television images. *The Black Scholar, 15* 10-20.

Stephenson, R. (1951). Conflict and control function of humor. *American Journal of Sociology, 56,* 569-574.

Suls, J. M., & Miller, R. C. (Eds.). (1977). *Social comparison processes: Theoretical and empirical perspectives.* Washington, DC: Halsted-Wiley.

Swartz, M. (Ed.). (1966). *Political anthropology.* Chicago, IL: Aldine.

Tajfel, H. (1982). Social psychology of intergroup relations. In M. R. Rosenzweig & L. R. Porter (Eds.), *Annual Review of Psychology. 33,* (pp. 1-39). Palo Alton, CA: Annual Reviews.

Taylor, S. C., & Falcone, H. (1982). Cognitive bases of stereotyping: The relationship between categorization and prejudice. *Personality and Social Psychology Bulletin, 8,* 426-32.

Van Sertima, I. (Ed.). (1983). *Blacks in science: Ancient and modern.* New Brunswick: Transaction Books.

Weber, M. (1964). *Theory of social and economic organization.* New York: Free Press.

White, R. (1959). Motivation reconsidered: The concept of competence. *Psychological Review, 66,* 297-333.

White, R., & Watt, N. (1981). *The abnormal personality* (5th ed.). New York: Wiley.

Wilder, D. (1986). Social categorization: Implications for the creation and reduction of intergroup bias. *Advances in experimental social psychology.* London: Academic Press.

Whorf, B. (1956). *Language, thought, and reality.* Cambridge: MIT Press.

Ziskind, E. (1967). Sociogenic models for mental disease. *British Journal of Medical Psychology, 40,* 283-292.

Zuckerman, M., Persky, H., & Link, K. (1968). Responses to sensory deprivation, social isolation, and confinement. *Journal of Abnormal Psychology, 73*(3), 183-194.

Zuckerman, M. (1979). Attribution of success and failure revisited, or: The motivational bias is alive and well in attribution theory. *Journal of Personality, 47,* 245-287.

Author

Carolyn B. Murray
Department of Psychology
University of California
900 University Avenue
Riverside, CA 92521-0426
Telephone: (909) 787-5243
Fax: (909) 787-3985

Part 4

Stress and Hypertension

Biobehavioral Perspective for Research on Stress and Hypertension in African American Adults: Theoretical and Empirical Issues[1]

Hector F. Myers, Norman B. Anderson, and Tony L. Strickland

Introduction

In the past decade we have witnessed a significant increase in basic, clinical, pharmacologic, epidemiologic and behavioral research on essential hypertension in African Americans (See Anderson, 1989; Anderson, McNeilly, & Myers, 1991; and Gibson & Gibbons, 1982, for a comprehensive bibliography and review on the subject). Most of the studies have focused on ascertaining the bases or causes of the observed differences in morbidity[2] and mortality from hypertension between African Americans and Whites. This research has been largely comparative in nature, and has focused primarily on identifying similarities and differences between African Americans and Whites on various factors relevant to this disease. Unfortunately, most of the studies to date have pursued their primary research questions within narrow disciplinary domains and have relied exclusively on the research tools specific to their disciplines. For example, pharmacologic and clinical studies have typically evaluated the impact of specific drugs, biochemical interventions or treatment procedures on specific biological mechanisms known to control blood pressure (Luft, Grim, & Weinberger, 1985; Weiner, 1979). On the other hand, epidemiologic and sociopsychological studies typically focus their attention on social status, health habits and psychological factors as potential contributors to differential risk, morbidity and mortality from essential hypertension in African American and White populations (Harburg, Erfurt, Hauenstein, Chape, Schull, & Schork, 1978a, 1978b; James, 1984; Syme, Oakes, Friedman, Feldman, Siegelaub, & Collen, 1974). Although these studies are addressing the problem of essential hypertension in African Americans, there is little comparability and overlap in the samples, in the measures taken, in the presumed causal mechanisms studied, or in the level of analysis conducted. Therefore, there is little opportunity for an integrative, synergistic perspective on the problem to emerge. A major obstacle faced by current research on essential hypertension is the absence of an integrated, multidisciplinary perspective that considers multiple contributing factors and different levels or domains of analysis within the same study (e.g., physiological mechanisms, neurohormonal processes, psychosocial factors and behavioral attributes).

This chapter reviews and discusses the empirical evidence for biological and psychosocial differences in the possible causes, in the course, and in the outcome of hypertensive disease in African Americans and Whites. Second, the basic rationale for an integrative, multi-domain, biobehavioral perspective for research on hypertension is presented, and the basic components of such a model outlined. Third, a brief review of current biobehavioral research addressing the question of African American-White differences in cardiovascular functioning is presented. And, finally, a brief discussion of new research directions, and the implications of their findings for improving the health status of African Americans are addressed.

African American-White Differences in Essential Hypertension

All of the available medical and epidemiologic evidence overwhelmingly identifies African American adults as running the greatest risk of developing essential hypertension, of suffering disproportionately from the pathological consequences of this disease, and of running the greatest risk of early mortality from this disease and its sequelae of all U.S. population groups (Finnerty, 1971; Gillum, 1991; Langford, 1981; National Center for Health Statistics Report [NCHS Report], 1981; Prineas & Gillum, 1985; Thompson, 1980). In the U.S., essential hypertension in some age groups of adults has been reported to be twice as prevalent in African Americans as compared to Whites. Further, African Americans have higher average resting blood pressures and higher prevalence of hypertension than Whites at all SES levels, all ages, and in both gender groups (Hypertension Detection & Follow-Up Program (HDFP), 1977; Syme et al., 1974). According to a recent report from the NCHS, African Americans were 1.23 times more likely to suffer from essential hypertension than Whites across all age groups. This excess morbidity rate is evident throughout the entire life span. For example, the African American excess morbidity rate for ages 1-24 was 1.62, for ages 25-44 it was 1.98, for ages 45-64 it was 1.70, for ages 65-69 it was 1.49, and for ages 70 and above it was 1.11. As these data indicate, the greatest African American-White discrepancy in morbidity

Table 1

Morbidity Rates by Race and Gender: U.S., 1979-1981 (Rates per 10,000 population)

Ages	White Men	Black Men	White Women	Black Women
1-24	799.64	998.68	823.14	1,606.51
25-44	7,860.88	111,163.09	5,743.67	15,184.56
45-64	21,835.73	32,937.57	23,132.68	42,812.12
65-69	30,327.36	43,166.84	38,661.45	58,079.25
70+	29,323.36	35,734.89	44,980.19	48,630.09
All	11,350.93	10,136.40	12,777.34	16,580.31

Relative Risk Based on White Morbidity

Ages	All Blacks	Black Men	Black Women
1-24	1.617	1.249	1.952
25-44	1.977	1.420	2.644
45-64	1.702	1.508	1.851
65-69	1.485	1.423	1.502
70+	1.113	1.219	1.081
All	1.231	1.120	1.298

Note: Data reported from the National Center for Health Statistics, Morbidity, U.S., HIS, 1979-1981. Selected Chronic Circulatory Diseases Database, 1985.

occurs among young and middle-aged adults (i.e., ages 25-44 and 45-64), and the lowest occurs among the aged (i.e., ages 70+). (See Table 1)

Evidence also indicates that there are different target end organ damage associated with more severe hypertension in African Americans and Whites. Hypertensive African Americans often show more cardiographic and radiographic evidence of left ventricular enlargement, yet run a lower risk of coronary heart disease than Whites. On the other hand, African American hypertensives run a greater risk of strokes, end-stage renal disease (i.e., severe kidney dysfunction requiring regular kidney dialysis), and are more likely to suffer from primary aldosteronism, pheochromocytoma, and coarctation of the aorta than their White counterparts (Curry & Lewis, 1985; Finnerty, 1971; Gillum, 1979; Shulman, 1985; Thompson, 1980). In the Gillum (1979) and the more recent Anderson (1989) reviews, researchers are warned against overinterpreting evidence that suggests that the biological mechanisms governing blood pressure in African Americans and Whites may be fundamentally different. The most reasonable hypothesis of the causes of African American-White differences in blood pressure, given the present state of knowledge, appears to be some combination of possible differences in renal

Table 2
Mortality Rate by Race and Gender: U.S., 1979-1981

Ages	White Men	Black Men	White Women	Black Women
20-24	0.08	0.49	0.05	0.40
25-29	0.27	2.12	0.10	1.62
30-34	0.48	5.63	0.23	3.05
35-39	1.02	11.83	0.45	7.21
40-44	2.52	26.01	1.15	15.63
45-49	4.86	39.85	2.59	28.20
50-54	9.03	62.76	4.47	44.26
55-59	16.05	88.60	8.24	62.54
60-64	24.67	113.32	14.94	88.24
65-69	38.84	146.81	26.28	124.12
70-74	59.20	194.75	47.37	177.47
75-79	95.45	238.73	85.60	244.34
80-84	150.62	323.77	157.47	343.40
85+	278.05	427.95	316.61	467.50
All	11.20	27.62	14.52	29.32

Note: Data reported from the National Center for Health Statistics, Mortality, U.S., HIS, 1979-1981. Selected Chronic Circulatory Diseases Database, 1985.

physiology interacting with differences in the impact environmental factors have on cardiovascular functioning (Anderson, McNeilly, & Myers, 1991).

The course of hypertension in African Americans also appears to be different in African Americans, with typically earlier onset, earlier development of the more pathological and severe forms of the disease, especially in African American men, and earlier mortality (Neaton, Kuller, Wentworth, & Borhani, 1984; Tyroler, Knowles, Wing, Logue, Davis, Heiss, Heyden, & Hames, 1984). Across all age groups, African American men are 2.47 times more likely to die from hypertensive disease than White men (i.e., 27.62 vs. 11.20) and African American women are 2.02 times more likely to die from this disease than White women (i.e., 29.32 vs 14.52). African American women are slightly more likely to die from hypertension than African American men (i.e., 1.05 times), but African American men are likely to die at a younger age. In fact, the mortality rate for hypertension is higher in African American men compared to African American women until age 80 (see Table 2).

Finally, there is some clinical evidence suggesting that compared to Whites, African American hypertensives respond differently to anti-hypertensive medications. African Americans often show comparatively greater blood pressure reduction to diuretics and comparatively lesser reduction from beta-adrenergic blockers

(Hall, 1985; Langford, 1981). These differences in treatment response have been attributed to the greater tendency of African American hypertensives to have lower plasma renin levels, especially older African American adults. This is further indication of differences in kidney function between the two ethnic groups (Chrysant, Danisa, Kem, Dillard, Smith, & Frohlich, 1979; Gillum, 1979; Langford, 1981; Luft et at., 1985).

It is this evidence of racial differences in morbidity and mortality, and the related differences in pattern of physiological functioning, in risk for end-organ damage, and in response to pharmacologic intervention that has stimulated the considerable interest in the causes of racial differences in hypertension that we now see. This research on the causes of racial differences in hypertension can be roughly grouped into four major categories; (a) studies of biological differences; (b) studies of genetic/familial differences; (c) studies of socioeconomic differences; and (d) studies of sociopsychological and behavioral differences.

Biological Differences

In two reviews of African American-White differences in hypertension (Anderson, 1989; Gillum, 1979), the empirical evidence of racial differences in renal physiology, endocrine function, autonomic nervous system function, and cardiac anatomy and function are discussed. The authors note that the most frequently cited explanation for African American-White differences in hypertension is the evidence of African American-White differences in renal physiology. These include the tendency of African American hypertensives to have lower circulating plasma renin levels, lower sodium and potassium excretion rates, and higher plasma volume levels than White hypertensives. The hypothesis has been offered that African Americans may have evolved more efficient mechanisms for renal sodium conservation (e.g., high sodium reabsorption in the distal tubules of the kidney), and therefore more African Americans than Whites may be "salt sensitive," and less able to excrete the excess sodium that is common to the modern diet (Luft et al., 1979, 1985). Results from the Evans County, Georgia study (Grim, Luft, Miller, Meneely, Batarbee, Hames, & Dahl, 1980), and from national dietary recall studies (Frisancho, Leonard, & Bollettins, 1984) also reported that while there are no consistent African American-White differences in sodium intake, African Americans consistently report lower dietary intakes of potassium and calcium. Thus, it is speculated that the greater prevalence of hypertension in African Americans may be due to both possible differences in sodium handling, but also to a relative deficiency in dietary intake of potassium which also affects renal handling of sodium (Langford, Langford, & Tyler, 1985).

The recent work by McCarron and his colleagues on the role of calcium in hypertension suggest that dietary intake of calcium and the mechanisms controlling calcium metabolism should also be included in the sodium-potassium equation (McCarron, Morris, & Cole, 1982). Evidence indicates that African Americans have lower dietary intake of calcium, and of vitamins C and A than Whites, and that calcium is an important factor in the metabolism of sodium and potassium (Langford, Langford, & Tyler, 1985).

Additional evidence of biological differences in African Americans and Whites that might be implicated in population differences in disease rates include differences in mineralocorticoid secretions by the adrenal cortex, and greater tendency in younger African Americans to develop hypertension when adrenal cortical abnormalities are present (Russel & Massi, 1973). Evidence has also been provided for possible differences in sympathetic tone as indicated by the higher prevalence of lower plasma renin levels in African Americans, lower heart rates in African American hypertensives, and lower DBH levels (dopamine-beta-hydroxylase) in both African American hypertensives and normotensives than in Whites (Lovenberg, Bruckwick, Alexander, Horwitz, & Kaizer, 1974).

Finally, Gillum (1979) reported evidence suggestive of greater pulse pressure, more left ventricular hypertrophy, and more cardiac enlargement at each blood pressure level in African Americans than in Whites. This author cautions, however, that much of this evidence of biological differences between African Americans and Whites is still inconclusive, and therefore, conclusions drawn from this evidence would be speculative at best. Nevertheless, this preliminary evidence provides interesting hypotheses about possible biological sources of racial differences in hypertension.

Genetic/Familial Sources of Differences

The preponderance of the scientific evidence to date supports the hypothesis of a strong genetic contribution in hypertension in both African Americans and Whites, and that the disease is probably polygenically determined (Grim, Luft, Weinberger, Miller, Rose, & Christian, 1984; Miller & Grim, 1983). Unfortunately, many investigators have taken the previously cited indications of possible biological differences in African Americans and Whites as convincing evidence of a genetic basis for African American-White differences in hypertension rates. Cooper (1984) and Watkins (1984) argue quite eloquently that several factors cast doubt on this proposition. First of all, "Black" is more of a sociopolitical category than a biological one. Ethnic similarity and identity should not be confused with unequivocal evidence of genetic homogeneity. In fact, the peculiar history of African Americans in the U.S. is one of considerable miscegenation, and therefore, the U.S. African American population is genetically quite heterogenous. Second, if the predisposition for higher blood pressure has a genetic basis, then dark-skinned people all over the world should share this common tendency towards elevated blood pressure. The world epidemiologic data on Africa and the Caribbean indicate no such consistent tendencies. In fact, the evidence seems to link high prevalence of hypertension in African Americans in these areas to environmental factors such as urbanization, diet, life-style and other by-products of the pressures of acculturation (Watkins, 1984).

Of equal importance in this discussion is the need to evaluate the evidence of genetic factors in hypertensive disease. Except for the compelling work on twins, most of the evidence of a genetic basis for this disease is based on indirect evidence. For example, there is ample evidence that a family history of hypertension is a major risk factor for this disease regardless of race, SES or gender (Epstein, 1984; Watt, 1986). This familial disease link is supported by evidence of moderate blood pressure concordance rates in families (Zinner, Rosner, & Kass, 1985), and moderate heritability estimates from population based, family aggregation studies of blood pressure (Hayes, Tyroler, & Cassel, 1971; Moll, Harburg, Burns, Schork, & Ozgoren, 1983). However, increased family concordance in blood pressure and increased risk for hypertension do not prove genetic transmission of the disease.

Somewhat more direct evidence for a genetic basis for African American-White differences in hypertension is provided by studies of the relationship between blood grouping, skin color and blood pressure in the U.S. These studies suggest that darker skin and purer African ancestry are associated with higher resting blood pressures and greater risk for this disease (Boyle, 1970; Harburg et al., 1973, 1978a, 1978b; Keil, 1981; Keil, Tyroler, Sandifer, & Boyle, 1977). African American theoreticians have also postulated theories that are somewhat consistent with this genetic model of determination. They argue that melanin, the factor that determines skin color and functions as a neurotransmitter, operates neurochemically to enhance physiological sensitivity and responsivity to environmental stimuli. Therefore, darker skinned African Americans are biologically more responsive to external stimuli, be they positive or negative (McGee, 1976). This theory, although not yet supported by empirical evidence, does recognize the significance of environmental factors even when a genetic predisposition is postulated.

Regardless of which theory is investigated, the conclusions drawn from these data must be treated with considerable caution. Investigators face considerable problems defining and measuring skin color, most fail to separate the biological attributes of race from their psychological and social meaning and from social class, and most studies use small, nonrepresentative African American samples (Cooper, 1984; Patterson, 1983; Tyroler & James, 1978). In addition, and as noted previously, these investigators ignore the fact that the association between skin color, racial admixture and blood pressure is not consistently evident in African American populations outside of the U.S. (Watkins, 1984).

The strongest and most compelling direct evidence of genetic influence in hypertension is provided by studies of White twins both adopted and reared together. These studies provide evidence of a very strong linear association between blood pressure concordance and genetic similarity (Annest, Sing, Biron, & Mongeau, 1979a, 1979b; Miller & Grim, 1983; Mongeau & Biron, 1981; Rose, Miller, Grim, & Christian, 1979, 1980). Preliminary results from a study of a small sample of African American twins indicated that blood pressure heritability estimates in African American twins are comparable to those reported for White twins (Grim & Cantor, 1986).

In sum, present evidence does support a genetic contribution in blood pressure. However, the available evidence falls short of supporting the hypothesis that there is a genetic basis for African American-White differences in rates of hypertension that are independent of and more important than socio-environmental factors. Future research should continue to pursue hypotheses about biological differences between the two groups, but care must be exercised in the definition of the groups (i.e., who is meant by African American and White), in the size and representativeness of the samples selected, and in the hypothesized relationships tested (i.e., simple direct effects vs multifactor interactions).

Socioeconomic Status Differences

Present epidemiologic evidence consistently point to an inverse relationship between socioeconomic status and both level of resting blood pressure and prevalence of essential hypertension (HDFP, 1977; James, 1984a). Since African Americans are disproportionately overrepresented in the low SES groups, a significant proportion of the variance in the observed African American-White differences in hypertension risk is undoubtedly attributable to their overall lower educational, income, and occupational status (James, 1984b; Keil et al., 1977; Syme et al., 1974).

However, this association between low SES, race and hypertension risk must be carefully evaluated. The tendency to treat socioeconomic status as a simple demographic descriptor on which subjects are classified only helps us to understand which groups are at greatest risk. It does not tell us much about *how* or *why* these characteristics are associated with enhanced risk. In an effort to clarify the latter two questions, several recent papers have suggested that socioeconomic and sociocultural factors that impact health should be subsumed under the generic construct of social status, and that this construct be conceptualized and measured multidimensionally. Distinctions between socio-structural factors and related sociopsychological attributes associated with social status are recommended (Myers et al., 1984; Watkins & Eaker, 1986). Socio-structural factors refer to such factors as race, education, occupation, income, marital status, and social mobility, all of which define social status through their social meanings, and through social institutions and practices that control life opportunities and obstacles faced by

African Americans. On the other hand, sociopsychological factors, include a host of individual differences in experiences, personal attributes, resources and liabilities that contribute to individual vulnerability or resistance in the face of external social conditions. In assessing the impact of SES on health, careful attention must be given to distinguishing between objective, concrete events and experiences that African Americans face from the subjective interpretations and meanings conferred on these experiences and events. Both individual and collective group meanings must be considered (Myers, 1982; James, 1984b; Kasl, 1984). Both the socio-structural and sociopsychological components of social status are believed to interact through biobehavioral mechanisms to define health status and illness risk (Anderson, McNeilly, & Myers, 1991). However, they also operate through social policy to impact the availability of health services, the quality of health care provided in the management of illness, and in the final analysis, they impact mortality risk (See Figure 1, Myers, 1985).

Recent evidence also indicates that race and gender mediate the meaning and role that SES has on health and well-being (James, Harnett, & Kalsbeek, 1983; James, 1984b; Kessler, & Neighbors, 1986). In the case of African Americans, it is difficult to completely separate the contributions of race/ethnicity from SES as attributable risk factors, especially when we recognize that institutional racism has insured a nonrandom distribution of educational and occupational status and income with respect to race (Hogan & Pazul, 1982; Washington & McCloud, 1982). Also, both race and SES exert their effects through a host of health beliefs, habits and behaviors that impact most detrimentally on the lowest SES groups, on darker skin African Americans, and on men (Jackson, 1981). However, Kessler and Neighbors (1986), argue rather convincingly that the relative contributions of each of these factors on health can be determined if the appropriate statistical procedures are used. For example, they demonstrated empirically that previous studies indicating that it was SES and not race that was the primary predictor of psychological distress were incorrect. When a more appropriate statistical treatment of the data was used, i.e., one that considers the possibility that race and SES could function interactively, the evidence indicate that the effect of SES on well-being was mediated by race such that low SES and African American was associated with greater psychological distress than either race or SES by itself. Taken as a whole, these data suggest that socioeconomic factors play an important role in the observed African American-White differences in risk and in the prevalence of essential hypertension. However, there is still additional research needed to disentangle the independent and joint contributions of race, gender and SES on the etiology, course and outcome of this disease.

Figure 1
**Conceptual Model of the Role of Social Status
in CHD Risk, CHD Morbidity and Mortality**

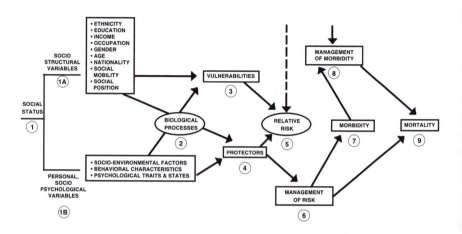

Sociocultural and Sociopsychological Differences

One of the major hypothesized sources of racial differences in hypertension has been the sociocultural, with particular attention focused on dietary habits. As noted earlier, primary focus has been on dietary abuses of sodium and unsaturated fats, and the resultant excess body fat and body weight as the major culprits. Research has consistently linked increased risk for essential hypertension to obesity, and this link is particularly evident in the poor and in African American women (Gillum, 1979, 1987a, 1987b). Data on the prevalence of obesity in African Americans and Whites, and in males and females between the ages of 20-24 years indicate that the obesity rate for White males and females and for African American males was 15%, while for African American females it was 23%. This pattern of excess weight in African American women continues with age such that by ages 55-64, 50% of all African American women are obese (Boham & Brock, 1985). Similar rates were observed in a national report by DHEW (1978), which noted that obesity rates among African American women ages 20-44 years of 25%, 45% among those ages 45-64 years, and 30% among those 65 years and older. In comparison, we find rates of 12.8%, 8% and a 5.8% among African American men in the respective age cohorts.

This tendency towards obesity among African American women has been attributed to both genetics and to dietary abuses of unsaturated fats and carbohydrates (Stamler, 1980). While some have offered primarily cultural explanations for these dietary differences (e.g., a predilection for soul food), social class and rural-urban residency factors are probably as significant in determining these dietary differences as is culture (i.e., relatively less access to more nutritious but more expensive foods among the poor).

It should be noted that the relationship between obesity and high blood pressure appears to be stronger and more direct in Whites than in African Americans (Boyle, Griffey, Nichaman, & Talbert, 1967; HDFP, 1979). Perhaps for African Americans, and especially for African American women, other biological (i.e., sodium intake) and socio-environmental factors (e.g., stress) play a more direct role in the etiology of hypertension, while obesity plays a more indirect, contributory role. In any event, additional research is needed to further specify the contribution obesity makes in this disease relative to other known dietary and non-dietary risk factors in African Americans.

The previously reported evidence of lower sodium excretion rate among African Americans despite no significant differences in sodium intake suggests that dietary sodium may be potentially more pathogenic for African Americans (Grim et al., 1980). Of course, support for this hypothesis does not prove that sodium is a cause of hypertension, but it would help to explain why excess dietary sodium appears to increase overall morbidity risk in *salt sensitive* African Americans and in those who possess other known risk factors. Additional studies are clearly needed to clarify this issue of salt sensitivity as a risk factor, and to consider the possible contributory role that dietary calcium and potassium intake might play in this regard.

Another major area in which considerable research interest has been demonstrated is in the exploration of socio-ecological and psychological differences between African Americans and Whites that might account for greater African American vulnerability to hypertension. This research emphasizes the role of socio-ecological and psychological stresses attendant to race and social status, to personality characteristics, and to coping styles as the central factors of interest. Sociopsychological studies have failed to demonstrate the existence of a specific *hypertensive personality* both in general and specific to African Americans (Harrell, 1980). However, provocative evidence has been reported in two large epidemiologic studies in Detroit and Charleston, North Carolina that indicate a strong association between elevated blood pressure, prevalence of hypertension and high level of community disorganization (Nesser, Tyroler, & Cassel, 1971), exposure to high socio-ecologic stresses, both alone (James & Kleinbaum, 1976) and in interaction with skin color and reactive anger management (Diamond, 1982; Gentry, Chesney, Fary, Hall, & Harburg, 1982; Harburg, Erfurt, Hauenstein, Chape, Schull, & Schork, 1973, 1978a, 1978b). These data indicate that sociopsychological factors interact to create a pattern of person-environment transactions that are more pathogenic in general, and specifically more pathogenic for hypertension (Lazarus, 1979; Lazarus & Launier, 1978; Myers, 1982).

More recently, James et al. (1983) also suggested that poorly educated African American men who believe that hard work and determination can overcome social obstacles despite their limited resources (i.e., high John Henryism) are at significantly greater risk for hypertension than better educated or less active coping African American men. This *high risk* coping style is conceptually consistent with observations that higher pressor responses occur under conditions of effortful coping with an uncontrollable behavioral stressor (Obrist, Gaebelein, Teller, Langer, Grignolo, Light, & McCubbin, 1978), and when neither flight not fight responses are available or appropriate (Ostfeld & Shekelle, 1967). Dohrenwend and Dohrenwend (1970), Syme (1979) and Myers (1982) suggest that this state of effortful coping under conditions of high uncertainty and perceived uncontrollability is the *normal* socio-structurally determined state of existence for a significant percentage of the African American population. This peculiar pattern of person-environment transactions is also likely to play an important role in the disproportionate risk for essential hypertension run by African Americans (James, 1984b).

Pitfalls of Racial Differences Research

Great care must be exercised in addressing the causes of African American-White differences. There is legitimacy to the pursuit of this knowledge, especially in light of the existing evidence of racial differences in risk, disease course, and in disease outcome. Unfortunately, however, the history of science is replete with evidence of gross abuses of racial differences research that has been used to justify racist and discriminatory social policies and practices. (See Thomas & Sillen's book *Racism in Psychiatry*, 1972 for a historical review of research on racial differences in psychiatry, and Robert Guthrie's book *Even the Rat was White*, 1976 for a review of the treatment of race in experimental psychology.) In addition, most of the studies of racial differences can be criticized for their small and nonrepresentative samples, their failure to control for social class or other sources of within-group variability, or to give adequate attention to the sociopolitical, economic and psychological dimensions of their variables. Thus, many investigators make faulty causal assumptions about the genetic and biological basis for the racial differences observed, and make unjustified generalizations to the population as a whole. A good example of this problem is the research on skin color and blood pressure. Researchers interested in questions about racial differences must recognize the complexity of the issues addressed, and the political underpinnings and implications of their research. Failure to do so raises serious questions about the scientific integrity and utility of such research.

To add to the complexity of the problem, we must also note that all of the available evidence point to multiple, interacting factors as causally implicated in hypertension (i.e., Page's [1982] mosaic theory of the hypertension), as well as in the observed racial differences in essential hypertension (Anderson, 1989). However, the evidence of racial differences in hypertension falls short of articulating any coherent pattern of relationships or mechanisms through which the hypothesized causes interact to result in different patterns of risk and different types of hypertensive disease in African Americans and Whites. One obvious missing link is the absence of a consistent pattern of racial differences in cardiovascular stress reactivity as measured by physiological, endocrine, behavioral and psychological indexes. Careful consideration of the role that race and social class might play in mediating stress-exposure, stress-reactivity and stress-coping should also be given (Anderson, McNeilly, & Myers, 1991).

The Biobehavioral Perspective on Essential Hypertension

In several seminal papers, the biological, clinical, and behavioral evidence in hypertension is reviewed, and an eloquent argument is made for taking an integrated, multidisciplinary and multi-domain approach in studying this disease (Krantz & Manuck, 1984; Lazarus, 1979; Matthews et al., 1986; Schwartz et al., 1979; Shapiro & Goldstein, 1982). Such an approach has been labelled biobehavorial to reflect the focus on the direct and concurrent effects of biological, psychological and behavioral processes in the pathophysiology of this disease. Essential hypertension is characterized as a disease of disordered homeostasis or disregulation of the biological mechanisms that control blood pressure. This disregulation is believed to result from frequent exposure to stress, and, in turn, frequent acute pressor responses are continuously being elicited over time. This pattern of hyperreactivity ultimately results in the resetting of the blood pressure control mechanisms to a higher resting level (i.e., chronically elevated resting blood pressure), which ultimately defines the disease of essential hypertension (Schwartz et al., 1979; Krantz & Manuck, 1984).

In recent years, biobehavioral researchers have focused their attention on the role that these short-term increases in cardiovascular activity during exposure to behavioral or environmental stressors play in the development of essential hypertension (See Krantz & Manuck, 1984, and Matthews et al., 1986 for a comprehensive review of this literature). This reactivity may be characterized by any of a number of adjustments occurring in various combinations or patterns. These cardiovascular adjustments, which are mediated by the sympathetic nervous system (SNS), may include increases in systolic and diastolic blood pressure, cardiac output, muscle blood flow, vascular resistance, and hormonal secretions. These adjustments are also directly affected by the emotional state and cognitive processes of the person as they act on, react to, and cope with their daily living environments. Therefore, the broad outlines of a biobehavioral model of essential hypertension can be depicted by linking the two major domains of influences, the biological and the sociopsychological or behavioral. In this model, stress is viewed as the catalyst that activates affective and cognitive processes, on the one hand, and biological (i.e., SNS) processes on the other (Kaplan, 1979).

Consistent with a biobehavioral perspective, it is hypothesized that individuals who exhibit exaggerated reactivity (i.e., those that are "hyperreactive") may be at greatest risk for the development of hypertension (Eliot, Buell, & Dembroski, 1982; Folkow, 1982; Obrist, 1981). Although this hypothesis has yet to be confirmed by prospective epidemiologic studies, it is supported by converging evidence from both animal (Schneiderman, 1983) and human experiments (Matthews et al., 1986). Laboratory experiments on humans have found that: (1) White hypertensives tend to exhibit cardiovascular hyperreactivity relative to normotensive subjects in response to laboratory stressors (Frederikson, Dimberg, Frisk-Hamber, & Strom, 1982; Hollenberg, Williams, & Adams, 1981; Steptoe, Melville, & Ross, 1984); (2) Whites with a parental history of hypertension frequently exhibit greater cardiovascular responses to stress than the offspring of normotensives (Ditto, 1986; Falkner, Kushner, Onesti, & Angelakos, 1981; Jorgenson & Houston, 1981; Manuck & Proietti, 1982); and (3) White adults display a different pattern of cardiovascular reactivity in different settings and while engaging in different activities (Mann, Miller-Craig, & Rafferty, 1985; Pickering et al., 1982). The latter evidence underscores the impact of the environmental setting or context on stress and cardiovascular reactivity.

If we extrapolate from this evidence in Whites to explain African American-White differences in hypertension, we would hypothesize that if cardiovascular hyperreactivity is in fact associated with a heightened susceptibility to hypertension, then African Americans should show a greater tendency to respond to stress with exaggerated cardiovascular reactions than Whites.

Biobehavioral Research on Hypertension in African Americans

Cardiovascular Stress Reactivity to Laboratory Stressors

Efforts are currently underway to apply a multidimensional, biobehavioral perspective to the question of what are the biological and psychological bases for the differences in hypertension disease risk between African Americans and Whites. The central focus of these efforts to date is primarily on laboratory stress reactivity measured on physiological, neurohormonal, behavioral and psychological parameters. Specifically, investigators often measure such physiological indexes of stress reactivity as changes in systolic and diastolic blood pressure, heart rate, pulse pressure, forearm blood flow, and skin conductance. Neurohormonal indexes frequently studied include serum electrolyte concentrations, urine electrolyte excretion rates (i.e., sodium, potassium, calcium, creatinine, etc.), and changes in plasma catecholamine concentrations (i.e., epinephrine, norepinephrine and cortisol).

The psychological parameters frequently investigated include anger response style (e.g., suppressed [In] vs. expressed [Out] anger; reflexive vs. reflective anger), trait anxiety, level of subjective distress, chronic life stresses and coping, life change stresses (life events), level of social supports, depression, Type A behavior pattern, and psychological defensiveness. Finally, the behavioral parameters are usually defined in terms of the types of stressor tasks faced, and include such varied stressors as active coping tasks (e.g., mental arithmetic, video games), interpersonal stresses and conflict (e.g., stressful interviews, role play, anger-arousing conflict interaction tasks), cognitive-perceptual tasks (e.g., the Stroop Color Conflict task, video games), dietary or chemical stresses (e.g., caffeine, alcohol, tobacco), passive physical stresses (e.g., cold pressor test), active physical exercise stresses (e.g., handgrip strength task, running in place, the step task, bicycle ergonometer, treadmill exercise stress), and finally, naturally occurring stresses (job stresses, driving on the freeway, arguing with a family member, etc.). (See also Light, 1987; Schneiderman, Kaufman, & Carver, 1990 for a review of these approaches.)

For purposes of organization and clarity, our review of the available studies of African American-White differences in cardiovascular reactivity will be organized into two major sections: (1) studies investigating differences in reactivity in normotensive adults; and (2) studies of differences in reactivity in hypertensives. In each section, distinctions between reactivity to physical and to psychosocial stresses will be made. Finally, the small body of research on African American-White differences in response to caffeine will also be reviewed.

Studies of Normotensive Adults

Physical Stressors

There have been comparatively few studies of ethnic differences in response to physical stressors in normotensive adults. In a study by Anderson, Lane, Muranaka, Williams, and Houseworth (1988), blood pressure, heart rate, forearm blood flow, and forearm vascular resistance were measured during the application of an ice pack to the foreheads of 10 African American and 10 White males (ages 18-22). This procedure has been shown to elicit profound peripheral vasoconstriction (Abboud & Eckstein, 1966). In response to the cold stimulus, African American subjects exhibited significantly greater increases in systolic and diastolic blood pressure and forearm vascular resistance. Since no ethnic differences were observed in heart rate, the hyperreactivity among African Americans was primarily vascular in nature rather than cardiac. In a second study by Venter, Joubert, and Styrdom (1985) heart rate and blood pressure responses to the head-up tilt were compared in sixteen South African Black and White adults matched on age, sex and body mass. Tilting from supine to 40 degrees, and from 40 degrees to 80 degrees caused significant increases in heart rate and diastolic blood pressure in both groups. White subjects had higher systolic pressures than African Americans when tilted to 80 degrees. No significant heart rate or diastolic differences were observed. The authors hypothesized that ethnic differences in systolic BP response to tilting might be due to quantitative and/or qualitative differences in cardiac beta-1 adrenoceptors.

Researchers at Indiana University have conducted an elegant series of studies on the effects on sodium loading in African American and White adult subjects (for review see Grim et al., 1984; Luft, Grim, & Weinberger, 1985). To investigate the effects of volume expansion and contraction in males (Luft, Grim, & Weinberger, 1979; Luft, Grim, & Weinberger, 1985), subjects were fed a 150-mEq/day sodium diet and given an intravenous infusion of 2 liters of normal saline (volume expansion). Sodium depletion was induced by a diet containing 10 mEq of sodium and three 40-mg doses of furosemide (volume contraction). Following sodium loading (expansion) African Americans excreted significantly less sodium in urine than Whites. In another study, blood pressure responses to six different levels of daily sodium intake (10, 300, 600, 800, 1200, 1500) were examined in African American and White males (Luft et al., 1979). At intakes of 600 mEq/day or greater, African American subjects showed consistently and significantly higher blood pressures than Whites. No significant blood pressure differences were observed at the lower intake levels. Thus, while research has failed to demonstrate racial differences in sodium intake (Grim et al., 1980), this study suggests that African Americans may be more susceptible to the deleterious effects of sodium on blood pressure (i.e., more African Americans may be salt sensitive than Whites).

Psychosocial Stressors

Few studies have compared the cardiovascular responses of normotensive African Americans and Whites during psychosocial stressors. In one recent study, Morell, Myers, Shapiro, Goldstein, & Armstrong (1988) measured heart rate, blood pressure and skin conductance responses to mental arithmetic (i.e., serial addition) in 34 African American and 42 White normotensive males, selected for a family history of hypertension. These groups were compared during screening, and at three experimental periods: at baseline or pre-MA period (5 mins.), during the mental arithmetic task (MA period) (5 mins.), and during recovery or the post-MA period (5 mins.). Although there were no differences in screening blood pressures, African Americans exhibited significantly higher diastolic blood pressures, and Whites exhibited higher heart rates and skin conductance levels during the baseline period.

African Americans also showed higher diastolic levels during the MA task. However, when the baseline differences were statistically removed, no significant diastolic differences remained, but higher systolic levels in the White subjects were uncovered. There were no significant race and family history interactions.

In an earlier report from that same study, Myers et al. (1985), compared SBP, DBP, and HR reactivity of African American and White normotensive males to a series of psychological stressors (i.e., mental arithmetic, Type A interview, the Stroop color conflict task, and a racial conflict film) and to two physical stressors (i.e., handgrip task and the exercise treadmill test). The preliminary results indicated few overall racial differences in reactivity. However, White males reacted to the acute psychological stressors with higher SBP and HR responses than African Americans, while African Americans evidenced greater SBP and DBP reactivity to the physical stressors than Whites. Contrary to expectations, neither group evidenced marked physiological reactions to the racially loaded conflict film. The latter may have been due to the passive nature of this stressful task which afforded the subjects ample opportunities to screen or to cognitively mediate the full impact of the events depicted in the film.

Caffeine and Stress

There has been increasing interest in the hemodynamic effects of caffeine, both alone and in combination with various psychological stressors (Shapiro et al., 1986). This drug, which is found in a wide variety of foods, and rivals nicotine and alcohol as one of the most frequently used psychotropic substances, has a variety of physiological effects on the central nervous system. The most relevant of these effects is small to moderate blood pressure increases in normotensives and mild hypertensives, especially when caffeine is combined with psychological stress (Goldstein & Shapiro, 1987; Robertson et al., 1978; Shapiro et al., 1986). The presence of a parental history of hypertension also appears to exacerbate the cardiovascular impact of caffeine and stress, at least in White and Chinese males who regularly consume caffeine (Greenberg & Shapiro, 1987; Greenstadt, Yang, & Shapiro, 1988).

To date, two studies have investigated whether caffeine, both alone and in combination with psychological stress would produce different patterns of blood pressure reactivity in African American and White adults. A study by Myers, Shapiro, McClure, and Daims (1989) examined blood pressure reactivity to caffeine (250 mg) and mental arithmetic stress in a sample of 40 healthy, normotensive African American and White male regular caffeine consumers. Comparisons on family history of hypertension were also made. These investigators found dose-related increases in systolic blood pressure (SBP) to 250 mg of caffeine and to the combination of caffeine and stress in both racial groups. However, there were no overall race or family history differences in reactivity observed. A second study by Strickland, Myers, and Lahey (1989) tested for race and parental history differences in reactivity to caffeine (250 mg) and mental arithmetic stress in 48 healthy, normotensive African American and White adult women who were not regular caffeine consumers. This investigator also failed to find any significant overall race or parental history differences in reactivity, but unlike in men, caffeine alone had no significant effect on blood pressure or heart rate in these young women. However, African American women with a parental history of hypertension reacted to the stress of the mental arithmetic task with significantly higher diastolic blood pressure (DBP) responses and slower DBP recovery than the other groups.

These results suggest that caffeine has different cardiovascular effects depending on whether it is consumed under stressful or non-stressful conditions; whether the consumer is male or female, or African American or White; whether they have a family history of hypertension, and whether they are regular or infrequent consumers of caffeine. At least among African American adults, the available evidence seems to indicate that African American men appear to be more reactive to caffeine and to stress, while African American women appear to react more to psychological stress than to caffeine. Having a parental history of essential hypertension seems to confer additional risk to African American women, but apparently not to African American men. Additional studies are needed to verify these preliminary results, as well as to investigate the long-term cardiovascular effects of regular caffeine use as a potential enhancer of risk for essential hypertension in African American adults.

Studies of Hypertensive Adults

Physical Stressors

Two studies compared African American and White hypertensives on cardiovascular reactivity to physical stressors. Rowland et al., (1982) evaluated blood pressure and heart rate reactivity in 16 African American and 16 White adult males and females with mild-to-moderate hypertension. In addition to gender, subjects were matched on age, blood pressure, and socioeconomic status. Tasks consisted of isometric handgrip, upright bicycle exercise, and the cold pressor test. No significant differences in heart rate or blood pressure responses between African American and White hypertensives were obtained on any of the tasks.

Dimsdale, Graham, Ziegler, Zusman, and Berry (1987) infused norepinephrine in African American and White normotensives and hypertensives on two extremes of dietary sodium intake: 10 mEq/day and 200 mEq/day. A highly significant dose-response relationship was found for norepinephrine dosage and blood pressure. Among hypertensives on the high salt diet, African American subjects had steeper dose-response slopes than White subjects.

Psychosocial Stressors

Several recent studies have also investigated ethnic differences in reactivity to psychosocial stressors among hypertensives or those with casual elevated blood pressure. Frederickson (1986) examined cardiovascular and non-cardiovascular reactivity in three groups of African American and White subjects: established hypertensives, borderline hypertensives, and normotensives. The task consisted of 16-signaled reaction time tasks where a 110 decibel White noise was delivered contingent upon poor performance, while measures of heart rate, blood pressure, respiration, skin conductance, and skin and muscle blood flow were obtained (muscle and skin vascular resistances were later calculated). Although resting cardiovascular activity was similar in African American and White hypertensives and normotensives, heart rate (HR) and systolic pressure (SBP) increased less in African American hypertensives and normotensives than in their White counterparts. Skin conductance changes were also attenuated in the African American subjects. Additionally, muscle and skin vascular resistance increased during the task in African American subjects irrespective of diagnosis, but not in Whites, suggesting enhanced vascular resistance among African Americans.

In another study of African American and White hypertensives, Nash, Jorgensen, Lasser, and Hymowitz (1985) examined heart rate and blood pressure responses of 98 African American and White mild hypertensives to the video game PACMAN and to the Stroop Color Conflict task. The investigators found that while no significant race or gender effects were observed on blood pressure, a significant heart rate effect emerged. African American subjects, regardless of gender, exhibited lower heart rate changes to the tasks. It was noted that the ethnic group differences could have been mediated by affective responding, since White subjects reported more task-related anxiety and frustration than did African Americans.

Schneiderman (1986) measured a variety of cardiovascular and humoral responses in African American and White male and female borderline hypertensives and normotensives to several challenging tasks (i.e., Type A interview, video game, bicycle ergonometer, cold pressor test). Also, ambulatory monitored blood pressure was assessed at home and at work. African American females and White males exhibited greater epinephrine and heart rate reactivity to the tasks than African American males or White females; this relationship was reversed on plasma renin reactivity. In an analysis of the predictability of home and work blood pressure by the laboratory responses, Schneiderman found that the best predictor of home or work blood pressures for all groups was the laboratory baseline blood pressure; blood pressure during the video game added significantly to the prediction of work blood pressure. Among Whites, the best predictor of ambulatory systolic blood pressure was the systolic responses during the video game. In African Americans, on the other hand, diastolic responses to the cold pressor test was the better predictor of ambulatory diastolic pressure.

Falkner, Kushner, Khalsa, and Katz (1987) examined the effects of sodium loading on cardiovascular responses to mental arithmetic in three groups of subjects: 45 representative African Americans, who were selected from a larger group of participants in an epidemiologic study; 45 borderline hypertensive African Americans who were also enrolled in the larger study; and 45 age-and gender-matched normotensive Whites. Cardiovascular reactivity to mental arithmetic and tilting was measured before and after sodium loading. Following sodium loading, African Americans showed the greatest increase in resting mean arterial pressure (MAP) indicating greater sodium sensitivity. The African American borderline hypertensives had the highest MAP levels at baseline and during stress, both before and after sodium loading. However, White subjects exhibited greater MAP changes from baseline to stress before and after the sodium intervention.

Light et al. (1986) have conducted perhaps the most comprehensive assessment of African American-White differences in stress reactivity. Cardiovascular and renal responses in African American and White subjects, selected for normal or borderline systolic blood pressure were examined in three studies. In the first study, they compared subjects on four stressors and found that African American borderlines showed greater increases in SBP to all four stressors than their White counterparts. Heart rate (HR) and DBP responses did not differ in the hypertensives, and the highest HR values were observed in the normotensive African Americans.

In a second study of ethnic differences in physiologic responses with and without beta-blockade during a competitive reaction task, Light et al., (1986) found increased cardiac output in the hypertensives prior to beta-blockade, but the increases were larger in the White hypertensives than in African American hypertensives. After beta blockade, however, cardiac output fell more noticeably in the African American hypertensives, and remained lower than in White hypertensives during stress. This indicates that there is less of an increase in beta-adrenergic activity in African Americans during stress, but greater beta-adrenergic activity at rest. Also, stress produced a greater decrease in total peripheral resistance in Whites than in African Americans prior to beta blockade. However, following beta-blockade, the greatest increase in peripheral resistance was observed in African American borderline hypertensives.

In a final study, Light et al. (1986) examined renal and cardiovascular responses in 8 African American and 8 White subjects under four experimental conditions following sodium and water ingestion; pre-task rest, competitive task, post-task rest 1, and post-test rest 2. These procedures were tested with and without beta-blockade. Light et al. found that without beta-blockade renal function fell in all groups, but the decrease was more marked in African Americans during post-task rest. Also, both with and without beta-blockade African Americans showed a significantly greater drop in their glomerular filtration rate during post-task rest. African Americans also excreted less fluid and less sodium during post-task rest both with and without beta-blockade. And, finally, while African Americans and Whites showed similar stress-induced SBP and DBP increases, the blood pressures of African Americans remained more elevated than in Whites during the post-task rest periods.

Within-Group Variability in Reactivity Among African Americans

As noted in the findings reported previously, there is considerable heterogeneity among African Americans in resting cardiovascular activity, particularly in blood pressure. For example, blood pressure levels in African Americans vary with SES, age, stress coping style, obesity, and other factors. It is probable then that the magnitude or pattern of cardiovascular responses to laboratory stressors also varies among African Americans. A substantial body of literature exists on White samples pertaining to reactivity differences in persons most at risk for cardiovascular disease compared to those at reduced risk (e.g., Type A vs. Type B adults, those with a parental history of hypertension vs. those without, etc.). Besides those studies that compared African Americans and Whites that were summarized in the last section, there are a few studies that have addressed individual differences in stress reactivity among African Americans.

At least three studies have investigated reactivity differences in African Americans as a function of Type A behavior. In a study of middle-aged African American women, Anderson et al. (1986) found Type A behavior assessed via structured interview to be significantly associated with SBP and DBP increases during the interview but not during mental arithmetic stress. Family history of hypertension did not predict cardiovascular response to either task, either alone or in combination with Type A. In a similar study with African American college-age women, and including forearm blood flow to BP and HR measures, Anderson et al., (1986) found that Type A behavior interacted with parental history of hypertension, such that in African American women with a parental history, Type A was significantly associated with increased SBP responses during the structured interview. Watkins and Eaker (1986) cite a study by Clark and Harrell (1982) which found a significant association between Type A behavior assessed using the Jenkins Activity Survey and diastolic blood pressure reactivity in African Americans.

Finally, Anderson, Williams, Lane, and Houseworth (1987) found that among college-aged African American women, those with a family history of hypertension exhibited significantly smaller SBP and FBF responses than their negative family history peers. This pattern of reactivity is somewhat contrary to that reported by

Light et al., (1986) and by Strickland et al., (1989), who found greater reactivity associated with a positive parental history of hypertension.

Summary and Future Directions for Research

Essential hypertension is one of the major health problems facing African Americans in the U.S. and in most industrialized societies. It is the leading contributor to the excessive rates of cerebrovascular, renal and cardiac disease morbidity and mortality in African Americans. The causes for the high morbidity rate is at present unclear. However, it is very doubtful that a comprehensive understanding of this problem can be attained by narrow biological explanations, but requires a more comprehensive examination of multiple interacting factors. In this chapter, we have reviewed the available literature on hypertension in African Americans, paying particular attention to the biological, socioeconomic and sociopsychological factors believed to be implicated in the excessive rates of hypertensive disease in African Americans. Current epidemiologic and clinical evidence identify racial differences in such factors relevant to hypertension as differences in renal function and in the metabolism of sodium; differences in dietary intake of potassium and calcium; differences in body mass, especially in African American women; differences in socioeconomic status, in exposure to insidious ecologic stresses, and in sociocultural experiences; and finally, differences in the impact of psychological responses to frustrating social obstacles (e.g., impact of reflexive anger, and an active, effortful coping style). These differences are believed to contribute to the observed racial differential in mortality and morbidity from hypertension.

We propose an integrative, biobehavioral perspective for investigating the problem of enhanced risk for hypertension in African Americans. This model seeks answers to this question in the interplay between factors and processes in the psychosocial, behavioral and biological domains rather than in any of these domains by themselves (i.e., seeking biological explanations to the exclusion of psychosocial contributors). The available evidence of African American-White differences in cardiovascular stress reactivity in laboratory experiments was reviewed as examples of studies investigating whether biobehavioral stress reactivity might be the mechanism underlying the racial differential in high blood pressure. This evidence indicates that although no firm conclusions can be drawn about racial differences in stress reactivity at this time, there are two noteworthy trends that have begun to emerge. The first concerns the possibility that African Americans respond to acute stressors with decreased cardiac reactivity (i.e., reduced heart rate or cardiac output) as compared to Whites (Frederikson, 1986; Light et al., 1986; Anderson et al., 1988). Although speculative at this time, these findings may indicate that cardiac influences, perhaps beta-adrenergically mediated, may be less significant to the development of hypertension in African Americans than in Whites. Biomedical evidence of lower plasma renin activity (Luft et al., 1985), decreased responsiveness to beta-adrenergic blockade in African American hypertensives (Hall, 1985), and lower resting heart rates in young African American normotensive adults provides partial support for this hypothesis.

A second trend suggests that African Americans may show a propensity toward blood pressure reactivity mediated by peripheral vasoconstriction (Anderson et al., 1988; Frederickson, 1986; Light et al., 1986; Strickland, Myers, & Lahey, 1989). Thus, alpha-adrenergic hyperreactivity, as indexed by peripheral vasoconstriction, may prove to be an important contributor to high blood pressure in African Americans.

Considerable additional research is needed to further elucidate these trends, including consideration of possible within-group differences due to gender, age, blood pressure group, family history of hypertension, and SES. Future biobehavioral studies must also venture beyond the safe but limiting confines of the experimental laboratory. Results of laboratory studies, although intriguing, suffer from built in constraints on external validity that are inherent in studying reactivity to acute stressors in a few individuals in the contrived settings of research laboratories. Life stresses that are most likely to contribute to the development of diseases such as hypertension are likely to be chronic and long term rather than acute, and they exert their effects during the normal daily lives and in the natural living environments of the individuals at risk (i.e., in African American communities).

Two exciting methodologies offer considerable promise as more naturalistic extensions of the biobehavioral research paradigm. These are the family interaction paradigm and the developments in the technology for ambulatory blood pressure monitoring. In recent years there have been several studies of blood pressure reactivity to interpersonal conflict stress in couples and families (Baer, 1983; Ewart et al., 1983; Hafner et al., 1983). These studies are based on the concept of family psychosomatics, which recognizes the powerful role that family context plays in shaping health beliefs and behaviors, in enhancing or buffering risk for a variety of psychological and physical illnesses, in shaping stress-coping and adjustment to illness, and in enhancing blood pressure concordance (Grolnick, 1972). This concept was subsequently elaborated by Baer (1983) into an appealing strategy for research on hypertension.

Research by Speers et al., (1986) on married couples reported moderate to high levels of concordance in health behaviors (e.g., eating habits) and in blood pressures. The blood pressure concordance rates in spouses were comparable to those reported for genetically related parent-offspring and sibling pairs. They also noted that BP concordance increased with length of marriage, which supports an environmental contribution in high blood pressure.

In a study of blood pressure reactivity in White couples, Ewart et al. (1983) demonstrated increased blood pressure reactivity in couples discussing a real marital problem. Their blood pressures increased as a function of the degree of marital distress experienced, the level of conflict expressed, and the degree of reliance on conflict avoidant coping strategies (i.e., anger-in). The latter has also been confirmed in studies with White hypertensive couples (Haffner et al., 1983), and in studies of family interactions in both African American and White families with a hypertensive father (Baer, 1983; Baer et al., 1980). These studies indicate that families with a hypertensive father evidenced more reactive blood pressures (i.e., greater pre-post BP changes) and a higher frequency of conflict-avoidant, nonverbal behaviors (i.e., gaze aversion) during a family conflict discussion and role play conflict task than normotensive families. These data suggest that families with a hypertensive father may develop, perhaps through parental modelling, a greater tendency to cope with conflicts by interpersonal distancing and avoidance (i.e., anger-in).

While this work was largely conducted on White couples and families, the focus on intrafamilial dynamics as a potentially powerful contributor to or protector against the development of hypertension in biologically at risk African Americans should make a significant contribution to the field. A recent study by McClure (1989) tested for differences in blood pressure reactivity and conflict coping styles in African American hypertensive and normotensive mother-daughter dyads during a family conflict discussion. These authors found low to moderate BP concordance in both hypertensive and normotensive dyads both during rest and in response to a family conflict task. These results may be accounted for by shared genetics and/or by shared conflict coping styles or other psychosocial attributes within families. Substantial additional work is needed using a family interaction model of stress reactivity to further elucidate the relative contribution of biological and sociofamilial factors in conferring risk for this disease.

The second exciting new development which promises to revolutionize stress reactivity research is the ability to measure blood pressure in the natural environment with ambulatory monitoring devices. Studies using this technology have shown that blood pressure varies greatly during a 24-hour period, with pressures tending to be highest while at work and lowest during sleep (Pickering et al., 1982). Studies by Pickering et al. (1982, 1985) indicate that clinic measures of blood pressure do not reliably reflect pressures at other times and in other settings, and that target organ damage secondary to high blood pressure appears to be more closely associated with 24-hour ambulatory blood pressures than with clinic pressures.

Given all of the evidence that African Americans and Whites differ in socioeconomic status, in exposure to socio-ecologic stresses, and in exposure to stresses associated with racism and discrimination, ambulatory monitoring of blood pressure over time and in the natural course of daily living could provide the necessary data to determine the extent to which these social differences contribute to the observed racial differences in hypertension morbidity and mortality. The one published study to date that compared 24-hour BP patterns in African Americans and Whites found no significant racial differences (Rowland et al., 1982). However, preliminary results of a recent study with a small sample of African American normotensives, on the other hand, suggested that African Americans may maintain higher resting blood pressures during sleep than those reported for Whites in other studies (Harshfield, personal communication, 1989).

Unfortunately, there are many conceptual and methodological problems that remain to be resolved in order to make full use of the ambulatory BP monitoring technology. Among them is the ability to reliably separate valid physiological responses from artifacts (e.g., due to noise, movement, etc.), the need to reliably link physiologic responses to identified stressors in the natural setting (i.e., what was the person reacting to at the time the reading was taken), as well as to link these responses to the psychological state of the respondent (i.e., how did the person feel at the time the reading was taken). Despite these technical complications, this is an exciting new approach to the biobehavioral study of blood pressure and it should be applied to the study of hypertension in African American adults.

In conclusion, biobehavioral studies of African American-White differences in stress-induced cardiovascular reactivity have gained prominence as a useful approach to identifying the bases for the observed racial differences in essential hypertension. Although present findings are inconclusive with respect to the causes of these racial differences, they suggest that perhaps decreased cardiac reactivity and increased peripheral vascular reactivity in African Americans compared to Whites may be part of the puzzle. Future biobehavioral studies on this question would be greatly improved by recognizing the heterogeneity of the African American population and exercising greater care in defining and selecting African American adult samples (e.g., including better gender, age, SES distributions in African American samples), by focusing more on differences among African Americans rather than on differences between African Americans and Whites, by using more interpersonally complex and personally meaningful stressor tasks that are likely to produce results that are more generalizable outside of the research laboratory, and by making better use of the available technology for ambulatory blood pressure monitoring to assess stress-reactivity to more chronic stresses and under more naturalistic conditions.

Notes

1. The preparation of this manuscript was supported in part by grant No. RO1-HL31707, NHLBI/NIH to the first author. An earlier version of this chapter was published in R. L. Jones (Ed.), *Black Adult Development and Aging*, 1989, 311-349. Berkeley, CA: Cobb & Henry Publishers.

2. A glossary of terms is included at the end of this chapter.

Glossary

Adrenal Cortex—A structure located within the adrenal glands that produces steroid hormones (e.g., cortisol, aldosterone) which are crucial to blood pressure regulation.

Aldosteronism—Abnormality of electrolyte metabolism (e.g., calcium, potassium, sodium, etc.) caused by excessive secretion of a aldosterone.

Alpha-adrenergic—Neurotransmitter receptor sites throughout the vasculature that when stimulated result in the constriction of the blood vessels. Vascular constriction results in increased blood pressure.

Autonomic nervous system (ANS)—The portion of the nervous system concerned with regulation of the activity of cardiac muscle, smooth muscle, and glands.

Beta-adrenergic—Neurotransmitter receptor sites located throughout the vasculature system that when stimulated result in the expansion or dilation. Vasodilation results in blood pressure reduction.

Beta-blockade—Introduction of chemical agents that prevent excitation of the beta-adrenergic receptors.

Biobehavioral—Research approach that investigates the concurrent effect of behavioral and psychosocial factors which influence biological mechanisms.

Catecholamines—Compounds that mimic the physiological effects of adrenergic stimulation such as norepinephrine and epinephrine. They facilitate "flight or fight" responses.

Coarctation—Refers to the stricture or contraction of a blood vessel (e.g., coarctation of the aorta).

Cold pressor test—Task involving the introduction of a hand or other body part into ice-water, and the measurement of subsequent physiological changes (e.g., blood pressure, heart rate).

Coronary Heart Disease (CHD)—Diseases of the heart and blood vessels.

Diuretics—Pharmacologic agents that promote the production of urine as a means of reducing blood pressure by decreasing body fluid volume.

Dopamine-beta-hydroxylase (DBH)—Enzyme involved in the biosynthesis of the catecholamine norepinephrine.

End-stage renal disease—Kidney disease marked by a loss of at least 80% of the kidneys' ability to filter waste products. This condition results in a buildup of toxic substances in the blood which can be fatal.

Endocrine—Pertaining to glands and other structures that produce and secrete hormones into the circulatory system.

Forearm vascular resistance—An index of vasoconstriction of blood vessels in the forearm skeletal muscle. This measure is obtained after the introduction of a stressor.

Glomerular filtration rate—The volume of waste formed by the kidney per unit of time (e.g., milliliters/minute).

Hemodynamic—Pertaining to factors (e.g., dimensions of vessels and the viscosity of blood) which influence the flow of blood through the cardiovascular system.

Hyperreactivity—Excessive or exaggerated physiological response to stress. This pattern of response is believed to be associated with enhanced risk for hypertension and other cardiovascular diseases.

Left Ventricular Hypertrophy—Enlargement of the left ventricle of the heart.

Mineralocorticoid—Group of corticosteriods, primarily aldosterone, which are principally involved in the regulation of electrolyte and water balance via their influence on ion transport in the kidneys.

Morbidity—Condition of being diseased or sick. Morbidity rate refers to the number of persons in a population who are afflicted by a specific disease in a given period of time (e.g., one year).

Mortality—Death rate in a population for a specific disease or for all diseases in a given period of time (e.g., CHB death rate in African Americans, ages 60-75 in 1985-1987).

Neurohormonal—Condition where both neural and hormonal factors influence a physiological outcome.

Pathophysiology—The physiological basis or processes underlying disordered functioning (e.g., the pathophysiology of hypertension).

Pehochromocytoma—Vascular tumor of the medulla of the adrenal gland. This tumor causes increased secretion of epinephrine and norepinephrine.

Plasma renin—Enzyme that is stored and secreted by the kidney. It plays a significant role in the regulation of blood pressure.

Pressor—Response to a stimulus or stressor indicated by increases in blood pressure.

Psychotropic Medication—Drugs that modify or affect mental states.

Radiographic—Pertaining to x-rays of internal structures of the body.

Renal functioning—Functioning of the kidneys.

Stress-reactivity—Hemodynamic (i.e., blood pressure) biochemical (e.g., catecholamines), and/or psychological (e.g., anxiety) responses to stressors which are generally introduced and measured in a controlled laboratory setting.

Type A behavior pattern—Behavior pattern characterized by hard-driving, aggressiveness, ambitiousness, restlessness, and functioning under self-imposed time pressure. This behavior pattern is associated with increased risk for coronary heart disease.

Vasoconstriction—The reduction of the diameter of a blood vessel, especially constriction of arterioles which result in decreased blood flow and increased blood pressure.

References

Abboud, F. M., & Eckstein, J. W. (1966). Active reflex vasodilation in man. *Federation Proceedings, 25,* 1611-1617.

Anderson, N. B. (1989). Racial differences in stress-induced cardiovascular reactivity and hypertension: Current status and substantive issues. *Psychological Bulletin, 105(11),* 89-105.

Anderson, N. B., Lane, J. D., Muranaka, M., Williams, R. B., & Houseworth, S. J. (1988). Racial differences in blood pressure and forearm vascular responses to the cold face test. *Psychosomatic Medicine, 50,* 57-63.

Anderson, N. B., McNeilly, M., & Myers, H. F. (1991). Autonomic reactivity and hypertension in Blacks: A review and proposed model. *Ethnicity & Disease, 1,* 154-170.

Anderson, N. B., Williams, R. B., Lane, J. D., Haney, T. S., Simpson, S., & Houseworth, S. J. (1986). Type A behavior, family history of hypertension and cardiovascular responses among Black women. *Health Psychology, 5,* 393-406.

Anderson, N. B., Williams, R. B., Lane, J. D., & Houseworth, S. J. (1987). Family history of hypertension and cardiovascular responses in young Black women. *Journal of Psychosomatic Research, 31,* 723-729.

Annest, J. L., Sing, C. F., Biron, P., & Mongeau, J. G. (1979a). Familial aggregation of blood pressure and weight in adoptive families. I: Comparisons of blood pressure and weight statistics among families with adopted, natural or both natural and adopted children. *American Journal of Epidemiology, 110*(4), 479-491.

Annest, J. L., Sing, C. F., Biron, P., & Mongeau, J. G. (1979b). Familial aggregation of blood pressure and weight in adoptive families. II: Estimation of the relative contributions of genetic and common environmental factors to blood pressure correlations between family members. *American Journal of Epidemiology, 110*(4), 492-503.

Baer, P. E. (1983). Conflict management in the family: The impact of paternal hypertension. *Advances in Family Intervention, Assessment and Theory, 3,* 161-184.

Baer, P. E., Vincent, J. Williams, B., Bourianoff, G. G., & Bartlett, P. (1980). Behavioral response to induced conflict in families with a hypertensive father. *Hypertension, 2,* 70-77.

Boham, G. S., & Brock, D. W. (1985). The relationship of diabetes with race, sex and obesity. *American Journal of Clinical Nutrition, 41,* 775-783.

Boyle, E. (1970). Biological patterns in hypertension by race, sex, body height and skin color. *JAMA, 213,* 1637-1643.

Boyle, E., Griffey, W., Nichaman, M., & Talbert, C. (1967). An epidemiologic study of hypertension among racial groups of Charleston County, South Carolina: The Charleston Heart Study, Phase II. In S. Stamler & T. Pullman (Eds.), *The epidemiology of hypertension* (pp. 193-203). New York: Grune and Stratton.

Chrysant, S., Danisa, K., Kem, D., Dillard, B., Smith, W., & Frohlich, E. (1979). Racial differences in pressure, volume and renin interrelationships in essential hypertension. *Hypertension, 1,* 136-141.

Clark, V., & Harrell, J. (1982). The relationship among Type A behavior styles used in coping with racism and blood pressure. *Journal of Black Psychology, 8,* 89-99.

Cooper, R. (1984). A note on the biological concept of race and its implications in epidemiological research. *American Heart Journal, 108*(2), 715-723.

Curry, C. L., & Lewis, J. F. (1985). Cardiac anatomy and function in hypertensive Blacks. In W. D. Hall, E. Saunders, & N. B. Shulman (Eds.), *Hypertension in Blacks: Epidemiology, pathophysiology and treatment*(pp. 61-70). Chicago, IL: Year Book Medical Publishers.

Diamond, E. L. (1982). The role of anger and hostility in essential hypertension and coronary heart disease. Psychological *Bulletin, 92*(2), 410-433.

Dimsdale, J. E., Graham, R., Ziegler, M. G., Zusman, R., & Berry, C. C. (1987). Age, race, diagnosis and sodium effects on the pressor response to infused norepinephrine. *Hypertension, 10,* 564-569.

Ditto, B. (1986). Parental history of essential hypertension, active coping, and cardiovascular reactivity. *Psychophysiology, 23,* 62-70.

Dohrenwend, B. S., & Dohrenwend, B. P. (1970). Class and race as status-related sources of stress. In S. Levine & N. A. Scotch (Eds.), *Social stress* (pp. 111-140). Chicago, IL: Aldine Publishing Co.

Eliot, R. S., Buell, J. C., & Dembroski, T. M. (1982). Blood pressure, ethnicity, and psychosocial resources. *Psychosomatic Medicine, 48,* 509-519.

Epstein, F. H. (1984). How useful is a family history of hypertension as a predictor of future hypertension? *Annals of Clinical Research, 16* (43), 32-34.

Ewart, C. K., Burnett, K. F., & Taylor, C. B. (1983). Communication behaviors that affect blood pressure: An A-B-A-B analysis of marital interaction. *Behavior Modification, 7*(3), 331-344.

Falkner, B., Kushner, H., Onesti, G., & Angelakos, E. T. (1981). Cardiovascular characteristics in adolescents who develop essential hypertension. *Hypertension, 3,* 521-527.

Falkner, B., Kushner, H., Khalsa, D. K., & Katz, S. (1987). *The effect of chronic sodium load in young Blacks and Whites.* Paper presented at the Annual Meeting of the Society of Behavioral Medicine, Washington, DC.

Finnerty, F. A. (1971). Hypertension is different in Blacks, *JAMA, 216,* 1634-1635.

Folkow, B. (1982). Physiological aspects of primary hypertension. *Physiological Reviews, 62,* 347-504.

Frederickson, M. (1986). Racial differences in reactivity to behavioral challenge in essential hypertension. *Journal of Hypertension, 4,* 325-331.

Frederickson, M., Dimberg, U., Frisk-Hambert, M., & Strom, G. (1982). Hemodynamic and electrodermal correlates of psychogenic stimuli in normotensive and hypertensive subjects. *Biological Psychology, 15*, 63-74.

Frisancho, A. R., Leonard, W. R., & Bollettins, L. (1984). Blood pressure in Blacks and Whites and its relationship to dietary sodium and potassium intake. *Journal of Chronic Disease, 37*, 515-519.

Gentry, W. D., Chesney, A. P., Fary, H. E., Hall, R. P., & Harburg, E. (1982). Habitual anger-coping styles: Effect on mean blood pressure and risk for essential hypertension. *Psychosomatic Medicine, 44*(2), 195-202.

Gibson, G. S. & Gibbons, A. (1982). Hypertension among Blacks: An annotated bibliography. *Hypertension, 4*(1), Part II.

Gillum, R. F. (1979). Pathophysiology of hypertension in Blacks and Whites. *Hypertension, 1*, 468-475.

Gillum, R. F. (1987a). Overweight and obesity in Black women: A review of published data from the National Center for Health Statistics. *Journal of National Medical Association, 79*, 865-877.

Gillum, R. F. (1987b). The association of body fat distribution with hypertension, hypertensive heart disease, coronary heart disease, diabetes and cardiovascular risk factors in men and women aged 18-79 years. *Journal of Chronic Disease, 40*, 421-430.

Gillum, R. F. (1991). Cardiovascular disease in the United States: An epidemiologic overview. In E. Saunders (Ed.), *Cardiovascular diseases in Blacks* (pp. 3-16). Philadelphia, PA: F. A. Davis, Co.

Goldstein, I., & Shapiro, D. (1987). The effects of stress and caffeine on hypertensives. *Psychosomatic Medicine, 49*(3), 226-235.

Greenberg, W., & Shapiro, D. (1987). The effects of caffeine and stress on blood pressure in individuals with and without a family history of hypertension. *Psychophysiology, 24*, 151-156.

Greenstadt, L., Yang, L., & Shapiro, D. (1988). Caffeine, mental stress and risk for hypertension: A cross-cultural replication. *Psychosomatic Medicine, 50*, 15-22.

Grim, C. E., Luft, F., Miller, J., Meneely, G. Batarbee, H., Hames, C., & Dahl, K. (1980). Racial differences in blood pressure in Evans County Georgia: Relationship to sodium and potassium intake and plasma renin activity. *Journal of Chronic Diseases, 33*, 87-94.

Grim, C. E., Luft, F., Weinberger, M., Miller, J., Rose, R., & Christian, J. (1984). Genetic, familial and racial influences in blood pressure control systems in man. *Australian & New Zealand Journal of Medicine, 14*, 453-457.

Grim, C. E., & Cantor, R. M. (1986, August). *Genetic influences on blood pressure in Blacks: Twin studies.* Paper presented at the American Federation of Clinical Research.

Grolnick, L. (1972). A family perspective on psychosomatic factors in illness: A review of the literature. *Family Process, 11*, 457-486.

Hafner, R. J., Chalmers, J. P., Swift, H., Graham, J. R., West, M. J., & Wing, L. M. (1983). Marital interaction and adjustment in patients with essential hypertension. *Clinical Experimental Hypertension*, *5*(1), 119-131.

Hall, W. D. (1985). Pharmacologic therapy of hypertension in Blacks. In W. D. Hall, E. Saunders, & N. Shulman (Eds.), *Hypertension in Blacks: Epidemiology, pathophysiology and treatment* (pp. 182-208). Chicago, IL: Year Book Medical Publishers.

Harburg, E., Erfurt, J., Hauenstein, L., Chape, C., Schull, W., & Schork, M. (1973). Socioecologic stress, suppressed hostility, skin color and Black-White blood pressure: Detroit. *Journal of Chronic Diseases*, *26*, 595-611.

Harburg, E., et al. (1978a). Skin color, ethnicity and blood pressure. II: Detroit Blacks. *American Journal of Public Health*, *68*(12), 1177-1183.

Harburg, E. et al. (1978b). Skin color, ethnicity and blood pressure. I: Detroit Whites. *American Journal of Public Health*, *68*(12), 1184-1187.

Harrell, J. P. (1980). Psychological factors and hypertension: A status report. *Psychological Bulletin*, *87*, 482-501.

Hayes, C. G., Tyroler, H. A., & Cassel, J. C. (1971). Family aggregation of blood pressure in Evans County, Georgia. *Archives of Internal Medicine*, *128*, 965-975.

Hollenberg, N. K., Williams, G. H., & Adams, D. F. (1981). Essential hypertension: Abnormal renal vascular and endocrine responses to a mild psychological stimulus. *Hypertension*, *3*, 11-17.

Hogan, D. P., & Pazul, M. (1982). The occupational earning returns to education among Black men in the north. *American Journal of Sociology*, *87*, 905-920.

Hypertension Detection and Follow-up Program Cooperative Group (1977). Race, education and prevalence of hypertension. *American Journal of Epidemiology*, *106*, 351-361.

Hypertension Detection and Follow-up Program Cooperative Group (1979). Five-year findings of the hypertension detection and follow-up program: Mortality by race, sex and age. *JAMA*, *242*, 2572-2577.

Jackson, J. J. (1981). Urban Black Americans. In A. Harwood (Ed.), *Ethnicity and medical care* (p. 37). Cambridge, MA: Harvard University Press.

James, S. A. (1984a). Socioeconomic influences on coronary heart disease in Black populations. *American Heart Journal, 108* (Suppl. 3, Part 2), 669-672.

James, S. A., (1984b). Psychosocial and environmental factors in Black hypertension. In W. Hall, E. Saunders, & N. Shulman (Eds.), *Hypertension in Blacks: Epidemiology, pathophysiology and treatment* (pp. 132-143). Chicago, IL: Year Book Medical Publishers.

James, S. A., Harnett, S. A., & Kalsbeek, W. (1983). John Henryism and blood pressure differences among Black men, *Journal of Behavioral Medicine*, *6*, 259-278.

James, S. A., & Kleinbaum, D. G. (1976). Socioecologic stress and hypertension-related mortality rates in North Carolina. *American Journal of Public Health, 66,* 354-358.

Jorgenson, R. S., & Houston, B. K. (1981). Family history of hypertension, gender and cardiovascular reactivity and stereotypy during stress. *Journal of Behavioral Medicine, 4,* 175-189.

Kaplan, N. M. (1979). Stress, the sympathetic nervous system and hypertension. *Journal of Human Stress, 4*(3), 29-34.

Kasl, S. V. (1984). Social and psychological factors in the etiology of coronary heart disease in Black populations: An exploration of research needs. *American Heart Journal, 108*(3)(2), 660-669.

Keil, J. E., Tyroler, H. A., Sandifer, S. H., & Boyle, E. (1977). Hypertension: Effects of social class and racial admixture: The results of a cohort study in the Black population of Charleston, South Carolina. *American Journal of Public Health, 67*(7), 634-639.

Keil, J. E. (1981). Skin color and education effects on blood pressure. *American Journal of Public Health, 71,* 532- 534.

Kessler, R. C., & Neighbors, H. W. (1986). A new perspective on the relationships among race, social class and psychological distress. *Journal of Health & Social Behavior, 27,* 107-115.

Krantz, D. S., & Manuck, S. B. (1984). Acute psychophysiologic reactivity and risk of cardiovascular disease: A review and methodological critique. *Psychological Bulletin, 96,* 435-464.

Langford, H. G. (1981). Is blood pressure different in Black people? *Postgraduate Medical Journal, 57,* 749-754.

Langford, H. G., Watson, R. L., & Douglas, B. A. (1980). Factors affecting blood pressure in population groups. *Transactions of the Association of American Physicians, 63,* 135-146.

Langford, H. G., Langford, F. P. J., & Tyler, M. (1985). Dietary profile of sodium, potassium, and calcium in U.S. Blacks. In W. D. Hall, E. Saunders, & N. B. Shulman (Eds.), *Hypertension in Blacks: Epidemiology, pathophysiology & treatment* (pp. 49-57). Chicago, IL: Year Book Medical Publishers.

Lazarus, R. S. (1979). A strategy for research on psychological and social factors in hypertension. *Journal of Human Stress, 4*(3), 34-40.

Lazarus, R. S., & Launier, R. (1978). Stress-related transactions between person and environment. In L. A. Pervin & M. Lewis (Eds.), *Perspectives in interactional psychology.* New York: Plenum Press.

Light, K. C. (1987). Psychosocial precursors of hypertension: Experimental evidence. *Circulation, 76* (1), 67-76.

Light, K. C., Sherwood, A., Obrist, P., James, S., Strogatz, D., & Willis, P. (1986). *Comparisons of cardiovascular and renal responses to stress in Black and*

White normotensive and borderline hypertensive men. Paper presented at the American Psychological Association Convention, Washington, DC.

Lovenberg, W., Bruckwick, E. A., Alexander, R. W., Horwitz, D., & Kaizer, H. R. (1974). Evaluation of serum dopamine-beta-hydroxylase activity as an index of sympathetic nervous activity in man. In E. Usdin (Ed.), *Neuropsychopharmacology of monoamines and their regulating enzymes.* New York: Raven Press.

Luft, F., Grim, C., & Weinberger, M. (1979). Effects of volume expansion and contraction in normotensive Whites, Blacks and subjects of different ages. *Circulation, 59,* 653-650.

Luft, F., Grim, C., & Weinberger, M. (1985). Electrolyte and volume homeostasis in Blacks. In W. D. Hall, E. Saunders, & N. Shulman (Eds.), *Hypertension in Blacks: Epidemiology, pathophysiology & treatment*(pp. 115-131). Chicago, IL: Year Book Medical Publishers.

Mann, S., Miller-Craig, M. W., & Raferty, E. B. (1985). Superiority of 24-hour measurement of blood pressure over clinic values in determining prognosis in hypertension. *Clinical Experiential Hypertension, 7*(2 & 3), 279.

Manuck, S. B., & Proietti, J. M. (1982). Parental hypertension and cardiovascular response to cognitive and isometric challenge. *Psychophysiology, 19,* 481-489.

Mathews, K., Weiss, S., Detre, T., Dembroski, T., Falkner, B., Manuck, S., & Williams, R. (Eds.). (1986). *Handbook of stress reactivity and cardiovascular disease.* New York: J. Wiley & Sons.

McCarron, D. A., Morris, C. D., & Cole, C. (1982). Dietary calcium in human hypertension. *Science, 217,* 267-269.

McClure, F. H. (1989). Blood pressure responses in Black hypertensive and normotensive families during interpersonal conflict. *Dissertation Abstract International.*

McGee, D. P. (1976). An introduction to African psychology: Melanin, the physiological basis for psychological oneness. In L. M. King, V. J. Dixon, & W. W. Nobles (Eds.), *African philosophy: Assumptions & paradigms for research on Black persons* (pp. 215-222). Los Angeles, CA: Fanon Research & Development Center.

Miller, J. Z., & Grim, C. E. (1983). Heritability of blood pressure. In T. A. Kotchen, J. M. Kotchen, & J. Wright (Eds.), *High blood pressure in the young* (pp. 79-90). Boston, MA: PSG.

Moll, P. P., Harburg, E., Burns, T. L., Schork, M. A., & Ozgoren, F. (1983). Heredity, stress and blood pressure, a family set approach: The Detroit project revisited, *Journal of Chronic Diseases, 36*(4), 317-328.

Morell, M. A., Shapiro, D., Myers, H. F., Goldstein, I., & Armstrong, M. (1988). Psychological stress reactivity to mental arithmetic stress in Black and White normotensive men. *Health Psychology, 7*(5), 479-496.

Mongeau, J. G., & Biron, P. (1981). The influences of genetics and of household environment in the transmission of normal blood pressure. *Clinical and Experimental Hypertension, 3*(4), 593-596.

Myers, H. F. (1982). Stress, ethnicity and social class: A model for research on Black populations. In E. E. Jones & S. Korchin (Eds.), *Minority mental health* (pp. 118-148). New York: Holt, Rhinehart & Winston.

Myers, H. F. (1985). Coronary heart disease in Black populations: Current research, treatment and prevention needs. *Health & Human Services Secretary's Task Force Report on Black and minority health, Vol. IV: Cardiovascular and Cerebrovascular Diseases .*

Myers, H. F. (Chair) (1984). Summary of workshop III: Working group on socioeconomic and sociocultural influences in coronary heart disease in Blacks. *American Heart Journal 108*(3)(2), 706-710.

Myers, H. F., & McClure, F. H. (1993). Psychosocial factors in hypertension in Blacks: The case for a interactional perspective. In J. C. S. Fray & J. G. Douglas (Eds.), *Pathophysiology of hypertension in Blacks* (pp. 90-106). New York: Oxford University Press.

Myers, H. F., Morell, M., Shapiro, D., Goldstein, I., & Armstrong, M. (1985). Biobehavioral stress reactivity in Black and White normotensives. *Psychophysiology Abstract, 22*(5), 605-606.

Myers, H. F., Shapiro, D., McClure, F., & Daims, R. (1989, May). Impact of caffeine and psychological stress and blood pressure in Black and White men. *Health Psychology, 8(5),* 597-612.

Nash, J. Jorgensen, R., Lasser, N., & Hymowitz, N. (1985, March). *The effects of race, gender and task on cardiovascular reactivity in unmedicated, mild hypertensives.* Paper presented at the Society of Behavioral Medicine meeting, New Orleans, LA.

National Center for Health Statistics Report (1981). *Hypertension in adults 25-74 years of age: United States, 1971-1975.* (Vital and Health Statistics, Series 11, No. 221. DHHS Publ. PHS 81-1671.). Washington, DC: Government Printing Office.

Neaton, J. D., Kuller, L. H., Wentworth, D., & Borhani, N. O. (1984). Total mortality and cariovascular mortality in relation to cigarette smoking among Black and White males followed up for five years. *American Heart Journal, 108*(3)(2), 759-769.

Nesser, W. B., Tyroler, H. A., & Cassel, J. C. (1971). Social disorganization and stroke mortality in the Black population of North Carolina. *American Journal of Epidemiology, 93,* 166-175.

Obrist, P. A. (1981). *Cardiovascular physiology: A perspective.* New York: Plenum Press.

Obrist, P. A., Gaebelein, C. J., Teller, E. S., Langer, A. W., Grignolo, A., Light, K. C., & McCubbin, J. A. (1978). The relationship among heart rate, carotic dp/dt and blood pressure in humans as a function of type of stress. *Psychophysiology, 15,* 102.

Ostfeld, A. M., & Shekelle, R. B. (1967). Psychological variables and blood pressure. In J. Stamler, R. Stamler, & T. N. Pullman (Eds.), *The epidemiology of hypertension,* New York: Grune & Straton.

Page, I. H. (1982). The mosaic theory 32 years late. *Hypertension, 7,* 177-185.

Patterson, O. (1983). The nature, causes and implications of ethnic identification. In C. Fried (Ed.), *Minorities: Community and identity* (pp. 25-50), New York: Springer-Verlag.

Pickering, T. G., Harshfield, G. A., Kleinert, H. B., Banks, S., & Laragh, J. H. (1982). Comparisons of blood pressure during normal daily activities, sleep, and exercise in normal and hypertensive subjects. *JAMA, 247,* 992-996.

Pickering, T. G., Harshfield, G. A., Devereaux, R. B., & Laragh, J. H. (1985). What is the role of ambulatory blood pressure monitoring in the management of hypertensive patients? *Hypertension, 7,* 171-187.

Prineas, R. J., & Gillum, R. (1985). U.S. epidemiology of hypertension in Blacks. In W. D. Hall, E. Saunders, & N. B. Shulman, (Eds.), *Hypertension in Blacks: Epidemiology, pathophysiology and treatment* (pp. 17-36). Chicago, IL: Yearbook Medical Publishers.

Robertson, D., Frolich, J. C., Carr, R. K., Watson, J. T., Hollifield, J. W., Shanel, D. G., & Oates, J. A. (1978). Effects of caffeine on plasma renin activity, catecholamines and blood pressure. *New England Journal of Medicine, 298,* 181-186.

Rose, R. J., Miller, J. Z., Grim, C. E., & Christian, J. C. (1979). Aggregation of blood pressure in the families of identical twins. *American Journal of Epidemiology, 109*(5), 503-511.

Rose, R. J. et al., (1980). Heritability of blood pressure: Analysis of variance in MZ twin parents and their children. *Acta Geneticae Medicae-Et Gemellological, 29,* 143-149.

Rowland, D., DeGiovanni, J., McLeary, R., Watson, R., Stallard, T., & Littler, W. (1982). Cardiovascular response in Black and White hypertensives. *Hypertension, 4,* 817-820.

Russel, R. P., & Massi, A. T. (1973). Significant associations of adrenal cortical abnormalities with essential hypertension. *American Journal of Medicine, 54,* 44.

Schneiderman, N. (1983). Behavior, autonomic function, and animal models of cardiovascular pathology. In T. Dembroski, T. Schmidt, & G. Blumchen (Eds.), *Biobehavioral bases of coronary heart disease.* Basel: Karger.

Schneiderman, N. (1986, August). *Race, gender and reactivity in the Miami Minority Hypertension Project.* Paper presented at the American Psychological Association Convention, Washington, DC.

Schneiderman, N., Kaufman, P., & Carver, C. (Eds.). (1990). *Research in cardiovascular behavioral medicine: A handbook of research methods, measurement and experimental design.* New York: Plenum.

Schwartz, G. E., Shapiro, A. P., Redmond, D. P., Ferguson, D. C. E., Ragland, D., & Weiss, S. M. (1979). Behavioral medicine approaches to hypertension: An integrative analysis of theory and research. *Journal of Behavioral Medicine, 2*(4), 311-364.

Shapiro, D., & Goldstein, I. (1982). Biobehavioral perspectives on hypertension. *Journal of Consulting & Clinical Psychology, 50*(6), 841-858.

Shapiro, D., Lane, J. D., & Henry, J. P. (1986). Caffeine, cardiovascular reactivity and cardiovascular disease. In K. A. Matthews, S. M. Weiss, T. Detre, T. M. Dembroski, B. Falkner, S. B. Manuck, & R. B. Williams (Eds.), *Handbook of stress, reactivity and cardiovascular disease* (pp. 311-328). New York: J. Wiley & Sons.

Shulman, N. B. (1985). Renal disease in hypertensive Blacks. In W. D. Hall, E. Saunders, & N. B. Shulman (Eds.), *Hypertension in Blacks: Epidemiology, pathophysiology and treatment* (pp. 106-112). Chicago, IL: Yearbook Medical Publishers.

Speers, M. A., Kasl, S. W., Freeman, D. H., & Ostfeld, A. M. (1986). Blood pressure concordance between spouses. *American Journal of Epidemiology, 123,* 818-829.

Steptoe, A., Melville, D., & Ross, A. (1984). Behavioral response demands, cardiovascular reactivity and essential hypertension. *Psychosomatic Medicine, 46,* 33-48.

Strickland, T. L., Myers, H. F., & Lahey, B. B. (1989). Cardiovascular reactivity to caffeine and stress in Black and White normotensive females. *Psychosomatic Medicine, 51,* 381-389.

Syme, S. L., Oakes, T. W., Friedman, G. D., Feldman, R. Siegelaub, A. B., & Collen, M. (1974). Social class and racial differences in blood pressure. *Public Health Briefs: American Journal of Public Health, 64*(6), 619-620.

Syme, S. L. (1979). Psychosocial determinants of hypertension. In E. Onesti & C. Klint (Eds.), *Hypertension: Determinants, complications and intervention.* New York: Grune & Stratton.

Thompson, G. E. (1980, May). Hypertension: Implications of comparisons among Blacks and Whites. *Urban Health,* 31-33.

Tyroler, H. A., & James, S. A. (1978). Blood pressure and skin color. *American Journal of Public Health, 68,* 1170-1172.

Tyroler, H. A., Knowles, M. G., Wing, S. B. Logue, E. E., Davis, C. E., Heiss, G., Heyden, S., & Hames, C. G. (1984). Ischemic heart disease risk factors and twenty-year mortality in middle-aged Evans County Black males. *American Heart Journal, 108*(3)(2), 738-747.

U.S. Department of Health, Education & Welfare: National Center for Health Statistics and National Center for Health Research (1978). DHEW Publication No. (PHS) 78-1232.

Venter, C., Joubert, P., & Styrdom, W. (1985). The relevance of ethnic differences in hemodynamic responses to the head-up tilt maneuver to clinical pharmacological investigations. *Journal of Cardiovascular Pharmacology, 7,* 1009-1010.

Washington, E., & McCloud, V. (1982). The external validity of research involving American minorities. *Human Development, 25,* 334-339.

Watkins, L. O. (1984) Worldwide experience: Coronary artery disease and hypertension in Black populations. *Urban Health, 13,* 30-35.

Watkins, L. O., & Eaker, E. (1986). Population and demographic influences on reactivity. In K. Mathews, S. Weiss, T. Detre, T. Dembroski, B. Falkner, S. Manuck, & R. Williams (Eds.), *Handbook of stress, reactivity and cardiovascular disease* (pp. 85-107). New York: J. Wiley & Sons.

Watt, G. (1986). Design and interpretation of studies comparing individuals with and without a family history of high blood pressure. *Journal of Hypertension,* 4(1), 1-7.

Weiner, H. (1979). *The psychobiology of essential hypertension.* New York: Elsevier.

Zinner, S. H., Rosner, B., & Kass, E. H. (1985). Significance of blood pressure in infancy: Familial aggregation and predictive effect on later blood pressure. *Hypertension,* 7(3)(1), 411-416.

Author

Hector F. Myers, Ph.D.
UCLA, Dept. of Psychology
Box 951563
Los Angeles, CA 90095-1563
Telephone: (310) 825-1813
Fax: (310) 206-5895
E-mail: Myers@psych.ucla.edu

Racism, Stress and Disease

Jules P. Harrell, Marcellus M. Merritt and Jimalee Kalu

Introduction

If he has not attained eminent status, David Levering Lewis is becoming one of the major historians in the United States. His books span topics ranging from recent European history to the Harlem Renaissance. Recently a biography on the first half of the life of W. E. B. Dubois, earned Lewis a Pulitzer Prize. The second volume of this weighty study of Dubois became available in 1996. Lewis is a meticulous scholar. His prose flows gently, but it sweeps the reader into a wealth of historical detail. We should not take lightly, his observations and his summary statements about history. Dr. Lewis is not given to wild speculation and overstatement.

In *The Race to Fashoda,* Lewis (1987) examines subtle contours of European and African history in the last three decades of the 19th century. In his introduction, he betrays that even he, a veteran historian, may have been rocked intellectually by the record of a prescient conversation that occurred in the last century. The famed adventurer and explorer, Henry Morton Stanley, reported the dialogue he had with people from a Central African ethnic group called the Buhaya. These Africans told Stanley that the Buhaya people believed Europeans were "those from the dead." They said this without malice and with great sincerity. Lewis, abandoning restraint, writes " . . . in African eyes, the coming of the Whites signified more than the menace of Remington repeaters. It presaged death itself" (p. 13). Lewis' words bring to mind those of clinical psychologist Hussein A. Bulhan (1985). "One of the tragic ironies in situations of oppression is that the oppressed submit to subjugation for fear of physical death, yet they die more frequently and at an earlier age than their oppressors" (p. 177).

"Post modern" racial oppression, in the last decade of this century results, in the same outcome that Africans "presaged" at the end of the last century. The psychologist of African descent cannot escape confronting racism's ultimate consequence. African American psychologists must uncover the social psychological mechanisms and the physiological pathways by which racism causes premature death in African people. Essentially, this is the focus of the present chapter, though we have narrowed our focus to African people living in the United States.

247

The health status and life expectancy of African Americans, though it never equaled that in the general population, had improved significantly for most of the century to the mid 1980s. However, recently life expectancy began declining. We can index the current health status of African Americans using two related health measures: leading indicators of death and prominent health behaviors. Leading causes of death for African Americans today include homicide, infant mortality, heart disease and stroke, cirrhosis, cancer, and diabetes (U.S. Department of Health and Human Services, 1985). Recent research shows significant disparities between White and African American adults in these diseases. African American rates of deaths are significantly higher than those of Whites.

Heart disease is the leading cause of death in the United States, accounting for 40% of all fatalities (National Center for Health Statistics, 1987). Hypertension or high blood pressure, results in 5,000 excess deaths a year in the African American population. Hypertension is an important risk factor for stroke and end-stage renal disease (National Research Council, 1989).

For African American males aged 15-34, homicide is the leading cause of death and disability (United States Department of Health and Human Services, 1985). In 1985 the homicide rate for African Americans aged 15-24 was six times higher than for Whites. Cultural, psychological, and social factors have been offered as precursors of homicide (National Research Council, 1989). For example, unemployment and use of alcohol and other illicit drugs have been associated with a significant percentage of homicides (Brenner, 1983; U.S. Department of Health and Human Services, 1986).

African Americans experience higher incidence and mortality from cancer than Whites. Cancers of the lung, prostate, and esophagus account for most of the cancers in African Americans (especially males) and are largely responsible for the higher rates for African Americans. Cigarette smoking, alcohol abuse, and poor access to preventive services are associated with high risks of cancer (National Center for Health Statistics, 1988).

Prominent health behaviors that adversely impact African Americans today include violent behavior, substance abuse, poor nutrition, and teenage pregnancy and poor reproductive health (National Research Council, 1989). These behaviors can lead to the disease outcomes mentioned above and possibly death. Substance abuse includes the use of alcohol, illicit drugs, and tobacco. Poor nutritional practices result in high sodium intake, high cholesterol and overeating. Although African American teen pregnancies are declining, teenage childbearing has some adverse consequences such as bearing low weight infants, reducing educational attainment, and increasing risk of contracting sexually transmitted diseases, and challenging African American family structure and functioning (National Center for Health Statistics, 1987).

Krieger, Rowley, Herman, Avery, and Phillips (1993) introduced their excellent discussion of racism, sexism, class and health with an overview of health statistics for some of the very youngest members of society. They looked at trends in infant mortality and low birth weight. The evidence is startling when viewed in terms of the ratio of African American/White rates of problematic births at different socioeconomic levels. Not only do African American women "fare worse than White women at every economic level, . . . their disadvantage persists even among the most highly educated African American women" (p. 82). Hence, death stalks even the youngest members of African American society.

To be sure, it should be noted that poor socioeconomic and physical environments play a major role in the current health status of some African Americans (U.S. Department of Health and Human Services, 1985). One might be tempted to see these, not racism, as the causes of poor health among African Americans. Many major health risks are linked to inadequate housing, limited access to health care services, unemployment, and exposure to environmental toxins. These factors appear to interact with personal health habits and lifestyle in affecting African American health status. Indeed, a lack of institutional viability in many African American communities today adversely affects the health status of many of its members. This has been the case since the early history of African contact with White racism. We must see the socioeconomic problems, institutional underdevelopment and poor health practices that are prevalent in the African American community for what they are. More often than not they amount to manifestations of racism and oppression. They are one of the avenues of influence through which racial oppression destroys the lives of African Americans.

This chapter takes up conceptual and empirical works related to racism and health. Initially, we examine the concepts of racism and stress. In both instances, the field has reached no real consensus on a definition. Therefore, for our purposes, we chart the parameters of each concept in some detail. We distinguish among various forms of racism and place it within a framework of social inequities and oppression, and cultural hegemony. The brief discussion of psychological stress entails a sketching of some of its known physiological concomitants.

We have partitioned the discussion of the empirical research into laboratory experiments, and field studies. The latter include survey studies of racism, stress and the health of people of African descent in the United States. Within the two bodies of empirical work there are several paradigms and approaches. These yield different qualities of information about the mechanisms and pathways involved in stress and disease. First, we provide a glimpse of the evidence from field studies. Observations about some of the principal findings from the laboratory investigations follow the discussion of the field studies. We conclude with a discussion of two models for understanding racism and health outcomes. These models point out promising leads and avenues for empirical studies.

What is Racism?

Defining Racism

A quarter of a century ago African American scholars insisted that the power to define was a crucial element in the liberation process. This notion is a truism among African American scholars today. Indeed, there is persistent tension between definitions of key social concepts put forth by progressive scholars from oppressed groups and those that individuals who identify with mainstream scholarship tend to propose. Nowhere is this more evident than in the tension over the definition of racism.

For example, in 1972, James Jones made a clear conceptual distinction between racism and prejudice. "Racism results from the transformation of race prejudice and/or ethnocentrism through the exercise of power against a racial group defined as inferior by individuals and institutions with the intentional or unintentional support of the entire culture" (p. 117). This definition has good currency within the African American community in the United States. Krieger et al. (1993) defined racism as an "oppressive system of racial relations justified by ideology" where one group receives advantages in the process of dominating the other (p. 85). This definition is compatible with Jones'. Nevertheless, mainstream scholars ignore or repress the distinction that Jones made. For example, Doob (1993) claimed that "racism is the ideology contending that actual or alleged differences between different racial groups assert the superiority of one racial group" (p. 5). The differences between these two definitional camps amounts to more than a case of the visually challenged men describing various parts of an elephant. The tension, that is, the intellectual battle, is between those who would place a power function at the core of the definition of racism and those who would not.

Some observers and scholars are outraged by the status of the power distributions across various groups and nations. Power differentials exist in a number of areas. In the United States, for example, Whites control or have the potential for influencing institutions that sustain life and enhance facets of human expression. Other groups, including African Americans, find that they depend on economic structures that are beyond their control for food, clothing and shelter. Their access to these institutions is very remote and indirect. Walter Rodney (1972) referred to this condition as underdevelopment.

There is a second level on which the outrageously uneven distribution of power is played out. Human societies go beyond structuring social mechanisms that meet survival needs. They invent cultural products that humanize members of the society. These include activities in the arts, sciences, technology and literature, both oral and written. In the face of racial oppression, the mainstream culture is able to deprecate, trivialize or exploit the cultural products other groups create as part of this humanizing function.

It becomes clear that the mechanisms that support racial oppression transcend individual attitudes and conjectures. Power and influence is at work in the oppression of one race by another. This power shapes the avenues by which people meet their essential needs. It also impacts the status and function humanizing cultural products that people produce. Therefore, racism cannot be defined in the absence of a discussion of power.

Racism is a multifaceted phenomena (Jones, 1972). Since, as we will discuss, it takes on individual, institutional and cultural forms, it saturates virtually every level of social commerce. Because of the success of wars against colonialism and more limited national human rights struggles, vulgar forms of racism have slipped out of vogue. Often, though not always, modern racism will take subtle forms. Racism creates conditions in the real world that are quite disturbing. Still, its role in creating these conditions will be cloaked. Hence, one might experience racism that may be damaging though the events themselves may not seem unpleasant. For example, many African Americans welcomed the presentation of African American characters on television programs. However, in many instances these characters are talented and entertaining, but constructed from a Eurocentric racist mythology. Hence, we must look for the impact of racism in circumstances that may or may not be distressing.

Racism includes, but rapidly goes beyond individual or interpersonal forms and manifestations. Individual forms of racism include interpersonal exploitation. Jones distinguished individual racism from institutional and cultural forms of racism. In the latter manifestations, pivotal socializing institutions support racism. Popular media, educational institutions, legal structures and practices, and economic conditions serve to block the human expression of the racially oppressed.

Mechanisms of modern racism seem to converge with the process of cultural hegemony. Cultural hegemony encroaches on those social forces that facilitate an ethnic group's institutional growth. Hegemony tends to place the oppressed in a position of dependency and economic displacement. Hegemonic forces promote self-destructive behaviors (Akbar, 1991), and institutional erosion and consequently, cultural denial. Cultural hegemony is a central instrument of systemic White supremacy. It shapes the human cognitive structures in such a way that they yield legitimacy or respect unconsciously to Eurocentric beliefs and desires. At the same time, these structures resist Afrocultural beliefs and desires (Semmes, 1995). That is, values and behavior automatically operate in a context of White supremacy. Carter Woodson (1933/1977) opened the first chapter of his classic book The miseducation of the Negro with a most compelling sentence. In it, he illustrates both the process and outcome of hegemony in the educational system. "The 'educated Negroes' have the attitude of contempt for their own people because . . . . Negroes are taught to admire the Hebrew, the Greek, the Latin and the Teuton and to despise the African" (p. 1).

Akinyela (1995) argued that hegemony involves the "gained consent" of a group to the controlling actions of another group (p. 35). This takes place even when the acquiescence offers no benefits to the consenting party. Institutions of civil society (such as churches and social clubs), rather than forces of domination enforce hegemony according to Akinyela. He sees the collective yearning for the fruits of the "American Dream" as the epitome of cultural hegemony.

Historically, hegemonic forces have preempted the capacity of African American people to define reality on their own terms. Hence, hegemony is a far-reaching if not all encompassing force. In fact, cultural hegemony can be thought of as the everyday social context in which the individual must cope with in order to maintain a healthy existence. If that context asserts and perpetuates the inferiority of African American cultural norms, practices and resources, then culturally hegemonic standards and habits are likely to prosper.

Racism and cultural hegemony potentially have distinct manifestations in the minds of the oppressed. Its many tentacles reach into at least three regions of cognitive activity. These are (1) body image, (2) one's sense of personal and group related competence and efficacy, and (3) cultural and historical attitudes and knowledge (Harrell, in press). The extent to which each will be affected will vary across people. However, the impact of the various forms of racism on the oppressed will be in one of these regions.

What is Stress?

Burchfield (1979) in a little-noticed article, argued that behavioral scientists should define stress as an interruption of "psychological homeostasis." Her discussion deserved more attention than it received because psychologists have long deferred to physiologists when defining stress. When Burchfield introduced it, psychological homeostasis was a relatively new concept. She defined it in terms of the regulation of moods and emotional states. She drew an analogy to regulation that takes place in the physiological domain. Humans tend to maintain moods and experiential states within set optimal limits. When an individual is confronted with a stressful situation, mood and affect tend to exceed the preset limits of normal psychological functioning. The physiological alterations that some have used to define stress (Selye, 1976, p. 55) are part of the larger picture of stress reactions. However, from the behavior scientist's perspective, they are not "pathonomic" of psychological stress. Burchfield argued that "by defining stress as an alteration of psychological homeostasis, differentiation is possible between those events which cause alterations of physiological responses and are psychologically stressful and those which are not" (p. 662). That is, psychological changes are not incidental or secondary manifestations in the matrix of events that make up a stress response. The psychologist defines the process of stress beginning with the psychological manifestation.

Burchfield (1979) did not take up a second facet of psychological homeostasis. This is the long-term manifestation of "optimal functioning." When approached from the longer temporal view, psychological homeostasis, ironically, is not a static process. Long term psychological homeostatic mechanisms regulate inherent growth tendencies in the human personality. Akbar (1991) and other humanists have argued that these growth tendencies include a dynamic unfolding of the human potential from conception to death. Akbar argued that human beings, under natural conditions, grow and expand continually across the lifespan in terms of their acceptance and awareness of the self. It is essential therefore, to expand the rubric of psychological stressors to include events that interrupt this long term or tonic growth process.

A variety of manifestations of stress in the human body can be delineated (Asterita, 1985; Cacioppo, 1994). Asterita suggested that there are 1,400 physiochemical changes associated with stress. Cacioppo argued that two branches of the response of the human body to stress are important to psychophysiologists. Figure 1 depicts two "axes" that help organize the myriad of changes that occur when human beings encounter a psychological stressor. The first is the sympathetic-adrenal medullary axis. Psychological stress activates the hypothalamus which, in turn, stimulates the sympathetic branch of the autonomic nervous system. The sympathetic nervous system (SNS) increases heart rate, dilates the bronchial tubes in the lungs and the arteries that serve the large muscles. These actions take place very rapidly. Also, the SNS activates the adrenal medulla. The adrenal medulla releases epinephrine into the blood stream. This sustains the arousal of the SNS.

The second axis, the hypothalamic-pituitary-adrenal cortical axis, responds more slowly. Many of the physiological changes involve hormones that are carried in the blood stream rather than the action of neurons. The hypothalamus secretes corticotropic releasing factor (CRF). CRF causes the pituitary gland to release adrenal corticotropic hormone (ACTH). ACTH stimulates the adrenal cortex of the adrenal glands to release cortisol and other steroids that help fight infection and build connective tissue. Researchers suspect that ACTH has the capacity to suppress the immune system by inhibiting the production of gamma interferon. Gamma interferon stimulates the natural killer (NK) cells of the immune system. These NK cells destroy tumors and fight infection. Thus stress influences the immune system through this second axis.

Berne and Levy (1993) in their basic physiology text, gave a modest amount of attention to the physiological consequences of psychological stress (p. 977). This reflects a growing acceptance among physiologists and psychologists that stress can influence an endless array of physiological processes. The relatively recent increase in our knowledge of stress and the cardiovascular system is striking. A decade and a half ago, a review of the psychophysiological pathways that might be involved in hypertension paid closest attention to the manner in which stress affected two physiological mechanisms (Harrell, 1980). These were cardiac output and periph-

Figure 1
Physiological Changes Associated with Psychological Stress Mapped Along Two Pathways

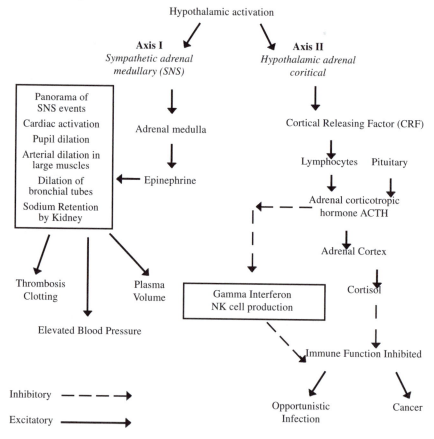

eral resistance. Then it was clear that stress could influence both directly through complex processes within Axis I. At that time it was also clear that blood volume, blood viscosity and arterial elasticity influenced blood pressure. There were very few published studies of the effects of stress on these physiological dispositions. Today, an adequate review of "psychological factors and hypertension" would have to involve a treatment of the impact of psychological stress on this trio of mechanisms.

For example, the influence of psychological stress on blood volume is mediated through the kidneys. Light (1993) provided a helpful summary of the evidence from studies of animals and humans that show the effects of stress on sodium excretion. Sodium excretion is one of the bodies principle mechanisms for regulating blood volume. Changes in blood viscosity as a function of stress are demonstrated in recent studies. Patterson, Krantz, Gottdiener et al. (1995) showed that changes in chemical processes that control blood clotting occur during stress. Patterson, Krantz, and Jochum (1995) showed that plasma volume decreases are a concomitant of psychological stress. In addition, Kaplan, Manuck, Williams and Strawn (1993) reviewed evidence from studies of primates showing psychological stress facilitates the build up of fibrofatty plaques as well as stiffening of the walls of the arteries. This condition is known as atherosclerosis. Thus Kaplan et al. provide evidence that the elasticity or compliance of arteries may be susceptible to stress factors. Obviously, the number of known pathways through which stress might influence blood pressure has increased appreciably in recent years.

One of the more exciting newer fields in stress research centers on identifying diseases that activation of stress Axis II influences. Kennedy, Glaser and Glaser-Kiecolt (1990) concluded that the early research into the manner in which psychological factors influence the immune system was encouraging. Both major and minor life events affect immune function. These authors called for longitudinal studies of the effects of stress on the activities of the immune system. The implication is that stress might play a role in this very important system's capacity to fight opportunistic infections as well as tumor growth.

Positing that psychological stressors alter physiological processes is not presenting an argument against the roles other factors play as determinants of physical dispositions. We are promoting a multicausal, interactional approach to disease. Modern studies of disease should acknowledge that stress influences mechanisms involved in diseases along with the panoply of other factors. These other, more established causal agents, include genetic predisposition, nutritional factors and environmental toxins. Indeed, an interactional approach reminds us that these causal factors can potentiate or moderate each other. An understanding of the etiology of diseases depends on our coming to understand this complex interplay among causes. We are arguing that psychological factors must be included in the mix.

Stress and Racism

Figure 2 depicts various manifestations of racism as events that might interrupt the short-term or long-term manifestations of psychological homeostasis. Thus, the figure shows how racism operates as a psychological stressor. The top portion of the figure lists the types of racism described above. It shows how these may be translated into forms of psychological stress. Institutional and individual forms of stress normally produce life stress and daily hassles. In addition, institutional racism can influence the more chronic and contextual environment. For example, institutional practices often influence the level of resources that communities receive.

Figure 2
Conceptual Model Describing the Relationship Among Racism, Mediating Variables, and Health Outcomes

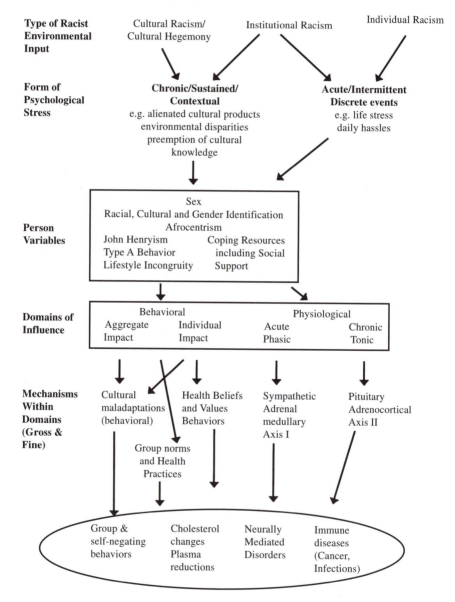

Frequently, businesses choose to locate away from inner city areas where there are large African American populations. Unemployment and decay are exacerbated by this practice. Finally, as L. Anderson (1991) showed, cultural racism and hegemony has its own stressful impact. He showed how cultural racism threatens ethnic identity development. One tends to manage challenging and oppressive life situations more effectively when ethnic identity has developed along positive lines.

Before these events and circumstances have their sordid impact on the individual however, they are filtered through a series of moderator variables. Ethnic identity is one of the moderators, but there are a host of others that researchers are studying presently. These moderators reside ultimately, in the person. These are depicted in the large oval at the middle of the figure. In a subsequent section we examine research findings related to the impact of some of these variables on stress reactions.

At the third level of the figure the impact of these events becomes the focus. This occurs when personal or cultural buffers fail to "filter" the negative impact of the stressful events. One can measure the impact in the domains of overt behavior and physiological process. We can think of the behavioral manifestations in terms of group tendencies as well as individual manifestations. The physiological manifestations tend to be thought of in terms of long-term and short-term impact. The physiological responses associated with Axis I and Axis II were described in Figure 1.

What Figure 2 fails to show is as important as the processes it outlines. The figure does now show the pathways leading from the various manifestations of stress to the mechanisms within a domain, and eventually, to disease. Some of these pathways remain speculative. However, as we mentioned, laboratory studies have made significant progress in identifying the almost innumerable sequelae of psychological stress. For example, we might think of individual racism as operating along Axis I. One is insulted by a security guard in a mall and becomes angry and physiologically aroused even at the thought of the incident. Blood pressure increases, plasma volume is altered and baroreceptors become less sensitive. This would represent a classic stress reaction to a socially noxious situation, one of life's hassles. However, we know that the lingering unpleasant emotion that may grow out of this encounter may dispose some individuals to "self medicate." That is, following the incident, individuals may consume alcohol or other psychotropic drugs to mitigate negative emotions. This may happen even as one seeks to obtain social support from friends. In this case, individual racism has reinforced a negative health practice that might lead to disease.

On the other hand, the tragic conditions at large urban hospitals often bring poor African American people in contact with the harried, over-worked African American health care providers. Interpersonal encounters within these overtaxed systems tend to be terse and detached, when they are not outright abrasive and belligerent. These encounters may lead the individual to neglect their health by avoiding contact with the health care delivery system. Obviously, this is one of the reasons many African American urban dwellers present with multiple symptoms or symptoms in a very advanced state.

However, poor health practices may not be the only outcome of this structural form of institutional racism. The individual, at some level, may be aware that these abject conditions are not universal. Suburban communities and wealthier parts of the city enjoy better health care facilities. This the individual knows at some level of cognitive processing. Experiencing this disparity will not facilitate psychological homeostasis in either the long-term or short-term form. That is, associating one's self with degrading conditions has the potential to impact both mood states and one's acceptance of self. There may be physiological consequences of experiencing this disparity. Could it be that the notion that one is associated with these squalid conditions impacts the physiological axes of stress? As researchers identify the subtle physiological alterations that are part of experiencing psychological stress, we must examine the consequences of processing the disparities that are an outgrowth of living in a racist environment.

Empirical Work

Research Paradigms in the Study of Racism and Health

We can group research on stress and disease among African Americans under three broad headings. This section will sample studies from two of the domains. We provide an overview of the kind of research that is available rather than an exhaustive review of the literature. The general methods and the quality of the data yielded by the paradigms differ markedly. The first heading includes field studies that are conducted at work sites, in residential communities or in clinics. A second approach is to conduct research in specialized laboratories, where investigators systematically control conditions and variables. The third form of research is a hybrid of these two. Here one strives to achieve some of the laboratory control in a field setting. We will look at research from the first two paradigms only. However, research from this third approach is of growing importance. Advances in physiological equipment now allow one to monitor activity as one engages in day to day activity. It is possible to monitor both blood pressure and cardiac activity for twenty-four hour periods with very small devices (Light, Obrist, & Cubeddu, 1988; Willemsen, De Geus, Klaver, van Doornen, & Carroll, 1996). We encourage the reader to follow the ambulatory monitoring literature carefully. In the coming years studies of racism and health should make use of these technological breakthroughs.

The field studies are an extension of survey research methods. Investigators measure demographics, personality variables and the environmental conditions in which participants are situated. In addition, they assess the health status of individuals using clinical records, self reports of symptoms or restricted physiological indices of diseases. The latter include causal measures of blood pressure and assays of biochemical variables. The studies determine the relationship between the measures of health status and the person and situational variables. An example of this kind of research is a large study conducted in Detroit. This study sought to determine if social economic factors, personality variables and skin color were related to the levels of blood pressure in African Americans (Harburg, Erfut, Haunstein et al., 1973). These studies establish the "real-world" correlates of disease states. Usually, they draw variegated samples compared to the ones used in laboratory studies. Hence, they help identify the role that age, income and life style differences may play in the onset and disposition of a disease. On the other hand, these studies provide us less information about the pathways of stress. That is, they cannot show *how* stressful and racist situations are translated into disease.

The laboratory studies impose carefully structured, stressful conditions on the participants. They measure the impact of these on any of the countless physiological or psychological variables that stress is known to affect. Sometimes these studies measure personality variables or manipulate physiological variables in order to uncover the pathways by which a given stressor is affecting the individuals. The literature is filled with studies where standard laboratory stressors like mental arithmetic or reaction time tasks served as stressors (see studies reported in Turner, Sherwood, & Light, 1992).

However, researchers can use more creative stimuli. For example, one could expose an individual to the hideous film of Los Angeles police criminally beating Rodney King. The researcher may choose to take measures of heart rate and blood pressure as indices of stress reactions. In addition, one might measure the impact of personality differences on the reactions to stress. Further, researchers use pharmacological agents to help identify the source of the physiological changes. That is, they give participants drugs that block certain branches of the nervous system. Subsequently, they determine the extent to which the physiological reactions to the stressors still occur when the drug is taken. If the responses fail to take place, it is assumed that the pharmacologically-blocked avenue was responsible for the stress responses. This is the important yield of the laboratory studies. Careful manipulations or assessments of situations and person variables allow the researcher to identify how stress impacts the psychological and physiological domains of individuals to cause diseases. This is the important work of identifying the chain of events leading from environmental situations to disease.

Field Studies and Survey Research

Social support, lifestyle incongruity and health outcomes. Ample research in the mental health domain establishes that social support acts as a stress buffer (Dressler, 1991a; Cohen & Wills, 1985; McAdoo, 1982). Dressler (1985a, 1991a) expanded the study of social support in regard to arterial blood pressure. Specifically, he examined the part social support played in buffering the risk of elevated blood pressure in a Southern African American community. His interpretation of social support stresses the process of social intercourse. Social support in the African American community is likely more elaborate than merely a function of different social organization because research suggests that extended family in the African American community serves as a buffer to stress (McAdoo, 1982).

Dressler (1991a) explored whether nonkin support would buffer the effect of incongruity among younger (< 40 years) African Americans, while kin support would moderate the effect of incongruity among older (> 40) African Americans. For the younger age group, the results indicate that nonkin support buffered lifestyle incongruity significantly for diastolic (not systolic) blood pressure. However, kin support had no buffering effect. Kin support in the older age group was significant in buffering the lifestyle incongruity in both systolic and diastolic blood pressures while nonkin support had no buffering effect. These results uphold the stress buffering model of social support. Cultural context must be accounted for in the interpretation of social support and the specification of outcomes of support in order to discern stressor effects on cardiovascular health.

Additionally, Dressler (1985a, 1985b, 1991b) found that culturally-based resistance resources are associated with depression in young African Americans in an urban Southern setting. The resistance resources that were investigated included coping styles and social support from extended family. A significant difference in the pattern of effects was evident for men and women. Men with greater extended kin support expressed fewer depressive symptoms. The men with high economic stressors and low extended kin support reported the highest level of symptoms.

Personality and health outcomes. African Americans experience higher rates of high blood pressure than Whites (National Research Council, 1989). Hypertension and SES (measured by education, occupation or income) appear to be negatively correlated. Moreover, African Americans and Whites have differential risk for hypertension by SES and by race (James, 1994). Relevant research suggests that the settings in which African Americans live and work produce unresolved psychosocial stress which, in turn, is principally accountable for increased propensity to hypertension (Livingston, 1987; Myers, 1976).

Active coping or prolonged attentional and affective engrossment with challenging psychosocial stressors likely generate considerable increases in systolic blood pressure and heart rate. Furthermore, these increases continue as long as individuals diligently work at eradicating the stressor (Anderson, McNeilly, &

Myers, 1992; Harburg et al., 1973; Kasl & Cobb, 1970). For example, blood pressure shifts of male, blue collar laborers whose factory was about to be shut down permanently was observed (Kasl & Cobb, 1970). As the factory closing date drew near the blood pressures of the men increased and stayed elevated over baseline levels until the men relinquished the active pursuit for new employment or found new jobs.

John Henryism is generally defined as sustained, active coping with challenging sociocultural stressors such as job insecurity, chronic economic strain, or racial discrimination (James, 1994; James et al., 1984). The John Henryism hypothesis proposes that low SES persons who score high on John Henryism will have the highest susceptibility for hypertension.

James, Hartnett, and Kalsbeek (1983) conducted a pilot study of the John Henryism hypothesis in North Carolina where death due to stroke and heart disease was among the highest in the country (see Mason et al., 1981; James, 1994). Research findings showed that men who scored high on John Henryism and low on education had significantly higher diastolic blood pressures (DBP) than men who scored above the median on both measures.

In another study of John Henryism and blood pressure differences in African American men, James et al. (1984) examined the role of job stressors. If individuals were high on John Henryism, DBP was also high regardless of job success. On the other hand, low John Henryism and high job success predicted low DBP. In addition, the belief that being African American actually helped in efforts to achieve job success was associated with lower DBP's for high John Henryism men. These results further emphasize the complex relationship between John Henryism and higher blood pressures in various populations of African American men.

In a third study testing the John Henryism hypothesis, education was not associated with blood pressure for African Americans and Whites (James et al., 1987). However, differences in blood pressure by SES was much larger for African Americans who were high on John Henryism than for African Americans who were low on John Henryism. Hypertension prevalence for the high SES/high John Henryism subgroup was uncommonly low for any group of African Americans, indicating that the combination of high John Henryism and high SES could be a safeguard against hypertension for African American adults .

In a southern and urban sample of African American adults, James et al. (1992) found hypertension prevalence was similar in the low (22.6%) and medium (22.8%) SES groups but greater in the high SES group (25.9%) for people with low levels of John Henryism. Adjusted prevalences decreased with increasing SES for people with high levels of John Henryism. James et al., (1992) argued that the largely weaker support for the John Henryism hypothesis found in this study, as compared to that of the previous investigations (James, Hartnett, & Kalsbeek, 1983; James et al., 1987), arouses doubts about the generalizability of the John Henryism hypothesis to urban, White-collar African American samples.

Jackson and Adams-Campbell (1994) reported John Henryism was not an independent predictor of blood pressure. However, John Henryism was associated with social support in females. The authors suggest that John Henryism may not be an accelerating determinant of elevated blood pressure in college students because of this group's access to specific socioeconomic resources.

Overall, the results suggest that John Henryism in African Americans has cultural as well as economic roots (James, 1987, 1994). A newly freed people (post Civil War) attempting to erect an American identity developed the strategy of John Henryism as a cultural adaptation. To be authentic, this true identity had to (1) recognize and come to grips with the significance in prior enslavement, (2) construct a culturally congruous manifestation of basic American values such as perseverance or self-sufficiency, and (3) offer a reasonable mechanism to confront modern forms of flourishing injustice. John Henryism incorporates all three elements. Certainly, its health consequences merit additional study.

Past research indicates that psychological and physiological functioning may not be examined sufficiently without considering racial or cultural identity. Several researchers have considered the sociocultural antecedents of psychological and physical stress (Anderson, 1991; Myers, 1981, 1983; Sutherland & Harrell, 1986). These studies show how culturally based appraisals significantly impact health outcomes.

Parham and Helms (1985a, 1985b) and Carter (1991) have found that being at a particular point in racial identity development has important implications for psychological health. Parham & Helms found that the Pre-encounter stage was associated with high anxiety. The Immersion-Emersion stage was linked to feelings of hostility. The Encounter stage was associated with low anxiety. Parham (1989) showed that the mental health consequences of the stages of identity change across the lifespan. Therefore, we should anticipate that the relationships among the stages and health outcomes will vary with age. Gary (1985), on the other hand, reported no relationship between racial consciousness and depression in study of urban African American men.

Merritt, Dixon, and Harrell (1995) investigated the relationship between racial identity and somatization in two samples of urban African American college students. The somatization dimension considers distress emanating from perceptions of bodily dysfunction. Pain, headaches, discomfort of the gross musculature and supplementary somatic equivalents of anxiety are constituents of the definition. In general, only the Pre-encounter stage was consistently and positively related to global somatization. The Internalization stage showed a modest, negative relationship with global somatization in sample one, but no relationship with global somatization in sample two emerged. Overall, the results suggest that advancement through the lower stages leads to freedom from somatic symptoms. However, the implications of the results are tempered by the fact that some of the significant correlations are at a modest level (approximately 0.20).

A separate preliminary analysis with the same population of urban African American college students examined the association between each of three cultural orientations, mainstream orientation, communalism (Boykin, 1986), and African Self-consciousness and alcohol use. African Self-consciousness denotes the endorsement of an African world-view that is based upon a set of biogenetic, social, and political principles (Baldwin, 1984). High mainstream orientation was associated with significantly more time drinking socially each week than low mainstream orientation. A similar, yet modest trend was evident for African Self-consciousness while an opposite relationship was evident for communalism. Therefore, communalism, a culturally-loaded personality variable, may act as a buffer against the social consumption of alcohol. The finding that a mainstream orientation is linked with drinking socially shows the pervasive effects of internalizing culturally hegemonic values.

Broman and Johnson (1988) reported that anger-hostility, a component of the Type A behavioral pattern, was a significant predictor of physical health problems and life stress. Dressler (1993) found two subscales of the Framingham Type A scale, time urgency and hard driving, were meaningful predictors of health outcomes. Time urgency was associated with higher systolic and diastolic blood pressure, while hard driving was associated with lower systolic blood pressure. High socioeconomic status significantly reduced the impact of time urgency when psychophysiological symptoms were analyzed. When bolstered by protective cultural resources, such coping patterns may have beneficial effects on health status.

Family cohesion and substance abuse, role strain and health. Pioneering studies (Dubois, 1967; Frazier, 1968) of urban African American migrants found that strong family organization with a suitable cultural ethic potentially had a moderating effect on the unhealthy repercussions of a poverty-stricken milieu. Consistent routine in family life (such as eating together regularly) could encourage health promotion. Thus, the family is a cultural institution capable of setting in motion activities and practices that are foundational for good health.

On the other hand, Bell (1990) argued that particular cultural factors can lead to substance abuse among members of the African American community. Historically, family stability, religion, and diet have been the principal lines along which African American people cope with stress (McAdoo, 1981; Neighbors, Jackson, Bowman, & Gurin, 1983; Semmes, 1983; Williams, Larsen, & Buckler, et al., 1991). However, when these culturally adaptive mechanisms are suppressed, two distinct maladaptive behavior patterns occur among African American youth: (a) They become more receptive to taking illicit substances as a coping mechanism (see also Myers, 1981); and (b) Their practice of alcohol or drug use subsequently inhibits development of productive coping mechanisms.

"Street values" result from such maladaptive coping (Bell, 1990). Street values divide people into two groups: predators and victims, conquerors and underdogs, or strong and weak. This primitive value system appears to be associated with the culturally hegemonic institutions such as the liquor industry, the drug trade, and the White dominated media and is reminiscent of a mainstream orientation. In addition, street values are similar to Akbar's (1991) notion of self-destructive disorders and appear antagonistic to an Afrocultural orientation (see also Boykin, 1986).

Again, the lack of proper socializing institutions in the area of health promotion can compromise the health values and behaviors of members of the African American community. Hegemonic processes weaken the institutions that once buffered the impact of stressful life conditions that are an outgrowth of oppression. In the breach, culturally hegemonic health values and orientations arise. These are often self-destructive and are symptomatic of such a process.

In a national survey of African Americans, Johnson and Broman (1987) explored the connection between psychosocial variables, anger expression, and physical health problems. African Americans who were unemployed were at a greater risk of experiencing health problems if anger was expressed overtly at an elevated level. Bowman (1990) discusses a role-strain adaptation model in which socially structured disparities enhance provider role strain which in turn, diminishes family life quality and psychological health. The employment status appears to be a significant, salient and pernicious predictor of health problems (see Dressler, 1991).

A causal chain begins in racism and cultural hegemonic forces, leads to stress and self-destructive coping, which in turn lead to disease processes (Akbar, 1991; Semmes, 1992; Williams et al., 1991). Personality factors appear to be moderating variables in this process, while health behaviors appear to be mediators of the relationship between cultural hegemony and health outcomes (e.g., Broman & Johnson, 1988; Dressler, 1993; James, 1994).

Appraisal and coping strategies appear to be the distinguishing factors in regards to the aversive impact of culturally hegemonic contexts. That is, values, beliefs, and behaviors that promote vulnerability to defective environments result in greater health breakdowns in those individuals with more traditional mainstream cultural values and coping strategies (Dressler, 1993; N. Anderson, McNeilly, & Meyers, 1992). Therefore, the lens that the person sees her/his environment has important implications for the stressful implications of exposure to hegemonic institutions.

Cultural hegemony tends to place African American people's health in the hands of individuals who have little regard for it. More proactive health strategies rooted in traditionally strong African American cultural traditions, values and mores will help offset this disturbing tendency. The survey evidence shows that traditional African American cultural resources and values protect African American people from the health debilitating influences of cultural hegemony.

Table 1
Paradigms for Laboratory Reactivity Studies

	Standard Controlled Task	Racist Scenarios
Sample Black		
Comparative (Blacks & Whites)		

Laboratory Studies

Table 1 depicts four quadrants in which we can place the laboratory reactivity studies that have employed African American samples. The studies have involved either all-African American samples, represented in the two upper quadrants, or they have included a White sample for comparative purposes (lower quadrants). The left quadrants of the table designate those studies where standard laboratory stressors were employed. These have included reaction time tasks, mental arithmetic, speech stressors, or the applications of cold to the face or limbs. The right columns identify studies where researchers employed analogs of racist social stressors. Mental imagery or video tape constituted the mechanism for importing these situations into the laboratory.

Any count of the published research would show that the bulk of studies reside in the bottom left quadrant. Researchers conducted a slew of comparative studies of cardiovascular reactivity from the mid 1980's to the mid 1990's. Researchers conducted these studies as part of a concerted effort on the part of the medical community to identify the reasons for the differences in the prevalence of hypertension and heart disease in African Americans and Whites. The investigators hoped to do this by examining group differences in the cardiovascular reactions to standard stressors. Far fewer published studies fit in the upper right and left quadrants though a modest body of research is available. Studies in the remaining quadrant would compare reactions of African Americans and Whites to racism. We could locate no published studies that fit this description. Indeed, the likelihood that Whites will encounter racism, even in its individualized form (Jones, 1972) is very remote. Therefore, comparisons between African American and White reactions to these events would be confusing and probably meaningless.

Studies from the left quadrants. Norman Anderson (Anderson, 1989; Anderson, Myers, & McNeilly, 1992) published two very fine review papers discussing empirical studies of cardiovascular reactivity in African American samples. The bulk of the experiments fit the lower left, with a few falling in the upper left quadrant. Researchers began reporting studies of cardiovascular reactions of African Americans to stress in the mid 1980's. A psychophysiological literature that had been virtually void of African American research participants, suddenly boasted of a full host of reports. Anderson's conclusions have stood the test of time. What follows is a summary of the evidence and critiques of the approach. Those who prefer a more detailed treatment of the individual studies should refer to Anderson's papers.

In the 1980's, African American people, old and young, entered these psychophysiological studies in comparatively large numbers. The bulk of the reports agreed that the cardiovascular systems of African Americans did not respond to the mental arithmetic tasks, the exposures to ice water and the video games in the same fashion that the systems of White participants responded. By 1992, Anderson located twenty-four papers showing that either cardiovascular activity at rest, or cardiovascular reactions to stress, were elevated in African American adults and children. These reports were published out of laboratories all over the country.

Further, the flurry of research localized the source of the differences in reactions. Recall that a search for the causes of high rates of hypertension in African Americans fueled the studies initially. A number of physiological factors influence blood pressure, including cardiac output, blood volume and peripheral resistance in the arteries. The findings suggested the constriction of peripheral blood vessels mediated the blood pressure increases in African American subjects to a greater extent than it did in White subjects. However, if the vascular activity of African Americans was "augmented," Anderson noted, that "African American adults tend to show either similar or diminished heart rate reactivity relative to their White counterparts" (p. 127). The findings for children regarding racial differences in cardiac reactivity however, were mixed and not as clear cut.

One last finding from these studies raises an interesting and contentious question. Many experiments have examined differences in cardiovascular reactivity between those with a family history of hypertension and those who have no such family history. A positive family history was almost invariably associated with larger blood pressure responses to stress in White samples. However, Anderson et al. (1992) concluded "most studies with African American males and females have shown no significant effects of family history on reactivity" (p. 129). It is this conclusion that the field appears to find incredulous. Researchers make an almost perseverative assumption that hypertension in African Americans is passed on from parent to child and therefore it is caused by some mysterious genetic fault.

For example, recently Wilson, Holmes, Arherat, and Alpert (1995) examined the blood pressure reactivity of siblings in order to ascertain the relative importance of genetic influence on blood pressure in African Americans and Whites. For diastolic blood pressure only, they found that African American siblings had larger intraclass correlations between their reactivity scores than the African American control and the White siblings. That is, the intraclass correlation coefficients that gauged the similarity of the reactivity scores for systolic blood pressure and heart rate across the African American and White siblings and controls were not significantly different between the two groups. These authors, in footnote, wrote that they "expected that African American siblings would show greater aggregation of CV reactivity" (p. 209). It is likely that they were aware of the conclusion by Anderson et al. (1992) regarding genetics and reactivity, since they cited the chapter as one source reporting high blood pressure is more prevalent and severe in African American populations. However, they ignored the major point Anderson et al. made in that review regarding familial aggregation of reactivity in African Americans. This conclusion speaks directly to the genetic hypothesis in which they were interested.

The reactivity studies that we would place in the lower left quadrant are problematic in several respects. The purpose of "acute psychophysiological" research where physiological reactivity is studied is to identify hyper-reactive individuals (Harrell, Morris, & Rasayon, 1996; Krantz & Manuck, 1984). Researchers suspect that these hyper-reactive individuals are the most likely candidates for cardiovascular disorders. Hyper-reactivity becomes a marker or predictor for disease. If this is the thrust of the racial comparative studies, the strategy is flawed. The appropriate control or normative group when trying to establish a marker of this kind would be a sample of less reactive people selected from the same population. If the hypothesis is correct, these hypo-reactive individuals are African American people who are less likely to develop cardiovascular disorders. Individuals selected from a different population (White or other groups) may differ from African Americans with respect to other physiological parameters that influence reactivity but are unrelated to the disease process. The cross-race comparison serves absolutely no purpose if one is trying to find those likely to become hypertensive in an African American population. It only confuses the matter.

Perhaps this bevy of studies was conducted to identify mechanisms that might be involved in hypertension in African Americans versus Whites. If this is the case, there was no reason to include individuals who did not have high blood pressure in the samples. One would simply study the cardiovascular and physiological dispositions of those with hypertension from both races. Racial comparative searches of this kind have a long and sordid history. Nineteenth century physicians were fascinated by differences in disease manifestations between African Americans and Whites (Krieger et al., 1993). This intrigue was rooted in the obsession within the racist scientific community with cataloging any difference between the races (J. H. Jones, 1991). Modern racial comparative studies of symptoms do well to be wary of this intellectual tradition. Clearly researchers risk sharing the morbid fascination with racial differences that their intellectual predecessors exhibited a century ago. Jones showed how the notorious Tuskegee syphilis experiment was an extension of this tradition.

A group of us at Howard University have conducted psychophysiological experiments where we used analogues of social situations involving racism as stressful stimuli. A desire to shed light on the mechanism through which racism affects health gave rise to these studies. Young adults of African descent constituted our subject population. Before we employed the analogues of racist events, we asked more general questions about the manner in which the heart adjusted to psychological challenges. Thus, the first set of studies are from the upper left quadrant of Table 1. The second set falls under the upper right quadrant.

The initial set of studies (Harrell & Clark, 1985; Harrell, Clark, & Sellers, 1987) used standard laboratory stressors including rotary pursuit and visual search task to challenge or stress participants. We found that when stress is mild, the heart may change its rate of pumping blood, but it compensates by reducing the volume of blood it pumps per beat. Cardiac output remained stable while heart rate tended to increase in response to stress (Harrell, Morris, & Rasayon, 1996).

However, we were struck by the large individual differences in the patterns of responses across participants. Some evidenced the compensatory adjustment quite nicely. Others showed massive increases in the force of the contraction of the left ventricle of the heart and large changes in the output of blood on each beat, even when stressors were relatively mild. Thus, we have a distribution of reactivity scores as one would expect in any sample. Are those on the high end of this distribution prone to cardiovascular diseases as prosed in "acute psychophysiology?" We did not pursue this longitudinal issue. Instead, we tuned our attention to the study of racism in the laboratory.

Studies from the upper right quadrant. Marcia Sutherland, as part of her doctoral dissertation, designed a study where the stressful manipulation included an analogue of a racist event (Sutherland & Harrell, 1987; Sutherland, Harrell, & Isaacs, 1988). Facial muscle activity in the region of the currogator or frowning muscles and pulse rate were very sensitive to the racist stressful scene. The findings encouraged us to use the imagery approach in setting up racist stimuli in the laboratory.

Sutherland's dissertation was multifaceted. She measured personality factors that had been associated with strong responses to stressors in previous studies. Measures of Type A behavior, anxiety and the capacity to generate vivid mental images all proved to have some limited utility in predicting subjective or physiological responses to the stressful scenarios. This rather involved study encouraged the use of the imagery procedure for generating stressful events in the laboratory that may have a counterpart in the real world. We were encouraged further when, from a separate laboratory, Armstead, Lawler, Gordon, Cross and Gibbons (1989) excerpted material from commercial films and used it in a psychophysiological investigation of the impact of racism. They reported that blood pressure increased when participants viewed the racist material. In addition, these authors reported that trait anger was positively correlated with increases in blood pressure as the racist material was observed. Trait anger is the tendency to exhibit anger frequently or in a large number of situations. Thus, the first two psychophysiological studies that examined the impact of racist events on physiological processes, demonstrated that personality variables moderate responses.

Denise Jones, (Jones, Harrell, Morris-Prather, Thomas, & Omowale, 1996) as part of her dissertation research at Howard used both mental imagery and video portrayals of racially noxious stressors in a psychophysiological study. Jones et al. (1996) replicated earlier findings that suggested the utility of both video and imagery procedures for eliciting reliable physiological and subjective reactions to stress. The more pronounced responses occurred when a blatantly noxious scene was encountered. The patterns of physiological changes differ depending on mode of presentation because the information processing requirements of the task differ. Jones used a measure of Afrocentricity as a predictor of reactions to this material. In general, Jones found that higher Afrocentrism scores were associated with stronger negative emotional reactions to the racist events. However, Afrocentrism was not related to physiological changes.

At this point we recognize that Afrocentrism will be related to reactions to racist stressors in complex ways. We might expect people who are high in Afrocentrism to be particularly sensitive to racism. Hence they may be very responsive to the scenarios we present. On the other hand, they may find encounters quite unsurprising and typical of life in a racist society. Hence they may not respond at all to them. Both speculations are reasonable. The predictive models using African American identity should include other personality measures that might moderate the manner in which it relates to stress reactions. In addition, we may find there are gender differences in the expression of behaviors related to Afrocentrism especially in younger samples. African American women experience sexism and racism in this society. Afrocentrism measures ideological postures related to oppression. A full accounting of the manner in which Afrocentrism influences the responses of those who frequently encounter "double-barreled" oppression is not yet available.

Another dissertation student, Cynthia Morris-Prather (Morris-Prather, Harrell, Collins, Leonard, Boss, & Lee, 1996) examined gender differences in reactions to social stressors. She scripted and supervised the making of four separate vignettes. In these, an African American or a White security guard or police officer accosted and falsely accused an African American man or woman of criminal behavior. Morris-Prather found that the stressors she developed were noxious enough to elicit increases in blood pressure, heart rate and negative moods regardless of the race of the perpetrator of the event. Men tended to show larger increases in systolic blood pressure when they encountered the stressors. The women, on the other hand, tended to report more negative affect than the men. This may be a result of gender differences in socialization. Parents and society may not encourage boys to express feelings and emotions. On the other hand, purely physiological actions of female hormones may have reduced the systolic blood pressure responses to these stressors. Female hormones tend to mitigate radical elevations in blood pressure in young women.

Two recent doctoral students examined the relationship between scores on Wade Boykin's Mainstream Orientation Questionnaire (MOQ) and responses to the laboratory analogs of racist events that we have used over the years. Bullard (1991) examined cardiac responses and subjective reactions to a wide range of laboratory manipulations. An interesting pattern of relationship between the MOQ scores and responses to the stressors emerged only when the participants viewed racist material. African American men reported being more fearful and tense, and experiencing less pleasant affect as their MOQ scores tended to be higher. With respect to the cardiac measures, the stroke volume responses tended to be positively correlated with MOQ scores as individuals viewed this material. The findings in Bullard's dissertation suggest that cardiac activation during the viewing of racist material was greater as individuals tended to endorse the values measured by the MOQ.

McManus (1992) executed a detailed study of the effects of viewing racist material on state anger responses. He reported that the MOQ scores were positively related to state anger. This relationship (r=.54) was comparable to the correlations between the various trait anger dimensions and state anger. Thus McManus provided support for Bullard's findings that acceptance of mainstream values is associated with stronger reactions to viewing racist material.

Clearly, cultural variables can have a complex impact on the manner in which one responds both physiologically and effectively to racist stressors. When an individual with a mainstream orientation confronts stark, individual racism in an undeniable form, the event runs counter to expectations and notions of the ultimate fairness of the society. This appears to heighten responses to the event. It is not clear whether the exacerbated response is a reaction to the failure of the circumstances to be consistent with expectations or increased anger because the situational elements themselves violate expectations. This is a viable area for further research.

Models for Racism and Health Outcomes

Anderson, McNeilly and Myers (1992) proposed a model showing how chronic stress might result in high blood pressure, that is hypertension, in African Americans. Their model was a comprehensive one. It traced stress pathways from the initiating environmental events to the physiological disease state. Thus, the model contains social, psychological and physiological facets. The physiological aspects were informed heavily by a body of research that identified peripheral vascular changes as principle mediators of high blood pressure in African American people. We will return to a discussion of some of this research in the next section.

The physiological aspects of the "contextual" model Anderson et al. outlined are complex. They are largely tangential to the present discussion. In general, they present evidence that chronic stress can lead to reductions in sodium excretion through sympathetic nervous system activation of the kidney. Retention of sodium is associated with increases in blood pressure. (A body of evidence suggests that African Americans tend to excrete less sodium than Whites [Luft, Grim, & Weinberger, 1985]. Some researchers propose that this capacity was advantageous in the hot and humid climate in Africa. Obviously this cross-racial comparative approach is vulnerable to the same confounds that we identified in the comparative reactivity studies. That is, it is quite possible to identify differences between racial groups that play no etiological role in the disease process.) Anderson showed that high levels of sodium "potentiate" both the release and action of norepinephrine. This leads to constriction in peripheral arteries and eventually, to chronically elevated blood pressure.

Thus the physiological mechanisms discussed in Anderson et al.'s model are specific to hypertension. However, the social and psychological facets of their model provide a more general framework for understanding the impact of stress on the health of African American populations. Anderson et al. placed the social factors under the general heading chronic stress. Their view of these events was forthright if restricted. They opined that though legislation in the 1960's ended legal forms of racism, "African Americans currently experience a greater array of chronic stressors relative to Whites" (p. 132). They listed among these poverty, unemployment, crowding and substandard housing. The psychological moderators of these social events included cultural and personality factors. Anderson et al. showed how traditional African cultural social orientations including spirituality, communalism and strong kinship ties might buffer stress reactions. Also, they reviewed evidence that the personality variables suppressed anger and hostility, as well as tendencies to strive in the face of formidable odds (John Henryism), are associated with elevated blood pressure.

This model is important for a number of reasons. It has remarkable heuristic value. Anderson et al. grounded the model in strong evidence and lit several paths for further studies of stress and hypertension in African Americans. Additionally, the authors addressed a nagging problem in the hypertension area. The question centers around the relative importance of genetic factors versus environmental causes in the hypertension of African American people. Anderson et al. reviewed the evidence that shows how intricately involved environmental factors are in many of the physiological systems that influence blood pressure. They show that simplistic genetic explanations are untenable. Anderson et al. show that kidney function, cardiovascular changes and a host of neurochemical mechanisms involved in blood pressure are impacted by psychological stress.

The model put forth in Figure 2 is of broader focus than Anderson's system. The approach to the social, psychological and physiological mechanisms is more general. Still the thrust is to show how these factors interact to endanger the health and longevity of African people. The survey and laboratory research findings we cited in the previous section account for the placing of specific elements that we have included in the model under the moderator variables.

The embellished version of Burchfield's definition of psychological stress undergirds our model. As noted in the previous section, this augmented definition holds that stress reactions have long-term or tonic as well as short-term or phasic manifestations. The phasic forms are those Burchfield identified as disruptions in mood states. It is axiomatic that countless physiological changes accompany these interruptions in psychological homeostasis. However, the tonic interruptions in psychological homeostasis involve changes of a more enduring nature. The events that lead to these cause individuals to veer from a generative psychological blueprint. The psychological changes extend into relatively permanent dispositional aspects of the personality. That is, they influence our perspectives, traits and views of the world.

For example, the Eurocentric education that most African American children in the United States receive results in a loss of what Hord (1991) called cultural memory. Others dating back to Carter Woodson agree with this position (see also Hilliard, 1995; Lee, 1994; Shujaa, 1994). On Figure 2, the events that lead to a loss of African cultural knowledge and perspective are placed under the heading of chronic, sustained, or contextual stressors. In many instances, Eurocentric education truncates the psychological growth of African people leaving legions of duped, highly cynical individuals who are plagued with a deep-seated suspicion of the intellectual and moral capabilities of other African people. These souls blame other African American people almost exclusively for the dispatches that exist between the economic and social conditions of African Americans and Whites. They have encountered stress and they are exhibiting stress reactions. In Taylor's (1991) framework, they have internalized racism.

Further, and this is the crux of our position, the tonic manifestations of psychological stressors in the form of cultural and institutional racism will have their physiological consequences. It is not only the life stress and hassles caused by racism that will have physiological effects, thought we agree with Anderson et al., that they will. The dispositional maladjustments that result from these subtler forms of racism will reverberate to the physiological domain. The poisoned perspectives and self-deprecating beliefs that cultural racism and cultural hegemony seek to instill will not limit their impact to the psychological and behavioral domains. Racism, like other forms of stressful events has its chronic and long-term dimensions. The psychological consequences, too, can be chronic. Much more than likely, these events and consequences have physiological effects. This is illustrated in the far left side of Figure 2. The right column of the figure shows the more traditional view of racism as a source of discrete stressors.

What is the empirical status of this claim? Physiological and personality measurement techniques are becoming sophisticated enough to give it a fair test. Some claim evidence shows that underlying physiological processes and mechanisms including arousal levels and inhibitory processes, are the basis of personality (Eysenck, 1967). Psychophysiologists have known for a long time that actively coping with stress tends to lead to beta-adrenergic activation of the heart (Obrist, 1981). In the previous two sections we cited studies supporting the notion that personality factors are associated with differences in physiological reactivity and various disease outcomes. The caution is that we must consider the manner in which various psychological state and situational variables moderate these effects. Our prediction here simply completes the possibilities for the relationship between physiological and personality dispositions. We are arguing that the relatively stable person orientation that might result quite readily from encounters with racism will have measurable physiological effects. Internalizing racist mythology and European perspectives will exact its physiological cost.

Conclusion

The bane of the stress researcher's existence remains the problem of individual differences in responses. This pest buzzes in the ears of those concerned with the impact of racism on health. Lewis (1987), Bulhan (1985) and the Buhaya were correct, but only in the general formulation of their thesis: racism does lead to premature death in a significant portion of oppressed groups. However, the mechanisms through which it executes this outcome vary. Some individuals will escape unscathed. What complicated concoction of situational, psychological and physiological factors account for the range of effects?

If the last thirty years of research on racism, stress and disease have not brought major breakthroughs, certainly they have brought advances. Conceptually, we understand racism to be an intractable, pervasive, and multifaceted set of practices and processes. It is much more than the attitudes of ignorant individuals. From the psychophysiological perspective, we are coming to appreciate the fact that cultural institutional manifestations of racism are as dangerous as the bothersome stressors that individual racism brings.

Additionally, researcher have developed measures of personality variables that will filter the environmental events one encounters. Some of these, including John Henryism and African American identity speak to the specific psychological makeup of people of African descent. There is a major advancement in knowledge on the research horizon. It will take the form of an increase in our understanding of the manner in which individual personality differences interact with situational variables to influence disease outcomes. The culturally sensitive measures will play an essential part in this new insight.

The final most astounding new development stems from the findings in the physiological domain. As we have seen, a psychophysiologist concerned with racism and disease can select from an innumerable set of physical systems and examine the effects of stress. The *interactions* among causes, and between causes and effects are staggering. Here lies the key to understanding the individual differences questions. Researchers must be mindful of the impact variables from one domain will have on the causal impact of variables from a second or third domain. Stress researchers cannot think exclusively in terms of main effects. The situational, psychological and physical domains are complex but our understanding of them is increasing. The manner in which they impact each other is even more complicated. We should not shrink from coming to an understanding of this complexity. The lives of people of African descent hang in the balance.

References

Akbar, N. (1991). Mental disorders among African Americans. In R. Jones (Ed.), *Black psychology* (3rd ed.). Berkeley, CA: Cobb and Henry Publishers.

Akinyela, M. M. (1995). Rethinking Afrocentricity: The foundation of a theory of critical Africentricity. In A. Darder (Ed.), *Culture and difference: Critical perspectives on the bicultural experience in the United States* (pp. 21-39). Westport, CT: Bergin and Gargey.

Anderson, L. P. (1991). Acculturative stress: A theory of relevance to Black Americans. *Clinical Psychology Reviews, 11*, 685-702.

Anderson, N. (1992). Racial differences in stress-induced cardiovascular reactivity and hypertension: Current status and substantive issues. *Psychological Bulletin, 105*, 89-105.

Anderson, N., McNeilly, M., & Myers, H. (1992). Towards understanding race difference in autonomic reactivity: A proposed contextual model. In J. R. Turner, A. Sherwood, & K. C. Light (Eds.), *Individual differences in cardiovascular response to stress* (pp. 125-146). New York: Plenum Press.

Armstead, C. A., Lawler, K. A., Gordon, G., Cross, J., & Gibbons, J. (1989). Relationship of racial stressors to blood pressure responses and anger expression in Black college students. *Health Psychology, 8*, 541-556.

Asterita, M. F. (1985). *The physiology of stress*. New York: Human Sciences Press.

Baldwin, J. A. (1984). African self-consciousness and the mental health of African-Americans. *Journal of Black Studies, 15*, 177-194.

Berne, R. M. & Levy, M. N. (1993). Physiology (3rd ed.). St. Louis, MO: Mosby Year Book.

Bell, P. (1990). *Chemical dependency and the African-American: Counseling strategies and community issues*. Center City, MN: Hazelden.

Bowman, P. J. (1990). Coping with provider role strain: Adaptive cultural resources among Black husband-fathers. *Journal of Black Psychology, 16*, 1-22.

Boykin, A. W. (1986). The triple quandary and the schooling of Afro-American children. In U. Neisser (Ed.), *The school achievement of minority children*. Hillsdale, NJ: Erlbaum.

Brenner, M. H. (1983). Mortality and economic stability: Detailed analysis for Britain and comparative analysis for selected industrialized countries. *International Journal of Health Services, 13*, 563.

Bulhan, H. A. (1985). *Frantz Fanon and the psychology of oppression*. New York: Plenum Press.

Bullard, C. (1991). *Psychophysiological and affective responses to stress by African American males: Situational and personological influences*. Unpublished doctoral dissertation, Boston University.

Burchfield, S. K. (1979). The stress response: A new perspective. *Psychosomatic Medicine, 41*, 661-672.

Cacioppo, J. T. (1994). Social neuroscience: Autonomic, neuroendocrine, and immune responses to stress. *Psychophysiology, 31*, 113-128.

Carter, R. T. (1991). Racial attitudes and psychological functioning. *Journal of Multicultural Counseling and Development, 19*, 105-114.

Cross, W. E. (1991). Shades of Black: Diversity in African-American identity. Philadelphia, PA: Temple University Press.

Doob, C. B. (1993). *Racism: An American cauldron*. New York: Harper Collins College Publisher.

Dressler, W. W. (1985a). Extended family relationships, social support, and mental health in a Southern Black community. *Journal of Health and Social Behavior, 26*, 39-48.

Dressler, W. W. (1985b). The social and cultural context of coping: Action, gender and symptoms in a southern Black community. *Social Science and Medicine, 21*, 499-506.

Dressler, W. W. (1990). Lifestyle, stress, and blood pressure in a Southern Black community. *Psychosomatic Medicine, 52*(2), 182-198.

Dressler, W. W. (1991a). Social support, lifestyle incongruity, and arterial blood pressure in a Southern Black community. *Psychosomatic Medicine, 53*, 608-620.

Dressler, W. W. (1991b). *Stress and adaptation in the context of culture: Depression in a Southern Black community*. Albany, NY: State University of New York Press.

Dressler, W. W. (1993). Type A behavior: Contextual effects within a Southern Black community. *Social Science and Medicine, 36*, 289-295.

Dubois, W. E. B. (1967). *The Philadelphia Negro: A social study*. New York: Schocken Books.

Eysenck, H. J. (1967). *The biological basis of personality*. Springfield, IL: Charles C. Thomas.

Frazier, E. F. (1968). Problems and needs of Negro children and youth resulting from family disorganization. In G. F. Edwards (Ed.), *E. Franklin Frazier on race relations*. Chicago, IL: University of Chicago Press.

Gary, L. E. (1985). Depressive symptoms and Black men. *Social Work Research and Abstracts, 21*, 21-29.

Harburg, E., Erfurt, J. C., & Haunstein, L. S. (1973). Socio-ecological stress, suppressed hostility, skin color, and Black-White blood pressure: Detroit. *Psychosomatic Medicine, 35*, 276-296.

Harrell, J. P. (1980). Psychological factors and hypertension: A status report. *Psychological Bulletin, 87*, 482-501.

Harrell, J. P. (In press). *Manichean psychology: Racism and the minds of people of African descent*. Washington, DC: Howard University Press.

Harrell, J. P., & Clark, V. R. (1985). Cardiac responses to psychological tasks: Impedance cardiographic studies. *Biological Psychology, 20*, 261-283.

Harrell, J. P., Clark, V. R., & Allen, B. A. (1991). That ounce of value: Visualizing the application of psychophysiological methods in black psychology. In R. Jones (Ed.), *Black psychology* (3rd ed.). Berkeley, CA: Cobb and Henry Publishers.

Harrell, J. P., Clark, V. R., & Sellers, R. (1987). Effects of posture on cardiac dynamics during visual search. *International Journal of Psychophysiology, 5*, 19-23.

Harrell, J. P., Morris, C. E., & Rasayon, N. K. B. (1996). Physiological measures in studies of psychological stress in Black populations. In R. Jones (Ed.), *Handbook of tests and measurements for Black populations*. Hampton, VA: Cobb and Henry Publishers.

Hilliard, A. (1995). *The Maroon within us*. Baltimore, MD: Black Classics Press.

Hord, F. L. (1991). *Reconstructing memory: Black literary criticism*. Chicago, IL: Third World Press.

Jackson, L. A., & Adams-Campbell, L. L. (1994). John Henryism and blood pressure in Black college students. *Journal of Behavioral Medicine, 17*, 69-79.

James, S. A. (1994). John Henryism and the health of African Americans. *Culture, Medicine, and Psychiatry, 18*, 163-182.

James, S. A., Hartnett, S. A., & Kalsbeek, W. D. (1983). John Henryism and blood pressure among Black men. *Journal of Behavioral Medicine, 6*, 259-278.

James, S. A., Keenan, N. L., Strogatz, D. S., Browning, S. R., & Garrett, J. M. (1992). Socioeconomic status, John Henryism, and blood pressure in Black adults: The Pitt County Study. *American Journal of Epidemiology, 135*, 59-67.

James, S. A., LaCroix, A. Z., Kleinbaum, D. G., & Strogatz, D. S. (1984). John Henryism and blood pressure differences among Black men II: The role of occupational stressors. *Journal of Behavioral Medicine, 7*, 259-275.

James, S. A., Strogatz, D. S., Wing, S. B., & Ramsey, D. (1987). Socioeconomic status, John Henryism, and hypertension in Blacks and Whites. *American Journal of Epidemiology, 126*, 664-673.

Johnson, E. H., & Broman, C. L. (1987). The relationship of anger expression to health problems among Black Americans in a national survey. *Journal of Behavioral Medicine, 10*, 103-116.

Jones, D. R., Harrell, J. P., Morris-Prather, C. E., Thomas, J., & Omowale, N. (1996). Affective and physiological responses to racism: The roles of Afrocentrism and mode of presentation. *Ethnicity and Disease, 4*, 291-326.

Jones, J. H. (1981). *Bad blood: The Tuskegee syphilis experiment.* New York: Free Press.

Jones, J. M. (1972). *Prejudice and racism.* New York: McGraw Hill.

Kaplan, J. R., Manuck, S. B., Williams, J. K., & Strawn, W. (1993). Psychosocial influences on atherosclerosis: Evidence for effects and mechanisms in nonhuman primates. In J. Blascovich & E. S. Katkin (Eds.), *Cardiovascular reactivity to psychological stress and disease.* Washington, DC: American Psychological Association.

Kasl, S. V., & Cobb, S. (1970). Blood pressure changes in men undergoing job loss: A preliminary report. *Psychosomatic Medicine, 32*, 19-38.

Kennedy, S., Glaser, R., & Glaser-Kiecolt, J. (1990). Psychoneuroimmunology. In J. T. Cacioppo & L. G. Tassinary (Eds.), *Principles of psychophysiology: Physical, social and inferential elements* (pp. 177-192). Cambridge, MA: Cambridge University Press.

Krantz, D. C., & Manuck, S. B. (1984). Acute psychophysiology reactivity and risk of cardiovascular disease: A review and methodologic critique. *Psychological Bulletin, 96*, 435-464.

Krieger, N., Rowley, D. L., Herman, A. A., Avery, B., & Phillips, M. T. (1993). Racism, sexism, and social class: Implications for studies of health, disease, and well-being. *American Journal of Preventive Medicine, 9*, 82-122.

Lee, C. D. (1994). African-centered pedagogy: Complexities and possibilities. In M. J. Shujaa (Ed.), *Too much schooling too little education: A paradox of Black life in White schools.* Trenton, NJ: African World Press.

Lewis, D. L. (1987). *The race to Fashoda: European colonialism and African resistance in the scramble for Africa.* New York: Weidenfelf & Nicolson.

Light, K. C. (1992). Differential responses to salt intake-stress interactions: Relevance to hypertension. In J. R. Turner, A. Sherwood, & K. C. Light (Eds.), *Individual differences in cardiovascular response to stress* (pp. 245-264). New York: Plenum Press.

Light, K. C., Obrist, P. A., & Cubeddu, L. X. (1988). Evaluation of a new ambulatory blood pressure monitor (Accutracker 102): Laboratory comparisons with direct arterial pressure, stethoscopic ascultatory pressure and readings from a similar monitor (Spacelabs Model 5200). *Psychophysiology, 25,* 107-116.

Livingston, I. L. (1987). Blacks, life-style and hypertension: The importance of health education. *Humboldt Journal of Social Relations, 14,* 195-213.

Ludescher, G., Nishiwaki, R., Lewis, D., Brown, E., Glacken, D., & Jenkins, E. (1993). Black male college students and hypertension: A qualitative investigation. *Health Education Research, 8,* 271-282.

Luft, F., Grim, C., & Weinberger, M. (1985). Electrolyte and volume homeostasis in Blacks. In W. Hall, E. Saunders, & N. Shulman (Eds.), *Hypertension in Blacks: Epidemiology, pathophysiology, and treatment* (pp. 131-151). Chicago, IL: Yearbook Medical.

McAdoo, H. P. (1981). *Black families.* Beverly Hills, CA: Sage Publications.

McAdoo, H. P. (1982). Stress absorbing systems in Black families. *Family Relations, 31,* 479-488.

McManus, C. H. (1992). *A study of anger in African American males: Issues of physiological reactivity, personality, and culture.* Unpublished doctoral dissertation, Howard University, Washington, DC.

Merritt, M., Dixon, P., & Harrell, J. P. (1995). *Dimensions of Physical Stress Symptoms Across Racial Identity Stages.* Paper presented at the 27th Annual Convention of the Association of Black Psychologists: Los Angeles, CA.

Morris-Prather, C. E., Harrell, J. P., Collins, R., Jeffries-Leonard, K. L., Boss, M., & Lee, J. W. (1996). Gender differences in mood and cardiovascular responses to socially stressful stimuli. *Ethnicity and Disease, 4,* 327-345.

Myers, H. F. (1976). Holistic definition and measurements of states of non-health. In L. King, V. Dixon, & W. Nobles (Eds.), *African philosophy: Assumptions and paradigms of research on Black persons* (pp. 139-153). Los Angeles, CA: Fanon Research Center.

Myers, H. F., Bastien, R. T., Miles, R. E. (1983). Life-stress, health, and blood pressure in Black college students. *The Journal of Black Psychology, 9,* 1-25.

Myers, H. F., & Miles, R. E. (1981). Stress, subjective appraisal and somatization in hypertension. *Journal of Human Stress, 7,* 17-29.

National Center for Health Statistics. (1987). *Health United States: 1986.* (DHHS Publication No. PHS 87-1232). Washington DC: U. S. Department of Health and Human Services.

National Center for Health Statistics. (1988). *Health United States: 1987.* (DHHS Publication No. 88-1232). Washington, DC: U. S. Government Printing Office.

National Research Council. (1989). Black Americans' health. In G. D. Jaynes & R. M. Williams, (Ed.), *A common destiny: Blacks and American society* (pp. 392-450). Washington, DC: Nautical Academy Press.

Neighbors, H., Jackson, J., Bowman, P., & Gurin, G. (1983). Stress, coping and Black mental health: Preliminary findings from a national study. *Prevention in Human Services, 2*, 5-29.

Orbrist, P. A. (1981). *Cardiovascular psychophysiology: A perspective.* New York: Plenum Press.

Parham, T. A. (1989). Cycles of psychological nigrescence. *The Counseling Psychologist, 17*, 187-226.

Parham, T. A., & Helms, J. E. (1985a). *The Racial Identity Attitude Scale (RIAS).* Unpublished manuscript.

Parham, T. A., & Helms, J. E. (1985b). Relation of racial identity attitudes to self-actualization and affective states of Black students. *Journal of Counseling Psychology, 32*, 431-440.

Parham, T. A., & Helms, J. E. (1985c). Attitudes of racial identity and self-esteem: An exploratory explanation. *Journal of College Student Personnel, 26*, 143-146.

Patterson, S. M., Krantz, D. S., Gottdiener, J. S., Hecht, G., Vargot, S., & Goldstein, D. S. (1995). Prothrombotic effects of environmental stress: Changes in platelet function, hematocrit, and total plasma protein. *Psychosomatic Medicine, 57*, 592-599.

Patterson, S. M., Krantz, D. S., & Jochum, S. (1995). Time course and mechanisms of decreased plasma volume during acute psychological stress and postural change in humans. *Psychophysiology, 32*, 538-545.

Rodney, W. (1972). *How Europe underdeveloped Africa.* Dar es Salaam: Tanzania Publishing House.

Selye, H. (1976). *The stress of life* (2nd ed.). New York: McGraw Hill.

Semmes, C. E. (1983). Toward a theory of popular health practices in the Black community. *The Western Journal of Black Studies, 7*, 206-213.

Semmes, C. E. (1992). *Cultural hegemony and African American development.* Westport, CT: Praeger.

Shujaa, M. J. (1994). Education and schooling: You can have one without the other. In M. J. Shujaa (Ed.), *Too much schooling, too little education: A paradox of Black life in White schools.* Trenton, NJ: African World Press.

Sutherland, M. E. & Harrell, J. P. (1986). Individual differences in physiological reposes to fearful, racially noxious and neutral imagery. *Imagination, Cognition and Personality, 6*, 133-150.

Sutherland, M. E., Harrell, J. P., & Isaacs, C. (1987). The stability of individual differences in imagery ability. *The Journal of Mental Imagery, 11*, 97-104.

Taylor, J. (1991). Dimensionalization of racialism. In R. Jones (Ed.), *Black psychology* (3rd ed., pp. 637-651). Berkeley, CA: Cobb and Henry Publishers.

Turner, J. R., Sherwood, A. & Light, K. C. (1992). *Individual differences in cardiovascular response to stress*. New York: Plenum Press.

U. S. Department of Health and Human Services. (1985). *Report of the secretary's task force on Black and minority health* (Vol. 1: summary). Washington, DC: Author.

U. S. Department of Health and Human Services. (1986). *Prevention of disease, disability, and death in Blacks and other minorities*. Annual Program Review. Centers for Disease Control, Public Health Service. Washington, DC: Author.

Willemson, G. H. M., De Geus, E. J. C., Klaver, C. H. A. M., van Doornen, L. J. P., & Carroll, D. (1966). Ambulatory monitoring of the impedance cardiogram. *Psychophysiology, 33*, 184-193.

Williams, D. L., Larsen, D. B., Buckler, R. E., Heckman, R. C., & Pyle, C. M. (1991). Religion and psychological distress in a community sample. *Social Science and Medicine, 32*, 1257-1262.

Wilson, D. K., Holmes, S. D., Arheart, K., & Alpert, B. S. (1995). Cardiovascular reactivity in Black and White siblings versus matched controls. *Annals of Behavioral Medicine, 17*, 207-212.

Woodson, C. G. (1933/1977). *The mis-education of the Negro*. Washington, DC: The Associated Publishers, Inc.

Author

Jules P. Harrell
Department of Psychology
Rm 256 C. B. Powell Blvd.
Howard University
Washington, DC 20059
Telephone: (202) 806-9458
Fax: (202) 806-4873

Part 5

Therapeutic Approaches

Toward a Psychology of Liberation and Restoration: Answering the Challenge of Cultural Alienation

Jerome Taylor, Chioma Obiechina, and Sherlyn Harrison

The purpose of this paper is to examine strategies for reclaiming and restoring values which enhance quality of life in the African American community. As such this paper is an extension of ongoing efforts to understand values formation and promotion through specialized program and policy initiatives (Burgess, 1995, 1996; Jackson-Lowman, in press; Taylor, Jackson-Lowman, Obiechina, & Lewis, in press; Taylor, Jackson-Lowman, Rogers, & Obiechina, in preparation; Taylor, Turner, & Lewis, in press; Taylor, Turner, Underwood, Franklin, Jackson, & Stagg, 1994). In part, the need for such program and policy initiatives is reflected in our first section which develops the case for liberation. For theoretical reasons, we argue that liberatory interventions should precede restorative interventions which are both described. We conclude by examining implications of this program of cultural habilitation for future research and policy development.

Case for Liberation

The historical and contemporary ubiquity of racism in our society is formatively related to what Taylor and Obiechina (in press) have referred to as *cultural alienation*—the tragic separation of African Americans from their culture of origin.[1] Typically, this is expressed in one of three ways: (a) identification with White racist stereotypes that African Americans are mentally defective and physically gifted; (b) unselfconscious identification with mainstream ideology or praxis;[2] or (c) passionate disaffection with African American nationalist ideology or praxis;[3] For empirical and theoretical reasons it has been argued previously that (a) is a more direct estimate of cultural alienation than (b) which is a more direct estimate than (c) see Taylor and Obiechina (in press).

While we do not have studies documenting the national incidence or prevalence of cultural alienation, our best estimate from local and regional studies is that about one in three African Americans may believe as White racists do that African Americans are *mentally defective*—intellectually, morally, emotionally—and *physi- cally gifted*—sexually, athletically, artistically. On a sample of 910 African American college students attending private and public institutions in 11 states, we found that 34 percent of the students who uncritically identified with mainstream ideology or praxis had the highest level of internalized racism (Taylor & Rogers, 1993). On a random sample of 600 African American women living in an inner city community, we found that about 35% endorsed racist stereotypes about African Americans (Taylor, Zhang, Stevens, in preparation). On either side of our estimate of one in three, the incidence of cultural alienation has been as low as 15 percent in a sample of African American married couples living in the inner city (Taylor, Andrews, Jackson-Lowman, Turner, Rogers, Logan, J., & Logan, R., submitted) and as high as 50 percent in a sample of single African American mothers living in public housing (Taylor & Tull, submitted). The "so what" question naturally arises within this context: What difference does it make? Table 1 provides a summary of studies relevant to this question. The first column identifies the indicator variable used to estimate cultural alienation, and the second column specifies the dependent variable utilized by investigators identified in the fourth column. The third column indicates the nature of the relationship between indicator and dependent variables.

Table 1 indicates that cultural alienation is directly related to a range of negative personal outcomes for African American adults: alcohol consumption (Taylor & Jackson, 1990 a/b), aggressive behaviors (Denton, 1985; Taylor, 1997a), mental health symptoms in general (Brown, 1976; Tong, 1993; Taylor & Jackson, 1991), and depressive symptoms in particular (Franklin, 1986; Taylor, Henderson, & Jackson, 1991; Tomes, Brown, Semya, & Simpson, 1990). Moreover, strident disaffection with nationalist ideology and praxis is directly related to severity of crimes committed against other African Americans (Terrell, Taylor, & Terrell, 1980). In relation to positive social outcomes, cultural alienation—indexed by internalized racism—is inversely related to marital satisfaction (Taylor & Zhang, 1990), disclosive disposition (Taylor & Tull, submitted), empathic capacity (Barrett, 1974), and structural attainment as indexed by educational level and annual income (McCorkle & Taylor, submitted; Murrell, 1989; Sturdivant-Anderson, in preparation).

Table 1 indicates that commitment to African American nationalist ideology and praxis—an inverse indicator of cultural alienation—is directly related to I. Q. scores of middle-school children (Asbury, Adderly-Kelly, & Knuckle, 1987). Mothers' identification with racist stereotypes about African American—a direct index of cultural alienation—is directly related to reports of psychological maladjustment of their children (McCorkle & Taylor, submitted). Internalized racism may also be directly related to gang violence (Evans & Taylor, 1995) and teenage pregnancy (Taylor & Franklin, 1994) among African American youths. For the African American community, Table 1 indicates that cultural alienation is directly related to the tendency to avoid participation in African American-oriented organizations (Cross, 1991).

Table 1
Effects of Cultural Alienation on Black Adults, Black Youth and the Black Community

Indicator of Cultural Alienation	Dependent Variable Evaluated	Nature of Relationship Between Indicator & Dependent Variables	Investigators
Internalized Racism	Alcohol Consumption	Direct	Taylor & Jackson (1990a, 1990b)
Mainstream Ideology	Aggressive Behaviors	Direct	Denton (1985): Taylor (in pressa)
Internalized Racism	General Mental Health Symptons	Direct	Taylor & Jackson (1991)
Internalized Racism	Depressive Symptons Health Symptons	Direct	Franklin (1986); Taylor, Henderson, & Jackson (1991); Tomes, Brown, Semenya, & Simpson (1990)
Internalized Racism	Marital Satisfaction	Inverse	Taylor (1992); Taylor & Zang (1990)
Internalized Racism	Disclosive Disposition	Inverse	Taylor & Tull (submitted)
Internalized Racism	Empathic Capacity	Inverse	Barrett (1976)
Nationalist Ideology	Black-on-Black Crime	Inverse	Terrell, Taylor, & Terrell (1980)
Internalized Racism	Structural Outcomes Education and Income	Inverse	McCorkle & Taylor (submitted); Murrell (1989); Sturdivant-Anderson (in prep)
Nationalist Ideology	I.Q. Scores	Direct	McCorkle & Taylor (submitted)
Mainstream	Black Involvement	Inverse	Cross (1991)

In summary, results of studies identified in Table 1 indicate that cultural alienation impairs the quality of personal, social, and political life within the African American community. These studies establish in the affirmative our case for liberation which must address presumptions of African American mental inferiority and physical superiority. Since African Americans conformed to racist stereotypes have lost their way culturally as well as spiritually (Jackson-Lowman, in press; Rogers, 1997), we feel a special urgency in designing, implementing, evaluating, and refining strategies of relevance to our spiritual and cultural redemption. Table 2 provides an overview of assumptions motivating our program of cultural habilitation, processes underlying liberatory and restorative interventions, and expectations issuing from ongoing implementation of these interventions. Table 2, then, provides the conceptual framework which guides our description of liberatory and restorative interventions.

Strategies for Liberation

Which interventions are effective in liberating African Americans from racist claims that African Americans are mentally defective and physically gifted? We believe three types of interventions are worthy of exploration: *awakening*, designed to heighten awareness of individual and communal implications of racist claims; *affirming*, proposed to highlight African American attributes which weaken and contradict racist claims; and *grounding*, structured to enhance cultural appreciation through lectures, readings, and discussions of African American history, politics, psychology, literature, and art. Together, these interventions are an instrument of what Akbar (1984) identified as the purpose of Africentric social science: human liberation.

Interventions proposed for awakening, affirming, and grounding are considered sequential and complementary. Awakening and affirming interventions are intended to expunge internalized representations of racist claims, and grounding interventions are designed to enhance appreciation of one's culture of origin. We believe that attempts to ground before awakening or affirming is akin to applying deluxe paint to a grimy surface: it won't stick. In this sense, we believe identified interventions are sequential. Moreover, we believe that awakening or affirming or grounding alone is insufficient to liberate African Americans from the claims of racism; all are needed. In this sense, we believe identified interventions are theoretically complementary and logically sufficient. Before introducing these interventions, we share an important note on perspective and usage.

On the matter of perspective, we believe that liberation is not a once-in-a-lifetime event. This is because the ubiquity of racism requires unceasing vigilance and courageous engagement. Within this context, we are clear that interventions proposed initiate but do not conclude this struggle of a life time. On the matter of

Table 2
Toward a Psychological Theory of Liberation and Restoration for Blacks Who Are Culturally Alienated

Assumptions

To the extent African Americans believe as racists do that Blacks are mentally defective and physically gifted, they will report poorer personal, social, and socio-econcomic outcomes.

To the extent African Americans believe as racists do that Blacks are mentally defective and physically gifted, they will report poorer communal outcomes -- political and economic

Interventions

If Awakening, Affirming, and Grounding are effective strategies of liberation; and

If Discovery, Engagement, and Maintenance are effective strategies of restoration,

Expectations

Immediate

Then there will be a significant reduction in racists beliefs that Blacks are mentally defective and physically gifted;

Intermediate

There will be a significant improvement in personal, social, and socio-economic outcomes; and

Long-range

There will be a significant improvement in communal outcomes -- spiritual, political, and economic usage, we believe our interventions can be adapted to different settings (churches, temples, schools, clubs, or community centers), to different combinations of settings (church, school, community center), and to persons of different ages (children, youths, and adults). We believe also that proposed interventions can be adapted to liberate Whites as well as African Americans. In all adaptations, the recommended structure of interventions would remain the same. The reader would consult examples provided for clues on how to adapt content to various targets of intervention.

Awakening

Three strategies are recommended to awaken persons to the seriousness of racist claims on African American lives. Cognitive insight is provided by hermeneutical training and affective insight by role play. Both types of interventions are used to support inoculation training which introduces skills for coping with some of the more than 360 forms of racial prejudice generated by the framework offered by Taylor and Grundy (1996).

Hermeneutical training. Our adapted purpose of hermeneutical training is to help participants understand and interpret "reality" in ways that liberate them from White racist claims. Toward this end our efforts here are directed toward helping persons become more critical, communal, and transcendent in their thinking.

To enhance *critical consciousness* is to help participants become inquisitive, probing, and relentless in their commitment to understand causes and implications of White racist conceptions of African Americans. Factual scenarios, negative sayings, and news articles provide primary methods to accomplish this objective. In scenarios, participants are presented with brief descriptions such as: "Black kids have a better chance of becoming a brain surgeon than a NBA player." They are then invited to discuss the "cause" question—"Why, then, do larger numbers choose basketball over medicine?" and the "implications" question—"What are consequences for the Black community?" Negative sayings such as "Don't bring me no niggah lawyer or doctor" or news items such as "Three Drive-Bys in One Night" will also be analyzed in terms of "cause" and "implications." In these and other instances the group leader will help participants see how identified behaviors which affirm White racist stereotypes about African Americans have ruinous implications for the African American community. Theoretically, the purpose of these exercises is to change the manner in which persons receive and interpret realities of relevance to White racist stereotypes about African Americans.

The objective of *communal consciousness* is to help participants appreciate communal implications of their behavior. Toward this end three strategies are recommended. First, it is important for participants to understand the nature of community from the perspective of ancestors, contemporaries, and progeny.

Defining and illustrating this community is a critical first task, especially for ancestors which may require historical supplementation. Second, participants are invited to assume the position of key actors identified under Critical Consciousness, e.g., to assume they were the person who said "Don't bring me no niggah lawyer or doctor." What would your African American ancestors who were early scientists, mathematicians, and diplomats say about this statement? How would this affect your peers who overheard you make this statement? How would it affect your children who overheard you make this statement? How would your children's children feel about you if they knew you made this statement? In what ways could your statement today affect your children's children? In general, how would this statement reflect on the African American community past, present, and future? Third, participants are instructed to maintain a daily log of personal behaviors or decisions. They then are assisted in examining personal behaviors and decisions from a communal perspective, that is, from the perspective of ancestors, contemporaries, and progeny—a familiar characteristic of African world view (Mbiti, 1970; Opoku 1972).

The objective of *transcendent consciousness* is to subject racist constructions of African Americans to transcendent principles.[4] For example, what does the claim "Don't bring me no niggah lawyer or doctor" mean in relation to transcendent principles? Does it mean African Americans were created intellectually inferior? If African Americans were involved in "Three Drive-Bys in One Night," does that mean they were created morally inferior? Since problems of African Americans sometimes affirm White racist stereotypes of African Americans, reference to a transcendent standard can be spiritually, psychologically, and politically liberating as well as reassuring.

Role play I. While hermeneutical training is designed to introduce a level of cognitive understanding of racist claims that African Americans are mentally defective and physically gifted, role play is structured to induce a measure of affective understanding of social roles which support or challenge these stereotypes. As such hermeneutical training and role play are complementary processes. Further, we suggest that affective learning will be richer to the degree cognitive learning has preceded it. Therefore, we recommend that hermeneutical training precede role play.

Identification of defining scenarios is the first challenge for implementing this version of role play. These scenarios which participants can help develop should be structured around *personalized expressions* of each of the six racist claims: African Americans are inferior intellectually (e.g., "You're dumb"), morally (e.g., "You're irresponsible"), and emotionally (e.g., "You're the class clown"); and gifted athletically (e.g., "You're nothing but a jock"), sexually (e.g., "Scoring is #1 in your life"), and artistically (e.g., "All you can do is dance"). Each scenario starts with Oppressor imposing the stereotype. Oppressed then shares how Oppressor's statements made him or her think or feel. The scenario concludes with Liberator refuting Oppressor's argument. Each member of the triad—*Oppressor, Oppressed, Liberator*—alternately plays each role with instruction to give special attention to what they think and feel while playing each role. A total of 15 minutes is required since roles are rotated every five minutes.[5]

Following each 15 minute module, members of the triad are given three minutes to write down their answers to three questions: While you were playing the role of Oppressor: (a) What thoughts raced through your mind? (b) What kind of feelings did you experience? and (c) What did your feelings and thoughts make you want to do? This same set of questions are raised successively for Oppressed and Liberator roles. After each group member has participated in each role, the instructor provides opportunities for sharing. In particular, the thoughts, feelings, and action tendencies of Oppressor, Oppressed, and Liberator are recorded publicly: What did the Oppressor think? How did Oppressor Feel? What did Oppressor want to do? Analogous questions are put to Oppressed and Liberator. From the instructor's charting of responses by role, participants are invited to analyze the results: What's common about how Oppressor thinks? Feels? Acts? What's common about how Oppressed thinks? Feels? Acts? What's common about how Liberator thinks? Feels? Acts? What's wrong with permitting yourself to be an oppressor? What's wrong with permitting yourself to be oppressed? And what are some of the problems and costs involved with being a Liberator? What are the rewards?

Finally, participants are asked to think about real life instances when they may have played roles of Oppressor and Liberator as well as Oppressed. Examples are solicited, analyzed. and discussed.

Inoculation training. When persons react to a mild but not overwhelming attack on their opinion, they tend to become more committed to that opinion. Research demonstrates that mild attacks stimulate defensive arguments which act to shore up that position against subsequent assault (Kiesler, 1971; McGuire, 1964). This has been referred to as an inoculation effect (McGuire, 1964) since a small "dose" of "the virus" fortifies against subsequent exposure to it. This approach has been used successfully to inoculate teenagers against peer-induced smoking (Flay, Ryan, Best, Brown, Kersell, d'Avernas, & Zanna, 1985) and school children against deceptive commercials (Feshbach, 1980). Given the likely exposure to peer pressure and misleading ads, inoculation training accommodates plausible reality. Whatever our level of success in removing the taint of racist claims from the mind of individuals, we are clear that this is not the same as removing it from the environment of individuals. We expect inoculation training might be of relevance to this reality. Assuming as we do that Herrmeneutical Training and Role Play I have been effective in challenging White racist beliefs and affirming culturally integrative beliefs, the immediate challenge here is to define the "attack dosage" which would inoculate participants against subsequent assaults on their newly discovered culturally integrative positions.

We would start out by identifying mild arguments that challenge culturally integrative beliefs: African Americans are inferior intellectually (e.g., "Blacks aren't as brainy as Whites"), morally (e.g., "Blacks can't be trusted"), and emotionally (e.g., "Blacks are silly"); and gifted athletically (e.g., "Blacks are stronger than Whites"), sexually (e.g., "Blacks can't control themselves sexually"), and artistically (e.g., "Blacks are natural entertainers"). We recommend seven strategies. First, the trainer leads the group in a discussion of what each racist claim means. Second, the trainer asks each member of the group to write down as many arguments as they can to refute each racist claim. Third, the counterarguments of the group are shared and discussed. Fourth, the trainer assigns reading materials which bolster and extend counterarguments offered by the group. Fifth, participants are instructed to write brief reports of their findings which are then shared with the class. Sixth, the group product is assembled and shared with each participant along with instructions to teach these materials to one person over the next week. Their teaching experiences are shared with the group. And seventh, the group participates in developing and performing a skit which incorporates their assembled materials and their experience teaching it. We expect that this training will help persons cope with—provide inoculation against recurring racist claims they are certain to encounter in daily living.

Affirming

Herrmeneutical Training, Role Play I, and Inoculation Training introduced in the previous section were designed to challenge racist stereotypes about African Americans. Role Play II and Counterattitudinal Training introduced in this section are designed to affirm culturally adaptive concepts of African Americans which we illustrate in the next paragraph. Together, these procedures which reduce cultural negatives and accentuate cultural positives are preparatory to grounding activities which are introduced in the next section. Since it's unlikely that cultural positives can be integrated fully before cultural negatives have been extruded systematically, we recommend that intervention procedures already described precede those about to be described. Before we introduce these interventions, it's important to illustrate what we mean by the phrase "culturally adaptive concepts."

For the racist presumption that African Americans are "mentally defective" we offer the culturally integrative concept that African Americans are "mentally competent"—intellectually (e.g., "Being Black is being smart"), morally (e.g., "Being Black is having integrity"), and emotionally (e.g., "Being Black is being mature"). For the culturally alienated view that African Americans are "sexually gifted," we offer the culturally adaptive concept that African Americans are sexually responsible (e.g., "Being Black is seeing the destructive effects of sexual irresponsibility"). For the racist presumption that "Blacks are athletically gifted and mentally defective," we offer the culturally integrative view that African Americans are intellectually and athletically competent (e.g., "Being Black is being 'smart' as well as athletic"). And for the culturally alienated view that "Blacks are artistically gifted and mentally defective", we offer the counterclaim that African Americans are intellectually and artistically competent (e.g., "Being Black is being 'smart' as well as musically talented").

Role play II. Here we use role play procedures to develop a belief calculus which generally is supportive of culturally integrative concepts. Through role play, which we now illustrate for the claim "being Black is being mature," participants develop a richly textured appreciation of this claim which supports the culturally adaptive concept of African Americans as mentally competent.

Experiences are structured around three roles: one participant who plays a culturally integrative belief, e.g., "being Black is being emotionally mature" which counters the culturally alienated belief "Blacks are emotionally immature." A second participant who plays the role of television anchor person whose assignment is to find out more about the first participant's belief, and a third participant who plays the role of observer and recorder. We shall refer to these roles as *Elder, Anchor,* and *Observer,* respectively. We now illustrate implementation of these roles for the culturally adaptive belief "being Black is being mature" which provides the template for processing other culturally adaptive beliefs.

Anchor to Elder: You have been quoted as saying, "Being Black is being mature." What do you mean by "mature"? Please complete the following sentence for me: "'Being Black is being mature' because. . . ." If young people believed that "being Black is being mature," how might this make their ancestors feel? If young people believed that "being Black is being mature," how might this affect relationships among young people? If parents believed that "being Black is being mature," how might this affect the way they raise their children? If people in general believed that "being Black is being mature," how might this affect the quality of life within our community? Between our communities? And where it is politically permissible, we would ask, how do you think the Divine would feel if people believed that "being Black is being mature"? The reader will note that most questions affirm key elements of critical communal and transcendent consciousness which we introduced under Hermeneutical Training .

We recommend that members of learning triads rotate roles every seven minutes such that at the end of 21 minutes each person will have played each role.[6] Rotation of roles—as *Elder, Anchor,* and *Observer*—provides multiple exposure to culturally adaptive beliefs which research demonstrates should heighten participant acceptability of these beliefs (Arkes, Boehm, & Zu, 1991; Cacioppo & Petty, 1989). Results of Role Play II are then shared with the full group which together develops a list of reasons why "being Black is being emotionally mature." This listing which is publicly recorded is combined with counterattitudinal training which we now review.

Counterattitudinal training. From the list of reasons generated by the full group, each participant is given the option of writing a rhyme, rap, song, poem, essay, mime, or skit or making a poster or creating a drawing which he or she is asked to present and defend over the following week with one friend and one stranger. To the extent participants have formerly endorsed racist stereotypes, this amounts to counterattitudinal training which can be quite effective when the activity is ego-involving (Baumeister & Tice, 1984) each student created it—and chosen voluntarily (Linder, Cooper & Jones, 1967)—each student decides with whom to share it if at all. Recent evidence on the effectiveness of counterattitudinal training is reviewed by Olson and Zanna (1993).

Grounding

We contend that awakening and affirming interventions should precede grounding activities which include systematic exposure to African American history, politics, psychology, literature, and art. Since this reasoning flies in the face of current practice which understandably opens with African American history lessons (Asante, 1987, 1988, 1990), we examine the theoretical basis for our position.

We sometimes assume that exposure to salutary messages transforms prior beliefs apodictically, e.g., the message "there were great kings and queens in ancient Africa" is expected to unsettle the view that "Blacks are mentally defective." While it is true that a history lesson which induces conflict between beliefs ("Blacks are great" vs. "Blacks are defective") stimulates cognitive dissonance which motivates efforts to reduce it (Festinger, 1957), research suggests there is more than one way to achieve this end: change one's beliefs in the direction of the instructor's message, seek more information to support one's existing belief, or minimize the importance of conflict between the instructor's message and one's existing belief.

So, then, Jahodi's response to lectures on African American kings and queens to counter the belief that African Americans are mentally defective may be processed in one of three ways. First, Jahodi might absorb these lectures in ways that fundamentally transform his view of African Americans in general and himself in particular. Second, Jahodi might reason that scholarship underlying the claim to African American royalty is suspect, and therefore his original position which affirms the racist claim is undisturbed. Or third, Jahodi might reconcile differences between racist and culturally affirming claims with a shrug: "Black kings and queens existed, but they don't today. So what's the big deal?" Thus while Jahodi entertains the culturally affirming claim, he is not transformed by it. In summary, lecture outcomes might be: (a) informative and transformative; (b) neither informative nor transformative; or (c) informative but not transformative. We note that while the message is believed in two of three instances (a, c), the message transforms in one instance only (a). These implications are basic to our argument.

African Americans who are culturally alienated are less open to transformation—option (a)—because initial beliefs they bring are so far removed from cultural lessons they're exposed to (cf. Kaplowitz, Fink, Malcrone, & Atkins, 1991, whose theoretical work provides the basis for this expectation). We suspect also that they might give the impression of accommodating culturally affirming viewpoints. Indeed, they might perform well on tests which tap these viewpoints which nonetheless fail to transform their cultural or self image (c). The purpose of awakening and affirming activities is to change initial beliefs in the direction of culturally affirming claims. In so doing, we enhance receptivity to culturally affirming claims and improve the likelihood of self and cultural transformation (a). These considerations provide the theoretical basis for our proposition that awakening and affirming interventions should precede grounding activities. This proposition applies as well to other types of grounding interventions—political, psychological, literary, artistic, or sermonic.

Proposals for Restoration

Once awakened, applied, and grounded, then what? While a complete discussion of this question is beyond the Scope of this paper, we identify three strategies we consider of relevance to a post-liberation agenda: discovery, engagement, and maintenance. Together these strategies are intended to normalize perspectives and values which enhance quality of life within the African American community. For theoretical reasons we will identify, unliberated persons are unable to participate fully in our post-liberation agenda. For these reasons, we argue that liberatory interventions should precede restorative interventions.

Discovery

Liberated persons should be helped to discover normative systems which enhance the viability of African American communities and families. While this may be distilled in part from grounding activities, we urge more directed and focused attention to normative systems which define the cultural soul of a community—its social ethic. What normative system is critical to the overall well-being of our community? Karenga's (1980) *Ngubo Saba* immediately come to mind: Unity, Self-Determination, Collective Work and Responsibility, Cooperative Economics, Purpose, Creativity, and Faith. What normative system helps African American children and families thrive against the odds? Objectives promoted by the *Values-for-Life Program* come to mind: Love and Respect, Interpersonal Skills, Learning Orientation, Self-Confidence, Self-Persistence, Self-Esteem, and Self-Reliance (Taylor, 1997b; Taylor, Turner, & Lewis, 1992; Taylor, et al., 1994). We believe these normative systems are complementary: the first primarily affirms communal principles which should be lived individually and the second primarily expresses individual values which should be lived communally.

While liberation interventions release the potential for growth, normative systems direct this potential along pathways of established relevance to the African American community. To borrow an analogy from physics, liberation is to discovery as potential energy is to kinetic energy. In relation to this analogy, we argue that unliberated persons—those whose aspirations have been constrained by racist stereotypes—are less able to affirm the agenda of the *Nguzo Saba* or *Values-for-Life*. Believing African Americans are mentally defective is incompatible with the principle of Self-determination or Communal Unity. Believing African Americans are mentally defective and physically gifted is incompatible with the values Learning Orientation or Self-Confidence. To fully release the potential of culturally alienated persons, to help them affirm the principles and values which enhance quality of life in the African American community, we believe liberatory interventions should precede discovery interventions.

Engagement

As liberated persons discover normative systems of relevance to the viability of African American communities and families, they must be provided planful opportunities to engage in activities and behaviors which affirm them. This requires ongoing collaboration of families with religious, social, educational, service, neighborhood, and cultural institutions around normative systems of relevance to the African American community. Unfortunately, we have few community collaboratives which provide systematic opportunities for engagement around the *Nguzo Saba* or *Values-for-Life*. At the Institute for the African American Family, we are developing policy and program models which we hope will correct this shortcoming (Taylor, Jackson-Lowman, & Obiechina, in press; Taylor, Turner, & Lewis, in press). The major challenge for these initiatives in relation to culturally alienated persons is summarized by the saying, "You can lead a horse to water but you can't make him drink." Unless persons are liberated, they may be unmotivated to invest personal resources of time and energy in otherwise excellent programs which may be quite accessible. For this reason we believe liberatory interventions should precede engagement interventions.

Maintenance

Maintenance refers to the development of communal culture which supports activities of awakening, affirming, grounding, discovery, and engagement—all critical elements of cultural habilitation. As with organizational cultures in general (Deal & Kennedy, 1982; Sackmann, 1991; Taylor, Prettyman, Cunningham,

Nelbourne, & Dixon, 1991), it would be critical to form cultural collaboratives which: (a) promote consensually identified normative systems throughout the community; (b) formalize procedures for training enrollees to standard within each level of the program—awakening through and engagement; (c) establish formal and informal means of recognizing enrollees who complete each level of the program; (d) establish formal and informal means of recognizing institutions involved in training enrollees to standard; and (e) provide a method for collecting process and outcome data which are broadly shared to deepen the sense of partnership and planfully utilized to make the program more effective. Maintenance, then, provides the institutional basis for achieving community through liberatory and restorative interventions. Because the success of maintenance interventions is likely to depend on level of cultural alienation in the community, it seems reasonable to argue that liberatory interventions should precede maintenance interventions.

Conclusion

Studies reviewed in this paper generally support the conclusion that cultural alienation undermines the viability of the African American community in general and African American adults and youth in particular. We have proposed liberatory and recovery interventions which we believe will reduce cultural alienation along with individual and systemic problems connected with this affliction. Several development, research, and policy implications follow from these considerations.

Implementation of proposed interventions will require a major development effort. Multidisciplinary input will be required to adapt recommended interventions to specific targets. Once developed, these interventions must be evaluated formally: Do liberatory interventions release African Americans from racist claims? Do restorative interventions enhance personal familial and communal integration? Should liberatory interventions precede all remaining interventions as we have argued? Moreover, how should psychological interventions recommended here be combined with spiritual, political, or economic interventions which may also have liberatory and restorative implications?

Finally, the question of who should be involved in implementing recommended or alternative interventions is really a question of cultural policy—the normalization of values and norms that enhance the viability of a people sharing common origin, experience, or location (Taylor, Jackson-Lowman, Obiechina, & Lewis, 1997). What's the role of families? Neighborhoods? Libraries? Schools? Social agencies? Churches, temples, or mosques? How should responsibilities for implementation be apportioned, and how should progress be monitored and results evaluated? Answers to these questions are likely to require formation of new collaboratives involving public and private sectors of community and state.

Notes

1. Although this refers generally to West African societies, we stress here more of a way of being than a place of being.
2. Refers to uncritical identification with materialistic and capitalistic values and practices of the dominant culture.
3. Entails a radical assertion of African American independence—culturally, economically, politically, ethically—across every life sphere.
4. Refers to principles revealed more by divine authority than by human deliberation.
5. This time proposal can and should be modified depending upon the age of participants and specific aims of the trainer.
6. See footnote 5 which applies here as well.

References

Akbar, N. (1984). Africentric social science for human liberation. *Journal of Black Studies, 14*, 395-414.

Arkes, H. R., Boehm, L. E., & Zu, G. (1991). Determinants of judged validity. *Journal of Experimental Social Psychology, 27*, 576-605.

Asante, M. K. (1987). *The Afrocentric idea.* Philadelphia, PA: Temple University Press.

Asante, M. K. (1988). *Afrocentricity.* Trenton, NJ: African World Press.

Asante, M. K. (1990). *Kemet, afrocentricity, and knowledge.* Trenton, NJ: African World Press.

Asbury, C. A., Adderly-Kelly, B., & Knuckles, E. P. (1987). Relationship among WISC-R; Performance categories and measured ethnic identity in Black adolescents. *Journal of Negro Education, 56,* 172-183.

Baumeister, R. F., & Tice, D. M. (1984). Role of self-presentation and choice in cognitive dissonance under forced compliance: Necessary or sufficient causes? *Journal of Personality and Social Psychology, 46,* 5-13.

Barrett, R. K. (1974). *A study of attribution of responsibility as a function of internal external locus of control and interracial person perception.* Unpublished doctoral dissertation, University of Pittsburgh.

Burgess, B. N. (1995). *Values for life day camp curriculum.* Institute for the Black Family, University of Pittsburgh, Pittsburgh, PA.

Burgess, B. N. (1996). *Values for life after-school curriculum.* Institute for the Black Family, University of Pittsburgh, Pittsburgh, PA.

Brown, A. B. (1976). *Personality correlates of the developmental inventory of Black consciousness.* Unpublished master's thesis, University of Pittsburgh, Pittsburgh, PA.

Cacioppo, J. T., & Petty, R. E. (1989). Effects of message repetition on argument processing, recall, and persuasion. *Basic and Applied Social Psychology, 10*, 3-12.

Cross, W. E., Jr. (1991). *Shades of Black: Diversity in African-American identity*. Philadelphia, PA: Temple University Press.

Deal, T. E., & Kennedy, A. A. (1982). *Corporate cultures: The rites and rituals of corporate life*. Reading, MA: Addison-Wesley Publishing Company, Inc.

Denton, S. E. (1985). *A methodological refinement and validation analysis of the developmental inventory of Black consciousness*. Unpublished doctoral dissertation, University of Pittsburgh, Pittsburgh, PA.

Evans, J. P., & Taylor, J. (1995). Why are contemporary gangs more violent than earlier gangs?: An exploratory application of the theory of reasoned action. *Journal of Black Psychology, 21*, 71-81.

Feshbach, N. D. (1980). *The child as "psychologist" and "economist": Two curricula*. Paper presented at the American Psychological Association Convention.

Festinger, L. (1957). *A theory of cognitive dissonance*. Stanford, CA: Stanford University Press.

Flay, B. R., Ryan, K. B., Best, J. A., Brown, K. S., Kersell, M. W. d'Avernas, J. R., & Zanna, M. P. (1985). Are social-psychological smoking prevention programs effective?: The Waterloo Study. *Journal of Behavioral Medicine, 8,* 37-59.

Franklin, A. T. (1986). *Influence of economic, social, religious, and cultural factors on depression in single Black women with male friends*. Unpublished doctoral dissertation, University of Pittsburgh, Pittsburgh, PA.

Jackson-Lowman, H. (in press). Using African proverbs to provide an African-centered narrative for contemporary African American parental values. In J. Adjaye & A. Andrews (Eds.), *Black popular culture*. Pittsburgh, PA: University of Pittsburgh Press.

Kaplowitz, S. A., Fink, E. L., Malcrone, J., & Arkins, D. (1991). Disentangling the effects of discrepant and disconfirming information. *Social Psychology Quarterly, 54,* 191-207.

Karenga, M. (1980). *Kawaida theory: An introductory outline*. Ingelwood, CA: Kawaida Publications.

Kiesler, C. A. (1971). *The psychology of commitment: Experiments linking behavior to belief*. New York: Academic Press.

Linder, D. E., Cooper, J., & Jones, E. E. (1967). Decision freedom as a determinant of the role of incentive magnitude in attitude change. *Journal of Personality and Social Psychology, 6*, 245-254.

Mbiti, J. (1970). *Introduction to African religion*. Garden City, New York: Anchor Books.

McCorkle, K. C., & Taylor, J. (submitted). A model for understanding the impact of parental cultural alienation upon the adjustment of African-American children.

McGuire, W. J. (1964). Inducing resistance to persuasion: Some contemporary approaches. In L. Berkowitz (Ed.), *Advances in experimental social psychology* (Vol. 1). New York: Academic Press.

Murrell, A. J. (1989). *Social support and ethnic identification as predictors of career and family roles of Black women.* Paper presented at the 21st Annual Convention of the Association of Black Psychologists, Fort Worth, TX.

Olson, J. M., & Zanna, M. P. (1993). Attitudes and attitude change. *Annual Review of Psychology, 44*, 117-154.

Opoku, K. A. (1978). *West African traditional religion.* Singapore: FEP International Private Limited.

Rogers, J. A. (1997). Spirituality: Questing for well-being. In R. L. Jones (Ed.), *African American mental health.* Hampton, VA: Cobb & Henry.

Sackmann, S. A. (1991). *Cultural knowledge in organizations: Exploring the collective mind.* Newbury Park, CA: Sage Publications.

Sturdivant-Anderson, M. M. (in preparation). *The role of parental level of aspiration in mediating the effects of structural and cultural variables on parenting behaviors and child outcomes.* Results from doctoral dissertation, University of Pittsburgh, Pittsburgh, PA.

Taylor, J. (1997a). Cultural conversion experiences: Implications for mental health research and treatment. In R. L. Jones (Ed.), *African American mental health.* Hampton, VA: Cobb & Henry.

Taylor, J. (1997b). Toward a purposeful systems approach to parenting. In R. L. Jones (Ed.), *African American children, youth, and parenting.* Hampton, VA: Cobb & Henry.

Taylor, J., Andrews, A., Jackson-Lowman, Turner, S., Rogers, J., Logan, J., & Logan, R. (submitted). *Control patterns in a sample of Black couples: The role of structural factors, spousal reciprocity, and cultural alienation.*

Taylor, J., & Franklin, A. (1994). Psychosocial analysis of Black teenage pregnancies: Implications for public and cultural policies. *Policy Studies Review, 13*, 157-164.

Taylor, J., & Grundy, C. (1996). Measuring Black internalization of White stereotypes about Blacks: The nadanolitization scale. In R. L. Jones (Ed.), *Handbook of tests and measurements for Black populations.* Hampton, VA: Cobb & Henry.

Taylor, J., Henderson, D., & Jackson, B. B. (1991). A holistic model for understanding and predicting depressive symptoms in African-American women. *Journal of Community Psychology, 19*, 306-320.

Taylor, J., & Jackson, B. B. (1990a). Factors affecting alcohol consumption in Black women: Part I. *International Journal of the Addictions, 25*, 1287-1300.

Taylor, J., & Jackson, B. B. (1990b). Factors affecting alcohol consumption in Black women: Part II. *International Journal of the Addictions, 25*, 1415-1427.

Taylor, J., & Jackson, B. B. (1991). Evaluation of a holistic model of mental health symptoms in African American women. *The Journal of Black Psychology, 18*, 19-45.

Taylor, J., Jackson-Lowman, H., & Lewis, M. (1997). Diunital policy: A proposal to enhance academic achievement in the inner city. In R. L. Jones (Ed.), *African American children, youth, and parenting.* Hampton, VA: Cobb & Henry.

Taylor, J., Jackson-Lowman, H., Rogers, J. A., & Obiechina, C. (in preparation). *Toward a science of cultural policy.*

Taylor, J., & Obiechina, C. (in press). Cultural alienation: Analytical and empirical implications. *Journal of Black Studies.*

Taylor, J., Prettyman, M. G., Cunningham, P., Newbourne, J. A., & Dixon, C. M. (1992). *CLEM: A leadership development plan for African American students in higher education.* Unpublished manuscript, Afro-American Studies Program, University of Maryland, College Park.

Taylor, J., & Rogers, J. A. (1993). Relationship between cultural identity and exchange disposition. *Journal of Black Psychology, 19,* 248-265.

Taylor, J., & Tull, E. (submitted). Cancer prevention orientation in single Black mothers: The role of disclosive disposition, depressive symptoms, and cultural alienation.

Taylor, J., Turner, S., & Lewis, M. (1997). Valuation: Definition, theory, and methods. In R. L. Jones (Ed.), *Advances in African American psychology.* Hampton, VA: Cobb & Henry.

Taylor, J., Turner, S., Underwood, C., Franklin, A., Jackson, E., & Stagg, V. (1994). Values for Life: Preliminary evaluation of the educational component. *Journal of Black Psychology, 20,* 210-233.

Taylor, J., & Zhang, X. (1990). Cultural identity in maritally distressed and nondistressed Black couples. *The Western Journal of Black Studies, 14,* 205-213.

Taylor, J., Zhang, X., & Stevens, S. (in preparation). *The factor structure of cultural alienation in a sample of inner city African American women.*

Terrell, F., Taylor, J., & Terrell, S. (1980). Self-concept of juveniles who commit Black-on-Black crimes. *Corrective and Social Psychiatry, 26,* 107-109.

Tomes, E., Brown, A., Semenya, K., & Simpson, J. (1990). Depression in Black women of low socioeconomic status: Psychological factors and nursing diagnosis. *Journal of National Black Nurses Association, 4,* 37-46.

Tong, L. (1993). *Impact of cultural, social, physical, and stress factors on the mental health of urban, elderly African American women.* Unpublished doctoral dissertation, University of Pittsburgh, Pittsburgh, PA.

Author

Jerome Taylor, Ph.D.
Exec. Dir., Center for Family Ex-
cellence, Inc., & Psychology in
Education and Africana Studies
University of Pittsburgh
5C01, Forbes Quadrangle
Pittsburgh, PA 16260
Telephone: (412) 392-4423
Fax: (412) 392-4545

Psychopharmacology and African American Mental Health

William B. Lawson

Introduction

Recent advances in psychopharmacology have greatly improved the prognosis for the mentally ill. Some of these agents have even been recommended as treatments for personality and behavioral problems not usually classified as mental disorders, and are presumed to improve the quality of life, not just treat the mental disorders. However the development of these agents has been perceived as both a boon and a threat to African Americans, who often do not have access to either optimal general health or mental health treatment, including psychopharmacology.

Diagnosis and Assessment

Recent research has shown that many severe mental disorders have biological as well as psychosocial determinants. However, to date no blood test or any other biological marker has been found to be useful in making psychiatric diagnoses. Yet new pharmacological treatments have been found to be as effective as somatic therapies such as penicillin when it is used to treat infections, if the proper diagnosis is made.

Historically, African Americans have been more likely than Caucasians to receive the clinical diagnosis of schizophrenia (Adebimpe, 1981; Jones & Gray, 1986). This disorder is characterized by hallucinations, delusions, or disorganization and generally has the worse prognosis of any psychiatric disorder. On the other hand, African Americans have been less likely to receive diagnoses of affective disorders, which are diagnoses of mood disorders such as depression or manic depressive illness. The prognosis for these disorders are usually more favorable. These ethnic differences in diagnosis may be either a consequence of "true" differences in prevalence, of misdiagnosis or diagnostic error, or the differences may reflect in phenomenology rather than prevalence, i.e., African Americans with the same disorder as Caucasians may have different presenting symptoms (Neighbors, 1984). However, when structured interviews are used, i.e., when the interview questions are predetermined, racial differences tend to disappear (Jones & Gray,

303

1986). Large scale studies such as the Epidemiological Catchment Area study, a five city door to door survey utilizing a structured interview to determine diagnoses, and the National Comorbidity Study (NCS), a recent national randomized survey using a structured interview that could generate DSM III-R diagnoses, found few consistent ethnic differences when socioeconomic status was controlled (Kessler, McGonogle, Zhao, Nelson, Hughes, Eshleman, Wittchen, & Kerdler, 1994; Robins, 1991). The NCS reported a lower prevalence of most mental disorders, including schizophrenia, when compared to non-Hispanic Whites (Kessler et al., 1994). However, that study did not survey institutional settings such as jails or inpatient psychiatric facilities where minorities are often overrepresented. Nevertheless, such findings suggest that previously reported ethnic differences in diagnoses were in large part due to diagnostic error rather than true differences in prevalence.

The overdiagnosis of schizophrenia in African Americans does appear to affect prescribing patterns. African Americans appear to inappropriately receive anti-psychotic medication (Lawson, 1986; Strickland, Ranganath, & Lin, 1991). Lithium and other anti-manic medications are recommended for maintenance treatment of manic depressive illness. Lithium salts appear to prevent the mood swings that characterize this disorder. Anti-psychotic medications may help to curtail acute manic attacks but have limited usefulness in maintenance therapy. Bell and Mehta (1980, 1981) reported that African American patients with lithium responsive bipolar affective disorder and excellent lithium response were often more likely to be initially diagnosed with schizophrenia than Caucasians and treated with anti-psychotics rather than lithium. The result was a poorer outcome for African American patients.

Sometimes patients with depression present with psychotic features although they do not have the full spectrum of features seen with schizophrenia. These patients do best with an antidepressant plus an anti-psychotic. Anti-psychotics alone are often ineffectual. We reported that Mexican American patients with English as a second language who met criteria for psychotic depression were often diagnosed with schizophrenia in the past (Lawson, Herrera, & Costa, 1992). They were usually treated with anti-psychotics alone and not given antidepressant medication (Lawson et al., 1992). The results were unnecessarily extended hospitalizations.

We have recently noted that anxiety disorders are also underdiagnosed and sometimes confused with schizophrenia. Combat veterans exposed to extraordinary stressors can develop a severe anxiety disorder called posttraumatic stress disorder (PTSD). They may experience persistent flashbacks, hyperreactivity, emotional blunting, and nightmares decades after the original stressor. Recent experience has indicated that PTSD is not limited to combat veterans. PTSD is common in rape victims and has been seen in inner city youth exposed to street violence (Paradis, Hatch, & Friedman, 1994). The presenting symptoms of PTSD, especially flashbacks and emotional blunting, may be easily confused with psychosis, especially in African Americans (Allen, 1986; Paradis, Hatch, & Friedman, 1994). While anti-psychotic drugs may have a role in PTSD, anti-manic, anti-anxiety, and anti-depressant agents are important as are non-medical interventions. Obsessive compulsive disorder is a disorder characterized by intrusive persisting thoughts (obsessions) or compulsive urges to carry out behaviors such as hand washing (compulsions). Some anti-depressant medication, especially the Specific Serotonergic Reuptake Inhibitors (SSRI), seem to have selective efficacy in this disorder. Behavioral techniques are also effective. Without proper treatment, the prognosis is poor and the disorder can be socially disabling. This disorder is often not diagnosed among African Americans (Paradis et al., 1994.). Yet multisite prevalence studies do not find significant ethnic differences in prevalence (Kessler et al., 1994; Robins, 1991). The ego dystonic thoughts or sometimes bizarre compulsive behavior could also be easily mislabeled as psychosis and treated only with anti-psychotics.

Differences in presenting symptoms may account for some of the misdiagnosing even though key symptoms used for diagnosis may not be different. African Americans tend to score differently on the MMPI, showing more paranoid type symptoms (Adebimpe, Gigardet, & Harris, 1979). More suspiciousness is seen compared to non-Hispanic White populations, which some have interpreted as a "healthy paranoia" (Jones & Gray, 1986). Affective disorders are more likely to present with psychotic symptoms, mania may present with more irritable symptoms, and depression may present with suspiciousness (Adebimpe, 1981; Adebimpe, Hedlund, & Cho, 1982; Adebimpe, Klein, & Fried, 1981). Moreover, therapists unfamiliar with African Americans may misrepresent cultural differences as psychopathology (Adebimpe, 1994). As a consequence, the risk for the misdiagnosing of schizophrenia is increased (Adebimpe, 1994; Lawson, 1990; Strickland, Ranganath, & Lin, 1991). Africans and perhaps African Americans are less likely to complain of guilt when they have an affective disorder (German, 1972). Presumably guilt is a more Western European concept because it assumes a more individualistic view of the world and focuses on individual responsibility. People from tribal cultures assume more communal responsibility. Shame rather than guilt is more likely to be experienced (German, 1972).

Attitudes Toward Mental Health Treatment and Psychopharmacology

African Americans may not receive appropriate treatment because of treatment seeking behavior and attitudes about mental health treatment and psychopharmacology. Over 50% of depressed African Americans may not receive treatment, partially due to racial differences in treatment seeking behavior (Sussman, Robins, & Earls, 1987). African American patients with panic disorder often do not seek treatment (Paradis et al., 1994). Those who do are often seen by general medical providers, where panic disorder is often worked up as a general medicine condition. As noted above, obsessive compulsive disorder and PTSD are often under-recognized as well as misdiagnosed. These disorders have an excellent prognosis when treated but very poor outcomes including the development of comorbid depression, loss of work, and social restriction when not treated (Paradis et al., 1994). Many racial and ethnic minorities are reluctant to seek treatment in the standard mental health system. African Americans may be more likely to seek treatment or support from friends, ministers, non-mental health professionals or no treatment at all (Adebimpe, 1994; Sussman et al., 1987). Treatment could be delayed until symptoms become intolerable. The individual may be more symptom-atic, resulting in a greater likelihood of hospitalization, involuntary treatment and the need for more medication (Lawson, 1986a; Strickland et al., 1991).

Ethnic differences in the perception of mental health services is a key issue in the avoidance or delay in mental health treatment seeking. African Americans are more likely to fear treatment and to fear hospitalization (Sussman et al., 1987). Distrust of standard mental health treatment is widespread, and as noted above, treatment is often sought from non-mental health professionals. The distrust of the system is further exacerbated by social economic concerns: providers are often of a higher socioeconomic class than the patients, especially for African Americans whose income is 60% that of Caucasians (Lawson, 1986b).

Pharmacotherapy may be viewed with special suspicion. Research in general medicine shows that many African Americans are deeply suspicious of drug treatment and especially chronic medical treatment, which is common in mental health (Daniels, Rene, & Daniels, 1994; Hildreth & Saunders, 1991; Saunders, 1991). Unfamiliarity with psychopharmacology, a lack of knowledge about the biological basis of mental illness and the relative lack of African American psychiatrists all exacerbate this suspiciousness (Lawson, 1986a; Lawson, Yesavage, & Werner, 1984). An active issue in the African American community is a strong awareness of the Tuskegee Study (Roy, 1995). This study, begun in the thirties, was federally sponsored and involved exclusively African American men who were diagnosed with syphilis. The men were never provided antibiotic therapy when it became available and were not informed. Partially due to a lack of knowledge or misinformation, psychotropic medications are perceived as being experimental like the syphilis experiments or unacceptably mind altering. We will note below that some of these perceptions of the mental health system may be based on reality. Nevertheless, unfairness and even racism characterize many institutions such as the educational system business community. However, none would seriously suggest that these activities and services should be avoided.

More recently, a former head of the National Institute of Mental Health in reviewing the literature on aggression tried to link inner city youth violence with aggressive rhesus monkeys (Marshall, 1994). This researcher is well known in psychopharmacology and for advocating psychopharmacological approaches to address mental disorders. Some community activists have linked stimulant medication to an insidious plot to reduce aggression in African Americans. As a consequence stimulant use has been avoided by some families as a treatment for attention deficit disorder (Safer & Krager, 1992). There is no doubt that hyperactivity/attention deficit disorder is a major problem for some youth that can lead to major problems in school performance. There is little doubt that stimulant medication seems to have a so-called paradoxical affect in these youth resulting in more normalized activity and/or improved attention. Stimulants have been overused in some African American communities, as have many psychotropic medications as noted above, often at the expense of psychotherapeutic approaches, or because of misdiagnosis. Affective disorders or obsessive compulsive disorders can be easily misdiagnosed by non-mental health professionals as hyperactivity or attention deficits. Also, stimulants do have a number of unpleasant side effects, including growth retardation, sleeplessness, weight loss, and increased risk of abuse. Nevertheless, stimulants are effective in African American youth when the proper diagnosis is made. The use of psychotherapeutic and behavioral approaches should not be looked upon as mutually exclusive to pharmacotherapy and should be utilized when effective. Newer treatments such as venlafaxine and other anti-depressants can be as effective as stimulants with fewer side effects, and when the youth is misdiagnosed, other psychopharmacological approaches may be useful in combination with psychotherapeutic approaches. Rather than rejecting the diagnosis and treatment, more needs to be done to improve diagnosis, treatment, and therapeutic options for African Americans.

Pharmacotherapy: Benefits and Risks

As noted above, African Americans are often treated differently from Caucasians in the mental health system. They may be more likely to be hospitalized, to be involuntarily hospitalized, sometimes to receive seclusion and restraints, and to be discharged earlier (Flaherty & Meagher, 1980; Lawson, Hepler, & Holladay, 1994; Paul & Menditto, 1992; Strakowski, Heather, & Sax, 1995). This differential treatment seems independent of degree of psychopathology and to some extent socioeconomic factors (Flaherty & Meagher, 1980; Lawson, 1986; Lindsey, Paul, & Mariotto, 1989). These differences extend to pharmacotherapy. As noted above, African Americans are more likely to receive anti-psychotic medication (Lawson, 1986; Strickland et al., 1991). African Americans receive more psychotropic medication, higher doses of anti-psychotic medication, more medication per nurse's request, and are more likely to be on depot or long lasting medication (Chung, Mahler, & Kakuna, 1995; Flaherty & Meagher, 1980; Price, Glazer, & Morgenstern, 1985; Segal et al., 1996; Strakowski, Shelton, & Kolbrener, 1993).

African Americans receive more oral doses of medication and more injections of medication. Careful trials have indicated that African Americans are, if anything, more responsive to anti-psychotic medication (Lawson, 1986a; Lawson et al., 1984; Strickland et al., 1991). Consequently, the risk of side effects are increased, which further contribute to suspiciousness, poor compliance, or active avoidance of treatment. Factors such as greater perceived dangerousness, and social distance may all play a part in the excessive use and dosing of anti-psychotics (Lawson et al., 1984). Therapists spend less time assessing African American patients and the tendency to overmedicate African Americans is lower when clinicians' efforts to engage patients were rated higher (Flaherty & Meagher, 1980; Segal et al., 1996). The tendency to prescribe depot medication, which is usually given when there are compliance problems, further suggests that problems in engagement between African American patients and predominately Caucasian therapists contribute to the differential treatment (Price et al., 1985).

Reports in the hypertension literature suggest that African Americans are more likely to be noncompliant with medication, perhaps due to socioeconomic factors, less access to care, and cultural beliefs about medication (Daniels et al., 1994; Hildreth & Saunders, 1991; Saunders, 1991). There are no definitive studies about this issue in psychiatry. However, African Americans tend to terminate or are terminated from psychiatric treatment sooner than Caucasians (Chung et al., 1995; Flaherty & Meagher, 1980) and are less engaged in therapy by Caucasian clinicians (Segal et al., 1996). Moreover, African Americans are more likely to get medication by injection, and African American males with schizophrenia are more likely to be on depot medication which implies that compliance may be an issue (Price et al., 1985; Segal et al., 1996; Smith, Lin, & Mendoza, 1993).

Recent studies suggest that Asians may require lower doses of tricyclic anti-depressants and anti-psychotics (Lin & Finder, 1983; Lin & Poland, 1995; Yamashita & Asano, 1979). Most psychotropic agents are "deactivated" or metabolized through the liver by microsomal enzymes. The P450 microsomal enzyme system is primarily involved in the metabolism of anti-depressant medication and anti-psychotic medication. In some ethnic groups this enzyme group had formed mutations such that their action is altered. As a result, some psychotropic agents are metabolized more slowly than in Caucasians (Bono, 1991; Lin & Poland, 1995). If an agent is metabolized more slowly, then plasma levels are higher and lower doses of the agent are needed to get the same effect. Differences in the pharmacokinetics of psychotropic agents in Asians vs. Caucasians are believed to lead to Asians requiring less medication for efficacy, having more side effects, and to an increased risk of toxicity than Caucasians even though both groups may be receiving the same oral dose. African Americans may also require lower doses of tricyclics, antidepressants and anti-psychotics because of a slower metabolization of these agents, although the evidence does not appear to be as consistent (Lawson, 1986a; Silver, Poland, & Lin, 1993; Strickland et al., 1991). African Americans may respond more quickly to anti-psychotic agents than Caucasians and may develop toxicity more easily on tricyclic antidepressants. Certainly there is no evidence that African Americans require more medication, despite the impressive evidence that African Americans are often prescribed more medication (Lawson, 1986a; Segal et al., 1996; Strickland et al., 1991). As a consequence the risk for untoward side effects is increased.

There are multiple reports of African Americans showing higher red blood cell to plasma levels (RBC to plasma ratio) of lithium than for Caucasians and Asians (Strickland, Lawson, & Lin, 1993). The clinical significance of this finding is unknown, but high RBC to plasma ratios are believed to be associated with lithium-neuroleptic toxicity (Strickland et al., 1993). Recently Strickland and associates (1995) reported that the high RBC to plasma ratios seen in African Americans is associated with more reported lithium related side effects. The basis for this altered lithium metabolism apparently is related to differences between African Americans and Caucasians in salt retention. African Americans tend to be sodium retainers, thereby increasing the risk for hypertension as well as a higher RBC to plasma lithium ratio. The ancestors of today's African Americans had high mortality rates while being brought across the Atlantic in slave ships. Many of these individuals died due to *hyponatremia,* as fluids were replaced but not salts. Those individuals who were sodium retainers on the other hand were more likely to survive, but also to have hypertension to pass on to their descendants (Hildreth & Saunders, 1991; Wilson & Grimm, 1991).

African Americans treated with Anti-psychotic medication may have a greater risk for tardive dyskinesia than Caucasians (Glazer, Morgenstern, & Doucette, 1994; Morgenstern & Glazer, 1993). Tardive dyskinesia is a persisting movement disorder consisting usually of involuntary movements of the mouth, tongue, facial muscles, or extremities. There is no reliable treatment. High doses of Anti-psychotics, long treatment duration, interruptions in treatment, and use of Anti-psychotic in those with affective disorder are all factors that increase the risk of tardive dyskinesia (Jeste & Wyatt, 1982). As noted above, these prescribing patterns are seen in African Americans. Whether there is an unspecified biological risk is unknown at present.

Newer treatments may be especially beneficial for African Americans. Newer antidepressants such as the specific Serotonergic Reuptake blockers may be beneficial for African Americans because of the reports of greater sensitivity or toxicity (Preskorn, 1995). Newer anti-psychotics such as clozapine and *risperidone* may offer increased efficacy and reduced risk of abnormal involuntary movements, including tardive dyskinesia (Kane, Honifield, & Singer, 1988; Marder & Meibach, 1994).

Cost limits the availability of many of these agents for African Americans (Revicki, Lou, & Weschler, 1990). African Americans often get treatment through the public sector but cost constraints necessarily cause these providers to be conservative in their treatment.

The new anti-psychotic clozapine has been shown to be more effective than standard anti-psychotics and to be better tolerated by patients (Kane et al., 1988). However its cost, the most for any anti-psychotic, greatly limited its availability. Medicaid sometimes made the agent available for the very poor. However, the working poor, not covered by Medicaid and frequently without health insurance, could not afford such medication. In fact, the cost of having a family member with schizophrenia would approach the median income of African American families even without clozapine (Lawson, 1986b).

Some of clozapine's high cost is due to its increased risk of causing the potentially lethal complication of agranulocytosis (Alvir, Lieberman, Safferman, 1993). As a result, Federal Drug Administration and Sandoz, Inc. (the agent's manufacturer) provide strict guidelines that require minimal leukocyte counts before treatment with the agent can be initiated or continued. However, African Americans tend to show a relative and benign leukopenia (Caramikat, Karayalcin, & Aballi, 1975; Karayalcin, Rosner, & Sawitsky, 1972). Thus, individuals who might benefit from clozaril would not get it if the clozaril prescribing guidelines were strictly followed.

Racial and ethnic minorities are less likely than Caucasians to have some medical procedures and to be included in pharmaceutical trials (Svensson, 1989; Wenneker & Epstein, 1989). We reviewed the psychiatric literature and found that most biological and pharmacological studies did not identify the ethnicity of the subjects (Lawson, 1990). When race or ethnicity was identified, African Americans were in a decided minority. Consistent with reports from other disciplines, less than 6% of subjects were identified as African Americans. As noted above, research is often viewed unfavorably in the African American community. Yet, inclusion of racial and ethnic minorities in drug trials is extremely important in order to fully understand the impact of pharmacological agents on the general population. Moreover, drug trials offer the additional benefit of making available new treatments at no cost.

More must be done to educate the public, including administrators, providers and patients about ethnic diversity in pharmacotherapy. Racial and ethnic minorities in particular must be included in any educational program or marketing efforts that promote the use of psychotropics. Most importantly, medications must be considered as part of an overall treatment strategy for African Americans who are seriously mentally ill. The newer agents especially can be a boon that can greatly improve the quality of life. But they can have serious side effects if not used with respect, and they can be worthless in the long run if not included in the context of a complete treatment program that offers respect to the African American patient as an individual, and as a treatment partner, within a positive cultural context.

References

Adebimpe, V. R. (1981). Overview: White norms and psychiatric diagnosis of Black patients. *American Journal of Psychiatry, 138,* 279-285.

Adebimpe, V. R. (1994). Race, racism, and epidemiological surveys. *Hospital Community Psychiatry, 45,* 27-31.

Adebimpe, V. R., Gigardet, J., & Harris, E. (1979). MMPI diagnosis of Black psychiatric patients. *American Journal of Psychiatry, 135,* 85-87.

Adebimpe, V. R., Hedlund, J. L., & Cho, D. W. (1982). Symptomatology of depression in Black and White patients. *Journal of the National Medical Association, 74,* 185-190.

Adebimpe, V. R., Klein, H. E., & Fried, J. (1981). Hallucinations and delusions in Black psychiatric patients. *Journal of the National Medical Association, 73,* 517-520.

Allen, I. M. (1986). Post Traumatic Stress Disorder among Black Vietnam veterans. *Hospital Community Psychiatry, 37,* 55-61.

Alvir, J. M., Lieberman, J. A., & Safferman, A. Z. (1993). Clozapine-induced agranulocytosis: Incidence and risk factors in the United States. *Journal of Medicine, 329,* 162-167.

Bell, C. C., & Mehta, H. (1980). The misdiagnosis of Black patients with manic-depressive illness. *Journal of the National Medical Association, 72,* 141-145.

Bell, C. C., & Mehta, H. (1981). The misdiagnosis of Black patient with manic-depressive illness: Second in a series. *Journal of the National Medical Association, 73,* 101-107.

Bond, W. S. (1990). Therapy update: Ethnicity and psychotrophic drugs. *Clinical Pharmacology, 10,* 467-470.

Caramikat, E., Karayalein, G., & Aballi, A. (1975). Leukocyte count differences in healthy White and Black children 1 to 5 years of age. *Journal of Pediatrics, 86,* 252-275.

linChung, H., Mahler, J. C., & Kakuna, T. (1995). Racial differences in treatment of psychiatric inpatients. *Psychiatric Services, 46,* 586-591.

Daniels, D. E., Rene, A. A., & Daniels, V. R. (1994). Race: An explanation of patient compliance—fact or fiction? *Journal of the National Medical Association, 86,* 20-25.

Flaherty, J. A., & Meagher, R. (1980). Measuring racial bias in inpatient treatment. *American Journal of Psychiatry, 137,* 679-682.

German, G. A. (1972). Aspects of clinical psychiatry in Sub-Saharan Africa. *British Journal of Psychology, 121,* 461-479.

Glazer, W. M., Morgenstern, H., & Doucette, J. (1994). Race and tardive dyskinesia among outpatients at a CMHC. *Hospital Community Psychiatry, 45,* 38-42.

Hildreth, C., & Saunders, O. (1991). Hypertension in Blacks: Clinical overview. *Cardiovascular Clinic, 21*, 85-96.

Jeste, D. V., & Wyatt, R. J. (1982). *Understanding and treating tardive dyskinesia.* New York: Guilford.

Jones, B. E., & Gray, B. A. (1986). Problems in diagnosing schizophrenia and affective disorders among Blacks. *Hospital Community Psychiatry, 37*, 61-65.

Kane, J., Honifield, G., & Singer, J. (1988). Clozapine for the treatment resistant schizophrenic: A double-blind comparison versus chlorpromazine. *Archives of General Psychiatry, 45*, 789-796.

Karayalein, G., Rosner, F., & Sawitsky, A. (1972). Pseudoneutropenia in Negroes: A normal phenomenon. *New York State Journal of Medicine, 72*, 1815-1817.

Kessler, R. C., McGonogle, K. A., Zhao, S., Nelson, C. B., Hughes, M., Eshleman, S., Wittchen, H. U., & Kerdler, K. S. (1994). Lifetime and 12 month prevalence of DSM III-R psychiatric disorders in the United States. *Archives of General Psychiatry, 51*, 8-19.

Lawson, W. B. (1986a). Racial and ethnic factors in psychiatric research. *Hospital Community Psychiatry, 37*, 50-54.

Lawson, W. B. (1986b). The Black family and chronic mental illness. *American Journal of Sociopsychology, 6*, 57-61.

Lawson, W. B. (1990). Biological markers in neuropsychiatric disorders: Racial and ethnic factors. In E. Sorel (Ed.), *Family, culture, and psychobiology.* New York: Leyas.

Lawson, W. B., Hepler, N., & Holladay, J. (1994). Race as a factor in inpatient and outpatient admissions and diagnosis. *Hospital Community Psychiatry, 45*, 72-74.

Lawson, W. B., Herrera, J. M., & Costa, J. (1992). The dexamethsone suppression test as an adjunct in diagnosing depression. *Journal of Associate Academic Minority Physicians, 3*, 17-19.

Lawson, W. B., Yesavage, J. A., & Werner, R. D. (1984). Race, violence, and psychopathology. *Journal of Clinical Psychology, 45*, 294-297.

Lin, K. M., & Finder, E. (1983). Neuroleptic dosage for Asians. *American Journal of Psychiatry, 140*, 490-491.

Lin, K. M., & Poland, R. E. (1995). Ethnicity, culture, and psychopharmacology. In F. E. Bloom & D. J. Kupler (Eds.), *Psychopharmacology: The fourth generation of progress.* New York: Raven Press.

Lindsey, K. P., Paul, G. L., & Mariotto, M. J. (1989). Urban psychiatric commitments: Disability and dangerous behavior of Black and White recent admissions. *Hospital Community Psychiatry, 40*, 286-294.

Marder, S. R., & Meibach, R. C. (1994). Risperidone in the treatment of schizophrenia. *American Journal of Psychiatry, 151*, 825-835.

Marshall, E. (1994). Anxiety hits mental health. *Science, 264*, 764-765.

Morgenstern, H., & Glazer, W. M. (1993). Identifying risk factors for tardive dyskinesia among chronic outpatients maintained on neuroleptic medications: Results of the Yale Tardive Diskinesia Study. *Archives of General Psychiatry, 50*, 723-733.

Neighbors, H. W. (1984). The distribution of psychiatric morbidity in Black Americans: A review and suggestion for research. *Community Mental Health Journal, 20*, 169-181.

Paradis, C. M., Hatch, M., & Friedman, S. (1994). Anxiety disorders in African Americans: An update. *Journal of the National Medical Association, 86*, 609-612.

Paul, G. I., & Menditto, A. A. (1992). Effectiveness of inpatient treatment programs for mentally ill adults in public psychiatric facilities. *Applied Prevention in Psychology, 1*, 41-63.

Preskorn, S. H. (1995). Comparison of the tolerability of bupropion, fluoxetine, imipramine, nefazodone, paroxexine, sertraline, and verlafaxine. *Journal of Clinical Psychiatry, 56 , 6*, 12-21.

Price, N., Glazer, W., & Morgenstern, H. (1985). Demographic predictors of the use of injectable versus oral antipsychotic medications in outpatients. *American Journal of Psychiatry, 142*, 1491-1492.

Revicki, D. A., Lou, B. R., & Weschler, J. M. (1990). Cost-effectiveness of *clozaine* for treatment resistant schizophrenic patients. *Hospital Community Psychiatry, 41*, 850-854.

Robins, L. N., Locke, B., & Regier, D. A. (1991). An overview of psychiatric disorders in America. In L. N. Robins & D. A. Regier (Eds.), *Psychiatric disorders in America: The Epidemiologic Catchment Area Study* (pp. 328-366). New York: The Free Press.

Roy, B. (1995). The Tuskegee syphilis experiment: Biotechnology and the administrative state. *Journal of the National Medical Association, 87*, 56-67.

Safer, D. J., & Krager, J. M. (1992). Effect of a media blitz and a threatened lawsuit on stimulant treatment. *Journal of American Medical Association, 268*, 1004-1007.

Saunders, E. (1991). Hypertension in African Americans. *Circulation, 83*, 1465-1467.

Segal, S. P., Bola, J. R., & Watson, M. A. (1996). Race, quality of care, and antipsychotic prescribing practices in psychiatric emergency services. *Psychiatric Services, 47*, 282-286.

Silver, B., Poland, R. E., & Lin, K. M. (1993). Ethnicity and the pharmacology of tricyclic antidepressants. In K. M. Lin, R. E. Poland, & G. Wallasaki (Eds.), *Psychopharmacology and psychobiology of ethnicity* (pp. 61-89). Washington, DC: American Psychiatric Association.

Smith, M., Lin, K. M., & Mendoza, R. (1993). Nonbiological issues affecting psychopharmacological therapy: Cultural considerations. In K. A. Lin, R. E. Poland, & G. Nakasaki (Eds.), *Psychopharmacology and psychobiology of ethnicity* (pp. 37-58). Washington, DC: American Psychiatric Association.

Strakowski, S. M., Heather, S. L., & Sax, K. (1995). The effects of race on diagnosis and disposition from a psychiatric emergency service. *Journal of Clinical Psychiatry, 56,* 101-107.

Strakowski, S. M., Shelton, R. C., & Kolbrener, M. L. (1993). The effects of race and comorbidity on clinical diagnosis in patients and psychosis. *Journal of Clinical Psychiatry, 54,* 96-102.

Strickland, T. L., Lin, K. M., & Fu, P. (1995). Comparison of lithium ratio between African American and Caucasian bipolar patients. *Biological Psychiatry, 37,* 325-330.

Strickland, T. L., Lawson, W. B., & Lin, K. M. (1993). Interethnic variation in response to lithium therapy among African American and Asian American populations. In K. M. Lin, R. E. Poland, & G. Nakasaki (Eds.), *Psychopharmacology and Psychobiology of Ethnicity* (pp. 107-123). Washington, DC: American Psychiatric Association.

Strickland, T. K., Ranganath, V., & Lin, K. M. (1991). Psychopharmacologic considerations in the treatment of Black American populations. *Psychopharmacology Bulletin,* 27, 441-448.

Sussman, L. K., Robins, L. N., & Earls, F. (1987). Treatment seeking for depression by Black and White Americans. *Social Science and Medicine,* 24, 187-196.

Svensson, C. K. (1989). Representation of American Blacks in clinical trials of new drugs. *Journal of American Medical Association, 261,* 263-265.

Wenneker, M. B., & Epstein, A. M. (1989). Racial inequalities in the use of procedures for patients with ischemic heart disease in Massachusetts. *Journal of American Medical Association, 261,* 253-257.

Yamashita, I., & Asano, Y. (1979). Tricyclic antidepressants: Therapeutic plasma level. *Psychopharmacology Bulletin, 15,* 40-41.

Author

Dr. William B. Lawson
Roudebush VAMC
Psychiatric Service (116A)
1481 W. 10th Street
Indianapolis, IN 46202
Telephone: (317) 635-7401 x5712
Fax: (317) 269-6333
E-Mail:WLAWSONPsy@aol.com

A Multisystems Approach to Home and Community Based Interventions with African American Poor Families[1]

Nancy Boyd-Franklin

The Multisystems Model is a problem solving approach that helps families with multiple problems to focus and prioritize their issues and to intervene effectively to produce change. It is a family and community based treatment approach that allows the psychologist to conceptualize and to intervene at multiple systemic levels. This approach is extremely helpful when working with urban poor families who may simultaneously confront a staggering number of problems such as poverty, unemployment, drug and alcohol abuse, teenage pregnancy, low educational attainment, poor health including AIDS, crime, and homelessness, among others. The Multisystems Model is particularly useful with African American families and communities because it recognizes the impact of the dual sociopolitical stressors of poverty and racism.

Psychologists who have not been adequately trained to address these issues, however, may become overwhelmed and withdraw from work in poor African American communities. Clinicians and researchers may mirror the hopelessness expressed by some urban poor families with their own sense of powerlessness. This sense of powerlessness must be challenged and changed by providing clinical and community intervention tools for psychologists so that they may effectively treat African American poor families.

This chapter will present a Multisystems Model that emphasizes the central concept of empowerment for both psychologists and the African American families they treat. The chapter will be divided as follows: (1) a brief review of the literature and explanation of the multisystems model; (2) an overview of the application of the model to strengths and survival skills of African American families; and (3) the Rutgers Counseling Project, a multisystems case example exemplifying the process of community and family interventions and empowerment. Although this model is appropriate for families of all cultural and racial backgrounds, this chapter will focus on an application of the model to the treatment of African American families living in poverty.

315

Review of the Literature

The Multisystems Model has a strong legacy as a conceptual approach as well as a sound intervention strategy. Proponents of this approach have included Bronfenbrenner (1979) who discussed these issues within a social ecology model; Minuchin, Montalvo, Guerney, Rosman and Schumer (1967), Minuchin (1974); and Aponte (1994), whose structural and ecostructural models provide intervention strategies for working with poor urban families. Borduin and Henggeler (1990) have provided a viable family therapy treatment intervention program. Empirical research and outcome studies have substantiated the viability of this approach with many complex psychosocial problems, including juvenile delinquency (Henggeler, Melton & Smith, 1992); adolescent aggression; and substance use and abuse in a juvenile offender population (Henggeler et al., 1991). All of these empirical studies targeted urban poor clients from families coping with multiple problems such as those described above.

A number of authors have also stressed the need for an Afrocentric perspective in the development of interventions for African American families and communities (Akbar, 1974, 1981, 1985; Boyd-Franklin, 1989; Nobles, 1976, 1985, 1986) . Boyd-Franklin (1989) has provided an Afrocentric application of the multisystems approach by focusing on these families' strengths, including powerful extended family bonds, spirituality and religious orientation, and an emphasis on education. These strengths and survival skills have been well documented in the literature on African American families (Billingsley, 1968, 1992; Hill, 1972, 1977; McAdoo, 1981, 1985; Nobles, 1976), and will be highlighted in the family and community intervention case example described in this paper.

The Multisystems Model

Parnell and Vanderkloot (1989, 1991), Aponte (1994), and Boyd-Franklin (1989) have documented that traditional individual and linear models of treatment have not been responsive to the needs of poor families with multisystemic problems. African American families are often complex and may frequently involve different levels of involvement such as:

-individuals
-subsystems in the family (e.g., the couple, the parents, and/or the siblings)
-family household members
-extended family
-friends and "nonblood" family
-Church family, spiritual supports and community resources (Boyd-Franklin, 1989).

In addition, outside agencies and systems often have a great deal of power to intrude in the lives of poor African American families. These multisystems agencies might include:

-schools

-hospitals, clinics, mental health centers and agencies

-police, courts child welfare and protective services

-social service agencies

The Multisystems Model incorporates sociopolitical and environmental factors (e.g., poverty and racism), addresses multiple levels of intervention, and helps the psychologist to organize these levels efficiently in an overall treatment plan by eliminating dichotomization of approaches and interventions, and emphasizing family and community strengths, and empowerment.

Empowerment

Many poor African American families are overwhelmed by the dangers facing them and their children and a sense of powerlessness in the face of racism and poverty. The agencies created to help them can be perceived to exacerbate these families' difficulties, especially when they are unduly intrusive. Unlike clinician-centered approaches that locate responsibility for change on the therapist, the Multisystems Model requires the therapist to empower the family members to take charge of their own destiny and to intervene with agencies to produce the desired results for themselves and their family members. Empowerment goes beyond traditional therapeutic concepts of "helping" families to the emphasis on self-determination as a treatment goal so that families will have learned the skills they need to produce change and not depend on therapists to perform essential tasks for them. This is particularly relevant for families negotiating other social systems.

Based upon structural family therapy concepts and interventions, Minuchin (1974), Haley (1976), and Boyd-Franklin (1989) recommended the following steps in an initial interview: (1) joining and engagement; (2) identifying the problems; (3) prioritizing the identified problems; (4) encouraging family members to actively discuss strategies and solutions with each other during the session; (5) assigning the client a task to be completed before the next session; and (6) contracting for a return session.

Henggeler (1994) has identified the following principles to be adhered to for multisystems therapy interventions:

1. Assessment within the Multisystems Model requires an understanding of the "fit" between the identified problems and their broader context. Thus, the assessment would explore the interface between different systems including the individual; the family; the extended family; peers and friends; school; church; and community organizations. Other

systems that may need to be considered in this analysis include hospitals; other treatment facilities; child protective services; and the police, courts, juvenile justice and/or the probation system.

2. "Therapeutic contacts should emphasize the positive and should use systemic strengths as levers for change" (p. 6).

3. "Interventions should be designed to promote responsible behavior and decrease irresponsible behavior among family members" (p. 7).

4. "Interventions should be present focused and action oriented targeting specific, well defined problems. . . . The therapist in collaboration with family members and using input from key informants such as probation officers and teachers, identifies specific problems that are targeted for change" (p. 7).

5. "Interventions should require daily or weekly effort by family members" (p. 9).

6. Empowerment: "Interventions should be designed to promote treatment generalization, and long term maintenance of therapeutic change" (p. 9).

7. Coordination of Care: Family members who are referred to different interventions and services may receive duplicated services and conflicting messages when these agencies do not communicate effectively. Centralizing care avoids redundant services and facilitates effective communication among the various agencies, thus increasing the possibility that positive change may be produced and maintained.

Therapists working within the Multisystems Model will need the flexibility to work with different constellations of family members and agencies. For example, a therapist may work with a whole family; see an individual family member for a session or a part of a session; include extended family members or other significant individuals in sessions, which will be helpful in clarifying roles and boundaries; and hold multisystemic meetings in which agencies involved with the family send representatives. This multisystemic intervention is an efficient method that may save hours of telephone time and systemic duplication and confusion.

Caution Against Stereotyping

Before discussing the application of this model to African American families, it is important to caution against the use of stereotypes. There are two levels on which this stereotyping may occur. The first stereotype consists of overgeneralizations, along the lines of a "culture of poverty." This approach is problematic because it assumes that poor people comprise a monolithic group. In reality, the poor consist of many cultures and racial groups. It is essential to go beyond simplistic approaches to recognize the combined impact of race and poverty in the lives of African Americans (Sanchez-Hucles, 1995).

The second level at which stereotyping most often occurs is the tendency to ignore the tremendous diversity within the African American community in terms of educational level, religious orientation or spirituality, family structure, place of origin, skin color, and class or socioeconomic level. The existence of middle and upper middle class African American families is frequently overlooked. Even among the urban poor African American families, there are many distinctions, e.g., working poor, unemployed, underemployed, and welfare recipients. Given this diversity, the material presented in this chapter should not be rigidly applied but rather viewed as a camera lens that must be adjusted for each new client and family.

The Application of the Multisystems Model to the Treatment of Poor African American Families and Communities

The Multisystems Model is a particularly effective treatment intervention for African American clients, families and communities for several reasons. First, many poor African American families are not self-referred. Treatment is often mandated by schools, hospitals, employee assistance programs, child welfare agencies, courts, and/or the criminal justice system. Second, the realities of racism together with the legacy of oppression and intrusion by agencies such as the welfare system have led to the development, in many African Americans, of a protective survival mechanism known as "healthy cultural suspicion" (Boyd-Franklin, 1989; Grier & Cobbs, 1968). Third, there are also cultural biases against therapy and counseling. It is not uncommon for African Americans to view this process as relevant only for "sick" or "crazy" people, "white folks," or the rich. In addition, discussing "family business in public" is discouraged from an early age (Boyd-Franklin, 1989).

Recognizing these issues, the multisystems model emphasizes the importance of joining with or engaging the family members first and building trust in the first few sessions *before* family history or genograms are explored. The initial focus is on the problem the family self-identifies. Since many African American poor families have multiple problems, this focus helps families to prioritize their concerns. It also assists in building credibility quickly by empowering the family through initial problem solving successes. Although gains may be small initially, they should be acknowledged and emphasized in family sessions. Therapists must be aware not to treat only the presenting problem and ignore the underlying causative factors of isolation, poverty and racism, lest they merely place a band-aid on a hemorrhaging wound.

Unlike the very close, tight knit and safe African American communities of previous years, many African American families living in inner city areas today perceive their communities to be so dangerous that they are afraid to go out after dark. Given the prevalence of drugs, gang violence, and crime, many families tend to isolate themselves. Many fear that they cannot effectively protect their children from the effects of drugs and violence. Homelessness has imbued some families with an even greater sense of isolation. This isolation leads to feelings of abandonment and depression.

In the past, African American communities provided support for children and parents in the process of childrearing reminiscent of the African proverb: "It takes a whole tribe to raise a child." Families, particularly those headed by single parents, frequently report feeling the loss of these community supports and role models. Some remember when adults of the community corrected children's misbehavior when their parents were not present. The case example discussed below illustrates how psychologists can utilize the Multisystems Model to develop interventions that empower African American communities to once again create a sense of connectedness, shared responsibility, and "community."

Resiliency and Strengths of African Americans

When African American poor families first present, their failures are often far more apparent than their successes and their weaknesses occupy the figure in their presenting picture while their strengths recede to the background. Psychologists must be aware of the cultural strengths and resiliency within these families that they can tap in treatment in order to offer a long term benefit to their clients.

Social scientists have historically viewed African American families from a deficit or pejorative framework (Deutsch & Brown, 1964; Frazier, 1950; Moynihan, 1965). In recent years, however, many scholars and researchers have focused on these families' resiliency and strengths (Billingsley, 1968, 1992; Boyd-Franklin, 1989; Hill, 1972; McAdoo, 1981, 1985), which include extended family, religion and spirituality, survival skills, and strong educational and work orientation (Boyd-Franklin, 1989). This chapter will focus on three of these strengths: (1) extended family supports; (2) religion and spirituality; and (3) strong educational orientation.

The role of extended family support systems in African American families is well documented (Billingsley, 1968, 1992; McAdoo, 1981, 1985; Hill, 1972, Boyd-Franklin, 1989). Even very poor African American urban families draw upon reciprocal help and support of grandmothers, grandfathers, uncles, aunts, cousins, and older siblings. In addition, in the African tradition of collective unity, "nonblood" relatives such as friends, neighbors and members of the "church family" are often incorporated into the definition of "family." Many poor African American families, however, are isolated and cutoff from these traditional supports. This isolation plays a central role in the mental health problems of families in treatment. Often, when a genogram or family tree is constructed, they report that they have "no one." At this point, the psychologist's knowledge of the cultural patterns of African Americans is essential. Instead of treating the client or family as an isolated entity, the therapist can explore areas of cutoff within the family's network. If reconnection with traditional sources of support is not indicated, the family can be empowered to create new supports. In order to reach extended family and community supports, psychologists must be prepared to do community outreach and home visits. The uses of the Multisystems Model to create family support programs that counter this isolation will be discussed in the case example below.

Religion and Spirituality

Although the role of religion and spirituality within African American families has been well documented (Billingsley, 1968, 1992; Boyd-Franklin, 1989; Hill, 1972), many clinicians have only a superficial understanding of the complexity of these issues in the psychological life of African Americans. There is also little knowledge of the central, all encompassing social service and mental health role played by African American churches. In these days of diminishing federal, state and city resources and funding, it is especially important for psychologists to be aware of the social services offered by many African American churches. Many African American ministers are powerful leaders within African American communities and have often started schools, day care centers, day camps, alcoholics and narcotics anonymous groups, tutoring, mentoring, rites of passage programs, after school programs, nursing home care, credit unions, and community development programs in their communities.

For an isolated African American client or family, they provide largely untapped resources that mental health providers must explore as potential community resources for persons who may not even be church involved. When African American clients state they have no church affiliation in response to intake questions the inquiry should not end there, but, rather, the clinician should probe further and ascertain the level of the person's spirituality and its role in their psychological life. In this way, the Multisystems Model empowers clinicians to look beyond the limited concept of service agencies to indigenous, culture specific community supports available to clients. It also makes the important cultural distinction between a strong sense of personal spirituality and religious or church involvement (Boyd-Franklin, 1989).

Educational Orientation

Strong educational orientation is another documented strength of African American families (Billingsley, 1968, 1992; Boyd-Franklin, 1989; Hill, 1972). As with poor families of other racial and cultural backgrounds, many African American families see education as the route out of poverty and a way for their children to have a better life. Although generations of African Americans have emphasized and passed on this value, many poor African American families today have experienced racism and other negative interactions with schools. The "failure system," described by Kunjufu (1985), engenders multiple senses of rejection and failure by mislabeling African American children, particularly males, in terms of intellectual potential and/or behavior. By high school, these youth may be so disaffected and discouraged that they drop out of school. In an effort to advocate for their children, African American parents and family members may exacerbate an already negative process by approaching schools in a very angry manner. This often results in the parent and child being further labeled and stigmatized. The Multisystems Model empowers psychologists and other therapists to intervene collectively on the community level and to help parents to learn to become even more effective advocates for their children. The following case example illustrates how the strengths of African American families were utilized through a Multisystems Model to address the issues of at-risk adolescents through a community and family intervention project in a community that was underserved in terms of mental health services. This intervention incorporated the three African American cultural strengths described above: (1) extended family supports; (2) religion in the form of a African American minister and his church; and (3) the strong educational orientation of these families. A multisystems intervention was designed that included: (1) community intervention; (2) home-based family therapy; (3) school consultation; and (4) parent and family support groups for the families of at-risk adolescents in middle school grades 6 through 8.

The Rutgers Counseling Project: A Case Example of a Multisystems Approach to Community and Family Interventions for African Americans

The Rutgers Counseling Project was begun in 1992 by the author Dr. Nancy Boyd-Franklin, and Dr. Brenna Bry (Boyd-Franklin & Bry, 1994; Bry & Greene, 1990), of Rutgers University. The population consisted of adolescent males and their families, who were residents of two predominantly African American low-income public housing projects. These projects were surrounded by a middle class suburb whose other residents were largely oblivious to the plight of these adolescents and their families.

An important tenet of the Multisystems Model is community intervention and outreach. Through a colleague Dr. Paulette Hines (Hines & Boyd-Franklin, 1982), we were introduced to the pastor of a large African American Baptist Church in the community, who was also a leader and a community activist. He, in turn, introduced us to parents, the principal of the middle school, and the head of the housing authority of one of the larger public housing projects. As we gained credibility in this community, we were later introduced to the principal of the high school and the head of a major social service agency. As a part of our entry into the community, this contact with the minister drew upon our knowledge of African American cultural strengths, i.e., spirituality and religion. This intervention was extremely important in the process of establishing the community's trust in our project.

Before we began the intervention and throughout the project we met regularly with parents in this community for input and feedback. Therapists and clinics working with poor African Americans cannot simply "hang out a shingle." They must join not just with each family, but with the community and build credibility. In addition, aware of the mistrust with which many African American families view therapy, we named the project The Rutgers Counseling Program. Members of this community found the term "counseling" less offensive than the term "therapy."

We established a liaison with the middle school principal and met with his counseling staff who referred at-risk adolescents to our program. In January, a small but determined group of parents braved a raging snowstorm to attend our first parent support group. As we began our first parent support group, we learned how isolated and afraid members of this community were. They began to spread the word in their community and became involved in family counseling. By March of that year, ten therapists, doctoral students in our Psy D program, were engaged in home-based family therapy; weekly behavioral reports were obtained from the schools; liaisons were in place between the therapists and teachers; and a parent and family support group had begun.

In April, a crisis struck. Eleven African American students and one Puerto Rican male student, involved in an incident which was termed "gang violence" by the principal and the police, were arrested and taken from the middle school "in shackles." All were subsequently indefinitely suspended. The Baptist minister immediately intervened, despite the fact that only one family with a child involved in the incident was a church member. The minister helped the families to obtain a lawyer and offered the church as the site of an alternative school for the boys. He started group counseling and mentoring programs for the boys and offered the services of Dr. Bry and myself to conduct home-based family therapy, parent and family support groups, and school consultation for these families. Home-based family therapy gave the counselors the opportunity to meet many of the figures who formed these boys' extended families, thus allowing us to draw on another cultural strength of African American families.

During our work with these families, we have interacted with many of the constituents that are a part of the Multisystems Model, i.e., individuals; families; extended family; church; schools; police; courts; probation department; and child protective services. There are currently 30 student counselors working with one family each, two liaisons in the school, and two parent support groups. A number of the adolescents have also been seen individually on an as-needed basis.

The families represent the diversity in our African American and ethnic minority communities. We have had to deal with the rage that these families feel when confronting the racism that they and their adolescents face in the schools and the criminal justice systems in their community. Through the parent and family support groups, however, these family members became empowered to redirect their rage toward achieving the positive outcomes they desired for their adolescents. Through collective unity in the family support group, the parents and family members discussed the changes they wanted and rehearsed presenting their positions on key issues to school officials. During the course of a year, various officials were invited to attend and present at a group session, including the principals of the middle school and the high school, counselors of the middle school and the high school, members of the Child Study Team (for children involved with Special Education services), a special education teacher, and eventually, the district's Superintendent of Schools. In addition to these key school officials, parent group meetings were held with the local police chief, a detective assigned to youth services, and a member of the probation department.

Training and Supervisory Issues

In the course of designing and implementing this program, a number of training issues arose. Many of the psychologists in training (doctoral students who served as family counselors and parent support group leaders) had never worked with poor families prior to this project. They needed training and preparation regarding the realities of their clients' lives, including the extent of outside agency intrusion. Counselors from middle-class families often required help in understanding the economic realities of the families they treated.

Fortunately, many of the counselors had taken courses on cultural diversity and on African American cultural patterns, which proved to be very helpful tools in understanding the complex extended family patterns in these families. It was particularly useful to the counselors to have a clear comprehension of how experiences with racism had shaped the families' suspicion of the schools, courts, and police and probation systems.

For many of the White psychologists, this was their first experience with cross-racial therapy. Careful work was done in supervision to explore their concerns and, often, feelings of inadequacy. If cultural stereotypes were discovered in supervision, they were addressed and discussed during this process.

Many of the African American psychologists involved were surprised to discover that they had countertransferential responses: They identified very strongly with the families they treated and identified their clients with members of their own families, which often caused them to lose therapeutic objectivity. When this occurred, it was addressed in supervision.

All of the counselors needed training in the process of "joining" or engaging with African American families in treatment. Since most of the counseling occurred in the families' homes or in community locations, such as the church or the community center of the housing project, psychologists who were used to a "clinic model" of service delivery with primarily self-referred clients had to be taught new methods of engagement. Many of the families involved in this project did not seek treatment voluntarily, and, in many cases, were reluctant to participate at first. This reaction is typical of the initial response to treatment by many African American families in other settings (Boyd-Franklin, 1989).

Clinicians had to be taught not to personalize this initial response but to connect with the families and build credibility. African American families, often suspicious and distrustful of therapy, will assess such issues as sincerity, trust, respect for clients when they meet with a counselor. Many of these families were not concerned about the psychologists' degrees or credentials. They were more interested in "who they were as people." Counselors had to learn the "therapeutic use of self" (Boyd-Franklin, 1989) in the treatment process. Both training sessions and the supervisory process focused on helping these psychologists to gain credibility with their clients through an effective use of themselves.

In order for a multisystems intervention of this type to be effective, the supervisory process must be "front line" and "hands on." Supervisors must be willing to go into the community with students and model effective community entry and family joining skills. Many of these families are involved in multiple crises and beginning counselors often need a supervisor "on call" for emergencies. Thus, the supervisory process becomes another level in the multisystemic process and a life line of support for the psychologists involved.

Finally, it is essential that programs attempting this type of intervention involve African American participation at all levels of the intervention, including faculty, trainers, supervisors, and, of course, the psychologists/counselors themselves.

Summary and Conclusion

This paper has presented an application of the Multisystems Model to African American families living in poverty. A number of important issues emerged in the course of this project. First, it became clear that therapists must be trained to fully understand the cultural strengths of African Americans. This is particularly essential when working with poor families who may feel overwhelmed by multiple problems. Secondly, psychologists must utilize a Multisystems Model in order to provide a conceptual framework to assess the multisystemic issues these families present. As demonstrated in the case example, psychologists must be trained carefully in the "use of self" (Boyd-Franklin, 1989) in order to effectively enter and join with African American families and communities.

It is clear from the case example presented that mental health agency directors must work to build relationships and credibility with African American church and community leaders before therapists can work directly with the families. This is particularly important given the "healthy cultural suspicion" (Boyd-Franklin, 1989; Grier & Cobbs, 1968) and the skepticism about therapy that exists among many African Americans. Within this context, psychologists must begin to recognize and utilize the power of African American churches and ministers and to work together with these leaders to develop meaningful and relevant mental health interventions that will truly empower African American communities and families.

Note

1. An earlier version of this chapter was originally presented as a Master Lecture at the American Psychological Association Annual Convention in August, 1995 in New York City.

References

Akbar, N. (1974). Awareness: The key to African American mental health. *Journal of Black Psychology, 1*, 30-37.

Akbar, N. (1981). Mental disorder among African-Americans. *Black Books Bulletin, 7*(2), 18-25.

Akbar, N. (1985). Nile valley origins of the science of the mind. In I. Van Sertima (Ed.), *Nile valley civilizations: Journal of African Civilization*. New York: LTD.

Aponte, H. (1994). *Bread and spirit: Therapy with the new poor*. New York: Morton Press.

Billingsley, A. (1968). *Black families in White America*. Englewood Cliffs, NJ: Prentice Hall.

Billingsley, A. (1992). *Climbing Jacob's ladder: The enduring legacy of African-American families*. New York: Simon and Schuster.

Borduin, C. M., & Henggeler, S. W. (1990). Multisystemic approach to the treatment of serious delinquent behavior. In R. J. McMahon & R. Peters (Eds.), *Behavior disorders of adolescence*. New York: Plenum Press.

Boyd-Franklin, N. (1989). *Black families in therapy: A multisystem approach*. New York: Guilford Press.

Boyd-Franklin, N., & Bry, B. H. (1994). *Rutgers counseling program.* Unpublished program proposal.

Bronfenbrenner, U. (1979). The ecology of human development: *Experiments by nature and design.* Cambridge, MA: Harvard University.

Bry, B., & Greene, D. (1990). Empirical bases for integrating school- and family-based interventions against early adolescent substance abuse. In R. McMahon & R. Peters (Eds.), *Behavior disorders of adolescence: Research, intervention, and policy in clinical and school settings* (pp. 81-97). New York: Plenum.

Deutsch, M., & Brown, B. (1964). Social influences in Negro-White intellectual differences. *Social Issues,* 27-36.

Frazier, E. F. (1950, Summer). Problems and needs of Negro children and youth resulting from family disorganization. *Journal of Negro Education,*.Vol, pages.

Grier, W., & Cobbs, P. (1968). *Black rage.* New York: Basic Books.

Haley, J. (1976). *Problem-solving therapy.* San Francisco, CA: Jossey-Bass.

Henggeler, S. W. (1994). *Treatment manual for family preservation using multisystemic therapy.* Charleston, SC: South Carolina Health and Human Services Finance Commission.

Henggeler, S. W., Borduin, C. M., Melton, G. B., Mann, B. J., Smith, L., Hall, J. A., Cone, L., & Fucci, B. R. (1991). Effects of multisystemic therapy on drug use and abuse in serious juvenile offenders: A progress report from two outcome studies. *Family Dynamics of Addiction Quarterly, 1,* 40-51.

Henggeler, S. W., Melton, G. B., & Smith, L. A. (1992). Family preservation using multisystemic therapy: An effective alternative to incarcerating serious juvenile offenders. *Journal of Consulting and Clinical Psychology, 60,* 953-961.

Hill, R. (1972). *The strengths of Black families.* New York: Emerson-Hall.

Hill, R. (1977). *Informal adoption among Black families.* Washington, DC: National Urban League Research Dept.

Kunjufu, J. (1985). *Countering the conspiracy to destroy Black boys* (Vol. 1). Chicago, IL: African-American Images.

McAdoo, H. P. (Ed.). (1981). *Black families.* Beverly Hills, CA: Sage Publications, Inc.

McAdoo, H. P. & McAdoo, J. L. (Eds.). (1985). *Black children: Social. educational and parental environments.* Beverly Hills, CA: Sage Publications.

Minuchin, S., Montalvo, B., Guerney, B. G., Jr., Rosman, B. L., & Schumer, F. (1967). *Families of the slums.* New York: Basic Books.

Minuchin, S. (1974). *Families and family therapy.* Cambridge, MA: Harvard University Press.

Moynihan, D. P. (1965). *The Negro family: The case for national action.* Office of Policy Planning and Research, U.S. Department of Labor.

Nobles, W. (1976). Extended-self: Re-thinking the so-called Negro self-concept. *Journal of Black Psychology, 11*(2), pages.

Nobles, W. (1985). *Africanicity and the Black family: The development of a theoretical model.* Oakland, CA: Black Family Institute Publishers.

Nobles, W. (1986). *African psychology: Toward its reclamation, reascension and revitalization.* Oakland, CA: Black Family Institute Publishers.

Parnell, M., & Vanderkloot, J. (1989). Ghetto children: Children growing up in poverty. In L. Combrinck-Graham (Ed.), *Children in family contexts* (pp. 437-462). New York: The Guilford Press.

Parnell, M., & Vanderkloot, J. (1991). Mental health services 2001: Serving a new America. *Journal of Independent Social Work, 5,* 183-203.

Sanchez-Hucles, J. (1995). Impact of the environment on families: Urbanicity's unique opportunities and challenges. In M. Harway, *Treating the changing family* (pp. 191-218). New York: John Wile & Sons.

Author

Nancy Boyd-Franklin, Ph.D.
Graduate School of Applied &
 Professional Psychology
Rutgers University
Busch Campus-P. O. Box 819
Piscataway, NJ 08855-0819
Telephone: (908) 274-0829
Fax: (908) 274-0997

A Cogno-Spiritual Model of Psychotherapy

Karen L. Edwards

Introduction

Over the past two decades African American psychologists have sought to formally establish the parameters of an African American psychology. The essence was to be found through the historical and cultural examination of Blacks' African heritage, which provided the linkage, foundation and philosophical framework for a psychology of African Americans. From this examination, the specific development of an Afrocentric worldview was elaborated (Nobles, 1980; White, Parham, & Parham, 1980), as well as an explanation of the philosophical aspects of cultural differences (Dixon, 1971; Nichols, 1976). There remains, however, the task of operationalizing the theoretical concepts, and applying them to the various areas of African American life. One such area of investigation, which is the concern of this paper, is a psychotherapeutic treatment orientation which addresses the specific concerns of African Americans. The purpose of this chapter is to describe a therapeutic orientation and intervention strategy which draws from the cognitive and Jungian (analytical-dynamic) approaches while building on the theoretical proposition of an Afrocentric worldview and, most importantly, to the incorporation of the quality of African American spirituality as a thaumatological enterprise, in proposing a "cogno-spiritual" orientation of psychotherapy with African Americans.

In seeking to develop psychotherapeutic paradigms consistent with the realities of African American existence, therapists and theorists alike have examined such factors as race of therapist (e.g., Helms, 1984, 1986; Jones & Seagull, 1977), political, social (e.g., Greene, 1985; Halleck, 1971a, 1971b; Hickling, 1988; Sager, Brayboy, & Waxenberg, 1972), familial, societal and ethnic identification influences (e.g., Boyd-Franklin, 1989; Comas-Diaz & Griffith, 1988; Griffith, 1977; Jones, 1978; McAdoo, 1988; McGoldrick, Pearce, & Giordano, 1982). It has been interesting to note, however, that while uniquely African American paradigms were sought, African American psychology in general, with the exception of Nobles (1972), Akbar (1979) and others, had been fairly consistent with Western psychol-

329

ogy in carefully veering away from or minimizing the role of religion in general, and "metaphysical spirituality" in addressing the psychological and emotional needs of African Americans in a therapeutic modality. Some have addressed the role of religion in the lives of African Americans as either facilitating (Smith, 1981) or hindering (Grier & Cobbs, 1971) African American development. Others have incorporated African American spirituality as it relates to an African worldview (Akbar, 1985; Myers, 1985; Nobles, 1980). However, little has been done to incorporate African American spirituality into a treatment modality. Even less has been done in applying the notion of spirituality as a thaumatological (Baer, 1984), power enhancing or empowerment strategy to be incorporated into either counseling or psychotherapy orientations.

Several interpretations could be made for this deficit such as the controversy regarding the validity of religion as a liberating/emancipatory or pacifying/accommodating philosophy (Baer, 1984; Marx, 1970; Marx & Engels, 1964) and/or the overriding perception of Western science that religion as the quest for meaning has no legitimate role and can contribute little in scientific or rational pursuits. However, it is unquestionable that whatever the valuation placed on religion by theoreticians and therapists, historically, religion in general, and spirituality and/or thaumatology in particular, has been (in Africa and America) a tremendous influence, having functioned as the essence of "Black beingness." A distinction is made for this paper between religion and spirituality (see Edwards, 1987), where the former is considered "creed," (Jung, 1964b) which binds its members to ritual as in the big business of institutional religion.

Spirituality, however, is defined as a transpersonal or metaphysical awareness and acknowledgment of a Higher Consciousness/Mind (Vaughan, 1985) Self or God within us (Jung, 1966a). Religion, is the/a basic structure through which one learns to develop spiritually. Spirituality, then, is the ultimate goal of religion (Edwards, 1987). The term religion, as its Latin expression, religare suggests, means to bind one's self to the transcendent, God, or Highest Consciousness. Spirituality presupposes a reverence for life, a willingness to confront life in its totality, e.g., good and evil, joy and suffering, and death, and a commitment to life generating forces (Davis & Weaver, 1982). Spirituality is here inclusive of what in traditional West African religions was called "magical-powers," more currently conceived of as metaphysical, transcendent or transpersonal (Baer, 1984). Spirituality as a magico-religious and thaumatological orientation, has a rich history, traced from antiquity through African American life in the Caribbean and South America, and indeed, in the "New World." It is alive today as a primary component of non-mainstream religious practices, some of which are of the African American Spiritual Movement (Alho, 1976; Baer, 1984). Within these practices, spiritualism and/or spirituality is seen as a power-enhancing, yet a non-manipulative and "non-ego-generated" strategy in which the individual benefits from the obtained power if and when the "collective good" (*all* inclusive) is of primary consideration or focus. It is not a power to be employed for personal ends. (Thus, a distinction is made between the use of "spiritual" power, or power informed by the "spirit," and the use of raw "energy." The latter is frequently employed as an exclusionary means of personal power enhancement, and as such, is often abused.) Indeed, Malcolm X (as cited in Breitman, 1967) proposed that the only true religion was one of the spirit.

This author recognizes that there have been several models proposed for working psychotherapeutically with African American/oppressed people (e.g., Boyd-Franklin, 1989; Jackson, 1980; Jackson, 1983; Jones, 1985; Mays, 1985; McAdoo, 1988). This model takes a nonspatial/transcendent, metaphysical/transpersonal stance which is a strong component of African heritage (Alho, 1976; Baer, 1984; Mbiti, 1970a). Specifically, the cogno-spiritual model combines Jungian concepts, and transpersonal and cognitive therapies with African American spirituality. Symbolic interactionist or phenomenological notions of defining situations/reality (McHugh, 1968) are also used to create a therapy orientation that addresses the psychological needs of oppressed African Americans, but the spiritual and political issues as well. Each area on which this orientation is based will be explained in the following sections. Case material will be presented regarding the operationalization of these notions in a therapy context.

Theoretical Foundation

The notion that spirituality can be considered the foundation of a therapeutic approach in the 20th century is not foreign to Western psychology. During the early history of Western psychology (300-500 A.D.; Middle Ages), philosophers such as St. Thomas Aquinas and St. Augustine thought psyche was soul and developed theoretical models for resolving moral crises and fostering spiritual development. The roots of psychology at that time were steeped in notions regarding good, evil and the religious aspects of human nature (which were thought to be sinful). Although Western psychology as a discipline was not formalized until the late 19th century, its development has been pendulous concerning the rational and suprarational, observable-non-observable, quantitative-qualitative, deterministic-teleological, and mind/spirit-body/matter issues. The predominate focus (at least in this century) has been on the deterministic, quantitative, objective and rational aspects of the field based on a Cartesian mechanistic philosophy. During most of its relatively brief history, psychology has sought to legitimize itself, by a cross-fertilization of concepts from classical physics, which are based on Newtonian/Cartesian assumptions about reality (Boorstein, 1980; Capra, 1982; Tart, 1983; Walsh & Vaughan, 1980). However, with the advent of quantum physics in the early 20th century, we have seen a paradigmatic shift to a greatly expanded vision of physics which more precisely reflects the nature of reality.

Many authors have turned away from philosophies and theories which are highly reductionistic in their attempts to describe the whole of nature. Seeing reality as two separate and warring factions has led to an over valuation of the rational, and locked us into a state of perception that at the very least is agentic and potentially destructive. The appositional thinking, so characteristic of the "religion" called Western science, has been challenged from within its ranks, as well as from without. The challenge was to develop a theoretical paradigm which sought to balance, or unite the dialectical opposites of rationalism. It has been proposed that an Afrocentric paradigm accomplishes this feat by acknowledging reality in its true multidimensional form, ontologically as both spiritual and material simultaneously (Myers, 1985). The key is that reality has many aspects that are separate, but together in the realization that they are all manifestations of the same phenomenon.

Jungian Conceptions of Spirituality

Jungian (analytical) psychology is particularly well-suited to an Afrocentric worldview and philosophy. Jung was one of the first to break away from a (Freudian) mechanistic view (Capra, 1982). Though it has been suggested that Jung held racist views regarding African Americans (Mays, 1985), we must not "throw the baby out with the bath water," and focus on the applicability of his ideas.

Jung "united the opposites" of mind/spirit and body/matter by formulating a theory which saw them as two aspects of the same reality (Clift, 1983). For example, symbolism and myth were sin qua non of meaning, on which he based his psychotherapy, the analysis of dreams for symbolisms. African epistemology suggests that the African American way of knowing is primarily through symbolism and rhythm (Nichols, 1976). Jung proposed that the psyche was both conscious and unconscious. The seat of consciousness was the ego, while the overriding, organizing principle of the psyche was the Self, also considered the God within (Jung, 1964b).

Jung's concepts of spirituality fit with the essence of an African American religious orientation in that religion to the African exerted the greatest influence upon the thinking and living of that people. Africans were (and are) extremely religious; there was no separation of the sacred and secular. According to Wilmore (1973):

> African religions know of no rigid demarcation between the rational and supernatural, the sacred and the profane. All of life is permeated with forces or powers which exist in some relationship to man's weal or woe. Man is, therefore required, for his own sake and that of the community, to understand and appreciate the spirit world which merges imperceptibly with immediate and tangible reality. (p. 20)

Traditionally, where the African was, even in America, so was his/her religion: they were inseparable (Mbiti, 1970a). So incorporated was the concept of religion within the African psyche and praxis that there was actually no word for it. It simply existed as a fact of life. In ancient Kemet (Egypt), the study of man (sic) was also the study of religion (Akbar, 1985).

Of particular relevance to the proposed model are other Jungian notions such as his belief in a supra personal function of the psyche, which is Godlike; his recognition that man/woman needed to feel connected to something larger than themselves; his belief in the existence of a transcendental reality which affected the psyche; and his constructs of the personal and collective unconscious. Jung's notion of the collective (or transpersonal) unconscious implies a link between the individual and humanity as a whole, and the individual and the universe (cosmos). In addition to this complimenting the Afrocentric worldview of connectedness, Jung made another very salient point regarding racial history. He felt that one can best study the religion of one's own culture. The implication is that for example, an African American might have difficulty reaching a higher level of consciousness, if the grounding images or the historical experiences are remote from her heritage.

Jung (1968) de-emphasized the rational, reductionistic and mechanistic Western notions, and focused on the supra rational, holistic notions of Self. The central, autonomous organizing function of this psychological construct expressed, according to Jung, an unknown essence that could not be deferred, which eluded human comprehension, but whose aim was to express wholeness, creativity, centeredness and meaning—the God within. The quest for this wholeness Jung called individuation (Jung, 1968).

In breaking away from Freud (determinism and mechanization of humans), Jung (1964a) also divested himself of the pathological stance (so rampant in the traditional psychiatric and psychological areas) toward religion. He certainly recognized that for some, religion and spirituality did in fact portend a psychological dependency and longing for abdication of responsibility onto parental or authority figures, but not by all. That we have a need for developing a "spiritual life," usually non-obtainable in our schools or churches, Jung saw as striving toward balance in the rational-suprarational dialectic (Jung, 1964a). Spirituality helped to give meaning to what could sometimes seem meaninglessness. Spirituality was something that allowed the transcendence (in consciousness to a higher interpretation of reality) of the boundaries of environment (however, not suggestive of a "denial of reality"). It has been proposed that political and social movements whose aim is the adherence of the people to their basic tenets (control), first attack the religious and spiritual foundation of the people. For they seem to know that the spirituality of a people, fortifies them against external control (Jung, 1964b). This charge has been leveled against Christianity by radical African American theorists (Wilmore, 1973), and against organized religions in general by feminists (Daly, 1978; Sjoo & Mor, 1987). They argue that during slavery, rather than take the

African slaves' religion away completely, the architects of slavery found it expedient to extend the boundary of social control by covertly converting the African slaves to a pro-slavery version of Christianity (Alho, 1976; ben-Jochannon, 1970; Raboteau, 1978), as many religions have been transformed by patriarchy (Daly, 1978; Reuther, 1974; Sjoo & Mor, 1987). Thus the dominant mode of the African religion was redefined (Wilmore & Cone, 1979).

More recently, there has been increased focus on Kemetic religion. As such, the emphasis has been on the nonphysical and transpersonal aspects of religion, or spirituality (Adams, 1988; Akbar, 1985; Asante, 1984; Edwards, 1987; Myers, 1985; Nobles, 1980). In this sense, the study of Kemetic religions has "reconnected" African Americans with the potential for empowerment within spirituality. Interestingly enough, parallel concepts are being discussed within the consciousness (Davidson, 1991; Jahn & Dunne, 1987; Pagels, 1988; Wilber, 1981), and transpersonal areas (Boorstein, 1980; Spretnak, 1982; Tart, 1983; Vaughan, 1985). However, the genesis of these concepts may be traced to the teachings and practices of those in ancient Kemet (Akbar, 1985). The ancient Egyptians understood the power inherent in "mind" and consciousness, as well as the power obtained from a spiritual knowledge of self (Akbar, 1985).

Traditional and Emergent Concepts of African Spirituality

The following presents in brief, the work of Mbiti (1971) on New Testament eschatology and African traditional concepts. Of significance is his discussion of the impact of Christianity on African traditional concepts. The goal is to highlight some practical and theological consequences of that interaction on African American conceptions of spirituality and religion. Important to this review, is the African conception of Time which as a two-dimensional phenomenon, has a long "past," and a dynamic "present." The "future" as we linearly conceive of it, did not exist. Time had to be experienced, thus the future was absent because future events have not been realized. What has taken place, or will occur shortly is more important than what is yet to be.

According to Mbiti (1970a) in traditional African religions, the concept of God was both immanent (close, near, or within) and transcendent, although decidedly more transcendent (meaning a concept of God that was far away—in the heavens). Traditional African religion could be summarized as "in theory God was transcendental, but in practice [God was] immanent" (Mbiti, 1970a). Mbiti (1971) in discussing New Testament corporate eschatology and mythology of the Akamba (Kenya, East Africa) and other African peoples, stated that there were three main strains of myths, practically all over Africa, concerning the first men and the coming of death which indicate that African peoples (at least according to mythology), support ideas about human resurrection and rejuvenation. In one strain of beliefs, it was proposed that man was originally given the gift of immortality so that he would never die; in another set it was supposed that if man did die, he would rise again; and in the third strain which Mbiti acknowledges is not as widespread a belief as the other two, that man would be rejuvenated if he did become old. However, according to mythology, the first men lost this original gift. The problem then, according to Mbiti (1971), is that:

> ... African mythology and wisdom for all their richness, have nothing to offer to remedy the situation or repair the loss. African myths look only "back-wards," to the tene period (past), and therefore all they can offer is an explanation of, but not the remedy for, the loss of immortality, resurrection and rejuvenation. Only by looking "future-wards" could they possibly reach at least a mythological remedy. But as we have argued all along, this is simply impossible since Time is traditionally conceived in primarily two dimensions of the mituki "present" and tene "past" periods. Therefore, the death of the individual only removes him towards what in fact has been lost; it cannot offer hope, since there can be no hope in what is lost. This contrasts very strongly with the biblical view that what was lost in Genesis, in the tene period, reappears in the eschatological scheme, placed no longer is the tene period but in an evidently distant future period (if we must use this three-dimensional view of Time). Therefore, with the resurrection (immortality and rejuvena-tion) placed "in front" of it, biblical eschatology does offer and provide a living hope. This is entirely absent in African religiosity, however rich and strong it might otherwise be. (p. 158-159)

This point is raised for two reasons: (1) to reflect a traditional African stance to better understand the more current mainstream African American view; (2) and to understand the political ramifications emanating from one stance over the other. Although traditional African religions have a transcendent aspect, their groundedness in the present and the past did not foster a conception of a messianic hope or spiritualism that extended into the unknown future, a redeemer-type of character (this was not true for all tribes however, e.g., as in Egypt or Kemet) as pronounced as it was during slavery.

The redeemer of the past for example, is present in the future, which is a circular type of eschatology (i.e., eternal, unending). However, to the extent that African American Africans lived in America as slaves, a change emerged in the tenor of their spirituality, such that more of the immanent aspects of God were emphasized. God was then likened to God the Liberator during slavery. A favorite theme within "slave religion" and in spirituals of the slavery period, was that of Moses as a messianic figure delivering his people from bondage to the promised land, and Jesus as a Messiah-King and saviour, spiritually delivering his people and bringing order to the world (Alho, 1976; Raboteau, 1978; Wilmore, 1973). According to Alho (1976), salvation in the theology of the spirituals is a messianic experience. Salvation could not be attained by the mere efforts of men; only through the intervening activity of Christ. Thus: "The 'sinner' of the spirituals is a passive being, greatly under the influence of Satan, and he has no means of his own for securing his salvation" (Alho, 1976, p. 77). As such, many African Americans developed a passivity with regard to God, e.g., the liberator who would deliver them, while they waited. Thus, the immanence was not fully empowering because they did not see themselves as manifestations of God's power. Interestingly enough, the philosophy espoused by many of those who practiced "spiritualism" in the African diaspora, included concepts of an empowering and powerful "God of spirit within" (metaphysical power) capable of redeeming Africans or Ethiopians in America (Baer, 1984).

Revisioning the traditional spirituality of Africans, and the extended linear future eschatology emphasized through slavery, spirituality can thus be redefined as not only immanent, i.e., within, but active as a verb form. God within or spirituality is active to the extent that we are active. Following in this same vein of thinking or the passivity vs. activity dimension of religion, and the dechristianization of African American radicalism which Wilmore (1973) addresses, it seems as though the very essence (spirituality of African peoples) of African American beingness, and other related Afrocentric qualities, have been falsely blamed for African American enslavement. Thus, African American spirituality had not been given the focus and benefit of incorporation into the mainstream of African American scientific thought that it deserved. Although polemics have been delivered regarding the virtue of spirituality as reflecting African American essence, how much of that essence is in actuality perceived as pallid in comparison to Western aggressiveness? African American spirituality has never been the culprit, only erroneous interpretations of it (Cone, 1975; Cone & Wilmore, 1979; Lincoln, 1984; Wilmore, 1973). Although in the traditional religion God could be called upon through prayers, ritual and the like for guidance, perhaps it became more of an issue that God be close and act as a deliverer under the oppression of slavery. Many of the mainstream African American churches currently hold to the more dominant transcendent emphasis, yet, the immanent aspect is still evidenced in the communications of African Americans as they have personalized God in such phrases as "I met Him the other day as I was walking along the street." According to Mbiti (1970b) there was a tribal saying (from one of the thousands of tribes in Africa) which spoke of when in times of trouble God would be so near that He would be "on my back"; here again is evidence of the more immanent focus. This could be considered immanent and personalized, the power of a God within, i.e., we are God manifest. As Mbiti (1970a) stressed, in traditional African religions, it was believed that " . . . everybody . . . [is] a spark or part of God . . . " and that God is "present to a greater or lesser degree in all things" (p. 17). This was not considered pantheism however.

Dimensions of Oppression: Implications for Effective Therapy

African Americans are still oppressed. The nature of the oppression has changed its character over the years, but its objective existence is experienced daily by the oppressed. However, it is the subjective belief in, and thus the co-creation of objective oppression which is of concern here. Of particular relevance, is the nature of oppression and the thinking of those who experience oppression in its duality. The cogno-spiritual model recognizes that the oppressed and the oppressors form a dialectical relationship in which one helps in the creation of the other (Freire, 1973; Myrdal, 1944).

Oppression has been described as a condition, a way of being, and a position one is forced to take with respect to one's self-in-environment-or-world, that one is limited, hopeless, helpless and expendable (Goldenberg, 1978). Oppression has four operative aspects: (1) containment, to limit the range of free movement e.g., isolation such as that resulting from tokenism; (2) expendability, the ability to be replaced or substituted with no loss to the whole; (3) compartmentalization, inability to feel a sense of personal dominion and completeness or integrated style of life; and (4) the ideological schema of a doctrine of personal culpability, to encourage or predispose the interpretation of shortcomings/failures as evidences of essential incompleteness and unchangeable personal deficit (Goldenberg, 1978).

Bulhan (1985) elaborated on Frantz Fanon's work on the psychology of oppression. He proposed that the concept of alienation was closely aligned with that of oppression. Proposed were five aspects of alienation: (1) from self (personal identity); (2) from significant others (family and group); (3) from general other (seen in race and gender relations); (4) from culture (one's language and history); and (5) from creative social praxis (denial and/or abdication of self-determining, socialized and organized activity) essential for the realization of human potential (Bulhan, 1985). Of particular relevance is the aspect of alienation in which there is denial and/or abdication of self-determining, socialized and organized activity (toward) the realization of human potential, i.e., creative social praxis.

It is all too common for African Americans to seek therapy in which one or more of the above are presented as underlying themes. Most of the models proposed for working with African American clients do in fact consider as key components, the recognition of the impact which environment and society, i.e., an oppressive environment, have on the psychological well-being of the African American psyche (Jackson, 1983; Jones, 1985). However, the social praxis aspect of alienation recognizes the role played by the oppressed in their own oppression. Critical to this discussion is the client's sensed degree of powerlessness, either by denial or abdication, and the failure to recognize the interactive nature and social construction of reality and one's role in shaping it (i.e., inherent power to create).

It is proposed that irrespective of the diagnostic classification given based on the specific clinical manifestation of difficulty, oppression is a component of the problem. Ready examples are depression, substance abuse and stress related disorders. Depression is often the result of sensed hopelessness and powerlessness to affect change; substance abuse may be viewed as an escape from this condition, and an attempt to "self-medicate"; and stress may be viewed as a perceptual distortion resulting in a sensed inability to cope with demands thought to exceed capabilities assessed as minimal and at the least, insufficient. The resulting thinking patterns of African American clients, relating strongly to negative interpretations of specific life events, self-reinforce an underlying oppressive thinking pattern with regard to their lives in general. Yet if the thinking pattern is corrected around just a specific event and/or presenting problem, the therapy is often considered success-ful. Yet, that would be only half of the therapy effort. For the therapy to be considered successful at that point might suggest in actuality, that both the therapist and client have an unconsciously conditioned "ceiling" on therapeutic expectations and gains; possibly reflecting the "reality of oppression" operating in the therapy. The thinking of both the therapist and the patient/client is important to this model. The therapist and client may actually collude in limiting the full manifestation of client potential by unconsciously holding an oppressive belief system.

Cognitive Therapy and Cognitions of Oppression

The importance of beliefs and thinking and their resulting influence on behavior is the hallmark of a cognitive therapy orientation (Arnkoff, 1980; Beck, 1971, 1976; Beck, Rush, Shaw & Emery, 1979; Wolpe, 1978). Cognitions and beliefs about one's world are seen as central components of effective therapy with African Americans and other pronounced ethnic persons, simply because African American thinking has been conditioned to reflect oppressive ideology. Baldwin (1980) in his work on the psychology of oppression postulated that race is a determining factor in the nature of definitional systems. He stated that definitions provide, and in fact dictate meanings and values; they determine what is and is not important, what is real and what is legitimate. Of significance then, is who controls the definitions; this he thinks is a racial issue. Baldwin's (1980) position is that "Euro-American culture has therefore attempted to force the legitimacy of the European system of social reality on African American people by superimposing their system on our African system of social reality" (p. 101). This is facilitated through the control of the formal processes of social reinforcements (Further elaboration on the power of definitions is offered below.)

The salience of the doctrine of personal culpability, can be seen as an underlying theme in presenting problems of African Americans in treatment. The theme of "I must have done something wrong," or "I am in someway damaged," at "fault," or "deficient" and "helpless" to affect my life/environment is common. Oppressed thinking of this nature readily leads toward alienation of self from self, and others, as well as a diminished "sensed ability" to engage in creative social praxis. According to Freire (1973): "[an] oppressive reality absorbs those within it and thereby acts to submerge men's consciousness" (p. 36). As therapists we seek to bring "reality" into the therapy session, and more times than not, reality is tainted by an oppressive ideology. Somehow, we have learned to equate reality with those things negative, formidable, and more important, incapable of change. For example, as therapists we may believe that we can help the client restructure his/her beliefs regarding a negative dynamic associated with a personal goal, such as getting on with one's life after a trauma. However, a pertinent concern begging for redress relates to the general sense of efficacy that is developed with respect to the ethnic client's more far reaching impact on his/her environment. My point here is that one can get so caught up in addressing what is "real," as to forget one's role in creating it.

Therapeutic Empowerment and Creating Reality

Several authors have addressed the political aspects of psychotherapy in general (Halleck, 1971a; Szasz, 1970), with African Americans (Bulhan, 1985; Cheek, 1977; Karenga, 1983; Mays, 1985), women (Chesler, 1972; Halleck, 1971b; Miller, 1986), and other pronounced ethnic persons (Inclan, 1985; Tyler, Sussewell & Williams-McCoy, 1985) in particular. A classic study by Broverman, Broverman, Clarkson, Rosenkrantz, & Vogel (1970) found that therapists held double standards and relatively stereotypic concepts of mental health for men and women, both based on an androcentric (male-centered) model. Therapy, like any other endeavor is not valueless nor without bias (Bart, 1971; Green, 1985; Kluckhohn & Strodbeck, 1961). The values, beliefs and attitudes of the therapist (counter transference issues) are operative in a therapeutic situation (Griffith, 1977; Jones, 1978). Therapy can be liberating or an instrument of oppression and the status quo (Halleck, 1971b). It cannot, and it is not, neutral. We know that total "objectivity" as was proposed to be possible in science based on Cartesian assumptions, does not exist; neither in a structured experiment in physics (Jahn & Dunne, 1987), nor in a client-therapist situation. Thus, as we speak of liberating a client from dysfunctional behavior, irrational ideas, emotional blocking, fixation and childhood trauma, we can also liberate them to manifest their highest potential, creativity, transcendent self—God within or "spiritual" power.

Within the humanistic and symbolic interactionist orientations, there is the notion that we participate in our own reality. Our thoughts and beliefs help to define reality which is taken as real. The often quoted statement by Thomas and Thomas (1970) is appropriate here: "if men define situations as real, they are real in their consequences" (p. 154). The basic view is that we are not separate, isolated entities, but that we live in a system of mutually conditioning relationships. We help to condition each other, as guided by our beliefs about others and our world. The Afrocentric, humanistic, transpersonal and analytical orientations represent systemic orientations to reality which recognize the interdependence and two-way flow of interaction. Thus we are not only conditioned by our environment, but we also help to shape and create it (Vaughan, 1985). However, a key point to be made is that oppressed people forget that they are conditioned to deny their power, are sometimes oblivious to, and do not fully utilize their participative power in this creation. Because they do not believe they can, their thinking is oppressed thinking or some would say "realistic." Does there exist an objective reality? As Thomas (Thomas & Thomas, 1970) stated above, the reality we create is real to us. Merleau Ponty (cited in Schur, 1971) stated that the whole spectrum of scientific investigation is built upon the world as directly experienced. Yet, our phenomenological interpretation of the world (second order) is what we know and have an opportunity to interpret.

Each time we aid a client in cognitively restructuring his/her thoughts, we are helping that person participate with the rest of us in creating a reality more self-enhancing. Cognitive therapy (as theory and technique) thus, in this view, helps the client to "define the situation," or create her own reality.

"By use of the phrase 'definition of the situation' (it is implied) that there is no one-to-one correspondence between an objectively real world and people's perspectives of that world; that something intervenes when events and persons come together, an intervention that makes possible the variety of interpretations called multiple realities" (McHugh, 1968, p. 8).

In any social interaction, people bring their beliefs/attitudes/values and conceptions and expectations regarding that interaction. Perhaps there is an objective reality to that situation, however, we also know that another very "real" reality is being unfolded, shaped and molded by the interacting persons. The pattern of thinking of oppressed people reduces and in most instances, negates their ability to help create an alternative reality of an interaction. However, the person aware of her higher consciousness (e.g., the Jungian "Self"), the transpersonal self-regulating system, or the God/spirituality within, has the psychological grounding to influence that interaction.

To the extent that one thinks and feels subjectively oppressed, then that oppression (i.e., patterns of thinking and resulting behaviors) is brought into that situation, and serves to define it, by conceding the power of overriding definition. Defining a situation is a process in which situations are assessed in terms of their limitations and behavioral possibilities. That is, prior to any self-determined act of behavior, there is a phase of examination and deliberation which is amenable to definition by the actor; one person can affect the definition into which another comes (Waller, 1971). Stated differently, it is possible for the oppressed person to get "caught up" in the oppressed role, and to the extent that it becomes highly salient in their overall personality, it becomes the definition for self, as well as the "master status determining trait" for others. Thus as persons become engulfed in the oppressed role (it is salient), they begin to define their "self" as others would define it. For Blacks/African Americans, Blackness is a "master status determining trait"; difficult to define in ways other than dominant group definitions if one uses those groups as a reference. Baldwin (1980) proposed that racism makes that possible through the promotion of social definitional systems of a Euro-American cultural reality. It is the task of the therapist to help the African American client to validate her self-enhancing identity, as well as to find or develop social support systems which will continue to help empower the person to self-define situations. Spirituality provides a constant and ever-present support which is immediate in this definitional process.

In cases where through culture, there are already configurational elements in existence defining a situation (e.g., racism), these elements tend to inhibit the formation of other configurations. The "important element of intelligence, [or knowledge of a God within,] is the ability to [deconstruct] the units of configurations from their context and to recombine them in different patterns" (Waller, 1970, p. 164). Intelligence is defined here as the higher "Self," the God/power within, the "energy" and attitude which according to the Afrocentric model connects African peoples by identity to nature, spirituality, and power of God manifesting. According to Waller (1970) this intelligence can be seen as the "incipient behavior resulting from the organization of the situation in the individual's mind and the concurrent organization of the individual with reference to the situation" (p. 164).

Cogno-Spiritual Model

The theoretical underpinnings of this model contain two central concepts: spirituality and oppression. Within these concepts are the issues of cognitions of oppression and empowerment.

The goal of cogno-spiritual psychotherapy is for the client to "know herself": to know the self is to know the Divinity or God within. The knowledge of a Self, or God within, connects one to the total power of the universe and creation. This goal is irrespective of religious orientation in that spirituality recognizes a "transcendent unity of all religions" (al-'Ashmawi, 1986; Schuon, 1975). Spirituality is an energy, which impacts the objective component of reality (which is dualistic) both transphysically (requires a physical substrate) and non-physically (no known physical substrate). Energy transfer and manifestation can be considered from any one of several models, such as would occur in a biogravitational field, emotional and ideational complexes, and electromagnetic interactions (Jahn & Dunne, 1987; Taub-Bynum, 1984). The point is that energy (e.g., particle or wave) created through our biochemical and physiological mechanisms, e.g., brain or mind, e.g., thoughts can create effects, change physical reality, and interact with other living and nonliving matter (Jahn & Dunne, 1987). The energy notion is not new to psychological theory. Psychodynamic and psychoanalytic theories applied energy concepts as well. The transphysical conceptualization of energy is somewhat comparable to the psychodynamic definition in that both are reductionistic and presume the necessity of a physical substrate to produce "mind." However, the nonphysical (spiritual) conceptualization applies to "mind-mind" interfaces of energy production and transfer, more like psi and thaumatological conceptualizations.

Spirituality then, is: a recognition of one's Divinity; is energy produced transphysically and non-physically; influences reality in its dualistic manifestations; is active; and is empowering. The empowering quality is significant, particularly when considering oppressed persons.

The model addresses the dynamics of oppression as they exist subjectively for the client. The essential point of the model is that irrespective of what may exist objectively, oppression is an illusion of dualistic reality; it exists to the extent that it is believed subjectively. The model proposes that there is only one true reality: that of God and one's Divinity within; all else is illusion. The illusion becomes real, when the client gives it power or energy to be real. Persons are oppressed when they believe in the oppression, and give their power over to the oppressor. Thus, belief in the power of the oppressor to oppress helps to create and sustain the oppressive condition. The cogno-spiritual therapy process teaches and allows the client to decathect from the oppressive illusion, and create a more healthy, non-oppressive reality.

It is essential that the client not hold (within) strategies similar to the oppressor for obtaining power or need gratification. The client learns to divest herself of all similar beliefs and strategies as those of the oppressor. In so doing, the "oppressed" will have no congruence (in behavior, thought or emotion) with the oppressor, thereby negating the potential power of "reality creation" of the oppressor. Congruence gives the "reality" substance, and hence makes its stance felt, and objectively "real." To hold the same or similar strategies (e.g., desire for personal "ego-generated" power vs. power for the collective good) as the oppressor, yet ostensibly for a different and no doubt "loftier" purpose, is to grant the legitimacy of, give power (energy) to, and help maintain those very mechanisms which are oppressive.

Oppression represents a state of imbalance, in that the oppressed are expressing an internal conflict between subjective beliefs of limitation, fear, anger, hostility, and a higher understanding (knowing) that the situation need not, nor does not exist (is an illusion). The client's internal conflict then serves to perpetuate itself externally in terms of manifestations of depression, helplessness, frustration, anxiety, paranoia and other clinical problems. The focus of the therapy is on the beliefs of the client perpetuating and helping in the creation of the oppressive conditions.

Assumptions and Goals of Model

The following assumptions and spiritual principles are representative of many philosophical, scientific, and psychological orientations (e.g., Kemetic, quantum physics, humanistic, transpersonal, Jungian).

Presupposition 1. Each person is a manifestation of a Higher Self or Divinity within; thus a task of life is to discover that (or one's) Divinity.

Postulates. As such:

a. each person has within, the power of self-knowledge or intelligence.

b. each person is inherently good, capable of love (receiving and expressing).

c. each person has an inherent capacity for wholeness and the experience of an integrated healthy self.

Therapy Goal: To facilitate and allow the client to discover her Divinity within through increased self knowledge.

Presupposition 2. The Self or Divinity within is connected to universal energy (spiritual power) far greater than the experienced self.

Postulates. As such:

a. each person has spiritual (nonphysical and transphysical) energy which is the power to create.

b. spiritual energy can effect material energy.

Therapy Goal: To facilitate the employment of the spiritual energy for wholeness and health.

Presupposition 3. There is one true reality, that of God and the Divinity within.

Postulates. As such:

a. everyone participates in the creation of "objective" reality (which is dualistic) through the projection of thoughts, beliefs, fears, ego-strivings and anxieties.

b. objective reality is an illusion because it depends on subjective interpretation (we assign meaning; events and situations have no meaning apart from that assigned), and social construction.

Therapy Goals: To facilitate clients' participation in the creation of a healthy, wholistic reality and to help release the client from cognitive bondage, to spiritual empowerment and healing spiritual power inherent in the knowledge of a Divinity within.

Model Application: The Case of Sandra

Sandra, a 35-year-old African American woman presented with several problems: (1) she reported a long-standing, almost debilitating depression of vague origins, by her assessment; (2) she felt like a victim and of a lesser quality than others, general unworthiness which she felt those in her environment responded to by harassing and berating her; (3) difficulties in managing her home life and ability to adequately address the needs of her two preadolescent male children (whom she had without benefit of a legal union, during the height of the civil rights struggles of the 60's); and (4) she felt different and alienated from her family, in particular her mother, whom she described as a demanding, controlling and very religious woman. In general, Sandra felt alienated, isolated, misunderstood, rejected and depressed.

Sandra was a very attractive, striking woman, yet the ravages of both depression and poverty were evidenced in the matted texture of her thick hair, in the unkempt and soiled quality of her clothes, and the lack of adequate attire for lower temperatures. Although worn and tattered, her clothing belied another dimension of Sandra, as one who leaned toward the flamboyancy and "bohemian/off-beatness" of the intellectual genre. Sandra was also a graduate student at a large predominantly White university. Sandra reported struggling with coursework and the "racism" of her professors. Overall, her dysphoria could be traced to the death of her father at a pubertal age, and to whom she was very close. She gradually noticed a growing emotional distance from her mother and sister and the beginnings of her feelings of alienation. Those feelings were accentuated by the series of events surrounding her tumultuous relationship with the father (her boyfriend) of her children; her active involvement in the civil and human rights struggles; and her tragic abandonment later by the father of her children. She perceived her life as empty with disappointments and rejections. She had a series of very low paying and menial jobs even though she possessed a college degree. She had all but retreated from the outside, to a world of her immediate home environment. However, she was rooted from this position by the threat of eviction from her landlord. She felt that there was no sphere of safety, peace and calm either within or external to herself.

Sandra came from a middle-class (economically and in terms of values) African American family, where the fruits of her father's position as a proprietor of a store were enjoyed by Sandra and her family until her father's death. At that point only reminiscences of a better life were available to her mother, sister and herself. Her elder sibling according to Sandra, suffered a difficult period of failure in her life, during which their mother looked to Sandra to "elevate" the family in status through educational achievements, the proper deportment and marriage to someone established. Sandra finished college, to her mother's pleasure, then became involved with the father of her children, and left home (which was an affront to the family conservatism and values regarding respectability) with this man. Her sister, however, recouped from her failures, got an advanced degree, married, and fulfilled her mother's dream. Sandra never regained her lost family status; in fact, by Sandra's own assessment, she sunk further into poverty, alienation, and rejection.

The first sessions with Sandra were difficult. There was constant testing of the therapist, and mistrust/suspiciousness of the therapist and agency in general. Dynamically, her behavior was facilitating to the therapy in that she was merely transferring her conflicts regarding her mother onto the therapist. The conflicts became components of the therapeutic relationship, and were addressed within the sessions. Paranoid features and low self-esteem associated with her depression could be evidenced in a written assessment of her treatment, in which she stated that:

> . . . the words I remember hearing most often in trying to find help were that it takes a great deal of strength to admit that you need help, but somewhere that feeling goes when you look at an office worker and internalize the strange looks she gives you, because your blouse doesn't match your skirt today or because in her mind you are a 'sick-o' . . . it's like you are an open book every time you walk through the door.

Sandra challenged the therapy and the therapist for almost six months. She imputed rejection from others in almost every interaction. In reflecting on these initial sessions Sandra was able to acknowledge her "anger, rebellion and paranoia" and the "destructive qualities of poverty, racism, isolation and age" on her thinking. Sandra was experiencing difficulties in many dimensions of her beingness, all relating to a sense of a nonintegrated self: fears of, yet simultaneous longing for dependency and nurturance; separation, individuation and loss issues; mastery issues; and elements of masochistic suffering and avoidant personality features.

Her family system was set up in a controlling, competitive fashion where the spoils (mother's approval and affection) would go to the sibling most adherent to mother's demands and conservatism. To derail her efforts at individuation, which threatened the structure, family mechanisms were set into motion to bring Sandra back into the fold. In many ways the family system represented the societal pressure to cease and desist, and to become a "good" citizen, which Sandra saw as contradictory to her philosophical adherence to subcultural admonitions to challenge the structure. However, it was through African American political activism, and the father of her children, that Sandra sought to establish her identity and independence. When that avenue was no longer viable, her false and superficial efforts in that direction were dissolved. Sandra was then left in an existential quandary regarding her legitimacy as a person. The self structure was never firmly established (only through another authority figure, the boyfriend and father of her children) hence the thin connectors were broken upon the dissolution of her only intimate bond toward selfhood.

The direction of therapy was conceptualized in light of the above factors. The "self-activity" referred to by Jenkins (1985) was acknowledged and accepted as instrumental to Sandra's attempts to find safety. Therapeutically, it was apparent that the intrapsychic issues could be handled with a dynamic strategy, while a cognitive-behavioral approach was utilized to help Sandra overcome her depression. Sandra responded well to the cognitive strategy which allowed her to restructure her thinking and interpretations of the events/people in her life, while concomitantly designing an orientation to the future which included recognition of her special skills. A modest behavioral program was agreed upon to add needed structure to both her thinking and behavior. The overriding framework of the therapy strategy, however, was cogno-spiritual in the following components of the therapy process.

Orientation of the therapist. Assumptions of the therapist are critical: the client is a manifestation of a Transcendent Beingness, and as such is basically good, desiring positive experiences, and worthy of respect; the therapist can project/elicit an acknowledgment and understanding in the client of a Higher Self as whole, healthy and integrated; that Self is connected to an Existence/Energy far greater than the experienced self; recognizing that spirituality is the very foundation of oppressed persons of African descent (irrespective of Western acculturation) and that it is impossible to define (i.e., to fully know) with certainty the inherent potential of the client. In the above case of Sandra, her thinking and assumptions about herself and her environment had been learned and thus could be unlearned and replaced by more functional or healthy ones. Therapy is seen as a learning environment where the therapist accepts the reality presented by the client, while creating an atmosphere which would allow the client to discover his/her own creativity and ability in shaping that atmosphere within the session as a model, with encouragement to explore that thinking and behavior outside the session. The client has the capacity to know herself better than the therapist, thus there is not the "I-Thou" or "Tu-Vous" status differential between the client and therapist. Therapy is to release the already existent healing power and intelligence from within the client. The therapy process combines the energy (spiritual) of the therapist (more of the therapist's initially) and client in discovery and exploration. There is an underlying assumption, however, that "you can't take someone to a place within themselves, where you have never been as a therapist." Jung (1966b) spoke to the necessity of the therapist to gain self-knowledge to work effectively. Therapy was viewed as a dialectical discussion between the therapist and client, where the therapist, in diminishing the status difference between the two, provided the client with the impetus or model to no longer remain a captive of infantile impulses or unbridled egocentric demands. Jung viewed treatment as a process, and the therapist as a healing agent. According to Jung (1966c) on: " . . . what the healing agent really is: it is the degree to which the analyst himself can cope with his own psychic problems. The higher levels of therapy involve his own reality" (p. 493).

Jung (1966c) basically felt that the therapist first had to make self corrections to gain self-awareness before hoping to correct those areas in the client. It was through the therapeutic alliance—the mutual confidence and confidence of the client in the therapeutic relationship, which would help the client gain psychic strength.

In working with African American clients, or other oppressed persons, it is critical that the therapist evaluate her/his own thinking and basic assumptions regarding the African American worldview as distinct from, but not less valued than, the Western view. This is a difficult task for living in this environment it is easy to be victimized by the agents of Western thinking, e.g., the media. The therapist herself, therefore, must be in constant touch with her own Higher Self to effectively project a "healing factor" (spiritual energy) for the client.

Therapy process. The goal of therapy is to release the client from cognitive, emotional and thus behavioral bondage, to personal and spiritual empowerment. The African American client may present with difficulties which call upon the therapist to intervene therapeutically on many levels, e.g., intrapsychic, social, existential, spiritual, etc. The therapist must initially make an accurate assessment to determine the primary level on which the client is functioning. It is impossible to separate the client from her environment and culture. Thus, therapy becomes not only a clinical enterprise, but a political one as well.

The goal of a cogno-spiritual therapy is to help the client to unfold and transcend (in consciousness) the immediacy (or illusion/distortion) of that environment, not escape it. In the cogno-spiritual process the client learns flexibility, e.g., having or developing the skills to shift when appropriate and synthesize from a rational mode to an intuitive mode. The goal is not to encourage the client to perceived reality exclusively at the transpersonal or suprapersonal level as according to Wilber's transpersonal paradigm (Wilber, 1977). Again, the original discussion of "uniting the opposites" or seeking a synthesis of orientation is relevant here.

Therapy techniques. The cogno-spiritual therapeutic model focuses primarily on the examination of the client's thinking regarding: intrapsychic conflict, interpersonal conflict, oppressed ideology and Higher consciousness and self-knowledge. Beck (1976) addresses in particular the subtle, almost subliminal conditioning which occurs with the client's "automatic thoughts" or "cognitions (verbal or pictorial events in the client's stream of consciousness) (which) are based on attitudes or assumptions (schemes) developed from previous experiences" (p. 3). Automatic thoughts can also be described as internal monologues and self statements made by the client. Working with African American and/or other oppressed clients, the techniques of the cognitive therapy orientation are thought to be essential for addressing issues of: (1) the specific presenting problem (the cognitive approach is not being proposed as the only approach for working with oppressed peoples); (2) oppressed ideology or conditioning; and (3) growth toward self-knowledge or spirituality/God within. Thus, cognitive strategies such as: cognitive restructuring and reattribution, seeking alternative conceptualizations, cognitive rehearsal, thought stopping and visual imaging may be employed.

The concept of reciprocal inhibition can be applied to the model. Rather than focusing on (and giving energy to) the mechanisms of oppression and the oppressor, it is emphasized that utilizing and giving energy to the spiritual aspect of self negates aspects unlike the Higher self. Reciprocal inhibition proposes that fear and anxiety are relieved to the extent that relaxation becomes central; so it is that fear and oppressive ideologies are relieved to the extent that spirituality (beliefs and practices) becomes central. Thus, it is not in struggling with oppression, but replacing it with more facilitating thoughts and energies, which eventually lead to its demise.

The concept of struggle is important. Within the act of struggle, there is the assumption that something has been taken away, or denied. Further, it is implied that one is at a deficit as a result, and must "struggle" to regain what has been denied. Those very assumptions or beliefs are limiting. However, to recognize that one's Self can be taken away, diminished or negated *only if we choose* to give it up, diminish it, or negate its power, is empowerment. Psychological oppression is a process of "denial, abdication, and diminishment" of one's power, based on the distorted belief that it has already been denied! The incorporation of religious and spiritual texts may be used effectively also, to stimulate thinking (learning) outside of the treatment sessions.

Case Summary

There were several conceptualizations possible regarding this case. The more traditional psychodynamic conceptualization would envision Sandra locked into a mode of attempting to establish a gratifying relationship: first with her father, who later traumatized her by his untimely death (emotionally perceived as abandonment), and who offered minimal and inconsistent nurturing; then with her mother, who demanded Sandra's foreclosure of self or of her individuation in order to obtain acceptance and emotional satisfaction; and finally, from her boyfriend, who represented a recapitulation of her parental struggles for a gratifying involvement thought to be necessary for selfhood and legitimacy as a person. Sandra brought to the therapy all of these struggles and her emotional outrage and defiance regarding her life.

The cogno-spiritual conceptualization of this case focused on: Sandra's understanding and forgiveness of her parents for their roles in her life; her understanding and forgiveness of herself for her need to compete with the female members of her family and her rage toward her parents for their not-good-enough-nurturing; her awareness of the same or similar aspects of personality, attitudes, and values held by family members, also within herself; awareness of the distorted beliefs she held regarding herself and of others; her distortions regarding her racial and gender identities; her special talents; the distortions of self necessitating a superficial desire for superiority; her recapitulation of her familial and parental struggles in all other relationships based on a desire for mastery over her traumas; and most important, her awareness of her uniqueness and specialness as a manifestation of a Higher Self.

In addition to Sandra's dynamic conflicts, there was the oppression which she felt from her racial and gender identities. The gender oppression was established early, as she learned that her father, and men in general had power over women: her mother's power was viewed as illegitimate, and obtained only after the death of her father (the real power). She learned that women gained power through men, and through manipulative means. She, as a woman, was powerless. For her mother to assume power over her (and withhold nurturing from her) only served to enrage Sandra. Her sense of a powerful self was again thwarted when she was abandoned with two male children, by her boyfriend. As a woman and an African American, Sandra felt incredible powerlessness and fundamental unworthiness.

In session the therapy focused on the inherent "power within," not subject to the vagaries of family, society or culture. Sandra learned that she held negative stereotypes about women and African Americans, which she enacted dysfunctionally, as she did her family conflicts. The important point of learning was that she held distorted beliefs about her racial and gender identities, irrespective of what others thought, and projected these expectancies in her interactions (she took on the role of a victim, abandoned by all those who "should" have loved her). She learned to reconceptualize from a more facilitating perspective. Meditation exercises helped Sandra to go "within" to her Higher Self for nurturing and acceptance. She learned to view herself holistically, rather than as separate identities (race and gender were aspects of a whole self). Cognitive strategies were helpful, in clearing her thinking about herself-in-relationship-to-the-world. Repeated exercises of "visual imaging" (and her understanding of the power inherent within thoughts and images) of herself as whole, fulfilled, and accomplishing goals, were practiced throughout the therapy.

It is important to make clear that the spiritual insights gained by Sandra were possible only after working through her anger, fears, and other clinical issues, using traditional psychodynamic and cognitive (some behavioral) strategies. It was necessary for her to first acknowledge the hostility and disappointment for example, prior to fully appreciating the spiritual interpretations. To do otherwise would require a total leap in faith without the necessary grounding. In Judeo-Christian language it would be considered "storming the gates of heaven." In psychodynamic terms, it would be related to the notion of "magical thinking" often associated with religious thought, in which issues and conflicts are presumed to disappear with insight alone, or because one "wishes" them to disappear. Spiritual empowerment requires that the principles are acknowledged, believed, developed, and practiced: "energy" (spiritual) must be expended in the desired direction to effect change.

The case of Sandra posed several therapeutic challenges. Sandra almost immediately formed a "distorted" bond with the therapist; and sought to show not only how unworthy she was, but how unworthy, incompetent, and powerless the therapist was as well. When Sandra met with total acceptance, understanding, and acknowledgment of her God self, she was at first determined to discredit that position. She learned however, that the therapist's position, was merely a reflection of that aspect of herself she had denied. After months of work (dynamically at first regarding issues of guilt, rage and abandonment; then more spiritually through meditation, visualizations, cognitive rehearsals or affirmations, and selected spiritual readings), Sandra began to feel a sense of her non-distorted, holistic beingness, and witnessed its power in her life. Sandra did not miraculously change: upon termination, she had learned to self-monitor her thinking, to spiritually reconceptualize events and situations in her life, e.g., through the recognition of how she participated in the creation of these events; and most important, she became acquainted with and empowered by, the knowledge of her true Higher Self.

Conclusion

The rationale for a cogno-spiritual model of psychotherapy is to focus on the thoughts (oppressed patterns of thinking) of African American clients, which impede the natural healing process, particularly when progress (to a Higher consciousness) is blocked by past events which render the client ineffectual in the present. The client learns to utilize both rational and intuitive processes. The cognitive approach clearly addresses, in the case of oppressed persons, the environmentally conditioned thinking or learned helplessness. In Batesonian (1972) terms, oppressed thinking is symmetrical in that for there to be an oppressor, at some level the oppressed has to believe in the power of the oppressor and behave accordingly. The therapist may find the client submitting in interactions because of his/her ability to understand the role of the other (the oppressor) and unconsciously take on the role of the oppressed.

It is also recognized that the manifestations of oppression result from many different factors—race/pronounced ethnicity is only one. People are oppressed on many dimensions: gender, age, poverty, familial past, beliefs, culture, sexual orientation and any number of imaginable factors used to establish dominance of one group over the other. It should be noted that oppressors, are themselves oppressed, by the very thought of the need to oppress. The distorted self which believes in oppression, is itself, oppressed. The end goal of cogno-spiritual psychotherapy is self-knowledge (knowledge of a God within/spirituality and spiritual power) and empowerment at an individual and collective level. The model proposes a cognitive and spiritual "re-awakening" from within, based on the knowledge of a "true self."

References

Adams, H. H., Jr. (1988, August). *Biophysics of creative states of consciousness: Towards a holistic theory of mind, behavior and the transcendent.* Paper presented at the annual conference of the Association of Black Psychologists, Washington, DC.

Akbar, N. (1979). African roots of Black personality. In W. D. Smith, A. K. Burlew, M. Mosley, & M. Whitney, *Reflections on Black psychology* (pp. 79-87). Washington, DC: University Press of America.

Akbar, N. (1985). Nile Valley origins of the science of mind. In I. Van Sertima (Ed.), *Nile Valley civilizations: Proceedings of the Nile Valley conference* (pp. 120-132). New Brunswick, NJ: *Journal of African Civilizations.*

al-'Ashmawi, S. (1986). Three cultures: Judaism, Christianity and Islam, *Jerusalem Quarterly, 38,* 138-144.

Alho, O. (1976). *The religion of the slaves.* Helsinki: Suomalainen Tiedeakatemia Academia Scientiarum Fennica.

Arnkoff, D. B. (1980). Psychotherapy from the perspective of cognitive theory. In M. J. Mahoney (Ed.), *Psychotherapy process: Current issues and future directions.* New York: Plenum.

Asante, M. K. (1984). The African American mode of transcendence. *Journal of Transpersonal Psychology, 16*(2), 167-177.

Baer, H. (1984). *The Black spiritual movement: A religious response to racism.* Knoxville: The University of Tennessee Press.

Baldwin, J. (1980). The psychology of oppression. In M. Asante, & A. Vandi (Eds.), *Contemporary Black thought: Alternative analyses in social & behavioral science* (pp. 95-110). Beverly Hills, CA: Sage.

Bateson, G. (1972). *Steps to an ecology of mind.* New York: Ballantine Books.

Bart, P. B. (1971). The myth of a value-free psychotherapy. In W. Bell & J. A. Mau (Eds.), *The sociology of the future* (pp. 113-159). New York: Russell Sage Foundation.

Beck, A. T. (1971). Cognition, affect and psychopathology. *Archives of General Psychiatry, 24,* 495-500.

Beck, A. T. (1976). *Cognitive therapy and the emotional disorders.* New York: International Universities Press.

Beck, A. T. Rush, A. J., Shaw, B. F., & Emery, G. (1979). *Cognitive therapy of depression.* New York: Guilford Press.

ben-Jochannon, J. (1970). *African origins of the major "western religions."* New York: Alkebu-lan Books.

Boyd-Franklin, N. (1989). *Black families in therapy: A multisystems approach.* New York: Guilford Press.

Boorstein, S. (Ed.). (1980). *Transpersonal psychotherapy.* Palo Alto, CA: Science & Behavior Books.

Breitman, G. (1967). *The last year of Malcolm X.* New York: Schocken.

Broverman, I. K., Broverman, D. M., Clarkson, F. E., Rosenkrantz, P. S., & Vogel, S. R. (1970). Sex-role stereotypes and clinical judgments of mental health. *Journal of Consulting and Clinical Psychology, 34*(1), 1-7.

Bulhan, H. A. (1985). *Frantz Fanon and the psychology of oppression.* New York: Plenum Press.

Capra, F. (1982). *The turning point.* New York: Simon & Schuster.

Cheek, D. K. (1977). *Assertive Black, puzzled White.* San Luis Obispo, CA: Impact Publishers.

Chesler, P. (1972). *Women and madness.* New York: Doubleday.

Clift, W. B. (1983). *Jung and Christianity: The challenge of reconciliation.* New York: Crossroad.

Comas-Diaz, L., & Griffith, E. (Eds.). (1988). *Clinical guidelines in crosscultural mental health.* New York: John Wiley.

Cone, J. H. (1975). *God of the oppressed.* Minneapolis, MN: Seabury Press.

Cone, J. H., & Wilmore, G. S. (1979). Black theology and African theology. In G. S. Wilmore & J. H. Cone (Eds.), *Black Theology* (pp. 463-491). New York: Orbis Books.

Daly, M. (1978). *Gynecology: The metaethics of radical feminism.* Boston, MA: Beacon Press.

Davidson, J. (1991). *Natural creation and the formative mind.* Boston, MA: Element.

Davis, J., & Weaver, J. (1982). Dimensions of spirituality. In C. Spretnak (Ed.), *The politics of women's spirituality: Essays on the rise of spiritual power within the feminist movement* (pp. 368-370). New York: Anchor Press/Doubleday.

Dixon, V. (1971). *Beyond Black or White: An alternative America.* Boston, MA: Little, Brown and Company.

Edwards, K. L. (1987). Exploratory study of Black psychological health. *Journal of Religion and Health, 26*(1), 73-80

Freire, P. (1973). *Pedagogy of the oppressed.* New York: Seabury Press.

Goldenberg, I. (1978). *Oppression and social intervention.* Chicago, IL: Nelson-Hall.

Greene, B. A. (1985). Considerations in the treatment of Black patients by White therapists. *Psychotherapy, 22*(2S), 389 -393.

Grier, W. H., & Cobbs, P. M. (1971). *The Jesus bag.* New York: McGraw Hill.

Griffith, M. S. (1977). The influence of race on psychotherapeutic relationship. *Psychiatry, 40,* 27-40.

Halleck, S. L. (1971a). *The politics of therapy.* New York: Harper & Row.

Halleck, S. L. (1971b). Therapy is the handmaiden of the status quo. *Psychology Today, 4(30).*

Helms, J. E. (1984). Toward a theoretical explanation of the effects of race on counseling: A Black and White model. *The Counseling Psychologist, 12,* 153-165.

Helms, J. E. (1986). Expanding racial identity theory to cover the counseling process. *Journal of Counseling Psychology, 33,* 62-64.

Hickling, F. (1988). Politics and the psychotherapy context. In L. Comas-Diaz & E. Griffith (Eds.), *Clinical guidelines in cross-cultural mental health* (pp. 90-111). New York: John Wiley.

Inclan, J. (1985). Variations in value orientations in mental health work with Puerto Ricans. *Psychotherapy, 22*(2S), 324-334.

Jackson, A. M. (1983). A theoretical model for the practice of psychotherapy with Black populations. *Journal of Black Psychology, 10*(1), 19-27.

Jackson, G. G. (1980). The emergence of a Black perspective in counseling. In R. Jones (Ed.), *Black psychology* (pp. 294-313). New York: Harper & Row.

Jahn, R., & Dunne, B. (1987). *Margins of reality.* New York: Harcourt, Brace, Jovanovich.

Jenkins, A. H. (1985). Attending to self-activity in the Afro-American client. *Psychotherapy, 22*(2S), 335-341.

Jones, A. C. (1985). Psychological functioning in Black Americans: A conceptual guide for use in psychotherapy. *Psychotherapy, 22*(2S), 363-369.

Jones, A., & Seagull, A. (1977). Dimensions of the relationship between the Black client and the White therapist. *American Psychologist, 32*(10), 850-855.

Jones, E. E. (1978). Effects of race on psychotherapy process and outcome: An exploratory investigation. *Psychotherapy, 15*(3), 226-236.

Jung, C. G. (1964a). Religion as the counterbalance to mass-mindedness. In H. Read, M. Fordham & G. Adler (Eds.), *The collected works of C. G. Jung: Civilization in transition* (Vol. 10, pp. 256-262). New York: Bollingen Foundation.

Jung, C. G. (1964b). The undiscovered self. In H. Read, M. Fordham & B. Adler (Eds.), *The collected works of C. G. Jung: Civilization in transition* (Vol. 10, pp. 256-262). New York: Bollingen Foundation.

Jung, C. G. (1966a). Two essays on analytical psychology. In H. Read, M. Fordham, & G. Adler (Eds.), *Collected works of C. G. Jung* (Vol. 10). New York: Bollingen Foundation.

Jung, C. G. (1966b). The practice of psychotherapy. In H. Read, M. Fordham, & G. Adler (Eds), *The collected works of C. G. Jung* (Vol. 16). New York: Bollingen Foundation.

Jung, C. G. (1966c). Symbolic life. In H. Read, M. Fordham, & G. Adler (Eds.), *The collected works of C. G. Jung* (Vol. 18). New York: Bollingen Foundation.

Jung, C. G. (1968). Natural transformation (individuation). In H. Read, M. Fordham, & G. Adler (Eds.), *The collected works of C. G. Jung* (Vol. 9). New York: Bollingen Foundation.

Karenga, M. (1983). *Introduction to Black studies.* Los Angeles, CA: Kawaida Publications.

Kluckhohn, F. R., & Strodtbeck, F. L. (1961). *Variations in value orientations.* Evanston, IL: Row, Peterson.

Lincoln, C. E. (1984). *Race, religion, and the continuing American dilemma.* New York: Hill and Wang.

Marx, G. (1970). Religion: Opiate or inspiration of civil rights militancy among Negroes. In M. Goldschmid (Ed.), *Black Americans and White racism* (pp. 366-375). New York: Holt, Rinehart & Winston.

Marx, K., & Engels, F. (1964). *On religion.* New York: Schocken.

Mays, V. M. (1985). The Black Americans and psychotherapy: The dilemma. *Psychotherapy, 22*(2S), 379-388.

Mbiti, J. S. (1970a). *African religions and philosophy.* Garden City, NY: Anchor Books/Doubleday.

Mbiti, J. S. (1970b). *Concepts of God in Africa.* New York: Praeger.

Mbiti, J. S. (1971). *New testament eschatology in an African background.* London: Oxford University Press.

McAdoo, H. P. (Ed.). (1988). *Black families.* Newbury Park, CA: Sage.

McGoldrick, M., Pearce, J., & Giordano, J. (Eds.). (1982). *Ethnicity and family therapy.* New York: Guilford Press.

McHugh, P. (1968). *Defining the situation.* New York: Bobbs-Merrill.

Miller, J. B. (1986). *Toward a new psychology of women.* Boston, MA: Beacon Press.

Myers, L. J. (1985). Transpersonal psychology: The role of the Afrocentric paradigm. *Journal of Black Psychology, 12*(1), 31-42.

Myrdal, G. (1944). *An American dilemma.* New York: Harper & Brothers.

Nichols, E. (1976, November). *The philosophical aspects of cultural differences.* World Psychiatric Association: Ibadan, Nigeria.

Nobles, W. (1972). African philosophy: Foundations for Black psychology. In R. Jones (Ed.), *Black psychology* (pp. 18-32). New York: Harper & Row.

Nobles, W. W. (1980). African philosophy: Foundations for Black psychology. In R. Jones (Ed.), *Black psychology* (pp. 23-36). New York: Harper & Row.

Pagels, H. (1988). *The dreams of reason.* New York: Simon & Schuster.

Raboteau, A. J. (1978). *Slave religion: The invisible institution in the antebellum south.* New York: Oxford University Press.

Reuther, R. (Ed.). (1974). *Religion and sexism.* New York: Simon & Schuster.

Sager, C. J., Brayboy, T. L., & Waxenberg, B. (1972). Black patient—White therapists. *American Journal of Orthopsychiatry, 42(3),* 415-423.

Schuon, F. (1975). *Transcendent unity of religions.* New York: Harper & Row.

Schur, E. M. (1971). *Labeling deviant behavior: Its sociological implications.* New York: Harper & Row.

Sjoo, M., & Mor, B. (1987). *The great cosmic mother: Rediscovering the religion of the earth.* New York: Harper & Row.

Smith, A., Jr. (1981). Religion and mental health among Blacks. *Journal of Religion and Health, 20,* 264-287.

Spretnak, C. (Ed.). (1982). *The politics of women's spirituality: Essays on the rise of spiritual power within the feminist movement.* New York: Anchor Press/Doubleday.

Szasz, T. S. (1970). The myth of mental illness. In G. P. Stone & H. A. Farberman (Eds.), *Social psychology through symbolic interaction.* Waltham, MA: Xerox College Publishing.

Tart, C. (1983). *Transpersonal psychologies.* El Cerrito, CA: Psychological Processes.

Taub-Bynum, E. B. (1984). *The family unconscious: An invisible bond.* Wheaton, IL: Theosophical Publishing House.

Thomas, W. I., & Thomas, D. S. (1970). Situations defined as real are real in their consequences. In G. P. Stone & H. A. Farberman (Eds.), *Social psychology through symbolic interaction* (pp. 154-155). Waltham, MA: Xerox College Publishing.

Tyler, F. B., Sussewell, D. R., & Williams-McCoy, J. (1985). Ethnic validity in psychotherapy. *Psychotherapy, 22*(2S), 311-320.

Vaughan, F. (1985). Discovering transpersonal identity. *Journal of Humanistic Psychology, 25*(3), 13-38.

Waller, W. (1970). The definition of the situation. In G. Stone & H. Farberman (Eds.), *Social psychology through symbolic interaction* (pp. 162-174). MA: Xerox College Publishing.

Walsh, R. N., & Vaughan, F. (1980). *Beyond ego: Transpersonal dimensions in psychology.* Los Angeles, CA: Tarcher.

White, J. L., Parham, W. D., & Parham, T. A. (1980). Black psychology: The Afro-American tradition as a unifying force for traditional psychology. In R. Jones (Ed.), *Black psychology* (pp. 56-66). New York: Harper & Row.

Wilber, K. (1977). *The spectrum of consciousness.* Wheaton, IL: The Theosophical Publishing House.

Wilmore, G. S. (1973). *Black religion and Black radicalism.* New York: Anchor Press.

Wilmore, G. S., & Cone, J. H. (Eds.). (1979). *Black theology.* New York: Orbis.

Wolpe, J. (1978). Cognition and causation in human behavior and its therapy. *American Psychologist, 33*, 437-446.

Author

Karen Lenore Edwards
Department of Psychology
M. L. #34
University of Cincinnati
Cincinnati, OH 45221-0034
Telephone: (513) 556-0648
Fax: (513) 556-2302
E-mail: karen.edwards@u.c.edu.

Spirit-Energy and NTU Psychotherapy

Frederick B. Phillips

Spirit and Energy

Spirituality is the core distinguishing principal in an African-centered philosophy of life and is the fundamental concept of healing in the NTU psychotherapy approach (Nobles, 1986; Phillips, 1988). With a keen acknowledgment that, at some level, the concept of spirituality becomes indefinable, I will nonetheless offer a working definition: Spirituality is a measure of the quality of one's relationship to the ultimate vitalizing life force. We will look more closely at this definition throughout this section of the paper.

The life force is a concept that is central to the worldview of many cultures and known by many names throughout the world. It is called "Prana" by the ancient Indians where it is seen as the basic constituent and source of all life (Brennan, 1988). Prana, the breath of life, moves through all forms and provides life; Yogis practice manipulating this energy through breathing techniques, meditation and physical exercise to maintain altered states of consciousness.

The Chinese in the 3rd millennium B. C., painted the existence of vital energy which they called *Ch'i*. All matter, animate and inanimate, is composed and pervaded with this universal energy. Thus *Ch'i* contains two polar forces the yin and the yang. When the yin and yang are balanced, the living system exhibits physical health; when they are unbalanced, a diseased state results. Overly powerful yang results in excessive organic activity. Predominant yin makes for insufficient functioning. Either unbalance results in physical illness. The ancient art of acupuncture therefore focuses on balancing the yin and the yang. Brennan has described this force as simply the Human Energy Field that exist around each of us (Brennan, 1988). Each life form has an energy field or aura that surrounds and interpenetrates the physical body and this energy field is ultimately associated with health. There are numerous variant procedures that involve rebalancing the energy field such as: laying on of hands, faith healing, and spiritual healing. Brennan further described the Human Energy Field as the manifestation of universal energy that is ultimately a representation of human life. It can be described as a luminous body that surrounds and interpenetrates the physical body, emits its own characteristic radiation and is usually called the "aura."

Within the African context, we will review the concept of the life force from the perspective of the Bantu peoples who principally reside in the central regions of Africa. For the Bantus, the life force is called NTU (pronounced "in-to") which is the universal force that makes everything. The Bantu cannot conceive of anything separate and apart from its NTU. NTU is the force (energy) which sustains everything. Equally important to Bantu (and all African) philosophy is that everything that there is, is considered a force, not substance. Viewing reality as a force rather than substance is a critical distinction in the framework of healing as force suggests dynamism and interaction as opposed to passivity and objectification. This ancient and indigenous worldview has present day Western cultural parallels in modern physics in which all matter can be conceived as either a particle (substance) or a wave (force) depending on the object's interaction with the observer (Copra, 1984). For the traditionally trained Western mind a brief review of the "new physics" is appropriate here before returning to the Bantu concept of NTU.

The quintessential physicist Albert Einstein, initiated two revolutionary trends of thought within Western science which allowed Western culture to better grasp ancient African philosophy. One thought was his special theory of relativity; the other was a new way of looking at electromagnetic radiation which was to become characteristic of quantum theory, the theory of atomic phenomena. Einstein strongly believed in nature's inherent harmony and, according to his concept of relativity theory, space is not three-dimensional and time is not a separate entity. Both are intimately connected and form a four dimensional continuum, "space-time." The most important consequence of Einstein's theory for our purposes herein is the realization that mass is nothing but a form of energy. Even an object at rest has energy stored in its mass and the relation between the two is given by the famous equation $E=MC^2$, C being the speed of light (Copra, 1983). As was stated earlier, all matter can be described as either a particle (matter) or a wave (force) depending on how we look at them (the interaction of the energy/force to the observer). To the traditional Western mind, this was a contradiction that gave rise to the koan-like paradox which formally led to the formulation of quantum theory. Most important to our discussion here is that quantum theory reveals a basic oneness of the universe. It shows that we cannot decompose the world into independently existing smallest units. As we penetrate into matter nature does not show us any isolated "basic building blocks" but rather appears as a complicated web of relations between the various parts of the whole. All of life is interconnected through the universal life force and life is dynamic so that reality as we have come to understand it in the popular culture does not really exist in a precise manner. The observer always has an influence on the observed; the therapist/healer has an influence on the client.

The quantum theory revelation of the oneness of the universe is the Western science lens on the African conceptualization of the harmony of life. The African philosophy of mutual compatibility and world harmony is best described by Adibayo Adensya, a Yoruba writer who is quoted by Janheinz Jahn in his book, *Muntu, the new African culture* (Jahn, 1961). "An African concept of harmony is not simply a coherence of fact and faith, nor of reason and traditional beliefs, nor of reason and contingent facts, but a coherence or compatibility among all the disciplines. A medical theory, e.g., which contradicted a theological conclusion was rejected as absurd and vice versa. This demand of mutual compatibility among all the disciplines considered as a system was the main weapon of Yoruba thinking. God might be banished from Greek thought without any harm being done to the logical architecture of it, but this cannot be done in the case of the Yoruba. In medieval thought, science could be dismissed at pleasure, but this is impossible in the case of Yoruba thought, since faith and reason are mutually dependent. In modern times, God even has no place in scientific thinking. This was impossible to the Yoruba since from the Olodumare an architectonic of knowledge was built in which the finger of God is manifest in the most rudimentary elements of nature. Philosophy, theology, politics, social theory, land law, medicine, psychology, birth and burial, all find themselves logically concatenated in a system so tight that to subtract one item from the whole is to paralyze the structure of the whole."

From the Bantu philosophy, all being, all essence, in whatever form it is conceived, can be subsumed under one of four categories which are:

I	Muntu	=	"human being" (plural; Bantu);
II	Kintu	=	"thing" (plural; Bintu);
III	Hantu	=	"place and time";
IV	Kuntu	=	"modality."

Everything there is must necessarily belong to one of these four categories and must be conceived of not as substance but as force (energy). Man is a force, all things are forces, place and time are forces and the modalities are forces. These forces are all related to one another, and the relationship of these forces is expressed in their very names, for if we remove the determinative the stem NTU is the same for all the categories. NTU is the universal force as such, which, however, never occurs apart from its manifestations: Muntu, Kintu, Hantu, Kuntu (Jahn, 1988). As we review the NTU philosophy of the Bantu, we are reminded of Einstein's "discovery" that all matter can be considered as either a force or as matter.

NTU is the cosmic universal force of the Bantu as Prana is the force described by the ancient Indians. NTU is a force, a spiritual energy, that manifests itself in man, beast, thing, place, time, beauty, etc. and is both immanent and transcendent.

In NTU *force* and matter are one as is particle and wave in the "new physics." The perspective of human beings as energy and spirit is not merely an academic discussion but has significant implications for mental health healing, and the practice of psychotherapy. These areas are more fully covered later in this paper but one brief example is appropriate now. Take the case of a middle aged women formally diagnosed as depressed. Therapeutic intervention can focus on medication to lift her depression or behavior modification to change her symptomatic behavior, or analysis that attempts to reconstruct her early childhood conflicts. All three approaches attempt to disconnect the therapist-healer from the client as well as they ignore the existence of the spirit in the healing process. NTU therapy, as do other spiritually-based approaches, recognizes that the depression is a constriction of the spirit-energy and that it is a reflection of a spirit disharmony and imbalance. Where is the spirit, or natural drive for health, being diverted? For what reason? To what effect? What is the experience of the client energy like for the therapist? What is the disharmonious energy communicating to the environment in terms of needs? What does the therapist see, hear, and feel as they co-exist and co-create reality in the energy exchange with the client? These are some of the directions that the NTU therapists explore as they function on the spirit-energy level of the client reality. The NTU orientation leads the therapist/healer to guide the client toward awareness of the spiritual disharmony and then to understand their emotions and behavior as expressions of a troubled spirit not at ease (or dis-ease). As the process unfolds and awareness of the spiritual disharmony is achieved, the client then has internal energy (NTU) that propels the mind/body toward healing. This process can then be further facilitated via behavior interventions and perhaps even medication, but what is key is the fundamental intervention which originated on the spiritual level.

As we have previously outlined, matter can be seen as energy and vice versa. Matter and energy are interchangeable and interconnectible and human beings are beings of energy. This perspective of humans as energy helps us to understand how a therapist or friend can provide a healing experience for a troubled client or associate by either touching (holding them) or just by mere physical presence and proximity. This is so because of the exchange of healing energy which can occur directly and without words. They are, quite simply, awakening the energy which has a calming effect. Similarly, one can also negatively influence another person's energy through the projection of negative thoughts and feelings which have a biochemical correlate and are therefore energy experienced by the other person through the interaction. We are all extensions of each other and are connected by the spirit-energy of the cosmos. Our body is not separate from the body of the universe and our human nervous system is capable of becoming aware of the information and energy from its surrounding environment. We, further, have the ability to influence and be influenced by, that energy. Energy systems are affected by other inner and outer forces whether those other forces may be emotions, spiritual balance, nutrition or the environment. It is well known in the medical community for instance, that a child's healing processes are positively impacted when their parent are in close proximity. For that reason, some hospitals allow the child's parent to stay overnight in the hospital room. The hope and love (emotions as energy) of the parent are conveyed to the child in a sustained verbal and non-verbal manner.

If we return to our initial definition of spirituality we find the word vitalizing. This is so stated since, in an African-centered context, the spiritual dimension is the energetic basis of all life. Spirit needs form and it is the energy of the spirit (NTU) which animates the physical framework. Energy, of course, never dies; it transforms into other forms and thus the African belief of human death as a transition of the spirit-energy which takes form as Orishas, ancestors, etc. These spirit energies are therefore available to the living and can be contacted, communicated with, and brought to bear in the present space time. We, for instance, all can gain real strength from the recall of an anchoring family ancestor into our consciousness. Though the "strength" may come into us through the emotional or spiritual level, it is available to us on the physical and mental levels also. We feel better, stronger, clearer and more empowered!

Consciousness itself can be viewed as a kind of energy that is integrally related to the cellular expression of the physical body (Gerber, 1988). This is a profound statement of the mind-body connection and of the African principle of consubstantiation which states that, "I am because we are" (Nobles, 1986). Viewing the link between consciousness as energy and the physical plane allows us to grasp the relationship between self-esteem, identity and health, for example. We are each from our own consciousness participating in the continuous creation of either health or illness. We are who we think we are in great part. We influence our reality and are influenced by the thoughts that we allow inside our consciousness. This view of consciousness suggests that "mind" is not just in the brain but throughout the body, within every cell. We are a holistic organism, body, mind and spirit where energy is interchangeable and interconnectible.

Because humans are elements of the divine we are a microcosm within a macrocosm. Throughout the macro-micro universe there are patterns of order that repeat themselves. This truth is aptly captured in the folk saying, "as above, so below," which is a recognition of the patterns of nature and the existence of a natural order and natural laws. Within an African-centered context, one can focus attention on the unique manifestation of spirit-energy that appears throughout nature whether that aspect is a tree, an eagle, or a rock since the spiritual person becomes increasingly able to see beyond the visible manifestation and into the very essence behind that form. By guiding your client to immerse himself in the essence of an eagle, he can gain the power to use the eagle's clarity of perspective (a manifestation of God's insight) to solve problems in his life that require profound awareness. In this example of spirit as transcendent and immanent, a client can learn to relate to the NTU spirit-energy in small comprehensible steps when each piece of creation is understood to manifest some separate quality of God and may be embraced as awareness in the client's own space-time.

An important component of the energy/spirit discussion is the understanding of the human senses and their contribution to awareness and health/illness. If we just take the traditional five senses that are generally accepted by Western society i.e. sight, sound, taste, touch, and smell we notice that they are receptors of energy that connect to the external environmental and that connection is experienced as a sensation. Remembering that matter is energy, the bodymind sees light waves, hears sound waves, etc. and transforms the energy into conscious images, experiences, and communication. The senses are the bodymind's way of assessing the environment and is an energy exchange. From an African-centered perspective, the most important of the senses, the so-called 6th sense is undervalued by Western culture and Western approaches to healing.

The 6th Sense is commonly referred to as intuition but also carries other names, some with positive connotation such as the "Mother's wit" and other names with either negative, or at least, guarded meaning such as clairvoyance, extrasensory perception, telepathy and the like. Intuition is defined in a Western context as a direct perception of truth, fact, etc. independent of any reasoning process. Africentrically, intuition is the bodymind sensation of spirit-energy in a more direct manner, less filtered by the cultural or learned information that becomes woven into the five senses and the senses' connection to the brain. Intuition is revelation, more spiritual and wholistic in its awareness. An intuitive experience is a sharpened awareness of the ongoing energy of consciousness and internal and external energy exchange. Adolescents and others, for instance, refer to this plane of knowing as vibes or feeling the vibrations. What, of course, is being depicted is a process of connecting to, and becoming aware of the frequency of the energy in the person's immediate environment. Intuition is also referred to as a gut feeling whereby the answer comes to us directly through our body part and not first in our brain. Our Western language limits our appreciation of the vibrational reality and we would generally describe the vibes as good or bad. Imagine, if you will, the increased human capability that would accompany the culture firmly accepting the reality of 'vibes' and intuition, creating more definitive language to interpret those experiences, and training people to access and utilize their intuitive power. Youth, for example, could be taught to access their intuitive awareness when in the midst of a developing negative situation and provided with behavioral skills of disengagement. Intuition is a byway to the spiritual dimension (NTU) and its affirmation and utilization would assist in preventive health and can be used in innumerable ways in the therapeutic encounter.

Central to our understanding of energy and its utilization from a psychotherapeutic perspective is knowing that energy emanates from the spiritual plane of existence and moves through the mental plane, then emotional, and lastly the physical (Stein, 1990). When the disease has symptomatically arisen on the physical level, we have had previous inner communication to alert us to a developing problem. Relevant questions are: Were we listening? What and how did we respond to the information presented? From an African-centered world view, human beings are multidimensional beings; we are more than flesh and bones, cells and proteins, we are in dynamic equilibrium with a universe of energy and light and we are composed of the "stuff" of the universe. It is this stuff, or the spirit-energy/ NTU, that provides both the power and the direction for healing.

NTU Approach to Healing

Let us first look at how the Akan people of West Africa approach healing in the larger world of medicine and health. Unlike Western technological medicine, which considers disease to be the result of outside agents such as microbes or impersonal biological processes, Akan medicine considers disease a state of disharmony in the whole body and even in the whole society. The Akan's recognition of the multiple factors causing disease is an asset in the treatment by traditional means. Etiological factors identified in the somatic, psychic, constitutional, and genetic makeup, as well as in the social and cultural environment, argue very strongly for the comprehensive approach, traditionally implored. Modern medicine's tendency is to isolate the patient. Since in the Akan view illness is derived from a sick or broken society, the community becomes the point of departure for individual diagnosis and treatment. To gain total health, participation of the family, clan group, or even the whole community is required. The healing sanctuaries and shrines of traditional Akan medical practitioners provide adequate room for the kin group to participate-in diagnosis, prognosis, and treatment. The healer, patient, and the patient's family make a unanimous decision for the healing of the patient. The group is involved at every stage. From the Akan culture springs the emphasis on wholism, family, community, and spirituality as anchoring principles of health and healing. These principles are integral to NTU psychotherapy, which revitalizes African cultural symbols, images, beliefs and values into a modern spiritual-intuitive philosophy and therapeutic approach. The spiritual-intuitive approach of NTU does not discard the rational-logical scientific world view but rather seeks to reintegrate the spiritual into consciousness and health, and establish harmony and balance with the rational-logical scientific world.

NTU psychotherapy, further, accepts and responds to the challenge of African-centered theorists such as Dr. John Bolling, Dr. Naim Akbar, Dr. Wade Nobles, and Dr. Linda Jones Meyer to return to the Center and have respect for the role of the soul in the health/healing process. In this new era of reintegration, therapists/healers of African descent must become more aware of the role of the soul as a vehicle of ethics, morals, and values in the therapeutic process (Bolling, 1986). Understanding this influence on the outcome of the healing process is critical as we must resist non-congruent Western cultural images, symbols, ethics, morals and aesthetic considerations. NTU therapy looks to create a healing model that arises from the cultural being and essence of persons of African descent.

NTU therapy is consistent with the African belief that the soul or inner self is the primary energy and ultimate healer. Healing comes from within and provides direction for mental and physical healing. When there is alignment of the inner spiritual law with the mind/body, the person/organism is engaged in the healing process. The more each of us is impelled by the intuitive, or rely upon the soul force within, the greater, deeper and more constructive may be the outcome. As Dr. Bolling states, "A heightening of awareness of the correct values and ethical considerations are necessary first to wake the healing energies of the inner self." NTU therapy facilitates this process through the exposure of clients to the Nguzo Saba principles and to the principles of MAAT (Truth, Justice, Balance, Harmony, Order, and Righteousness).

The inner self is also represented as a composite of the concepts of unconscious, preconscious and paraconscious and its energy is ever available to us. At all times the inner self, or soul, is connected to, informed by, and given great assistance and guidance from the invisible spirit world of the ancestors and Orishas [Orishas are forces of the soul, similar to the archetypes of Carl Jung and serve as the bridges between the human and non-human worlds and between the invisible and the visible world (Bolling, 1986)]. The ever presence of the ancestral energy is made conscious through the African ritual of libation among other processes. Libation, briefly, is conducted through the pouring of liquid into the earth for circular connectedness and accompanied by the calling forth of the names of family and historical ancestors. The libation ritual is prominently used in NTU Psychotherapy within group processes for centering, empowering, and healing purposes.

NTU Psychotherapy organizes its approach to healing around four basic principles that incorporate the African centered philosophy of health, life, spirituality and energy (Cherry, 1994; Foster & Phillips, 1993; Phillips, 1990). The four principles are: Harmony, Balance, Authenticity, and Interconnectedness. These principles are essentially the dimensions of how a person, or a family's life energy should manifest for optimal health. That is, a measure of the quality of one's relationships to the ultimate vitalizing life force is the assessment of the direction and quality of their energy along the four principles of NTU. For example, is one's energy in harmony? Is the energy balanced? Is the person's energy clear and authentically flowing from their essence? We will explain each of these principles of healing and their assessment and therapeutic implications in the following sections. On your review of these principles, you are encouraged to acknowledge them as circular rather than from a linear logic perspective. The NTU principles are tantamount to viewing the energy from a different vantage point as opposed to seeing a different energy; therefore, there is significant overlap in the context of each principal with the other.

Harmony

The African concept of natural order implies that our life energy should be characteristically purposeful, orderly and in tune within our internal and external environment. As our energy comes more attuned with natural order spirit-energy, healing and health become more of a natural process. Within the African principles of the extended family and community it is vitally important to sustain right relationships with our family and our community since relationships are the vessels of spirit-energy. Harmony is both cooperative and integrative. It is cooperative in that harmony is reciprocal in energy exchange and the bodymind must adjust itself to appropriately, and positively connect, to the ongoing environment (Note: The other NTU principles provide balance to this concept as previously stated). Harmony is integrative in that a healthy bodymind seeks to become one with the environment and integrates the ongoing experience inside its being and essence. When the bodymind is in optimum harmony, the energy flows in, among, and between the environment peacefully and energetically. The individual, group, family, or community is increasingly empowered since the energy available is maximized. When the organism/client is in disharmony, then there is a disconnect between and among internal and external systems and the energy is thwarted, misdirected and unstable. There is a need to restore *wholeness* and *integrity* to the bodymind to receive healthy balance. The right relationship of a person to the environment is one of synchronous rhythm in which the integrity of the relationship is whole yet free flowing. When an organism is in functional, if not optimal, harmony there is a confluence and congruence of energy that allows for peak attunement of the bodymind capacity to access information from, and be responsive to, the environment. One *sees* better both physically and psychologically. That is, a person is better able to see the whole picture and experience the connections and togetherness of the ongoing experience whether that *seeing* is of an athlete "seeing the whole court," a business person "seeing the whole deal," or a therapist "seeing the whole system." Seeing makes a person happiest as the experience of things together is wholesome and joyful. Witness the experience of positive, harmonious family time during holiday periods or the experience of communities that come together to manage a natural or human disaster. Being at one accord is rhythmic and has a particular energy frequency not unlike the experience of listening to a singing group, a band, or an orchestra which achieves musical harmony. The experience of harmony is also the felt experience of being in love. Studies have demonstrated, for instance, that when two people are in love, there is more synchronism between the rhythm of their heart beats. The emotional and physical state of love has a spiritual quality and a heightened exchange of positive energy which is both cause and effect of the deepening harmony.

The perspective of the direction and degree of energy and harmony within and among the bodymind provides clear and fruitful clinical assessment information as well as opportunity for insightful intervention. This idea is expanded upon in the section on NTU therapeutic processes.

Balance

The NTU principle of balance is essentially the equilibrium of opposites from an African-centered perspective, that is, there are no absolute realities and everything is, to some degree, a matter of perspective. Similarly, balance illustrates that the polarities of life are not absolute, detached existences but rather are relative. Inherently connected positions that are dependent on each other for meaning and also represent points an a circular continuum. For example, the opposite ends of a magnet need each other for their power or electrical charge; the concept of day needs the concept of night; good needs evil, etc. Clinically, balance is a concept that suggests that we had a continuous need to mediate the seemingly conflicting or opposing forces of life. Balance suggests a centering of the spirit and energy in the manner that Chinese healers use acupuncture to balance the positive and negative energy in the body. As Chopra has stated, "When you quietly acknowledge the exquisite coexistence of opposites, you align yourself with the world of energy— the material non-stuff that is the source of the material world. This world of energy is fluid, dynamic, resilient, changing, forever in motion. And yet it is also non-changing, still quiet, eternal and silent."

When an organism is not in balance, it oscillates at a different or less-harmonic frequency. Since we each have a biofield (energy field) which surrounds and penetrates the physical body, a person, particularly a NTU therapist skilled in energy work, can knowingly and directly experience the unstable energy of another person (client) which provides invaluable assessment information. Since energy is not bounded by the physical skin we are always in contact with the biofield or vibrations of others. The questions become: to what extent are we aware of the influence of this energy on us; and, what do we do when we have become aware? NTU therapy encourages awareness of one's energy qualitatively and facilitates an inner search for processes that are contributing to the energy imbalance. The next step, of course, is a healthy rebalancing of the energy. This step is called Realignment in the NTU therapeutic process.

Interconnectedness

Human beings are more than flesh and bones, cells and protein: Rather, we are composed of the same stuff of the universe and are in dynamic equilibrium with a universe of energy. We are connected to all life and from an African world view, connected across time and space in the spirit world. This interconnectedness and healing are sustained through the vessels of healthy relationships, relationships that are congruent with the principles of MAAT (Truth, Justice, Order, Righteous, and Balance). Relationships are the part of the axiology of the African culture and truth is entrusted to relationships as exemplified by the emphasis on oral history in the African tradition. Further, good mental health in the African community is enhanced or diminished through the quality of one's relationship with the community. Relationships allow us to experience interconnectedness as a mutual dependency, a unity or oneness. It allows and facilitates sensitivity to others and to the larger environment. When interconnectedness is experienced more intensely it is called love. Love has regenerative powers and sustains and enhances spirit-energy. When the concept is used more generically, love can also represent the connectedness between all of life.

In the clinical relationship, there is critical bond between the clinician/healer and the person that reveals themself to you. This bond becomes increasingly sacred as the relationship generates the spirit-energy necessary for healing. Understanding this sacredness provides the mutual protection that both the therapist/healer and the client needs for harmony, balance, and integration. Appreciating the sacredness of the relationship allows the therapist to maximize their connection to client energy, but also will serve as a internal guide for therapeutic direction and boundaries.

Authenticity

Authenticity corresponds to the MAAT principle of truth in the sense of a genuiness of a person's spirit-energy. For similar reasons already stated, relationships are the vessels of spirit-energy and truth and necessitate the authentic representation of the bodymind spirit-energy for harmony, balance, and interconnectedness. It is the relationship that we build within the larger family/community that defines the quality of our being. Projecting ourselves in truth is a key component of that task. When we are authentic, the spirit-energy is clear and crisp. We are aware of our needs and wants and have increased ability to communicate those needs and wants without psychological interference. We are more creative and spontaneous when we exist and project from an authentic inner core. The organism functions from a place of integrity since it is sharing and receiving honestly and openly. The bodymind is trusting the spirit-energy for guidance and protection and not sustaining dysfunctional barriers to health and optimal living.

When a person is authentic they are "for real" and their genuineness of their energy is felt by those around them. They are sincere and trusting yet aware of potential harmful energy that is transgressing into their biosphere and better able to disarm the threat through insightful response. Authentic energy is self-directed (Kuji Chagulia) yet appropriately loving and accepting of others. It is sustained through the balancing mechanism of continuous self awareness and openness to feedback from others. It is achieved through a process of self-knowledge, self-acceptance, and self-actualization. Authenticity is the process of being real through accessing your inner self and following through with integrity. It is the process of being true to your self. Things (life) can often go wrong when we do violence to ourselves by not being either self-aware or true to self.

Role of the NTU Therapist

The goal of NTU psychotherapy is to restore harmony, balance, interconnectedness, and authenticity to the bodymind in order to facilitate the internal healing spirit-energy. Succinctly, the role of the NTU therapist in this process is that of a spiritual guide assisting the organism or collective to become aware of, and stimulate their self-healing mechanism. In order to accomplish this task the therapist must:

1. Be in harmony with the spirit-energy of the client system;
2. Be aware of their own energy and balance;
3. Stay centered in the interconnected time and space of the healing
     relationship; and
4. Experience authentic love for the client system.

To the extent that the therapist/healer is in harmonious relation to the spirit-energy of the client system, they become able to access and experience the imbalanced energy in a manner deeper than the verbal communications. The healer is able to perceive the inconsistency or unauthentic quality of the client's bodymind and, with emphatic technique, intervene toward bringing the client into awareness of their own blocks to health. The healer, in the African tradition, heals through *inspiration,* creating the healing medicine through their own authentic energy. The healer inspires and energizes the client system through the infusion of positive healing energy within the framework of authentic human love. Inspiration stands in contrast to manipulation which is the use of negative energy. Manipulation is a most potent poison and potentially destroys people, plants and all life. Therapy is a search for the true self, the natural self, and the therapist/healer empowers the true self of the client's bodymind to reveal itself and follow it's natural course. It is imperative to avoid force, deception, and manipulation in the healing relationship. Instead, the NTU therapist relies on inspiration to do the work of the spirit. The therapist engages the client with rituals of cooperation (inspiration), not rituals of competition (manipulation).

Again, in the African tradition, the NTU therapist/healer counters the despair of the client by giving them hope which liberates the soul. The therapist works to purge the falsehoods out of the abused self of the client bodymind, flushing out the poisons from the body and soul. This process allows for the client to regain contact with the true self and to rediscover their authentic self. It allows for the unfolding of the NTU healing spirit-energy.

The NTU therapist understands that evil exists only with your consent; that diseases need a receptive host to thrive and that unity creates and division destroys. It is further understood that evil (disease) borrows on a person's strength and that the client system can deny it strength through awareness and positive energy. The healer assists the client system to synthesize all their scattered energies thereby empowering the bodymind. The therapist's work, then, is one of seeing, hearing, and knowing the spirit-energy of the client system bodymind and helping with the awareness, realignment, and integration process. The spiritual and healthy functioning therapist develops a shadow i.e., when the therapist develops their spiritual abilities to see and hear the energy around them, that knowledge follows them. In order to do this work, the NTU healer must be prepared to see and hear at the spirit-energy level and this mandates authenticity and a continuous process of self-awareness, rebalancing, and personal growth.

NTU Phases and Techniques

The phases of the NTU Psychotherapy have been more robustly articulated in a previous article (see Phillips, 1990) and will only be summarized herein. In addition, the reader is directed to a matrix of NTU phases and techniques developed by Dr. Pamela Foster and Dr. Frederick Phillips at the Progressive Life Center in Washington, D. C. that appears on the following pages (see Table 1).

The initial phase of NTU therapy is *Harmony,* defined as the developing coherence or compatibility between therapist/healer and client system such that the therapist is experienced as a positive extension of the client system. In this phase, the major task of the healer is to experience the spirit-energy of the client system and to develop a healing anchor for the troubled energy of the client biosphere. From the client's perspective, they would want to feel good while being in the therapist's energy. The client should feel an increasing comfort and personal security that would allow them to deepen their sharing of barriers to healing. This phase, (harmony) although being the primary focus of the initial component of NTU therapy, is manifested throughout the entire healing relationship albeit at lesser intense levels. Since the therapist, at this point, knows little about the client system in terms of information, it is the therapist heightened ability to see with his/hers spirit-energy eyes that will guide him/her to a successful conclusion of this phase. As a matter of fact, in some ways it is disadvantageous for the healer to have information on the client system because those "facts" tend to orient the therapist's perception in a particular manner thereby placing the harmony phase within a prescribed contact. While soliciting information is certainly indicated, it is more a

Table 1

NTU Psychotherapy: Phases and Techniques

PHASE	DEFINITION	MANIFESTATION	OUTCOMES	TECHNIQUES
HARMONY	A developing coherence or compatibility between therapist and client system such that the therapist is experienced as a positive extension of client system.	Shared essence, belonging, nurturance, love, interdependence, developing trust, relation.	Shared consciousness, therapist joins with system, Therapeutic Bridge.	Being real/authenticity, Selfdisclosure, Use of Rituals, Acceptance of where client is, Therapist composure and relaxation, Accentuation of the positive in all components of the client system.
AWARENESS	Having or showing realization, perception or knowledge of self and of self in relation to others. *Cognitive awareness* of issues allows a sensitivity to the "facts" and the definable aspects of a situation, and makes available a process for defining or knowing reality. *Affective awareness* of issues allows a sensitivity to the subjective aspects or feeling generated by a situation or experience.	Differentiation between thoughts and feelings; process vs. content focused, clarify discrepancy between reality and expectation, acknowledgment, ownership and respect for feelings. Developing feeling of NTU energy.	Identification and expression of thoughts and feelings. Clarification of significant factors which influence functioning.	Reframing, Relabeling, Visualization techniques, Use of I statements, Talking directly, Awareness wheel, Feedback of thoughts and feelings, Present centered, empty chair, self-awareness.
ALIGNMENT	The synergism of beings and of beings; material and psychic forces toward a central point of existence. The adjustment or arrangement of people and/or things in relation to each other so that healing force (NTU) becomes operative.	The sharing of feelings and experiences, introspection, role, clarification, corrective, recapitulation, catharsis, interconnectedness, restoration, and revitalization. The experience of NTU, appropriate responsibility for self and for system.	Restructured client system, reinforcement and emphasis of indigenous strengths. New energy available to client system.	Peel the onion, Exploration of worse fear, own projections, Confront fear, Accept responsibility, share self; take risks.
ACTUALIZATION	The materialization of potential. Utilization of new attitudes and behavior in a system's life space.	Identification of goals, tasks, roles, behaviors, process and resources. Behavior change.	Increased confidence, re: problem-solving abilities.	Practice new behavior record new establish tasks/ objectives, Homework assignment.
SYNTHESIS	The balancing integration and appropriate use of all functional resources available to the system; spiritual, psychic and material. The delineation and availability of a problem-solving process indigenous to the client system.	Realistic expectations and goal setting, personalization of the problem solving process, system stability and flexibility, proactive involvement and investment in systemic well-being.	Need fulfillment, empowerment, reciprocal nurturing, authentic, supportive relationship, a unified resilient and self-correcting system. The absorption of the NTU Force throughout the system.	How have you responded differently to life situations? Q. What do others say about you? How do you resolve stressful situations? Q. What is your process for psychological problem-solving.

function of the needs of an information driven society than it is by the need to achieve harmony. Within a traditional African healing context, for example, the healer has the mentally ill person spend the day with him for the expressed purpose of observing his spirit as the patient interacts with others. Harmony, and diagnosis, can be achieved with little reliance on information as such. Rather, the healer/ therapist utilizes their spiritual sense, their intuitive sense, to access and connect to the energy field of the client and develops an initial hypothesis. During this phase the therapist's flexibility is key since the patterns of the client's needs are unknown to them and the particular expression of the client's need may require an unplanned deviation from their agenda. At this point, the client system is attempting to "feel" the authenticity of the healer energy so that they can determine the expected quality of the developing healing relationship. How much can we trust? And is this going to be real experience, are the primary underlying client questions of the harmony phase.

The second phase of NTU therapy/healing is *awareness* whereby the focus is on developing self knowledge and knowledge of the self in relation to others. The self knowledge is ultimately a developing awareness of the blocks or barriers that the client system has created and sustained that is preventing the natural healing process from becoming operative. What are the thoughts and feelings that we are generating that are in conflict with the natural rhythm of our healing energy is the predominate quest of the awareness phase. Another way to view the same objective is assisting the client system to take responsibility for the production of their thoughts, feelings, and behaviors. What, for example, is the psychological gain that the client derives from thinking a certain thought, feeling a certain emotion, performing a certain behavior? These, and other interventions, have as their primary objective facilitating the client's awareness of their own energy patterns and the impact of their energy on others and vice versa. Is the client's energy congruent with their verbal statements? If not, why not? Or if not, is the client aware of the inconsistency. Through various techniques, and a focus on the spirit-energy of the client system, the healer therapist can effectively guide the client system through deepening levels of self awareness of their blocks to healing.

The *Alignment* phase is the reintegration process of healthy thoughts and feelings that impels the healing NTU force throughout the bodymind experience. It is the phase where the psychological impasses are "worked through" so that available energy is released within the client system. It is the phase of cleansing, self renewal, and regeneration. We have walked through the darkness and into the light; we have faced the psychological fears/anxieties that have immobilized us and integrated their energy into our being. We are more whole as we have reincorporated our previously disparate parts; we are empowered.

Normally, the major task of the alignment phase is the reconciliation of our fears and anxiety whether either stated as fears, or can'ts, or should's. It can be a fear of letting go, a distrust of self ability, a fear of intimacy or a fear of losing control. Invariably there is an energy of fear/anxiety that is sustaining the block of the healing energy although the fears may be covered in different terms and occur on multiple levels. The healer's role, therefore, is to guide the client system to reclaim the energy that is being misdirected by the anxiety since it is that misdirected energy that is creating the system disharmony and imbalance and promoting the disease of the bodymind.

The NTU phase of *Actualization* refers to the building process of realizing one's potential through the initiation of new behavior. The emphasis here is on behavior and the process of experimenting with the new behavior that has arisen from the release of the NTU healing energy. The act of behaving differently in one's life space will necessarily influence the life space of those with whom the client is in contact thereby inviting a qualitatively or quantitatively different response. While the external environment, whether family members, work colleagues, or others may react in various ways along the continuum of healthy (supportive) through unhealthy (manipulative) behaviors, it is the healing client system that needs to remain centered and anchored in their unfolding new alignment. New awareness may, and often does, occur during this phase since the client energy system has shifted thereby allowing the client to see their environment and relationships from a different and hopefully, healthier perspective.

The final NTU phase of healing is *Synthesis* which a more advanced and complete reintegration of the client's spiritual and psychic energy. The key outcome of this phase is that the person or client system has an overall healthier process that will enable them to reconcile their future life stresses into opportunities for personal growth. Assuring that the client system has a healthy process to rebalance their energy or keep themselves communicating authentically are areas of inquiry during this phase. The client system not only has resolved the initial presenting problems but also has a process and direction for healthy living.

Case Example

OT, a 42-year-old African male, was referred by his Employee Assistance officer. His presenting symptoms included a long history of compulsive and irresponsible behavior. OT would, for example, stop off from work to visit friends, not call his girlfriend, and stay out late sometimes overnight. Both he and his fiancee agreed that there was no suspicion of infidelity just failure to communicate even though OT understood intellectually the need to communicate. Further, OT had mild to moderate problems with following through on commitments and decisions and at times, was untruthful. Related to the above behaviors was his tendency to spend large sums of money usually gambling. Otherwise, OT was viewed as friendly, intelligent, warm, and caring. OT described his behavior as compulsive, sometimes, and irresponsible. He stated that he didn't understand me because this is not how he wanted to be and he "knew better." He was motivated to address these issues at present because he didn't want to lose his current relationship and stated that truthfulness and respectable behavior is what his fiancee demanded. OT stated he initially experienced symptoms in 1968 as a Vietnam era veteran. He was raised on a country farm; his parents separated at age 3; and he had an older sister that he never really new. OT thought that, "I had a happy childhood," but he always carried with him the question of why his parents divorced. He further wondered why his mother kept him so close to her and away from his sister. His mother had since died.

His father was still alive but suffering from Alzheimer's Disease, and he was suspicious that his sister was manipulating the father and the estate. OT had been married twice and was presently engaged. His first marriage ended with a spat of violence culminating with his wife stabbing him in the throat while he was asleep. He has a 15-year-old daughter from the second marriage and he describes the relationship with his daughter as good.

Diagnosis

From an NTU therapy framework Mr. OT was perceived along the following dimensions:

Harmony - OT was substantially disharmonious within himself and between his environment. His spirit energy was confused, conflicted and it was experienced as very disconnected by the therapist-healer. His sense of purpose, or NIA, was fragmented, diffused, and rather than providing a healthy anchor, was mostly a source of nagging frustration and anxiety. His energy was very agitated and did not flow freely; rather it was very disjointed. It was clear that OT was neither at peace with himself nor did he feel a sense of wholeness.

Balance - OT was extremely off-center and this was experienced as very unstable energy by the therapist. His behavioral pattern of engaging in sustained play activities such as visiting a friend and staying all night was a clear example of a life imbalance. Relative to his roles as husband, father, worker, friend, etc., OT was able to articulate, albeit just intellectually, his recognition of his spirit imbalance and was aware, further, that this signified a major problem. He also self described that he didn't have sufficient control over his behaviors, thus his explanation (in reality, an excuse) for his imbalanced actions and decisions.

Interconnectness - OT's spirit energy was classically conflictual in that it would alternatively attract and repel. His energy was very engaging at the surface level and then his energy would function to thwart developing emotional closeness on the deeper level of authentic relationships. This unhealthy interactive pattern was equally evident in both his male as well as his female relationships. For example, OT experienced significant difficulty in sharing negative feedback with male colleagues which contributed to his difficulty with extracting himself from unhealthy situations. OT's spirit-energy was experienced by the therapist-healer as an energy that was seeking connectedness though fearful of finding it.

Authenticity - Related to Mr. OT's global difficulty with personal relationships was his relative inauthenticity within those and other relationships. Though his energy was usually vibrant and engaging it would become forced and strained especially when he himself became the subject of inquiry. OT's diminished authenticity suggested a fundamental fear or avoidance as it usually does diagnostically. He was unable to access his true self and, behaviorally, always looked for convenient escape routes rather than risk movement toward being in tune with his genuine self.

The initial phase of NTU, *harmony*, was rapidly established in great part through the continuous reinforcement by the therapist of OT's inherent desire to address and correct his behavior and, his inner power that would guide him through the conflict that was blocking his healing energy. The therapist conveyed an authentic belief that OT ultimately wanted to change his behavior and that, perhaps more importantly, he had the power to do so. OT was told that the role of the therapist healer was to guide him through his own unique healing process and to provide verbal and emotional sustenance through the difficult points and times along his path. The challenges to establishing harmony included the widespread African American male protective attitude that guards against the vulnerability of personal sharing and emotional exposure and therefore interprets external assistance as intrusive. The therapist-healer deepened the developing coherence by sharing his own Vietnam era military experiences, consequent moral and cultural conflict, and residual emotions.

As the *awareness* phase of the NTU therapy process developed, O.T. became cognizant of his own emotional themes of alienation; insecurity; embarrassment; feelings of inadequacy; and anger feelings toward his father and sister. From the NTU paradigm, OT experienced the pain of his spiritual disconnectedness that had been prevalent since childhood. The therapeutic relationship between the healer and OT was itself used as the stage for the acknowledgment of and confirmation of OT's spirit-energy, and through the NTU process OT became increasingly cognizant of the quality of his spirit-energy and more authentic in his communication. The therapist, for instance, would ask OT at the beginning of each session, and also at appropriate intervals during a session, to reflect on the quality of his spirit energy by simply asking him, "How is your spirit today," or, "Describe your energy at this moment." The mere focus of the question encouraged and allowed OT to be within himself and to contact his inner self or inner voice.

As OT became more aware of his own energy he increased his ability to discriminate between authentic responses and fictitious responses and, perhaps even more importantly, he developed an increased disdain for non-authentic responses. In other words, it felt better to OT to be truthful, honest and authentic within himself and in his communication to the healer and that positive feeling was labeled by the healer to be the NTU healing energy. Through the principle of authenticity and its healing powers, OT became increasingly aware of the connectedness of prior events in his early life and, thereupon, was able to uncover the meaning of those events as they related to his present spirit energy impasse. The synthesis of authenticity and connectedness provided him a real life platform in which to understand the essence of his troubled energy. Specifically, he was able to see the impact on him of his family house burning down at age 11; his loss of all his material belongings; the significance of its occurrence on Christmas Eve; and his running out of the house into the snow only clad in his underwear. More meaningful than the facts of this event was the connection OT made to his spirit within those events so that through the experiencing of that dynamic process he was able to become more aware and reintegrate his splintered energy. With the developing awareness of his authentic spirit energy within each event, OT was able to integrate the available NTU energy into his being thereby becoming healthier and having more energy to more fully negotiate the next unresolved issue. In the house fire, for example, OT became more empowered through reorganizing and accepting that it was his unresolved anger energy at the manner in which his father responded to him after the fire, rather than the trauma of the fire itself that was the critical impasse. Similarly it was the acknowledgment of the reaction of his spirit-energy to his father's "boring existence" rather than the denial of any feelings that allowed OT more energy for his own healing. OT's connection with his spirit energy's intuition that there had been an incestuous relationship between his father and his sister (with the aftermath result being a fractured family of two dyads; the mother and OT being one pair, and the father and OT's sister being the other) was an important point in the treatment. An awareness technique of re-creating the past in the present experience by using verbs that are present centered ("I am *saying* to my dad..." rather than "I *said* to my dad...") was used. This awareness technique utilized prominently in gestalt therapy manifests that time and consciousness is a continuous dynamic and we can easily connect to the so-called past because all experience is a present experience. When we acknowledge past experiences in the present as OT did, then we are able, as he was, to experience the critical moment fully with the richness of the emotions of the spirit energy that existed within that event.

As the NTU healing process transitioned more into the **Alignment** phase OT had indeed become increasingly and authentically aware of his spirit energy in relationship to his sister and father but had not, as yet, dissolved his impasses between them. He was therefore still operating from blocked or fragmented energy; he was not at peace. His anger energy toward his father had been identified and acknowledged but not reconciled nor in alignment. The primary technique that was used to facilitate realignment of OT's spirit energy was a visualization experience with an ancestor. OT was assisted to achieve a relaxed mental and physical state through a deep breathing method while listening to an African rhythm relaxation tape. As OT was experiencing the pleasantness of his relaxed state, he was guided into three images. First, he was assisted to connect to an image of himself as a younger child; second he was guided to see and feel the spirit energy of one of his ancestors coming into contact with his own energy; and third, it was suggested to OT that the ancestor knew of the source of his troubled energy and that they would share with OT what they wanted for him and also provide a path for him to seek peace. When OT returned from this spiritual experience, he was tearful yet relieved. He had experienced the spirit-energy of his grandmother with his mother behind her. According to OT, his grandmother in a calm and reassuring manner said to him,

"Let it go, we'll take care of her." OT felt a tremendous relief and stated that it was a most powerful, real, and full experience. Through the incorporation of his grandmother's spirit-energy into his being, he became more enlightened, powerful, and healthy. The impasse was dissolved for him.

OT was presented with an immediate opportunity to *actualize* his realigned spirit energy as he interacted with a number of his family members over the next two weeks. He reported that now his relatives had, "...begun to come over to his side," as they discussed both the immediacy of his father's future and the relationship with OT's sister. He reported that he began to have more substantive and healthy 'talks' with his other family members and with his own daughter. Overall OT stated that he felt that, "...a burden has been lifted," after he made the decision to "let go" and he felt as though he was on track. OT demonstrated the *Synthesis* phase of NTU psychotherapy when, at a later time, a crisis developed within his part-time business, a business which he ruminated had excellent upside potential but one in which there were always nagging problems. The crisis (opportunity) occurred when his business partner stated to OT that he wanted to "drop out" whereupon OT was then faced with the critical decision of where he was going with the business, whether he was going to continue, or whether he was going to drop out also. OT engaged in a clean and healthy process of personal and business reevaluation, he communicated effectively with his ex-partner on the termination issues associated with his departure from the business; and he initiated a process to both refocus and restructure the business into a healthier operation.

Summary

Traditional African philosophy is anchored by the concept of spirituality, herein defined as a measure of the quality of one's relationship to the ultimate vitalizing life force energy. This life force which is manifested as both energy and matter is known to the Bantu people of Central Africa as NTU and discussed by Western scientists as a particle (substance) or a wave (force) depending on the object's interaction with the observer. African philosophy has a singular appreciation of the harmony of life which also undergirds the NTU perspective of force and matter, body and mind, being an integrated whole. This force/matter, known in NTU as spirit-energy, becomes the operational framework through which the therapist-healer both understands and facilitates the healing process. The diagnostic constellations of NTU are: Harmony, Balance, Authenticity, and Interconnectedness. The major circular phases of NTU Therapy are: Harmony, Awareness, Alignment, Actualization, and Synthesis. The goal of NTU psychotherapy is to assist the client system in realignment of their spirit-energy toward a more authentic and healthier process of being within the principals of Nguzo Saba and MAAT.

References

Ackerman, D. (1990). *A natural history of the senses.* New York: Random House.

Armah, A. (1978). *The healers.* Portsmouth, New Hampshire: Heinemann Educational Books LTD.

Bolling, J. (October, 4, 1986). *Ori: The personality/character soul and the practical inner healer.* Unpublished paper presented at the third Orisha Conference.

Brennan, B. (1988). *Hands of light.* New York: Banton Books.

Chopra, D. (1990). *Quantum healing.* New York: Bantam Books.

Dossey, L. (1991). *Meaning and medicine.* New York: Bantam Books.

Foster, P., Phillips, F., Belgrave, F. Z., Randolph, S. M., & Brarthwaite, N. (1993). An Afrocentric model for AIDS education, prevention, and psychological services within the African American community. *Journal of African-American Psychology, 19(2),* 123-141.

Gawain, S. (1986). *Living in the light.* San Rafael, CA: New World Library.

Gerber, R. (1988). *Vibrational medicine.* Sante Fe, NM: Bear and Co.

Hay, L. (1984). *You can heal your life.* Santa Monica, CA: Hay House, Inc..

Jaffe, D. (1986). *Healing from within.* New York: Simon and Schuster.

Jahn, J. (1961). *The new African culture.* New York: Grove Press.

Myers, L. J. (1988). *An Afrocentric world-view: Introduction to an optimal psychology.* Dubuque, IA: Quintal - Hunt.

Nobles, W. W. (1986). *African psychology: Towards its reclamation, reascension, and revitalization.* Oakland, CA: African-American Family Institute.

Nwosu, O. (1979). *The Indiangenous African culture.* Unpublished Paper.

Phillips, F. (1990). NTU Psychotherapy: An afrocentric approach. *Journal of African-American Psychology. 17,* (1) 215-222

Stein, D. (1990). *All Women are Healers.* Freedom, CA: The Crossing Press.

Author

Frederick B. Phillips
1123 11th Street, NW
Progressive Life Center
Washington, DC 20001
Telephone: (202) 842-4570
Fax: (202) 842-3510
Email: ntufred@aol.com

Upwardly Mobile African American Adults: Reflections on Rootedness, Psychotherapy and Identity

Arthur C . Jones

In recent years much has been accomplished with respect to our awareness of a need for a genuine psychology of African peoples, both in America and throughout the diaspora. However, those of us who are actively involved in clinical work with African Americans must ask ourselves what this new understanding has contributed concretely to the assessment and amelioration of emotional disorders in our clients. It is certainly true that awareness of race and culture as factors affecting the therapy and counseling situation is no longer considered novel. Still, the question arises whether there has been any substantial impact (beyond the theoretical stage) on the way daily clinical work with African Americans is actually conducted. Some time ago, Enrico Jones, addressing this very question, concluded:

> The appreciation of diversity has led to a greater realization of how culture generates among individual members specific behaviors consonant with the main cultural themes and how these behaviors are comprehensible only if one understands, and understands sympathetically, the ethnic culture. It has led us to accept that without the understanding of the cross-cultural framework of individual behaviors—whether sympathetic, attitudinal or treatment-related—change-oriented interventions with ethnic populations will be of limited effectiveness; and finally, it has fostered a greater sensitivity to the role that values play in the study of ethnic people. . . . All well and good. *But how has our acknowledgment of cultural differences helped to guide our conduct of psychotherapy with the Black patient? So far, I think, very little.* (1984, p. 63, emphasis added).

My own observations have led me to conclude that much of what Enrico Jones wrote in 1984 still remains accurate, for both African American clinicians and clinicians from other ethnic backgrounds. It has been difficult for many in the clinical arena to take the leap beyond elaborate theories of Afrocentricity and African American psychology to the development of concrete clinical interventions that apply those interesting, but difficult to concretize, theoretical ideas. One factor which I believe has impeded our progress in the clinical arena is the prevalent assumption of cultural homogeneity in much of the African American psychology literature (A. C. Jones, 1985; E. E. Jones, 1984). Within this misdirected focus, the question asked is how to understand or treat *the* African American client. This question, of course, has no useful answers and necessarily leads to vague, trite generalities that have little practical utility in daily clinical work. The relevant focus, of course, is how to treat *this* African American person, with *this* particular set of values, living in *this* current situation, asking for help with *this* particular problem. When clinical material is approached in this way, significant and sophisticated work becomes possible. In the absence of any such specific focus in much of the clinical literature concerning African Americans, it is not surprising that clinicians are at a loss when it comes to the practical application of their newly acquired knowledge about ethnic issues. Fortunately, there are at least the beginnings of such a specific focus in some of the recent writings addressed to African American psychology and psychotherapy (e.g., Boyd-Franklin, 1989; Jackson & Westmoreland, 1992; Tatum, 1987). Clearly, much more remains to be accomplished with respect to identifying *specific* situations in which African American psychological theory can be applied clinically.

One specific group of African Americans has been seen with increasing frequency in clinical settings around the country: upwardly mobile, middle-class adults who are successful (often highly successful) professionally but nevertheless emotionally distressed. These adults, along with their sometimes equally distressed children (A. C. Jones, 1992) often present with psychological concerns in which cultural and ethnic factors are especially prominent. In order to reflect on some of the issues affecting this *specific* group of clients, it will be helpful to review a scenario reflecting a typical initial psychotherapy session. Following that review, and some further discussion of the kinds of concerns these clients bring into therapy, I'd like to draw on some examples of fictional and autobiographical writings by prominent African American authors to discuss some of the specific cultural and psychological issues I believe are important in understanding more clearly the lives of the clients who come from this particular segment of our community. My hope is that these reflections will be helpful in our collective attempt to develop specifically effective clinical strategies for work with these clients.

A Group of "Successful" Psychological Casualties

Many of us who work in psychotherapy practices have been struck with the startlingly increasing frequency of economically and professionally successful African Americans whose psychological symptoms are, in effect, a byproduct of their "success" (A. C. Jones, 1992). In many cases, their malaise is vaguely defined but nonetheless sufficiently intense to prompt them to seek professional help. At the core of many of these clients' difficulties is the inability to retain a sense of personal integrity while pursuing a track of professional success. In some cases, their inner discontent is avoided while they focus instead of the psychological problems they perceive their children to be experiencing. In fact, some of these adults are unaware of any significant problem in their own lives except their children's unhappiness (A. C. Jones, 1992). However, many are subjectively distressed and seek help for themselves independent of concerns about other members of their families.

In many typical cases, a woman or man has become singularly invested in a quest for success and power, frequently as a result of new opportunities which have finally become available in the wake of the civil rights and Black power movements of the 1960's and 1970's. Astutely aware that the persistence of racism renders such opportunities painfully precarious, many of these women and men have adopted a strategy of neglecting other areas of their lives in the interest of establishing professional and economic security for themselves and their families. For many, such a one-sided focus is adaptive, as they are able to maintain clear sight of the continuing realities of racism and are able as well to return to other life tasks once they have achieved some semblance of security. However, many others have either lost sight of the continuing influence of societal oppression or have become obsessed with professional achievement to the exclusion of other personal and family needs. In either case, their paths towards success have been accompanied, ultimately, by a sense of disillusionment and emptiness. An example is B, a 35-year-old executive with a small corporation who had attained a position of vice-president within the company. He came for help because he felt depressed and unhappy in his marriage and felt he was "missing" something:

Therapist: What brings you here? What is it that I can help you with?

B: I don't know exactly. I'm unhappy . . . no, not really . . . well, I really am unhappy, although I shouldn't be.

Therapist: Wow, there's a lot going on there. You're unhappy, but you shouldn't be?

B: I know that sounds confusing . . . I just know that I had always thought that what I wanted was to make it as an executive in this damn company I'm working for. Well, I finally made it, but now I don't care. I know that doesn't make any sense.

Therapist: There is obviously something which is preventing you from experiencing this promotion in the way you thought you would.

B: I don't know, Man, seems like you can never win. I spent so many years hoping and dreaming and working hard to be seen as not *just* a Black man . . . I just don't know if it was all worth it. I don't know what I'm saying. . . . I'm just tired.
. . .

B's predicament is similar to that of numerous other middle class African Americans who come for therapy. The system has opened up just enough to permit them the attainment of certain goals which would have been closed to African Americans just a generation ago. Yet, actual attainment of these goals leaves them confused, empty and angry. In part, of course, their experience is not unlike that of many Caucasian Americans who find that attainment of the American Dream leaves them still unsatisfied, forcing them to engage in a cycle of more and more material acquisition in an effort to satisfy their unmet personal needs (Wachtel, 1983). But for many African Americans, the problem goes even deeper. In the process of reaching for the American Dream, they have also sacrificed a large part of their souls. They don't feel connected in any meaningful sense to what they have been reaching for and they are uncertain that they can recover what they have given up. The Black power movement of the 60's and 70's provided a chance for many middle class African Americans to recover meaning in their lives. In undergoing a "Negro to Black conversion" (Hall, Cross, & Freedle, 1972), they reconnected with important aspects of their identities. However, for many of these individuals the metamorphosis was incomplete. Faced with the task of retaining their newly developed sense of identity while forging ahead to develop a niche in the larger society, they had difficulty sustaining their inner satisfaction.

An often unrecognized element in this problem is the general importance of ethnicity in the mental health of all people. The ability to feel part of a defined group with a proud history is an important but sometimes missing component of identity development. McGoldrick, in an important discussion of the clinical significance of ethnicity, underscores this point:

> Ethnicity describes a sense of commonality transmitted over generations by the family and reinforced by the surrounding community. It is more than race, religion, or national and geographic origin (which is not to minimize the significance of race or the special problems of racism). It involves conscious and unconscious processes that fulfill a *deep psychological need for identity and historical continuity* (1982, pp. 4-5, emphasis added).

For African Americans, the importance of ethnicity is heightened by the experience of racism. Ties to community and to ethnic history assume crucial roles in dealing with external stress. But for clients like B, the nature of the stress is the subtle but deadly demand that if one desires success, one must also downplay Blackness. This removes the important resource of ethnic rootedness as a buffer against the subtle daily insults of racism. Thus, despite the important social transformation which occurred in the 60's and 70's, many successful individuals in the 1980's and 1990's have become casualties; people who started out feeling that "Black is beautiful," but have ended up feeling mostly empty and angry. Ethnic rootedness has still further significance in African cultures, which stress the importance of ties to the community as a part of personal identity (Nobles, 1991a, 1991b). Thus, the key to the ability of African Americans to attain "success" without sacrifice of self is the maintenance of ongoing connections with family, community and history.

Essentials of a Productive Clinical Focus

There are many directions which a discussion of clinical work with any particular subpopulation of African Americans might take, and a number of writers have addressed issues of technique and approach with African American clients (Acosta et al., 1982; Boyd-Franklin, 1989; Jones & Block, 1984; Paster, 1985; Ridley, 1984; Shipp, 1983; Sue & Sue, 1990). However, an important issue, independent of technique, is the underlying orientation and value system which guides a particular piece of clinical work.

Jenkins (1982, 1985) has described how a humanistic approach or orientation is particularly effective in work with some African Americans. Core within this orientation is the concept of a person as an active, striving being who struggles to adopt ways of viewing the world which are most compatible with survival and growth. Within this framework, the choices which individuals make determine to a large extent the nature and effectiveness of particular adaptation styles. This frame of reference, it seems to me, is a good starting point for viewing psychological adaptation (Jones, 1985). In addition, the humanistic tradition includes the notion of psychological growth as a natural process, the importance of which can only be discovered if one removes impediments to natural growth. As Akbar (1977) has illustrated, this concept is also compatible with African cultural tradition which, in contrast to Western, mechanistic psychology, emphasizes natural growth, spontaneity and union with nature as important elements of human existence. If one listens carefully to many disgruntled middle class African American clients, it is just this spontaneity and "natural" living which appears missing in their lives.

An important question which arises in this context is how one goes about establishing the missing link in many clients' lives. Some clinicians (e.g., Jackson, 1983; Shipp, 1983), noting the communal nature of African American culture, have stressed the use of group and community foci in clinical work as a way to bolster natural growth. In many cases, such a focus may be important and may provide the basis for significant growth in some clients. However, the depth of the malaise which we often see clinically speaks to an inner imbalance which, it seems to me, requires working from within, to restore connections with one's inner self, which then in turn can result in productive connections with others in the community. Thus, in working with clients like B, a core part of the therapeutic work may include assistance in discovering within themselves the sense of direction which is missing in their lives.

Of course, the issue being discussed really concerns human potential, much of which has been obscured and distorted by the mechanistic, competitive emphasis of the behavioral and psychoanalytic schools of Western psychology (Akbar, 1977). This mechanistic emphasis often impedes the ability to help individuals who have lost touch with themselves and with their families and communities.

Striving and Rootedness: The Precarious Balance: Three Lives and Three Solutions

An analysis of three works by African American authors—two autobiographies and a novel—serves to illustrate the diversity of adaptation in achievement-oriented African Americans as well as the central importance of rootedness in finding satisfactory adaptation solutions. The three books—*A Man's Life*, by Roger Wilkins; *Brothers and Keepers*, by John Edgar Wideman; and *Praise Song for the Widow*, by Paule Marshall—all deal with striving, with dreams and hopes and with "success" in the lives of African Americans.

Roger Wilkins' (1982) autobiography is a readable account of Wilkins' persistent struggle for identity in the context of the highest levels of professional achievement. Roger Wilkins is the nephew of the late Roy Wilkins, Executive Secretary of the NAACP. Roger grew up in Kansas City, New York, and Grand Rapids, Michigan, and eventually came to have a distinguished career in law, government and journalism. With amazing candor and openness, Wilkins describes achieving success after success, yet becoming more and more despondent as time progressed. At several points in the book, he expresses his ambivalence: He was proud on the one hand of the many personal achievements and especially the powerful people with whom he worked and partied. On the other hand, he was aware of more and more distance from his Blackness as time progressed. Looking back, he was aware that this separation from his roots began in childhood. At age 12, when his family moved from New York's elite Sugar Hill community in Harlem, he was happy that he would no longer have to deal with bullying and harassment from envious Harlem street kids. Yet, he was still aware of a connection with these kids and this community, and experienced a certain sadness in his "escape":

> As I sat on that train, staring out the window hour after endless hour, sitting next to my grandmother, I felt glad that Harlem was behind me. But my relief had been purchased at a real and quite substantial cost. Though I was not again to know such terror, I had also, at the age of 12, moved beyond the last point in my life when I would feel totally at peace with my Blackness. (p. 33)

Later, he was to become a successful lawyer, Justice Department administrator, and Pulitzer Prize-winning journalist. But he was also to feel alienated and chronically discontent. During the Civil Rights Movement, he became the conscience of his colleagues in the federal government and provided the impetus for action in support of the movement. He also made friends with people whom he felt were loyal and supportive. However, these experiences failed to provide any sustained personal satisfaction. Wilkins became increasingly depressed and appeared to seek more power and prestige in his attempts to overcome his malaise. As time grew on, he became bitter and, the book hints, also developed a serious drinking problem. Painfully, he became more conscious of important parts of himself that were being sacrificed in the midst of his power seduction:

> Because I was viewed as the *different* and the high African American, I was afforded opportunities to socialize with the brass. But sometimes a transaction was expected to occur, even when my superiors were not conscious of it. In a subtle way, I was being told that I was different from the other African Americans who worked around the place. I was being told I was like the White people who owned or ran things. It was the gentlest seduction in the world because, by and large, they were all nice and enjoyable people to be with. Whether they knew it or not, I could see it . . . in the end, the Black has to give up a little bit of himself that is valuable or, at some point, there is a fight and he does indeed become a wretched ingrate in the eyes of the people who have feted him. (pp. 354-355)

Wilkins did in fact fight the fight he alluded to, in editorials, in arguments with colleagues, in his commitment to less fortunate African Americans. But he never seems to have found a way to regain that "little bit of himself." Towards the end of the book, he portrays his life as much improved and happy, with a new loving wife after two failed marriages. However, his attempt to persuade the reader is not convincing. One is left with the impression that Wilkins has lost in the difficult struggle to be successful in the larger society while maintaining his self-integrity. Ultimately, his power seduction seems to have prevented him from recovering his core self.

In some ways, John Wideman (1984) presents, in *Brothers and Keepers,* a more successful resolution of adaptation conflicts faced by high-achieving African Americans. Wideman, a former Rhodes Scholar, is a university professor and prize-winning novelist. *Brothers and Keepers* is a moving report of the dialogue between John Wideman and his younger brother, Robby, who, coming from the same family in the Homewood section of Pittsburgh, ended up with a life prison sentence for his role in a crime which ended in the killing of a man. In his dialogue with his brother, the elder Wideman also deals with parts of himself, seen through Robby. John Wideman's personal adaptation strategy is to establish distance, both geographically and psychologically, from the brutality of life for African American people in his hometown, while maintaining a psychological and spiritual connection through writing and home visits. However, one senses that his strategy has not worked as effectively as he would have liked and that he, like Wilkins, has lost "a little bit of himself." The reader is left with the continuing tension of an artificial dichotomy. One choice, Wideman seems to suggest, is the self-imposed isolation of the ivory tower, with protection from the victimization of urban street life but also a certain loss of personal vitality. The other choice, reflected in Robby, is the creativity, vibrancy and spirit of a man immersed in the African American community at home, but inevitably becoming a victim of the most oppressive aspects of street life. One

senses that Wideman is somehow struggling to merge the two parts of himself—
English professor and Homewood street boy—but he never seems to pull it off.
Ironically, the book almost becomes two books. When the younger brother speaks,
the lively rhythm and creativity of African American life and language come
through. When the older brother speaks, the reader is left bored and uninterested.
Inadvertently, Wideman conveys the impression that immersion in the community
carries a high risk of victimization and that ivory tower distancing results in the loss
of "down home" vibrancy. This beginning dialectical struggle is never really
resolved. Wideman's adaptation solution, therefore, is only partially satisfactory.

Paule Marshall's (1984) allegorical novel, *Praisesong for the Widow,* completes the struggle in a way which is only hinted at in Wilkins' and Wideman's life
stories. Marshall's central character, Avey Johnson, is a middle-aged African
American widow who is at a transition point in her life. Nostalgically, she recalls
the early years of her marriage to a man with whom she had shared love, warmth and
spontaneity. Slowly, however, Avey became suspicious and jealous of her husband.
Even though the two of them sense the real target of Avey's discomfort—racism—
the jealousies and suspicions eventually result in the death of their spirit together as
husband and wife. Avey's husband then invests all of his energy in professional
pursuits, looking for a way to heal their marriage. He obtains a degree in accounting
and establishes his own business. In the process, he undergoes, in Avey's eyes, a
transformation from the alive, spirit-filled "Jay" to the stiff, distant "Jerome
Johnson," preoccupied with his own success and disdainful of others whom he
regards as lazy and unambitious. Avey undergoes a similar transformation.

Marshall uses her character's emotional recollection of this painful past to set
the stage for a second, healing inner transformation. The process begins with a
dream of a great aunt, Cuney, whom Avey had visited as a child during summer
vacations on the sea island of Tatem, off the coast of South Carolina. During those
visits, Aunt Cuney had made a point of taking the young Avey [1] out on a spit of land
where the river met the ocean and had told her, repeatedly, the story of the original
African Ibos who had come to the island as slaves. Aunt Cuney had always insisted
that the Ibos, visionary in their abilities to see what lay ahead, had simply turned
around and walked across the water back to Africa. As a young child, Avey could
not grasp the symbolic significance of what her aunt was telling her. Instead, she
would ask a question that missed the whole point; for example, why the Africans
hadn't drowned. She was unable to understand that Aunt Cuney derived spiritual
and psychological sustenance from the ritual of retelling the Ibo story: "Her body
she always usta say might be in Tatem but her mind, her mind was long gone with
the Ibos . . . ."

It is in the dream that Avey first begins to understand the true meaning of her
childhood experiences. In the dream, Aunt Cuney appears again, but this time Avey
is an adult, dressed in her fine clothes, annoyed that Aunt Cuney wants her to dirty
herself by going out to the Ibo landing. Avey struggles to resist, but eventually is

dragged violently by the old woman out to the landing. Following this emotionally wrenching dream, Marshall's character finds herself, through a strange set of coincidences, journeying to an island in the Caribbean where a group of island natives return home to participate in an annual ritual of music and dances. Slowly, Avey finds herself experiencing a transformation as she is cared for by the islanders, accepted as one of them and invited to participate in their dance celebration. At first, Avey is resistant. However, there is something in the ritual of the dance which forces her to shed her staid and protected outer shell, much as she had been forced by Aunt Cuney in the dream to the sea shore:

> ... she found herself as the time passed being drawn more and more to the scene in the yard. The restraint and understatement in the dancing, which was not even really dancing, the deflected emotion in the voices were somehow right. It was the essence of something rather than the thing itself she was witnessing. Those present—the old ones—understood this. All that was left were a few names of what they called nations which they could no longer even pronounce properly, the fragments of a dozen or so songs, the shadowy forms of long-ago dances and the rum kegs for drums. The bare bones. The burnt-out ends. And they clung to them with a tenacity she suddenly loved in them and longed for in herself. Thoughts—new thoughts—vague and half-formed slowly beginning to fill the emptiness. (p. 240)

And later, as she is drawn more and more into the magic of the music and the dance, she recognizes more clearly the source of the compulsion under whose grip she has fallen:

> ... feelings that were beyond words, feelings and a host of subliminal memories that over the years had proven more durable and trustworthy than the history with its trauma and pain of which they had come. After centuries of forgetfulness and even denial, they refused to go away. The note was a lamentation that could hardly have come from the rum keg of a drum. *Its source had to be the heart, the bruised still-bleeding innermost chamber of the collective heart*. (p. 245, emphasis added)

Avey leaves the island a changed person, feeling an inner peace which she had not felt since the beginning years of her marriage, before "Jay" had become "Jerome" and before she had made the change from a lively, vibrant young African American woman to a stiff, staid old Negro woman. She now understood the urgency of the message in the dream to restore, through the power of ritual, one's spiritual connection to self through one's people, present as well as past.

The message in *Praisesong* is powerful and moving, and points to a direction which fills the gap in the life stories of striving African Americans like Roger Wilkins and John Edgar Wideman. It is a message also relevant to clients like B, whose struggles for success have left a void which seems worse in some ways than the economic poverty of childhood. The difficulty faced by these individuals is the seeming irreconcilable choice between professional success and prestige on the one hand and ties to oneself and one's community on the other. The character sketched by Marshall stands as a symbol of the potential for resolving that conflict:

> Would it have been possible to have done both? That is to have wrested, as they had done over all those years, the means needed to rescue them from Halsey street and to see the children through, while preserving, safeguarding, treasuring those things that had come down to them over the generations, which had defined them in a particular way. *The most vivid, the most valuable part of themselves!* . . . What would it have taken? . . . Awareness. It would have called for an awareness of the worth of what they possessed. Vigilance. The vigilance needed to safeguard it. . . . And strength. It would have taken strength on their part, and the will and even cunning necessary to withstand the glitter and the excess. To take only what was needed and run. And distance. Above all, a certain distance of the mind and heart had been absolutely essential. . . . "Her body she usta say might be in Tatem, but her mind, her mind was long gone with the Ibos." (p. 139, emphasis added)

Directions

It seems to me that we have had available to us for some time the beginning outlines of what is needed in work with achievement-oriented clients like B who have ended up as spiritual and emotional casualties of their newly acquired success. For example, it seems as if Na'im Akbar (then Luther X) might almost have had a premonition of Paule Marshall's allegorical message when, over twenty years ago, he stressed the need for awareness of, and reconnection with, roots in dealing with clients who have been seduced into maladaptive aspects of the European American cultural value system (Luther X, 1974). Akbar (1977, 1991a, 1991b) has continued his thinking on these issues in some of his more recent work. Similarly, much of what Nobles (1991a, 1991b) has written about the spiritual and communal nature of African American traditions is also relevant.

A large part of what appears to happen in the lives of some upwardly mobile African Americans is that their rapid ascent into the upper middle class is forged at the expense of their ability to hold on to important cultural traditions, traditions that over the years (centuries) have formed not only a core of African American identity, but also a central element in psychological adaptation for African Americans, regardless of their economic status (A. C. Jones, 1985, 1989, 1993). While it is true that, as Cross (1991) has shown, levels of racial identification are not always directly correlated with levels of self esteem, it has been my experience as a psychotherapist that for many women and men who have climbed the economic ladder at a rapid pace, the correlation is frequently both high and positive. That is, the ability to retain a strong core African American identity appears to be highly correlated with positive mental health, for both high achieving adults and their children (A. C. Jones, 1992).

Paule Marshall's powerful symbolism takes us even one step further, beyond the pioneering theoretical frameworks begun by such thinkers as Akbar and Nobles. Marshall's psychological portrait illustrates how the inner world can dictate its own direction. For people who undergo rapid changes in their external circumstances (e.g., material success, changes in the make-up of ones neighborhood environment), the ability to listen to the inner voices guiding such direction may be particularly important. For example, Marshall's character Avey is spiritually and psychologically dead *until* she begins a dramatic inner transformation, directed by the emotional pull of her significant dream. It was her willingness to *listen* to the dream (even before she knew anything about its ultimate meaning) that made her transformation possible.

Marshall also lays out for us the symbolic importance of rituals, particularly music and dance rituals, in the African American cultural experience. These rituals serve to strengthen connections to significant spiritual and psychological processes. Those who are nurtured and bathed in African American communities often take such rituals for granted, as in the case of those who participate regularly in traditional African American church ceremonies. However, the opportunity, for the first time, for a segment of our community to enjoy the benefits of rapid economic and professional growth has resulted in many of the participants in this process finding themselves, sometimes inadvertently, stripped from their access to the power of these long-standing African and African American rituals.

One very poignant example of the loss of cultural rituals in our communities is the waning access to our traditional religious folk music, most frequently referred to as "the spirituals," or "Negro spirituals." In the case of these songs (which were created in slavery but are often confused with their twentieth century progeny, gospel songs) it is not only members of the new class of upwardly mobile African Americans who have lost touch, but the African American community generally. The result has been the potential loss of a uniquely powerful array of tools for psychological and spiritual survival (and even excellence) in an environment that would otherwise have killed our spirits as a people long ago. Increasingly, children as well as adults in all segments of our community have begun to regard the spirituals as needless relics from a time when we were both the physical and psychological victims of our enslavement. Sadly, the now commonplace perception of the spirituals as outdated and no longer psychologically useful prevents people from appreciating the timeless ability of these songs to promote and support spiritual and psychological grounding *as well as* effective action in the ongoing fight against the forces of racism and oppression (A. C. Jones, 1993). Marshall's character Avey's deeply spiritual experience with traditional dance and music is reminiscent of the power of the spirituals, originally sung within the structure of the African ceremonial dance ritual known as the ring shout. Throughout the decades such rituals have provided critical nurturance and support for cultural rootedness, psychological centeredness and effective action (Jones, 1993; Stuckey, 1987).

A potentially potent ingredient in working effectively with clients like B, whose success has been wrought with negative psychological consequences, is our assistance in helping them to re-access the culturally grounded rootedness they have unwittingly lost. Within such a framework, the clinician's role is to provide the support and direction for such a reconnection, facilitating an inner process for the client in which a natural reliance on these resources assumes a life of its own (A. C. Jones, 1989). Like Avey in *Praisesong,* many African American people who find themselves in the psychological predicament of alienation from themselves are able, with support, to reconnect with aspects of their cultural roots that have provided them emotional and spiritual nurturance at earlier times in their lives. When they are open to it, they find themselves supported and nourished in any number of situations. For example, such support might be found in their singing or listening to the spirituals or other traditional African American music, or in the communal fellowship of the African American church. There are in fact numerous situations and settings in the African American community where the force of connection with other African American people (living as well as ancestral souls) functions like a "tonic" (Thomas, 1971) in reviving weary and lost souls. Spiritually and psychologically renewed, they are able to retain a sense of themselves in hostile psychological environments, and even to transcend the potentially negative psychological impacts of those environments.

Carl Jung, one of the few cross-culturally sensitive European psychological theorists and therapists[2] recognized the importance of self-anchoring in healthy psychological development. His blueprint for *all* people was the emergence of what he called the "transcendent function":

> The transcendent function does not proceed without aim and purpose, but leads to the revelation of the essential man. It is in the first place a purely natural process, which may in some cases pursue its course without the knowledge or assistance of the individual, and can sometimes forcibly accomplish itself in the face of opposition. The meaning and purpose of the process is the realization, in all its aspects, of the personality originally hidden away in the embryonic germ plasm; the production and unfolding of the original, potential wholeness. (1966, p. 110)

For Jung, the development of this process could best be tracked in dreams, which reflected the underlying wisdom of the Self. However, it is important to recognize that although Jung highlighted the importance of this inner process, he was certainly not the first to recognize it. Centuries-old African and African American cultural structures have accessed the manifestations of this powerful process, in music and dance rituals, in the rich oral storytelling tradition, and in the spiritual bonds flowing from the collective spiritual power of African people wherever they are found in the diaspora (A. C. Jones, 1993; Nobles, 1991a). It is in paying attention to and nurturing connections to this power that self-alienated individuals are assisted in their own growth processes and in their ability to reconnect with important people in their present and past experience. Inevitably, clients like B are able to discover that their own individual "success" is empty and meaningless without continued awareness of forces and people outside of themselves. When they do develop (re-develop) such awareness, they can easily resonate to Marshall's character Aunt Cuney: "Her body she usta say might be in Tatem, but her mind, her mind was long gone with the Ibos." In fact, Aunt Cuney's comments might receive some fresh new meanings: "His body, he says, might be in corporate America, but his mind, his mind is always with his people."

Hopefully we have exhausted our need for deconstruction of European psychological theory and are now at a stage where we can begin to construct positive and effective elements of theoretical framework for psychotherapeutic work with specific segments of the African American community, who present with particular kinds of difficulties. This chapter represents the beginnings of a sketch of such ideas for one group of clients, adults who suffer from a set of psychological symptoms which are byproducts of a path of rapid economic and professional success. There is a need for much more dialogue, research and creative thinking about this group of clients and any number of other groups of problems presenting themselves to those of us who work in the psychotherapeutic arena. And as Nancy Boyd-Franklin (1989) has shown persuasively in her work with African American families, we will also need to begin to detail both the strengths and the liabilities of the cultural patterns of our clients.

Notes

1. Aunt Cuney had insisted that Avey be called by her full proper name, Avatara. It is instructive that the word "avatar" refers to the incarnation of another person. In Marshall's novel, which is concerned largely with spiritual connections to persons present and past, Avey Johnson becomes a living symbol of her ancestral past.

2. As a European psychiatrist, Jung was not altogether immune from the influences of racism and prejudice. See Mays (1985) for a discussion of this point. However, there is also no doubt that Jung, more than any other Western psychological theoretician, understood the importance of spiritual connections to self and community. See, for example, Akbar (1984).

References

Acosta, F. X., Yamamoto, J., & Evans, L. A. (1982). *Effective psychotherapy for low income and minority patients.* New York: Plenum Press.

Akbar, N. (1977). *Natural psychology and human transformation.* Chicago, IL: World Community of Islam in the West.

Akbar, N. (1984). *Chains and images of psychological slavery.* Jersey City, NJ: New Mind Productions.

Akbar, N. (1991a). The evolution of human psychology for African Americans. In R. L. Jones (Ed.), *Black psychology* (3rd ed.). Berkeley, CA: Cobb & Henry.

Akbar, N. (1991b). Mental disorders among African Americans. In R. L. Jones (Ed.), *Black psychology* (3rd ed.). Berkeley, CA: Cobb & Henry.

Boyd-Franklin, N. (1989). *Black families in therapy: A multisystems Approach.* New York: Guilford Press.

Cross, W. E., Jr. (1991). *Shades of Black: diversity in African-American identity.* Philadelphia, PA: Temple University Press.

DeVos, G. A. (1982). Adaptive strategies in U.S. minorities. In E. E. Jones & S. J. Korchin (Eds.), *Minority mental health* (pp. 74-117). New York: Praeger Publishers.

Jackson, A. M. (1983). A theoretical model for the practice of psychotherapy with Black populations. *Journal of Black Psychology, 10,* 19-27.

Jackson, H. L., & Westmoreland, G. (1992). Therapeutic issues for Black children in foster care. In L. A. Vargas & J. D. Koss-Chioino (Eds.), *Working with culture: Psychotherapeutic interventions with ethnic minority children and adolescents.* San Francisco, CA: Jossey-Bass.

Jenkins, A. H. (1982). *The psychology of the Afro-American: A humanistic approach.* New York: Pergamon.

Jenkins, A. H. (1985). Attending to self activity in the Afro-American client. *Psychotherapy, 22*(2S), 335-341.

Jones, A. C. (1985). Psychological functioning in Black Americans: A conceptual guide for use in psychotherapy. *Psychotherapy, 22,* 363-369.

Jones, A. C. (1989). Psychological functioning in African American adults: Some elaborations on a model, with clinical applications. In R. L. Jones (Ed.), *Black adult development and aging.* Berkeley, CA: Cobb & Henry.

Jones, A. C. (1992). Self-esteem and identity in psychotherapy with adolescents from upwardly mobile middle-class families. In L. A. Vargas & J. D. Koss-Chioino (Eds.), *Working with culture: Psychotherapeutic interventions with ethnic minority children and adolescents.* San Francisco, CA: Jossey-Bass.

Jones, A. C. (1993). *Wade in the water: The wisdom of the spirituals.* Maryknoll, New York: Orbis Books.

Jones, E. E. (1984). Some reflections on the Black patient and psychotherapy. *The Clinical Psychologist, 37,* 62-65.

Jones, J. M., & Block, C. B. (1984). Black cultural perspectives. *The Clinical Psychologist, 37,* 58-62.

Jung, C. G. (1966). *Two essays on analytical psychology* (2nd ed.). Princeton, NJ: Princeton University Press ([1972] Paperback Edition).

Luther X (Weems). (1974). Awareness: The key to Black mental health. *Journal of Black Psychology,* 1, 30-37.

Marshall, P. (1984). *Praisesong for the widow.* New York: E. P. Dutton, Inc.

Mays, V. M. (1985). The Black American and psychotherapy: The dilemma. *Psychotherapy, 22,* 379-388.

McGoldrick, M., Pearce, J. K., & Giordano, J. (Eds.). (1982). *Ethnicity and family therapy.* New York: Guilford Press.

Nobles, W. (1991a). African philosophy: Foundations of Black psychology. In R. L. Jones (Ed.), *Black psychology* (3rd ed.). Berkeley, CA: Cobb & Henry.

Nobles, W. (1991b). Extended self: Rethinking the so-called Negro self concept. In R. L. Jones (Ed.), *Black psychology* (3rd ed.). Berkeley, CA: Cobb & Henry.

Paster, V. (1985). Adapting psychotherapy for the depressed, unacculturated, acting-out, Black male adolescent. *Psychotherapy, 22,* 408-417.

Ridley, C. R. (1984). Clinical treatment of the nondisclosing Black client. *American Psychologist, 34,* 1234-1244.

Shipp, P. L. (1983). Counseling Blacks: A group approach. *The Personnel and Guidance Journal, 62,* 108-110.

Stuckey, S. (1987). *Slave culture.* New York: Oxford Press.

Sue, D. W., & Sue, D. (1990*). Counseling the culturally different: Theory and practice.* New York: Wiley.

Tatum, B. D. (1987). *Assimilation blues: Black families in a white community.* Northampton, MA: Hazel-Maxwell Publishing.

Thomas, C. W. (1971). *Boys no more.* Beverly Hills, CA: Glencoe Press.

Wachtel, P. L. (1983). *The poverty of affluence: A psychological portrait of the American way of life.* New York: Free Press.

White, J. L. (1984). *The psychology of Blacks: An Afro-American perspective.* Englewood Cliffs, NJ: Prentice Hall.

Wideman, J. E. (1984). *Brothers and keepers.* New York: Holt, Rinehart & Winston.

Wilkins, R. (1982). *A man's life.* New York: Simon & Schuster.

Author

Arthur C. Jones, Ph.D.
Department of Psychology
University of Denver
2155 S. Race Street
Denver, CO 80208
Telephone: (303) 871-3795
Fax: (303) 871-4747
E-mail: arjones@du.edu.

Invisibility Syndrome in Psychotherapy with African American Males

Anderson J. Franklin

One of the reasons African American men resist psychotherapy is part of their broader struggle to establish a personal identity in a society where they are the object of considerable prejudice and discrimination. Finding the people, and social setting, that accept and embrace your contribution as an African American man compensates for pervasive experiences of being insufficiently recognized as a person of worth. Frequently in the day-to-day experiences of African American men, they are seen as the stereotypes that others hold about them. They are threatening, aggressive, violent, irresponsible, undependable, and less capable (Gordon, Gordon, & Nembhard, 1995; Hammond & Yung, 1993; Hutchinson, 1994; Oliver, 1994).

Studs Terkel in his book on *Race* (1992) conveys the epitome of racial misunderstanding when a White respondent noted how his wife continued incorrectly driving down a one-way street misinterpreting the waving arms of young African American men as threatening. These images far outweigh the image of the African American man as competent, compassionate, responsible and dependable (Billingsley, 1992; Edwards & Polite, 1992). But many African American men are victimized by these stereotypes and distorted attributions (Cose, 1993; Feagin & Sikes, 1994). Their genuine personality often gets enveloped, and made invisible by these caricatures.

It becomes a challenge to not internalize those negative presumptions held by others, into personal behavior (Franklin, 1993; Grier & Cobb, 1968). It becomes a personal task of determining how reactive you want to be towards the way others see you; how much you pay attention to what others think. You must regulate the degree you allow it to affect you. Each African American man seeks, within their own personal style, to resolve their inner emotional and cognitive tension that comes from racial slights.

An example of this is the case of Sam, a young African American lawyer who worked his way up from the hardships of inner city life. One day in his office building he encountered a not atypical African American male incident which alarmingly rattled his sense of self and almost caused him to totally lose it:

395

Sam was taking the court house elevator when a young White woman joined him at another floor. He was dressed impeccably as usual and gave her a slight smile as she entered. But when the door closed she looked at him and said, "You're not going to hurt me are you." Stunned by her comments, and stinging from its audacity and presumptions, Sam felt angry. An urge to strike back swelled in his gut. Feeling he could not let her get away with this insult, stretching his frame to its fullest height, and narrowing his eyes, Sam slowly growled, in a thinly veiled intimidating manner, "no, not today." At the next floor they went their separate ways.

Sam knew this woman was lumping him with her stereotyped notions that all African American men are threatening and aggressive predators. But the experience just the same reminded him how much appearances—or success—can be overwhelmed by the attributions from biased attitudes about African American men. It was not that Sam was naive about such experiences, but that on this occasion, it nearly touched the "last straw" depths of his tolerance for racial slights.

Invisibility as a Psychological Context

Invisibility is a psychological stressor from perceived acts of prejudice and discrimination where one feels as an African American person that the person you are—one's talents, gifts, skills, and persona—are not really seen. There is a greater feeling of tolerance rather than acceptance. There is a greater pressure towards conformity to behave in ways that replace African American ethnic behavior, if not racial identity. There is a sense of one's identity being rejected or denied. One feels that people do not see, much less understand, or care to know who you are, what you think, or how you genuinely feel, except for their own psychological construction of you.

Or, as Ralph Ellison explains in his classic novel *Invisible Man* (1947) " . . . When they approach me they see only my surroundings, themselves, or figments of their imagination—indeed, everything and anything except me" (p. 3). This experience is stressful, and forces each person into reducing the stress associated with it. Classic ways African Americans have handled the discomfort of Whites with our presence, or our mistrust of their intents, were to cover up our genuine person by putting on the "mask," such as the obsequious "Uncle Tom" behavior. In other words becoming invisible. Putting on the mask, and becoming something other than our "authentic self" is still a major adaptation style for African Americans (Graham, 1995). It reduces the stress from confronting and rejecting the expectations of others.

Stress developed from acts of perceived racism has physical and mental health implications for African Americans. Studies of African American males have documented how their unique life experiences lead to greater anxiety, anger, and frustration levels than the general population (Anderson, 1989; Johnson, 1989b; Scherwitz, Perkins, Chesney, & Hughes, 1991; Sutherland & Harrell, 1987). Stress from inability to fulfill gender and family roles produces role strain for African American men creating a host of personal and community problems (Bowman, 1989a, 1989b).

Reducing the stress from experiences that deny your genuine person or self is a matter of struggling with the dynamic elements in achieving a self defined visibility—such as racial identity—countervailing the acts of racism pulling to make you invisible—such as an imposed nonracial identity acceptable to society. The crucial dynamic elements in an invisibility—visibility intrapsychic struggle include competing experiences of recognition, satisfaction, legitimacy, validation, respect, dignity, and identity (Figure 1).

Each African American person, mindful of race, seeks to achieve a visibility and sense of identity-in-the-world by a self determining process that brings personal comfort. That personal comfort includes meeting those dynamic elements of visibility. But this is further influenced by society's determination of how African Americans should be, in contrast to the African American person's individual choice. For African Americans, society's racism and the personal comfort of White people denies or dilutes racial self definition—making it invisible—and pulls for conformity to an imposed identity more acceptable to society's "personal comfort," such as a racially neutralized identity.

The crucial dynamic elements such as recognition, rewards, validation are sought by the individual in every day interpersonal encounters and social environments. We seek to extract from diverse psychological contexts an internalization of these interdependent elements in a configuration that is reinforcing and cultivates a sense of genuine visibility built on identity and self respect. Historically, the African American church has been a primary social environment providing the African American person a place to be most genuinely ourselves (Lincoln & Mamiya, 1990). In contrast, the world of work has been a context where our African/ African American persona is frequently suppressed.

Therefore, when Sam stepped off the elevator after the infuriating incident his efforts at immediate "micro repair" of his psyche entailed discrediting the woman's attributions by self affirmations and seeking validation from his fellow African American colleague that his indignation over this racial slight was justified. The individual's desire to achieve inner peace must be consistent with their chosen path to be visible—such as a person of African descent, or a White-identified African American. Therefore, whatever reduces the inherent tension and conflict for achieving comfort with "who you are" is a resolution of the dilemma. It can take many forms. Evolving a racial identity is one way in which African Americans choose to resolve the inherent conflicts and tension presented by circumstances designed to deny their ethnic visibility.

Figure 1
The Persona Dilemma for African Americans

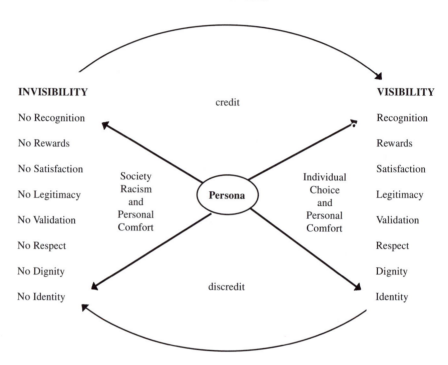

Dysfunctional Behavior from Invisibility

Stress from the inner turmoil of being Black and African American continues to be best summarized by what W. E. B. DuBois (1903) called a "twoness, an American, a Negro; two souls, two thoughts, two unreconciled strivings; two warring ideals in one dark body, whose dogged strength alone keeps it from being torn asunder" (p. 45).

The struggle to achieve an identity that brings an inner peace and personal level of comfort is demanding upon the psyche. In the process of achieving the acceptable persona are racial circumstances which attempt to negate it such as what Dr. Chester Pierce, an African American professor at Harvard, calls "micro-aggressions." Micro-aggressions are perceived small acts, behavior, or attitude which fit a pattern, and history of slights that the person considers hostile and inconsiderate. They are interpersonal interactions or social circumstances that are deliberate or mindless acts of disrespect.

An individual's response to racial slights produces a myriad of emotions and thoughts such as anger, guilt, anxiety, frustration, confusion and disillusionment. It is the "accumulated unresolved indignations" from a life time of reconciling racial slights, or "come-uppance," that build psychological scar tissue within the emotional world of the African American man. Furthermore, there are limited peer accepted emotional outlets for the pain inflicted by racial slights among African American men. Nevertheless, its resolution must be handled in a way that is consistent with notions of African American masculinity such as being "cool."

Being "cool," that is masking true thoughts and feelings under a public veneer of unflappability and being in complete control, is deeply rooted in African American male culture (Anderson, 1990; Majors & Billson, 1992). Therefore internalizing emotions from micro-aggressions and displacing them often in self destructive behavior is frequently a pattern of resolving racial slights among African American men. Even those occasions where it is immediately acted upon, such as a retaliatory outburst of anger at the person perpetrating the indignation, it is often inadequate to resolve totally the residual feelings after the precipitating event has passed.

Over time, individual efforts to achieve visibility in a genuinely acceptable manner for the African American man must withstand resistance to it. Slights, and the indignation from perceived acts of racism, are acts of resistance to an image of a powerful and efficacious African American male presence. Unsuspecting and persistent racial slights tear away at personal confidence and competence. The most characterizing but still meaningful cliches among African Americans still have truth. "As soon as you think you've made it, they change the rules." Moreover, "You have to be twice as good in order to get half as much."

The disassembling of belief, if not hope, when prejudice and discrimination compromises the individual's chosen path to visibility and sense of efficacy, promotes disillusionment and confusion. This cultivates within the individual frustration, anger, feelings of personal betrayal from second guessing oneself—such as questioning judgment about the way you chose to live your life. One can be beset with chronic indignation originating from mistrust of interpersonal interactions with Whites and little faith in their genuineness.

The emotional turmoil from confusion and disillusionment can convert episodic anger into chronic internalized rage by pervasive disorientation and sense of powerlessness to control one's destiny against incidents of prejudice and discrimination no matter how much you achieve (Cose, 1993; Edwards & Polite, 1992; Feagin & Sikes, 1994). Chronic feelings of powerlessness not only breeds disillusionment but sows hopelessness. Reaching these depths of emotional distress brings immobilization. Despair and depression, aided by the narcotizing effects of substance abuse, can exacerbate these symptoms.

All of the above behaviors can combine into a cluster of symptoms to form an "invisibility syndrome," whose etiology is from chronic unresolved indignation and emotional upset from acts of perceived racism. Symptoms of this syndrome among African Americans are worsened by the individual's growing dysfunction from incapacity to psychologically resolve inner conflicts over being the object of perceived acts of racism. Efforts to choose and maintain a path towards an acceptable identity and personal comfort zone is undermined by disillusionment and disorientation. Promotion of an African American racial identity therefore is designed to lessen the "persona dilemma" by providing a focus.

Racial Identity Development

In the development of personal identity one achieves a sense of self by resolving inner conflicts from doubts and tension over acceptance and self worth. Therefore, the behavior in our chosen places to be, and the people we choose to associate with, become crucial to our feelings of acceptance and affirmation of self image. Personal identity therefore refers to our feelings, thoughts, and attitudes about ourselves. Reference-group orientation involves our use of a particular group such as African Americans, and ascribed identity is the conscious and deliberate affiliation and commitment to a particular racial group. These distinctions help delineate the complexity in understanding any individual's personal racial identity development (Cross, 1991; Helms, 1993).

Theory and research on racial identity development has continued to explore various stages and factors in a process of being and becoming identified as African American (Carter, 1995; Cross, 1991; Helms, 1993). Cross's early model of five stage development remains the focus of primary research and writing in this area. He hypothesized racial identity development initially begins at a *preencounter stage* which is characterized by dependency on White society for definition and approval. Next is the *encounter stage* when one has a personally profound racial experience which challenges your sense of relationship and order to Whites and African American society. As a result of confusion, and a greater significance and meaning of race, the individual wants to move closer to African American culture and in turn an African American identity. Consequently the individual can move to an *immersion-emersion stage* which is characterized by a period of idealization of African American culture coupled with negative feelings toward Whites and their culture. *Internalization stage* follows where the person transcends racism and acquires a view that both African Americans and Whites have strengths and weaknesses. A last stage is *internalization-commitment* represented by the person evolving to embrace active commitment and involvement in advocating for the welfare of African American people.

What racial identity development theory and research provide is a model showing a possible path for resolving intrinsic conflicts of the invisibility syndrome for African Americans. It describes and implies some of the social experiences, milestones, and developmental tasks but insufficiently details the person's intrapsychic and cognitive dynamics facilitating or inhibiting achievement of a given stage. There are many implications drawn from the numerous factors related to and predictive of racial identity status (Carter, 1995). However, there remains a great need for continued research and theory on the individual's internal process in racial identity development.

Resolution of Invisibility Through Racial Identity Development

The process of racial identity development helps the individual resolve the social and psychologically marginalizing dilemmas that make the genuine person feel invisible and not worthy. It compensates for detached feelings and a confused or diffused sense of self by bringing coherence and purpose to personal identity. It resolves inner conflict from pseudo-assimilation in reference groups and ambivalence about ascribed identity. Maintaining perpetual disorientation, such as keeping you off balance by intensifying personal frustration and anger from changing rules, is an intrinsic dynamic of the invisibility syndrome. Fundamental to the process of keeping African American men invisible are experiences which attack his sense of competence, worth, and inevitably psychological well being (Franklin, 1993). Being immersed in the racial identity development process can counterbalance the perceived acts of racism and the internalization of their intentions. It provides a perspective and context for interpreting, understanding, and responding to the marginalizing experiences that make you feel invisible.

Take our earlier example of Sam, the young lawyer. His first inclination after the comments of the young White woman was to transform into "street" behavior, and exploit the African American male stereotype by saying in an intimidating manner, "no, not today." In my work with Sam I would place his racial identity development in transition between the immersion-emersion stage and the internalization stage. Parenthetically, for some people this incident could have been the pivotal encounter stage experience. However, for Sam his race consciousness had evolved from his leadership and activism in the African American Student Union of his college days to his present participation in the National Association of Black Lawyers. This allowed him to normalize the incident within the framework of how these reference groups viewed racism and the treatment of African American men.

As he subsequently admitted, these experiences do not happen every waking moment but enough to verify racism is alive and well. His level of racial identity development also allows him to see exceptions in his treatment, both in terms of his success, as well as acknowledging the White people who have supported him throughout his professional development.

Pressure Upon Racial Identity Development

Racism's obligation to maintain African American men socially marginal and psychologically invisible require repeated experiences of slights provoking indignation. They must wear and tear defenses down, to force compliance and acceptance of how society's racism wants African Americans to behave and think. What Sam also confronts in the development of his identity is how the invisibility syndrome marginalizes that which is different. A successful, intellectually competent, empowered African American man is different from the stereotyped conceptions of the African American male. Implicit within the microaggression directed at Sam was a discrediting of his accomplishments promoting confusion and disillusionment about criteria for acceptance. Unless the person is very resilient, chronic experiences of disillusionment from capricious and systematic undermining by racism make the individual dysfunctional.

Therefore, what the elevator incident does is to attack worthiness and sow self doubt. An underlying message in the scenario is that African American men no matter what their status can only be seen as their stereotypes. It forces Sam to reaffirm his legacy of positive experiences which have made him the person and professional other than the stereotype he encountered in the elevator. He has to draw upon his source of resilience. Sam in part achieves this by reinforcing his present sense of self, and to reaffirm the progress in his racial identity development. Consequently, Sam sought out Rich, his fellow African American office mate, to recount the elevator incident as a release for his anger, and get validation for the righteousness of his indignation and manner of handling the incident as an affirmation of appropriate identity behavior.

The insidious nature of invisibility is its attack upon self esteem, chosen personal identity, reference group, and ascribed identity. Racism's pervasive manipulating or denying of recognition, rewards, and sense of legitimacy around people and in places underlies the indignation of African Americans. It can challenge efficacy as worker, partner, parent and friend. How much our racial identity is generalized and infuses our other personal identities is also central to resisting the deleterious consequences of psychological marginalization.

Sam's behavior is more "Black" and ethnic among his fellow African American lawyers' meetings than he is in the predominately White District Attorney's Office. It is the well known bicultural code switching behavior employed by African Americans. However, how he thinks of himself, and his personal comfort with being an African American are central to how he behaves, and what he internalizes.

Entering Therapy

When Sam entered therapy at the urging, and insistence of friends to deal with his perpetual anger, he did so with great reluctance and skepticism. An inviolable requirement was the therapist must be African American and male. It was a classic African American male approach to help—increase the ante to reduce the possibility of coming, and control the process with important conditions before commitment.

Request by African Americans for a therapist reflecting their race and gender is common. The therapist's link to the patient's ethnic group and familiarity with cultural and racial issues facilitates understanding and efficacy of therapeutic technique (Boyd-Franklin, 1989; Carter, 1995; Franklin, Carter, & Grace, 1993; Sue & Zane, 1987). Although these therapist's attributes may be apparent to the patient, it does not automatically make the African American man any less resistant to the process. It helps to get him to the initial treatment session—through the door, so to speak.

There are a number of barriers to getting African American males into therapy but overcoming them is essential for demonstrating the potential worth of the service, as well as achieving effective treatment. The reasons for low participation in therapy by African American males are many. Certainly the stigma to seeking mental health services is one explanation; in addition, the perception of the field of mental health, and how it is viewed as a service is another (Boyd-Franklin, 1989; Ruiz, 1990). A prominent explanation is based on gender differences in attitudes towards help seeking behavior. Males in general do not seek help for personal problems in the same way or frequency as females (Meth & Pasick, 1990).

However, to attribute attitudes towards mental health, and gender role differences as the primary explanation for the lack of African American males' participation in therapy is overly simplifying the issue. Clearly there is a more complex interaction, and their comprehension must consider psychological, social, and historical contexts (Jackson, 1991; Neighbors, 1991).

Trust, Power, and Control

Developing trust between a therapist and an African American man is necessary to keep them engaged in the therapeutic process and be effective in achieving therapeutic goals. The invisibility syndrome in its cultivation of chronic indignation, anger, disillusionment and confusion has undermined trust, confidence in self empowerment, and efficacy in controlling personal circumstances in one's life. This is an outcome from perceived acts of repeated prejudice and discrimination across the life span.

African American men are often very sensitive and reactive to themes of trust, power and control in their lives, whether it is at home, work, or leisure activities. It is embedded in rules and codes of interpersonal behavior governing their relationships with African American men, African American women as well as White men and women (Hecht, Collier, & Ribeau, 1993; Kochman, 1981; Majors & Billson,

1992; Russell, Wilson, & Hall, 1992). Also powerfully linked to his life themes is the concern about betrayal and the ability to rely upon integrity of intent in others.

Betrayal, whether in the form of a trusted friend reneging on confidentiality, or the world of work reneging on employment opportunities, is at the source of African American men's skepticism. And racism has had a multitude of betrayal experiences for the African American man not the least of which is the denial of our historical legacy (Franklin & Moss, 1994; Sertima, 1976).

Therefore, the essential reliance of therapy upon trust in self disclosure for effective therapeutic intervention is competing with many African American men's proclivity to mistrust the motives of others. Moreover, personal guardedness, as epitomized by the cherished masked persona, is a common means for maintaining a sense of powerfulness and control over interpersonal interactions. It is crucial to achieving a self determined personal identity and genuine visibility with acceptance, recognition, rewards and legitimacy intricately woven into everyday experiences.

Therapy's Threat to Visibility

The openness intrinsic to therapy does not have viability for African American men when their survival has been tied to not disclosing or trusting intent. Consequently, African American men will not likely, or be quick, to share personal vulnerabilities. Any disclosures will be censored by the need to preserve fragile personal identities frequently manipulated and undermined by the indignities of racial slights.

Seeking help from a therapist for an African American man is perceived as admitting loss of control over one's life. The disillusionment intrinsic to the invisibility syndrome is in part due to the individual's having expectations of treatment or opportunity result in unexpected disappointment. Being "blind sided" insinuates a momentary loss of control. For example, in the brief encounter on the elevator Sam was expecting the conventional benign greeting but instead was confronted—"blind sided"—with him being the object of fear. The interaction was as disruptive to his confidence about controlling his image as it was emotionally disconcerting. Control is an essential dynamic dimension of manliness. Control suggests power, demonstrates ability to have authority over the diverse forces and pressures acting upon the everyday life of being an African American man.

For African American men, therapy is not perceived as an activity that reinforces one's sense of personal control and power, but rather as a process that exposes one's weakness and powerlessness. Consequently, therapy, perhaps more than other contexts, can be perceived as being a greater threat to the African American man's survival instincts because trust, power, and control are viewed as entrusted to the process. For many African American men, that requires more confidence in a person and a process than life experiences have taught. This is captured by the behavior of a reluctant African American father whose son was in therapy:

> Interrupting a therapy session unannounced, the father came into the office stating he was in the neighborhood and wanted to see how things were going. He wanted his son to know he supported him, and expressed his love for him, and had confidence he would make something of himself as a Black man— "like me, and I don't want your therapy to change my influence."

Or, another example is an African American man in couples therapy:

> "Shut up, bitch!" was one of the first demonstrative statements the husband had made since sessions began. His startled wife objected, after tearfully disclosing her husband was unable to find another job since being laid off, and their relationship had not been intimate for a while. She turned to him and insisted he discuss his problem with the doctor. "You don't understand anything, or understand what I'm going through," her husband said. "Doc is a Black man, he knows . . . talking about it is not going to help us, or help me get a job."

Both African American men mistrusted the therapeutic process and felt insecure in their ability to control and influence the process as they possessed in their daily life. It was important for the father to feel that he controlled his son's destiny. The therapist was lumped with other influential people and circumstances in the life of the father that competed with his conception of how to conduct his personal affairs. Intruding on the therapy session was his was a way of inserting and maintaining his visibility in the life of his son which he perceived as threatened by the strength of the therapeutic bond established by the therapist. The father's behavior was also motivated by his persistent struggle to be different from his own father who epitomized the haunting images of "absent Black fathers."

For the African American man in couples therapy, his wife's emotional disclosures were humiliating. He felt they stripped him of his dignity. Her sharing their private thoughts and feelings about his inability to perform sexually, intensified his sense of powerlessness. He did not view therapy as the place to solve his problems. Her disclosures had preempted his carefully guarded defenses, and he faulted himself for this embarrassing predicament as much as his wife. His survival instincts as an African American man, that is, "to not let another person or circumstance get the better of you," had failed him. Intuitively he knew that he should not have placed himself in a position to be coerced into "counseling." Having his problems exposed to a therapist, another African American man, was demeaning and compromising to him. His appeal to the therapist's race was to abbreviate discussion by projecting into the session the therapist's connection to the "Black male experience," particularly around codes of conduct for "saving face."

Therapeutic Strategies

Bridging the trust gap between therapist and the African American male patient is most important (Franklin, 1992; Franklin, 1993; Pinderhughes, 1989). Without it there will be no therapy. During the initial sessions, the African American man is earnestly evaluating whether he can trust the therapist and the process. The skepticism brought into therapy is often sufficient for him to maintain intentions of limiting the trust he will extend to it.

Carrying this attitude does not mean that trust between therapist and the African American man cannot be established. It only characterizes the context in which trust must be earned. In general, their attendance indicates a degree of openness that can be capitalized upon. The therapist therefore needs to carefully assess the reason (both verbal and nonverbal) for his coming, and the source instrumental in his attendance.

For example, Sam's initial reason for seeing a therapist was to learn stress management skills which would help him manage his hypertension. The concern of his mother and close friends about him repeating his family's poor cardiac history was reasonably convincing. But also significantly anchoring his justification to come was a compelling belief in "his destiny" to make a contribution to the African American community. This was closely tied to the continued evolution of his racial identity development. He did not want his dismissal of a medical risk to eclipse his future prematurely.

Likewise, the father's intruding upon the therapy session was an act of monitoring a process he held in great suspicion. However, his willingness to allow his son to attend was governed by his passionate desire for his son to follow in his "hard earned Black upper middle class footsteps." His wife convinced him that therapy was the way White middle class families helped their sons to succeed. This clearly was an appeal to his values as well as racial identity.

African American men do not walk into a session proclaiming their underlying beliefs and motivations. Many African American men who agree to a therapy consultation mask it's real necessity with grudging participation, or engaging conversation unrelated to the purpose of the meeting. On the other hand, some will keep the focus of the consultation solely on the presenting problem, exclusively censoring inquiry beyond those boundaries. This constrains the therapeutic process and makes it superficial. However, these behaviors in therapy are simply manifestations of mistrust in the process.

To achieve trust from the African American male in therapy the therapist must have the willingness to allow some of their skepticism to be expressed freely without overly interpreting, or exploring them initially. One of the pitfalls in therapy is engaging the process faster than it is desirable and necessary to gain the trust and bonding that reassures the patient.

Moreover, the therapist's training and experience often allows for quick formulation and insight into the patient's problems. Thrusting such therapist's insight into the process too soon may be received as intolerant, not willing to allow the patient to disclose at their own pace. Disregarding the patient's need for personal pacing of disclosures by premature formulations and interpretations is perceived as professional arrogance, disrespectful, and an unfortunate display of "magical powers" that deepens distrust. If premature formulations or interpretations reinforce a patient's belief in "therapist magical power" (e.g., "you can read my mind"), then bridging the trust gap may be completely compromised.

In addition, premature disclosing of uncanny insight can also play into the African American man's suspicion that the therapeutic process is linked to the "know-it-all" mentality of White people. Such assumptions very likely will stir his feelings around power and control issues he confronts in a racist society. Nevertheless, showing insight which conveys knowledge, understanding, and empathy remains an effective agent to gaining trust, and can be seen as a sign of the therapist's competence.

The fundamentals of bridging the trust gap with African American men are not unique to the therapy context but are critical to being successful with this patient population. Conveying respect, projecting genuineness and integrity are important therapist attributes. These virtues, obvious as they are, reflect the therapist's humanity, a key component to demonstrating empathy and understanding about the patient's needs.

It is the African American man's need to feel that the therapist is a genuine person that will bridge the trust gap. The therapist as a model of personal genuineness fits the needs of African American men who struggle to achieve visibility with self integrity in a duplicitous society. Acknowledging the importance and significance of his coming to, and participation in therapy will facilitate this endeavor. This should be done in a supportive fashion. Beware of verbal and nonverbal expressions of amazement that the man showed at all. Because African American men come to therapy infrequently, surprise at their appearance can inadvertently be manifested in many unconscious behaviors by the therapist. This is condescending, and alienates him from the process. Clearly, the more therapy is seen as affirming the man's power to make life decisions the more accepting of it he will be. Furthermore, this is initiating a process of empowerment in therapy, a key element towards personal self-fulfillment that many African American men need and desire support in.

Therapeutic Support Groups

Therapeutic support groups for African American men can also serve as an important outlet for sharing feelings, thoughts, and concerns about being African

American, and male in today's world (Franklin, in press).

Most African American men do not talk about personal issues, or share vulnerabilities with each other. It is what further makes therapy a strange and alienating experience for African American men. This is not all together uncommon for men in general. But for African American men there is a special peer accountability for surviving a universal set of experiences that cannot manifest as vulnerability in a barely tolerant racist society.

The stress and pressure from projecting an image of emotional invulnerability to the indignation from racial slights create the need for a support group focused upon such masculine intransigence. There is a need to evaluate, in a safe group forum, how "bravado in the brotherhood," impacts the way African American men achieve recognition, emotional stability, and fulfillment of personal life goals.

African American men engage in "buddy chatter" which is light, social and business discussions, but not genuinely honest talk which exposes uncharacteristic emotions, immobility, struggle with weaknesses, or lack of knowledge. There is almost no discussion of emotional issues which suggest weakness since that is counter to the male image of strength.

Managing the psychological effects from African American male invisibility in this society, and its consequences to mental health is by itself a single important reason for support groups. They become instrumental in validating these experiences as members learn they are not alone, but rather share similar emotional dilemmas as other African American men. Moreover, they acquire insight into how others cope with these issues, and learn new ways of resolving their emotional conflicts. This becomes particularly important for such emotions as anger and rage which among African American men are often internalized to later manifest in self destructive behaviors. How to interpret and manage the indignation and anger provoked by episodic racial slights is crucial to the psychological well being and mental health of African American men.

References

Anderson, E. A. (1990). *Streetwise: race, class and change in an urban community.* Chicago, IL: The University of Chicago Press.

Anderson, N. B. (1989). Racial differences in stress induced cardiovascular reactivity and hypertension: Current status and substantive issues. *Psychological Bulletin, 105,* 89-105.

Billingsley, A. (1992). *Climbing Jacob's ladder: The enduring legacy of African American families.* New York: Simon & Schuster.

Bowman, P. J. (1989a). Research perspectives on Black men: Role strain and adaptation across the adult life cycle. In R. L. Jones (Ed.), *Black adult development and aging* (pp. 117-150). Berkeley, CA: Cobb & Henry.

Bowman, P. J. (1989b). Marginality, ethnicity and family life quality: National study of Black husband-fathers. In H. P. McAdoo (Ed.), *Family, ethnicity and diversity*. Newbury Park, CA: Sage Publications.

Boyd-Franklin, N. (1989). *Black families in therapy: A multisystems approach*. New York: The Guilford Press.

Carter, R. T. (1995). *The influence of race and racial identity in psychotherapy*. New York: John Wiley & Sons, Inc.

Cose, E. (1993). *The rage of a privileged class*. New York: Harper Collins Publishers.

Cross, W. E. (1991). *Shades of Black: Diversity in African American identity*. Philadelphia, PA: Temple University Press.

DuBois, W. E. B. (1903). *The souls of Black folks*. Chicago, IL: McClurg.

Edwards, A., & Polite, C. K. (1992). *Children of the dream: The psychology of Black success*. New York: Doubleday.

Ellison, R. (1947). *Invisible man*. New York: Vintage Books.

Feagin, J. R., & Sikes, M. P. (1994). *Living with racism: The Black middle-class experience*. Boston, MA: Beacon Press.

Franklin, A. J., (1992, June). Therapy with African American men. *Families in Society: The Journal of Contemporary Human Services*, 350-355.

Franklin, A. J. (1993, July/August). The invisibility syndrome. *The Family Therapy Networker*, 32-39.

Franklin, A. J., Carter, R. T., & Grace, C., (1993). An integrative approach to psychotherapy with Black/African Americans: The relevance of race and culture. In G. Stricker & J. R. Gold (Eds.), *Comprehensive handbook of psychotherapy integration*. New York: Plenum Press.

Franklin, J. H., & Moss, A. A. (1994). *From slavery to freedom: A history of African Americans* (7th ed.). New York: Alfred A. Knopf.

Franklin, A. J. (in press). Therapeutic support groups for African American men. In L. E. Davis (Ed.), *African American males: A practice guide*. Newbury, CA: Sage Publications.

Gordon, E. T., Gordon, E. W., & Nembhard, J. G. (1995). Social science literature concerning African American men. *Journal of Negro Education, 63*(4), 508-531.

Graham, L. O. (1995). *Member of the club: Reflections on life in a racially polarized world*. New York: Harper Collins Publishers.

Grier, W. H., & Cobb, P. M. (1968). *Black rage*. New York: Basic Books.

Hammond, R., & Yung, B. (1993). Psychology's role in the public health response to assaultive violence among young African American men. *American Psychologist, 48*(2), 142-154.

Hecht, M. L., Collier, M. J., & Ribeau, S. A. (1993). *African American Communication: Ethnic identity and cultural interpretation*. Newbury Park, CA: Sage Publications.

Helms, J. E. (Ed.). (1993). *Black and White racial identity.* Westport, CT: Praeger.

Hutchinson, E. O. (1994). *The assassination of the Black male image.* Los Angeles, CA: Middle Passage Press.

Jackson, J. S. (Ed.). (1991). *Life in Black America.* Newbury Park, CA: Sage Publications.

Johnson, G. J. (1989b). Underemployment, underpayment, and psychosocial stress among working Black men. *Western Journal of Black Studies, 13*(2), 57-65.

Kochman, T. (1981). *Black and White styles in conflict.* Chicago: The University of Chicago Press.

Lincoln, C. E., & Mamiya, L. H. (1990). *The Black church in the African American experience.* Durham, NC: Duke University Press.

Majors, R., & Billson, J. M. (1992). *Cool pose: The dilemmas of Black manhood in America.* New York: Lexington Books.

Meth, R. L., & Pasick, R. S. (Eds.). (1990). *Men in therapy: The challenge of change.* New York: The Guilford Press.

Neighbors, H. W. (1991). Mental health. In J. S. Jackson (Ed.), *Life in Black America.* Newbury Park, CA: Sage.

Oliver, W. (1994). *The violent social world of Black men.* New York: Lexington Books.

Pinderhughes, E. (1989). *Understanding race, ethnicity, & power: The key to efficacy in clinical practice.* New York: The Free Press.

Ruiz, D. S. (1990). *Handbook of mental health and mental disorder among Black Americans.* New York: Greenwood Press.

Russell, K., Wilson, M., & Hall, R. (1992). *The color complex: The politics of skin color among African Americans.* New York: Harcourt Brace Jovanovich, Publishers.

Scherwitz, L., Perkins, L., Chesney, M., & Hughes, M. (1991). Cook-Medley hostility scale and subtests: Relationship to demographic and psychosocial characteristics in young adults in the CARDIA study. *Psychosomatic Medicine, 53*(1), 36-49.

Sertima, I. V., (1976). *They came before Columbus.* New York: Random House.

Sue, S., & Zane, N. (1987, January). The role of culture and cultural techniques in psychotherapy: A critique and reformulation. *American Psychologist,* 37-45.

Sutherland, M. E., & Harrell, J. P. (1987). Individual differences in physiological responses to racially noxious and neutral imagery. *Imagination, Cognition and Personality, 6,* 133-150.

Terkel, S. (1992). *Race: How Blacks and Whites think and feel about the American obsession.* New York: Anchor Books.

Author

Anderson J. Franklin, Ph.D.
Department of Psychology
The City College of New York
Convent Ave. @ 138th Street
New York, NY 10031
Telephone: (212) 650-5666
Fax: (212) 650-5673
E-mail: ajfcc@cunyvm.cuny.edu

African Americans in Behavioral Therapy and Research: The Need for Cultural Considerations

Russell T. Jones, Renee Brown, Mary Davis, Rosell Jeffries, and Uma Shenoy

Introduction

The rate of growth of ethnic minority populations continues to climb, presently representing 24.4% of the entire United States population (U.S. Bureau of the Census, 1990). The need to enhance the quality of functioning among members of these groups presents a major challenge for mental health professionals. The magnitude of this challenge is heightened given the lack of attention to people of color within the traditional boundaries of psychology. The exigency to broaden our borders with reference to our service toward these often underserved groups is evident given our less than spectacular track record in the areas of research and therapy. Innovative methods of conceptualizing, assessing and treating "problem behavior" among these individuals may well determine the continued growth or rapid demise of our discipline.

The clarion call for proactive thinking and action to meet the demands of the growing numbers of ethnic minorities has been made over the past two decades (e.g., Bernal, 1990; Bernal & Padilla, 1982; Stricker, Davis-Russell, Bourg, Duran, Hammond, McHolland, Polite, & Vaughn, 1990; Sue, 1982; Turner & Jones, 1982). Ethnic minority is being defined as those individuals who represent the following groups: African Americans, American Indians, Asian Americans and Latino Americans. Given that the quality of life of many members of these groups is seriously threatened by poverty, lack of education, unemployment, racism, and health problems, the urgency for attention is paramount. However, by several indicators, the need is yet to be met. The age old adage "the harvest is ripe but the laborers are few," appears to accurately summarize the current state of the art.

413

The goal of this chapter is to obtain a preliminary, empirical measure of the extent to which African Americans have been represented and benefited from research and therapeutic efforts carried out by behavior therapists. Additionally, the extent to which these investigations addressed the needs of African Americans in culturally-sensitive ways is also critically examined. Behavioral therapists are being defined as those individuals typically trained in departments of psychology where the primary model for behavior change is cognitive behavioral. While we recognize the importance for such attention to all four ethnic groups, such a comprehensive review goes beyond the scope of this chapter. However, we feel that the findings and recommendations are beneficial to many individuals in each ethnic group. In carrying out this review a perusal of eight journals from the years of 1985 to 1995 was undertaken. Only those investigations which employed adults and which were specified as treatment outcome studies were targeted. Journals reviewed included: *The Journal of Consulting and Clinical Psychology, Behavior Therapy, Behavior Modification, American Journal of Community Psychology, Journal of Traumatic Stress, Child and Family Behavior Therapy, Journal of Behavior Therapy and Experimental Psychiatry, and Clinical Psychology Review.* Those investigations which had any percent of African American representation were included. Studies were critically evaluated on the following variables: assessment, treatment, and process. This examination revealed that a dearth of research and clinical efforts have targeted African Americans as well as other ethnic diverse groups. Surprisingly little attention has been given to a number of variables related to race, ethnicity and culture. Critical evaluation of existing efforts revealed that authors rarely analyzed or controlled for these factors. These results strongly argue for increased attention to the variables of race, ethnicity and culture in both research and clinical endeavors. Our findings are summarized in Table 1. Explanations for the current state of the art, guidelines to increase cultural sensitivity, and empirical attempts to incorporate culturally competent practices will also be discussed.

Brief History of Behavior Therapy

Behavioral Therapy emerged from the doctrine of behaviorism and represented a shift from the dominant focus of psychology on introspection. Due in part to the innovative efforts of Watson (1913) and his advocacy for methodological behaviorism, the ground rules for objectively defining problem behavior, determining conceptually-based etiologies, articulating assessment methods and implementing empirically-based treatment plans were set into motion. The major emphasis of the behavioral approach on environmental, situational and social determinants as causes of behavior rather than inferred motives, traits, impulses and

Table 1
Critique of Reviewed Studies

Author/ Date	% AA	Cultural Specific Assessment	Target Behavior	Techniques	Effective Relative to AA only	Match		
						Race	Gender	Age
Abramowitz & Coursey (1989)	31% of 48	not mentioned	management of schizophrenic patients, social support and community services	group session with families of schizophrenic patients	nm	nm	nm	nm
Alexander, Neimeyer, Follette, Moore, & Harter (1989)	24% of 65	nm	treatment for adult survivors of sexual abuse	a) interpersonal transaction group b) process group	nm	nm	nm	nm
Baker & Kirschenbaum (1993)	11% of 56	nm	weight control	self-monitoring	nm	nm	nm	nm
Ball, Carroll, Rounsaville (1994)	50% of 355	nm	cocaine & sensation	interviews	nm	nm	nm	nm
Baucom, Sayers, & Sher (1990)	3% of 60	nm	marital therapy	behavioral marital, cognitive restructuring, emotional expreivness	nm	nm	nm	nm
Beck, Baldwin, Deagle, & Averill (1994)	7% of 70	nm	panic disorder	cognitive therapy, relaxation therapy, minimal contact	nm	nm	nm	nm
Benson, Johnson-Rice, & Miranti (1986)	52% of 54	nm	anger management with MR subjects	relaxation group, self-instruction, problem solving	nm	nm	nm	nm

* not mentioned (nm)

Table 1 (Continued)
Critique of Reviewed Studies

Author/ Date	% AA	Cultural Specific Assessment	Target Behavior	Techniques	Effective Relative to AA only	Match Race	Match Gender	Match Age
Blount, Powers, Cotter, Swan Free (1994)	67% of 3	nm	Medical regimen compliance	coping techniques	yes	nm	nm	nm
Boczkowski, Zeichner, & DeSanto (1985)	53% of 36	nm	neuroleptic compliance	behavioral tailoring intervention & psychoeducational intervention				
Brown & Coursey (1989)	2% of 287	nm	pain coping & depression	passive and active coping	nm	nm	nm	nm
Burgio, Engel, McCormick, Hawkins, & Scheve (1988)	50% of 4	nm	urinary incontinence	behavioral treatment	nm	nm	nm	nm
Burling, Bigelow, Robinson, & Mead (1991)	44.6% of 411	nm	smoking cessation	letter absent smoking and it's effects directive stop smoking advice	nm	nm	nm	nm
Butters & Cash (1987)	3% of 32	nm	body image dissatisfaction	cognitive behavior therapy	nm	nm	nm	nm
Caplan, Weissberg, Grober, Sivo, Grady, & Jacoby (1992)	90% of 206	nm	social adjustment, social alcohol use	stress management	nm	nm	nm	nm

* not mentioned (nm)

Table 1 (Continued)
Critique of Reviewed Studies

Author/ Date	% AA	Cultural Specific Assessment	Target Behavior	Techniques	Effective Relative to AA only	Match		
						Race	Gender	Age
Chambless & Williams (1995)	24% of 75	nm	agoraphobia	in-vivo exposure	yes	nm	nm	nm
Cooper & Clum (1989)	14% of 4	nm	post traumatic stress disorder	flooding	nm	nm	nm	nm
Cordova, Andrykowski, Kenady, McGrath, Sloan, & Redd (1995)	7% of 55	nm	post traumatic stress disorder and breast cancer	phone interview	nm	nm	nm	nm
Darkes & Goldman (1993)	3% of 74	nm	drinking	expectancy challenge of alcohol effects/alcohol info sessions	nm	nm	nm	nm
DeRubeis, Evans, Hollon, Garvey, Grove, & Tuason (1990)	9% of 108	nm	depression	cognitive therapy, Becks cognitive therapy pharmaco-impromine	nm	nm	nm	nm
Dolan, Black, Penk, Robinowitz, & DeFord (1985)	71.4% of 21	nm	illicit drug use	contracting for Tx termination for methodone maintenance Tx	nm	nm	nm	nm
Foa, Riggs, Massie, & Yarczower (1995)	33% of 12	nm	post traumatic stress disorder	imagery desensitizaton fear activation	nm	nm	nm	nm

* not mentioned (nm)

Table 1 (Continued)
Critique of Reviewed Studies

Author/ Date	% AA	Cultural Specific Assess- ment	Target Behavior	Techniques	Effective Relative to AA only	Match		
						Race	Gender	Age
Follette, Follette, & Alexander (1991)	24% of 65	nm	adjustment of incest survivors	interpersonal transactional group	nm	nm	nm	nm
Grant & Cash (1995)	9% of 23	nm	body dis- satisfaction	cognitive behavior therapy in group ther- apy vs modest con- tact cognitive behavior therapy-self directed form				
Hall, Tunstall, Ginsberg, Benowitz, & Jones (1987)	6% of 139	nm	smoking cessation	aversive smoking, ed- ucational materials, re- lapse preven- tion skills, written exer- cises	nm	nm	nm	nm
Hanson & Gidycz (1993)	4% of 346	nm	sexual assault	cognitive be- havior ther- apy	nm	nm	nm	nm
Hare, McPherson, & Forth (1988)	.4% of 521	nm	criminal activity	checked computer for convictions and prison times	nm	nm	nm	nm
Horowitz, Rosenberg, Baer, Ureno, & Villasenor (1988)	4% of 103	nm	inter- personal problems	therapy psycho- therapy	nm	nm	nm	nm

* not mentioned (nm)

Table 1 (Continued)
Critique of Reviewed Studies

Author/ Date	% AA	Cultural Specific Assessment	Target Behavior	Techniques	Effective Relative to AA only	Match		
						Race	Gender	Age
Jamison & Scogin (1995)	15% of 80	nm	depression	cognitive bibliotherapy	nm	nm	nm	nm
Jason, McMahon, Salina, Hedecker, Stockton, Dunson, & Kimball (1995)	28.5% of 283	nm	smoking	self-help group incentives	nm	nm	nm	nm
Jenson, Turner, & Romano (1994)	2% of 94	nm	chronic pain	multidisciplinary pain program cog. coping strategies	nm	nm	nm	nm
Kalichman, Kelly, Hunter, Murphy, & Tyler (1993)	100% of 106	nm	AIDS knowledge	video tape information	effective	yes	yes	nm
Kelly, St. Lawrence, Hood, & Brasfield (1989)	13% of104	nm	AIDS risk activities	behavioral intervention	nm	nm	nm	nm
Kidorf, Stitzer, & Broomer (1994)	54% of 84	nm	drug use	1) take home incentives 2) methodone maintenance	nm	nm	nm	nm
Kivlahen, Marlatt, Fromme, Coppel, & Williams (1990)	4% of 43	nm	drinking	alcohol skills training, alcohol intervention class	nm	nm	nm	nm

* not mentioned (nm)

Table 1 (Continued)
Critique of Reviewed Studies

Author/ Date	% AA	Cultural Specific Assessment	Target Behavior	Techniques	Effective Relative to AA only	Match		
						Race	Gender	Age
Lucic, Steffen, Harrigan, & Stuebing (1991)	4% of 48	nm	relaxation	muscle contraction before progressive relaxation training versus relaxation w/o muscle contraction	nm	nm	nm	nm
Martelli, Auerbach, Alexander, & Mercuri (1987)	57% of 46	nm	stress and coping during oral surgery	problem focused, emotion focused or mixed focus coping strategies	nm	nm	nm	nm
Michelson, Mavissakalian, & Marchione (1988)	1% of 73	nm	agoraphobia	cognitive behavioral, psychophysiological, graduated in-vivo exposure, paradoxical intention, progressive dmr	nm	nm	nm	nm
Michelson, Mavissakalian, & Marchione (1985)	3% of 31	nm	agoraphobia	cognitive behavior treatment	nm	nm	nm	nm
Michelson, Mavissakalian, Marchione, Dancu, & Greenwald (1986)	3% of 31	nm	agoraphobia	self-directed in vivo exposure	nm	nm	nm	nm

* not mentioned (nm)

Table 1 (Continued)
Critique of Reviewed Studies

Author/ Date	% AA	Cultural Specific Assessment	Target Behavior	Techniques	Effective Relative to AA only	Match		
						Race	Gender	Age
Middleton & Cartledge (1995)	100% of 5	nm	direct observation	social skills instruction: modeling, role playing, parental involvement	yes	nm	nm	nm
Monti, Rohsenow, Rubonis, Niaura, Sirota, Colby, Goddard, & Abrams (1993)	6% of 40	nm	alcoholism	exposure, coping skills training.	nm	nm	nm	nm
Morin, Kowatch, Barry, & Walton (1993)	8.3% of 24	nm	insomnia knowledge	cognitive behavior therapy	nm	nm	nm	nm
O'Malley, Foley, Rounsaville, Watkins, Sotsky, Imber, & Elkin (1988)	8% non-white of 35	nm	depression	interpersonal psychotherapy	nm	nm	nm	nm
Porzelius, Houston, Smith, Arfken, & Fisher (1995)	7% of 54	nm	weight loss	standard behavioral weight loss vs. binge eating weight loss	nm	nm	nm	nm
Roerich & Goldman (1993)	16% of 80	nm	alcoholism treatment	cognitive stimulation procedures	nm	nm	nm	nm

* not mentioned (nm)

Table 1 (Continued)
Critique of Reviewed Studies

Author/ Date	% AA	Cultural Specific Assessment	Target Behavior	Techniques	Effective Relative to AA only	Match		
						Race	Gender	Age
Lucic, Steffen, Harrigan, & Stuebing (1991)	4% of 48	nm	relaxation	muscle contraction before progressive relaxation training versus relaxation w/o muscle contraction	nm	nm	nm	nm
Martelli, Auerbach, Alexander, & Mercuri (1987)	57% of 46	nm	stress and coping during oral surgery	problem focused, emotion focused or mixed focus coping strategies	nm	nm	nm	nm
Michelson, Mavissakalian, & Marchione (1988)	1% of 73	nm	agoraphobia	cognitive behavioral, psychophysiological, graduated in-vivo exposure, paradoxical intention, progressive dmr	nm	nm	nm	nm
Michelson, Mavissakalian, & Marchione (1985)	3% of 31	nm	agoraphobia	cognitive behavior treatment	nm	nm	nm	nm
Michelson, Mavissakalian, Marchione, Dancu, & Greenwald (1986)	3% of 31	nm	agoraphobia	self-directed in vivo exposure	nm	nm	nm	nm

* not mentioned (nm)

Table 1 (Continued)
Critique of Reviewed Studies

Author/ Date	% AA	Cultural Specific Assess-	Target Behavior	Techniques	Effective Relative to AA only	Match		
						Race	Gender	Age
Rothbaum & Foa (1991)	100% (case study of one)	nm	post traumatic stress disorder with conversion mutism	imaginal and in vivo exposure	yes	nm	yes	nm
Sharp & Foreman (1985)	31.7% of 60	nm	anxiety	a) stress inoculation b) classroom management training	nm	nm	nm	nm
Snyder & Wills (1989)	15.9% of 79 couples	nm	interspousal and intraspousal functioning	a) behavioral marital therapy vs b) insight oriented marital therapy	nm	nm	nm	nm
Taras, Matson, & Felps (1993)	25% of 4	nm	independence training with visually impaired men	modeling instruction, corrective feedback, self-evaluation, trainer feedback, reinforcement	nm	nm	nm	nm
Wilfey, Agras, Telch, Rossiter, Schneider, Golomb-Cole, Sifford, & Raeburn (1993)	5% of 56	nm	binge eating	group cognitive behavior therapy, group interpersonal therapy	nm	nm	nm	nm

* not mentioned (nm)

drives, has enhanced significantly the ability to explain, predict and change behavior (Kazdin, 1984). The assumption that the majority of behavior (normal and abnormal) is a function of three primary types of learning (i.e., classical conditioning, operant, and observational learning), has provided an empirical, theoretical base for the large majority of behavior change efforts. While the rich history of behaviorism and the behavioral model has been summarized by several writers (Hersen & Van Hasselt, 1987; Kazdin, 1978), suffice it to say here that the field has advanced rapidly and the benefits to human functioning have been enormous.

One of the most significant contributions to the field of psychology was made by B. F. Skinner. His functional analysis of behavior provided a means for determining factors which lead to the development and maintenance of behavior. While a host of behavioral treatments were developed during the two decades following Skinner's functional analysis, many of the changes produced were of relatively short duration. Therefore, in the 1970's, efforts were undertaken to discover methods to enhance the persistence and/or maintenance of desired behavior following treatment withdrawal. While several noble efforts were carried out (Jones & Kazdin, 1975; Kazdin 1984), the need to examine the potential role of cognitive processes (i.e., thoughts, perceptions and memory) in not only the development of behavior, but also its long term maintenance of such behavior was obvious. The early work of Bandura (1971), Meichenbaum (1977), Staats (1971), and Mahoney and Thoresen (1974) did much to integrate aspects of the various learning paradigms with cognitive processes. Treatment strategies stemming from the combination of these efforts are often referred to as cognitive behavioral. Within this model the conceptualization, assessment and treatment of problem behavior has been greatly improved.

In sum, behavioral therapy involves the systematic assessment of behaviors, feelings and thoughts, the determination of causes of problem behavior, and the development and implementation of treatment strategies. Cognitive behavior therapy attempts to more fully involve the cognitive processes that underlie behavior. The primary goal of cognitive behavioral therapy is to effect change by exposing the cognitive processes that contribute to behavior and altering the content of these processes as a means of altering the behavior. This approach typically entails both the client and therapist taking an active and directive role in the therapeutic process. Among several of the most successful strategies employed are systematic desensitization, cognitive restructuring and flooding.

Adequacy of the Cognitive Behavioral Conceptualization for African Americans

The studies included in this review targeted a wide range of psychological problems ranging from body-image distortion to substance abuse. Generally, the etiological factors contributing to the development of such problems fell within the scope of the major categories of causation of behavioral problems. The majority of the treatment regimens evaluated were consistent with a cognitive behavioral orientation. Many multi-cultural theorists maintain that research among ethnic groups should acknowledge the viability of cultural orientations and incorporate relevant factors into the conceptualization and treatment of psychological problems (Acosta, Yamamoto, & Evans, 1982; White & Parham, 1990). They assert that the cultural values and qualities of individuals' ethnic groups do influence functioning; and that failure to incorporate such factors results in incomplete understanding and treatment of the ethnic client's overall functioning. One means to ensure such culturally-based features into one's framework is to engage in cultural competent practices. Cultural competence is defined as "an awareness of, sensitivity to, and knowledge of the meaning of culture." It includes one's openness and willingness to learn about cultural issues, including one's own cultural biases. Cultural competence is an evolving process that depends on self-reflection as well as on the contributions of people from other cultures, (p. 722) (Dillard, Andonian, Flores, and Lai, 1992). Cross and his colleagues maintain that cultural competence is achieved when a therapist possesses key attitudes, knowledge, and skills to work effectively with clients from various cultural backgrounds (Cross, Bazron, Dennis, & Isaacs, 1989).

More broadly, the discipline of psychology has been frequently criticized for not engaging in culturally competent practices with African Americans (Bernal & Castro, 1994; Sue, 1977; Turner & Jones, 1982). One reason for this criticism stems from the lack of recognition of a viable distinct African American culture which significantly impacts the functioning of African Americans. Additionally, the consequent skepticism toward the existence of psychosocial phenomena that may differentially impact the psychological functioning of African Americans has precluded empirical investigation and has fostered the belief that the prevailing psychological theories are equally relevant for African Americans. Further, the assumption that treatment modalities generated by these theories are equally effective for this group has often gone uncontested.

Several African American researchers, however, recognized the limited utility of the prevailing psychological paradigms and related assessment and treatment strategies in providing effective psychological care for African Americans. They argue that in the absence of the incorporation of culturally relevant factors which may differentially impact African Americans and members of the dominant society, efficacy is compromised. They have also begun to articulate the nature of these culturally-relevant variables and to delineate the manner in which they may influence the conceptualization and implementation of effective treatment strategies to this group. One line of thinking stems from the theory of Afrocentrism. This theory asserts that there are unique characteristics of the world-view of African Americans, whose roots of origin can be traced back to original civilizations in ancient Africa (Nobles, 1980; White & Parham, 1990). There are several distinct components of this theory which impacts the behavior of African Americans including: a holistic view of man and the universe, a group ethos which incorporates a collective sense of responsibility and extended family kinship bonds, circular conceptualization of time, strong emphasis on the oral tradition, and an unending life cycle which includes ancestors and those yet to be born (Nobles, 1972). Further, this model asserts that the world-view and resultant behavior of African Americans are heavily influenced by these values and should be considered when evaluating members of this group.

Other African American researchers have purported that any theory which attempts to explain the psychological functioning of African Americans must incorporate the impact of their status within the dominant society and the stressors that are derived from their acculturative experiences (Anderson, 1989). These stressors are purported to result from the inconsistencies that are present between the cultural values of African Americans relative to European Americans. Also, the subsequent pressure African Americans experience living in a society that primarily reflects the social characteristics of the dominant society must be considered. As such, theories that attempt to explain maladaptive behavior of African Americans that underpin formulations of treatment strategies should incorporate the moderating impact of unique stressors and other factors encountered.

One of the goals of this review is to determine the extent to which behavioral researchers and therapists have considered these unique factors in their conceptualization, assessment and treatment of problem behavior with this target group. What follows is a critical evaluation of assessment practices with African Americans followed by attempts to treat problem behavior. The extent to which relevant process variables have been considered and a priori incorporated into research and therapeutic strategies will be examined. Explanations for the current state of the art and guidelines to achieve desired ends with African Americans will also be presented.

Critical Review: Assessment, Treatment, and Process

Assessment Practices with African Americans

The assessment measures most frequently used in these studies were the Beck Depression Inventory (BDI), the Diagnostic Interview Schedule (DIS) and the State-Trait Anxiety Inventory (STAI), the Hamilton Rating Scale for Depression, the Structured Clinical Interview for DSM-III-R (SCID-R), the Symptom Checklist-90-Revised (SCL-90) and the Anxiety Disorders Interview Scale-Revised (ADIS-R). While many of the aforementioned instruments have been determined to be psychometrically sound, studies indicate that several have been found particularly problematic for use with African Americans. For example, some researchers have maintained that instruments such as the Diagnostic Interview Schedule, utilized to diagnose mental illness have less validity for African Americans than for other groups (Hendricks, Bayton, Collins, Mathura, McMillian, & Montgomery, 1983; Lopez & Nunez, 1983).

In the past, traditional measures of assessing the psychological functioning of African Americans has been regarded with suspicion by the African American community. Many of the measures used in psychological assessment are shrouded in controversy concerning multicultural appropriateness. This is largely because traditional assessment measures are designed for the dominant culture and normed primarily on this population (Neighbors, Jackson, Campbell, & Williams, 1989). Consequently, many have questioned the validity of utilizing instruments normed on Caucasians with other racial and ethnic groups (Neighbors et al., 1989; Paniagua, 1994).

Neighbors et al. (1989) suggests that two assumptions are commonly made when comparing diagnoses of African Americans and Caucasians. The first assumption is that the groups manifest symptomology in the same manner but are often diagnosed differently because of biases by clinicians. For example, African Americans are less likely than Caucasians to be diagnosed with an affective disorder but more likely to be diagnosed with schizophrenia. This occurs even when symptomatology presentation is similar. The second is that, although the groups differ, clinicians erroneously believe that their expression of symptoms are identical. This suggests that clinicians often do not consider how cultural differences may impact symptom expression. For example, assuming that depression will manifest itself in the same way and have identical etiologies may lead to faulty conclusions. While there are arguments to support and refute each of these claims, our perusal of the literature suggests that the latter assumption may be more widely endorsed by behavior therapists.

In this review of only fifty-one cognitive behavioral studies found to employ some proportion of African American adult subjects, a range of major assessment instruments were employed. However, none of these studies employed culturally specific instruments nor discussed the potential benefits of using such instruments with African Americans. Even in those studies where samples consisted of entirely African Americans, culturally-specific assessment instruments were not used. In neither instance were the potential limitations of assessment devices nor the absence of culturally-sensitive instruments discussed. It is important to note however, that in the majority of the studies reviewed, the proportion of African Americans comprising the sample was so small that the utilization of culturally specific instruments would likely not be warranted. Additionally, the authors in these studies did not appear to consider race a distinguishing variable and may have assumed that symptom expression of targeted behavior was identical across race.

More generally, within the broad disciplines of psychology and psychiatry several instruments have been used to determine the rate of mental health illness in the African American population. Many studies employing these instruments have consistently found a higher rate of mental illness in African Americans than Caucasian (Adebimpe, 1981; Jones & Gray, 1986). Particularly, studies have shown that African Americans are more likely to be diagnosed with schizophrenia than an affective disorder (Collins, Rickman, & Mathura, 1980; Jones & Gray, 1986). The Epidemiological Catchment Area (ECA) study was one of the most comprehensive efforts conducted on the epidemiology of psychiatric disorders (Neal & Turner, 1991; Regier, Myers, Kramer, Robins, Blazer, Hough, Eaton, & Locke, 1984). This study has been criticized because rates of some anxiety disorders as well as other forms of psychopathology may have been inflated (Horwath, Lish, Johnson, Horning, & Weissman, 1993; Neal & Turner, 1991; Williams, 1986). These discrepancies leave one wondering about the accuracy of some diagnostic instruments with African Americans. In fact, because of such discrepancies, some researchers have called for a transcultural diagnostic system (Lopez & Nunez, 1987). These investigators reviewed the Diagnostic Statistical Manual of Mental Disorders (DSM-III), and accompanying assessment instruments, such as the Diagnostic Interview Schedule (DIS), the Structured Clinical Interview for DSM-III Personality Disorders, and the Schedule for Affective Disorders and Schizophrenia (SADS) and concluded that they minimally addressed the significance of cultural factors in symptom expression of affective, personality, and schizophrenic disorders.

For example, as alluded to earlier, the Diagnostic Interview Schedule (DIS) has been found to have questionable validity by some researchers (Hendricks et al., 1983). In fact these researchers suggested that this instrument may have low content-validity for low socioeconomic status African Americans. Although it is predicated on the DSM, not until recently did this source adequately address cultural differences in symptom expression of particular disorders. They asserted that all diagnostic criteria and concomitant interview schedules should have statements acknowledging and alerting clinicians to the possibility of cultural influences on the expression of mental disorder.

Additionally, it is important to consider applicability of current diagnostic criteria to disorders manifested by African Americans. In that the DSM-IV (American Psychiatric Association, 1994), does address cultural concerns with reference to diagnostic criteria and provides information on cultural formulations and culture-bound syndromes, it affords substantial benefits over past editions. This edition attempts to remedy problems noted in past diagnostic manuals and the multicultural nature of our society as well as variability in the expression of psychopathology. For example, Appendix I of this manual gives an outline that details factors that should be considered when a clinician is attempting to formulate a disorder within a cultural framework. The second part of the appendix is devoted to defining indigenous disorders. While this information may provide insight to those who may have never considered cultural influences on the expression of a disorder, one's biases, norms and socialization will likely impact the extent of consideration given to cultural influences. In light of Tharp's (1991) assertion that Eurocentric norms are institutionalized and therefore hinder psychocultural under-standing, the need for continued consideration to issues related to assessment is essential.

In summary, considering that assessment often precedes treatment, it is obvious that inadequate assessment could lead to undesired treatment outcomes. It is important for clinicians to be aware of how cultural/contextual issues affect the interpretation and treatment of problem behavior. We feel that the engagement of specific, culturally, sensitive assessment instruments is paramount. Consistent with this thinking, Pearson (1994) suggests that it is essential that investigators and clinicians examine the following factors when attempting to carry out culturally-sensitive assessment:

1. The client's current and past life experiences.
2. The client's beliefs, behavior, and family interaction, particularly those related to health.
3. The impact of illness on the family's overall functioning.
4. The cultural background, including religious and spiritual perspective of the client, and
5. The client's financial situation (p. 93).

The need to become aware of culturally-relevant questionnaires and to determine their relative merit is an important next step. For example, in the area of Child Psychology, Jones and Herndon (1994), reviewed the literature and found a number of culturally-relevant alternative assessment instruments for African Ameri-can children and adolescents. Similar quests should be undertaken in the adult area. We strongly encourage investigators targeting African Americans to creatively develop and integrate culturally sensitive assessment instruments when possible. In those instances where this cannot be done, due to the nonexistence of such measures, some discussion regarding the limitations of existing measures would be in order.

Treatment Findings

The representation of African Americans and other ethnic groups in the studies reviewed was extremely low. Only fifty-one outcome studies published in a ten year span across seven major journals bodes poorly for the field's efforts with this group. The small number provides little power to draw meaningful conclusions. Obvi-ously, the need for greater representation of African Americans in empirical investigations is great. Of those studies reviewed, few specifically tailored their interventions to African Americans. In most of the investigations, the data analysis precluded interpretation of the differential effects of treatment on race. In most instances, this appears to be due to no attempt to analyze data by race. As indicated earlier, we do recognize that such analyses may be unnecessary given the small numbers of racially diverse subjects in most studies reviewed. As a result, however, we gained little knowledge on the effectiveness of specific behavioral techniques on changing behaviors of African Americans from this review.

Therefore, from our review, direct evidence of the effectiveness of treatment strategies is scant. Most of the studies provide only indirect evidence to support the effectiveness of behavior therapeutic interventions with African Americans. However, it should be noted that while these studies did not specifically examine the efficacy of treatment solely with African Americans, the overall levels of effectiveness suggests that particular treatment strategies may be quite useful with this target group. Additionally, positive results from studies employing relatively large proportions of African Americans further validate this claim. For example, Boczkowski, Zeichner and DeSanto (1985) found that a Behavioral Tailoring (BT) intervention was effective in increasing neuroleptic compliance among chronic schizophrenic outpatients. It should be noted that their sample was 47% African American. Dolan, Black, Penk, Rabinowitz, and DeFord (1985) found that contingency contracting was an effective intervention for increasing treatment compliance among problem patients in methadone maintenance programs. In this study, 75% of their sample was African American. Alexander, Neimeyer, Follette, Moore, and Harter (1989) conducted a comparison of group treatments for women sexually abused as children and found that interpersonal transaction and process groups, were effective in reducing depression and alleviating distress. Twenty-four percent of this sample was African American. Kidorf, Stitzer, and Brooner (1994) examined the characteristics of methadone patients responding to take-home incentives, and found that contingent take-home privileges could be integrated successfully into standard methadone maintenance treatments. Specifically, they found that those patients who may succeed on a take-home incentive program could be differentiated from those who may not improve without additional treatment intervention. Over half of the subjects in this investigation were African Americans.

In summary, these studies certainly imply that behavior therapy may be an effective treatment modality for African Americans. However, given the limited representation of African Americans and the fact that most of these findings only indirectly suggest high levels of efficacy, what is needed are more investigations which target African Americans and other ethnic groups to better determine effectiveness of behavior therapy approaches. While the data seem to suggest favorable outcomes, the final verdict awaits more empirical efforts targeting this population.

Process Issues

While several process variables were examined (e.g., race, age and gender) across change-agents (therapists, researchers), and participants (subjects, clients, patients) to determine the degree of match between these two variables, few matches were found. In no study was there mention of racial or age matching between change-agents and participants. Concerning gender, there were a few attempts where gender of therapist and subject were matched. This was most likely in cases of a sexual nature (e.g., rape, incest). In general, this information was difficult to ascertain because methods sections did not consistently provide such information. Consequently, the extent to which racial, gender and age match is a meaningful predictor of outcome cannot be determined. Obviously, the need for continued research in this area is essential. We are certainly aware of the fact that there were many instances where the need to "match" was totally inappropriate. For example, in those studies where no experimenter, researcher or therapist was required (i.e., self-help groups), no such matches were necessary. We also recognize the fact that suggesting that matching be carried out in studies where only small numbers of African Americans or other ethnic minorities are represented, would be overly demanding. However, we do feel that attention and sensitivity to such issues should be provided during the early formulation and conceptualization of the effort.

While early claims speculated that little or no relationship existed between client-therapist's similarity or complementary therapeutic effectiveness (Berzins, 1977; Garfield, 1978), more recent research targeting ethnically diverse clients in clinical analog studies have provided at least tentative findings to suggest that matching by race results in more positive outcomes (Sue, 1988). While support for therapist-client ethnic match was a very important consideration for White, Asian American and Mexican American clients in predicting premature termination, this relationship was not found for African Americans. However, there was a significant relationship between ethnic-match and number of sessions for African Americans as well as Asian Americans, Mexican Americans and Whites (Sue et al., 1991). These authors concluded that these data do partially support the cultural responsiveness hypothesis which maintains that "the efficacy of psychotherapy is, among many factors, a function of the extent to which therapists can communicate in the language of clients and understand the cultural background of clients" (Flaskerud, 1986; Sue et al., 1991, p. 34). Unfortunately, given the relatively small numbers of African Americans represented in the studies reviewed and lack of information reported within the method sections, the extent to which match is a meaningful predictor of outcome cannot not be determined. Obviously, the need for continued research in this understudied area is essential.

Given the importance of race and gender as psychological variables, we suggest that further examination of each may well strengthen our knowledge base of these two seldom studied variables. Rather than analyzing data by race and gender as an apparent afterthought, or not at all, we advocate, as do others (Scarr, 1988), the need to analyze these variables on a consistent basis. In the context of this investigation it would have been valuable to analyze results by race and gender to determine potential variation in functioning relative to these two variables. Although each is viewed as highly sensitive by members of our discipline, the need for forthright study of racial and gender differences is obvious if the quality of life of all individuals is to be enhanced (Scarr, 1988). For example, within the context of psychopathology, several investigators have made compelling cases for the examination of racial differences. One group of disorders where such a case can be made is the anxiety disorders. General survey data showed that these disorders were the most frequent diagnoses rendered to African American women who sought psychiatric treatment and the second most common diagnoses given to African American men (Jones & Gray, 1986). Furthermore, there are also data to suggest that the expression of anxiety symptomology may be different across White and African American clients (Neal & Turner, 1991). The knowledge to be gained from studying the variable of race may aid significantly in our ability to assess, conceptualize and treat anxiety disorders as well as related problems suffered by African Americans.

The need for both "mainstream" and African American researchers to investigate further the variables of race and gender is particularly germane given the personal values that investigators bring to the research setting. "The positive or negative value attached to particular observations is often very much in the eye of the beholder" (Scarr, 1988, p. 57). Asking the right questions and interpreting conclusions objectively may do much to enhance skill development and adaptive functioning across a variety of contexts for those African Americans who seek out counsel. In light of the fact that there is "very little research on the strengths of underrepresented groups in the social science literature" (Scarr, 1988, p. 57), the call for additional research attention by researchers with different racial backgrounds and gender status is of paramount importance.

Explanations for the Current State of the Art

The small number of African Americans represented in the studies reviewed may be a function of a number of factors ranging from historical perception of African Americans by mental health professionals to practical issues on the part of African Americans. What follows is a brief overview of several factors which may have contributed to the state of the art regarding African American participation in psychology-related endeavors.

Historical Perceptions of African Americans

A primary reason for a lack of participation of African Americans, not only in research-related endeavors, but also in the therapeutic setting is the field's negative view of African Americans. When tracing many historical accounts of psychologists' attitudes and perceptions of African Americans, numerous negative allegations were made in regards to the intellectual ability, societal contribution or potential to obtain even a minimal level of optimal functioning. Maultsby's (1982) informative account of "African American's Distrust of Psychiatry" sheds much light on this topic. He states that "Black Americans have a deeply rooted, long-standing distrust of American psychiatry" (p. 39). One of the earliest and most devastating blows against African Americans was by American physicians who maintained popular beliefs of African American inferiority. Maultsby (1982) states that many of these early physicians "willingly fabricated pseudoscientific evidence" (p. 39) in support of African American inferiority. For example, he cites the work of Samuel G. Morton, professor of anatomy at the Pennsylvania Medical College during the early 1840's, who stated that "the brains of people become progressively smaller as one descends from the Caucasian to the Ethiopian" (p. 41). These data were said to be based on unreplicated findings (Stanton, 1960). G. Stanley Hall, the first president of the American Psychological Association and founder of the American Journal of Psychology, depicted African Americans and Indians as "members of the adolescent races in an arrested stage of development" (p. 41).

Yet another negative ploy which no doubt did much to increase the gap between African Americans and the mental health profession was the 1840 census where White census takers engaged in "bungled fraud" as reported by Jarvis (1844, 1852). For instance, these census takers reported that there were 27 insane African Americans, two deaf and dumb African Americans, and one blind African American in eight towns in Maine that had no African American residents. Maultsby also cites similar evidence of racially-based thinking following the Civil War. R. B. Bean, a professor of Johns Hopkins University, wrote in the Journal of Anatomy in 1906 that "the Negro's brain is smaller than the brains of Whites and that explains the Negro's lack of willpower, self-control, self-government, ethical and esthetic faculties" (p. 379). He went on to state that he was "forced to conclude it is useless to try to elevate the Negro by education" (Thomas & Sillen, 1972). Unfortunately, such thinking reinforced the distrust of African Americans toward mental health professionals. Many of these negative perceptions have persisted into the twentieth-century. Among notable instances are several claims by A. R. Jensen which were based on the questionable work of Sir Cyril Burt. Jensen's classic paper "Intelligence and Social Mobility" (1969), seemed to reinforce the notion that IQ is genetically determined and that people who have low scores are mentally inferior to those who have higher scores. Leon Kamin (1974) at Princeton University produced evidence to strongly suggest that Burt had probably falsified his data but, the damage had already been done. Maultsby goes on to state that several of the most influential mental health professionals throughout history believed that African Americans were inferior and had abnormal personality structures (Thomas & Sillen, 1972; Willie, Kramer, & Brown, 1973).

Early conceptualizations of the psychological functioning of African Americans' often adhered to an inferiority or deprivation/deficit orientation (White & Parham, 1990). This also contributed toward African Americans' negative perceptions of psychology. The inferiority model posited that African Americans were intellectually, physically, and mentally inferior to Whites. This belief was supported by theories of genetics and heredity which asserted that the development of humans was biologically determined through genetic encoding. Support for this orientation included studies of genetic inferiority. The assertions of racial and intellectual inferiority such as the one below posited by Jensen (1969), reinforced such thinking:

> The deficiency/deficit orientation emerged around the late 1950's to the early 1960's. Primarily this orientation involves the expectation that African Americans have been prevented from developing into healthy psychological people due to the deleterious effects of racism, oppression, and negative stereotypes that has characterized their history within our society. Thus, within this framework it is assumed that African Americans are inferior in terms of cognitive functioning, family structure, and other psychological factors due to negative environmental factors. This model emerged primarily as a way of dispelling models that posited African Americans being inadequate due to biological determinants and genetic heredity. An essential component of this conceptualization is the acceptance of European cultural standards as the normative standard and the resultant cultural deprivation of African Americans as a result of not being adequately exposed to these European American values (p. 8).

The most notable application of the deficiency/deprivation model is to the African American family. According to White and Parham (1990):

> The deficit-deficiency model assumes that, as a result of [a] background of servitude, deprivation, second-class citizenship, and chronic unemployment, African American adults have not been able to develop marketable skills, self-sufficient, future orientation, planning and decision-making competencies, and instrumental behaviors thought to be necessary for sustaining a successful two-parent nuclear family while guiding children through the socialization process" (p. 9).

Similarly, the body of research which posited that African Americans had dysfunctional family systems characterized by a strong matriarchal leader and the absence of male heads of households (Boyd-Franklin, 1989; Moynihan, 1965) is also supported by this model.

Unethical Practices

Other historical accounts of gross violations of ethical standards and human rights loom large in the minds of many African Americans. For example, the Tuskegee experiment where African American men, without their knowledge, were infected with the syphilis virus and never treated, did much to lessen African Americans' enthusiasm toward becoming involved in research endeavors. While much has been done to prevent such violations through regulations of the Department of Health and Human Services and institutional review boards and the ethical standards written by organizations such as the American Psychological Association; traumatic memories of such experiences are not easily forgotten.

Lack of Representation of African Americans within Psychology

With reference to the African American client/patient, several practical factors may be operative in lessening their participation in psychologically related activities. For example, the lack of financial resources to afford therapy or even the time to become involved in research projects may hinder participation. An African American student recently took the first author's undergraduate abnormal psychology course. After she acquired knowledge of the etiology, assessment and treatment of Attention Deficit Hyperactivity Disorder (ADHD), she felt that she may have been suffering from this disorder. However, she refused to be assessed because she felt "it cost too much." Similarly, many African American parents of young children who we see in our clinic often shy away from therapy opportunities for their children because of a lack of finances to pay for such services. A related concern is the perceived stigma that often accompanies "visits to a psychologist." Many African Americans often seek out other sources when faced with problems including physicians, members of the clergy, and members of their extended families (Neighbors, 1988; Sue, Zane, & Young, 1994). Many well-meaning, White therapists, have often told us that they have met with little success in attracting African Americans to the therapeutic setting. In those instances where they do, their level of success in treating their problems is often minimal. While we believe that such failure is frequently due to a lack of training in culturally competent practices, it has been documented for over two decades that improper stereotyping of the poor by psychotherapists has led to problems in treatment as well as diagnosis (Goldstein, 1971). Many Eurocentric therapists may not view their African American clients as "good clients" because they perceive them as nonYAVIS (young, attractive, verbal, intelligent, and successful) as initially described by Schofield (1964). Consequently, the level of success in therapy is hindered. One of several documented sources of this fact is the report by the President's Commission on Mental Health (1978), which concluded that many clients from ethnic groups experienced premature termination rates and ineffective treatment at the hands of traditional mental health services. Such occurrences may have done much to lessen African American involvement in research and therapy.

Small Number of African American Researchers and Therapists

A final reason for the low representation of African Americans in research and therapy efforts is the small number of African American researchers and therapists. Bernal and Castro (1994) have made this point more broadly in that they maintain there is a gross under-representation of ethnic minorities in psychology (psychology doctoral enrollments, doctoral recipients, APA members, and faculty in graduate departments). More specifically, they conclude that the initial rise in psychology doctoral enrollments, doctoral recipients, APA members, and faculty in graduate departments between 1970 and 1980 appears to have leveled out. Among psychology faculty in graduate departments, African Americans make up only approximately 3%. Given that many of these individuals and their graduate students are often more likely to engage in research projects targeting African Americans than their White counterparts, the lion's share of such research may fall on the shoulders of this small group. These authors conclude, "There is clear indication that the need for mental health services and research on ethnic minority populations will increase at a greater rate than will the availability of qualified professionals to address these needs," (p. 798). The need for greater representation of African Americans in the field is clear.

Guidelines to Achieve the Goal of Increasing Research and Therapy Efforts with African Americans

As first voiced in 1977 at a symposium at the annual meeting of the Association of African American Psychologists, held in Los Angeles, California, the need for cultural sensitivity toward ethnic diverse groups within the field of psychology was essential to the involvement of greater numbers of African Americans and other people of color in the therapeutic process and related research endeavors. Since that time, numerous recommendations have been made, and positive steps taken to promote the quality of interaction between psychologists and ethnic minorities. For example, Sue (1977), after reviewing the files of 14,000 clients in the mental health system in Seattle, where the effectiveness of therapy was found to be quite dismal, made the following recommendations: (a) equipping mental health professionals, through training, to work with culturally dissimilar clients; (b) a greater representation of employed bilingual and bicultural mental health workers; and (c) the development of parallel services which are uniquely devoted to ethnic minority groups.

More recently, Locke (1992) spelled out key characteristics which should be considered when interacting with African Americans and other ethnic minorities in psychologically-related endeavors (including therapy and research) to ensure maximal effectiveness. These characteristics include: acculturation; poverty and economic concerns; history of oppression; language; racism and prejudice; childbearing practices; religious practices; family structure; and cultural values and attitudes. Paniagua (1994) also stressed the need for taking into consideration certain culture-specific factors. Specifically, he noted that African American clients expected quicker solutions to problems and were less assertive than other groups. For this reason, he suggested that problem-solving and assertiveness training may be potentially effective for African American clients. He also added that, since the extended family played an important role in the life of many African Americans, family therapy may be an effective treatment modality. Paniagua (1994) commented upon the fact that the long history of slavery, racism, and discrimination experienced by African Americans also makes empowerment an important component for effective therapy.

Wu and Windle (1980) reported that the quality of mental health services to ethnic minorities has improved considerably as a result of more "ethnic-specific" mental health centers, more service providers from diverse groups hired and encouragement to fund innovative intervention programs for ethnic communities. O'Sullivan, Peterson, Cox, and Kirkeby (1989) concluded that because more cultural responsive interventions and outcomes of community mental health services for ethnic minority groups is evident, the years of attempting to be "culturally responsive" have met with some level of success. Notwithstanding these positive initial steps, the need for continued strides in these areas is essential. A critical examination of many hypothesized relationships among client and therapist variables should also be undertaken. For example, with respect to therapist knowledge of clients' culture, no rigorous tests have ever been conducted to see if therapists' understanding of culture is related to therapy outcomes," (Sue et al., 1991, p. 534). Similarly, there are few hard data to substantiate the claim that ethnic minority clients are better due to culturally responsive strategies. Further insight into these issues is essential.

Future Directions

While several studies have documented varying levels of success with behavioral techniques with African Americans (see Rothbaum & Foa, 1991), future research should engage more fine grained analyses to determine the relative impact of specific techniques with African American versus Caucasian clients/patients. One such study cited in this review was carried out by Chambless and Williams (1995) which examined the differential effects of a specific technique on Caucasians and African Americans. Specifically, they examined the effectiveness of in-vivo exposure for treating agoraphobia for these two racially different groups. Their findings showed that African American clients remained more severe on measures of phobia following treatment. They also found that African Americans evidenced less change on frequency of panic attacks, and on one measure of avoidance. These authors concluded that exposure alone was an insufficient treatment for both African Americans and Caucasians, but especially for the former. They recommended that more effective treatment programs be devised for African Americans. A logical next step seems to be the carrying out of studies where culturally-specific measures are taken to enhance the effectiveness of interventions with African Americans. The following study provides an excellent example of such an undertaking.

In a case-study targeting a severely socially phobic African American woman, Fink, Turner, and Beidel (1996) reported the effectiveness of including culturally sensitive factors in the context of behavior therapy. They noted, as have others, that culturally sensitive components of intervention efforts have often been ignored in the treatment of anxiety disorders. As a treatment strategy, they used Social Effectiveness Therapy, where they incorporated racially relevant factors in both the imaginal and in-vivo exposure sessions. They reported a marked decrease in social anxiety and associated distress following this treatment. "This case presentation should serve to alert therapists to the importance of culturally sensitive factors in the acquisition of fear states and to the need to address these issues within the context of behavior therapy. Failure to take these issues into account has the potential to result in less than optimal benefits from treatment" (Fink et al., 1996, p. 8).

Another novel attempt to incorporate culturally relevant components into treatment strategies with African Americans was presented by Rowe and Grills (1993). They maintain that one area that African Americans have not faired well is substance abuse treatment programs. They have been shown to have greater dropout and recidivism rates than do their Caucasian counterparts (Longshorem, 1992).

Factors contributing to these unfortunate patterns include the perception by African Americans that the change-agents in traditional programs are not effective and often use techniques which are irrelevant and even damaging to the client's well-being (Butler, 1992; Terrell & Terrell, 1984). Consequently, these authors have presented an alternative research model to examine the role of ethnicity and racism in substance abuse treatment. The major premise of this model was that the current model for treating this target problem failed to "appreciate a unique perspectives." A primary component of the program was a consistent and positive ethno-cultural identity in African American males. It was reasoned that a positive ethno-cultural identity would enable these individuals to not only set meaningful expectations but also increase their perceived capacity to perform desired behaviors. The conceptual underpinnings of this view is based in the work of Boykin (1991), who maintains that African ancestry is viewed as a source of motivation, strength, and pride and that those individuals who define their behavior by the standards and interests of African and African American people are better able to reject negativistic, dismissive beliefs and expectations resulting from social-political definitions. While this approach has heuristic appeal, it awaits empirical validation.

The need for novel ways of training cross cultural competence is evident given the above findings. One model for such training stems from the work of LaFromboise and Foster (1992), who maintain that throughout each phase of clinical and research training in scientist-practitioner programs, attention to needs of ethnic and culturally different groups is essential during doctoral study. To respond skillfully and with appropriate sensitivity to ethnic and cultural diversity steps beyond the Boulder Model must be taken. Bernal, Barnum, Martinez, Olmedo, and Santisteban (1983), nicely summed up the shortcomings of this model in the following statement, "The scientist-practitioner model has produced research methods with little relevance to studies of ethnic minority concerns and outcomes that have limited application to non-White populations" (p. 473). The ability to respond to clients from many cultures and to evaluate and conduct research across cultures necessitates the integration of cross-training within the scientist-practitioner model. While several models presently exist (e.g., separate course model, area of concentration model, and interdisciplinary model), the integration model places responsibility on the training program as a whole rather than on a single faculty member, a mentor, or a single ethnic group. The understanding of individual, cultural, and contextual differences are viewed as essential components for social change within this research training model. Specific recommendations by these authors included institutional modifications at the departmental level, specific additions to research and clinical work, information on available resources for curricular reform in each area, and an apprenticeship continuum from prepracticum to internship.

From a community perspective, several investigators have argued for a more proactive role of African Americans improving their own quality of life through several means (Neighbors, Braithwaite, & Thompson, 1995). Among recommendations put forth are the following:

1. Based on needs-analyses, health education interventions should be designed and implemented.

2. Mental health providers and educators should strongly encourage African American clients to take personal responsibility for their own health actions. These messages should be culturally sensitive and foster self-help, self-reliance, empowerment, and self-pride among other positive attributes.

3. Specific skill-oriented training should be acquired which would hopefully lessen the usage of alcohol, tobacco, illegal substances and other harmful practices.

4. Becoming more culturally-competent when working with people of color should be a major goal of those professionals who most often interact with these individuals. Behaviors, attitudes, and skills that characterize cultural competence should be taught to all mental health professionals.

5. Greater exposure of members of the health profession to norms, values, and lifestyles of ethnically-diverse groups is paramount if greater levels of productive interaction and desired outcomes are to be obtained.

6. Mental health professionals need to be trained to have a healthy respect for African Americans' perceptions of causes and potential treatment of problem behavior, and be willing to incorporate such information into the formulation and implementation of intervention efforts.

These and related suggestions should do much to enhance the quality of functioning of African Americans. It is important to note that, just as both African Americans and the behavior therapists have contributed to this less than desirable state of the art, each must take an active and aggressive role in reversing and correcting current trends in the field.

Conclusion

Our review over a ten year period reveals a rather dismal picture concerning the involvement of African Americans in psychological research and the related therapeutic process. Of the investigations reviewed, it appears that the majority failed to incorporate culturally-competent practices in the conceptualization of etiologic factors, assessment of problem behavior, and the formulation of treatment strategies to address problem behavior.

Although our power to make firm conclusions concerning the adequacy of the cognitive behavioral conceptualization for African Americans is limited (given the limited numbers of studies in the literature), we maintain our initial hypothesis that its potential to effect desired change across a variety of problem behaviors with this group is excellent. We remain in agreement with those researchers who have postulated that behavioral and cognitive behavioral approaches provide the most effective strategies for assessing and treating members of multi-cultural groups (Acosta et al., 1982; Paniagua, 1994; Turner & Jones, 1982). The utility of such approaches for these groups lies not only in the fact that they are authoritative, concrete, action oriented, and emphasize immediate, focused learning, but also objectively functionally analyzes behavior and complex cognitions. While we remain sympathetic to the assertion by Maultsby (1982), who maintains that behavior and cognitive behavior therapies present the most culture-free types of psychotherapy, the need for greater culturally competent practices with African Americans, other ethnic groups, by White change-agents is essential if effective long term changes are to be produced. Concerning the area of assessment, we strongly encourage the continued use of behavioral assessment strategies given that these methods seem particularly suited for African American clients. In fact, as mentioned earlier, some studies have shown that African Americans find behavioral assessment preferable to traditional forms of assessment (Jones & Herndon, 1994; Paniagua, 1994; Tarnowski, Simonian, Park, & Bekeny, 1992; Turner & Jones, 1982). However, the need to critically examine frequently used assessment instruments remains vital. Regarding treatment, it is vital that more fine-grained analyses be carried out with African American clients/patients to determine the extent to which factors including race, gender, social class, and chronic levels of stress, may moderate outcome in research and therapy endeavors.

Process issues provide a rich source of future research among behavior therapists given that the cultural background of African Americans is an important aspect of the therapeutic relationship. African Americans living in the United States face discrimination, stress, and often economic hardship which create difficulties not faced by the typical, White, affluent therapist (Acosta et al., 1982). It is evident that a better understanding of the role of race, culture, and gender in the therapeutic relationship is vital. We must first begin by reporting the impact of such factors on outcome. In those areas in which differing patterns emerge, additional research must be encouraged and reported. Instead of ignoring or dismissing cultural, racial, and gender differences, we should embrace this knowledge as it may assist therapists in more effectively treating this diverse group.

Note

1. Special thanks is extended to the following members of the "team" who assisted in the evaluation of research articles: Kathy Adkins, Catarina Aldi, Alison Carmack, Shelly Ellison, Christina Faraone, Jennifer Ferris, Anne Hastings, Whitedove Mays, Mary O'Flaherty, Stacy Phillips, Anton Puckham, Valerie Shepherd, and Duane Thomas.

References

Abramowitz, L. A., & Coursey, R. D. (1989). Impact of an educational support group on family participants who take care of their schizophrenic relatives. *Journal of Consulting and Clinical Psychology, 57,* 232-236.

Acosta, F. X., Yamamoto, J., & Evans, L. A. (1982). *Effective psychotherapy for low-income and minority patients.* New York: Plenum Press.

Adebimpe, V. (1981). Overview: White norms and psychiatric diagnosis of African American patients. *American Journal of Psychiatry, 138,* 279-285.

Alexander, P. C., Neimeyer, R. A., Follette, V. M., Moore, M. K., & Harter, S. (1989). A comparison of group treatments of women sexually abused as children. *Journal of Consulting and Clinical Psychology, 57,* 479-483.

American Psychiatric Association (1994). *Diagnostic and statistical manual of mental disorders* (4th ed.). Washington, DC: Author.

Anderson, N. B. (1989). Racial differences in stress-induced cardiovascular activity and hypertension: Current status and substantive issues. *Psychological Bulletin, 105,* 89-105.

Baker, R. C., & Kirschenbaum, D. S. (1993). Self-monitoring may be necessary for successful weight control. *Behavior Therapy, 24,* 377-394.

Ball, S. A., Carroll, K. M., & Rounsaville, B. J. (1994). Sensation seeking, substance abuse, and psychotherapy in treatment-seeking and community cocaine abusers. *Journal of Consulting and Clinical Psychology, 62,* 1053-1057.

Bandura, A. (1971). *Social Learning Theory.* New York: General Learning Press.

Baucom, D. H., Sayers, S. L., & Sher, T. G. (1990). Supplementing behavioral marital therapy with cognitive restructuring and emotional expressiveness training: An outcome investigation. *Journal of Consulting and Clinical Psychology, 58,* 636-645.

Beck, J. G., Stanley, M. A., Baldwin, L. E., Deagle, E. A., & Averill, P. M. (1994). Comparison of cognitive therapy and relaxation training for panic disorder. *Journal of Consulting and Clinical Psychology, 62,* 818-826.

Benson, B. A., Johnson Rice, C., & Miranti, S. V. (1986). Effects of anger management training with mentally retarded adults in group treatment. *Journal of Consulting and Clinical Psychology, 54,* 728-729.

Bernal, M. E., & Padilla, A. M. (1982). Status of minority curricula and training in clinical psychology. *American Psychologist, 37,* 780-787.

Bernal, G., Barnam, M. E., Martinez, A. C., Olmedo, E. L., & Santisteban, D. (1983). Hispanic mental health curriculum for psychology. In J. Churn, P. Dunston, & F. Ross-Sheriff (Eds.), *Mental health and people of color* (pp. 65-94). Washington, DC: Howard University Press.

Bernal, M. E., & Castro, F. G. (1994). Are clinical psychologists prepared for service and research with ethnic minorities? *American Psychologist, 49*(9), 797-805.

Berzins, J. l. (1977). Therapist-patient matching. In A. S. Gurman & A. M. Razin (Eds.), *Effective psychotherapy. A handbook of research* (pp. 222-251). Oxford: Pergamon Press.

Blount, R. L., Powers, S. W., Cotter, M. W., Swan, S., & Free, K. (1994). Making the system work: Training pediatric oncology patients to cope and their parents to coach them during BMA/LP procedures. *Behavior Modification, 18,* 631.

Boczkowski, J. A., Zeichner, A., & DeSanto, N. (1985). Neuroleptic compliance among chronic schizophrenic outpatients: An intervention outcome report. *Journal of Consulting and Clinical Psychology, 53,* 666-671.

Borkovec, T. D., & Costello, E. (1993). Efficacy of applied relaxation and cognitive-behavioral therapy in the treatment of generalized anxiety disorder. *Journal of Consulting and Clinical Psychology, 61,* 611-619.

Boyd-Franklin, N. (1989). *Black families in therapy: A multisystems approach.* New York: Guilford.

Boykin, A. W. (1991) . Black psychology and experimental psychology: A functional confluence. In R. Jones (Ed.), *Black psychology (3rd ed.).* Berkeley, CA: Cobb & Henry.

Brown, G. K., Nicassio, P. M., & Wallston, K. A. (1989). Pain coping strategies and depression in rheumatoid arthritis. *Journal of Consulting and Clinical Psychology, 57,* 652-657.

Burgio, L., Engel, B. T., McCormick, K., Hawkins, A., & Sheve, A. (1988). Behavioral treatment for urinary incontinence in elderly inpatients: Initial attempts to modify prompting and toileting procedures. *Behavior Therapy, 19,* 345-357.

Burling, T. A., Bigelow, G. E., Robinson, J. C., & Mead, A. M. (1991). Smoking during pregnancy: Reduction via objective assessment and direct advice. *Behavior Therapy, 22,* 31-40.

Butler, J. P. (1992). Of kindred minds: The ties that bind in M.A., perspectives on Black drug use. *Youth and Society, 11,* 449-473.

Butters, J. W., & Cash, T. F. (1987). Cognitive-behavioral treatment of women's body-image dissatisfaction. *Journal of Consulting and Clinical Psychology, 55,* 889-897.

Caplan, M., Weissberg, R., Grober, J., Sivo, P., Grady, K., & Jacoby, C. (1992). Social competence promotion with inner-city and suburban young adolescents: Effects on social adjustment and alcohol use. *Journal of Consulting and Clinical Psychology, 60,* 56-63.

Chambless, D. L., & Williams, K. E. (1995). A preliminary study of African Americans with agoraphobia: Symptom severity and outcome of treatment with in vivo exposure. *Behavior Therapy, 26,* 501-515.

Collins, J. L., Rickman, L. E., & Mathura, C. B. (1980). Frequency of schizophrenia and depression in a Black inpatient population. *Journal of the National Medical Association, 72,* 851-856.

Cooper, N. A., & Clum, G. A. (1989). Imaginal flooding as a supplementary treatment for PTSD in combat veterans: A controlled study. *Behavior Therapy, 20,* 381-391.

Cordova, M. J., Andrykowski, M. A., Kenady, D. E., McGrath, P. C., Sloan, D. A., & Redd, W. H. (1995). Frequency and correlates of postraumatic-stress disorder-like symptoms after treatment for breast cancer. *Journal of Consulting and Clinical Psychology, 63,* 981-986.

Cross, T. L., Bazron, B. J., Dennis K. W., & Isaacs, M. R. (1989). *Towards a culturally competent system of care* (Vol. 1). Washington, DC: Child and Adolescent Service System Program Technical Assistance Center.

Darkes, J., & Goldman, M. S. (1993). Expectancy challenge and drinking reduction: Experimental evidence for a mediational process. *Journal of Consulting and Clinical Psychology, 61,* 344-353.

DeRubeis, R. J., Evans, M. D., Hollon, S. D., Garvey, M. J., Grove, W. M., & Tuason, V. B. (1990). How does cognitive therapy work? Cognitive change and symptom change in cognitive therapy and pharmocotherapy for depression. *Journal of Consulting and Clinical Psychology, 58,* 862-869.

Dillard, M., Andonian, L., Flores, O., & Lai, L. (1992). Culturally competent occupational therapy in a diversely populated mental health setting. *American Journal of Occupational Therapy, 46,* 721-726.

Dolan, M. P., Black, J. L., Penk, W. E., Robinowitz, R., & DeFord, H. A. (1985). Contracting for treatment termination to reduce illicit drug use among Methadone maintenance treatment failures. *Journal of Consulting and Clinical Psychology, 53,* 549-551.

Flaskerud, J. H. (1986). The effects of culture-compatible intervention on the utilization of mental health services by minority clients. *Community Mental Health Journal, 22,* 127-141.

Fink, C. M., Turner, S. M., & Beidel, D. C. (in press). Culturally relevant factors in the behavioral treatment of social phobia: A case study. *Journal of Anxiety Disorders.*

Foa, E. B., Riggs, D. S., Massie, E. D., & Yarczower, M. (1995). The impact of fear activation and anger on the efficacy of exposure treatment for post traumatic stress disorder. *Behavior Therapy, 26,* 487-499.

Follette, V. M., Follette, W. C., & Alexander, P. C. (1991). Individual predictors of outcome in group treatment for incest survivors. *Journal of Consulting and Clinical Psychology, 59,* 150-155.

Friedman, S., & Paradis, C. (1991). African American patients with panic disorder and agoraphobia. *Journal of Anxiety Disorders, 5,* 35-41.

Garfield, S. L. (1978). Research on client variables in psychotherapy. In S. L. Garfield & A. E. Bergin (Eds.), *Handbook of psychotherapy and behavior change* (2nd ed.). New York: Wiley.

Goldstein, A. P. (1971). *Psychotherapeutic attraction.* New York: Pergamon.

Grant, J. R., & Cash, T. F. (1995). Cognitive-behavioral body image therapy: Comparative efficacy of group and modest-contact treatments. *Behavior Therapy, 26,* 69-84.

Hall, S. M., Tunstall, C. D., Ginsberg, D., Benowitz, N. L., & Jones, R. T. (1987). Nicotine gum and behavioral treatment: A placebo controlled trial. *Journal of Consulting and Clinical Psychology, 55,* 603-605.

Hanson, R. A., & Gidycz, C. A. (1993). Evaluation of a sexual assault prevention program. *Journal of Consulting and Clinical Psychology, 61,* 1046-1052.

Hare, R. D., McPherson, L. M., & Forth, A. E. (1988). Male psychopaths and their criminal careers. *Journal of Consulting and Clinical Psychology, 56,* 710-714.

Hendricks, L. E., Bayton, J. E., Collins, J. L., Mathura, C. B., McMillian, S. R., & Montgomery, T. A. (1983). The NIMH diagnostic interview schedule: A test of its validity in a population of African American adults. *Journal of the National Medical Association, 75,* 667-671.

Hersen, M., & Van Hesselt, V. B. (Eds.). (1987). *Behavior therapy with children and adolescents: A clinical approach.* New York: Wiley.

Hollingshead, A. B., & Redlich, F. O. (1958). *Social class and mental illness.* New York: Wiley.

Horowitz, L. M., Rosenberg, S. E., Baer, B. A., Ureno, G., & Villasenor, V. S. (1988). Inventory of interpersonal problems: Psychometric properties and clinical applications. *Journal of Consulting and Clinical Psychology, 56,* 885-892.

Horwath, E., Lish, J. D., Johnson, J., Horning, C. D., & Weissman, M. M. (1993). Agoraphobia without panic: Clinical reappraisal of an epidemiologic finding. *American Journal of Psychiatry, 150,* 1496-1501.

Jamison, C., & Scogin, F. (1995). The outcome of cognitive bibliotherapy with depressed adults. *Journal of Consulting and Clinical Psychology, 63,* 644-650.

Jarvis, E. (1844). Insanity among the coloured populations of the free states. *American Journal of Medical Science, 8,* 71-83.

Jarvis, E. (1852). Insanity among the coloured populations of the free states. *American Journal of Medical Science, 8,* 268-282.

Jason, L. A., McMahon, S. D., Salina, D., Hedeker, D., Stockton, M., Dunson, K., & Kimball, P. (1995). Assessing a smoking cessation intervention involving groups, incentives and self-help manuals. *Behavior Therapy, 26,* 393-408.

Jensen, A. R. (1969). How much can we boost I.Q. and scholastic achievement? *Harvard Educational Review, 39,* 1-123.

Jensen, M. P., Turner, J. A., & Romano, J. M. (1994). Correlates of improvement in multidisciplinary treatment of chronic pain. *Journal of Consulting and Clinical Psychology, 62,* 172-179.

Jones, B. E., & Gray, B. A. (1986). Problems in diagnosing schizophrenia and affective disorders among blacks. *Hospital and Community Psychiatry, 37,* 61-65.

Jones, R. T., & Herndon, C. (1994). The status of black children and adolescents in the academic setting: Assessment and treatment issues. In C. E. Walker & M. Roberts (Eds.), *Clinical Child Psychology* (pp. 901-917). New York: John Wiley & Sons.

Jones, R. T., & Kazdin, A. E. (1975). Programming response maintenance after withdrawing token reinforcement. *Behavior Therapy, 6,* 153-164.

Kalichman, S. C., Kelly, J. A., Hunter, T. L., Murphy, D. A., & Tyler, R. (1993). Culturally tailored HIV-AIDS risk-reduction messages targeted to African American women: Impact on risk sensitization and risk reduction. *Journal of Consulting and Clinical Psychology, 61,* 291-295.

Kamin, L. (1974). *Science and politic IQ.* Potomac: Erlbaum.

Kazdin, A. E. (1978). *History of behavior modification: Experimental foundations of contemporary research.* Baltimore, MD: University Park Press.

Kazdin, A. E. (1984). *Behavior modification in applied settings.* Homewood: The Dorsey Press.

Kelly, J. A., St. Lawrence, J. S., Hood, H. V., & Brasfield, T. L. (1989). Behavioral intervention to reduce AIDS risk activities. *Journal of Consulting Clinical Psychology, 57,* 60-67.

Kidorf, M., Stitzer, M. L., & Brooner, R. K. (1994). Characteristics of methadone patients responding to take-home incentives. *Behavior Therapy, 25,* 109-121.

Kivlahen, D. R., Marlatt, G. A., Fromme, K., Coppel, D. B., & Williams, E. (1990). Secondary prevention with college drinkers: Evaluation of an alcohol skills training program. *Journal of Consulting and Clinical Psychology, 58,* 805-810.

LaFromboise, T. D., & Foster, S. L. (1992). Cross-cultural training: Scientist-practitioner model and methods. *The Counseling Psychologist, 20,* 472-489.

Locke, D. C. (1992). *Increasing multicultural understanding: A comprehensive model.* Newbury Park: Sage Publications.

Longshorem, D. M., Hiseh, S., Anglin, S., & Annon, T. A. (1992). Ethnic differences in drug abuse treatment and utilization. *Journal of Mental Health Administration, 19,* 268-277.

Lopez, S. R. (1989). Patient variable biases in clinical judgment: Conceptual overview and methodological considerations. *Psychological Bulletin, 106,* 184-203.

Lopez, S., & Nunez, J. A. (1987). Cultural factors considered in selected diagnostic criteria and interview schedules. *Journal of Abnormal Psychology, 96,* 270-272.

Lorion, R. P. (1973). Socioeconomic status and traditional treatment approaches reconsidered. *Psychological Bulletin, 179,* 263-270.

Lorion, R. P. (1974). Patient and therapist variables in the treatment of low-income patients. *Psychological Bulletin, 81,* 344-354.

Lucia, K. S., Steffen, J. J., Harrigan, J. A., & Stuebing, R. C. (1991). Progressive relaxation training: Muscle contraction before relaxation? *Behavior Therapy, 22,* 249-256.

Mahoney, M. J., & Thoresen, C. E. (1974). *Self-control: Power to the person.* Monterey, CA: Brooks-Cole.

Martelli, M. F., Auerbach, S. M., Alexander, J., & Mercuri, L. G. (1987). Stress management in the health care setting: Matching interventions with patient coping styles. *Journal of Consulting and Clinical Psychology, 55,* 201-207.

Maultsby, M. C. (1982). Historical view of Black's distrust of psychiatry. In S. M. Turner & R. T. Jones (Eds.), *Behavior therapy and black populations: Psychosocial issues and empirical findings.* New York: Plenum Press.

Meichenbaum, D. (1977). *Cognitive-behavior modification: An integrative approach.* New York: Plenum Press.

Michelson, L., Mavissakalian, M., & Marchione, K. (1985). Cognitive and behavioral treatments of agoraphobia: Clinical, behavioral and psychophysiological outcomes. *Journal of Consulting and Clinical Psychology, 53,* 913-925.

Michelson, L., Mavissakalian, M., & Marchione, K. (1988). Cognitive, behavioral, and psychophysiological treatments of agoraphobia: A comparative outcome investigation. *Behavior Therapy, 19,* 97-120.

Michelson, L., Mavissakalian, M., Marchione, K., Dancu, C., & Greenwald, M. (1986). The role of self-directed in vivo exposure in cognitive, behavioral, and psychophysiological treatments of agoraphobia. *Behavior Therapy, 17,* 91-108.

Middleton, M. B., & Cartledge, G. (1995). The effects of social skills instruction and parental involvement on the aggressive behaviors of African American males. *Behavior Modification, 19,* 192-210.

Monti, P. M., Rohsenow, D. J., Rubonis, A. V., Niauru, R. S., Sirota, A. D., Colby, S. M., Goddard, P., & Abrams, D. B. (1993). Cue exposure with coping skills treatment for male alcoholics: A preliminary investigation. *Journal of Consulting and Clinical Psychology. 61,* 1011-1019.

Morin, C. M., Kowatch, R. A., Barry, T., & Walton, E. (1993). Cognitive-behavior therapy for late-life insomnia. *Journal of Consulting and Clinical Psychology, 61,* 137-146.

Moynihan, D. (1965). *The Negro Family: The case for national action.* Washington, DC: Office of Policy Planning and Research, U. S. Department of Labor.

Neal, A. M., & Turner, S. M. (1991). Anxiety disorders research with African Americans: Current status. *Psychological Bulletin, 109,* 400-410.

Neighbors, H. W. (1988). The help-seeking behavior of Black Americans: A summary of findings from the National Survey of Black Americans. *Journal of The American Medical Association, 80,* 1009-1012.

Neighbors, H. W., Braithwaite, R. L., & Thompson, E. (1995). Health promotion and African-Americans: From personal empowerment to community action. *The Science of Health Promotion, 9,* 281-287.

Neighbors, H. W., Jackson, J. S., Campbell, L., & Williams, D. (1989). The influence of racial factors on psychiatric diagnosis: A review and suggestions for research. *Community Mental Health Journal, 25,* 301-311.

Nobles, W. W. (1972). African philosophy: Foundations for Black psychology. In R. Jones (Ed.), *Black psychology.* New York: Harper & Row.

Nobles, W. W. (1980). African philosophy: Foundations for Black psychology. In R. Jones (Ed.), *Black psychology* (pp. 99-105). New York: Harper & Row.

O'Malley, S. S., Foley, S. H., Rounsaville, B. J., Watkins, J. T., Sotsky, S. M., Imber, S. D., & Elkin, l. (1988). Therapist competence and patient outcome in interpersonal psychotherapy of depression. *Journal of Consulting and Clinical Psychology, 56,* 496-501.

O'Sullivan, M. J., Peterson, P. D., Cox, G. B., & Kirkeby, J. (1989). Ethnic populations: Community mental health services ten years later. *American Journal Of Community Psychology, 28,* 17, 17-30.

Paniagua, F. A. (1994). Guidelines for the assessment and treatment of African Americans. In F. Paniagua (Ed.), *Assessing and treating culturally diverse clients.* Thousand Oaks: Sage Publications.

Porzelius, L. K., Houston, C., Smith, M., Arfken, C., & Fisher, E., Jr. (1995). Comparison of a standard behavioral weight loss treatment and a binge eating weight loss treatment. *Behavior Therapy, 26,* 119-134.

President's Commission on Mental Health (1978). *Report to the President.* Washington, DC: U. S. Government Printing Office.

Regier, D. A., Myers, J. K., Kramer, M., Robins, L. N., Blazer, D. G., Hough, R. L., Eaton, W. W., & Locke, B. Z. (1984). The NIMH Epidemologic Catchment Area program: Historical context, major objectives, and study population characteristics. *Archives of General Psychiatry, 41,* 934-941.

Roehrich, L., & Goldman, M. S. (1993). Experience-dependent neuropsychological recovery and the treatment of alcoholism. *Journal of Consulting and Clinical Psychology, 61,* 812-821.

Rothbaum, B. O., & Foa, E. B. (1991). Exposure treatment of PTSD concomitant with conversion mutism: A case study. *Behavior Therapy, 22,* 449-456.

Routh, D. K. (1994). *Clinical psychology since 1917: Science, practice, & organization.* New York: Plenum Press.

Rowe, D., & Grills, C. (1993). African-centered drug treatment: An alternative conceptual paradigm for drug counseling with African American clients. *Journal of Psychoactive Drugs, 25,* 21-35.

Scarr, S. (1988). Race and gender as psychological variables. *American Psychologist, 43,* 56-59.

Schofield, W. (1964). *Psychotherapy: The purchase of friendship.* Englewood Cliffs, NJ: Prentice Hall.

Sharp, J. J., & Forman, S. G. (1985). A comparison of two approaches to anxiety management for teachers. *Behavior Therapy, 16,* 370-383.

Snyder, D. K., & Wills, R. M. (1989). Behavioral versus insight-oriented marital therapy: Effects on individual and interspousal functioning. *Journal of Consulting and Clinical Psychology, 57,* 39-46.

Staats, A. W. (1971). *Child learning, intelligence, and personality.* New York: Harper & Row.

Stanton, W. (1960). *The leopard's spots: Scientific attitudes towards race in America* (pp. 1815-1859). Chicago: University of Chicago Press.

Stricker, G., Davis-Russell, E., Bourg, E., Duran, E., Hammond, W. R., McHolland, J., Polite, K., & Vaughn, B. E. (1990). *Toward ethnic diversification in psychology education and training.* Washington, DC: American Psychological Association .

Sue, D. W. (1982). Position paper: Cross-cultural counseling competencies. *Counseling Psychologist, 10,* 45-52.

Sue, S. (1977). Community mental health services to minority groups: Some optimism, some pessimism. *American Psychologist, 32,* 616-624.

Sue, S. (1991). Community mental health services for minority groups: A test of the cultural responsiveness hypothesis. *Journal of Counseling Psychology, 59,* 533-540.

Sue, S. (1988). Psychotherapeutic services for ethnic minorities: Two decades of research findings. *American Psychologist, 43,* 301-308.

Sue, S., Zane, N., & Young, K. (1994). Research on psychotherapy with culturally diverse populations. In A. E. Bergin & S. Garfield (Eds.), *Handbook of psychotherapy and behavior change* (4th ed., pp.783-817). New York: John Wiley & Sons.

Taras, M. E., Matson, J. L., & Felps, J. N. (1993). Using independence training to teach independent living skills to children and young men with visual impairments. *Behavior Modification, 17,* 189-208.

Tarnowski, K. J., Simonian, S. J., Park, A., & Bekeny, P. (1992). Acceptability of treatments for child behavioral disturbance: Race, socioeconomic status, and multicomponent treatment effects. *Child and Family Behavior Therapy, 14,* 25-37.

Terrell, F., & Terrell, S. L. (1984). Race of counselor, client sex, cultural mistrust level, and premature termination from counseling among African American clients. *Journal of Counseling Psychology, 31,* 371-375.

Tharp, R. G . (1991). Cultural diversity and treatment of children. *Journal of Consulting and Clinical Psychology, 59,* 799-812.

Thomas, A., & Sillen, S. (1972). *Racism and Psychiatry.* New York: Brunner/ Mazel .

Turner, S. M., & Jones, R. T., (Eds.). (1982). *Behavior modification in African American populations: Psychosocial issues and empirical findings.* New York: Plenum Press.

U.S. Bureau of the Census (1990). *The Hispanic population in the United States: March 1989* (Series P-20, No. 444). Washington, DC: U.S. Government.

U.S. Department of Health, Education, and Welfare. (1979). *Health status of minorities and low-income groups* (Public Health Service, Health Resources Opportunity Publication No. HRA79-627). Washington, DC: U.S. Government Printing Office.

Watson, J. B. (1913) . Psychology as the behaviorist views. *Psychological Review, 20*:158-77-4.

White, J. L., & Parham, T. A. (1990). *The psychology of Blacks and African American perspective.* Englewood Cliffs, NJ: Prentice Hall.

Wilfey, D. E., Agras, W. S., Telch, C. F., Rossiter, E. M., Schneider, J. A., GolombCole, A., Sifford, L., & Raeburn, S. D. (1993). Group cognitive behavioral therapy and group interpersonal psychotherapy for the nonpurging bulimic individual: A controlled comparison. *Journal of Consulting and Clinical Psychology 61,* 296-305.

Williams, D. H. (1986). The epidemiology of mental illness in Afro-Americans. *Hospital and Community Psychiatry, 37,* 42-49.

Willie, C. V., Kramer, M. B., & Brown, B. S. (1973). *Racism and mental health.* Pittsburgh, PA: University of Pittsburgh Press.

Wu, I. H., & Windle, C. (1980). Ethnic specificity in the relative minority use and staffing of community mental health centers. *Community Mental Health Journal, 16,* 156-168.

Author

Russell T. Jones, Ph.D.
Department of Psychology
4092B Derring Hall
Virginia Tech
Blacksburg, VA 24060
Telephone: (540) 231-5934
Fax: (540)231-3652
E-mail: rtjones@vt.edu

Part 6

Symposia on Therapeutic Approaches

Does Insight Serve a Purpose: The Value of Psychoanalytic Psychotherapy with Diverse African American Patients

Cheryl J. Thompson

The purpose of this paper is threefold: First, to establish a picture of the psychological concerns of African Americans in general, many of whom do not seek psychotherapy. Secondly, to present two cases that highlight some of the concerns that have impacted my clinical work. The purpose of the cases is to present the merger of the experience of discrimination and psychopathology and finally, to encourage psychoanalysts to apply their craft to a wider population of minority patients, in this instance African Americans of various histories and social classes. Psychoanalytic thought is uniquely positioned to explain and address both the adaptation and maladaptation of individuals in society. It is the one discipline that has the conceptual framework that enables us to evaluate the impact of social, institutional, familial and personal issues at a microscopic level. The unique ability of psychoanalysis to understand and to empower should be available to all segments of our society. It is clear that the literature is in increasing need of data regarding diverse populations. However, in focusing on the African American population, especially around the specific topic of race, resistance on both sides must be addressed. For Blacks, the struggle to be acknowledged as human beings has been so painful that discussions about psychopathology foster fear that only inhumanity will be acknowledged. For Whites there is often a combination of guilt, anger and denial that forces the dialogue to become truncated before there can be any understanding between the groups.

Race

For Black America, the problem of race is twofold. There are external uncontrollable issues that are sometimes clear and sometimes so foggy that one cannot be sure of the nature of the problem. The end result is that there are things that can be addressed as a person, as an activist, or on a community level and there are some things that are so insidious that they go unacknowledged. Many patients don't even report their experiences around discrimination because these are not experiences that Blacks would consider remarkable enough to pay money to someone to listen. However, if Whites experienced some of these events they would be outraged, and these experiences would become therapeutic material. Shopping in department stores or looking for housing are two such examples. These are often painful experiences for middle class Black people.

Black America is essentially no different from White America. Black people would like to be judged for who they are. They would like the freedom to live where they can afford or feel comfortable living. They would like to feel safe, they would like to feel that their work is meaningful, that they can contribute to society; and that their children can rely on parental achievement as a stepping stone for their own lives. The wish is a simple one, to be seen as human beings by the larger society.

Some Black people come close to the experience of acceptance, of appreciation for accomplishment, of being able to pass a legacy to the next generation, but most don't. The struggle for Black America is to have the freedom to achieve desired and socially acceptable goals without external encumbrances.

We live in a country with a fantasy that by the third generation enculturation becomes complete. This is true for some people, but for those ethnic minorities with visible differences that process does not occur. Even when members of the visible minorities enjoy reasonable adaptation or mental health, there remain real and pervasive limitations in achievement, housing and financial security. Black America has an increasing middle class now into its second clear generation and many who are middle class for a fourth or fifth generation. However, there remains a large group, approximately 70%, who are collectively members of the working class, the working poor or the underclass. The tragedy of the situation is that the country as a whole believes that poor people have deliberately chosen to live at a level of bare survival rather than to live with some degree of comfort. It is the American belief that the victim is responsible for being in a victimized position that confounds psychotherapeutic intervention and often results in treatment that does not end with a person equipped to address the real problems of life.

Race has been a split-off part of the American psyche since the founding of this nation. The founding fathers wrote a magnificent doctrine defining all people as equal. However, Black people were not included. It was the removal of humanity from this group that justified slavery and indentured servitude in this new land where Europe's persecuted could find new life and self-expression unavailable in their homelands. Our nation began with the identification with the persecutor carried to a new extreme. A group of people were robbed of their humanity. From that time until now Black America has struggled to regain control over self-definition.

I think if any of us have watched the fall of communism we see that a veneer can be forced onto a people but issues that are not negotiated do not get settled. It is clear, as we watch Central Europe, that time has no impact on the wounds of subjugation. We see that pain that is centuries old can be a force of destabilization which could propel the world into yet another round of mass destruction. It is this awareness that time alone cannot change the internal or intrapsychic environment that is unique to psychoanalysis. All of the other therapeutic modalities are based on the assumption that people can change fairly easily.

It is this belief that time alone should change things that seems to result in what is observed between Blacks and Whites. That is, Blacks are perceived as whining and Whites are convinced the problem is no longer significant. There are many well-meaning people in this country, people who feel that something should he done but can't figure out what to do. There are others who feel helpless simply because the problem appears insoluble. There are people who feel that if there is a problem, they had nothing to do with the problem. Finally, there are others who believe the problem has been unfairly redressed and now many decent White people have been displaced because of the rise of the Black middle class (Comer, 1969).

We live in a country that believes that any acquisition by one person has been at the expense of another. This belief creates a climate of distrust. It does not allow for inequity to be addressed. Many Black people have learned to accommodate to the implications of these ideas. Usually, the result is that Blacks work and often live in isolation. That is, it is not unusual for Black professionals to be the only Black worker at their level or for the Black middle class family to live in a community where they are the only Black family. This combination of tokenism and isolation results in a less than full expression of the self and often results in difficulty in accurate assessment of internal and external experiences. Thus, Black achievement comes at a price that many people might experience as neither fair nor reasonable. The end result for many Black professionals is the inability to accurately evaluate their work or lifestyle because much of it is in reaction to real or perceived discrimination.

These are the problems of people who do not come to the psychotherapist's office. However, this is the backdrop. There are true, profound and subtle limitations to self-development and achievement that are extremely painful for Black Americans but that continue to exist. To a great extent these limitations remain outside of the awareness of many people both—Black and White.

It is my contention that the issues patients bring to therapy are reflective of the confluence of their personal pain and the social price paid for existence. Thus, the issues that Black patients raise about race must be given careful analytic consideration because these are often the issues that reverberate through many aspects of the patients internal and external experience.

Race permeates existence for Black America. Many neutral activities become dichotomized as Black or White so that work, language, dress, lifestyle, and education become reflective of racial identity (Steele, 1990) rather than reflections of self-definition. The inability to define oneself can result in disruptions of the self-experience as well as unreliable self-esteem. There is often a heightened level of self-consciousness and defensiveness encountered in patients about what is and what is not part of the self-definition and part of the group definition. For many there is lingering self-doubt, shame and guilt around the racial aspects of identity specifically.

The profundity of the shame and self-doubt a people feel because of their history can be best captured for me by the experience I had with my then 7-year-old son. He came home from school one day filled with tears and sadness saying to me, "Did you know about slavery? How bad must we have been to be slaves?" This was probably my second-worst worry about questions children ask parents. I responded to my son, that all people all over the world have a time in the sun and a time in darkness. Power is the sun and it changes periodically. He had come from an ancient people whose time in the sun was long ago. I wanted him to know that power and powerlessness are not absolute and are variable. I did not want him to feel ashamed of what he is because of what he was being taught. I wanted him to feel proud of what he could become because of his ability and that slavery was not his only history. In his face, I saw the power of information that is often used to wound. Slavery is not a unique experience for African Americans. Slavery continues to exist today. It is the dehumanizing of those in American slavery that serves to erode self-esteem and to encourage the pain of feeling victimized. The historical reality continues to affect self-perception. The history of oppression must be experienced in the context of culture (Butts, 1964) as well as within the individual in order to help alleviate the pain that results from a history of oppression.

Despite the pain, people live, work and die with the hope that their lives matter to their families, friends and country. The pain brings with it strength and a sense of communion that may not always exist in other groups.

Psychoanalytic Psychotherapy

The issues involved in the treatment of Black patients have been evolving over the last 40 years. Initially, there were questions as to whether Black patients could be treated psychoanalytically because there was such obvious oppression (Kardiner & Ovesy, 1951). Over the last four decades the issues have shifted as more Black mental health professionals entered the treatment arena and as more Black patients entered treatment. Race does impact treatment. Holmes (1992) and writers preceding her (Brantly, 1983; Calnek, 1972; Carter & Hazlip, 1979; Cohen, 1974; Flowers, 1972; Griffin, 1977; Jones, 1974; Jones & Seagull; Krantz, 1972; Mayo, 1974; Myers, 1984; Phillips, 1990; Ridley, 1984; Schacter & Butts, 1969; Thompson, 1987; Thompson, 1989; Thomas & Sillen, 1974) report on the impact race can have on the issues that emerge as well as the impact of race on the speed with which transference unfolds. Some of the most recent contributions to minority treatment suggest that new conceptualizations are necessary to work effectively with minority patients (Jones, 1990; Lee, 1990; Parson, 1990; and Watkins-Duncan, 1992). The need for new frames of reference may reflect the belief that the constructs now in place are pejorative or that without a new reference point, therapists may respond out of cultural stereotypes rather than with the creativity that is ordinarily used to understand every patient that comes to treatment.

In my own work, Ego psychology (Hartmann, 1951) continues to serve as a basic frame of reference. However, I have also found the work of other theorists to be especially helpful in informing work with patients. Specifically, Fairbairn (1954), Winnicott (1965), and Kohut (1977) are extremely helpful because their foci lend power and understanding to the issues that are often problems my Black patients struggle with. It is the emerging synthesis of drive psychology, ego psychology, self-psychology and object relations theory as demonstrated in the work of Pine (1990), that seems most effective in working through the issues presented in psychoanalytic psychotherapy with minority patients.

Within the discipline there are marked intellectual disagreements. Sometimes these disagreements result in fragmentation of organizations. However, it appears to me that the area of basic agreement is the use of the patient's personal history, the unfolding of a transference relationship, understanding dreams and deriving meaning from data patients choose to share in the service of assisting the patient in expanding self-awareness. It is important to focus on the ideas and constructs that bring psychoanalysts together lest the divisions destroy a frame of reference that offers the broadest and deepest understanding of human beings currently available.

The cases that follow have been chosen to represent a range of issues that frequently emerge in psychoanalytic psychotherapy with minority patients. Their treatment includes some of the more recent ideas in theory construction that has served to broaden the base of psychoanalytic treatment.

Case One

The first patient is a 42-year-old college educated carpenter. He had been separated from his wife for over one year when we began our work together. He is now divorced. They had been married for 6 years although they have been together for the last 12 years. Steven, a pseudonym, is a tall somewhat thin but large-framed, light-skinned man with a face and features that makes his ethnic origin a curiosity. Steven is the offspring of a White mother and a Black American father. He has lived most of his life in suburban New Jersey. He has one brother who is two years his junior. His parents, both of whom completed college, have worked as research scientists. His parents are together and are described by Steven as being very close.

However, when Steven was faced with a serious crisis in his marriage, his mother told him it would be best if his father were never made aware of the problem. Steven at age 42 has had two relationships with women. His first was in his early 20's after graduation from college. He met a white woman that he dated for about five years. This woman is described as depressed. She never wanted to go out so most of their time together was spent in either her apartment or his apartment. He now understands that she was an alcoholic but at the time of their dating he felt that she was uncomfortable about his ethnicity. The relationship ended when he found himself unable to cope with her drinking. He believed that his ethnicity exacerbated her drinking.

When questioned about dating before this woman, Steven tearfully talked about being seen as a friend by women but never someone to date. He had lots of friends, many of whom were female, but he never went to a movie or any other activity with any of them. When it was time for his senior prom, he asked a White girl from the neighborhood to go with him. This girl was a friend, a girl whose parents he knew and whose home he had been in many times. The girl accepted the date and then came to him tearfully saying that she could not go because her father would not allow her to date him. Steven did attend the prom with another girl but felt that he had accepted a date with someone who wanted him, not his own choice. He continues to experience himself as essentially unacceptable. At this point, he describes himself as a Black man who only dates black women. His dating Black women has only involved his wife from whom he is now divorced. She is a volatile and demanding person. She does not trust men in general and has had long standing issues of deprivation that have helped to truncate the marital relationship.

When further questioned about his isolation and experience of rejection since adolescence, Steven explained that everyone liked him from a distance and that during adolescence he did not identify himself as a Black man or a White man but as a human being. He only became a Black man after going to college and being unable to succeed in his chosen major, geology. His chosen major seems to be a clear attempt to identify with and gain approval from his parents. When he switched to liberal arts he did feel as if he had found himself. He experienced true pleasure learning but he also felt that he had failed. Steven's identification with being Black appears to be an identification with failure and rejection. For him, blackness is both resistance and defense.

Steven has a brother who is two years his junior who graduated from the same high school, went to the prom with the woman of his choice, has dated for many years, has dated Black women and White women but has expressed a preference for White women. The brother married a young White woman and now is a successful middle level executive in a large corporation. The second son is that family's star. Steven sometimes speculates that his brother's success is related to his having paved the way for him. He denies being envious of his brother, but is sad for his inability to stand up to his full measure. It was Steven's brother who was pivotal in the crisis that occurred in his marriage. Before Steven met his wife, she had seen his brother many times. They lived in the same neighborhood and took the commuter bus at the same time. She found his brother very attractive but was never able to spark a conversation with him. At a later time, she met Steven while jogging. She was aware of the striking resemblance between Steven and the man she found attractive so she had a positive response toward him. Once they started dating, she became aware that he was the brother of the man to whom she was initially attracted. She and Steven's brother became friends and confidants. The brother would spend many hours with Steven's wife whenever he had no one to date. When he found a girlfriend he would stop hanging out with her. She would in turn become depressed and Steven would assume that he had done something to precipitate her depression. The brother eventually met the woman he would marry. He tried then to create an atmosphere where each of the couples could spend time together.

Steven's wife responded to this shift in the relationship by slashing the woman's car tires, by scratching the paint on her car, by sending anonymous hate mail and by making threatening telephone calls. Steven's wife was quickly discovered and confronted by the brother. Although she finally admitted what she had done, and apologized, she did not tell the brother of her feelings of rage and disappointment. She kept to herself her feelings that the only reason the brother rejected her as an intimate was because she was Black. Steven responded to this crisis by sticking by his wife. He accepted responsibility for her behavior by saying she did this because he had not been home enough and that he knew his brother had a better personality than he did.

Steven and his wife attempted to resolve the crisis by leaving the country. After living abroad for approximately 2.5 years, their separation was precipitated by another crisis. Steven's mother-in-law died. Again, Steven felt that he was solely responsible for the breakup of the marriage because he did not fully participate in the funeral plans for his mother-in-law.

Blackness and defeat tie Steven and his wife together. He is the son who defines himself as Black but sadly reports that he has found no comfort in his associations with Black people because they question whether he is one of them. He does not feel that he belongs anywhere. He is neither Black nor White. His self-experience is that of a pilgrim seeking a place of acceptance. Steven has no home internally and for part of treatment had no real home externally. He has an internal dialogue of race that prevents him from learning about himself. There are issues around his development that leave him feeling unacceptable, that have left him terrified of women, of rejection, of performance, and of self-expression. Black and White can be seen as an internal conflict between passivity and aggression. He is afraid to stand out, to assert himself, if he does so he becomes a "little nigger" in his father's eyes. He understands intellectually that his father came from a time when being a Black man was fraught with pain and rejection. Because this perception is not fully integrated into Steve's sense of himself, he is tied in knots and experiences himself as fragmented. His adaptation has resulted in his living in a netherworld where he cannot find a home. Racial identity has become the mechanism of denial, a veil of helplessness that has partly convinced Steven that he should accept his feelings of loneliness and unacceptableness as simple reality. Because this dialogue for Steven is both internal and external he is acutely aware of race as he travels between groups as an invisible being, always reaffirming his rejectability.

He is aware of the differences between the levels of acceptance of the two sons but has not become able to explore this area. At this point, I suspect that his pain may be a result of some of the parental anxiety for their first born. However, it appears complicated by their being a bi-racial couple who experienced tremendous rejection from the mother's family and some rejection from the father's family. It is also complicated by a family secret. Steven may have been conceived prior to the parental marriage. The premise that there may be such a secret is based on two exchanges that have occurred with Steven. When asked when his depression began, he stated 42 years and 9 months ago. Secondly, he reports that whenever the parents try to figure out how long they have been married, they ask Steven his age and giggle when he responds to their question.

In my work with him, we began with the data as he presented it. Then we looked together for meaning in these experiences. The work moves from the global to the specific. The goal is to foster Steven's ability to see himself more accurately so that he is free to evaluate the true consequences of his relationships. Currently, ethnicity is used by him to describe most of his experiences rather than race simply serving as an aspect of his personality. It is not to his or any patient's advantage to accept external definitions, especially those around race, when the result is psychological distress.

He is painfully aware that the identity he now claims is one that he feels has been thrust upon him. He saw his ex-wife as the clear indicator of his identity. Because of her brown skin, he became identified as a Black man. His need to use her to define himself made their relationship a volatile and fragile one. The goal of clarifying her role in his life was seen as a function of establishing a self identity that belongs to him. Some of the more recent practitioners with a psychodynamic frame suggest that psychotherapy utilize different modalities to assist Black patients with their pain. It is not clear to me that it is necessary to develop a new modality.

What is necessary is to look at the issue of race in terms of the purpose it serves at that moment in the patient's life. The neurotic aspects of race may look very different for each patient. Further, the choice that people make about how they will address the issue of race needs to emerge freely from the enhancement of the self. For the therapist to have a fixed idea about self-expression or self-direction in minority patients is to maintain race as caste, that is, something that one must acquiesce to or accept as limiting as the social order currently defines it to be. This view is not empowering. For Steve, race served as a metaphor for his hurt relationship with his mother. He resolved his feelings of competition with his father by choosing to see himself as Black thereby affirming that his mother had no value to him. This view was enhanced by a social milieu that required his identity formation to reject her input into his life and development. When Steven began to have the freedom to acknowledge that he truly has a heritage that reflects distinctly different ethnic identities, he became able to evaluate potential dates based on their compatibility with him. He is now involved in a serious relationship that appears to be successful for him and his partner. It seemed to me that the need to deny his mother and her reality served to constrict his experience of himself and limited the possibility of finding a person with whom he could share his life experience. Race in this instance had served to deny a significant part of Steven's existence.

Case Two

Amy is a 35-year-old, obese, Black single woman with a bachelor's degree in social work. Amy entered treatment 6 years ago complaining that she had no life, no friends and no reliable family. Amy resides with her maternal grandmother. She was never clear about her parents marital status as this was maintained as a family secret. However, when we began our work each parent was married to someone else. Amy was often left to wonder about her parentage as each parent would often deny knowledge or simply renounce any responsibility toward her.

In the beginning, it was difficult to get her to tell her story. She resented being asked to repeat anything. She felt that one telling should be sufficient. My requests for repetition were seen as evidence of my disinterest and inadequate memory. While Amy was often hostile and rejecting of my requests for information, I felt that my role was to provide a safe and predictable environment, a "holding environment" (Winnicott, 1965).

Amy revealed a story of painful rejection and abandonment. She was the second child in a family of seven children. Her parents were 17 years old at the time of her birth. The parents separated during her infancy. Her mother became deeply depressed and is alleged to have tried to kill Amy. Amy's father then took her to live with him and his mother. Amy has no idea how long she lived with her father, but at age four she was diagnosed as failure to thrive. She was hospitalized and released in the care of her maternal grandmother where she has remained.

The grandmother and Amy had no contact with each other and Amy felt she could not have contact with the paternal grandmother and maintain her relationship with her maternal grandmother. By the time Amy was firmly placed with her grandmother, each of her parents had established other relationships and began to rear new families. Amy was excluded from each of these families.

Her grandmother was experienced as a good custodial parent. The grandmother reminded Amy regularly that she was her only caretaker and that no financial assistance had ever been provided for her care. The grandmother is a deeply religious woman who rarely allowed Amy any social activity that did not revolve around their church. As a result, Amy experienced her childhood as very lonely.

The source of her deepest distress was experienced whenever she talked about her mother and the six other children the mother kept with her. Amy resented them and felt that she had been treated more harshly than her siblings. The situation with her father was essentially the same. He had a son with whom he maintained a close relationship and only saw Amy on irregular occasions.

Amy recalls painfully spending holiday times with her siblings in which they were given many gifts while she received one gift. Her gift was usually something that either didn't fit or something she disliked. Amy has experienced most of her childhood as a time when she had to be both vigilant and compliant. If she misbehaved, who would take care of her? Her fears of further abandonment and her multiple experiences of rejection have left her angry, hostile, deprived and depressed.

Her treatment opened with her telling me that she had been in therapy before and the treatment failed. She stated that she had little faith in me as a therapist and only came to see me because I came highly recommended. In the beginning, I dreaded seeing Amy. She was ever watchful for evidence of disapproval or rejection. Informational questions were experienced as attacks. It was clear that interpretation was out of the question (Eissler, 1953). Amy mostly needed to know that I would be a reliable person in her life. We moved through this phase of treatment because everything was held constant; her session time, the length of the session, and even the positioning of items in the treatment room. We remained in this mode of interaction: my questioning, her resentment and everything held constant, for two years.

She began every session by stating that she was aggravated. In seeking clarification of the source of her aggravation, she would share a litany of narcissistic injuries. For example, co-workers would come to her desk and take candy from her, but ignored her when they went to lunch or when she needed help with a visit to a specific home.

Amy was unable to understand that she presented an angry, hostile posture that created a climate of rejection. Amy believed that she was simply the victim of rejection as usual (Miller, 1981).

Another painful and repetitive experience was an argument she and her grandmother had every summer. Amy explained that for almost ten years, she, her grandmother and an aunt who resides with them would have a serious verbal altercation that would result in Amy being told to move. This argument often started over Amy's small flower garden or over the management of her dog. Amy lived in fear of being homeless. She also began to associate these arguments with the therapy because they happened in August while I was on vacation. Amy felt that my pleasure was at expense of her losing her world. As we explored these issues, it became clear to Amy that her aunt and her mother were resentful of the care Amy received from the grandmother. Rather than responding to Amy as a daughter or a niece, their response reflected a perception of her as a pampered sibling. As this idea became comfortable for Amy, she began to ask about her mother's history and her grandmother's history. Amy discovered that none of the women in her family reared their own children (Boyd-Franklin, 1989). This understanding allowed Amy to see herself as less destructive. Amy's prior conception of the family was that only she had been reared by someone other than her mother.

It was during this time that Amy could acknowledge that I meant something to her. She became able to say that I represented her link to the outside world. She also allowed herself to say that she was often afraid that I would tell her to leave. I responded to her acknowledgment of our relationship by telling her that I would be there with her until she wanted to leave even though she was sometimes a very difficult person. This was the first time Amy laughed and cried in the treatment room.

As we worked together, Amy very slowly came to understand that she played a significant role in eliciting anger from many sources. She became able to observe herself become rigid and demanding. With a slight softening of her inflexible expectations, Amy became able to assess her role in these experiences of hostile rejection. Because Amy's contact with others was so limited, changes were seen in the treatment room before they were described in conjunction with others. Amy began to tolerate my asking for clarification. She also became able to see humor in her usual opening sentence in the treatment which was, "I'm aggravated." These changes in her interaction with me allowed for changes in her interaction with her grandmother. As this woman became a person to Amy, she became able to accept the grandmother's caretaking as an expression of genuine concern. With awareness that her grandmother cared about her, Amy allowed herself to explore her relationship with her birth mother and began to understand that her biological mother was unavailable as a parent. While Amy continues to feel hurt when her mother visits, Amy can now accept her mother's immaturity and competitiveness.

The mother remains resentful of Amy's relationship with her grandmother. Deprivation is a central and recurring theme in this family.

In the fourth year of her treatment, Amy began to talk about her relationship with God. She had returned to the church of her childhood and even though she had many complaints about the way in which she felt treated at church, she managed to find solace there. As her comfort increased, Amy felt a need to provide ministerial services to others. This was really the first time that Amy felt a desire to give to others. Her ability to look outside herself was experienced by me as a very positive step toward better mental health. Amy decided that she wanted to become a minister. This decision changed her perspective on many facets of her life.

Amy was initially very fearful that she could not complete an advanced degree. She believed that her difficulty in undergraduate school was reflective of her ability.

After two years with excellent grades, she now has a feeling of competence and an understanding that her undergraduate performance was related to her emotional state. Amy is now an active member of her church and as part of seminary training is beginning to minister to sick and shut in church members.

In the classes in seminary, she tells people that she never smiled before. Her classmates have never seen her without a warm face so that they respond with disbelief. Her achievement and her feelings of acceptance have allowed her to be more open to contact with other people.

She now has made friends in her church and has found that people like her and enjoy her company. She was however, quite surprised to realize that her grandmother is not very pleased that Amy spends so much time away from home. Amy was surprised by her grandmother's reaction. In the past, Amy would have interpreted her grandmother's reaction as meaning she was unacceptable to others and should remain at home. However, this time, the grandmother's reaction further enhanced feelings of self-worth. She now understands that she is important to her grandmother.

Amy, like many other African American patients I've treated, opened up to a spiritual domain (Robinson & Ward, 1991) that was shut off in anger. Amy has been able to talk about a changed relationship to God as she became able to depersonalize some of her interactions with significant people. Her initial premise that she was being punished by God for some unknown violation has changed to a perception that God cares for her. A return to spirituality is seen by me as an important part of this patient's success. Psychology cannot address all of life's questions and having an organized means of addressing spiritual need is a tradition in the Black community.

Finally, Amy has come to a place where she can give to her grandmother. She now recognizes the grandmother as a frail and needy elder. Amy reports feeling pleased that she can provide comfort to her grandmother as she expresses concern about the time remaining for their improved relationship.

Amy continues in treatment. She has a small circle of friends and is very successful in school. She has started to look at some of the men in her church and timidly flirts. She has also begun to wonder about the meaning of obesity in her life. I remain optimistic about the final outcome for her.

Amy's treatment was a particular challenge to me. She needed to grow to trust me, to believe that her life could be better and to evaluate the effects of deprivation (Mahler, 1975; Meers, 1972) on her character development. This case was initially very difficult because of the hostility and the conviction that pain and rejection were all that could be available to her.

Outside of a psychoanalytic frame, l wonder how a patient with Amy's history could be treated. We had to develop an aspect of her life that could be experienced as a strength before we could explore any of the issues that hurt her.

Amy's need for a relationship that was stable and reliable were compelling. She needed to learn that her hate could be tolerated (Fairbairn, 1954). When she really understood that I survived each session, she became able to allow the wounded child to emerge and to help herself heal.

It is the affective component of race that often prevents its exploration in psychotherapy. Some of the affects involved in approaching the issue of race serve as complimentary resistances. The anger that is often a major affect of Black patients is often met with equally strong feelings of guilt experienced by the White therapist. Sometimes the feelings are so powerful that White therapists feel unable to treat Black patients. This is often addressed by a White therapist saying the patient should be treated by a Black therapist because they don't know what it feels like to be Black. Sometimes the Black therapist is made to feel that the very ability to function as a therapist is evidence of rejection of blackness. It seems helpful to understand that this anger is the intrinsic anger that exists between privilege and deprivation in our culture. When therapists accept the reality of the therapeutic relationship—that it is one of privilege (often painfully earned) to one of deprivation (unpredictably bestowed), the therapy relationship becomes a powerful vehicle for mutual expansion and self-understanding. Because therapy essentially involves an intimacy of an unequal dyad, constructs that divide people often emerge in the treatment. Race becomes one such construct when either member of the treatment dyad represents a racial difference.

The essence of the work is the process of self-discovery in a safe environment. In the cases that were presented, each had issues that are specific to race as well as specific psychopathology. In Case two, the combination of race and social status could have served as a sufficient explanation for her current level of functioning. When people are poor in addition to being Black, the focus away from psychopathology becomes more comfortable. However, that does not help the patient grow in understanding or allow for expanded areas of autonomous function. Case two represents the expanded base of psychoanalytic treatment. Amy would not have been seen as an acceptable patient prior to the acknowledgment of pre-oedipal and narcissistic pathology as amenable to psychoanalytic psychotherapy.

In the first case, the issues of race are palpable. But this patient presents his pain in such a way that race could be denied and other aspects of his psychopathology could be addressed and could even result in a successful treatment. However, the price for not integrating the issue of race would result in continued fragmentation of the self. In each instance a balance must be struck so that an integrative self-definition emerges from the treatment. It is this balance managed in the context of a therapeutic dyad that allows for the development of stable self-identity for people whose definitions of self have previously been primarily external and defensive.

I think Black patients do present with special concerns that are experienced as both group and individual problems. These psychological problems coexist with unique strengths requiring the therapist to keep a balanced perspective between weakness and strength. However, the problem in psychotherapy is to help patients discern the differences between those problems that are unique to them as individuals and those that are related to the concerns of the group. In order for these distinctions to be made, therapists must have a wide variety of patients representing the mix that is American. There can be no vehicle for analytic theory construction about the vicissitudes of ethnic identity development if psychoanalysts treat only a narrow band of rigidly selected patients.

Black people have much to contribute to psychoanalytic thinking as theorists, therapists and patients. One of the special qualities psychoanalysis offers is that these roles are interchangeable—patient can become psychoanalyst. Theory construction exists with each interchange between patient and analyst. The analyst must always seek to understand the individual's experience of universal analytic constructs. It is the acceptance of diversity in the context of universality that allows each of us to experience our uniqueness as well as our shared humanity. It is the role of the psychologist/psychoanalyst to foster appreciation and acceptance of our individual selves through acknowledgment of sameness and difference.

Black patients present with many interesting polarities that are a result of the position of deprivation as a result of the racial climate in the United States. However, the external climate often reverberates with prior experience to increase the level of maladaptation. The purpose of this chapter is to demonstrate the entanglement of racial and neurotic issues in Black patients in psychoanalytic psychotherapy.

References

Babcock, C., & Hunter, D. (1967). Some aspects of the intrapsychic structure of certain American Negroes as viewed in the intercultural dynamic. *Journal of the American Psychoanalytic Association, 4*, 124-169.

Boyd-Franklin, N. (1989). *Black Families in Therapy: A Multisystems Approach.* New York: Guilford.

Brantley, T. (1983). Racism and its impact on psychotherapy. *American Journal of Psychiatry, 140*, 1605-1608.

Butts, H. (1964). White Racism: Its origins, institutions and the implications for professional practice in mental health. *International Journal of Psychiatry 8*, 914-928.

Calnek, M. (1972). Racial factors in the countertransference: The black therapist and the black client. *American Journal of Orthopsychiatry, 42*, 865-871.

Carter, J. H., & Haizlip, T. M. (1979). Frequent mistakes made with black patients in psychotherapy, *Journal of the National Medical Association, 71*, 1007-1009.

Cohen, A.L. (1974). Treating the black patient: Transference questions. *American Journal of Psychiatry, 28*, 137-143.

Comer, J.P. (1969). White racism: Its root, form and function. *American Journal of Psychiatry, 128,* 802-806.

Davis, G., & Watson, C. (1982). *Black life in corporate America.* New York: Anchor Press/Doubleday.

Eissler, K. (1953). The effect of the ego on psychoanalytic technique. In R. Langs (Ed.). *Classics in psychoanalytic technique.* New York: Jason Aronson.

Erikson, E. (1959). *Identity and the life cycle.* New York: International Universities Press.

Fairbairn, W. (1954). *An object-relations theory of the personality.* New York: Basic Books.

Flowers, L. K. (1972). Psychotherapy: Black and White. *Journal of the National Medical Association, 64,* 19-22.

Fromm, E. (1955). *The sane society.* Greenwich, Conn: Fawcett Pubs.

Griffin, M. S. (1977). The influence of race on the psychotherapeutic relationship. *Psychiatry, 40,* 27-40.

Guntrip, H. (1969). *Schizoid phenomena object relations and the self.* New York: Basic Books.

Hacker, A. (1992). *Two nations: Black and White, separate, hostile, unequal.* New York: Charles Scribner & Sons.

Hartmann, H. (1951). Ego psychology and the problem of adaptation. In D. Rapaport (Ed.), *Organization and pathology of thought.* New York: Columbia University Press.

Holmes, D. (1992). Race and transference in psychoanalysis and psychotherapy. *International Journal of Psycho-Analysis, 73,* 1-1 1.

Jenkins, A. (1990). Dynamics of the Relationship in Clinical Work with African American Clients, *Group, 14,* 36-43.

Jones, A., & Seagull, A. (1977, October). Dimensions of the Relationship between the Black Client and the White Therapist. *American Psychologist,* 850-855.

Jones, E. (1974). Social class and psychotherapy: A critical review of research. *Psychiatry, 37,* 307-320.

Jones, N. (1990). Black/White issues in psychotherapy: A framework for clinical practice, *Journal of Social Behavior and Personality, 5,* 305-322.

Kardiner, A., & Ovesey, L. (1951). *The mark of oppression.* New York: World Publishing.

Klein, M. (1975). *Love, guilt and reparation.* London: The Hogarth Press.

Kohut, H. (1977). *The restoration of the self.* New York: International Universities Press.

Lee, C. (1990). Psychology and African Americans: New perspectives for the 1990's. *The Journal of Training & Practice in Professional Psychology, 4,* 36-44.

Mahler, M. (1975). *The psychological birth of the human infant.* New York: Basic Books.

Mayo, J. A. (1974). The significance of sociocultural variables in the psychiatric treatment of black outpatients. *Psychiatry, 15,* 471-482.

Meers, D. (1992). Sexual identity in the ghetto. *Child and Adolescent Social Work Journal, 9,* 99-116.

Miller, A. (1981). *Prisoners of childhood.* New York: Basic Books.

Myers, W. A. (1984). Therapeutic neutrality and racial issues in treatment. *American Journal of Psychiatry, 141,* 918-919.

Parson, E. (1990). Post-traumatic psychocultural therapy (PTpsyCT): Integration of trauma and shattering social labels of the self. *Journal of Contemporary Psychotherapy, 20,* 237-259.

Penderhughes, C. (1969). The origins of racism. *International Journal of Psychiatry, 8,* 929-933.

Phillips, F. (1990). NTU Psychotherapy: An Afrocentric approach. *The Journal of Black Psychology, 17,* 55-74.

Pine, F.(1990). *Drive, ego, object, & self.* New York: Basic Books.

Ridley, C. R. (1984). Clinical treatment of the nondisclosing black client: A therapeutic paradox. *American Psychologist, 39,* 1234- 1244.

Robinson, T., & Ward, J. (1991). "A belief in self far greater than anyone's disbelief": Cultivating resistance among African American female adolescents. *Women & Therapy, 11,* 87- 103.

Schacter, J. S., & Butts, H. F. (1968). Transference and countertransference in interracial analysis. *Journal of the American Psychoanalytic Association, 16,* 792-808.

Steele, S. (1990).*The content of our character.* New York: Harper Collins Publishers.

Sullivan, H. (1953). *The interpersonal theory of psychiatry.* New York: Norton.

Thomas, A., & Sillen, S. (1974). *Racism and psychiatry.* Secaucus, New Jersey: The Citadel Press.

Thompson, C. (1987). Racism or neuroticism: An entangled dilemma for the black middle class patient. *Journal of the American Academy of Psychoanalysis, 15*(3), 395-405.

Thompson, C. (1989). Psychoanalytic psychotherapy with inner city patients. *Journal of Contemporary Psychotherapy, 19*(2), 137-148.

Watkins-Duncan, B. (1992). Principles for formulating treatment with Black patients. *Psychotherapy, 29,* 452-457.

Winnicott, D. W. (1965). *The maturational processes and the facilitating environment.* New York: International Universities Press.

Author

Cheryl L. Thompson
PPFT- College of Education &
Human Services
400 South Orange Avenue
South Orange, NJ 07079
Telephone: (201) 761-9451
Fax: (201) 762-7642
E-mail:
Thompsee@LANMAIL.shu.edu

Psychoanalysis and African Americans

Enrico E. Jones

The value of psychoanalytic treatments for African American patients has been greatly underestimated. It has unfortunately been argued, from a variety of standpoints, that psychoanalytic models of intervention are inappropriate for the African American population. For their part, non-minority psychologists have often concluded that psychoanalytic therapies are not useful for African American patients because they allegedly do not possess the attributes required for insight-oriented therapies. Of course, one cannot help but wonder whether those who hold that African Americans are unsuitable for psychoanalytic therapies continue to be influenced by stereotypes now slowly being discarded (Jones, 1974). Still, many African American psychologists have frequently agreed with the conclusion that psychoanalytic therapies are unsuitable for African American patients, but for other reasons. They argue that because of important cultural differences between African Americans and European Americans, traditional psychoanalytic approaches to psychotherapy are inadequate, and they call for the development of new models of intervention for African Americans.

There is, for very obvious reasons, a strong tendency to view the intrapsychic, interpersonal and behavioral problems of African Americans as deriving from the experience of social stress, economic disadvantage and oppression, and to believe that their amelioration is to be sought not in psychotherapy, but in community intervention and social and political action. From this point of view, psychotherapy is at best a palliative; at worst it detracts from recognizing the true source of the problem. It is argued that society, not the patient, is sick and blaming the victim for difficulties caused by a social order that distorts an individual's life locates the problem incorrectly. The locus of the problem is instead the social system; the reality of social stress, economic disadvantage and racial discrimination is self-evident. This is the context in which psychotherapy must occur and, as a result, will often fail since the individual who may have in fact benefited from psychotherapy is often forced to return to a pathogenic environment of discrimination or community disorganization (Jones & Matsumoto, 1982). At the heart of this argument is the concern that traditional models of psychotherapy can contribute to minimizing social problems that are involved in the individual's malaise about him or herself, and can in this sense participate in the maintenance of the status quo.

471

This perspective contains a kind of social reductionism; that is to say, it implies that all psychological problems derive in some way from social conditions in every instance. While it is unquestionably true that racial discrimination and economic deprivation are often factors contributing to psychological disturbance among African Americans, these are not the only stressors. The fact that people from all economic and racial backgrounds can experience psychological difficulties suggests that other factors clearly contribute to their etiology. This view, then, neglects to take into account that African Americans can suffer from psychological disorders that are associated only minimally with social conditions. While a longer-term goal for improving the psychological health of African Americans must include social change, there remains the problem of treating those who are in psychological distress now, whatever the presumed origin of their difficulties. The focus on educative, advocacy and community mental health approaches needs to be supplemented by psychotherapies that treat problems of psychological (cognitive and emotional) structure (Jones & Korchin, 1982).

The political and social change emphasis in thinking about African American mental health has contributed, beyond the usual psychological resistances to psychotherapy, to an unwarranted antagonism particularly towards psychoanalytically-oriented treatments. In her refreshing essay, Thompson (1997) underscores psychoanalysis' potential to understand and empower. A psychoanalytic psychotherapy that improves the functioning of an African American does not adapt the person to the existing social order or preempt a desire for social change. On the contrary, the individual is likely to become more effective in focusing on the insufficiencies of their social environment, and become increasingly effective in efforts to change their condition. The real dilemma is that too many individuals in fact defeat themselves in reaching out for desirable social objectives. Psychotherapy may enhance an individual's capacity to assert what control he or she can over their personal existence, however this control might be limited by external forces. Psychotherapy can promote greater effectiveness and satisfaction in living for African Americans despite an often unfavorable social context (Jones & Matsumoto, 1982).

Trauma and Its Effects in African American Patients

Thompson (1997) presents clinical material with the intention of illustrating the merging of the experience of discrimination and psychopathology. She touches on what is a sensitive topic among African American mental health professionals: the role of trauma, including the trauma of experiencing racial discrimination, in the etiology of psychological disorder in African American patients. Thompson points out that in the struggle to be acknowledged as human, a discussion of trauma and psychopathology fosters fears that, like the debate over the intellectual abilities of

African Americans, this will simply bring attention to one more characteristic by which African Americans will be viewed as inferior or deficient. The "deficit hypothesis," of course, posits that African Americans have historically experienced isolation and economic and cultural deprivation and that impoverishment, powerlessness and disorganization find expression in psychological deficits in the domains, among others, of intellectual performance and mental health. The deficit hypothesis has by now been subject to important critiques and corrections (Banks, 1982; Jones & Thorne, 1987).

Nevertheless, it is in fact true that many African Americans have experienced significant trauma, often through an early family life of economic hardship and struggle for survival, within a social context of discrimination and poverty. The Case of Amy presented by Thompson is a poignant illustration: Amy's parents were 17 when she was born, one of seven children. Her parents separated in infancy; her mother became severely depressed, and possibly tried to kill Amy, and she was excluded from her family of origin. Amy was diagnosed as a failure to thrive baby. The point is that Amy was severely traumatized in infancy and early life. I would argue that many African American patients who present themselves in the consulting room have had traumatic early experiences. These experiences most often have a distal origin in poverty and racial discrimination, and are more proximally mediated and shaped by early family experience. In a recent consultation of mine, Ms. A, a 22-year-old African American university student presented with a severe depression. She was very intelligent and hard-working, had an outstanding academic record, was a superior athlete, and had founded and managed a campus organization for African American students. As a child, her father had been in the military and as a consequence the family relocated frequently. When she was four years old, her parents divorced, and she and her sister were sent to a distant state to live with her father and a stepmother. There she was treated like a maid, and frequently beaten. She was also regularly sexually abused by a relative over a period of several years. Finally, when she was 14, after a physical fight with her stepbrother, she and her sister ran away to live with their biological mother, who had since remarried. Despite this young woman's exceptional strengths and competencies, her traumatic early life resulted in significant emotional distress and inhibited the development and expression of her considerable talent. Many African Americans feel that if the collective experience of trauma is acknowledged, it will be used, as Thompson phrases it, to dehumanize African Americans and be counted as yet another deficit. Like Ms. A, however, the talents and capacities of African Americans are often inhibited by early traumatic experiences caused by racism and poverty either directly or as mediated through early family experience.

An important point to be made here is that psychoanalytic theory is virtually the only theory that has addressed itself to the role of trauma and of early childhood and family experience in the etiology of emotional problems, and has provided the conceptual tools for understanding and treating such problems. I would agree with

Thompson that there is no other treatment available that has a compelling model for understanding and ameliorating emotionally damaging early life experiences.

Problems of Self-Definition

Thompson comments in passing about what might be termed narcissistic problems among African Americans concerning self-definition, disruptions of self experience, and difficulties in the maintenance of self-esteem fostered by the preoccupation with race that permeates American social life. This has been an important theme in African American literature. In Ralph Ellison's (1947) classic, *The Invisible Man*, the hero experiences difficulty in seeing himself, a difficulty that stems from his ambivalence toward African Americans' divisions of class and diversities of culture. A more recent statement of this often shared dilemma is provided by onetime Black Panther Party leader Elaine Brown in her autobiography, *A Taste of Power* (1992). "Why was I flying away, then? . . . I was terrified of being with myself; I had no self. . . . Even my own voice frightened me. . . . I realized I was a fragmented being who could not choose a favorite color, much less a lover or a life work. It was not simply black or white." She describes how alienation and identity conflicts were the source of much of her psychological distress, and openly acknowledges the importance to her of a lengthy psychotherapy.

The African American social and political movement of the 60's and 70's had, for very important psychological reasons, racial identity, pride and a renewed interest in cultural and historical roots as central themes. This movement provided a context for the transformation of identity, the amelioration of alienation, and the enhancement of self-esteem (Jones, 1985). Although this experience provided a kind of communal therapeutic, for many African Americans there is lingering self-doubt, shame and guilt around racial aspects of identity (Thompson, 1995). Thompson notes the isolation that many African Americans experience results in a less than full expression of the self and in difficulty in accurately assessing internal and external experience. In these circumstances it is difficult for them to accurately evaluate their work or life because much of it is in reaction to real or perceived discrimination. Identity, after all, is to a large extent what we make of what others make of us (Erikson, 1968). A recent African American patient of mine, age 35, complained that he tended to accept and believe any gossip or criticism that was directed at him. He was born to teenage parents, and was cared for during his first three or four years by his father, who was a heroin addict. He was adopted at age five by a single older woman. This patient had been married three times, twice to African American women, once to a White woman. The patient had enrolled in college twice, but did not finish because he really had no clear idea about what he wanted to do in life. He had established a successful business, but sold it after he lost interest in it. He then worked successfully for a period of time in a management position at a major corporation in which few African Americans were employed; there he was being groomed for a high level position. However, he had difficulties with what he felt to be untrue criticisms of him and his work which he felt might have been racially motivated, and which, despite evidence to the contrary, he tended to believe. This patient had difficulty consolidating a sense of self, probably stemming from both the absence of early stable figures for identification, as well as his perhaps resulting tendency to accept external definitions based on race. As Thompson notes, such a patient's self-definition is primarily external and defensive.

Problems of self-esteem, self-definition, and identity are, I believe, not uncommon among African American patients. Psychoanalytic theory, especially the self-psychological approaches (Kohut, 1971), is the only approach that offers the conceptual and clinical tools for understanding and treating such difficulties. Some African Americans explain their problems exclusively in terms of its racial aspects (Holmes, 1992); that is, they use race defensively, and problems are considered only in terms of environmental and social context. Psychoanalytic theories help to understand how race and identity concerns can serve a variety of psychological purposes, and how they are most often interwoven with the patient's other important psychological conflicts.

Empathy and Countertransference in Treating African American Patients

Thompson touches briefly on the emotional reactions that psychotherapists, both White and African American, may experience in their work with African American patients. I would like to conclude with a few remarks about empathy, countertransference and the therapy relationship (Blumenthal, Jones, & Krupnick, 1985; Jones, 1978, 1982). It is often believed that in the act of empathy—the self-conscious awareness of the consciousness of others, or the sensitive perception of others' thoughts and feelings—one's own feelings are used as an index of what another is experiencing. Since you are judged by my perception of my own feelings, if we are too different, I cannot feel what you feel. Empathy, then, depends on a bond based on the similarity of individuals. Psychoanalysis with those who are different in terms of race, gender or culture would necessarily be problematic, since *empathy* defined in terms of understanding of others on the basis of shared qualities cannot occur. I do not think that similarity is a necessary, or even sufficient, basis of empathic understanding. Empathy can be based on differences as well. Empathy in this form would focus the imagination in a way that would transpose oneself into another, rather than upon one's own feelings, and in this way achieve a more complete understanding of culturally or gender varied predispositions and experiences. It is a kind of outward movement of empathy, which actively attends to the subjective life of another.

Any patient can invoke in a therapist an emotional response that might interfere with the most effective conduct of the treatment. I think that African American patients may evoke more complicated countertransference reactions, and more frequently (Griffith & Jones, 1978). The reason for this seems to be that social images of African American people make them easier targets for therapists' projections; the culturally or racially different patient provides more opportunities for empathic failures (Leary, 1995). A psychotherapist's self-knowledge and continual self-awareness are the means to prevent personal reactions from intruding in unhelpful ways. The importance of the role of *self-understanding* in countertransference and the empathic understanding of the patient who is different from us is not given sufficient attention. Although race and culture, as well as gender, are important definers of the self, they should not be emphasized in a way that obscures the unique individuality of the person. Psychoanalysis serves to remind us that in the realm of mental health it is a mistake to emphasize these characteristics at the expense of the individual.

References

Banks, W. C. (1982). Deconstructive falsification: Foundations of a critical method in Black psychology. In E. E. Jones & S. J. Korchin (Eds.), *Minority mental health* (pp. 59-73). New York: Praeger.

Blumenthal, S., Jones, E. E., & Krupnick, J. (1985). The influence of gender and race on the therapeutic alliance. In R. Halas & A. Francis (Eds.), *Psychiatry update: Annual review, 4,* 586-606. Washington, DC: American Psychiatric Press.

Brown, E. (1992). *A taste of power: A Black woman's story.* New York: Doubleday.

Ellison, R. (1947). *Invisible man.* New York: Random House.

Erikson, E. (1968). *Identity: Youth and crisis.* New York: W. W. Norton & Co.

Griffith, M., & Jones, E. E. (1978). Race and psychotherapy: Changing perspectives. *Current Psychiatric Therapies, 18,* 99-109.

Holmes, D. E. (1992). Race and transference in psychoanalysis and psychotherapy. *International Journal of Psychoanalysis, 73,* 1-11.

Jones, E. E. (1974). Social class and psychotherapy: A critical review of research. *Psychiatry, 37,* 307-320.

Jones, E. E. (1978). The effects of race on psychotherapy process and outcome: An exploratory investigation. *Psychotherapy: Theory, Research and Practice, 15,* 226-236.

Jones, E. E. & Korchin, S. J. (Eds.). (1982). *Minority mental health.* New York: Praeger.

Jones, E. E. (1982). Psychotherapists' impressions of treatment outcome as a function of race. *Journal of Clinical Psychology, 38,* 722-731.

Jones, E. E., & Matsumoto, D. (1982). Psychotherapy with the underserved: Recent developments. In L. Snowden (Ed.), *Reaching the underserved: Mental health needs of neglected populations* (pp. 207-228). New York: Sage.

Jones, E. E. (1985). Psychotherapy and counseling with Black clients. In P. Pederson (Ed.), *Handbook of cross-cultural counseling and therapy* (pp. 173-179). Westport, CT: Greenwood Press.

Jones, E. E., & Thorne, A. (1987). Rediscovery of the subject: Intercultural approaches to clinical assessment. *Journal of Consulting and Clinical Psychology, 55,* 488-495.

Kohut, H. (1971). *The analysis of the self.* New York: International Universities Press.

Leary, K. (1995). "Interpreting in the dark": Race and ethnicity in psychoanalytic psychotherapy. *Psychoanalytic Psychology, 12,* 127-140.

Thompson, C. L. (1995). Self-definition by opposition: A consequence of minority status. *Psychoanalytic Psychology, 12,* 533-545.

Thompson, C. L. (1997). Does insight serve a purpose: The value of psychoanalytic psychotherapy with diverse African-American patients. In R. Jones (Ed.), *African American Mental Health.*

Author

Enrico E. Jones
University of California, Berkeley
Department of Psychology
3210 Tolman #1650
Berkeley, CA 94720-1650
Telephone: (510) 642-2055

Psychoanalysis into the 21st Century

W. Henry Gregory

Thompson makes strong points for the use of psychoanalysis with African Americans. It seems to me that she encourages us not to throw the "baby out with the bath water" as we attempt to avoid the discomfort of acknowledging pathology. A clear acknowledgment and statement of the problem (or issue of concern) is indeed necessary to focus any intervention. The choice of terminology and conceptualization that may be used to attend to the pathology is relative to the chosen modality. I suggest, however, that we as helpers be cautious in the pathological labeling of our clients. Too often these labels have been applied too liberally with African Americans and consequently created more hardship and obstacles than appropriate treatment.

The individualistic orientation of psychoanalysis is another issue of concern. It may be impossible to understand the context and experience of being African American in twentieth century America without understanding the orientation of African Americans to the extended self (Nobles, 1980). The extended self is the larger self that sees itself in relation to others. Self-esteem for African Americans indigenously is less about individual achievement and more about relationship or how one fits into the valued community. Even if this were not a natural and historic orientation for African Americans, the artificial grouping of African Americans by race in the dominant culture makes group (race) membership a constant issue in the unconscious if not the conscious experience of being African American. This grouping for exclusionary purposes is supported by the scarcity model that presumes that there are not enough resources to go around. The scarcity model is akin to the pathological orientation on which traditional psychoanalysis is based. The point is that strong forces within the race and external to the race promote definitions of self and ideas of esteem and worth that are group based. For example, while Thompson, seems to recognize the "a sense of communion" among African Americans as important, she nevertheless encourages her son to look to "what he could become" or accomplish as an antidote for the hurt associated with his learning about slavery. This interaction seems to represent a common paradox resulting from the triple quandary (Boykin, 1986) that African Americans experience as they negotiate their experience: (1) as indigenous Africans; (2) as members of an oppressed minority, and (3) as those who are socialized into Western mainstream.

479

While the indigenously African part is attracted to the extended self, the Western part is socialized to appreciate individual achievement as salvation. True understanding of the African American experience must include an understanding and processing of the self as an extension of the larger group/race.

Thompson's concern about looking beyond race to understand the difficulty that African American clients experience is also well taken. The implication is that therapists, no matter what race, must be aware of and deal with their own racial orientation (bias) in order to help the client effectively explore the therapeutic issues relating to race and those that are independent of race. Differences can be used by the client (and the therapist) in the therapeutic process to support resistance. When separation is tolerated it sabotages the therapeutic process. Keys to dealing with attempts at separation include the therapist:

1. being aware of his/her feelings and issues relevant to race

2. being culturally sensitive; to understand the context of the client's experience

3. being culturally competent; to hear and respond to specifically what the client is saying and meaning (cultural competence requires the therapist to (a) value diversity, (b) have the capacity for cultural self-assessments, (c) be conscious of the dynamics inherent when cultures interact, (d) have institutionalized cultural knowledge and (e) have developed adaptations to diversity.

4. being process focused and understanding resistance as part of the process.

5. having good joining skills (joining is the process of connecting with another and establishing a relational bond that by definition provides access to the real person).

When we expand the definition of culture to include a broader perspective on differences, we become more vigilant in honoring diversity. The definition of culture in this context must also include differences within race such as class, religion, age, education, gender etc. to keep us in touch with "the creativity that is used to understand every patient" as a unique entity; otherwise it becomes easy to make unfounded assumptions about people.

There is need for balance in recognizing the internal as well as the external factors that influence one's behavior. To look at the life of any individual as chiefly determined by external factors is to minimize that person's personal power. However, to ignore the effects of institutional racism, discrimination and oppression on the psyche and behavior of African Americans is to be equally naive; there are universal themes that play out in the lives of all members of the human species, the manifestation of these themes is relative to the circumstance of their lives, which include factors like race, class and ethnicity.

There is a chronic sensitivity to labeling behavior as pathological in the African American community. Perhaps the sensitivity to this practice would not be so great if labeling had a history of a more even handed application and had not been used so often in perpetuating negative stereotypes, blaming African Americans for the conditions under which many struggle. This labeling of behavior as pathological undermines not only African Americans but society as a whole. When looked at it the larger context, the process of being obsessively critical, looking for deficits, inconsistency, and contradictory or illogical findings, feeds the depression (that has become so pervasive in this Western society) by creating feelings of inadequacy. inferiority and unworthiness. It also seriously inhibits risk taking, which is the prerequisite for creativity. When creativity wanes a society's ability to produce innovative and effective solutions is hampered.

When Thompson calls for a "new reference point" for psychoanalysis, I agree and hope that it will include both a competency focus and larger definition of self. The focus on unconscious process, transference and dreams need not be limited by a pathological focus and a restricted idea of self that is a carry over from an outdated positivistic paradigm. To be a relevant participant in the shaping of the new paradigm, psychoanalysis will have to grow beyond the confines of the Eurocentric world view where ten years of therapy (three times a week) is considered necessary. It seems to me that psychoanalysis could use a marketing strategy to clean up its image. Many of its conceptualizations are rooted in the patriarchal sexual politics of 19th century Europe. This is not to say the conceptualizations have no validity. On the contrary, to some degree we are talking about matters of perspective, terminology and the implications thereof.

Another issue that caught my attention was the statement that "all other modalities assume change (is) fairly easy." Change is a natural process whose direction and momentum can be assisted by a skilled facilitator. Each treatment model offers a different role for the therapist in the change process. Change is not an option. Everything is in dynamic flux, changing in one direction or another. The option is in how change will occur. Different treatment models match the processing styles of different people. For instance, some people are not satisfied until they understand "why." Others simply want relief. In fact, I think that our attraction as therapists to different models is more a product of our temperament and personality (as well as the emphasis of the school we attended) than any genuine superiority of one model or another. The need to see one's model as superior to another may be more the product of dichotomous thinking that promotes a choosing of one over the other than anything else. Repeated findings have demonstrated all major schools of psychotherapy to be equally effective (Omer & London, 1988). The effectiveness of treatment seems to be determined by how one applies whatever model one chooses. Empathy, the ability to demonstrate understanding of the client's viewpoint may be the most influential factor in whatever model one chooses (Berger, 1987). Empathy includes what Strupp (1988) refers to as the three determinants of psychotherapy: (1) the healing effects of a good relationship; (2) the re-experiencing of painful memories in the therapeutic context; and (3) communications by the therapist that demonstrate understanding and are thus contributory to the patient's growing understanding of his or her inner world in its continuity from past to present.

While psychoanalysis certainly has a valid place and well deserved status among treatment modalities, I see psychoanalysis as part of a continuum of approaches. Psychoanalysis' focus on unconscious process and early life experience argue to make it the approach of choice for abuse and other trauma issues. When people are emotionally constipated it takes a greater amount of energy to free them. When time and resources permit the psychoanalytic approach may be a preferred method for eliminating the emotional blocks that can clog and inhibit our emotional circulatory systems as the result of trauma. Healing emotional wounds that block the flow of life force (love) is critical to optimal health and functioning. The human continuum of needs (and managed care) require that we also perform other functions in the treatment process.

Each of the major schools of psychotherapy offers a perspective on change that has relevance. The humanistic/existential school provides a vision of human potential. The reflective methodology predominant in humanism supports a perception of humans as evolving beings capable of choice and empowered with will. Vision is the unique contribution of this approach as it defines humankind by what can be and gives direction to aspirations. The cognitive/behavioral schools provide skills in thinking, communicating, negotiating, parenting, anger management etc. The cognitive/behavioral approach easily lends itself to psychosocial presentations which are particularly helpful with groups. Skills are the tools that are used to manifest the vision. The special offering of psychoanalysis, of course, is in the development of insight and the raising of consciousness. Insight, as freeing as it is, requires the exercise of will and effort in order to change behavior. All this and more can happen within the context of a pluralistic continuum of treatment. The psychoanalytic process requires the most energy from the client of any approach. Clients sometimes need to develop strength before they are ready to explore pain. This development of strength can come, in my opinion, from the proper application of another approach. This concept of treatment continuum is consistent with pluralism (the application of different schools of psychotherapy in context). Pluralism differs from eclecticism (the use of what works) to which as many as 70% of psychotherapists in some studies (Jensen, Bergin, & Greaves, 1990; Norcross & Prochaska, 1982) say they ascribe, in that pluralism requires a reconciliation between practice (methodology) and theory (philosophy). In other words, each of the schools promotes a perspective on change, human nature, the purpose of behavior etc. that cannot be reconciled with other schools. Pluralism resists, for example, integrating psychoanalytic conflict model's view of behavior with humanistic theory that sees humans as acting to fulfill potential. The two, as currently defined, have basic irreconcilable differences. The pluralist prescribes an organized usage of one school then another as the context of treatment changes.

Pluralism is very applicable for the large range of issues that African Americans face in this current social-political environment. African Americans are a diverse grouping of people who also experience the regular stresses of high paced twentieth century living, must face racism, oppression, and the internalized self-hate that has often resulted. Pluralism offers diverse and varied options with which to tackle these issues. It allows African Americans with different interpersonal styles (Bell & Evans, 1981) and in different stages of self discovery to partake of the benefits of therapy in proportion to their readiness. For certainly, the temperament and treatment needs of an urban juvenile offender, substandardly educated, paranoid of system intervention and mandated to therapy by the justice system would be different than an accomplished African American professional who is accustomed to interacting in the dominant society. The differences may reflect their levels of acculturation and comfort with themselves as African American people.

The challenge in pluralism is for psychotherapists to be competent is several schools of psychotherapy simultaneously, thereby being able to appropriately fulfill the role of therapist as prescribed by various schools. Culturally competent treatment demands that therapists be skilled in various methodologies to accommodate the learning and communication styles of an increasingly diverse population. The glue for African Americans is in the understanding and honoring of the Africentric world view (Meyers, 1988; Nichols, 1976) that offers insight into the process and content issues of people of African descent. For instance, any treatment of African Americans—understanding that African Americans are relationship oriented—must place special attention on the joining process as a prerequisite to addressing the treatment issues. Further, issues of primary concern to African Americans like spirituality (which Thompson addressed so appropriately) should be given attention. To exclude a processing of issues of spirituality when working with people of African descent is to ignore a major motivational system in their lives. Care, however, needs to be taken not to mix a processing of spirituality with a promoting of a religion.

Summary

The key to psychoanalysis' relevance in the treatment of African American people relates more to how it is applied than what it is. Competently applied psychoanalysis can be an optimal approach to healing emotional wounds and freeing psychic energy. Psychoanalysis' poor reputation in the African American community is to some extent the product of its pathological orientation and focus on the self as an individual. Its prominence in the emerging paradigm of the twenty-first century may depend on its ability to evolve and to a competency orientation that views the self as a collective experience.

Psychoanalytic treatment to be relevant to African Americans and others whose world views are non-Eurocentric must conform to rules of cultural competency. The culturally competent psychoanalytic psychotherapist must be able to (1) generate a wide variety of verbal and nonverbal responses in adapting to the interpersonal styles of the client; (2) send and receive both verbal and nonverbal messages accurately and appropriately; (3) be aware of their own interpersonal communication style, recognize their limitations and anticipate their impact upon the client whose background differs from theirs; (4) acknowledge their own ignorance and ask consumers to be their teachers and adopt the role of student; and (5) comprehend consumers' definitions and understandings of an experience, are familiar with indigenous strategies of problem intervention, and are able to incorporate this knowledge into their practice (Green, 1982).

The practitioner who masters a pluralistic approach will have a larger arsenal of weapons with which to attack the multifaceted problems many African Americans endure. The psychoanalytic approach is an essential component of a pluralist's repertoire.

References

Bell, P., & Evans, J. (1981). *Counseling the Black client: Alcohol use and abuse in Black America.* Center City, MN: Hazelden.

Berger, D. M. (1987). *Clinical empathy.* Northvale, NJ: Jason Aronson.

Boykins, A. W. (1986). Triple quandry and the schooling of Afro American children. In U. Neisser (Ed.), *School achievement of minority children.* Hillsdale, NJ: Erlbaum.

Green, J. W. (1982). *Cultural awareness in the human services.* Englewood Cliffs, NJ: Princeton Hall.

Jensen, J., Bergen, A., & Greaves, D. (1990). The meaning of eclecticism: New survey and analysis of components. *Professional psychology: Research and practice, 21,* 124-130.

Meyers, L. J. (1988). *Understanding an Afrocentric world view: Introduction to an optimal psychology:* Dubuque, IA: Kendall/Hunt Publishing.

Nichols, E. (1976, November). *The philosophical aspects of cultural differences.* Paper presented at the World Psychiatric Association. Ibadan, Nigeria.

Nobles, W. (1980). Extended self: Rethinking the so-called Negro self-concept. In R. L. Jones, *Black psychology* (2nd ed.), New York: Harper and Row.

Norcross, J., & Prochaska, J. (1982). A national survey of clinical psychologists: Affiliations and orientations. *Clinical Psychologist, 35,* 4-6.

Omer, H., & London, D. (1988). Metamorphosis in psychotherapy: End of the systems era. *Psychotherapy, 25*(2), 171-180.

Strupp, H. (1988). Commentary on Omer and London: Metamorphosis in psychotherapy: End of the system era. *Psychotherapy, 25*(2), 182-184.

Author

W. Henry Gregory
Progressive Life Center
1123 11th Street, N.W.
Washington, DC 20001
Telephone: (202) 842-4570/2016
Fax: (202) 842-1035
E-mail: ntuhenry@aol.com

The Expansion of Psychoanalytic/ Insight Therapy To Be More Effective with Diverse African Americans (Africentrism/DCT)

Howard King

This paper is a response to the chapter by Cheryl T. Thompson, Ph.D., ("Does Insight Serve a Purpose: The Value of Psychoanalytic Psychotherapy with Diverse African American Patients"). Thompson stated that her purpose was to establish psychological concern regarding African Americans who don't seek psychotherapy, present a couple of cases, and to encourage psychoanalysts to apply their craft to African Americans of varied social classes.

While this paper will be, almost by necessity, critical of the Thompson chapter, I have a professional as well as a personal need to preface critical comments with some introductory statements. First and professionally, I have considered myself to be an eclectic clinician as far back as 20-25 years ago, when eclecticism was not a popular or well accepted position to hold. In fact, it was during my internship training as an army psychologist, in 1979 through 1980, that my supervising psychologist made perfectly clear to me that one can only treat clients using a modality or modalities where the therapist is an expert. Since I was astute enough to discern the drift, and since his area of expertise was essentially behavioral, my behavioral skills increased. In the military, the application of classical and operant behavioral techniques had wide range practical application. Needless to say, my interest and competence levels in humanistic and cognitive areas, in which I had knowledge, became temporarily dormant, if I may use a psychoanalytic term. My point here is that the eclecticism to which I have subscribed over the years has tended to focus on behavioral, humanistic, cognitive, and now Africentric concepts and ideas. While I understand basic psychoanalytic concepts due to the college level courses I teach, and while I use them to a minor degree with clients I see in private practice, I acknowledge that I am not an expert in the areas of psychoanalysis. At the same time, I understand the chapter, "Does Insight Serve a purpose: The Value of Psychoanalytic Psychotherapy with Diverse

African American Patients," and feel able to make some constructively critical comments.

Second and personally, I am persuaded that more good can emerge from cooperative efforts that tend to build, rather than tear down the ideas of others, which tends to separate and destroy — similar to Thompson's comment that, "It is important to focus on the ideas and constructs that bring psychoanalysts together lest the divisions destroy a frame of reference that offers the broadest and deepest understanding of human beings currently available." Though I do not concur with the last part of the above quote, I do believe that psychologists/therapists from different schools and perspectives must apply, in therapy, those aspects of modalities that have the most potential for assisting clients. I believe this from both a humanistic perspective which sees man as good and gravitating naturally toward self-actualization, and from an Africentric perspective whose axiological concepts or values center around people working together through cooperation and interdependence. The African saying, " I am because we are, and because we are, therefore I am," captures this idea. Consequently, from the perspective of professional psychology, I believe we must consider how different approaches facilitate the therapeutic process resulting in positive client change.

Over the balance of this paper, my intent is twofold. First, I will identify and address comments/positions by Thompson that I either disagree with, or am at variance with, from my perspective. Secondly, I intend to outline a therapeutic approach that is truly applicable to diverse African American clients. By the way, the reader will note that the humanistic term "client," will be used in this article in place of the comparable psychoanalytic term "patient." Most mental health professionals agree that the term "client" reduces the negative connotations connected with individuals in counseling or therapy and sounds much less psychopathological than the term "patient."

It would be difficult for any rational or solidly grounded therapist to disagree with the need for therapy or counseling to address the dual issues of race and psychopathology as described quite capably in the Thompson article. Additionally, I certainly agree that racial issues need addressing from external as well as internal perspectives. However, whether insight serves as a prerequisite for change is an altogether different issue. Certainly behavioral therapy based on reinforcement of desirable behaviors, or punishment of undesirable behaviors that leads to behavioral change, albeit temporary at times, needs no documentation. Structure based and brief family therapy models evolving in the 1980's (Haley, 1963, 1976; Minuchen, 1972; Minuchen & Montalvo; Satir, 1967, 1972; Walzlawick, 1972) that shook the existing family system through the use of such revolutionary techniques as paradoxing, prescribing the symptoms, taking sides, reframing, etc., demonstrated the change process within families without the occurrence of insight. So, while insight may serve a purpose, I question whether or not it is necessary in therapy with diverse populations.

Beyond insight as a necessary ingredient for change in psychotherapy is my concern regarding treating diverse African American clients. Some diversity was noted through Thompson's cases in that one was male and one was female. However, both were middle-class, middle-age, seen individually, employed, and amenable to insight development. Thompson acknowledges that about 30% of African Americans are middle-class, which means that the majority, or 70%, are not middle-class. This concern that I am addressing, extends far beyond the two cases presented by Thompson, it is about both the availability of psychoanalytic/insight oriented therapy to African Americans as well as their amenability to it.

From its beginnings with Sigmund Freud, psychoanalytic therapy has been a treatment of choice for middle-class, intelligent, insight oriented individuals suffering from neurotic disorders more contemporarily referred to as anxiety disorders. In recent years Schneidnan has referred to these types of preferred clients as YAVIS (young, attractive, verbal, intelligent, and single). Such is not the case for most African American clients in need of treatment who are more often referred to with a less desirable acronym HOUND (homely, old, unattractive, nonverbal, and dumb). While this acronym is one that is biased against African Americans, there are some realities inherent in it, that must be considered. They include such realities as payment for services, by clients as well as insurance companies, length of treatment, type of treatment the client is amenable to, and responsibility for treatment.

As an insight therapeutic modality where successful treatment often requires years, coupled with lots of money, psychoanalysis as a treatment of choice, presents a serious problem for most African Americans. More specifically, the vast majority of African Americans fall within the 70% blue collar or unemployed range. Additionally, insurance companies are looking increasingly for opportunities to cut costs. Many insurance carriers require candidates for therapy to go through pre-authorization procedures to determine need for treatment, and frequent updates requiring progress to be shown almost immediately for continued treatment to be approved. Many insurances grant very limited treatment in terms of number of sessions over the course of a year, or even the lifetime of a policy. In addition to insurance company limitations that are likely to make psychoanalytic therapy prohibitive, many clients, African Americans included, are not amenable to insight oriented therapy. Their attitudes, sociocultural experiences, or cognitive processes may not predispose them to the internal operations required over time that produces breakthrough experiences culminating in insight, change, and success in psycho-analytic psychotherapy. Finally, slow or even inhibited insight development in psychoanalytic psychotherapy may be attributable in part, to a process inherent in psychoanalysis. For example, the therapist is the professional with the knowledge residing in a position superior to the patient, in psychoanalysis. It is only after several stages are worked through and the subserviently stationed patient, on whom the responsibility for change rests, is able to go through the necessary changes, that treatment can be successful. In other approaches, successful treatment outcome centers less around the responsibility of the patient than in psychoanalysis. For example, successful therapy outcome using behavioral techniques is more directly related to the application of reinforcers. From a humanistic perspective, characteristics of the therapist such as genuineness, accurate empathy, and offering unconditional positive regard, are presumed to be most associated with successful therapy outcome. From an Africentric perspective, it is the therapist's assisting the client to get to know and understand himself often through gaining an historical perspective, that results in heightened self-knowledge, self-esteem, and even more of a spiritual awareness, that results in successful therapy outcome.

While insight may or may not occur with the application of behavioral, humanistic, or the Africentric approach, progress in psychotherapy is highly probable. This change can occur relatively fast so as to conform to the time constraints of insurance companies or the limited resources of many without coverage. In psychoanalytic therapy, the responsibility for change rests on the patient while in other modes of therapy, additional factors contribute to or are responsible for the change process as well. Moreover, therapy offering a combination of behavioral, humanistic and Africentric aspects, can be completed briefly in many cases, and offered to a diverse African American client population. While such therapy does not preclude insight development if it emerges relatively fast in treatment, it can be accomplished over a brief period of time and therefore, economically. This type of therapy can be offered to the young and the old. It can be offered to the attractive and the unattractive. Additionally, it can be offered to the verbal as well as the nonverbal to the intelligent and the dumb, and even to the single and those who are homely. If what has been presented is correct, then psychotherapy with diverse African American client populations is available whether insight serves a purpose or not.

The therapeutic approach that follows, will be presented from a conceptual model perspective with a few illustrative examples. This approach incorporates behavioral, affective, and cognitive components, while consisting of the application of Africentric concepts and principles to the Developmental Counseling and Therapy model of therapy. An interesting comparison can be offered at this juncture. Psychoanalysis is a Eurocentric approach to therapy created by one individual, Sigmund Freud. Developmental counseling and therapy is a much broader based approach growing out of the work of an international group of mental health professionals (Ivey, 1986, 1991; Ivey & Goncalves, 1988; Ivey, Goncalves, & Ivey, 1989). Moreover, Africentric concepts are based, for the most part, on the Africentric Ethos or what has constituted the world view of a people whose origins is in Africa. Given this information and combining it with the belief that two heads are greater than one, and the wisdom associated with the passing on of customs and values through tradition that has stood the test of time, it makes rational and intuitive sense that combining Africentric theory with Developmental Counseling and

Therapy would have broader application than psychoanalysis alone. Furthermore, the pairing of Africentric concepts with Developmental Counseling and Therapy should be made clear by the therapist through each stage (structure/orientation) as treatment unfolds. Africentric Theory has emerged today through the writings of African American Psychologists such as Myers (1993), White (1991), Cross (1991), Akbar (1991), and Parham (1990), and others, designed for the most part to help African Americans combat the insidious effects of racism in America. In so doing, understanding the proud African traditions, seeing ourselves from a positive perspective, and understanding the processes we have gone through, or need to go through, contribute to high self-concept development. Africentric Theory is diverse enough to be applicable to all African Americans. The purpose of Developmental Counseling and Therapy, on the other hand, was to come up with a therapeutic approach that can be applied across populations (Capuzzi and Gross, 1995).

While Developmental Counseling and Therapy consists of two approaches, Developmental Cognitive Therapy (DCT) which focuses on the individual, and Systemic Cognitive Development and Therapy (SCDT) which focuses on the family and larger units, for brevity, both will all be referred to as DCT. While addressing individual, family, and larger group issues, DCT is built on two essential concepts. One is a variation of the cognitive developmental constructivism of Piaget's stage theory approach to development. The second involves the impact of societal and cultural values on the development of the person.

DCT has adopted a spherical approach whereby people move within (horizontally) or between (vertically) cognitive developmental structures. The cognitive developmental structures are similar to Piaget's four cognitive developmental stages. In DCT however, they include the sensorimotor (visual, perceptual) structure or orientation, the concrete operational (belief) structure or orientation, the formal operational (abstract thinking) structure or orientation, and the dialectic/systemic (world awareness) structure or orientation. According to DCT, one operating within the sensorimotor orientation copes from an essentially behavioral perspective where knowing is connected with perception derived from sensory modality stimulation. Movement within this orientation or structure is horizontal. If one operates from the concrete operational orientation or structure, knowledge emerges on the bases of one's belief system which has significant affective connectedness. An individual, or family, may operate on the formal operational level. If so, knowledge or cognition is connected with abstract capabilities such as the ability to engage in hypothetical deductive reasoning. Finally, individuals, families, or larger groups, may operate out of the dialectic/systemic orientation or structure. In such cases, learning, understanding and cognitions emerge as a result of awareness of worldly things.

While movement within either of the four orientations or structures is horizontal and comparable to what Piaget called decalage, movement between structures as seen through going from one structure to another, is considered to be vertical.

Movement results in adaptation and it is caused by disequilibrium or imbalance in any cognitive developmental structure that results in activity such as assimilation or accommodation, which results in subsequent balance or equilibrium or homeostasis. When this occurs, adaptation is achieved. According to DCT, movement within one structure is not considered to be preferred to or better than movement within any other structure. The essential task of the therapist is that of co-construction. Co-construction is a process that leads to the goal of adaptation. As such, the therapist and client (family) interact in ways that result in vertical and/or horizontal movement. Specifically, the therapist's role is to assist the client, through co-construction, to move within and between structures or orientations where disequilibrium results in equilibrium. In facilitating the change process, the therapist must identify the cognitive developmental orientation within which the client (family) is operating. Comments and statements must be made by the therapist within that cognitive developmental orientation that precipitate movement (triggers disequilibrium).

DCT, as a treatment modality, requires a therapist to recognize the structural level or orientation within which the client is operating whether it is behavioral, affective, abstract, or world awareness. Abstract and world awareness orientations require insight, that which is required for successful psychoanalytic treatment. On the other hand, treatment of individuals or families operating out of the behavioral or affective orientations, do not require insight. For these reasons, DCT can be effective with diverse African American client populations. Moreover, this approach provides special therapeutic options to the astute therapist who is grounded in Africentric concepts and principles.

In closing, specific applications of the DCT approach with African Americans, will be discussed. Research reported by Shade (1991) has shown that African Americans exhibit preferred sensory modalities to their Caucasian counterparts. Specifically, the data show African American to learn more effectively through the auditory modality while Whites prefer visual stimulation. The research reported by Shade also reveals, with regard to sensory cues, that African Americans focus on relational cues in pictures such as faces that convey feeling. Caucasians, on the other hand, tend to focus on information and specifics in presented pictures. Given this knowledge, the therapist places him or herself in a unique helping position when able to facilitate co-construction with a client operating within the sensorimotor cognitive developmental orientation. Additionally, if the therapist is able to facilitate vertical movement through cognitive developmental orientation, the aforementioned change process described, can occur.

Africentric concepts and principles can be addressed through DCT or any cognitive developmental orientation. The work of Linda James Myers (1991) where the Africentric Ethos or world view is compared to other world views could be used by a therapist assisting a client operating within the dialectic/systemic cognitive developmental orientation. When a client is experiencing conflict related to their belief system, DCT would consider them to be operating out of the concrete operational cognitive developmental orientation. The Africentric oriented theorist could help the client through this area, if it is racially loaded, by presenting the stages of nigrescence as developed by several authors (Cross, 1991; Helms, 1990; Parham, 1990). Africentric theory contends that its people are spiritually based though many are confused consequent to the breakdown of the family and societal ills. In such situations where the spiritual belief system is in question, the Africentric theorist grounded in Christian doctrine, has the unique opportunity to present the salvation plan according to the gospel, if the individual is in the concrete operational cognitive developmental orientation where belief system problems center around spirituality.

I have attempted to explain that the Africentrically knowledgeable therapist who understands the DCT conceptual model, is in a position to engage the client or family on whatever cognitive developmental orientation/structure in which he, she, or they are operating. As co-construction which leads to adaptation or progress in therapy occurs through horizontal and or vertical movement, the therapist introduces Africentrically based ideas, concepts and principles that are on the client's structural or orientation level. Again, insight may result in this mode of therapy, or it may not. When sensorimotor or concrete operational cognitive developmental orientations are in operation, insight may not result. Progress in therapy may take place nevertheless. Similarly, when the abstract operational or the dialectic/systemic level of cognitive developmental orientations is in operation, insight is involved in the therapeutic change process. The use of Africentric concepts, ideas, and principles in DCT can be an effective approach for all African Americans, thereby making it one applicable to diverse African Americans.

I acknowledged myself to be eclectic at the outset of this paper. It takes little imagination by now, to recognize how comfortably the application of Africentrism to the DCT approach fits with my theoretical frame of reference which includes, behavioral, humanistic, cognitive, and Africentric concepts. Although this approach may appear to be somewhat complicated and complex, I believe that it has tremendous utility when used therapeutically with all African American who seek counseling.

References

Akbar, N. (1991). The evolution of human psychology for African Americans. In R. Jones (Ed.), *Black psychology* (3rd ed.). Berkeley, CA: Cobb & Henry.

Capuzzi, D., & Gross, D. (1995). *Counseling and psychotherapy.* Englewood Cliffs, N J: Merritt/Prentice Hall.

Cross, W., Parham, T., & Helms, J. (1991). The stages of Black identity development: Nigrescence models. In R. Jones (Ed.), *Black psychology* (3rd ed.). Berkeley, CA: Cobb & Henry.

Haley, J. (1963). *Strategies of psychotherapy.* New York: Grune & Stratton.

Haley, J. (1976). *Problem-solving therapy.* San Francisco: Jossey-Bass.

Haley, J., & Madanes, C. (1986). Structural, strategic, and systemic family therapies. In F. Piercy & D. Sprenple et al., *Family therapy sourcebook.* New York: The Guilford Press.

Minuchin, S. (1974). *Families and family therapy.* Cambridge, MA: Harvard University Press.

Minuchin, S. (1986). Structural, strategic, and systemic family therapies. In F. Piercy & D. Sprenple et al., *Family therapy sourcebook.* New York: The Guilford Press.

Minuchin, S., & Fishman, H. C. (1981). *Family therapy techniques.* Cambridge, MA: Harvard University Press.

Minuchin, S., Montalvo, B., Guerney, B. G., Rosman, B. L., & Schumer, F. (1967). *Families of the slums.* New York: Basic Books.

Myers, L. (1984). The psychology of knowledge: The importance of world view. *New England Journal of Black Studies, 4,* 1-12.

Myers, L. (1988). *Understanding and Afrocentric world-view: Introduction to an optimal psychology.* Dubuque, Iowa: Kendall/Hunt Publishers.

Myers, L. (1991). Expanding the psychology of knowledge optimally: The importance of world view revisited. In R. Jones (Ed.), *Black psychology* (3rd ed.). Berkeley, CA: Cobb & Henry.

Nobles, W. (1972). African philosophy: Foundation for Black psychology. In R. Jones (Ed.), *Black psychology* (1st ed.). New York: Harper & Row.

Rigazio-DiGilio, S., Goncalves, O., & Ivey, A. (1995). *In Counseling to Psychotherapy.* Columbus, OH: Merrill/Prentice Hall.

Satir, V. (1967). *Conjoint family therapy.* Palo Alto, CA: Science & Behavior Books.

Satir, V. (1972). Family systems and approaches to family therapy. In G. Erikson & T. Hogan (Ed.), *Family therapy: An introduction to theory and technique.* Monterey, CA: Brooke/Cole.

Shade, B. (1991). African American patterns of cognition. In R. Jones (Ed.), *Black psychology* (3rd ed.). Berkeley, CA: Cobb & Henry.

White, J. (1991). Toward a Black psychology. In R. Jones (Ed.), *Black psychology* (3rd ed.). Berkeley, CA: Cobb & Henry.

Author

Howard R. King Jr.
Psychology Department
Hampton University
Hampton, VA 23668
Telephone: (757) 727-5875

Healing the African American Collective Requires More than the Psychoanalysis of Individuals

Maisha Hamilton-Bennett

The paper "Does Insight Serve a Purpose: The Value of Psychoanalytic Psychotherapy with Diverse African American Patients" contained an appreciable number of very cogent insights. Although Dr. Cheryl L. Thompson was drawn to the conclusion that psychoanalytic psychotherapy may be a much needed panacea for Africans in America, her arguments drew me to a contradictory conclusion. My paper will critique the strengths and the weaknesses which I noted in Dr. Thompson's theoretical formulations, propose an alternative model, and provide discussion which supports my approach.

The legacy of slavery and oppression and its consequent impact on the African American psyche is well presented in her paper. It was not just the removal of identity as a man or as a woman of African descent, but the removal of identity as even a human being which was successfully used to justify and perpetuate slavery. Further, it has been the imposition on African Americans of a foreign and degrading identity by enemies of their freedom and self-determination that has maintained chattel slavery, neo-slavery, racism, and oppression up to and including present times.

Dr. Thompson states very eloquently that "People all over the world have a time in the sun and a time in darkness." She points out very accurately that power and powerlessness are variable rather than absolute phenomena. With time and effort people as well as circumstances can and do change. Therein, Dr. Thompson establishes a compelling basis for hope, justification for struggle, and motivation for change.

Very correctly, Dr. Thompson points out that the mere passage of time is not sufficient to eradicate the pains that have been inflicted on Africans in America. Despite popular opinion by many Whites, the legacy of slavery is still extraordinarily significant. African Americans are not just whining, but are expressing the pains of their reality as the victims of racism. She further states that centuries old pains which are not healed can eventually become forces of sociopolitical destabilization. The pains of slavery and racism have not healed. The drug addiction, interpersonal violence, disrupted families, high rates of incarceration, poor health status, and high rates of mortality and morbidity which are commonplace in urban environments have certainly destabilized significant segments of American society.

Statements were made by the author which raise questions regarding whether or not White psychoanalysts can even treat African Americans due to the generalized feelings of guilt, anger, and denial associated with race which are so prevalent in the White community. On one hand, Dr. Thompson states that race is a split-off part of the American psyche, not readily accessible to most Whites or Blacks for examination or resolution. On the other hand, she states that race is a variable which influences the content, speed, and success of the treatment process, and the generation of cultural stereotypes which could influence both transference and clinical interpretations. Dr. Thompson further points out that race is a central issue for most, if not all, African American clients. The difficulty that most Whites have facing the issue of race juxtaposed with the centrality of race as a therapeutic issue for most African Americans would seemingly render all but the most exceptionally well integrated White analysts incapable of delivering effective psychoanalysis to clients of African descent.

Although I agree that the struggle to regain self-definition is paramount, that cathartic healing is crucial, that correct insights are imperative, and that the strategic and purposeful use of time is necessary for resolution of these centuries old racial problems, I am not convinced that psychoanalysis is the best approach for carrying out that agenda. My primary criticisms of psychoanalysis are related to its focus on the individual rather than the group, the number of years of treatment typically required in order to achieve even moderately effective outcomes, the reality that the overwhelming majority of analysts are members of the oppressor group and therefore disadvantaged as therapists for African Americans, and my conviction based on my experiences that the desired insights, self-definition, and healing for Africans in America can be achieved more effectively and efficiently in other ways.

Catharsis is an important component of psychoanalysis. In psychoanalysis, however, the catharsis is always individual and primarily emotional. Since psychoanalysis is individually oriented, it demands the eradication of individual and personal pathology. However, the problems which have emanated from racism are primarily social. These pathologies are so pervasive in American society that it is difficult, if not impossible, for either the perpetrators or the victims of racism to be mentally healthy. A very powerful group catharsis is needed to heal and eradicate the racial pain and the consequent pathology which characterizes America.

Techniques and approaches which transform American values, beliefs, and practices in regards to race are necessary to produce truly effective and lasting solutions. Individuals must become enlightened and strengthened so that they can be full participants in the social transformation process that is necessary to produce a social context conducive to mental healthiness. Psychoanalysis is too narrowly focused on the individual to accomplish the mammoth social task which is necessary.

The foundation for the isolation and tokenism to which so many African Americans subject themselves is their exploited egocentrism which teaches them to place a greatly distorted priority emphasis on the personal pursuit of American materialism. African Americans move into segregated communities and into corporate positions where they are isolated from their culture in order to pursue the American dream. They have learned to define the financial and material aspirations that they hold for themselves personally above the social, physical, mental, emotional, and spiritual aspirations that they hold or should hold for themselves, their families, and their ethnic community. Depression is primarily a western phenomenon related to perceived failures and shortcomings in acquiring or maintaining physical beauty and/or material and financial successes.

As Amy, one of Dr. Thompson's case studies demonstrated, one straight path to mental health is self definition as a member of a community, followed by focus on understanding what is good for that community group, and then by engagement in regular efforts to give benefits to other members of that group. Amy became active in her church; she then began to provide ministerial services to others. When Amy started to attend to the spiritual dimension of her life, in addition to the material, physical, emotional, and mental dimensions, the consequent balance and wholeness which she was then able to create in her life allowed her to begin to heal.

Dr. Thompson touches an important key but fails to turn it to open the lock when she writes, "Amy, like many African American patients I've treated, opened up to a spiritual domain that was shut off in anger." Embracing her spiritual dimension allowed Amy to change her relationship with God. She was enabled to release her anger by allowing herself to forgive, love, and serve others. She changed her self-perceptions and therefore her relationships with herself and with others. She started to become whole.

The therapeutic process which is most effective for resolving the individual and group pathologies which are the result of racial oppression is a group healing process. Clinicians must search and must help clients search for meaning in collective rather than individual experiences. If the problems are collective, then the solutions must also be collective. It is out of the collective wisdom that the correct understanding and resolution will evolve. Solutions created by the collective rather than imposed by experts have greater likelihood of being accepted and internalized by individual members of the collective as well as accepted, implemented, sustained, and enforced by the group.

Identity is one of six basic human drives in my own theoretical formulation of mental/emotional wholeness and health. The other drives are for worth, security, affiliation, stimulation, and joy. An individual establishes identity in each of five dimensions: Material, Physical, Emotional, Mental, and Spiritual. The Material dimension refers to the things an individual owns, controls, or uses that are incorporated into his or her self-definition. Examples include income, credit, housing, automobile, clothing, jewelry, a profession or business. The Physical dimension refers to aspects of an individual's body or beauty which are salient in his or her self-definition. Examples include gender, ethnicity, age, body build, skin color, hair color-length-texture, height, weight, and strength.

The Emotional dimension refers to the ways that an individual expresses his feelings and relates to others which are central to his or her self-definition. Examples include personality, moods, ease of expressing feelings, family memberships, family roles, friendships, and social activities. The Mental dimension refers to the ways and the extent that an individual uses his or her mind which are incorporated into his or her self-definition. Examples include intelligence, level of education, scholarly pursuits, common sense, and problem solving skills. The Spiritual dimension refers to the ways that an individual understands and expresses his or her life purpose, values, talents, aspirations, and relationship with God or some other divine power. Examples include religious affiliation and conforming one's life to moral and ethical values, principles, and standards.

Biological identity is based on genetic inheritance from the father and from the mother. If one does not know one's parent or if one cannot see truth, beauty, or strength in one or both parents, then an individual will have extreme difficulty knowing or esteeming himself or herself. Social identity is based on the groups to which one can legitimately claim membership and the consequent roles that one is called upon to perform as a member of that group. If one is blocked from legitimate fulfillment of assigned social roles, then one will again have extreme difficulty defining or valuing oneself.

In one of the case studies presented by Dr. Thompson, Steven rejects his Black father (as his father appears to reject himself) as well as the entire ethnic group to which his father belongs. At the same time Steven is angry with and hurt by his White mother. Unsuccessful with White women, Steven declares himself to be Black, marries a Black woman in order to get even with his White mother and punish his Black father. He is fiercely competitive with his brother who has apparently been successful in coupling with White women and immersing himself in the White community.

Steven's story is one of self-hatred, loneliness, and unacceptability. His racial identification as a Black man has seemingly evoked in himself strong denial of that reality, as well as feelings of helplessness, hopelessness, and rejectability. Reportedly Steven is terrified of defeat, rejection, performance failure, and self-expression. He uses his Blackness as a defense mechanism and a form of resistance. Steven's disdain for himself based on his disdain for his race is so consuming that reportedly he has come to describe all of his experiences in terms of race, rather than race as an aspect of his identity.

I have serious concerns about the true nature of the cure which Steven is achieving through psychoanalysis. In the absence of a group process including at least his own family and their significant others as group participants, and culminating in a group catharsis, Steven will not be able to resolve the deep seated racial issues that envelope him, preventing him from achieving internal balance and harmony.

Dr. Thompson described success for Steven as gaining ". . . the freedom to acknowledge that he truly has a heritage that reflects distinctly different ethnic identities. . . ." She wrote that he has overcome ". . . the need to deny his mother and her reality that had served to constrict his experience of himself. . . ." It was in this context that she wrote, "He is now involved in a serious relationship that appears to be successful for him and his partner." My educated guess is that psychoanalysis has merely enabled Steven to turn his back more fully on the American political definition of himself, a biracial man, as a Black man, and strengthened his resolve, justification, and ability to couple with a White woman as a means of escaping his Blackness.

In my extensive work treating African descent men and women, I have encountered many variations of Steven's story. These are men of African descent, both pure and biracial, whose fathers were either absent, weak, or unacceptable. Biologically or functionally, their fathers were unable to help these men to define purpose, strength, or competence in their roles as African American men.

The transmission of identity is a family/community process and responsibility. Our African ancestors have ritualized identity formation at all human developmental milestones, including birth, naming, rites of passage from childhood to adulthood, marriage, parenthood, elderhood, and death. The collective community must transmit and reinforce a healthy and balanced sense of identity to all members of the community.

Psychoanalysis has many benefits for many people– the evocation of personal insights and the stimulation of individual catharsis being primary. But the challenges that face Africans in American can only be resolved through community insights and group catharses sufficient to transform the collective. The right answers and correct solutions lie in the collective wisdom.

Therefore, therapeutic techniques which mobilize the collective wisdom as well as collective energies that produce positive change are most effective. Such approaches include brainstorming, debating, discussing, reading, reflecting, storytelling, writing, chanting, singing, and movement incorporated into rituals, ceremonies, and celebrations. The good of the group can only be achieved through collectively healing the collective.

Author

Maisha Hamilton-Bennett, Ph.D.
President and CEO
Hamilton Wholistic Healthcare, Ltd.
7425 South Shore Dr., Unit 1B
Chicago, IL 60649
Telephone: (773) 731-1733
Fax: (773) 731-1910
E-mail: maisha@earthlink.net

Psychoanalytic Psychotherapy With African American Patients: Yes and/or No

Cheryl Thompson

Before I begin to respond to the papers written in reaction to my essay, it is necessary to state that I do not hold that psychoanalytic theory is superior to other treatment modalities, nor do I believe it to be a treatment of choice for every patient. My concern is that psychoanalysis is a powerful treatment that is specifically able to address some of the mental health concerns of Black Americans, and yet is not offered to minority patients for a variety of reasons, by mental health professionals of all ethnic origins. Many Black mental health professionals have rejected this treatment because of the time, the expense of training and because of its elitist and rejecting attitude toward the poor, the disenfranchised and people of color. It is a theory that has often been used to explain the plight of Black Americans through deficit hypotheses without offering any hope or means of redress.

As we move toward the next century, we also bear witness to a fundamental shift in the American population. This shift involves movement away from a Eurocentric explanation of psychological well-being to a set of theory constructions that change the centricity of the autonomous self as the ideal outcome of psychodynamic psychotherapy. The field is responding to the differing needs of patients who have self-definitions that differ from the former ideal because they are not subscribers to this view of mental health. The shift in understanding of mental health is a result of inclusion of people from cultures that have very different definitions of mental health. However, even without the population shift that is currently underway, we are experiencing the American ideal of the individual, independent of social need and connection as a questionable entity. As a reference point, the "rugged individual" who has no need of other human beings has taken our society to the point of fragmentation. It is a construct that is in need of reexamination in order for society to continue. Reconstruction of societal ideals is necessary. As this reconstruction occurs, inclusion of definitions of health and family from perspectives not formally considered will be necessary if there is to be any hope of maintaining social order.

Reaction to Enrico Jones

Dr. Jones' response to the paper reflects his current work and understanding of psychoanalysis. It is always easy to respond to a paper or idea that agrees with you. His paper was supportive of psychoanalysis as an effective treatment for African Americans and it acknowledges some of the reasons for limited involvement on the part of Black Americans in this treatment modality both as patients and as therapists. He states that "The political and social change emphasis in thinking about African American mental health has contributed, beyond the usual resistances to psychotherapy, to an unwarranted antagonism particularly to psychoanalytically-oriented treatments" (Jones, 1997). This antagonism appears to be a direct result of the deficit hypotheses usually associated with psychoanalytic theory with regard to treatment of Black and poor patients. This model appeared most vulnerable to the very issue Black people wrestle with, that is, to address legitimate concerns about mental health without being further described as inferior or deficient. It is the deficit hypotheses, or the pathological definition of many of the issues faced by Black Americans that make many African American students reject psychoanalytic theory as a means of organizing and understanding patients of African descent. There is tremendous resistance to discussion of trauma and early history because of the possibility of such data being used to further discriminate against African Americans. The deeply embedded idea of blaming the victim in American psychology makes any oppressed group avoid constructs which exacerbate an already beleaguered position. With the entrance of more mental health professionals into the psychoanalytic movement, the constructs will change. There will be wider application of already existing constructs but most importantly, there will be shifts in theory construction that address concerns of non-European people. The expansion of theory to include wider populations strengthens the theory and assures it of continued vitality. Without this kind of expansion and inclusion the theory would die and a useful tool for understanding and empowering people would be lost.

In avoiding the use and understanding of psychoanalytic theory for treatment of minority patients, we lose the use of a powerful tool in clarifying the role of trauma and the development of the personal strength that comes from a deep understanding of the self. This model is one that fully addresses issues of self, self-development and self-organization as Dr. Jones points out in his case descriptions. In his paper there are many references to the concerns Black mental health professional have regarding psychoanalytic theory and application. These concerns are legitimate and need to be addressed before there can be greater acceptance of psychoanalytic theory among minority mental health professionals.

The final point that Dr. Jones addresses in his paper is most important, that is, the role of the therapist and the need of the therapist to be aware of his/her impact on the patient. The power of the therapy relationship is often ignored. The greater the movement away from psychoanalytic theory the greater also is the lack of awareness of the power of the therapist in the relationship. This is a variable that raises the question for me of the need for psychoanalytic training for all mental health professionals regardless of the treatment modality ultimately chosen. It is an orientation that teaches the therapist about the power, and responsibility that exists in the most intimate relationship most people would ever experience.

Reaction to W. Henry Gregory

This paper was also primarily supportive of psychoanalytic intervention. Gregory clearly addresses the concern that nonanalytic practitioners have regarding psychoanalytic treatment, that is the pathological labeling of patients. Because of the individualistic orientation of psychoanalysis, and the denial of the impact of reality on psychological development, Gregory states and quite aptly so, that psychoanalysis, "Could use a marketing strategy to clean up its image."

These criticisms of psychoanalysis are valid and will need to be addressed by the psychoanalytic community before it can gain wider acceptance among minority practitioners and patients. Psychoanalysts are often surprised to hear about the pathological labeling of patients because with the movement patients are highly regarded. The differentiation between analyst and patient is only based on who is on the couch at that moment. Many analysts acquire their own sense of well-being from the patients they treat. In this regard, the analytic movement is not that difference from Black Americans of an earlier time. Black people often derived their self-esteem from the white people they served. The richer, the more powerful, the greater status the Black person was able to claim for him/herself. The elitism of the analytic movement in this country may stem from a source similar to the social class development that occurred among Black Americans. The pathological labeling may reflect nothing more than aspects of self-hatred or reactions to a deep sense of exclusion or envy of rich and powerful patients who need the psychological services of an "Outsider" to alleviate their pain and suffering.

The second assessment of psychoanalysis, the individualistic orientation, is another construct that is under attack within the analytic movement. A basic construct of psychoanalysis, psychosexual development based primarily on internal issues and not very much impacted by external reality, was consistent with the American construct of the "rugged individual." The initial idealizations of American culture with its belief that anyone can become anything they want without regard to race or birth or national origin had great appeal to analysts who came in large numbers to the U.S. because of the danger and the restrictions they experienced in Europe. This idea coupled with the elitist control which the medical profession had on the American psychoanalytic community led to little desire to address the social impact of such a world view. Within the psychoanalytic movement, a profound paradigm shift occurred. It started with the movement away from the centrality of the Oedipal conflict as the definer of psychological development to a deeper understanding of the importance of dyadic relationships in forming personality. This shift has affected treatment. It has expanded the definition of who is treatable (Guntrip, 1969; Kohut, 1977; Mahler, 1975; and Winnicott, 1965). The shift has also shifted the functioning of the psychoanalyst in the treatment room and reflects the reality of human beings as social beings with a profound need to maintain human relationships (Bowlby, 1969). In fact, at this point in the psychoanalytic movement, it is within the relationship that the self is experienced and defined. That is the self, the human being comes into existence because of interpersonal relationships. These shifts have not been without pain and have sometimes resulted in the small but significant psychoanalytic movement becoming even more fractured. This movement is not without its tensions from within and some of the very criticisms from without have resulted in an assortment of schools or orientations. The movement is not immune to criticism or reconstruction.

The third criticism of psychoanalysis, essentially, that only intrapsychic reality matters is another feature of the movement that is filled with controversy. There are many believers in psychoanalysis that see environmental factors as more important than intrapsychic issues. The movement is broad enough to tolerate a range of viewpoints from those holding that intrapsychic issues are all that is relevant (Klein, 1975) to those who hold that environmental issues define the personality (Fromm, 1955; Sullivan, 1953) to a more centrist view that holds that the human personality is a complex blend of inner and outer experiences (Erikson, 1959; Mahler, 1975; Pine, 1990; and Winnicott, 1965).

The point is that within the movement there is much vitality and room for greater understanding of diverse populations. It requires, however, willingness to engage in the philosophy of psychoanalytic psychology in order to find both a place that provides ideational comfort and a place that challenges the practitioner to ask new questions.

The next two papers are critical of psychoanalytic work with African American patients. Both writers disagree with the treatment from a philosophical viewpoint. King acknowledges the need for psychologists to be inclusive. It was my hope that psychologists would begin to see that psychoanalytic constructs can very successfully be used with Black patients.

I do not believe that psychoanalysis or any other specific form of psychotherapy can be monolithically applied to all patients. Psychotherapy as a treatment involves adherence to a belief system. The decision to become one kind of therapist or another kind of therapist is based on the belief system of the therapist. That is, students of psychology choose either consciously or unconsciously a treatment modality that is consistent with the conviction of the therapist as to either what is healing or what explains human nature to that person. Therapists treat patients based upon that belief system. Although this may be too reductionistic, one can believe that humans come to the fullness of being either through action, thought or feeling. All treatment modalities have as meta-psychology one or a blend of these ideas as the basis for change in human behavior. Psychoanalytic theory has as its basic premise that feeling is the starting point of knowledge and therefore feeling precedes cognition and action.

Reaction to Howard King

King's paper presents an "eclectic treatment style." However, his basic premise is that cognition defines the person and through cognitive processes human beings change. King's criticism of psychoanalytic treatment is that the treatment is elitist, too expensive and too time consuming. He further states that insight is not necessary for change to occur and he states that many African American patients are not inclined toward insight as a basis for understanding.

I agree fully with him; I do not believe psychoanalysis is for every patient but I do believe it is a treatment that could be offered more widely than most practitioners believe. I strongly disagree with King's contention that his form of Africentric, Developmental Cognitive Therapy is a treatment form that is suitable for all African American patients. I also do not believe that any therapist can treat any patient. King points out that his Africentric approach is a treatment developed by Black clinicians as they have contributed to the field of psychotherapy. So too, are Black psychoanalysts contributing to psychoanalytic theory and affecting definitions of health, illness and culture (Holmes, 1990; Parson, 1990). As different groups with different perspectives move into the arena of mental health service delivery, the voices of health and healing will reflect their inclusion.

King notes that his form of cognitive theory ascribes to the hypotheses of cognition developed by Piaget. Piaget, like Freud was European and developed his theories in work with his own children and other European, primarily middle class children. Piaget's understanding of cognition is no less Eurocentric than Freud's understanding of emotional development.

Treatment should begin with the patient. The patient presents his/her understanding of development. Some patients define themselves through their histories, some through their current life situation and some through behavior that causes distress. The treatment should fit the person's explanatory style. Treatment will be unsuccessful if the therapist has one world view and the patient another.

To think that all Black people should have a "One size fits all" treatment is to do a disservice to any person seeking relief from psychological distress. People are not the same and what cures varies from person to person.

King states that the two patients presented as case examples are both middle class. One patient, Steve is clearly middle class. He would probably not have been seen as acceptable for psychoanalysis 20 years ago because of the severity of his depression. Expanded understanding of pre-oedipal conditions provides a basis for understanding and helping him.

Amy, while college educated, is not quite middle class in terms of values and behavior. She is the only college graduate in her family and is often ostracized because she wants to share her acquired knowledge to help solve family problems. Her situation is not unique. In many African American families, the first person to become educated often struggles with achievement and maintenance of family relationships. Her psychotherapy also includes assisting her in achieving a lifestyle that is more consistent with her ideals. Amy is being seen at a much reduced fee. She is not a patient who could afford to pay a full fee for any form of treatment. Amy is however, a patient who believes that her current struggles are a result of her history. She has a world view that is consistent with an analytic orientation and is a patient who can benefit from insight based treatment.

King also raises the issue of insurance and the movement into an era of managed care as being a further limitation to the possibility of psychoanalytic therapy. He is correct, however, there are many short-term psychodynamic models that are effective treatment tools and are often employed by psychoanalysts.

Finally, I think it is important to state that the patient dictates the treatment in that patients often decide when they have reached a point at which they feel no longer troubled by an issue or symptom and end the treatment. Many patients become skillful self-analysts and become able to apply their insights to many varied problems encountered as their life proceeds. This ability often precludes the necessity for further treatment.

Reaction to Maisha Hamilton-Bennett

Dr. Hamilton-Bennett does not believe that psychoanalysis is equipped to address the large social problems that African Americans need to address. I agree with that premise. However, psychotherapy is not intended to be a vehicle for addressing social issues but should instead be a means of self-development so that any person who chooses to address social problems is not so tied with neurotic issues that they can not help themselves or anyone else.

As Dr. Hamilton-Bennett points out in her discussion of Amy, regarding the development of greater spirituality, this occurred not inspite of her treatment but because of her treatment. I believe that my criticism of Dr. Hamilton-Bennett is much the same as my criticism of King. That is, one's belief system creates the treatment modality offered. Dr. Hamilton-Bennett believes the group produces the individual and through the group healing can occur. Philosophically, I think I feel more kinship with Dr. Hamilton-Bennett's approach but not every person seeks the group. Again we must meet the patient at the patient's starting point.

Dr. Hamilton-Bennett questions the outcome of Steven's treatment particularly around the issue of racial identification. Steven now acknowledges himself as a bi-racial person. I think the demand in society to claim only half of an identification when one has a Black parent is to wreck havoc on identity. Bi-racial people often find no greater welcome in the black community as the white community. This rejection in the black community often goes unacknowledged but many bi-racial individuals are fully aware of it.

Dr. Hamilton-Bennett states that Steven must accept a political definition of his identity in order not to escape his blackness. Blackness cannot be escaped, what I believe to be important is to be able to define oneself and to create an environment that supports the person's self identification. Many young Black men and women do not achieve anything near their potential because the community or even the family discourages achievement. While Dr. Hamilton-Bennett states that the community/family is the source of identity development, it should be remembered that not all families are healthy enough to deliver a fully functioning human being to the society. My patients have been hurt or thwarted in the family and in the community, and as a therapist it is my goal to help people find themselves and a place in the society that affirms them.

Just as with King's paper, I hope that we expand the field, offer many choices and not attempt to force people to accept a monolithic world view because someone has decided what is best for all African Americans and once again denied us the heterogeneity that we are. Dr. Hamilton-Bennett's approach is one that would work for those people who believe that the group is the source of well-being but would not work for the person who believed the group was the source of difficulty. It would take considerable preparation for that person to want to engage in a group effort.

I hope that we can begin to allow each of us the freedom to experience individual reality and to come into society in manner that supports differences within the community. Again, I think psychotherapy should be offered based on the patient's assessment of concern and should not be dictated by the therapist's idea about what is good or right for others.

Author

Cheryl L Thompson
PPFT-College of Education and
Human Services
400 South Orange Avenue
South Orange, New Jersey 07079
Telephone: (201) 761-9451
Fax: (201) 762-7642
E-mail:
Thompsee@LANMAIL.shu.edu

Rootwork and Voodoo in the Diagnosis and Treatment of African American Patients

Kwabena Faheem Ashanti

Introduction

There are clearly understandable reasons why contemporary, Western trained mental health professionals are ineffective, and even dysfunctional, in the diagnosis and treatment of African American patients. This is particularly salient with patients who present the Rootwork and "Voodoo" syndrome. Among many reasons for the ineffectiveness of Western-trained professionals are: (1) the hegemony of the European worldview being applied to African patients, (2) the secularization and de-emphasis of religion and spirituality in psychological theory and therapeutic methods; (3) lack of knowledge of African American culture and beliefs, and little or no clinical education and training for African American professors with expertise in "cultural-Bound Syndrome" (DSM IV, 1994), Rootwork and Voodoo. These points are particularly salient in the treatment of patients who present the Rootwork and "Voodoo" syndrome. If not examined in a cultural context, these syndromes may be misconstrued as psychotic episodes.

It is crucial to note that there have been positive development since I first called for the inclusion of Rootwork and Voodoo syndrome as a diagnosis in the *Diagnostic and Statistical Manual of Mental Disorders* (DSM-III-R) (Ashanti, 1990). Both the Association of Black Psychologists endorsed and the authors of DSM-IV have come to support my position. The DSM-IV (1994) now includes culture-bound syndrome. This term denotes "locality-specific patterns of aberrant behavior and troubling experience that may or may not be linked to a particular DSM-IV diagnostic category." There is seldom a one-to-one equivalence of any culture-bound syndrome with a DSM diagnostic entity (DSM-IV, 1994). Among the glossary of the best-suited culture-bound syndromes within the DSM-IV are now the syndromes of *Rootwork* and *spell*.

The style in which this chapter is written departs in several ways from the scholarly orientation reserved for the academy. Specifically, much of what I present will be absent of literature support. This is due to the lack of literature written by those with expertise on the subject. In addition, this topic will have a broad audience, including those not having a formal background in psychology or mental health. I am attempting to communicate with this audience.

I give thanks to my Nsamanfo (ancestors) who maintained a stubborn presence of African traditional healing and religion in my family. My great great grandfather Bright, was descended from the Fon ethnic group of Dahomey, West Africa, the source of the Vodu religion. My great grandfather, Osei Ashanti, was from Mampong Ashanti, in Ghana, West Africa, the source of the Abosome religion. My grandfather Kofi (Fred), was a first generation African American. He was a Rootdoctor who specialized in "talking out the fire" of burned patients. I am a descendent of a long line of African healers and American Rootdoctors.

My formal training and initiation in African Traditional healing and Rootwork began at age twelve, in a small town in southern North Carolina. After the completion of my Ph.D. degree in counseling psychology, I continued my training in African Traditional medicine in Africa, and Rootwork here in America. I have obtained the highest rank of an African Traditional Healer and I am an African American Root Doctor. In addition, I am the founder and Okomfohene (Chairman) of the *American Abusua of Traditional African Priests, Healers, and Rootdoctors Board*. This is the certification organization for professional practice, education, and clinical training.

I have used the collective terms "Rootwork and Voodoo Syndrome" to include other names of the same illness. For example, in the Caribbean, the African tradition of belief in spiritual healing survives in Haitian Vodu, Puerto Rican and Cuban Santeria, Jamaican Obeah and Pukumina, and Trinidadian Shango. In Brazil, it survives in candomble. The proper spelling of the religion in Benin (Dahomey) and Ghana, West Africa, is Vodu, a term that will be used on occasion in this chapter. Here in America it may also be referred to as Hoodoo and or mojo. There are many African nationals who refer to it in terms from their own languages. In addition, there are African peoples from South and Central America who use their own terminology for the syndrome. All of these groups are living, working, or studying here in the United States of America.

Africentric Conceptualization of Illness

The African and African American believers in Rootwork and Vodoo priests have an African conception of human functioning, illness, and disorders. It is different from that of fully acculturated Eurocentric Blacks.

Every race has its Social Galaxy Traditional system that determines its world-view and ideology. African peoples throughout the yapete (diaspora) have theirs.

There are radical differences in the epistemologies and paradigms which exists in Western psychology and Africentric psychology.

In African psychology there is a dimension of health which overlaps physical reality, and includes a moral or spirtual aspect. These aspects exist with respect to illness. This Africentric perception of illness contrasts sharply with the mechanistic tradition of the European tradition defining illness either as a chemical, physical, or biological condition to be manipulated by mechanical techniques, or a psychological condition (Montilus, 1989).

The African conception of illness is more complex and unified than its European counterpart in that it includes factors such as individuality, family, society, nature, and mysticism. The European division of the real into physical as opposed to the metaphysical, and mental as opposed to physical contrasts with the complexity of the Africentric world-view. The African approach is inclusive, while the European American system is fragmentary. Thus, the African traditional practices of healing and therapy are a product of a philosophy that significantly searches for elements which provide answers and meaning rather than searches for mechanistic regimens that produce physical effects, i.e., psychotrophic drugs.

From an Africentric perspective, the concept of illness is dynamic; it is violence released by some power. As a form of violence, illness threatens the individual, social, and cosmic order. Illness is energy. As energy, illness may be released by benevolent powers such as the ancestors, the good spirits, and even God. In such cases the illness is directed at improving moral behavior. Illness may also be released by malevolent powers, such as sorcerers hired by enemies, bad spirits, or witches. In such cases the illness is undeserved and physically, spiritually, and socially destructive. It is set in motion by jealousy, envy, and selfishness of the malevolent power. This type of illness and its concomitants exist as things or objects triggered by malevolent forces (Montilus, 1989). It should not be surprising that many African Americans, especially those less acculturated to the white conceptual frame of practicing the dichotomy between the physical and the spiritual, retain the African holistic conception of the unity of the supernatural and the natural perspective of the universe. It is for this very significant reason that Eurocentric psychology is inappropriate for large segments of African people.

The inappropriate nature of European psychology as a tool for understanding Africans strongly suggests that the diagnosis of mental illness must not be made on the basis of standard DSM-IV criteria alone. Physicians and psychologists must ask patients directly and sincerely if they believe their disorders to be the result of Voodoo or Rootwork. It is important for health professionals to be aware of the beliefs of their patients; it would be a great error to assume that only low socioeconomic African Americans from rural areas hold these beliefs. An estimated fifty percent of the patients and clients of professional Voodoo priests and root doctors have some college education, and are from urban areas. In certain areas, about one fourth of these patients and clients are white.

Patients coming to university-trained health professionals are often very reluctant to talk about Voodoo and Rootwork; they fear ridicule and rejection . If a patient seems to be implying that there may be something out of the ordinary involved with her symptoms, the health professional should ask for direct clarification. Statements such as, "You mean that someone may have worked roots on you?" or "You think someone may have put something down for you?" are good questions to elicit the beliefs. These questions will lessen the embarrassment of the patient, because he/she can transfer the burden of the topic onto the health professional who first introduced the subject.

Definition of African Traditional Healing

African traditional healing is the sum total of all knowledge and practice, whether explicable or not, used in diagnosis, prevention, and elimination of physical, spiritual, mental, or social imbalance and relying exclusively on practical experience, written documents, symbols, and observation, handed down from Imhotep, the father of kemetic (Egyptian) medicine, from generation to generation, whether orally or in writing. This knowledge is obtained only through initiation, and is protected by oaths of secrecy of the Mystery system. It is African-Centered (Africentric) (Ashanti, 1990).

Few physicians and psychotherapists understand or are aware of the cultural beliefs or treatment methods appropriate for patients who present symptoms of Voodoo possession or Rootwork. Patients presenting these complaints and symptoms are at risk for misdiagnosis of psychosis, and do not typically respond to modern medical or psychological treatment. Traditional healers, whose treatments are the most effective, are impossible to find in Europe (Veyrat & Ferrier, 1989).

Western psychiatry and medicine have scarcely begun to understand Voodoo and Rootwork possession (Davis, 1985), even though anthropologists have documented this type of behavior in 360 out of 488 societies around the world, including the United States. From the ancient African Ethiopians and Egyptians, European Greeks and Romans, to modern Asians, Europeans, and Americans, possession by a spirit has been accepted as a normal phenomenon that occurs when and where appropriate, and usually within a religious worship context. Here in America, spirit possession is manifested at its highest among the Pentecostal White believers. In West Virginia's snakehandling churches, members hold live rattlesnakes to show faith in the power of God while in states of possession. Suffering holds a high honor for these people with their serpents. On occasion, worshippers engage in even more spectacular displays of faith, downing solutions of lye, strychnine, and battery acid known as salvation cocktails. These followers of a unique faith have changed little since the 1940s (St. John, 1987). Pentecostal Black church members are also a hotbed of Voodoo beliefs and Rootwork practices.

Brief Features of African Traditional Religion

To understand what I call "Rootwork and Voodoo Syndrome" it is first necessary to understand traditional African religion. More significantly, it is necessary to have a basic understanding of what I have named Nyansa Tumi Sankofa *(Social Galaxy Traditional System)*. The Social Galaxy Traditional System is composed of race, philosophy, ideology, theology, ethnic group, culture, and rituals. Obviously, this chapter could not possibly cover extensive treatment of these basic building blocks of society. Therefore, for additional information on my perspective, I recommend that you read the following books: *Rootwork and Voodoo in Mental Health* (Ashanti, 1990), *Psychotechnology of Brainwashing: Africentric passage* (Ashanti, 1993), and *Taking Back your African Mind and Culture: Sankofa* (Ashanti, 1996).

To refer to African religion as "traditional" is not to infer that it is something of the past; it is only to indicate that it has its own structure, with its own philosophy, ideology, theological, cultural and ritual historical inheritance from the past. African traditional religions such as Orisha (Yoruba), Abosom (Akan), and Vodu (Fon) are over 5,000 years older than Judaism, Christianity, and Islam. In fact, they are the modern descendants of the classical pharaonic (Ra, 1995) periods of Kemet (Egypt), Ethiopia, and Nubia in structure and the Medu Netchers (gods). At the same time, African traditional religion is a contemporary reality which also connects the present with infinite time; is Africentric. The languages and metaphors used to describe African religions are less descriptive of the religions than they are reflective European efforts to maintain European hegemony, and an unfortunate manifestation of European prejudice.

When African people were transported, against their will, and in the holes of White merchant ships to the West, they brought with them their religions and cultures. I estimate that approximately eighty percent of the enslaved Africans practiced Traditional African religions, and twenty percent were Muslims. They were physically forced and psychologically brainwashed to convert to Christianity by White slave owners. Our African enslaved ancestors did not give up their religion and beliefs without a struggle. Instead, their religion and beliefs were often incorporated within Christianity, practiced "underground"—or special aspects were reserved in the hands of elders to be called upon in times of crisis by the believers. After 400 years of oppression, most African Americans are now Christians with almost no knowledge of their traditional African religion or spirituality. However, most still recognize or believe in supernatural powers. And even if they do not believe in non-Christian supernatural forces, they will often be referred to someone who has knowledge in this area when all else fails in a major crisis. Many African Americans have elder relatives who keep the tradition alive and well.

Unfortunately, African Americans, and others with African heritage, have been made to feel ashamed, embarrassed, or to even deny identity with their

African cultural religion. This is true even when they accept other parts of African culture.

According to the great religious scholar, Kofi Asare Opoku (1978), African religion is often described as *Animism.* This word is derived from the Latin word anima which means "breath," and has come to be associated with the idea of soul or spirit. Africans' own ideas about the soul and their attitudes toward nature will prove that it is not animism. To Europeans, animism is the lowest form of evolution of religion. For them religion evolved through polytheism to monotheism, the most advanced form of religion.

The term *polytheism,* which means the belief in, and the worship of more than one God is also used to describe African traditional religion. However, those familiar with African religion, know that God, or the supreme Creator, is above and outside of the pantheon of the lesser gods. The God of all creations within the universe is male and female in one, and is the eternal Creator of the lesser gods. God is differentiated from the lesser gods in having a special name which is always singular. The lesser gods, on the other hand, have group names like Abosom (Akan), Orisha (Yoruba), or Vodu (Fon). These group names are Africans' way of showing there is only one God of Creation, and all the lesser gods are the essence of the Creator and are answerable to God.

African religion is also called *paganism.* Originally, a pagan was a person who was not a Jew, Christian, or Muslim. The term was also applied to people who had no religion. Presently Paganism is used to refer to Africans who practice an African traditional religion (Opoku, 1978). In fact, African people were the first humans to have a religion. This is documented in the written history found in the book, *Chapters of Coming Forth by Day* (Book of the Dead), the pyramids of Kemet (Egypt), and the Papyrus of Ani (Budge, 1960). The book *Coming Forth By Day is* about 5,000 years older than the Christian Holy Bible. In fact, the Ten Commandments appear to have been lifted from 42 of the 147 Negative Confessions found in the *Chapters of Coming Forth By Day.* To describe African religion as paganistic is to misconstrue and downgrade African spirituality and to support White superiority.

Fetishism is also used to describe African religion. Fetish is from the Portuguese word *fetico,* which referred to any work of art or such man-made religious objects as talismans, or amulets that Africans make use of for good luck or harm. This suggests that African religion is nothing more than the use or worship of charms.

African religion means much more than what the word fetishism implies. There is a distinct discrimination against African religion as though it is the only religion that uses man-made religious objects. White, Arab, and Asian people also use man-made religious objects, but their objects are never referred to as fetish, but by their actual names. Jews wear the Star of David; Christians wear crosses, light candles, symbolically eat the body of Jesus (bread) and drink his blood (wine), carry special bible verses, and believe that one can be possessed by the devil and must be exorcised by a preacher; and many Muslims wear objects to avoid the "Evil Eye," wear silver instead of gold, and carry leather amulets with holy verses from the Koran for protection. It appears then, that race becomes the determining factor for the degradation of fetishism, but not however, when Africans practice other peoples religions.

African religion is also referred to as *ancestor worship.* The ancestors have important roles in the religion and spirituality of Africans, but the term ancestor worship is oversimplified and incorrect. There are rites performed in connection with the ancestors, such as libations and the offering of food to the ancestral spirits. These are religious acts, but not worship. These acts only show the firm belief in the unbroken relationship that exists between the living and those who have transformed from physical life. It is only God and the lesser gods who are worshipped. Are Jews worshipping an ancestor when they honor David; are Muslims worshipping an ancestor when they honor Mohammed (PBIH), and are Christians worshipping ancestors when they honor St. Anthony, St. Acquinas, St. Joseph, Mark, Luke, and John? Are they worshipping ancestors when they place flowers annually on relatives graves?

The above descriptions and definition of African religion are the result of the scholarship of White theologians, anthropologists, sociologists, historians, and psychologists, among others, and even Blacks who have followed their lead. This misinformation has a purpose. Part of this purpose is to mentally encapsulate African Americans in the hegemony of White supremacy. The word *Vodu,* which has been corrupted to Voodoo, is from the Fon language ethnic group of the former Dahomey (Benin). It means to serve God and the gods. It was the enslaved Fon and Ewe ethnic groups, from West Africa, who carried the Vodu religion to Haiti and the Americas. So when you are afraid of the Vodu (Voodoo) religion, you are in fact afraid of and running away from God, your protector. This is the power of the psychotechnology of brainwashing (Ashanti, 1993) in White supremacy.

There is no such thing as a Vodu (Voodoo) spell or curse. When one hears that someone can work Vodu, he/she becomes afraid; yet we never hear of someone working Judaism, Christianity, or Islam on someone. Vodu is a religion, just as these other religions are, and it is opposed to evil and witchcraft. However, racism and ignorance have transformed this holy name, Vodu, the religion of many of our enslaved ancestors is now associated with evil and the devil.

All religions and all cultures recognize good and evil, and forces of negativity and positivity. We even hear of White magic (good) and Black magic (bad). The concept of witchcraft (Halloween) and sorcerers is found in most societies of the world. African people are no different in this regard. There are individuals who, because of special training and beliefs, perform rituals or services for good or for evil purposes. Therefore, they are able to help or to hurt others. As a result, people seek their services for good fortune, or to harm, hurt or destroy something or someone. In fact, during African American enslavement, our ancestors regularly used rituals of malvolition against White slave masters to free themselves or to wage war. This occurred in Haiti during the war against the French. It was under the banner of the Vodu religion that Haitian people won their independence in 1804. They are the only African people in the Western world to militarily defeat a White European nation.

African religions, including culturally African Islam and their rituals, were also the driving force that energized and sustained African Americans to free themselves from enslavement in America (Ashanti, 1993). This is the main reason that Vodu came to be associated with evil, destruction, and witchcraft by Whites in the Western world. In most cases, our enslaved ancestors only hid their African religion under the varnish of Christianity. Most of their preachers were actually Vodu priests or priestesses. Wholesale adoption of the Christian religion by African Americans only occurred during the late 1930s in the South.

The term "Rootwork" is originally derived from the traditional folk medicine of African Americans and Native Americans. It is a system of using natural herbs, roots, minerals and animal products (pharmacopoeia) in the preparation of medicinal medicines to treat physical and psychological pathology. The term Vodu priest comes from the Benin in West Africa. These professionals are known as "Root Doctors," Vodu priests, or African Traditional Healers. They are engaged in an ancient medical tradition derived from Classical Kemet (Egypt). They undergo a minimum of 3 to 4 years of rigorous training and internships. Root doctors may be male or female, however many are female. They pass their knowledge of traditional healing to their selected children, or members of their families. It is a system closed to outsiders. Vodu priests and root doctors take oaths of secrecy upon initiation. Anyone who is not a root doctor or Vodu priest will find it almost impossible to learn the secret rites used by these professionals.

There are individuals, with limited knowledge of natural pharmacopoeia, or African theology, who use their skills for destructive and evil purposes. Some are highly skilled in using methods or preparations to cause someone harm or even death. They are generally known as sorcerers, or they practice "witchcraft." Unfortunately, these individuals have been mistakenly confused as true Vodu priests or root doctors when they actually are not. These sorcerers are truly afraid of the powers of real Vodu priests and root doctors who are vastly superior to them. Only priests and root doctors are able to treat and cure the victims of sorcerers. Therefore, sorcery and witchcraft should never be confused or identified with the Vodu religion.

The members of *National Association of Black Psychologists* have taken the lead in recognizing that their education and training in European and American psychology has not equipped them to treat African American patients who still maintain elements of African cultural and religious beliefs. The Association has endorsed and supported the idea that indigenous African culture acts as an agent of strength and support. To address this need, they have established an official Covenant with the Traditional Healers Association in Ghana, West Africa (*Psych Discourse*, June, 1995) to become trained in Traditional African Healing.

Many African Americans, especially college graduates, are attempting to relearn their African culture, and to practice African spirituality and religion. Unfortunately, some are being taken advantage of and hurt by a few, unscrupulous and untrained "fake" traditional African healers and root doctors. I often have been sought out by individuals, throughout the nation, to assist them when this has occurred. There is a great need for more professional mental health service providers, with knowledge of the *African Social Galaxy Traditional System* (Ashanti, 1996), to heal their patients' psychological, spiritual depression, and physical dysfunction. This holistic approach to healing and psychotherapy is the most effective treatment for "voodoo and rootwork syndrome," regardless of the race of the patients.

For nonbeliever scientists, there is something profoundly shocking about spirit possession. Its power is strong, quick, and undeniably real, devastating in a manner completely unknown to those who have a different belief and value system. Physicians and psychologists encountering patients with spirit or root possession who attempt to understand possession from a scientific perspective often dismiss the symptoms as magical superstitions, or merely the outward appearance of some underlying disease.

Mental health professionals should not take their patients' belief in supernatural powers lightly. Among Whites, according to a *New York Times* article, the last few years have seen "a new kind of customer for readers of cards, palms, and minds . . . people in their 20s and 30s for whom old questions about love, money, and success are often posed in terms of marriage or divorce, investing in commodities or condominiums." [Van Biema (1987), reported that Michael Goodrich, New York City founder and chief officer of Cosmic Contact Psychic Services, is a full-time agent for over 30 "Practitioners of the Paranormal."] These developments point to the dissatisfaction with standard mental health practices and treatments and indicate that some individuals are looking for alternatives.

In popular White newspapers such as the *Enquirer, Examiner, Star,* and *Globe,* the classified advertising section is full of services offered by psychic astrologers and religious healers. They claim to solve all problems of money, love, health, and bad luck. Even in corporate White America, one is hard pressed to find a thirteenth floor in a hotel or an office suite with the number thirteen. In hospitals one will not find a patient room with the number thirteen. In White cultural philosophy the number thirteen is considered to bring bad luck. In politics, it has been reported that former front runner Democratic presidential contender Gary Hart had for a number of years a native American spiritual adviser, Marilyn Youngbird *(People,* 1987). It is well known that President Reagan had a personal astrologer.

A limited number of articles in scientific journals have also appeared in an attempt to explain the phenomenon, and have recommended treatments for patients with symptoms of Voodoo possession or Rootwork (Campinha-Bacote, 1992; Cohen, 1988; Hounkpatin, 1991; Jacobs, 1990; Morse, Martin, & Moshonov, 1991; Ness & Wintrob, 1981; Veyrat & Ferrier, 1989; Turner, 1986). These articles, written for the most part by White researchers and physicians (outsiders) who are sensitive to the need for expanded expertise in treating patients, are woefully off-course. African American physicians and mental health professionals appear to be equally distant from developing expertise in treating these patients, relying instead on standard treatment modalities. Both groups of professionals, with a few exceptions, do not understand the philosophical basis, etiology, and treatment of patients with Rootwork or Voodoo syndrome (Golden, 1977; Hayatt, 1970; Hilliard, 1982; Snow, 1974; and Whaten, 1962).

The belief in supernatural powers, therefore, is by no means limited to low income African Americans. However, there are significant differences in origin and expression of the belief between African Americans and European Americans. It is also important to understand that the technology of modern medicine and mental health has not rendered professional practitioners and providers immune to the same beliefs as their patients; many professionals simply hide their spiritual beliefs behind the veneer of scientific objectivity.

Over the past nineteen years I have had the opportunity to assess and treat many patients who have presented various complaints of physical and mental symptoms of Voodoo possession and Rootwork. In addition, l have presented seminars to the medical departments of Duke University, the University of North Carolina at Chapel Hill (Ashanti, 1975, 1976, 1986) and several other medical schools. These medical schools have shown an interest in increasing their knowledge and skills in treating "Rootwork syndrome."

The art and science of Voodoo and Rootwork is held so closely by the providers, and so confidentially by their patients, that very little is actually known to the medical and mental health professions. This is true in spite of the large number of patients seen in hospitals and private practices with "Rootwork syndrome."

The general assumptions are that only a minority of the lower socioeconomic class of African Americans subscribe to the belief in Rootwork and Voodoo. The truth is that the belief has no socioeconomic or racial boundary. However, the vast majority of believers are of African heritage.

Mental and physical health professionals tend to overlook, to a large extent, the folklore and religious belief systems of their patients, other than the obvious manifestations of the Judeo-Christian ethic. Nevertheless, these belief systems play an important role in the lifestyles of troubled patients. Any belief or custom that is in conflict with or different from the dominant culture is generally assumed to be superstition or a product of ignorance. This arrogant attitude of health professionals is often counterproductive in the treatment of Rootwork or Voodoo syndrome. To arrive at an appreciable understanding and conceptualization of this syndrome, one must obtain a knowledge of the background of the subject in question, the hexed patient.

Traditional concepts still form the essential background of many African American peoples, though obviously, the degree differs from individual to individual and from place to place. Even if African Americans do not subscribe to all of the religious and philosophical practices and ideas described here, the majority of people, regardless of formal education, still hold on to some of the traditional corpus of beliefs and practices. Anyone familiar with small town gossip cannot question this fact, and one will also notice evidence of it in the urban areas (Ashanti, 1976). The recent influx of new citizens from the European, Asian, Middle Eastern, West Indies, Central American, South American, and African countries added to the existent believer population and in the future will only increase the number of patients presenting Rootwork and Voodoo, or other cultural syndromes.

A conflict often exists between the belief and value system of Voodoo patients and modern scientific thinking. God and magic might be banished from scientific thinking without any harm done to its logical structure, but this cannot be done by Rootwork and Voodoo syndrome patients. To these patients, religion, philosophy, social theory, law, medicine, psychology, birth, marriage, and burial, are all logically connected in a system so tight that subtraction of any one item from the whole would break down the structure of their world. Patients may determine their current state of being in at least five categories: sight, bodily experience, inference, reasoning, and hearsay. All five make up the category of knowledge as opposed to conjecture (Levi-Strauss, 1967). When individuals are not able to resolve their problems either physically or mentally, or understand the relationship of the knowledge obtained by one or all five of the categories, they seek the advice and treatment of Voodoo priests and root doctors, even though they may at first seek assistance from physicians and mental health professionals.

Voodoo priests and root doctors serve a valuable role in the treatment of these patients. Most knowledgeable physicians and mental health professionals appear to agree that therapy practiced by Voodoo priests and root doctors who are familiar with the beliefs and environments of their patients often has positive results. Their treatment methods and overall management are vastly superior to what is offered and practiced by modern psychiatry and psychology. Their success rate with psychological disorders is estimated at ninety percent, in a much shorter time period, compared to modern traditional methods of psychiatry and psychology. The methods of the Voodoo priests and root doctors deserve respect (Veyrat & Ferrier, 1989).

While their methods of treatment are dissimilar in all respects to modern Western psychiatrists and psychologists, the criteria used to distinguish particular types of disorders are similar to those used by Western health professionals. Individuals are diagnosed according to symptoms, and degree of disorder. I believe that if not for Vodu priests and root doctors, the streets of America would be filled with even more Black patients than the already large number released by the state mental hospitals.

Patients seen in hospitals and private clinics with Voodoo or Rootwork syndrome will often present the following indications and diagnostic criteria that mimic: organic brain syndrome (delirium, personality, delusional, substance-induced, and affective), schizophrenic disorders, paranoid disorders, affective disorders, somatoform disorders, fictitious disorders, adjustment disorders, and personality disorders. Mental health professionals easily misdiagnose psychosis and utilize improper treatment with these patients. Voodoo and Rootwork syndrome is found in none of the above diagnostic classes.

University trained physicians and mental health professionals must not view and treat humans as mechanical objects. Humans are very complex, and proper diagnosis demands taking in strong consideration of the social, racial, and cultural backgrounds of the patients. Further, I believe that humans are four dimensional—physical, psychological, spiritual, and transcendental (above material existence). Unlike animals, humans are concerned with then, now, and there. They do not always act in response to their immediate needs. For example, a patient may be physically sick, and go to the doctor for treatment. When the doctor makes her (his) diagnosis and offers the patient medicine in a very cold mechanical manner, he (she) is rebuffed by the patient. Even though the patient's immediate need is medicine for his sickness, he (she) in fact responds to the then, now, and there. He does not like the way the doctor talked down to him, as his father once did. He does not feel the doctor would look after his best interest in the future--then. The difference between treating an animal and a human being is that animals are treated scientifically and mechanically (diagnosis and medicine), and humans should be treated on a four-dimensional level. Humans should be asked questions such as "How are you feeling?"; "What is worrying you?"; "Are you happy?"; "Do you have pleasant thought about your deceased aunt?"; and "Do you think someone has caused you bad luck or worked roots on you?" Humans are very complex, and proper diagnosis demands strong consideration of the social, racial, and cultural backgrounds of the patients.

Let me be clear on the problem of diagnosis. The culturally determined system of Voodoo and Rootwork syndrome may appear to be a personality disorder, and may involve strange delusions (e.g., lizards living under the skin, frogs in the stomach, one's thoughts being influenced by another with magic power). These beliefs and symptoms may not represent a loss of contact with reality, but may represent instead an interpretation of reality in relation to an extensively accepted belief not shared by the physician or mental health professional.

Here, one must be very careful before he or she refers to patients' belief as superstitions. As Dr. Daryl Rowe stated, "Superstition is just a word that the ignorant give to their ignorance" (personal communication, 1996). There are significant epistemological, and conceptual frames of difference between patients and Western trained physicians and mental health professionals.

A physician or psychologist who has not been trained in the treatment of Voodoo or Rootwork syndrome should never attempt to perform his own counter-spell ceremony. This act will not only backfire on the health professional, it will also drive the patient away. Most patients would have already sought a counter-spell from a root doctor, long before coming to the health professional for new treatment. Patients never respect a professional provider who pretends to be something he is not. Moreover, in my training seminars I have found that medical and psychological interns are afraid of the "rootbags" and rituals of Rootwork and Voodoo.

Symptoms of Voodoo and Rootwork Syndrome

Voodoo and Rootwork syndrome is known by several names among believers—hoodooed, handicapped, tricked, goofered, and rooted. The principles on which Voodoo spells and Rootwork are based are explained scientifically by Frazer (1959) in his Law of Similarity, and Law of Contact or Contagion. According to the former, like produces like, or an effect resembles its cause; the latter states that things that have once been in contact continue to act on each other at a distance after the physical contact has been severed.

No physical or mental disorder in America manifests as many strange or unusual symptoms as Voodoo and Rootwork syndrome. The most significant symptom is the suddenness of the attack. Common symptoms are sharp pains, lizards and snakes in the body, patient making strange animal sounds (e.g., dog barks, cat sounds, cow moos, chicken crows, etc.), eating endlessly, not eating at all, walking on hands, and knees, fearful of other people, amoral thoughts and acts, leaving a spouse suddenly, a string of misfortunes, being fired from a job, sores that are difficult to heal, bowels constipated, interpersonal problems, paralysis, not responding to medical or psychological treatment, and sudden death. Patients with Bibles in their possession should be suspect.

An individual who is aware that he is the object of Voodoo spells or Rootwork is completely convinced that he is doomed unless a counter power is found. His friends and relatives share this certainty. Even when the patient does not expect or share this belief, friends or members of his family may convince him of this "unearthly power." From then on his support group may withdraw from him, as though he were a danger to them or already doomed. Unless the patient seeks and receives the appropriate treatment from a Voodoo priest or root doctor, his support group will believe he cannot escape his fate.

As a result of a Voodoo spell that may have been administered miles away, the individual can become physically ill, lose his personality, become insane, or even die. The physical body cannot withstand the destruction of the social personality.

The treatment by an untrained physician or psychologist will be useless in this case. This is a fact that must be accepted by health professionals.

Context and Symptomatology

A patient becomes physically or mentally sick as a result of a "charm," "trick," "mojo," "grigri," "fix," "hand," or "hoodoo" being placed where he will come in contact with it or them. It may be placed in the path where he normally travels, or even in locations on the job, i.e., office, chair, or desk.

Mojos are made from many unusual objects—minerals, herbs, bones, grave yard dirt, hair, and animal parts. These materials are placed in bags of red flannel, in bottles, or wrapped in paper. When an individual sees the mojo he becomes frightened and desperate. He will often become depressed and develop physical symptoms. There are thousands of ways of putting a "charm" on someone. Charms can be put in an individual's shoes, clothes, car, bed, home, buried in the ground or placed in food or drink. Some of the physical sickness of patients is due to actual poisoning. In these cases, the medical doctors may be at a loss because low order poisons are not listed in American pharmacopoeia. Root doctors have secret prescriptions of poisons made from secret herbs, insects, and reptiles. Most doctors may never suspect their presence, and would not be prepared to treat the patients even if they did.

A patient can be taken to a hospital emergency room for an electrocardiogram and the EKG may be read by the hospital staff as normal. They may conclude that the patient is just anxious or stressed. The patient is then sent home and the next morning found dead in bed. An autopsy may not reveal a clear cause. No heart disease, drugs, or alcohol. The report will be written that the patient died of cardiac arrhythmia, but could not say why.

In the case of Voodoo spells and Rootwork acts, the clinical facts are that the proximity or, worse, contact with the phobogenic objects (roots or mojo) generates intense anxiety of the unknown, and fear of the known. A Voodoo spell generates a combination of insecurity and feelings of helplessness. The patients are not always conscious of this. They will no longer be able to analyze their feelings, especially when the anxiety and fear become too intense. The victims of Rootwork and Voodoo spells appear to sense intuitively that the mojo or spell gets its morbid power, not from within itself, but from somewhere else.

The "placebo experiments" of scientific research have demonstrated the power of the belief systems of individuals. Placebo is the term given to an indifferent substance which contains no helpful remedy, but looks, tastes, and is packaged to look like the medicine it is imitating. In placebo experiments, patients, without knowing it, are given the fake, placebo, instead of the real medicine. Many times these patients receive the same expected cure as the patients given the actual medicine. The point here is that if patients believe in the power of a substance, and have faith in the doctor, cures are often accomplished. This is even more true of believers in Rootwork and Voodoo spells. In reference to the belief system of these individuals, all medicines and treatments are highly effective in connection with the genuine power of the word of God and the Voodoo priest or root doctor.

In the treatment of Rootwork syndrome, it is important to understand the context of the disability and its relationship to the physical and psychological system. The first order, and one of the most significant aspects of the onset, is the social environment. If the believer is aware that he is the object of Rootwork, he is thoroughly convinced that he is in fact doomed according to the most solemn traditions of his social group. His relatives and friends even share this certainty. From this point on his social group withdraws from him, to avoid self contamination. By the act of group withdrawal, the patient is viewed as a source of danger to all his relatives and friends, or is already dead waiting to be buried. By every action, and every occasion, the social group suggests doom to the patient, who has no hope of escaping his fate. The group withdrawal becomes the catalyst for the destruction of the patient's personality, i.e. self esteem, self confidence, motivation, will, and a depressed soul. The physical body (chemicals, muscles, and organs) cannot resist the destruction of the personal and social personality.

On a physiological level, Cannon, as early as 1942, demonstrated that fear, like rage (and I may add AIDS) is associated with a particularly intense activity of the sympathetic nervous system. The activity of fear and excitement is ordinarily useful, involving organic modifications which enable the individual to adapt himself to a new situation. However, if the individual cannot avail himself of any instinctive or learned response to an extraordinary situation (or to one which he thinks is such), the activity of the sympathetic nervous system becomes intensified and disorganized. Sometimes within a few hours, it may lead to a decrease in the volume of blood and a concomitant drop in blood pressure, which results in irreparable damage to the circulatory organs. Cohen (1988) discusses the relationship between "voodoo spells" and AIDS deaths in Haiti and suggested a biopsychosocial model for AIDS research instead of the reductionist medical model.

"Patients with Rootwork syndrome frequently reject food and drink, which precipitates the damage to the circulatory system. Dehydration acts as a stimulus to the sympathetic nervous system, and the decrease in blood volume is accentuated by the growing permeability of the capillary vessels. Similar cases have been confirmed by the study of several cases of trauma resulting from bombings, battle shock, and even surgical operations; death resulted, yet the autopsy revealed no lesions (Levi-Strauss, 1967)."

Voodoo death has been commonly reported, and extensively verified and documented by scientific researchers, and its existence is not subject to doubt. According to Davis (1985), the first scientists seriously to consider the phenomenon of Voodoo death were physicians. They saw a connection between Voodoo death and the shock death of certain traumatized soldiers of World War I. These soldiers, who had not suffered any wound, inexplicably died of shock. Scientists have suggested that individuals terrified by Voodoo spells suffered, like the soldiers, from an overstimulation of the sympathetic-adrenal system, which led to a form of fatal shock.

Other explanations have been offered for Voodoo death, but the psychological process appears to be most salient. The emphasis here is on the power of suggestion (Morse, Martin, & Moshonov, 1991). Just as people can be cured by faith, they can also be killed by fear. Psychologists have demonstrated that the individuals state of mind plays a significant role in whether s/he becomes ill or dies. Depression, despair or feelings of hopelessness make one more susceptible to diseases. A large number of husbands and wives often die within a year of the death of a spouse due to loneliness and depression. This phenomenon has been termed by psychologists the "giving up/given up complex." According to the psychological view of Voodoo death, the individual becomes entangled in a vicious web of belief that indirectly kills him. Once the individual knows that a death curse has been worked on him, he and all his close associates believe he is doomed to die. The individual will develop physical symptoms of pain that he finds unbearable. He will become depressed, anxious, fearful, and guarded. His physical and psychological reactions will be expected by his close friends as proof of the death sentence. They will often come to the aid of the victim to suggest likely individuals who had the death curse performed or determine how much longer he may have to live. Once a decision has been made as to who did it and how much longer the victim has to live, his friends or relatives will often leave him, treating him as though he were already dead socially. Over a period of time the victim will either kill himself to relieve his suffering or will slowly, but certainly, die. All as a result of psychological suggestion and group withdrawal of emotional support. Scientists still do not fully understand the process of Voodoo death, and a standard mechanism to account for it has still not been identified. Voodoo deaths, however, are not typical of Rootwork or Voodoo spells. More typical is the following case study.

This case is a typical example from my experience of treating patients in a mental health center of a major state university. This relatively brief description of a real patient is edited to focus on information relevant to differential diagnosis. It would be useful for clinicians to get experience in applying the principles of the DSM-IV to patients with Rootwork or Voodoo syndrome. This case will be followed by a brief discussion of my diagnosis. I will not go into detail about treatment, but the case material may serve as a useful point of departure for discussion.

A 24-year-old African American male graduate student asked for a consultation with me because of poor academic performance and relationship concerns. The counseling center had a staff of eleven psychologists, four consulting psychiatrists, and several interns, yet this patient requested an appointment specifically with me. This student was an officer on leave from the United States Army. He was to complete his master's degree in communications. He, the youngest of fifteen children, was from a rural area of North Carolina. Upon graduation from high school, he attended community college and was trained to be a radio announcer. He went on to complete a bachelor's degree, and worked for 6 months as a radio announcer before entering the army. During this first year his academic performance had consistently been above average.

A Case of Rootwork

DSM-IV Diagnosis:

Axis I:	V62-3	Academic Problem
	V62-81	Relational Problem Not Otherwise Specified
Axis II:	301-22	(Rule out) Schizotypal Personality Disorder. Odd beliefs?
Axis III:		None
Axis IV:		Discord with teachers and inadequate school environment, difficulty with acculturation, racial discrimination
Axis V:		GAF = 75 (current)

Eight months before the consultation, the patient, broke off a romantic relationship with his girlfriend, had his car repossessed, narrowly escaped a house fire that took his uncle's life, and failed two courses. During consultation, this patient revealed that he: (1) never had close friends, and his social contacts were limited to essential course work in class; (2) was suspicious of other people; (3) was very intelligent; (4) revengeful toward anyone who caused him problems; (5) was hypersensitive to criticism; and (6) had bizarre ideations surrounding the death of his father.

The patient noticed a poster sign of Voodoo on my office wall and asked me if I believed in Rootwork. I answered him cordially, "Yes I do, why do you ask?" The patient said that his father died as a result of Rootwork, when he was ten years old. I asked him to tell me more about the circumstances of his father's death. Here is the story, which the patient believed to be true. When the patient was nine years old, his father sought a position as a deacon in a Baptist church. However, another man sought the same position. After the patient's father was selected as the deacon, the mother of the other man became very angry and hostile toward the father. After attending church services one morning, the rival candidate walked up to the passenger side of the patient's father's car and threw a white powder substance through the window. Soon the father became ill and had to be hospitalized. He didn't respond well to the medical treatment. After a week in the hospital, the rival candidate came to visit the father and gave him a "gift" of several old silver coins. Soon after the visit, the father developed complete paralysis of his limbs. The patient's mother, who believed in Rootwork, went to see a root doctor who told her that a spell had been placed on her husband and not to accept any more gifts or visits from the rival candidate. The root doctor told her also that a live snake and a frog were in the stomach of her husband, eating his insides, slowly killing him.

The root doctor gave the mother instructions and an antidote for the spell. He told her that the snake must leave the body through her husband's anus, and the frog by way of the mouth. She would know that the snake had been destroyed by her husband's feces; it would be hard, dark, and scaly, and the frog, by a large lump in the side of his neck, attempting to leave the mouth. When she gave the antidote to her husband at home, true to prediction, the symptoms appeared. However, the frog tried but was not able to leave through his mouth, and he began to choke to death. Before he died, he told his son (patient) to take care of his mother; these were the last words spoken to the patient.

A few weeks after the father's death, his mother became weak and sick. One day while working in the field she threw her hands up and prayed to God to take her evil burden away, and felt instant relief. Soon after her prayer, her oldest daughter called her to come to the house. When the mother arrived, she was told that the old mother of the rival candidate had just died.

I asked the patient if he thought that someone had placed a bad spell on him causing all the problems he had been having. The patient said yes, he thought that was a strong possibility. There was more information provided which is not reviewed here. However, the patient did not have hallucinations or disorganized speech, but he did have unusual perceptual experiences. There were impairments in his social and academic functioning, even though he felt brilliant and wanted to be recognized as someone important. He believed that someone from his hometown was working roots on him, and that his professor was out to get him. He didn't trust anyone. Socially he was passive-aggressive.

Discussion

Possible diagnoses for this case are (DSM-IV) adjustment disorder (309-9), narcissistic personality disorder (301-81), paranoid personality disorder (301-0), mixed personality disorder (301-19), or schizophrenic residual type (295-60).

There are symptoms of maladaptive reactions to an identifiable stressor, which occurred within three months (house fire). There is impairment of his social and occupational (student) functioning. He lacks empathy for other people and displays interpersonal exploitativeness. His relationship with his girlfriend went between overidealization and devaluation. He expected others to harm him, was secretive, and ready to counterattack when any threat was perceived. His story regarding the death of his father appears to fit schizophrenia. The content is patently absurd and appears to have no possible basis in fact. He believes that root doctors can cast spells, control one's actions, cause snakes and frogs to live in one's stomach. Would further assessment be warranted in this case—administer the MMPI or Rorschach?

With a clinical background in Voodoo or Rootwork, the diagnosis and treatment of this case would be quite simple. This patient is quite normal in all respects; however, he does suffer from stress and anxiety. None of the diagnoses based on DSM-IV would be correct and testing would be of little value. This is because Eurocentric world-views and testing protocols are incapable with Africicentric world-views and diagnostic protocols.

Treatment of patients with Voodoo and Rootwork syndrome involves an antagonism inherent in the curing process. The patient is depressed, self-alienating, and passive, while on the other hand, the root doctor is positive, self-confident, projecting, and active. The cure is partially effected by interrelating these opposite terminals, transferring the psychic universe of the physician or healer to the psychic and social universe of the patient.

The belief of the patient and, in certain cases, the traditional healer, is that illness is often caused by possession (spell, mojo, etc.). Either the illness is itself an evil spirit which has seized the patient, or it has been brought by an evil being which has caused the illness. The evil spirit must be cast out or destroyed to effect a cure. In certain cases a combination of evil spirits and toxins must be eradicated.

The passive patient is often put into a trance, much like hypnosis, by the active healer, and the Voodoo priest may also go into a trance. With or without a trance, the healer tells the patient why he became ill—perhaps from a moral wrong he did to someone else, or the result of a spell or toxin which a rival paid another root doctor to administer. The root doctor or healer then attempts to expel the evil spirit or toxin from the patient and, if the healer is successful, the patient emerges from the trance mentally and physically healed. In the clinical practice of a Voodoo priest or root doctor, cures of this type actually work, especially with illnesses incorrectly diagnosed as schizophrenia.

From a psychologist's perspective, what happens is that in trance the patient is able to admit his moral wrongs and pour out his problems, stresses, and anxieties in the same manner as a patient in a university-trained psychotherapist's chair. This process has a real treatment value for many reasons; most significantly, the patient responds to suggestions and completely believes the evil spirit which possessed him has been driven out or destroyed. From the Vodoo priest or healers perspective the cure is achieved by achieving balance in the spirit, mind, and body.

Patients who believe or are actual victims of Rootwork are very seldom cured by modern physicians and psychologists because these health providers do not have the expertise and power to heal these patients, nor do they come close to bearing the prestige of a Voodoo priest or root doctor in treating this disorder.

The treatment methods of Voodoo priests and root doctors seem crude and strange to untrained health providers and consumers. They cure their patients by utilizing multifarious therapeutics. For example, a cure for conjure poisoning is "Maybutter" (made on the first day of May) mixed with saltpeter, and the yolk of a brown egg which is rolled into small pills and taken two times a day. With each pill the patient must read a special passage in the Bible. If a patient is having major setbacks of misfortune and mental depression for some unknown reason, the doctor may bring about a positive change in her life by boiling a special root (High John, the Conqueror) tea. In addition, he may tell the patient to carry a special "hand" (charm) in his/her purse/wallet.

To the Voodoo priests and root doctors, the condition of the spiritual state of the patient is very important because it determines the physical status of the body. To be healthy, one must have a balance between the physical, mental, and spiritual elements of life. Sickness is the imbalance of these elements, and may reflect the effects of evil forces or objects within the body.

Voodoo and Rootwork treatments work on three different levels: physical, psychological, and spiritual. The treatment level is determined by the nature of the illness. An unlimited range of relatively minor physical disorders (first level) are treated symptomatically, as they would be in establishment medicine. However, treatment is achieved only with medicinal roots, herbs, plants, animal products, and minerals (natural folk medicines). The knowledge of these preparations is part of the basic education of the Voodoo priests and root doctors. Treatment on the psychological second level often includes allowances for the accompanying physical problems and is much more difficult to treat. These cases include marital problems, financial and legal problems, and educational and work-related issues, among others.

To cure on the third level of treatment for restoring balance within the patient, a number of techniques may be employed by the priest or root doctor (if trained to do so—many are not). At the physical level these may include special diets, doses of medical potions, and body massages. The amazing thing to those who are unfamiliar with Voodoo and Rootwork is that it works. A strong faith in the religious Voodoo priest's or root doctor's treatment most often brings a cure on this third level. While the psychological processes involved within the cures are not fully understood, the power of belief or faith is recognized by medical science, and it is a fact that cures do actually occur. I have obtained many cures personally. Faith in the treatment and the priest or root doctor will, in fact, almost guarantee a cure. It does matter what the healer gives or tells the patient, however.

Faith in the remedy actually hastens the cure (Puckett, 1969). Faith in the good produces the positive behavior and results. Faith in the harmful, likewise, will produce the harmful, negative behavior and results. If a patient believes that snake-dust has been placed in his food, he will actually feel and see the symptoms of small snakes growing within him (just as in the movie *The Believers*). Does this mean that the patient is mentally ill? The answer is no; he in fact is reacting to his sane reality of religious belief, and must be treated accordingly.

Although no two are the same in cases of marital conflicts, legal problems (civil and criminal), educational performance, job related stresses, and psychological disability, I have brought about relief and cures utilizing Voodoo and Rootwork treatment methods. No questions exist in the minds of the clients and patients of the value of the treatment; sometimes cures are almost instantaneous.

The most serious and difficult cases to treat are those on the fourth level—the spiritual decay of the soul. In these cases (each different), the presenting symptoms cover physiological and psychological problems, in addition to loss of spiritual vital energy in the here and now, and the life after death. To treat these patients, intervention and adjustments must be made on the physical level by traditional medicinal potions, diet, baths, and massages. To bring about change on the psychological level, special counseling and psychotherapy, and physical environmental change must be rendered within the context of the belief of the Voodoo priest, in a proactive manner. Patients with this fourth order syndrome feel always passive, hopeless, and doomed. They will not, generally, respond to modern western medical treatment in hospitals or their homes. They are, in fact, prime candidates for Voodoo death syndrome, wasting away slowly or committing suicide.

Only the Voodoo priest's intervention at the vital spiritual-soul level will ultimately save and cure a patient with fourth level Voodoo or Rootwork syndrome. By administering the appropriate treatment, the Voodoo priest becomes the humble earthly servant of God and the lesser gods of the Voodoo religion. The priest must perform the sacred ceremonial sacrifice of an animal (only) to wet the ground with blood, and invoke the proper God. The spirit of the God must possess the physical body of the priest in order to give the knowledge of the cure for the patient. In most cases, a lesser God or spirit will also possess the patient while the treatment is administered by the priest.

Only Voodoo priests possess the authority and power to call upon God and the lesser gods for explanations that lie beyond common sense and Western scientific reasoning. The explanations permit the believers and priests to identify the "roots" and treatment for sickness and suffering.

Voodoo and Rootwork beliefs are more common in the United States than is generally appreciated by physicians. A patient's belief that he is the victim of Rootwork may be the result of many different biological, psychological, and social problems. Treatment must be based on a carefully maintained alliance with the patient and his family, and on a careful biopsychosocial formulation. No one form of treatment will be appropriate for all patients, but most patients can benefit from therapy until an appropriate referral is made to a qualified Root doctor or African traditional healer. In some cases, joint treatment may be necessary (Hilliard, 1982).

Physicians and mental health professionals will find the clinical approach outlined here to be helpful with patients of Rootwork syndrome. This model suggests that patients can best be understood from a design that recognizes a cultural connection to Africa. Gerald G. Jackson (1980) and I suggest specific strategies that are more advantageous in the treatment process of patients.

The Patient

Before the patient enters the door, s/he must be viewed as a worthy human being. The dominant cultural group, by its rejection of many patients' religion and culture (C. Thomas, 1973), implies that those unlike themselves are inferior, deprived, culturally disadvantaged, and superstitious. However, even though the doctrine of color blindness suggests avoidance of race differences in our work with Rootwork syndrome, this concept, along with the European perspective of mental health, has no value even with white Rootwork patients. Voodoo and Rootwork syndrome is an Afrocentric illness.

The problems many psychiatrists, psychologists, and health professionals have with patient assessment are the result of their own socialization or the acceptance of many false concepts in Voodoo and Rootwork. Errors are committed in diagnosing because of failure to understand the peculiar life circumstances of the patients by medical personnel (Chess, Clark, & Thomas, 1953). A more positive treatment outcome will occur if the provider conveys to the patient his understanding of the racial, cultural, and religious aspects of his problem.

A generally accurate assessment can be obtained by evaluating three major aspects which the patient presents; (1) the mogya (her physical body), (2) her sunsum, and (3) her environment (Opoku, 1978).

The mogya—The patient has a body and a body concept which the provider must remember no matter how psychologically or culturally biased s/he becomes. His/her perception of her mogya (body) as a source of pleasure or discomfort, and how s/he sees and experiences reality in terms of this mogya concept are significant to all her thoughts and imagery. If the patient feels small snakes in her body, they must be acknowledged, although only in the context of Rootwork symptoms.

Even more important, the provider must recognize the impact which various bodily illnesses have on the patient's self-concept. These illnesses will have subjected him/her to interpersonal experiences with others which will be relevant in his/her approach to the health provider.

Sunsum—Sunsum refers to the patient's interacting goal striving—defense system; that is, how she organizes, differentiates, and mediates her external world and her internal desires. The weakness or strength of his/her sunsum impacts significantly on his/her ability to withstand anxiety and reality frustrations as the healing process germinates. A weak sunsum will fail his/her in one or all of these functions, and the provider's treatment will be useless. The sunsum is the part of humans which is open to attack by witchcraft (Opoku, 1978).

Environment—The geographical location, living conditions, religion, and values of her/his social community must be taken into account. Family, friends, job, and church all exert force. They provide the pathways for obtaining material and emotional resources. These resources come together to regulate self-esteem and status within the environment. Environmental factors are significant determiners of the impact of the reaction of the patient to negative Rootwork and Voodoo spells. With positive environmental support, the prognosis for cure will be excellent. With negative environmental support, the outcome of treatment will be long term, and of questionable value.

I have recommended these three aspects for assessment when evaluating a patient presenting Voodoo and Rootwork syndrome. I also recommend that medical and psychological providers think in these terms first, rather than in those of the *Diagnostic and Statistical Manual of Mental Disorders,* to avoid misdiagnosis.

I and other healers are now called upon for consultation by psychiatric providers, mental health centers, and social service agencies. Unfortunately however, the treatment expertise of most mental health providers has not been developed to match the new DSM-IV cultural-bound syndrome recognition. This lack of expertise is not likely to change in the future, due to their unwillingness to accept the Africentric world-view. Priests will not train or teach outsiders due to the oaths of secrecy taken by Rootdoctors and African Traditional Healers. However, collaboration between these two professions can become a reality. It must be understood that true Rootdoctors or Traditional Healers will not allow themselves to be "pumped" for their knowledge or to be exploited.

The Psychotherapist and Treatment

The general requirements and qualifications of providers who treat patients with "Voodoo and Rootwork Syndrome" follow. The DSM-IV (1994) refers to this under the rubric of Culture-Bound syndromes:

1. A knowledge of the African-centered world-view and spirituality.

2. A knowledge of normal and pathological thought and behavior of Voodoo and Rootwork believers.

3. A knowledge of African American psychology and theoretical concepts of treatment.

4. Technical experience or classroom instruction in therapeutically integrating observations with clinical work with patients.

5. Practiced and controlled ability to read and understand the hidden meanings behind spoken words and body language.

6. Awareness of personal anxieties, and defenses and their influence on the treatment techniques.

"Voodoo and Rootwork Syndrome" are classified by Western medicine as representing psychopathology, and treatment reflects a biomedical orientation (Campinha-Bacote, 1992). This classification is incorrect in the majority of cases, and the biomedical orientation is patently contraindicated. Such classification only complicates the treatments.

The psychotherapist must exercise extreme prudence before attempting to diagnose and treat patients with "Rootwork or Voodoo Syndrome." Eurocentric or Western psychological theories of personality, and methods of treatment, are patently inappropriate with these presenting patients. There is no similarity in the style or methods used by Western trained therapists, and Vodu priests and Root doctors. In fact, there are epistemological and paradigm shifts between Western psychology and Africentric psychology.

Individuals come for psychotherapy for several reasons. They may be referred by their physicians after consultation for physical symptoms determines that there are no organic bases for treatment. Many patients with physical symptoms of Rootwork are resistant to the idea of psychotherapy, and its implications of psychological disability. As a result, they may terminate the relationship after only one or two interviews. Relatives and friends may also influence patients to come for psychotherapy. In many cases, more educated patients may have some doubts about the reality of Voodoo and Rootwork spells, and come for psychotherapy. Even though they suffer from unusual symptoms, they may think they are connected in some form to their own psychological makeup and that with counseling, the unpleasant symptoms will be cured. An even smaller group of patients are referred for psychotherapy by Voodoo priests and root doctors. These patients are often referred because they are psychotic, violent, ill, intellectually dull, or had poor references.

With all cases, patients coming for psychotherapy have conscious and unconscious fears of the Rootwork spell. They also fear the put-down or contempt of the provider. They fear being found crazy. However, they naturally hope for the answers, and quick cures with little effort on their part; they are passive.

Patients feel they have little reason to trust psychotherapists. The therapist must therefore, be prepared for a period in which his words, "I am not as the others who harm you" are measured against his or her acts. In the initial sessions, the patient's contribution will stem from the character structure, and the amount of "counter power" the patient attributes to the therapist.

With children, nervousness, timidness, and nightmares maybe the result of superstitious beliefs held and practiced by their parents and peer group. Rarely is negative Rootwork practiced against children, but it does occur sometimes.

The African and African American believers in Rootwork and Vodoo priests have an African conception of human functioning, illness, and disorders. It is radically different from fully acculturated Blacks, and White patients.

Every race has its own Traditional Social Galaxy system that determines its world view and ideology. African peoples throughout the *yapete* (diaspora) have theirs. There is a dimension of health which overlaps the physical reality, and comprehends a moral or spiritual aspect. The same aspect exists in the notion of illness. This Africentric perception of illness contrasts sharply with the mechanistic tradition of the European tradition defining illness either as a chemical, physical, or biological condition to be manipulated by mechanical techniques, or a psychological condition (Montilus, 1989).

The specificity of African healing and psychotherapy must take into account the two elements of order and power. Illness, suffering, and death call for effective power to stop the threat of chaos and reestablish order (McGuire, 1982). The Traditional Healer's treatment regimens with patients with Rootwork or Voodoo syndromes may include one or all of the following:

1. Divination to determine origin of illness
2. Consulting lesser gods and nature spirits
3. Sacrifices and purification rites
4. Ancestor consultation and offerings for atonement
5. Invocations and antispells for sorcerer
6. Grigris
7. Herbal preparations
8. Family group treatment,
9. Individual treatment
10. Environmental and or career change, and
11. Spiritual realignment

As one readily observes from the above list of treatment regimens and qualifications of mental health or health providers, there are indeed epistemological and paradigm shifts.

There are, however, temporary and supportive techniques that Eurocentric health providers and mental health professionals may employ with these patients. The psychotherapist should demonstrate a strong sense of caring also the therapist may initiate family counseling. In addition, therapist may, if properly trained judiciously manipulate the environment. This may entail botanical and pharmacological empiricism. For example, botanical and pharmacological preparations can be used for safe and gentle effectiveness in reducing emotional and psychological stress. Wild flower preparations (used for hundreds of years by Voodoo priests and root doctors), such as the Bach Flower Remedies, have been found effective in improving self-image, confidence, and deep suicidal depression. Dr. John L. Bolling, a former psychiatrist at New York University's Bellevue Medical Center, has conducted extensive studies with "wild flower preparations." In fact, Bolling (1987) recommends moving away from the overuse of synthetic drugs toward more natural approaches such as the Bach remedies. Many health food stores and pharmacies carry these preparations.

In very general terms, therapy should be directed toward self-concept, and self-confidence improvement and the resolution of conflicts regarding what is important in the patient's life. This can be difficult, because a pivotal portion of the patient's self image and confidence already will have been damaged by the Rootwork object or spell. The patient has to contend with that reality, as well as with the unreal. The therapist's second task is to develop willpower within the patient. If there is no willpower, there is nothing that the psychotherapist, the medical treatment, or the patient can do but be a victim of Rootwork doom.

Significant others in the patient's life, i.e., spouse, family, friends, should be frequently involved in the counseling process. To move forward, without these essential support people, would encourage the patient to make self-centered decisions without considering the feelings of his or her support group members. The success of the traditional African healer has been related to the patient's familiarity with the treatment environment (Lambo, 1964) , the presence of another member of the family, and an open-door policy (Laosebikan, 1973).

In terms of counseling techniques, a dyadic method is recommended only in the early phases of treatment. As willpower develops within the patient, group approaches are advocated because they coincide more with the group orientation of the believers. When dyads are used, a directive approach is much more appropriate. The directives should be rather subtle and complex and not merely suggested. Change in perception and behavior should be attempted from the moment of the first contact with the patient. Emphasis should be placed on the patient's present symptoms and circumstances. Exploration of the patient's childhood is not necessary in the early phases of treatment. The therapist must quickly gain the information he or she needs.

While obtaining the information needed, the therapist should immediately establish the context of therapeutic change. The idea should be implanted that progressive improvement is occurring in the patient, and work should be conducted within the context of continuing improvement. The encouragement of a patient's commitment to a positive change should be established as soon as possible. During treatment, the patient should be asked to follow specific directions which involve her/him in a participating endeavor to remove the rootwork spell and to change his/her symptoms. The symptoms and behavior of the patient must be accepted by the therapist, but only in a manner producing change. For example, a therapeutic directive can be added to the existing symptoms of the patient to bring about change.

The patient can be told to perform a simple ritual, three times a day, when Rootwork thoughts enter his mind. The purpose of the ritual is to destroy the negative thoughts.

The client-centered (non-directive) approach of Carl Rogers is threatening to patients and may result in their withdrawal. More specifically, non-directive Eurocentric therapy as a form of treatment is not suitable to patients with Rootwork syndrome because the patients believe that evil forces which are beyond their control are the causes of their problems. These methods only encourage patients to engage in introspection for self-blame. Behavior therapy, extensively modified to fit the culture of the patient, can be quite effective with Rootwork syndrome. Concerted efforts must be made to locate, bring in or refer patients to qualified Root Doctors and or African Traditional Healers. It is quite possible for these two classes of health professionals—Western trained and traditional healers—to work together in providing the most appropriate treatment.

Conclusion

There is more room for dispute between Western style university-trained physicians, psychologists, mental health professionals, and root doctors and Traditional Healers in the area of the diagnosis of psychological disorders, than with treatments involving herbal medicines. After all, herbal medicine's effects are always open to testing and validation by Western scientific methodology.

In the areas of psychological illness, Western trained providers often tend to reject out of hand, the diagnosis and treatments of root doctors, and Vodu priest healers. Many refer to the treatments of patients by Traditional Healers as "magic" and "quackery." However, many Whites are now having second thoughts about African healers and root doctors, and are attempting to learn their techniques. Unfortunately, most African American providers are being left behind because of their own indoctrination in Western philosophy. Dr. Addul Alim Muhammad, Minister of Health and Human Services for the Nation of Islam, made the following observations, "Chinese doctors use their traditional medicine with their patients, but, what do we (Black doctors in America) know about African traditional medicine?" Dr. Levi Watkins, an associate dean at John Hopkins University of Medicine said, "I agree with Dr. Muhammad." He argued that the American medical profession must "dare to dream and challenge" in order to accomplish its goals. Dr. Henry Foster, senior advisor to President William Clinton on the reduction of teenage pregnancy said, "Black doctors must go beyond the norm and get antibiotics from the jungles of South America." Finally Dr. Betty Williams, President of the National Black Nurses Association, said "Health problems for Blacks go beyond medicine" (Muhammad, 1996). These statements suggest that health care professionals are becoming increasingly aware of a need to explore alternatives to Western medical practices.

Root doctors and African Traditional Healers use of physical, psychological, and spiritual methods for diagnosis and treatment represents a *paradigm shift* from Western methods. This paradigm shift is firmly rooted within the healers' Social Galaxy Traditional System. This paradigm shift is prevention-oriented, unlike Western methods of treatments. These paradigms of diagnosis and treatments are not open to Western laboratory evaluation, and the methodologies are quite unknown to Western mental health professionals. Hence, these important aspects of African Traditional Healing and medicine are often characterized as "magical" or pejoratively referred to as "voodoo therapy." However, in the Western world, many African ideas and practices are viewed as primitive and inferior. These negative descriptions are expressions of racism, discrimination, and ignorance.

On the other hand, there is acceptance, and often imitation, of Chinese and East Asian traditional healing arts and sciences by the Western medical establishment. For example, practitioners of acupuncture and acupressure believe energy, called Qi, flows through pathways (called meridians) in the body, and that illnesses are the result of energy being blocked in these pathways. By stimulating certain points with finger pressure or needles, they believe they can clean out energy imbalances and prevent and or treat problems. These methods have been used for more than 4,000 years in China and East Asia. The same is true of African traditional healing. Not only do African healers use acupuncture and acupressure, but body massage and hypnotherapy, among many other forms of treatment and prevention.

It is important to understand that not everyone can become a Traditional African Healer or root doctor. A candidate, male or female, must be deemed by Master Priests Healers to have the nature and personality of a healer before acceptance into the long, demanding, and difficult period of education, training, and internship.

Traditional African Healers and Rootdoctors must be viewed and accepted from their own Social Galaxy Traditional System of culture. This is the only way that useful dialogue and cooperation between them and modern Western health care providers can be achieved. Traditional healing *will not* fade away in America. In fact it will be increasing, because now many races and ethnic groups in America, including Whites, are recognizing, respecting and observing their own cultures and traditions.

There is a desire and need to develop a system for more cooperation between orthodox and traditional healers. These systems are in place and working well in Africa, India, and China. We need to do likewise in America. There is need and room for both orthodoxy and tradition in our efforts to provide the best health care for the public. Every system of medicine and healing has its own limitations. Even with the specialized and sophisticated Western medical systems, people still die of diseases and illness.

African American scholars who are knowledgeable about theses subjects should be hired as regular full time professors within departments. According to the

National Institutes of Health Office of Alternative Medicine, as many as half of all U.S. physicians refer patients for "unconventional" treatments, usually in conjunction with conventional medicine. Given the obvious need for effective alternative to Western medical practice. Psychology, mental health, and medical schools should include knowledge and training relating to African healing in their curricula of alternative healing and medicines, and mental health training programs.

The present practice of locating and bringing in old root doctors and herbalists, for one day seminars must cease. Little gain comes from this outdated practice, because of the magnitude of knowledge to be mastered and the specialized skills required. Given these requirements, the present chapter must be viewed as only a brief introduction to the subject.

References

Ashanti, K. F. (1975). Voodoo, superstition and the black patient. Paper presented at the *Grand Round, Department of Psychiatry, Duke University.*

Ashanti, K. F. (1976). Voodoo superstition and the black community. Paper presented at the *National Association of Black Psychologists Convention,* Chicago.

Ashanti, K. F. (1976). Black superstition sects came from Europe: Doctor. *Jet Magazine,* September 30, *51* (2), 33.

Ashanti, K. F. (1986). Rootwork and folk healing. Paper presented to the Consultation Liaison Service, *School of Medicine Department of Psychiatry, University of North Carolina,* January 22.

Ashanti, K. F. (1990). *Rootwork and Voodoo in Mental Health.* Durham, N.C.: Tone Books.

Ashanti, K. F. (1993). *Psychotechnology of brainwashing*: Africentric passage. Durham, N.C.: Tone Books.

Ashanti, K. F. (1994). From traditional healing to brainwashing. Paper presented to the 8th World Melanin Conference, University of the District of Columbia, Washington, D.C

Ashanti, K. F. (1996). *Taking back your African mind and culture: Sankofa.* Durham, N.C.: Tone Books.

Bolling, J. L. (1987). Wild flowers healing Harlem: Study shows promise in stress relief. Louis C. Young (Ed.), *The Carolina Times,* June, 6.

Budge, W. E. A. (1960). *The book of the dead.* New York: Bell Publishing Co.

Campinha-Bacote, J. (1992). Voodoo illness. *Perspectives in Psychiatric Care.* January-March, Vol. 28 (1) 11-17.

Chess, S., Clark, K., and Thomas, A. (1953). The importance of cultural evaluation in psychiatric diagnosis and treatment. *Psychiatric Quarterly, 27,* 102-114.

Clegg, L. H. (1986). Black rulers of the golden age. In Ivan van Sertima (Ed.), *Journal of African Civilization.*

Cohen, S. I. (1988). Voodoo death, the response to stress, depression and AIDS. *Psicopatologia,* January-March, *8* (1) 1-15.

Diagnostic and Statistical Manual of Mental Disorders - IV (1994). Washington, D.C.: American Psychiatric Association.

Davis, W. (1985). *The serpent and the rainbow.* New York: Simon and Schuster.

Frazer, J. G. (1959). *The newgolden bough.* T. H. Gaster (Ed.), Chicago: Mentor Book.

Golden, K. M. (1977). Voodoo in Africa and the United States. *American Journal of Psychiatry, 34,* 1425- 1427.

Hayatt, H. M. (1970). *Conjuration, witchcraft, rootwork.* Hannibal, MI: Western Publishing Company.

Hillard, J. R. (1982). Diagnosis and treatment of the rootwork victim. *Psychiatric Annuals,* July, 127.

Hounkpatin, L. (1991). The function of the object in therapeutic Yoruba thought (Benin). *Psychologie-Francaise, 36*(4) 363-370.

Jackson, G. G. (1980). The African genesis of the, black perspective in helping. R. C. Jones (Ed.), *Black psychology* (2nd ed.). New York: Harper and Row.

Jacobs, C. F. (1990). Healing and prophecy in the Black spiritual churches: A need for re-examination. *Medical-Anthropology, 12*(4), 349-370.

Lambo, S. (1964). The village of Aro. *Lancet, 11,* 513-514.

Lamy, L. (1981). *Egyptian mysteries, new light on ancient spiritual knowledge.* New York: Crossroad.

Laosebikan, S. (1973). Mental health in Nigeria. *Journal of Black Studies,* 4, 221-228.

Levi-Strauss, C. (1967). The sorcerer and his magic. In J. Middleton (Ed.), *Magic, witchcraft and curing.* Garden City, New York: The Natural History Press.

Makinde, M. A. (1988). *African philosophy, culture, and traditional medicine.* Ohio: Center for International Studies, Ohio University.

McGuire, M. B. (1982). *Pentecostal catholics: Power, charisma, and order in a religious movement.* Philadelphia: Temple University press.

Montilus, G. (1989). *Dompim: The spirituality of African peoples.* Nashville, TN: Winston-Derek Publishers, Inc.

Morse, D. R., Martin, J., & Moshonov, J. (1991). Psychosomatically induced death: relative to stress, hypnosis, mind control, and Voodoo: Review and possible mechanisms. *Stress-Medicine.* October-December, *7*(4), 213-232.

Muhammed, D. (1996). Health Summit focuses on AIDS, saving black lives. *The Final Call,* Chicago: Nation of Islam. p.8, May 21.

Ness, R. C., & Wintrob, R. M. (1981). Folk healing: A description and synthesis. *American Journal of Psychiatry, 138* (11), 1477-1481.

Opoku, K. A. (1978). *West African traditional religion.* Accra, Ghana: FEP International Private Limited.

People Weekly. (1987). Donna Rice: *The woman in question*, May 18, 37.

Psych Discourse. (1995, June). *Covenant with traditional healers association in Ghana, West Africa*. Washington, DC: The Association of Black Psychologists (June).

Ra, A. M. (1995). *Let the ancestors speak*. Temple Hills, MD: JOM International Inc.

Snow, I. F. (1974). Folk beliefs and their implications for the care of patients: A review based on studies among Black Americans. *Annual of Internal Medicine, 81,* 82-96.

St. John, P. (1987). Snake-handling churches keep the faith. *Durham Morning Herald,* Durham, North Carolina, p. 6E, March 8.

Thomas, C. (1973). The system-maintenance role of the white psychologist. *Journal of Social Issues, 29,* 57-65.

Turner, E. L. (1986). Encounter with neurobiology: The response of ritual studies. *Zygon-Journal of Religion and Science.* June, *21,* (2), 219-232.

Van Biema, D. H. (1987). Michael Goodrich offers himself. *People Weekly,* May 18, 113-118

Veyrat, J. G., & Ferrier, J. (1989). From Haitian-Voodoo and Brazilian Candomle to European Hyperpnea: Applications to psychosomatic medicine. French Tunisian Meeting of the Medico-Psychological Society. Jerba, Tunisian Meeting of the Medico-Psychological Society (1988). *Annales-Medico-Psychologiques. May-June, 147*(3) 341-347.

Whaten, N. (1962). Contemporary patterns of malign occultism among Negroes in North Carolina. *Journal of American Folklore, 75,* 31 1-325.

Author

Kwabena Faheem Ashanti, Ph.D.
Counseling Center
North Carolina State University
Raleigh, NC 27695-7312
Telephone: (919)515-2425
Fax: (919) 515-8525
E-mail:
kwabena-ashanti@ncsu.edu

The Dilemma of the Double-Consciousness: Understanding Voodoo from a Eurocentric Perspective

Na'im Akbar

> . . . the Negro is a sort of seventh son, born with a veil, and gifted with second-sight in this American world, a world which yields him no true self-consciousness, but only lets him see himself through the revelation of the other world. It is a peculiar sensation, this double-consciousness, this sense of always looking at one's self through the eyes of others, of measuring one's self by the tape of a world that looks on in amused contempt and pity. One ever feels his twoness, an American, a Negro; two souls, two thoughts, two unreconciled strivings; two warring ideals in one dark body whose dogged strength alone keeps it from being torn asunder [W.E.B. DuBois (1903) *The Souls of Black Folk).*

This often quoted passage from Dr. DuBois' classical piece which so succinctly characterizes the psychological functioning of African people in America is an excellent description of the dilemma which Ashanti encounters in this effort to describe *"Rootwork and Voodoo in the Diagnosis and Treatment of African American Patients."* Of course, it takes considerable courage necessary to take on this "Shaka Zulu type" task and Dr. Ashanti deserves the commendation of the scholarly world for his willingness to rush in where wise men fear to tread. This subject matter is seldom discussed with serious scholarly interest among Eurocentrically trained social scientists and mental health practitioners. The fact that the entire arena has been dismissed as superstitious nonsense at worst, and an anthropological curiosity at best, represents the European-American trained scholar's approach to phenomena such as this. In short, these phenomena have no place in European American paradigms of science or their ontology of reality.

Simultaneously speaking in two separate realities is difficult at best and impossible at worst. In Ashanti's effort to bridge the chasm of these "two souls" he encounters many of the inevitable difficulties of synthesizing two mutually exclusive concepts of reality. As a result, there are several errors of translation which affected this discussion.

543

Rootwork and Voodoo as Derogatory Concepts

Since the Euro-American scholar has traditionally had only a limited appreciation for the phenomenological worlds of these concepts, the concepts have been dismissed as aspects of the paganism and superstition of non-European people. Within the scholarly literature and the media such practices have been offered as evidence of the scientific deficiency of non-Western people. For the Western scholar the idea that people believe in phenomena that have so little "empirical" demonstrability is sufficient to explain why these people lack the material and technological sophistication of European scholars. These practices are held aloft as examples of poor understanding of the universe.

With such underlying assumptions about *"Rootwork and Voodoo,"* it is rather difficult to introduce the topic in a serious scholarly context without automatically being thrust into an intellectually defensive posture. This defensive posture is reflected in the author's effort to normalize the characteristics of this belief system by referencing the widespread interest in so called "psychic" phenomena among growing numbers of White people. Unfortunately, such a normalizing effort simply permits the practices to be included within the domain of White "lunatic fringe" behaviors. Dr. Ashanti's argument for the validity of traditional beliefs regarding Rootwork and Voodoo in the African American community cannot be legitimized by suggesting that growing numbers of European American people are considering it to be valid. Instead, it would appear that the African American scholar/practitioner must accept the validity of his indigenous ideas and validate them within the parameters of his own paradigm. For example, it should be sufficient to state that the majority of the world's people, from Africa to Asia and throughout the Native American world, accept comparable phenomena of spiritual healing and spiritual disorder. That minority of the earth's population which overwhelmingly rejects this reality should be required to justify *their deviance* rather than the other way around. When we assume the need to normalize our ideas by invoking the examples of the deviant, then we degrade our concepts and alienate ourselves from both historical precedents, as well as consensus among the earth's longest-standing and largest examples of civilized life.

The Generic Brand of Rootwork and Voodoo

The second consideration which complicates Dr. Ashanti's discussion is the characterization of rootwork and voodoo as generic phenomena. This means that if one entered this discussion without prior preparation the observer would assume that there is a clear and delineated package of what rootwork and voodoo is really all about. Dr. Ashanti's discussion places into these categories everything from herbal treatments to the spiritual conjuring requiring years of training and connectedness with centuries of related practitioners. As the author observes, voodoo itself is a westernization of the traditional religious practices of Dahomey called *Vodun* (Thompson, 1984). Rootwork and its attendant practices represent a bastardization of a wide range of African spiritual practices which were corrupted by the disruption of the *Maafa* (Ani, 1993) or the slavery, captivity and oppression of African people. This so-called "Rootwork" was one of the vestiges of what was maintained by the captive Africans in their effort to hold on to the traditional healing and scientific principles of their cultures and their heritages. Dr. Ashanti provides an excellent review of this in his discussion of traditional African religions.

These vestiges took on different forms in different environments. They remained most intact in environments where there was minimal disruption of the cultural life of the captive Africans. The greater the disruption, the less prevalent the practices. In areas where there were large Maroon or runaway colonies (Hilliard, 1994) these practices remained more intact as did the language and many other aspects of West African cultural practices. So rootwork and such activities persisted strongly around the Maroon colonies of the Carolinas and the Sea Islands of Georgia. It also found a prominent presence in Louisiana, in the Caribbean and in Central and South America where the Maroons were prevalent. The reality is that the practices differed tremendously from one area to the other. Even though we accept a common basis to all of the practices which make them generic in terms of their origin, the prevalence and the likely occurrence of Ashanti's "Rootwork syndrome," is likely to take on very different expressions in different parts of the USA where African retentions differed considerably. An African American who has grown up in New Orleans would have no difficulty accepting the kind of interviewing which asked an African American client if they think "someone has caused them bad luck or worked roots on them." An African American client raised in urban Atlanta would be baffled somewhat by such a question. However, this same urban-reared dweller would have no problem relating to a question as to whether they thought prayer could help them in their condition, or to the suggestion of transpersonal causation for some of their difficulties.

The characterization of all these diverse phenomena as rootwork as if it were a generic occurrence could be seriously misleading. It would seem that either a new terminology would be necessary in order to raise the occurrences from the pejorative or to place them in a context that they could be understood in the general sense that African descendants would be able to relate to them. The writer characterizes his "Rootwork syndrome" as if it were a homogeneous occurrence and that any or at least most African-Americans would be able to relate to it. There are serious questions as to whether or not this is the case. Dr. Ashanti is correct in both his characterization of the common origin of the multiple manifestations of these phenomena and in terms of its broad presence in *some form* in the African-American community. If we are going to refer to it as a generic phenomenon then it should be given a terminology that provides a general recognition. Our analysis is easily misled by the use of an alien language to describe another reality. This is a manifestation of the double-consciousness described by Dr. DuBois in our opening quote.

African Spirituality as a Holistic System

Another source of error in discussions such as this is the failure to fully grasp the significance of a *holistic* concept of health and healing. The African spiritual system assumes an interconnection between mind, body and spirit and between the individual self and the collective community self. These interconnections are foreign to traditional conceptualizations of the Western thinker and medical practitioners. As Dr. Ashanti asserts in his characterization of humans as four dimensional (physical, psychological, spiritual and transcendental) and as transtemporal, i.e. living simultaneously in the "then, now and there," he identifies the difficulty in making his own analysis. In his description of Rootwork syndrome he illustrates a presenting concern of a patient who has been ''influenced by another with magic power." This is an expression of the African-based consciousness whereby individuals both see themselves as integrally connected with other people, and understand that spiritual (i.e., invisible and transcendental) phenomena are real. Since time and space are not limitations in such systems, the perpetrator's physical proximity is not a consideration.

In the Western context, a person suffering from an illness of any form would go to his doctor and leave his Bible (i.e., spiritual prescriptions) at home, or go to church and pray without drinking teas and/or rubbing him/herself with oils since these arenas are considered separate and often contradictory. In the African context such separations are not considered legitimate. Dr. Ashanti's description of the symptoms of Rootwork and Voodoo syndromes describes "patients with Bibles in their possession (as being) suspect." The synthesizing of the two world views is not a symptom of the illness, but a recognition that the causation is of multi-dimensional origin. Such an expression of self-diagnosis represents a more sophisticated understanding of the African person's disorder than that of the Western trained practitioner who views mental or physical disorders in a fragmented way.

The African spiritual system is not essentially negative or destructive. It is, in fact, a health care maintenance system that is intended to maintain the person's relationship with other people, and facilitate harmony with the rest of nature. As a holistic system it is not only (or even primarily) manifested as a malevolent act from an enemy or a form of retribution sent from the spirit world. First and foremost the "Rootwork and Voodoo" system is a set of practices related to health maintenance or health restoration. The system acknowledges that disruption of the interconnection between people, nature or the moral order of nature results in a tension which can be manifested in physical illness, spiritual disturbance or even bizarre symptoms of experiencing nature out of order (e.g., lizards under the skin and snakes in the stomach). Such experiences are a part of the recognition, on a higher level of consciousness, that when one steps outside of nature's order by a moral infraction or a violation of the social order, then the consequence, in obedience to the (Asian called) "Karmic" law, is a disruption of one's relationship to nature, the social and/ or spiritual community.

The problem presented by classifying such reactions as a component of the American Psychiatric Association's *Diagnostic and Statistical Manual of Mental Disorders* (4th ed.) is that this classification system emanates from another reality altogether. The DSM IV, as is all of Western medicine, is rooted in a system which assumes pathology as the model to classify health (Akbar, 1994). The use of rootwork in the generic way that we have discussed above, implies that any aspect of these reactions constitutes a manifestation of mental disorder. Though there are expressions which represent disorder, there are many expressions which are clearly healthy within the context of genuine African consciousness. If Rootwork syndrome is left to mean everything about this spiritual system rather than some very specific manifestations of a disrupted *whole* system, then we put our entire reality into the category of Western mental disorder. This is definitely not the intention of Dr. Ashanti, but it represents another pitfall of the dual paradigm which this critique assumes as fundamental in the problem of this entire discussion.

Perhaps a more appropriate term would be "nature disruption syndrome" or something to that effect. The identified patient may have been the disrupter or someone may have disrupted it for him. The "Root worker" or priest is fundamentally a healer who specializes in restoring order. Again, the negative characterization of this spiritual system by Western thinkers has made the root worker take on the appearance of a perpetrator rather than a healer. When someone approaches a root worker to do harm or good they are seeking an expert on the spiritual order, and are seeking their expertise in correcting disruptions in their order or disrupting the order of others because of some infraction of social or moral principles. The presenting symptoms are the expressions of the disordered person.

The Dis-ease of Disrupted Nature

Dis-ease is quite literally a disturbance of "ease," peace or order. Rootwork is a healing system, not a military system. The condition which must be healed is one which has disrupted the person's harmonious relationship with nature, the social and/or spiritual communities. Within the African cosmology or conceptual system, all sickness comes from some disturbance in this order. The ultimate cause of illness is the consequence of fragmentation of separation from the order which connects and contains all life. The source of such separation can be physical, mental or spiritual. The order can be restored by utilizing physical, mental and/or spiritual methods. Similarly the symptoms can be spiritual, mental or physical. Whether the person is experiencing somatic symptoms, psychological symptoms or spiritual symptoms is incidental since all components of the self are impacted in these syndromes of disruption. Life requires a harmony with spirit. If the relationship with spirit is severed then certainly death results. This description of what Dr. Ashanti refers to as "Voodoo death" as a consequence of the "power of suggestion" is another relapse to the Western paradigm which sees life as fundamentally physical/ mental rather than one that is fundamentally spiritual. This is an example of the Cartesian Conclusion: "*I think therefore I am*" rather than the African Ontology of "*We are therefore I am.*"

Dr. Ashanti characterizes the healing process in his case study as a matter of the "antagonism in the curing process between the depression, self-alienation and passivity of the patient confronting the all positive self-confidence, projection and activity of the root worker." One might more appropriately see the disordered victim (patient) restored to ease by the expertise of one who has mastered the rituals and processes of restoring order. This expert in order restoration may use a variety of methods from the physical (roots and herbs), mental (suggestion or active instruction in ritualistic behavior), and/or spiritual (incantation, Biblical or Quranic scriptures or amulets). The priest is a student of not just techniques but of processes of personal transformation or initiation. This does not correspond with the description of requirements and qualifications of the "psychotherapist" given by Dr. Ashanti. These qualifications essentially describe a Western practitioner as opposed to an "African healer." This distinction is the difference between the concept of African holistic health and Western therapy which is a technique to alter behavior rather than to facilitate the restoration to order.

Summary

As African American social scientists and healers, we are faced with a dual reality: we must develop a culturally grounded system for identifying disorder in our communities while operating under the coercion of an alien philosophical system which requires our compliance. We are better equipped than Western practitioners because we possess the double-consciousness which is both an asset and a burden. This double-consciousness is a burden in that we have the cumbersome task of trying to make sense in a nonsensical world, as well as the task of adapting to an alien reality that does not take account of what is real for us. It is an asset because we have been forced to master both systems in order to survive. We know the Western way, and those who claim to be psychologists, psychotherapists or social scientists were forced to master the ways of the culture in which we find ourselves, i.e., Eurocentric culture. However, we are of the direct lineage of those people who knew and lived for thousands of years in another reality. We have been forced to perpetuate that lineage not only in our genetic memory, but in the social conditions of exclusion from effective control of resources in an environment that has defined us and our reality as nonexistent at worst, and as degraded and inferior at best. This isolation has required us to keep essential elements of our reality intact in order to find a reason and basis for being. The manifestations of the African spiritual system are evidence of that mechanism of our true beingness which we dare not relegate to the implicit distortion of a Western mental health (illness) system. The conundrum described by Dr. DuBois continues to challenge our best minds for a resolution. Accolades are due to Dr. Ashanti for his efforts to remove the "mojo" from our collective condition here in the West.

References

Akbar, N. (1994). *Light from Ancient Africa*. Tallahassee, FL: Mind Productions & Associates.

Ani, M. (1994). *Yurugu*. Trenton, NJ: African World Press.

DuBois, W. E. B. (1903/1989). *The Souls of Black Folk*. New York: Viking Penguin.

Hilliard, A. (1995). *The maroon within us*. Baltimore, MD: Black Classic Press.

Thompson, F. (1984). *Flash of the Spirit*. New York: Vintage Books, Random House.

Author

Na'im Akbar, Ph.D.
324 N. Copeland Street
Tallahassee, FL 32304
Telephone: (904) 222-6417
Fax: (904) 224-5331
E-mail: mindpro@polaris.net

The Role of Possession and Other Spiritual Phenomena in Understanding Psychopathological States: Comments on Ashanti

Samuel M. Turner

The treatise by Ashanti combines a discussion of voodoo, rootwork, humanism and spirituality in relation to problems of diagnosis and treatment of African American patients with emotional disorders. Embedded in this rather free wheeling exposé are a number of important issues that modern psychology generally has neglected in its attempt to understand the forces that shape human behavior, both normal and psychopathological states. In particular, relatively little attention has been devoted to understanding unique cultural patterns within the African American culture that may be important in understanding mental disorders among this group.

A particularly noteworthy point contained in Ashanti's writing is the fact that there is a reciprocal relationship between "mind" and body. Despite advances in understanding the role of psychological parameters in disease processes, modern psychology still is largely operating under the tenets of Cartesian dualism, or separation of mind and body. Ashanti's discussion reminds us of this reciprocal relationship by highlighting the dramatic influence of beliefs on emotionality and physical health. This treatise also serves to remind us of psychology's failure to consider as important what appears to be powerful cultural factors and their relationship to the development of psychopathological states. In the age of cognitive psychology, it particularly is surprising that this area remains neglected because it appears to be fertile ground for the study of the effect of strong belief systems in shaping human behavior.

According to Ashanti, there is a specific syndrome particularly identifiable among African Americans that he labels "Rootwork and Voodoo Syndrome." This syndrome ostensibly results from the victim's belief that someone has used "roots," "charms" or various other methods of the occult to cast a spell on them. One limitation of Ashanti's description is that it is not entirely clear exactly what behaviors constitute rootwork and voodoo syndrome. Although he mentions a number of symptoms that might be manifested by such patients, it still remains uncertain that one can identify a consistent and cohesive cluster of symptoms (behaviors) that is implied by use of the term syndrome. A second limitation is that there are no empirical studies provided to document the existence of the syndrome. Although empirical studies are mentioned, no specific data are presented.

In examining Ashanti's discussion of this "syndrome," it is not entirely clear whether Ashanti views these behaviors to be the result of the powerful influence of culturally held beliefs (i.e., the emotional reaction occurs because the patient believes in the concept of possession), or whether he views them as "real." Clearly, the symptoms are real to the patient. But the question remains, does Ashanti believe, for example, that such patients have snakes in their stomachs and frogs in their throats. His position seems to wax and wane between these two positions at various times, making it difficult to discern his position or to interpret exactly what he views as modern psychology's failure in this area. Has modern psychology failed to study the impact on behavior of powerful cultural belief systems, or has modern psychology failed to realize that demonic or other types of possession are "real"? This is a critical issue because if it is the former, the type of behavior described in his paper is a powerful illustration of the " mind" body interface, and a vivid illustration of the critical role of cultural belief patterns in shaping human behavior. This behavior could be studied scientifically, and represents an entire arena that modern psychology has neglected. Also, if the behavior is subject to scientific study, then we should be able to develop an understanding of it and develop methods of treatment to help patients so afflicted. If on the other hand it is the latter, we perhaps may no longer be within a psychological purview but rather may have traversed to a spiritual plane that may not be subject to scientific inquiry.

Although Ashanti mentions a number of DSM diagnoses in his discussion, he does not tell us how to differentiate voodoo syndrome from DSM psychotic conditions or severe personality disorder. Moreover, it is unclear whether he thinks the diagnoses mentioned are in addition to rootwork and voodoo syndrome, conditions for which rootwork and voodoo syndrome are in his view mistaken, or if they typically are concurrent conditions. In general, there is not much information provided that clinicians can use to guide their diagnostic decision making or in their selection of an intervention strategy. The case material provided does not help because it basically is experiential and the methods and rules used to identify the condition are not delineated.

Although belief in voodoo, root doctors and other "spiritual" beings is thought to be more prevalent in African American and other cultural groups from the Caribbean and Central and South America, similar belief patterns can be found in all cultural and ethnic groups. In fact, Ashanti goes to some length to make this point but then rather curiously concludes that rootwork and voodoo syndrome is an Afrocentric condition. This appears to be contradictory, but if he does believe it to be an Afrocentric condition, it would have been helpful to have a discussion of why this is so.

In summary, the points raised in Ashanti's article are important because they illustrate an area that psychology has neglected, and one that appears to be fertile ground for examining the effects of cultural belief patterns in some psychopathological states. At the practical level, if indeed there are patients suffering from rootwork and voodoo, psychologists, African American or others, are not prepared to recognize the condition, nor to treat it. This highlights the need for psychology training programs to develop methods to adequately train students with respect to these and other cultural belief patterns and their potential effect on behavior. Finally, this piece is heuristic because little research has been done in this area, and in actuality, it is unreasonable to expect training programs to seriously address this issue if we do not have an empirically based literature from which to draw. Thus, a significant missing part of this discussion is how research might be conducted to elucidate the parameters governing these and other cultural belief systems that may be related to maladaptive behavior patterns.

Author

Samuel M. Turner, Ph.D.
Dept. of Psychiatry & Behavioral Sciences, Medical Univ. of S. C.
Anxiety Prevention & Treatment Research Center
615 Wesley Drive, Suite 200
Charleston, SC 29407
Telephone: (803) 852-4190
Fax: (803) 852-4195
E-mail: turnersm@musc.edu

Bridging Spirituality and Psychotherapy

Jacqueline S. Mattis

"In Rootwork and Voodoo in the Diagnosis and Treatment of African American Patients," Dr. Faheem Ashanti provides us with a provocative discussion of the treatment issues which are raised by Voodoo poisoning and Rootwork Syndrome. Dr. Ashanti correctly notes that "there is something profoundly shocking about spirit possession. Its power is strong, quick, and undeniably real, devastating in a manner completely unknown to those who have a different belief and value system." It is precisely because of its potential to shock that Dr. Ashanti's work requires context. First, there is a need to place the discussion of Voodoo and Rootwork in its proper context. That is, there is a need to situate the discussion in a broader discussion about spirituality. Second, there is a need to provide a framework for understanding the rift between "spirituality" and psychology. Third, there is a need to place Rootwork and Voodoo in social context as healing traditions. Finally, there is a need to provide a framework for bridging spirituality and psychotherapy. An important part of this work involves a discussion of specific ways in which psychotherapists can work with matters of spirit. Contextualizing the discussion of Rootwork and Voodoo in these ways is necessary because this nation is inundated with myths about these activities. When we initiate a decontextualized discussion of Rootwork and Voodoo, we run the risk of reinforcing dangerous myths about these practices. This response addresses each of these concerns about context and, in doing so, raises questions and possibilities about the effective treatment of spiritual dis-eases, including Rootwork Syndrome and Voodoo Poisoning.

My perspectives on these topics develop, in part, out of my identity as a Jamaican woman who grew up in a culture where spirit possessions are within the bounds of the cultural norms. While the overwhelming majority of Jamaicans are Christian, many hold strong and complex beliefs about the power of such secular spiritual practices as Obeah, Pukumina, Rootwork and Voodoo. These beliefs and the involvement with these practices are as common among Jamaicans in the United States as they are on the island. My perspectives on the psychotherapeutic treatment of individuals who suffer from spiritual dis-ease are shaped by my work as both a clinical psychologist and as a researcher. In my work with diverse clients, spirituality often emerges as an important part of their identity and experience. The spiritual concerns and perspectives which these clients bring to the therapy relationship are profoundly important, but are mundane when compared to the

555

shocking nature of Rootwork Syndrome and Voodoo poisoning. However, these more shocking presentations are a part of a vast continuum of spiritual dis-eases. It is necessary, therefore, to ground ourselves in a discussion of spirituality, and to use that grounding as a point of departure for discussions of the treatment of spiritual dis-ease.

On Spirituality

In the American academy the mention of spirituality[1] often stirs anxieties about zealotry and fundamentalism. Among the society's intellectual elite, spirituality is generally treated as the antithesis of rational (scientific) thought. As such, spirituality and religion are not accepted as a viable topics for critical inquiry and/or research. What is lost in the frenzy of anxiety and misrepresentations which surround spirituality is the fact that it plays a crucial role in human efforts to explain and resolve adversity. It is a focal part of human efforts to render life meaningful (Lehmann & Myers, 1989).

Despite the important role of spirituality in the lives of humans, psychologists have resigned themselves to treating spirituality with a measure of ambivalence. Clinical psychology training programs tend to ignore the topic, or to invoke the words "religion" and "spirituality" only in brief discussions which occur under the rubric of multicultural issues in psychology. However, clinical intake procedures commonly include questions about the religious/spiritual identification of potential clients. In addition, while religion and spirituality are rarely the primary topics of psychological research, researchers do routinely ask respondents about their religious affiliation and participation. These data are often included as important independent variables in statistical analyses. The end result of this schizoid approach to spirituality is the failure on the part of training institutions to define a clear, thoughtful and meaningful relationship between spirituality, psychological research and psychotherapy.

Psychology's ambivalent relationship to spirituality is emblematic of a fundamental rift in Western conceptualizations of religious/spiritual and scientific epistemology. William Clements (1995) cogently notes that Western thinking has become dichotomized such that "[e]ither reality is scientific—materialistic and quantifiable—but without existential meaning and incapable of transmitting personal or cultural values that do not fit the scientific paradigm, or it is religious—rationalistic, aesthetic, affective and paradigmatic—but without possibility of quantification or establishing itself as factually based. What a choice!" (p. 503)

In short, an unfortunate consequence of Western dualistic thought is that science and spirituality are positioned as forces which are inherently antagonistic to each other. As such, psychologists, in their on-going search to establish themselves as scientists, have generally accepted that the serious study of spirituality is the appropriate fare of religious leaders and religious institutions. The irony in this thinking is that the psychotherapeutic enterprise often centers on clients' questions of existence and their search for meaning—issues which are clearly associated with spirituality.

Faheem Ashanti suggests that psychologists can play an important role in treatment of individuals who suffer from dis-eases caused by spirit possession (e.g., Rootwork Syndrome and Voodoo Poisoning). He identifies several roles which psychotherapists must assume if they are to successfully treat these dis-eases. He recommends a directive, dyadic approach in the early phases of treatment and an eventual transition into a group modality. Dr. Ashanti indicates that the goals of the early phase of the treatment are to improve the client's self-concept, facilitate his/her willpower, and to reintegrate the client into his/her network of support. The model of treatment which Dr. Ashanti proposes is an attractive synthesis of professional and cultural competence.

However, none of the aims which Dr. Ashanti describes are possible until we first give psychologists a framework for understanding spirituality. Only when we extricate spirituality from the web of misrepresentations that surround it can we begin to see the powerful connections between clinical psychotherapy and matters of spirit. Until we lay this foundation, the work that psychotherapists do with individuals who define themselves as spiritual will be unnecessarily constrained, and the notion that psychotherapists can be effective in the treatment of dis-eases of the spirit will be rhetorical.

All spiritual systems are concerned with the uses of power and with the organization of power within the cosmos. Within many spiritual systems there is a notion of a hierarchy of power in which deities hold the greatest power to create, destroy, maintain or influence life. Lower on the hierarchy are spirits which inhabit the space between the material and spiritual world, and even further outside of the core valence of power are humans and other animals. In addition, the metaphors of spirituality use power as a constant reference. For example, the language(s) of spirituality make constant references to a "Higher power," to "the power to heal/create etc.," to metaphysical "energies," powers and abilities and the like.

These powers and many of the entities (spirits) which possess these powers are outside of the dominion of human will. The notion of a world of entities and powers over which humans have no control can be threatening to some. Further, this world of spirits operates by standards which do not readily adhere to scientific constructions of logic. The knowledge claims made by individuals who are religious and or spiritual cannot be verified by reliance upon the familiar senses. For example, individuals may derive information from dreams, they may respond to positive or negative "energies," or may call upon ancestors/spirits to intercede in earthly events. These individuals may rely upon intuition, perceptions and faith as well as the translation of signs and cues which are unfamiliar to those who require material/empirical proof.

Individuals who define themselves as "spiritual" often attach a great deal of intensity to that self-definition. That monolithic intensity may be mistaken for power. That is, the more intense the experience of spirituality, the more potent a role the individual may believe spirituality plays in his/her life. However, intensity is not power. Spirituality is powerful and functional insofar as individuals are able to use it agentically and intentionally to address crucial existential questions, or to effectively manage adverse life circumstances.

Therefore, it is not sufficient to simply know the system of beliefs which comprise an individual's spirituality. Therapists also must understand the "functional significance"[2] of spirituality for the client. Therapists must understand spirituality as an organic aspect of identity; as a "doing thing." That is, they must understand the ways in which individuals use spirituality. They must identify the circumstances under which individuals invoke their spiritual beliefs, and the circumstances under which they do not. They must cull information about the rituals in which individuals engage and the goal(s) of those rituals. The therapist must determine how effective these strategies are in achieving the prescribed goal(s). These concerns are important because individuals are often unclear about the specific ways in which spirituality operates in their lives. Psychotherapists can assist their clients in moving towards increasingly specific, mature and coherent uses of spirituality. The way in which this kind of movement can be achieved is demonstrated in the following case example.

Case

The client, C., is a 27-year-old African American woman who is a survivor of a physically and emotionally abusive relationship. She and her former partner are the parents of a 15 month old boy. Since leaving the abusive relationship she has had tremendous financial difficulties and has been struggling with depression, a feeling that she cannot trust her own judgment, and a paralyzing sense of confusion. She has wondered from time to time if she made the wrong decision in leaving the relationship. On several occasions she suggested that perhaps she has been "cursed," and that she may be destined to seek out abusive relationships. She has cast herself as a woman who has no control over any facet of her life.

Therapist: You didn't survive by accident. How have you made it this far?
C: I don't know . . . I don't have anything except God. God and my baby.
T: Do you see yourself as a spiritual person?
C: Yes! Yes! I don't go to church. I haven't gone for years, and I have to be honest, you probably won't see me passing anybody's collection plate or singing in anybody's choir anytime soon (T&C laugh). But I pray. I pray everyday. I talk to God every day. That's really what gets me through!

T: How do you see God? What's God like?

C: Ahm . . . Well . . . I say 'Him" when I talk about God, but sometimes I think God is a She, or maybe an It. But mostly I say He. So, . . . He is kind of like . . . the ultimate friend, you know. Gentle, easy to talk to. You can count on Him to be there to give you what you need. The kind of person who, when something is going on, you just automatically think to call on them first. Wise. Non-judgmental. I mean, you can take anything to Him, you know. You can just say it cause he already knows and he won't judge you, you know. And, it's nice to have someone in your life like that.

T: So when you talk to God, what do you say?

C: I tell him what I'm feeling. I tell him how hard it is. And I ask for strength, you know. Just to make it through today—to make it to another day.

T: Is that what you want most? To feel better?

C: No, I want to get out of the situation. But feeling better doesn't hurt, you know.

T: That's true. But, let's go back for a moment. You said that God is always there to give you what you need, (C: Yeah) but you don't ask Him for what you need.

C: God already knows what you need, so you shouldn't ask for things.

T: But you are already asking for things from God. You ask for strength. And do you get that?

C: Yeah, I sure do. I guess I never thought about it that way.

T: So God is not offended by you asking.

C: No, I guess not.

T: So, let's think about what you need . . . . Let's talk to God, let's tell Him what you really need . . . .

This dialogue grew first into an exploration of the ways in which C. has learned to be silent about her needs in relationships. By practicing new ways of being in her relationship with God, she was able to explore new and more effective ways of being in her relationships with her family and with herself. Second, we introduced the notion of power more directly in an effort to challenge and reframe C.'s belief about the magnitude of power which her partner had over her life.

T: You said [partner] was stronger than you. In what ways was he stronger?

C: Physically! He was stronger than me physically.

T: Are there other ways of being strong?

C: Yeah, I guess there's emotional strength. There's spiritual strength. It takes a lot of courage and strength to raise a child, or to love someone in a good way. It takes a lot of strength to face up to who you really are, and change . . . [C. was asked to generate a list of strengths which were written down during the session.]

T: Looking back over the list . . . How many of those strengths describe who you are? [C. noted with surprise that many of those strengths described her.] Okay, now let's go back to what you said you wanted to do—how can you use these strengths to get the things that you want?

C. believed that her strengths were given to her by God, and that she could call on God to build on those when needed. These beliefs helped her to achieve a vision of herself as more powerful (i.e., stronger) than she had previously thought herself to be. It also allowed her to reframe and diminish the strength which she believed her partner had over her life.

Psychotherapy can be used as a place in which clients can clearly formulate ideas about their needs, and as a site in which to identify novel ways in which they might call upon powers which they already possess, as well as the power of God, ancestors, and spirits in their effort to fulfill those needs. Individuals who have learned to utilize spiritual rituals (e.g., prayer) in stagnant ways may use psychotherapy as a place in which to think more clearly about their relationship to God and or spirits, and may learn how to use prayer as a vehicle for building that relationship. Individuals can learn to use meditation, prayer etc. as vehicles for empowerment— for developing more authentic and meaningful understandings of their needs, responsibilities, capabilities and choices.

Critical Considerations for Working With Rootwork and Voodoo

Again, it is important that we place Rootwork and Voodoo in the context of the role which they traditionally serve—that is, they are forces of empowerment. Rootwork and Voodoo are healing traditions. Practitioners of these traditions are principally concerned with the healing and prevention of illnesses whose causes are organic ("natural"), supernatural, social or cultural. In keeping with their focus on healing, Rootwork and Voodoo are also used to inoculate individuals against the potential effects of negative forces in their lives (e.g., from the jealousy of neighbors or the ill-intentions of rivals). Root doctors and Voodoo priests dedicate themselves to a lifetime of disciplined, intensive study of ethnobotany—the study of the medicinal effects of plants, herbs and roots—and other means for restoring health. In some cultures Root doctors and Voodoo priests receive training in divination practices. Divination techniques allow them to communicate with God or with spirits who provide important information about the causes and nature of illnesses, and the appropriate treatment protocol to be used to remedy those illnesses.

Despite the healing, protective and empowerment foci of traditional Rootwork and Voodoo practices, American popular culture has insisted on equating these traditions with witchcraft, malice, evil and destruction. Karen McCarthy Brown, an anthropologist who has conducted extensive studies of Voodoo practices in the United States and in the African diaspora reiterates this point. She states:

American popular culture dwells on images of Vodou's malevolence, an attitude as nonsensical as equating Catholicism with Satanism. The understanding most North Americans have of Vodou is derived mainly from its portrayals in novels, films, and television, where images of sorcerers, zombi, snakes, blood and violence abound. In the United States the word Voodoo is used in a casual and derogatory way to indicate anything on a spectrum from the deceptive to the downright evil. If it were not so clear that racism underlies these distortions, it would be hard to understand why this kind of stereotyping is tolerated for an African-based religion when it would not be tolerated for other religions" (1991, pp. 110-111).

It is important to clarify that "Voodoo" and Rootwork do not name a uniform set of practices. Rather, these terms name a vast array of culturally distinct practices which are shaped by the history of the people within a particular culture, the ideologies and illnesses which are endemic to that culture, as well as by the resources (e.g., the plants) which are indigenous to or available in the environment. As such, Haitian Voodou is distinct from Jamaican Voodoo (properly known as "obeah"), and these practices are distinct from the practice of Voodoo in North America. Further, the Voodoo and Rootwork practices which are seen in particular regions of the United States are likely to be a synthesis of the traditions of the various groups which have immigrated to that region over time. The histories, ecologies and the cultural beliefs in these various sites are distinctly different, and as such, the healing traditions are very different and are always changing.

Ashanti (this volume) notes that "[m]ost patients would have already sought a counter-spell from a root doctor long before coming to the health professional for new treatment." This assertion forces us to address an important question: what is the role of a health professional who encounters a patient such as this? Ashanti effectively rules out one potential role. He cogently argues that untrained therapists should not attempt to effect a "cure" for such conditions as Voodoo poisoning or "Rootwork syndrome." However, we are still left to determine the appropriate role for the health professional (psychotherapist) in working with victims of Rootwork syndrome and Voodoo poisoning.

Assessment

The goal of assessment in work with clients who are suffering from Voodoo poisoning or Rootwork syndrome is three-fold. First, the term Rootwork Syndrome is misleading. A syndrome is a group of symptoms which together are characteristic of a particular disease. The behaviors which Dr. Ashanti describes (e.g., strange animal sounds, lizards and snakes in the body etc.) are among an infinite list of "symptoms" which may be seen in people who have been subjected to Rootwork. I believe that the use of the term Rootwork syndrome is inappropriate because it mistakenly implies that there is one specific disease which is caused by Rootwork. It is best to think of Rootwork and Voodoo in etiological terms. That is, it is appropriate to speak of Rootwork and Voodoo not in terms of specific syndromes, but in terms of practices which can be used to induce varied symptoms and varied forms of dis-ease in others. By thinking of Rootwork and Voodoo in this way, psychologists are freed to see that victims of the negative uses of these practices may manifest any of an infinite list of symptoms.

Second, it is important to remember that Rootwork and Voodoo poisoning are never random acts. They are deliberate acts which are waged against specific people for very specific reasons. As such, an individual who believes that s/he is the victim of such an act will have developed some theories about who might have poisoned her/him, and for what reasons. This fact has an important consequence for diagnostic work. That is, it forces us to shift our focus from attention to symptoms, to a focus on issues of causality. Rootwork doctors and Voodoo priests often use divination techniques to identify who has poisoned the patient and why. This information then becomes an important part of the treatment which the doctor or priest prescribes. Likewise, this information may be useful to a mental health professional. A clinician may use this information to make an assessment of the nature and integrity of the client's support system. For example, the client may suspect that the poisoning was initiated by a jealous friend. In this case, the client would not be able to rely on this friend or members of their network of mutual friends for support. The client and therapist would have to work together to identify or build other sources of support.

Dr. Ashanti asserts that "patients with Bibles in their possession should be suspect." The reasons for this are unclear. Certainly, as Dr. Ashanti notes in the beginning of his chapter, many Christians believe in (or practice) Rootwork and Voodoo. It is plausible, then, that an individual who is frightened by the possibility that s/he is suffering from this kind of poisoning may turn to religion and to the Biblical verses for solace and or help. It is not unusual for people to turn to religion in times of crisis. Particular passages of the Bible may give them hope or may inspire them to cope. In addition, the Bible may represent the presence of the ultimate form of protection and power (God's power). As such, it may function as a protective "charm" (i.e., as a "lucky object").

Third, it is necessary to assess the client's expectations of the therapy and of the therapist. A client may come to a therapist because of particular qualities which the therapist possesses (the therapist may be of the same cultural or language background, or the same gender). Or the client may come to a particular therapist because of her/his hopes and fantasies about the efficacy of the therapist in dealing with particular dis-eases. The client may also come to therapy with particular intentions in mind. S/he may come with the intention of verifying that s/he is the victim of spirit possession. S/he may come to therapy intending to find a way to become comfortable with the finality of impending doom, or with the state of living death. The client's expectations must be explicitly identified and discussed because they will greatly shape the nature and direction of the work that the client and therapist do together.

Dr. Ashanti suggests that a correct assessment of the client requires an evaluation of the client's "khat" (physical body), selido-fa (balance and synthesis of the demands of her external world and her internals desires), and environment. However, it is unclear how a mental health professional might assess either the client's khat or selido-fa. It would be useful to know what kinds of questions a mental health practitioner might ask in his/her effort to assess these two aspects of the client's life. In addition, it would be advantageous to have specific information on how to use this information to generate a treatment plan.

Treatment Concerns

The African ethnomedical techniques which are used by Root doctors and Voodoo priests share a commonality with modern Western medical practice. Researchers such as Robert Edgerton (1989) suggest that the success of traditional African enthnomedical techniques is dependent upon four factors: catharsis, group support, suggestion, and the pharmacological effects of the medicines which are used. Dr. Ashanti cogently notes that modern Western medicine depends on the same four methods for its success. Western psychological practices also rely on these factors for their success.

An appropriate treatment plan might include referring the client to a Rootwork or Voodoo healer. This healer might work collaboratively with the therapist and client to determine whether or not the client is a victim of Rootwork or Voodoo poisoning. If it is determined that the client's symptoms are the result of Rootwork or Voodoo, then the healer can take a lead role in orchestrating the appropriate remedy(ies).

However, if, as Dr. Ashanti argues, it is the client's ability to have faith in the healer and not the "remedy itself" which often results in successful cure, it is crucial that a reputable and trustworthy healer be identified. An individual's self-identification as a Rootwork or Voodoo practitioner does not automatically establish her/his credibility or efficacy. The client must have some criteria for determining the credibility of a healer. Certainly, the individual's reputation within the community serves as one means of determining his/her authenticity and credibility.

Referral to a trained and qualified Rootwork or Voodoo practitioner need not signal the end of a psychotherapist's involvement with the client. In fact, the therapist's decision to use the referral as a basis for terminating his/her involvement with the client may constitute poor and perhaps unethical practice. In standard psychotherapy practice we are aware that there is often a gap of time between the time that a referral is made and the time when a client can actually be seen. When a client is in great distress, it is good practice for therapists to continue to work with the client until the new therapy relationship is established. Given the level of distress which may be associated with a diagnosis of Rootwork syndrome, it may be best that the therapist continue to work with the client until the healer begins to work with the client.

Indeed, a client who leaves a therapist's or a healer's office with the (confirmed) notion in mind that s/he is indeed the object of Rootwork, may experience extreme dysphoria and fear. Dr. Ashanti observes that "an individual who is aware that he is the object of Voodoo spells or Rootwork is completely convinced that he is doomed unless a counter-power is found. . . . If the believer is aware that he is the object of Rootwork, he is thoroughly convinced that he is in fact doomed according to the most solemn traditions of his social group . . . . Over a period of time the victim will either kill himself to relieve his suffering, or will slowly, but certainly die." Given the real possibilities for suicidal ideation and action, a therapist would be remiss to refer the client to a healer without a clear plan for ensuring the client's safety. Continuity of care is no less important in these cases than in other cases.

Dr. Ashanti notes that therapists working with victims of Voodoo poisoning and Rootwork Syndrome should focus on improving the client's self-concept, and will power, and on social network/environment. However, there are other important roles which the therapist must play in this work. For example, the therapist must play a role in bridging the gap left by family members, friends and loved ones who desert him/her when they discover that he has been "hexed." If it is the case that the client has been abandoned by his/her crucial support network, then the therapist can serve as a crucial ally in a time when the client needs social contact. In addition the therapist can serve as a bridge between the client and his/her family and friends. This bridging work may be used to allow the client to address feelings of rejection and loss which s/he experiences as a result of her/his abandonment by friends, family and loved ones.

Summary

The work of synthesizing spirituality and psychotherapy requires us to abandon the dichotomous thinking which represents psychology and spirituality as intrinsically antagonistic disciplines. This work also requires us to abandon the myths and misrepresentations which surround the beliefs and practices which are associated with (African and African American) spirituality. Mental health professionals cannot work effectively with spiritual dis-eases if they associate spirituality with irrationality or malevolence. Instead of seeing spirituality and psychotherapy as opposed forces, Dr. Ashanti correctly notes that there are similarities in the methods used by university trained therapists, Voodoo priests and Root doctors (e.g., in their mutual belief that by reliving past experiences, individuals can change the course of their lives). Likewise, there are similarities between the intellectual concerns of psychotherapy and spirituality in general. Both are concerned with addressing existential concerns, both are concerned with individual's efforts to change, and both use and value people's interpretations and perceptions of experience. In short, spirituality and psychotherapy are each a part of the continuum of ways of knowing.

Psychotherapists can profit from spirituality's explicit attention to power. They can use this focus on power to raise questions about the client's (mis)perceptions of his/her personal power and/or powerlessness. This process can be used to empower clients to think more clearly about their spiritual beliefs and practices, and to define increasingly meaningful and effective ways of using spirituality. This attention to power is compatible with Dr. Ashanti's suggestion that psychotherapy be directed towards addressing the client's self-concept and willpower. However, by attending explicitly to power, the therapist may avail him/herself of a metaphor through which to address a broad range of issues including self-concept, the potential for change, the capacity to identify and achieve one's needs, and the subjective value of spirituality.

Endnotes

1. James Chaffers' (1994) definition of spirituality is privileged here. He notes that the word "spirituality" derives from the Latin root "spiritus" which means "the force of life." Chaffers states:

"Spirituality . . . [is] derived from our uniquely personal tie to energies of the Cosmos; specifically the source of our identity, our individuality and our individual creative powers within a larger universe; i.e., the source of our inherent capacity to be self-validating; self-motivating, and self-directing . . . As such, it is the source of our capacity for optimism, personal enthusiasm, and passionate conviction.

"In sum, 'spirituality' can be understood as an essential 'inner-wellspring of energy' having the capacity to sustain our active participation in the whole of ever-evolving human and ecological systems. As such, it awakens us to the essence and greater potential of life as a self-transformative journey."

In keeping with this definition, religion is seen as one expression of spirituality, but is not assumed to be the only or most viable expression of human spirituality. Chaffers' recognition that spirituality is both individual and communal makes his definition particularly appropriate for a discussion of spirituality in the lives of African American people (for whom communalism has been identified as a defining characteristic).

2. This phrase was coined by Dr. Robert Jagers and is borrowed with his permission.

References

Brown, K. McCarthy (1991). *Mama Lola: A Vodou Priestess in Brooklyn*. Berkeley: University of California Press.

Chaffers, J. (1994). *Spirituality — the missing "i" in mass product(i)on: or why "Mass quality" need not be an oxymoron*. Proceedings of the Association of Collegiate Schools of Architecture European Conference: The Urban Scene and the History of the Future.

Clements, W. M. (1995). Science and religion in dialogue. In M. Kimble, S. McFadden, J. Ellor, & J. Seeber (Eds.), *Aging, spirituality and religion: A handbook*. Minneapolis: Fortress Press.

Edgerton, R. B. (1989). A traditional African psychiatrist. In A. C. Lehmann & J. E. Myers (Eds.), *Magic, witchcraft, and religion: An anthropological study of the supernatural*. Mountain View, CA: Mayfield Publishing.

Lehmann, A. C. (1989). Eyes of the Ngangas: Ethnomedicine and power in Central African Republic. In A. C. Lehmann & J. E. Myers (Eds.), *Magic, witchcraft, and religion: An anthropological study of the supernatural*. Mountain View, CA: Mayfield Publishing.

Lehmann, A. C., & Myers, J. E. (1989). The anthropological study of religion. In A. C. Lehmann & J. E. Myers (Eds.), *Magic, witchcraft, and religion: An anthropological study of the supernatural*. Mountain View, CA: Mayfield Publishing.

Levi-Strauss, C. (1989). The sorcerer and his magic. In A. C. Lehmann and J. E. Myers (Eds.), *Magic, witchcraft, and religion: An anthropological study of the supernatural*. Mountain View, CA: Mayfield Publishing.

Author

Jacqueline D. Mattis, Ph.D.
Department of Psychology
University of Michigan
525 E.University Ave.
Ann Arbor, MI 48909-1109
Telephone: (313) 764-3662
Fax: (313) 7474-3520
E-mail: jmattis@umich.edu

Taking Back Your Mind and Health: A Reaction Paper

Kwabena Faheem Ashanti

The subject of Root Doctors and African Traditional Healing, has rarely been addressed by mental health practitioners in a scholarly and open forum. It has been, therefore, a pleasure to have been selected to be among scholars like Drs. Na'im Akbar, Jacqueline S. Mattis, and Samuel Turner to address this relatively unexplored area. Observations and reactions to my paper that were proffered by Drs. Akbar, Mattis and Turner are presented below.

African people will never be free and independent of the hegemony of others as long as they think, believe, and behave in the manner of those who oppress them. Africans were first deceived and defeated with the assistance of rival African soldiers. In America they were enslaved, culturally aborted, totally contained, and then brainwashed by Eurocentric psychotechnology. They were asked to sing in strange lands, and still they rise. The hot flames of their African spirits remained high, while their tongues stuck to the roofs of their mouths for forgetting and rejecting Africa. But the African God of Creation, the lessor gods, and the curse of the Ancestors never broke the covenant with Africans in the *yapete* (diaspora). Even though they were forced and brainwashed into serving a foreign God and religion, their own Traditional Spiritual System merely stooped to survive, and is now beginning to rise to the levels of the great religions of the world once again.

Dr. Na'im Akbar's reaction paper is excellent and his analysis is "right on target." Of course this is to be expected from such an esteemed scholar and clinician. I should point out that Akbar essentially completed most of his reaction paper before he received my addendum. However, his broader concerns remain.

Dr. Akbar is quite correct when he points out the "difficulties of synthesizing two mutually exclusive concepts of reality," and that the Africentric perspective "has no place in their (European) paradigm of science and their ontology of reality." He is also correct when he pointed out the "intellectually defensive posture . . . reflected in the author's effort to normalize the characteristics of this belief system by suggesting the widespread interest in so-called 'psychic' phenomena among growing numbers of White people." Here, however, I intentionally described the widespread interest and participation of Whites in psychic phenomena for three important reasons, but not from a "defensive posture," as Dr. Akbar has interpreted.

The first reason was to address the very concern that Dr. Akbar described as the "White lunatic fringe behaviors . . . " which "are no more valid within the Eurocentric framework." The reason I called attention to the fact that there are hardly any "thirteenth" floors in five-star, White conservative, owned hotels, or rooms in hospitals, is to call attention to the *mainstream*, and not the "lunatic fringe." The second reason was the recognition that, due to the *psychotechnology of brainwashing*, many Eurocentric African Americans do, in fact, need the legitimization of Whites to validate their own behaviors and beliefs. This may be observed, for example, in African Americans' accepting: White standards of physical beauty (especially hair styles), names, religions, holidays, lifestyles, superstitions (black cats), and even sororities and fraternities (black Greeks?). The third reason was to forcefully open the myopic lens of those Whites who utilized their Eurocentric standards to "normalize" African peoples perspectives and beliefs. I was making an attempt to level the playing field.

Dr. Akbar is in error when he refers to Rootwork as a " . . . bastardization . . . of African spiritual practices which were corrupted by the disruption of the *Maafa*." Instead, Rootwork is actually an African American syncretical practice. It is a fusion of various systems of traditional healing methods: Africans, Native Americans, Christianity, and European witchcraft. This is also true of the Haitian Voodoo religion, with the exception of European witchcraft. Haitian Voodoo is not a pure form of the Vodu religion of Benin (Dahomey), and Togo, West Africa, the very origin of this ancient African religion. There indeed was a disruption of African culture and personality, caused by the horrors of African enslavement. Dr. Akbar, and Ani (1994), refers to these enslavement horrors as the *Maafa*.

The word *Maafa* is from the Kiswahili language of East Africa. This is a multiethnic language, which has been named after the Swahili ethnic group on the Kenya Eastern Coast. It is not a "power" language, in the sense of having a distinct African history, culture, religion, art, and technology (Ashanti, 1995). It was, and still is, a language to communicate across ethnic and racial lines or groups. It was a trade language that was heavily influenced by the language of Arabic, Portuguese, German, French, and English. Kiswahili was the language extensively used in Eastern, Central, and Southern Africa to trade and buy African men, women, and children for enslavement in the West, the Middle-East, and India (Mazuri, 1986; The Horizon History of Africa, 1971). Too much negative baggage comes with the term *Maafa*. It is well known that the African American population is heavily composed of peoples from West Africa. For these reasons I prefer to use a "power word" that more accurately describes the destructive horrors of African enslavement. The word is *)sennya* (voo-sen-yah). That comes from the Akan ethnic group of the former Gold Cost, now Ghana, West Africa. It is here that we find, still standing to let us know, "Never, Never Again," Elmina, and Cape Coast Slave Forts. *)Sennya* means a long brutal fire of destruction and disease, killing everything for many years. It is a term that is so horrible it is not used in general conversation. It more accurately describes the *cultural and psychological abortion* of enslaved Africans in the West. I am very much aware, of the significance of the intent of Dr. Akbar's use of the term *Maafa,* however.

Dr. Akbar, again, correctly points out the problems "presented by classifying such reactions (Rootwork and Voodoo syndrome) as a component of the *American Psychiatric Association's Diagnostic and Statistic Manual (IV)*." However, it is very important to understand that mental illness does not explain the behavior of all individuals with the syndrome characteristics. This is an important fact that I attempted to demonstrate. Conversely, there are also individuals who present the syndrome who are in fact mentally ill, and think it is due to "rootwork" when it is not. However, before a DSM-IV classification should be assigned, an evaluation by an African Traditional Healer or Rootdoctor is essential, and ethically required.

Here, I offer my dissent with Dr. Akbar's application of Dubois' "Double-consciousness" thesis, to his "Dilemma of the Double-consciousness: Understanding Voodoo from an Eurocentric Perspective." My alternative analytical paradigm of African American psychological dynamics to the one presented by Professor Na'im Akbar, differs substantively, rather than contextually. We both agree that the environment, circumstances, mis-education, religious indoctrination, as well as the treatment, had psychological consequences for African Americans. This is not the proper forum to have this exchange, but I believe it is necessary to at least open this critical psychological issue. I believe that the issues of "The Dilemma of the Double-consciousness" have salient implications for the diagnosis and treatment of Rootwork and Voodoo syndrome.

When Dr. W. E. B. Dubois published his book, *The Souls of Black Folk* in 1903, a ship load of enslaved Africans had arrived in Charleston, South Carolina just 15 years earlier, in 1888. These enslaved Africans had a single consciousness and it was African. They looked at themselves through their own eyes, not those of White people. They did not identify themselves as American or Negro. Instead, they felt themselves to be Ashanti, Ibo, Yoruba, Ewe, Zulu, or one of the many other African ethnic groups.

The single consciousness, however, did evolve into the peculiar sensation of a double-consciousness for those Africans who were first through fourth generation (1903) Africans enslaved in America. The *Psychotechnology of Brainwashing* (Ashanti, 1993) and its attendant partial psychological and cultural abortion, i.e., religions, names, languages, rituals, and physical standards of beauty, negatively affected.

By definition, the term "conscious" means being cognitively deliberate, intentional, and internally aware of some known fact or object. Within Dubois' context, the facts were African religions, names, languages, rituals, ethnic groups, and standards of physical beauty. The objects were African tools, stools, musical instruments, clothes, and etc. The term "double" means two together. In this context, the other conscious is composed of similar facts and objects of the White (European) race and culture, imposed upon them by enslavement and brainwashing.

The later generations of Africans in America, about the period of 1903, were the beneficiaries of the single African consciousness of their enslaved elders and relatives, in addition to the White consciousness. Thus, the "double-consciousness." From emancipation from legal enslavement in 1865, through Reconstruction, Jim Crow, segregation, the Civil Rights Movement, and the hegemony of the White (European) social system erased the double conscious of most African Americans. Their racial identities during these periods were known as: Blacks, coloreds, Negroes, and now, African Americans. During these periods, African people in America were induced, indoctrinated, and seduced, to reject Africa, not only by Whites, but also by the "educated class" of African Americans.

However, many Africanisms (beliefs and behaviors) remained and are still practiced by African Americans (Holloway, 1990). These Africanisms are no longer consciously identified, recognized, and in many cases, not accepted to be African. This includes the beliefs and practices of Rootwork, Voodoo, and spiritualism. These are the salient issues that mental health professionals must be aware of, when interviewing and evaluating patients with Rootwork and Voodoo Syndrome. This is also true when consulting with many African American Traditional healers, and Root doctors. To misunderstand or misinterpret these issues of Dubois' concept of the "Double Conscious" is to invite distrust, and even rejection, by the patients, and sometimes, the healers themselves. There are many Rootdoctors who identify themselves with Native Americans and Christianity, and not with Africans, and African spirituality (religions). My research indicates, an alternative to the Double Consciousness thesis, that *Brainwashopherenia* (Ashanti, 1993) is more descriptive of African American psychology than Dr. Akbar's concept of the "dilemma."

Dubois' concept of "double consciousness," and Dr. Akbar's "dilemma," in analyzing the psychological behaviors of present day African Americans, will have to be re-examined and adjusted to today's reality. To do so would be in the great tradition of Dubois himself. After all, it was Dubois who wrote the book that rejected his own "Talented Tenth" thesis. He changed his position in light of the realities.

African culture is amazingly resilient; in spite of culturally destructive forces (enslavement and brainwashing) in history, it has not disappeared. The most powerful indication of our African ancestry lies in our spirituality. However, our Africanness exists primarily on an *unconscious level*. It is the strength and depth of African spirituality and humanism that has allowed for the survival of African Americans (Richards, 1980).

All too often, illness is a surface expression of our deep spirituality, the results of our inability to deal with racism and oppression. Too often, deep spirituality implies an overabundance of faith in people and institutions that do not deserve it (Richard, 1980).

Regardless of religious dogma, many of us still believe in "spells," "roots," and "charms," i.e., Christian crosses. We still believe that some people may have knowledge which can be used for good or bad. We recognize the Traditional Healers and their rituals and medicines as effective weapons against illness and bad luck. We believe that illness can be caused by curses of elders, spiritual and emotional imbalance. We believe in spiritual power.

Dr. Jacqueline S. Mattis' response, *Bridging Spirituality and Psychotherapy* is germinal and powerful. It provides the contextual foundations of African Traditional Healing, as well as the "healing traditions" of Rootdoctors. It also explains the underpinnings of the patient believers. Dr. Mattis correctly observes that "Clinical psychology training programs tend to ignore the topic, or to invoke the words 'religion' and 'spirituality' only in brief discussions which occur under the rubric of multicultural issues in psychology." Her points of clarification, under Assessment, regarding the term "Rootwork Syndrome" correctly points out "that victims of the negative uses of these practices may manifest any of an infinite list of symptoms." The treatment concerns that Dr. Mattis raises should be well heeded by any mental health providers with patients suffering from Rootwork and Voodoo syndrome. This is especially so during the referral and co-therapist phases.

Dr. Samuel Turner, of the Medical College of South Carolina also raises some of the points that concerned Dr. Mattis. Again, I did not present an exhaustive list of symptoms that form a "consistent cluster of behaviors that are implied by the use of the term syndrome." Dr. Turner poses this observation, "It is not entirely clear whether Ashanti views these behaviors to be the result of the powerful influence of culturally held beliefs, or whether he views them as "real" . . . does Ashanti believe . . . that such patients have snakes in their stomachs and frogs in their throats? If (he does) then we no longer are within a psychological purview. . . ." My response to Dr. Turner's observation and question is absolutely *No*, most of the time, and *yes, in rare cases*. As Dr. Mattis correctly pointed out in her paper, "Rootwork and Voodoo (attacks) are never random acts. . . . They are deliberate acts which are waged against specific people for very specific reasons. . . . This fact has important consequences for diagnostic work." There are indeed "secret" ways for small snakes to enter a patient's stomach, and the patient can feel them move. Is it not true that medical doctors have found long worms in their patients? These worms have not "traversed to the spiritual," they are in fact "real" medical and psychological problems.

Drs. Turner, Mattis, and Ashanti all recognize, agree, and recommend " . . . the need for psychological training programs to develop methods to adequately train students with respect to these and other cultural (and spiritual) patterns and their effect on behavior."

African American Medical Schools (Howard, Morehouse, and Mehary) and Universities such as: Florida A&M, North Carolina Central, Howard, Tuskegee, and Norfolk State University, should take the lead in developing these training programs and should also be awarded large federal research grants from the National Institutes of Health Office of Alternative Medicine for this purpose.

Some practices might appear archaic and deceptive, however, the study of illness and healing in this context shows that the African and African American tradition have many of the values that Western society is seeking (Montilus, 1989). We must no longer look to others to validate our world view. Rather than defining emotional disturbances as "mental illness" we need to adopt terms independent of psychiatric and psychological labels and to introduce traditional African healing methods into the health care system where appropriate.

There is still much the West could learn from African cultures. To disregard and insist that African peoples in the West abandoned their culture and the intrinsic wisdom they contain, is at best the height of foolishness and at worst pure evil. Rather, Africans should revere that which is true and wise in their traditional religions and cultures, even while they take advantage of all that the technological age has to offer them.

References

Ani, M. (1994). *Yurugu*. Trenton, NJ: Africa World Press.

Ashanti, K. F. (1993). *The psychotechnology of brainwashing: Africentric passage*. Durham, NC: Tone Books.

Ashanti, K. F. (1995). *Asaase Yaa: Black women's self-empowerment*. Durham, NC: Tone Books.

Holloway, J. E. (Ed.). (1990). *Africanisms in American culture*. Bloomington, IN: Indiana University Press.

The Horizon History of Africa. (1971). American Heritage Publishing Co., Inc. New York, N. Y.

Mazuri, A. A. (1986). *The Africans: A triple heritage*. Boston, MA: Little, Brown and Company.

Montilus, G. (1989). *Dompim: The spirituality of African peoples*. Nashville, TN: Winston-Derek publisher, Inc.

Richards, D. M. (1980). *Let the circle be unbroken: The implications of African spirituality in the diaspora*. Lawrenceville, NJ: The Red Sea Press.

Author

Kwabena Faheem Ashanti, Ph.D.
Counseling Center
North Carolina State University
Raleigh, NC 27695-7312
Telephone: (919)515-2425
Fax: (919) 515-8525
E-mail:
kwabena-ashanti@ncsu.edu

Author Index

Author Index

Subject Index

Subject Index